Specifying and Diagnostically Testing Econometric Models

Specifying and Diagnostically Testing Econometric Models

HOUSTON H. STOKES

QUORUM BOOKS
New York • Westport, Connecticut • London

Library of Congress Cataloging-in-Publication Data

Stokes, Houston H.
   Specifying and diagnostically testing econometric models / Houston
H. Stokes.
     p. cm.
   Includes bibliographical references and index.
   ISBN 0-89930-632-2 (alk. paper)
   1. Econometric models—Computer programs. I. Title.
HB141.S85 1991
330'.01'5195—dc20   91-8399

British Library Cataloguing in Publication Data is available.

Library of Congress Catalog Card Number: 91-8399
ISBN: 0-89930-632-2

First published in 1991

Quorum Books, One Madison Avenue, New York, NY 10010
An imprint of Greenwood Publishing Group, Inc.

Printed in the United States of America

The paper used in this book complies with the
Permanent Paper Standard issued by the National
Information Standards Organization (Z39.48-1984).

10 9 8 7 6 5 4 3 2 1

Copyright Acknowledgments

The author and publisher gratefully acknowledge permission to use the following:

Extracts from Lehrer-Stokes, "Determinants of the Female Occupational Distribution: A Log-Linear Probability Analysis," *The Review of Economics and
Statistics* 67, no. 2 (August 1985): 120-125.

Extracts from Thornber, Houston, "Manual for B34T (8 Mar 66) A Stepwise
Regression Program," *University of Chicago Business School Report* 6603 with
supplements 1967 and 1968.

Contents

Tables

Preface

In the late 1960s, I became aware of the enormous gap between the appropriate statistical procedures suggested by econometric theory and the then availability of options in statistical packages. My research interests comprised estimating equations using generalized least squares (GLS) with more than first-order serial correlation in the error (Sinai and Stokes 1972). To my amazement, I discovered that few statistical packages were able to perform GLS estimation, and the ones that could were restricted to first-order GLS. An exception was the B34T program, which was developed by Hodson Thornber (1966) at the University of Chicago in the middle 1960s to estimate up to ninth-order GLS. B34T consisted of 3,000 FORTRAN II statements for an IBM 7094 and represented an enhancement of the UCLA BIMED34 regression program.

In the 1960s, applied econometricians were hampered by researchers developing single-purpose statistical packages, each of which required data in a different form. Many of the statistical routines in these packages were unable to identify matrices that were almost rank deficient and thus unexpectedly gave poor results.[1] The research reported in this book originated from the perceived need to implement on the computer a number of statistical methods and specification tests for econometric models.[2] This book documents a variety of econometric diagnostic and specification tools and provides illustrations of their use with actual econometric examples in a number of fields using the B34S® Data Analysis program.

The reader <u>does not</u> need to have access to the B34S program to use this book effectively. All results are completely documented in the text and illustrated with computer output. Readers desiring to apply the indicated techniques could use B34S, or program the techniques in a higher level programming language such as the SPEAKEASY® system or the SAS/IML® system. The techniques illustrated have been used in economic analysis, in financial modeling, in health economics, in energy modeling, in environmental economics, in sociology, in political science and in industrial research. Many of the problems in these areas have been used as illustrations in this book.

Each chapter in this monograph will indicate briefly the statistical problem, what specific calculations are available, the routines to be used to make these calculations and, wherever possible, provide an example of this procedure. When more common procedures are being discussed (such as two-stage least squares), the technical discussion will be reduced and the reader will be referred to appropriate textbooks. When procedures use code developed by others, the reader will be directed to the original source for additional detail.

A project the size of this book incurs numerous debts. My

father, W. E. D. Stokes, Jr., first introduced me to signal
filtering as applied to economic problems and stimulated my
interest in graduate work in economics. I am deeply in debt to
Henri Theil and Arnold Zellner who introduced me to econometrics
in the late 60s at the University of Chicago and provided
encouragement for this project at many stages. Their classes led me
to question whether the assumptions of the usual OLS model were met
by the data for the problem at hand. They stressed the importance
of model specification and diagnostic checking of the results.

Next, I would like to thank the numerous reviewers of my
scientific papers who have corrected my analysis and suggested many
improvements. While any remaining errors or shortcomings of the
B34S system are the sole responsibility of the author, certain
individuals deserve special mention during the software development
aspects of this project. In the early days, Ron Golland, at the
University of Illinois, was especially helpful in pointing me to
the finest available utility routines (LINPACK, EISPACK) and in
developing other useful utility routines that I have incorporated
into B34S. The University of Illinois Computer Center has
generously provided computer time for the project and George Yanos,
Associate Director, has been most helpful when serious design
problems had to be solved. In recent years Paul Setze and Jim
O'Leary have made contributions. Professor Lon-Mu Liu, the
developer of SCA, has made many suggestions and has worked with me
on the design of the B34S to SCA and SCA to B34S data interchange.
Professor Barry Chiswick has made suggestions involving changes in
the B34S to make it easier to use, such as the development of the
new syntax and the implementation of the SAS/B34S interface. My
research colleagues, Richard Kosobud, Allen Sinai, Hugh Neuburger,
John McDonald, Evelyn Lehrer and Melvin Hinich, all played major
roles in pointing out econometric problems whose solutions required
the development of procedures that later found their way into B34S.

Ali Akarca has assisted me with the testing of the program,
particularly in the area of time series analysis. I have received
many helpful suggestions from former students, such as Terry Elder,
Linda Manning, Dimitri Andrianacos, John Sfondouris and Ron
Usauskas. I am grateful to Hodson Thornber who has given me
permission to adapt material from his manual for B34T and whose
program was the basic building block for B34S and to the Review of
Economics and Statistics, which is published by North Holland and
from which I adapted material from my papers. Individual code
contributions are acknowledged throughout this book. Most
important, I owe a large debt of gratitude to my wife, Diana, who
not only gave me encouragement and support while I was building the
code and fixing elusive "bugs," but, in addition, provided valuable
editorial help on the manuscript. Individual acknowledgement to
others who have contributed to B34S is given in the individual
chapters where procedures are discussed and in the two on-line help

manuals.[3] Any remaining errors or design limitations are, of course, my responsibility.

Houston H. Stokes
Department of Economics
University of Illinois at Chicago
11 January 1991

NOTES

1. In a now classic study of statistical program accuracy, Longley (1967) found that the percentage error in the price coefficient of a multicollinear data set ranged from .03% to 375%. Four of the nine programs tested did not agree even in the first digit, two were accurate to 1 digit, two to 3 digits and one to 4 digits. Further detail on this paper is contained in chapter 10, which discusses the QR approach to OLS estimation. Modern computer programs such as SAS® and SPEAKEASY® have built-in accuracy checks.

2. The basic B34S code, which was developed from the B34T program, now consists of over 120,000 FORTRAN 77 statements and runs on IBM 370/MVS and IBM 370/CMS. It is available for lease from the author (312-643-4383) or from Scientific Computing Associates, P. O. Box 625, De Kalb, IL 60115 (708-960-1698).

3. B34S contains two on-line help manuals (Stokes 1988a, 1988b). The B34S command

```
B34SEXEC HELP=MANUAL NEWPAGE$ B34SEEND $
```

prints the B34S command reference manual. If the keyword OLDMANUAL is substituted for MANUAL, the B34S "native" command manual is printed. Since complete help is available in these manuals, no attempt is made in this book to provide complete command references. The purpose of this book is to document the calculations and illustrate their use with actual econometric research. This book is not a computer manual, nor is it meant to be a text.

1. Applied Econometric Modeling

1.0 Introduction

This book illustrates the use of model specification and diagnostic tests applied to a variety of econometric modeling techniques. The techniques discussed include simple, one-equation OLS models with continuous variables on the left-hand side. These models can be tested for the appropriate specification and for changes in the parameters over time and for different levels of the right-hand side variables using recursive residuals and BLUS residual tests. Extensions of the simple, one-equation model include models in which the left-hand side is a 0-1 variable (probit and logit procedures) or models in which the left-hand side variable is bounded (tobit procedure).

If we relax the assumption of exogenous variables on the right-hand side of a model, the appropriate estimation technique is either two-stage least squares or limited information maximum likelihood. Sets of equations should be estimated with three-stage least squares if there is covariance among the error terms. If the data set consists of pooled data (time-series and cross-section), error-components models are appropriate. In more limited cases where market share analysis is desired, Markov probability models are a viable alternative. Forecasting extensions of the simple OLS model include modeling only the error (ARIMA analysis) or specifying the dynamics of the mapping of the exogenous variables on the endogenous variables and modeling the error (transfer function modeling). The VAR and VARMA models are shown to be a time series generalization of three-stage least squares and full information maximum likelihood models. Transfer function and ARIMA modeling is a special case of these more general VARMA forms. VAR models can be viewed in the frequency domain for added insight. More specialized techniques include orderly searches for the appropriate equation specification, using the Leamer SEARCH program; optimal control analysis; nonlinear analysis and the QR approach to computation. The purpose of this monograph is to illustrate the above techniques, using actual research data. To facilitate the calculations, the B34S Data Analysis program was developed. Sample output for all procedures discussed in the text has been provided so that the availability of the B34S program is not required to benefit from this book.

1.1 Outline of the Book

Chapter 2 discusses options involving regression analysis and specification tests. These options are accessed from the REGRESSION command and include ordinary least squares, weighted least squares, generalized least squares, heteroskedasticity, normality, and serial correlation tests. Additional features

include BLUS residual analysis, BAYES analysis options, and other
residual analysis options (RA option).

Chapter 3 is devoted to a discussion of logit, probit and
tobit models, all of which involve restrictions on the range of the
dependent variable. The basic code for the logit routines, which
are accessed with the LOGLIN command, was obtained from Nerlove
and Press (1973, 1976). The tobit and probit code was obtained from
Mathematica Policy Research Corp[1] and is accessed by the PROBIT and
TOBIT commands. The multinomial logistic code, which is accessed by
the MLOGLIN command, was initially obtained from Kawasaki (1978,
1979). XLOGLIN, a revision of this program, based on the prior B34S
version, MLOGLIN, was obtained from Klein and Klein (1988a,
1988b). The multinomial probit procedure, which operates on ordered
probit data and which is accessed with the MPROBIT command, was
developed from code originally written by McKelvey and Zavoina
(1971, 1975).

Chapter 4 discusses the use of routines built by Les Jennings
(1980) that calculate ordinary least squares, limited-information
maximum likelihood, two-stage least squares, three-stage least
squares, iterative three-stage least squares and full-information
maximum likelihood estimation for systems of equations. This code
is accessed by the SIMEQ command. Advantages of the Jennings code
are the speed and accuracy of the algorithms used (QR approach) and
the option of obtaining the constrained reduced form of a system of
simultaneous equations.

Chapter 5 is devoted to problems that arise in the
distribution of the error term when pooled time-series and cross-
section data are used in a regression.   The error-components
procedure is a solution that avoids either the assumption being
made that the constant is the same in the cross section as through
time or the loss of degrees of freedom if this assumption is
relaxed and multiple dummy variables are entered into the equation
for each time period or for each cross section observation.   The
code used in this section is an extension of the Freiden (1973)
program by Houston H. Stokes, following suggestions by Henry and
McDonald. The basic reference is Henry, McDonald, Stokes (1976) and
is accessed with the ECOMP command.

Chapter 6 discusses an extension of the basic Lee, Judge, and
Zellner (1970) Markov probability model, following suggestions
contained in Theil (1972, chap. 5). The basic Markov code was
first extended to allow more states, and many of the linear algebra
routines were replaced with LINPACK matrix routines. The code was
next extended to include decomposition of the transition
probability matrix into the fundamental matrix, the exchange
matrix, the mean first-passage matrix, etc. These extensions,
which are all available with the TRANSPROB command, were used in a
number of articles by Kosobud and Stokes   (1978, 1979, 1980)
modeling OPEC behavior and Neuburger and Stokes (1979a) modeling

economic history.

    Chapters 7 and 8 are devoted to the time series capabilities
of B34S.   Chapter 7 discusses the use of the autocorrelation and
cross correlation function in building OLS models, autoregressive
integrated moving-average models (ARIMA) and transfer-function (TF)
models. The commands BJIDEN and BJEST are used to identify and
estimate these models, respectively. The basic code used in these
commands was originally built by David Pack (1977), following
suggestions made by Box and Jenkins (1976) and Box and Tiao (1975).
Suggestions of Neuburger and Stokes (1979b), Stokes and Neuburger
(1979) and Stokes (1990) for additional diagnostic specification
tests have been incorporated. A simplified treatment of the ARIMA
modeling process is contained in Nelson (1973).   The Pack code has
been extensively modified to include many features not found in the
original, such as spectral analysis and further diagnostic tests,
to improve accuracy.

    Chapter 8 discusses vector autoregressive moving-average model
building (VARMA). The BTIDEN and BTEST commands are used to
identify and estimate a VARMA model.   These commands were based on
a heavily modified version of the Wisconsin WMTS-1 program, which
was developed by Tiao and Box (Tiao, Box, Grupe, Hudak, Bell, Chang
1979). Enhancements to the code include tests on the residuals
suggested by Hinich (1982), Hinich and Patterson (1985, 1986),
Hinich and Wolinsky (1988), and Stokes and Hinich (1989) and a
decomposition of the covariance matrix to study instantaneous
causality suggested by Granger and Newbold (1977, p. 223).

    Chapter 9 discusses how to use the recursive-residual analysis
technique to test an equation for parameter stability.   The RR
command code was written by Houston H. Stokes, following the
suggestions in the seminal article by Brown, Durbin, and Evans
(1975) and Dufour (1979, 1982).   Since the recursive residual
technique involves repeated calculation of regressions as new
observations are added, a great deal of effort has been devoted to
making the code execute quickly and accurately. Modifications of
the recursive residual technique have been made to allow it to be
used with cross-section samples to test for both variation of the
coefficients for different levels of the explanatory variables and
for interaction effects.   The code has been improved by the
inclusion of LINPACK routines, particularly in updating and
downdating the Cholesky decomposition.

    Chapter 10 discusses the QR approach to OLS estimation, a
technique particularly suitable in cases of multicollinearity.
While the ridge estimation procedure attempts to deal with the
multicollinearity problem via investigating the effect on the OLS
coefficients of a perturbation of the X'X matrix, the QR procedure
factors the N by K X matrix directly such that X=QR, where the K
vectors in the N by K matrix Q are orthonormal and the K by K
matrix R is upper triangular. Although a Cholesky decomposition of

X'X into R'R is an alternative approach to get R, the disadvantage
of the latter procedure is that the condition (ratio of the largest
to smallest eigenvalue) of X'X is the square of the condition of R.
When X'X is close to singularity, problems will arise that would
have been avoided if one could get R directly (via the QR method)
without forming the more rank-deficient matrix X'X.[2]   The QR
factorization code in B34S is taken directly from LINPACK and, by
use of a pivoting option, allows the user to detect dependencies
among the columns of X. The QR command performs the above
procedures, can optionally calculate principal-component
regressions and, in addition, allows a branch to the Leamer (1978)
SEARCH program, which provides extensive equation specification
diagnostic tests. Since SEARCH is documented extensively in Leamer
(1978), only a brief discussion is given here. The SEARCH command
structure has been maintained.

Chapter 11 concerns nonlinear estimation, which is accessed by
the NONLIN command.   The basic code was originally written by
Meeter (1964a, 1964b) to implement the Marquardt (1963) algorithm.[3]
The code has been improved via the addition of LINPACK routines and
the use of a dynamic calling option (DYNCAL), which allows the user
to code his own models and create a library of programs that B34S
can branch to during execution. The flexibility and speed of the
B34S system is maximized over other possible implementations that
would have involved either relinking B34S each time the model is
changed or coding the functional form of the model in a program-
level syntax.

Chapter 12 contains a discussion of the VARFREQ and KFILTER
commands, which allow decomposition of a VAR model into the
frequency domain, following methods suggested by Geweke (1982b,
1982c), and state space estimation, following suggestions by Aoki
(1987). The MTSM program developed by Geweke (1982a) was
modified for B34S by Stokes (1986) and forms the basis for the
VARFREQ command. The KFILTER command uses the code developed by
Aoki (1987) and is only discussed briefly.

Chapter 13 contains a brief treatment of the OPTCONTROL
command, which implements the Chow (1975, 1981) optimal control
code into B34S. Since the use of this approach is extensively
discussed and documented in the seminal references by Chow (1975,
1981), only a brief discussion of the program is given here. The
B34S implementation of the Chow program uses the DYNCAL procedure
to allow researchers to build a library of subroutines containing
their models to which B34S can dynamically branch at the time of
the execution. An example using the Klein-Goldburger model is
provided.

It is the firm conviction of the author that one learns
econometrics by application of techniques. Only by systematically
testing the specification of a model can one truly begin to
appreciate how sensitive results may be to the initial

specification. While many programs require the user to "run blind," because they do not provide adequate diagnostic tests, B34S allows the user to subject his/her model to a battery of test procedures, which will demonstrate how sensitive the results are to alternative specifications of the functional form. The remaining chapters discuss some of these procedures and their use in greater detail. Most chapters contain B34S control setups to run sample programs that use the procedures discussed in the chapters. Readers are encouraged to run these sample programs in their entirety.[4] Edited versions of the output of these control programs are contained in the text and are briefly discussed. Before moving to a discussion of the regression specification tests, a brief discussion of the B34S software is provided to give the reader an overview of the model specification and diagnostic testing options available.

1.2 B34S Overview

The B34S Data Analysis Program is a collection of econometric procedures that are useful in the analysis of both cross-section and times-series models. While it is assumed that the reader has a good background in econometrics, obtainable from study of such books as those by Johnston (1963, 1972, 1984), Theil (1971), Pindyck and Rubinfeld (1981), Chow (1983) and Kmenta (1971, 1986), many of the more advanced statistical procedures involve techniques that are just beginning to appear in econometric textbooks.[5] To aid the reader, the treatment of all techniques discussed in this book is meant to be self-contained.

The B34S program, which was developed to analyze the examples in this book can be run as either a SAS procedure, which is recommended, or as a stand-alone program. When running as a stand-alone program, B34S will read data in a number of ways, the most common being from a sequential file that can be either in E format, F format, Z format, A8 format or double-precision unformatted.[6] B34S can create and read an SCA FSAVE data file library (Liu, Hudak 1986a, 1986b) and can create and read its own DATA step within a B34S MACRO library. These options facilitate data interchange between B34S and SCA, which are complementary programs. In addition, B34S will support a random-access data-bank format, which uses an IBM FORTRAN DEFINE FILE statement. The design of the data bank is based on the Wharton Econometric Forecasting System and allows the user to read a subset of economic time series in any order from the data bank. The form of the data bank requires two random-access data sets, one for data and one for documentation. Further information concerning the construction of the data bank and the B34S DATA step is contained in <u>The B34S On-Line Help Manual</u> by Stokes (1988b) and <u>The B34S Data Analysis Program: A Short Writeup</u> by Stokes (1988a), which is available on-line and which documents the "native" B34S command language. As an alternative to loading data into B34S directly, use of the SAS PROC CB34S, which is discussed later, allows B34S to be seen as a SAS

procedure. Because of the wide availability of SAS, most B34S users
at the University of Illinois at Chicago run B34S as a SAS
procedure.

The B34SII (hereafter referred to as the B34S) command
structure involves the specification of multiple <u>paragraphs</u> or
<u>commands</u>, each containing <u>sentences</u>. The first sentence in each
paragraph begins with the keyword B34SEXEC, which starts the
parser. The last sentence in each paragraph, which turns off the
parser, must be either B34SEEND$ (B34S EXEC END) or B34SRUN$. Each
sentence must end with the delimiter $ or optionally the delimiter
;. The B34SEEND$ sentence is used in batch operation. The B34SRUN$
sentence is used in an interactive environment to force B34S to
execute the command. Its use is similar to that of the SAS RUN;
command. If the B34EEND$ sentence is used, B34S will parse all
commands prior to attempting to execute. In this book, the term
"B34S command" and "B34S paragraph" will be used interchangeably.
More detail on the B34S command structure is contained in Stokes
(1988b). A list of currently supported B34S commands or paragraphs
is given in Table 1.1.

The B34S control language is completely free format and is in
many ways similar to that of SAS. The SAS PROC CB34S, distributed
with B34S, allows B34S to be seen by a SAS user as a SAS procedure
(Stokes 1986a). An example of this mode of operation is illustrated
in Table 1.2. The developer of B34S recommends running B34S under
SAS since it allows the user to utilize the powerful SAS data step
to load and process the data prior to the call to the more
specialized B34S procedure. The same job could be run in B34S
stand alone. This job is illustrated in Table 1.3. In this mode of
operation, the B34S DATA paragraph is required, while in the
SAS/B34S job, the B34S DATA paragraph does not have to be
explicitly supplied.

The complete B34S command reference manuals (Stokes 1988a,
1988b) are available on-line. While these manuals may be used as
the sole references for B34S, they contain little documentation of
the statistics calculated and no examples of their use. Just as
B34S is an outgrowth of the B34T program, this book can be thought
of as a major extension of the original B34T manual written by
Hodson Thornber (1966, 1967, 1968). Sections of Thornber's
original manual have been included in chapter 2 of this book with
the author's permission.

Table 1.1 B34S Commands

Command	Description
HELP	Provide help, generate on-line manual.
OPTIONS	Set B34S run-time options.
REGRESSION	OLS and GLS estimation. BLUS and RA analysis.
LIST	Display data in B34S data file.
PLOT	Plot and graph series in B34S data file.
PROBIT	Probit analysis on (0-1) dependent variables.
TOBIT	Tobit analysis on truncated dependent variables.
LOGLIN	Logit analysis on up to four equations at once.
ECOMP	Error-components analysis.
AUTOC	Autocorrelation and cross correlation analysis.
RR	Recursive-residual analysis.
QR	QR factorization & principal component analysis.
DATA	Load data into B34S without SAS/B34S interface.
MPROBIT	Multinomial probit analysis.
MLOGLIN	Multinomial logit analysis.
SIMEQ	2SLS, LIML, 3SLS, I3SLS, FIML, SUR estimation.
TRANSPROB	Estimate Markov probability model.
BJIDEN	Box-Jenkins identification. Spectral analysis.
BJEST	Box-Jenkins ARIMA, transfer-function estimation.
BTIDEN	Identification of VAR and VARMA models.
BTEST	Estimation of VAR, VARMA and VMA models.
NONLIN	Estimation of user-specified nonlinear models.
VARFREQ	Spectral decomposition of VAR models.
PGMCALL	Branch to SAS, SPEAKEASY, SPSS, SCA, TSP and LIMDEP.
POLYSOLV	Solution of polynomials.
DTASSM	Data-manipulation utilities.
OPTCONTROL	Optimal control analysis.
CALL	Call user procedure.
KFILTER	Estimate state-space model.
SOURCE	B34S FORTRAN source manager.
SCAINPUT	B34S/SCA input option.

Table 1.2 B34S RUN Under SAS for Probit Analysis

```
* SAS JOB to load DATA;
DATA TEST;
INPUT Y X1 X2;
CARDS;
1 22 33
0 122 66
0 12 55
1 22 33
0 2 66
;
PROC CB34S DATA=TEST;
VAR Y X1 X2;
PARMCARDS;
B34SEXEC PROBIT $
    MODEL Y = X1 X2  $
    B34SEEND$
;
```

Table 1.3 B34S Run Stand Alone for Probit Analysis

```
B34SEXEC DATA NOOB=5 $
INPUT Y X1 X2$
DATACARDS$
1 22 33
0 122 55
0 12 66
1 22 33
0 2 66
B34SRETURN$
   B34SEEND$
B34SEXEC PROBIT $
   MODEL Y = X1 X2  $
   B34SEEND$
```

1.3 Conclusion

Depending on the specific econometric problem, the chapters in this book do not necessarily have to be read in chronological order. Probably chapter 2 should be read to get some idea of the assumptions of the basic OLS model.

NOTES

1. The TOBIT code was very old and possibly is the original Tobin source code. The PROBIT code most likely was originally developed by John Cragg, but has been changed by a number of others. All three programs (LOGIT, PROBIT and TOBIT) were converted to double precision and extensively improved by the addition of the LINPACK matrix subroutines (Dongarra, Bunch, Moler, and Stewart 1979).

2. Strang (1976) contains an excellent discussion of this approach.

3. The GAUSHAUS routine, developed by Meeter (1964a, 1964b), has passed the test of time and three variants are used: in the nonlinear estimation section, in the Box-Jenkins ARIMA and transfer function model-building section, and in the Box-Tiao VARMA model-building section.

4. The B34S code can be typed in or obtained from the B34S libraries that are distributed with the B34S program. Since most sample setups are B34S MACROS, they can be selectively run with the B34S OPTIONS command.

5. Epstein (1987) contains a good discussion of how current econometric practice has evolved over time.

6. For a discussion of these formats, see any basic FORTRAN textbook or IBM (1972, 1988a, 1988b).

2. Regression Analysis With Appropriate Specification Tests

2.0 Introduction

The options discussed in this chapter concern testing for appropriate functional specification, ordinary least squares (OLS) models, generalized least squares (GLS) models, and weighted least squares (WLS) models. The appropriate syntax for running these options is contained in the REGRESSION command section of Stokes (1988b). It is assumed that the user has entered his data in B34S and is ready to estimate his/her model.[1] After a detailed discussion of the statistics available, a number of examples are shown.[2]

2.1 Standard Regression Model With a Constant

Assume a set of T observations on (K+1) variables denoted

$$
\begin{bmatrix} y_1 \\ \cdot \\ \cdot \\ \cdot \\ y_T \end{bmatrix}
\quad
\begin{bmatrix} x_{11} & \cdots & x_{1K} \\ \cdot & \cdots & \cdot \\ \cdot & \cdots & \cdot \\ \cdot & \cdots & \cdot \\ x_{T1} & \cdots & x_{TK} \end{bmatrix}
. \tag{2.1-1}
$$

It is supposed that these variables are related by a set of stochastic equations that can be written in matrix notation as:

$$
\begin{aligned}
Y &= (X, i)\beta + \sigma\varepsilon \\
&= (X, i)\beta + e,
\end{aligned} \tag{2.1-2}
$$

where Y is the Tx1   vector of observations on the dependent variable, or regression;

X is the TxK   matrix of independent variables, or regressors, corresponding to the regression coefficients;

i is a Tx1   vector of 1's, the regressor corresponding to the constant, β_{K+1};

β is the (K+1)x1   vector of fixed, but unknown, regression coefficients;

σ is the standard deviation of the disturbance term e;

ε is a Tx1   vector of independent, identically distributed random variables with mean = 0 and variance = 1, $\sigma\varepsilon$ = e = population residual; and

e is a Tx1   vector of population residuals.

The least-squares estimate of β may be computed in either of two equivalent ways, the difference being in the handling of the constant term. First, we might actually consider the matrix (X, i) and compute the <u>regression coefficients</u>

$$\hat{\beta} = [(X,i)'(X,i)]^{-1}(X,i)'Y, \qquad (2.1-3)$$

where (') denotes the operation of matrix transposition. This approach treats the constant like all other coefficients. Second, we could use the deviation of the data from their means, get the coefficients $(\hat{\beta}_1, \ldots, \hat{\beta}_K)$, and then use the equation relating the means to compute $\hat{\beta}_{K+1}$. To do this, let

$$\overline{X} = X'i / T \text{ and } \overline{Y} = Y'i / T \qquad (2.1-4)$$

so that $\overline{X}$ is the Kx1 vector of means of the independent variables $\{\overline{x}_1, \ldots, \overline{x}_K\}$ and $\overline{Y}$ is the mean of the dependent variable, then

$$\begin{bmatrix} \hat{\beta}_1 \\ \cdot \\ \hat{\beta}_K \end{bmatrix} = (((X'X)/T) - \overline{XX}')^{-1} \; (((X'Y)/T) - \overline{XY})$$

$$(2.1-5)$$

and

$$\hat{\beta}_{K+1} = \overline{Y} - (\overline{x}_1, \ldots, \overline{x}_K) \begin{bmatrix} \hat{\beta}_1 \\ \cdot \\ \cdot \\ \cdot \\ \hat{\beta}_K \end{bmatrix}. \qquad (2.1-6)$$

This approach takes advantage of the special structure of the last regressor, i, and requires the inversion of a KxK instead of a (K+1) x (K+1) matrix. Each approach has its advantages, but rather than working both out completely (Johnston 1963, 134-135) we will use here only the first one.

For convenience we will now redefine X to include i, so we can rewrite the basic model as

$$Y = X\beta + \sigma\varepsilon$$
$$= X\beta + e, \qquad\qquad\qquad\qquad (2.1\text{-}7)$$

where $\quad E(e) = 0, \ E(ee') = \sigma^2 I$

and the least squares estimator of β as

$$\hat{\beta} = (X'X)^{-1} X'Y . \qquad\qquad\qquad\qquad (2.1\text{-}8)$$

Given $\hat{\beta}$, we can compute the estimates of the sample disturbances, or the <u>residuals</u>

$$\hat{u} = Y - X\hat{\beta} \qquad\qquad\qquad\qquad (2.1\text{-}9)$$

and from them an unbiased estimate of σ^2, the residual variance

$$\hat{\sigma}^2 = \hat{u}'\hat{u} \ / \ (T\text{-}K\text{-}1) \qquad = (Y'Y - Y'X \ \hat{\beta})/(T\text{-}K\text{-}1). \qquad (2.1\text{-}10)$$

The square root of $\hat{\sigma}^2$ is the <u>standard error of estimate</u> $S_{y.x}$.

If X is independent of e (Goldberger 1964, 164, 167, 267-268), the <u>covariance matrix of regression coefficients</u> is estimated by

$$\hat{\sigma}^2 (X'X)^{-1}. \qquad\qquad\qquad\qquad (2.1\text{-}11)$$

The square roots of the diagonal elements of the covariance matrix are the <u>standard errors of the coefficients</u> (SE_i). The <u>t-ratios</u> of the coefficients, t_i, are defined as

$$t_i = \hat{\beta}_i \ / \ (SE_i) . \qquad\qquad\qquad\qquad (2.1\text{-}12)$$

<u>The partial correlation</u> between y and x_j, given all the other variables, is given the same algebraic sign as $\hat{\beta}_j$ and is defined as

$$t_j^2 \ /(t_j^2 + T - K), \qquad\qquad\qquad\qquad (2.1\text{-}13)$$

where we assume there are K right-hand-side variables. The equivalence of this formula to the standard definition of partial correlation is given in Gustafson (1961, appendix 1, 365). The <u>elasticities</u> estimated at the mean are

$$\beta_i \overline{x}_i \ / \ \overline{Y} . \qquad\qquad\qquad\qquad (2.1\text{-}14)$$

The <u>squared coefficient of multiple correlation</u>, R^2, is

$$R^2 = 1 - (u'u \ /(v_y \ (T\text{-}1))), \qquad\qquad\qquad (2.1\text{-}15)$$

where v_y is the variance of the dependent variable. Theil (1971,

179) recommends the <u>adjusted multiple correlation coefficient</u>

$$R_a^2 \quad = \quad R^2 - ((K-1)/(T-K))(1-R^2),\qquad\qquad (2.1\text{-}16)$$

which is preferred to equation (2.1-15) since it is adjusted for the number of independent variables in the regression.

The <u>F-statistic</u> to test the hypothesis that $\beta_1 = \ldots = \beta_k = 0$ is

$$F = (R^2)(T-K-1) \ / \ (1-R^2)(K) \qquad\qquad (2.1\text{-}17)$$

and has $(K, T-K-1)$ degrees of freedom.

Additional diagnostic statistics provided include $-2 * \ln(\text{ maximum of the likelihood function})$, which is defined as

$$T \ln(2\pi) + T \ln((u'u)/T) \ + T. \qquad\qquad (2.1\text{-}18)$$

Akaike's Information Criterion (AIC) (1973) is defined as

$$AIC = T \ \ln(2\pi) + T \ \ln((u'u)/T) \ + T + (2(K+1)) \qquad (2.1\text{-}19)$$

and the Schwartz Information Criterion (SIC) (1978) is defined as

$$SIC = T \ \ln(2\pi) + T \ \ln((u'u)/T) + T + ((K+1) \ Ln(T)). \qquad (2.1\text{-}20)$$

The smaller the AIC and SIC, the better the model.

It can be shown that the OLS estimators $(\hat{\beta}_1, \ldots, \hat{\beta}_K)$ are in fact maximum likelihood estimators. Let $f(y_i)$ be the probability density of the left-hand variable. The maximum likelihood method of estimation attempts to select values for the estimated coefficients and σ^2 such that the likelihood $\mathcal{L}$

$$\mathcal{L} = f(y_1)f(y_2),\ldots,f(y_T) \qquad\qquad (2.1\text{-}21)$$

is maximized. Kmenta (1971, 213) cites the change of variable theorem, "If a random variable X has probability density $f(x)$, and if a variable Z is a function of X such that there is a one-to-one correspondence between X and Z, then the probability density of Z is $f(z) = |dx/dz| f(x)$, $dx/dz \neq 0$." Using this theorem and the model specified in equation (2.1-7), we write

$$f(y_i) = |de_i \ / \ dy_i| \ f(e_i). \qquad\qquad (2.1\text{-}22)$$

Since from equation (2.1-7), $|de_i \ / \ dy_i| = 1$, then

$$f(y_i) = f(e_i) \qquad\qquad (2.1\text{-}23)$$

or the distribution of the left-hand variable is equal to the distribution of the error. Equation (2.1-23) implies that equation (2.1-21) can be written

$$\mathcal{L} = f(e_1)f(e_2),\ldots,f(e_T). \tag{2.1-24}$$

Assuming the distribution of the error term is normal,

$$f(e_i) = (2\pi\sigma^2)^{-.5} \exp(-.5e_i^2\sigma^{-2}) \tag{2.1-25}$$

or taking logs,

$$\ln(f(e_i)) = -.5 \ln(2\pi\sigma^2) - .5e_i^2\sigma^{-2}. \tag{2.1-26}$$

Maximum likelihood estimation selects values for β_i and σ such that L is maximized where $L \equiv \ln(\mathcal{L})$ or

$$L = \Sigma_{i=1}^{T} \ln(f(e_i)) . \tag{2.1-27}$$

It follows from substitution of equation (2.1-26) in equation (2.1-27) that

$$L = -.5T \ln(2\pi) \quad -.5T \ln(\sigma^2) \quad - .5\sigma^{-2} \Sigma_{j=1}^{T} (y_i - \beta_i x_i)^2. \tag{2.1-28}$$

Differentiation of L in equation (2.1-28) with respect to β_i and σ gives the OLS estimates of β_i and an estimate of σ^2 as $T^{-1}\Sigma_{i=1}^{T}e_i^2$. Multiplication of equation (2.1-28) by -2 gives equation (2.1-18). Note that the OLS estimation of σ^2 uses the large sample T rather than T-K.

2.2 Regression Model Without a Constant

When it is known a priori that β_{K+1}, the constant, is zero, one often wants to impose that constraint on the estimation procedure to gain efficiency in the estimation of $(\beta_1,..,\beta_K)$. With $\beta_{K+1}= 0$, equation (2.1-2) reduces to

$$Y = X\beta + \sigma\varepsilon, \tag{2.2-1}$$

where β is now a Kx1 vector containing only $(\beta_1,\ldots,\beta_K)$ and X is the TxK matrix of regressors, not including the column of ones, i.

Under these two redefinitions, formulas (2.1-8) and (2.1-9) apply to model (2.2-1). From equation (2.1-9) the residual variance becomes

$$\hat{\sigma}^2 = (u'u) / (T-K). \tag{2.2-2}$$

Using equation (2.2-2), formulas (2.1-11) to (2.1-14) carry over.

The formula for the coefficient of multiple correlation given in equation (2.1-15) must be reinterpreted as simply a measure of efficiency of estimation relative to the mean of y, in that it can now be negative. Heuristically, without a constant, the algebra no longer guarantees that the u'u will be less than the variance of

the dependent variable times (T-1) since the mean of the residuals
is no longer forced to equal zero. If the R^2 is found to be
negative, it indicates that a better prediction of y could be
obtained by using its mean and forgetting about the regression.
This might lead the user to reconsider his specification that β_{K+1}
= 0 or to alter the functional form of the independent variables.
The F-statistic for test of the hypothesis that $\beta_1 = \ldots \beta_K = 0$ is
now

$$F = (R^2)(T-K)/(1-R^2)(K) \qquad\qquad (2.2-3)$$

with (K, T-K) degrees of freedom (see Roy 1957, 82).

If no constant is estimated, the regression line is forced
through the origin instead of the mean, i.e., the mean of the
computed residuals will no longer = 0. Details concerning this
calculation are contained in Johnston (1963,   131-132).

2.3 Generalized Least Squares

In this section, we will consider a generalization of the
specification (2.1-7), or (2.2-1), if the constant is being
suppressed. In equation (2.1-2) the disturbance term is

$$e = \sigma\varepsilon \qquad\qquad (2.3-1)$$

so that the covariance matrix of the disturbances becomes

$$Cov(e) = E(ee') = \sigma^2 E(\varepsilon\varepsilon') = \sigma^2 I, \qquad\qquad (2.3-2)$$

where "E" denotes mathematical expectation and "I" is the TxT
identity matrix.   This model is said to have a scaler covariance
matrix. The specification of a scaler covariance matrix is often
felt to be too restrictive, so we will develop a linear regression
model with an arbitrary covariance matrix and then consider two
useful applications of it: weighted least squares and least
squares with autoregressive disturbances.

Instead of equation (2.3-1), let us suppose that

$$e = P\varepsilon, \qquad\qquad (2.3-3)$$

where P is an arbitrary, TxT, lower triangular, positive definite
matrix that is assumed to be known up to a scale factor; then

$$Cov\ (e) \equiv \Omega = PP'. \qquad\qquad (2.3-4)$$

Since Ω must be a positive definite symmetric matrix and any such
matrix can be factored as in equation (2.3-4), it follows that
allowing P to be arbitrary is sufficient to allow Ω to be
arbitrary. The generalized linear regression model may now be
written as

$$Y = X\beta + P\varepsilon, \tag{2.3-5}$$

which may be transformed to the standard model (2.1-1) by multiplying each side of the equation by a matrix, R, proportional to P^{-1}, or

$$R = cP^{-1} \qquad (c > 0). \tag{2.3-6}$$

We may remove the arbitrary scale of the transformation by imposing the constraint

$$i'R'Ri = T \tag{2.3-7}$$

so that for any P we find

$$c^2 P'^{-1}P^{-1}i = T. \tag{2.3-8}$$

This implies that

$$R = (i'P'^{-1}P^{-1}i)^{-.5} \quad T^{.5} \quad P^{-1}. \tag{2.3-9}$$

Applying the transformation, R, to equation (2.3-5) and replacing the original data, Y and X, by the <u>weighted data</u>,

$$Y^* = RY \text{ and } X^* = RX, \tag{2.3-10}$$

we find that the relationship among the weighted data is

$$Y^* = X^*\beta + \sigma\varepsilon, \tag{2.3-11}$$

which satisfies the standard model. The constraint (2.3-8) is exactly what is required to preserve the equivalence of the two computational techniques outlined at the beginning of section 2.1, and using it implies that all the equations of sections 2.1 and 2.2 hold for the general model given in equation (2.3-5) after the transformation given in equation (2.3-10). For instance, the means and variances of the weighted data are exactly the same as the weighted means and variances of the original data; similarly, the regression coefficients and standard errors are unchanged. <u>Weighted</u> <u>residuals</u> may be computed by

$$\widehat{u}^* = Y^* - X^*\widehat{\beta} \tag{2.3-12}$$

and will be estimates of random variables, $\sigma\varepsilon_t$, which are independently and identically distributed.

In practice, only relatively simple forms of P are used. The following sections discuss two such forms.

2.4 Weighted Regression Model

For simple weighted regressions, P is a diagonal matrix, the tth element on the diagonal being proportional to the standard deviation of the disturbance term in the tth observation. This yields what should really be called the <u>heteroskedastic model</u>:

$$
\begin{bmatrix} y_1 \\ \cdot \\ \cdot \\ \cdot \\ y_T \end{bmatrix} = \begin{bmatrix} x_1 \\ \cdot \\ \cdot \\ \cdot \\ x_t \end{bmatrix} \beta + K \begin{bmatrix} P_{11} & & \\ & \cdot & \\ & & \cdot \\ & & & P_{TT} \end{bmatrix} \varepsilon \quad (K > 0),
$$

$$(2.4\text{-}1)$$

where x_i is the ith row of X. The transformation $R = cP^{-1}$, required to reduce this to the standard model, is fully determined by the matrix P and the constraints (2.3-7) and (2.3-8). In the language of weighted regression, the "weights" are the T variables $\{c^2(P_{tt})^{-2}\}$ (t=1, ..., T) in spite of the fact that from (2.3-10), it is clear that the observations are weighted by $\{c(P_{tt})^{-1}\}$ (t=1,T). In deference to custom, we will call this last quantity the "square root of the weight." For example, assume that in the B34S DATA paragraph the WEIGHT option was specified as WEIGHT=X3. This means that for all OLS regressions run with the B34S REGRESSION command, the data have been transformed such that $NEWX_i = OLDX_i * (X3_i)^{.5} * Z$, where Z is $(1/MEAN(X3))^{.5}$. If B34S is run under SAS, the WEIGHT option on the SAS PROC CB34S will accomplish the same thing. The B34S WEIGHT option on the DATA PARAGRAPH allows quick experimentation with various weights in an attempt to remove heteroskedasticity.

2.5 Autoregressive Disturbances Model

Another simple specification for the P matrix is used to take account of autocorrelated disturbances following a stationary autoregressive process. Suppose that instead of

$$e_t = \sigma\varepsilon_t \quad (t=1, ..., T), \tag{2.5-1}$$

as is implied by equation (2.3-2), the disturbances are assumed to have been generated by the stationary autoregressive process

$$e_1 = \sigma(1 - \Phi^2)^{-.5}$$

$$e_t = \Phi\, e_{t-1} + \sigma\varepsilon_t \quad (t=2,T), \tag{2.5-2}$$

where $|\Phi| < 1$. For standard discussions of this model, see Goldberger (1964, 236-238), and Johnston (1963, 185-187). Both of these authors omit the above specification of e_1 and are led to a (T-1) x T transformation, which "almost completely" satisfies equation (2.3-4) for the required Ω (Johnston 1964, 186). Using the more complete specification (2.5-2), one can, as below, derive the transformation under which equation (2.3-4) is satisfied exactly for all T observations. The textbook analyses referred to can be interpreted as proceeding conditional on the observed y_1, while the following analysis uses the marginal distribution for y_1. These two approaches to the problem are described more fully in Thornber (1965, 2-9).

The GLS algorithm in the B34S REGRESSION paragraph is the more traditional approach, which does not estimate Φ and the β's jointly. Its main advantage is its simplicity and the fact that one does not get the convergence problems associated with methods such as maximum likelihood that estimate Φ and the β's jointly. The B34S REGRESSION command allows extensive diagnostic tests that are not available in other packages. Once the correct model is determined, the user may wish to try the ML approach to estimate Φ and the β's jointly, which is available in SAS PROC AUTOREG (SAS 1984). If convergence can be achieved, the ML approach is to be preferred. Johnston (1984, 291-293), Maddala (1977, 277-284) and Kmenta (1986, 311-322) are basic references on possible ways to proceed. Since the GLS model is a special case of the more general transfer function (TF) and VARMA models, if complex lags are found with the GLS option in the REGRESSION command, these alternative approaches should be investigated. The advantages of these approaches will be covered later in chapters 7 and 8.

Equation (2.5-2) may be written in matrix form as

$$P^{-1}e = \varepsilon,$$
(2.5-3)

where P^{-1} is the TxT matrix

$$P^{-1} = \sigma^{-1} \begin{bmatrix} (1-\Phi^2)^{.5} & & & & \\ -\Phi & 1 & & & \\ & -\Phi & 1 & & \\ & & \cdot & \cdot & \cdot \\ & & & \cdot & \cdot & \cdot \\ & & & -\Phi & & 1 \end{bmatrix}.$$
(2.5-4)

To show that equation (2.5-4) gives the proper covariance matrix (see Johnston 1963, 185), use equation (2.3-4) and compute

$$\Omega^{-1} \;\; = p'^{-1}p^{-1} = \; \sigma^{-2} \begin{bmatrix} 1 & -\Phi & 0 & \cdots & & 0 \\ -\Phi & 1+\Phi^2 & -\Phi & & & 0 \\ & \cdot & \cdot & \cdot & & \\ & & \cdot & \cdot & \cdot & \\ & & & \cdot & \cdot & \cdot \\ & & -\Phi & 1+\Phi^2 & & -\Phi \\ 0 & \cdots & 0 & & -\Phi & 1 \end{bmatrix},$$

(2.5-5)

which is exactly what is required by Johnston. We can now write the "autoregressive disturbances" model as

$$\begin{bmatrix} y_1 \\ y_2 \\ \cdot \\ \cdot \\ \cdot \\ y_T \end{bmatrix} = \begin{bmatrix} x_1 \\ x_2 \\ \cdot \\ \cdot \\ \cdot \\ x_T \end{bmatrix} \beta + \sigma \begin{bmatrix} (1-\Phi^2)^{.5} & & & \\ -\Phi & 1 & & \\ & \cdot & \cdot & \\ & & \cdot & \cdot \\ & & -\Phi & 1 \end{bmatrix}^{-1} \varepsilon$$

(2.5-6)

or

$$Y = XB + P\varepsilon$$

(2.5-7)

subject to

$$c^2 i'P'^{-1}P^{-1}i = c^2\sigma^{-2}[(T-2)\Phi^2 - 2(T-1)\Phi + T] = T.$$

(2.5-8)

This determines the transformation $R = c\,P^{-1}$, which reduces the data to one of the standard models, equation (2.1-1) or (2.2-1), as was done in the heteroskedastic model above.

The transformation recommended by Goldberger and Johnston is

$$\begin{bmatrix} -\Phi & 1 & 0 & \cdots & & 0 \\ 0 & \cdot & \cdot & & & 0 \\ \cdot & & \cdot & \cdot & & \cdot \\ \cdot & & & \cdot & \cdot & \cdot \\ & & & & \cdot & \\ 0 & & & & -\Phi & 1 \end{bmatrix}.$$

(2.5-9)

The exact solution embodied in equation (2.5-8) differs from that in equation (2.5-9) in that it uses the initial observation (y_1, x_1), giving it a weight proportional to $(1-\Phi)^{.5}$, which maintains the sample size nominally at T; the textbook procedure takes (y_1, x_1) as unexplained data, giving it a weight of zero, which reduces the sample size to (T-1). Also, while the transformation implied by equation (2.3-8) is adjusted for scale, equation (2.3-9) is not. As T goes to ∞ or $|\Phi|$ approaches 1, the distinction between the two becomes negligible, but for "small" samples with $|\Phi| << 1$, the increase in precision due to having one more observation may be well worth the slight additional computing cost involved in using specification (2.5-8).

Model (2.5-2) for the disturbance may be generalized to higher-order autoregressive processes in a straightforward way. However, deriving the distribution of the initial values of $\{e_t\}$ now involves the manipulation of generating functions. These manipulations, like those of matrix inversion, are easy to do numerically, but awkward to exhibit algebraically, except in simple cases like equation (2.5-2). No attempt will thus be made to give here the exact analyses for higher-order processes, but it is quite feasible to do so. The solution analogous to equation (2.5-9) for the qth-order case

$$e_t = \Phi_1 e_{t-1} + \ldots + \Phi_{t-q} e_{t-q} + \sigma \varepsilon_t \qquad (2.5-10)$$

is the (T-q) x T transformation

$$\begin{bmatrix} -\Phi_q, & \ldots, & -\Phi_1, & 1 & & \\ & & & & \ddots & \\ & & -\Phi_q, & \ldots, & -\Phi_1, & 1 \end{bmatrix}, \qquad (2.5-11)$$

which reduces the last (T-q) observations to the standard model.

The transformation used in B34S uses the textbook transformation (2.5-11), with an adjustment for scale:

$$(1-\Phi_1-\ldots,-\Phi_q)^{-1} \begin{bmatrix} -\Phi_q, & \ldots, & -\Phi_1, & 1 & & \\ & & & & \ddots & \\ & & -\Phi_q, & \ldots, & -\Phi_1, & 1 \end{bmatrix}. \qquad (2.5-12)$$

At some future time, equation (2.5-12) may be replaced in the program by the exact solution described above. In the meantime, the user who feels it important not to lose any initial observations may do the exact transformation by transforming the data prior to running GLS with the REGRESSION command.

In practice, the parameters $\{\Phi_j\}$ (j=1, ..., q) are, of course, unknown and are estimated by a two-stage procedure (Goldberger 1964, 245-246). Stage 1 regresses y on X, giving consistent estimates of the residuals. Stage 2 fits a qth-order difference equation to these residuals, transforms the data from (y, X) to (y^*, X^*), using equation (2.5-12), and regresses y^* on X^* to get the final regression coefficients. The second stage is executed initially with q = 1, then q = 2, etc., until the autocorrelation in the weighted residuals falls below a specified tolerance. The procedure used does not iterate for a given q. For a given q, the computation is exactly analogous to the second and third stages of three-stage least squares, and has the same motivation.

This two-stage procedure gives consistent estimates of the regression coefficients only if each regression variable, x_{tk}, in a given observation is independent of the disturbance, e_t, for that observation (Goldberger 1964, 278-280). <u>This means that X may not include lagged values of the dependent variable</u>. The ML procedure available in SAS does not have this problem, since the β's and the Φ's are estimated jointly. (For a complete explanation and an example, see Goldberger 1964, 274-278.)

The maximum order of the GLS regression is controlled by the parameter MAXGLS, which is specified in the REGRESSION sentence of the REGRESSION command. The present maximum order for GLS is 9. The parameter TOLG controls whether the maximum order of GLS is reached. Assume MAXGLS=n. The tolerance supplied with the TOLG parameter is applied to the maximum of the absolute value of the first n autocorrelation coefficients (calculated using equation 2.8-5) of the residuals of the previous step. If the maximum of the absolute value of the n autocorrelation coefficients is less than TOLG, the calculation of GLS will be terminated. Although the GLS stopping rule will look at the first n autocorrelation coefficients, the parameter NTAC can be used to set the maximum number calculated. Thus, a user can check to see if there is higher-order serial correlation. If such correlation is found, the user might consider changing methods of estimation to vector autoregressive moving- average models (see chapter 8) or altering the variables in the GLS regression. The advantage of the B34S REGRESSION design is that the user can set up for the worst case (highest-order GLS model) but only report lower-order GLS models if serial correlation is found not to be a problem. The Goldberger GLS approach is very cost- effective in comparison with the more modern ML approaches and thus facilitates experimentation to test the sensitivity of the results to the order of GLS selected.

Serial correlation only affects the distribution of the standard errors of the coefficients, not the asymptotic distribution of the coefficients. It is often erroneously thought that after correction for serial correlation, the SEs are always raised in absolute value. This is not always the case. An example of the second-order GLS model, using the Sinai-Stokes (1972) data, is shown later in this chapter.

If TOLG is not specified, B34S will use $T^{.5}$. In most empirical work, where serial correlation is a potential problem, the usual practice is to set MAXGLS = 2 and let B34S decide whether GLS is needed (i.e., whether there is sufficient serial correlation of the residual to warrant going to first- or second-order GLS). Since the user may wish to switch off printing for some options, the options NOBLUSPLOT, NOGLSPLOT and NOCOV can be used to save paper. If residual analysis without plots is desired, the option RESIDUALA should be used, <u>without</u> RESIDUALP being set, to give compact output.

B34S allows the user to perform a grid search on Φ_1. Since the statistical properties of this approach are not known, its use is not recommended, except for experimental purposes. The parameter GLSGRID is used to specify the number of steps in the search between PHO (default=.4) and PHI (default=.95). In contrast to the usual method of searching, B34S will give results for every step, allowing the user to either select the Φ_1 desired or see how sensitive the estimated SE's are to the Φ_1 used.

2.6 Estimation Control Options

The B34S REGRESSION command requires model specification with the MODEL sentence in a manner similar to the SAS PROC REG command. If the keyword STEPWISE is given in the REGRESSION sentence, the REGRESSION command will list the steps as the variables are entered. If the ORDER sentence is used, the user can specify variables that should be placed in the regression first. For example, assume it is desired that all equations should have the constant and X1 and X4, but that the data should select the order of the other variables in the model. The correct setup would be:

```
B34SEXEC REGRESSION STEPWISE$
ORDER CONSTANT X1 X4$
MODEL Y = X1 X2 X3 X4 X5 X6 X7 X8 X9 $
B34SEEND$
```

The REGRESSION sentence options EFIN and FOUT control the minimum level of F for inclusion and exclusion, respectively. The default value for EFIN is .01 and for FOUT is .005. The default settings imply that a variable will enter a regression if the square of its t value is > .01 and will be removed if the square of its t value falls such that it is < .005. Usually, EFIN > FOUT. For example, a variable might enter into the model first, but when other variables enter into the model, it may be removed because it was multicollinear with these new variables. Even if the STEPWISE option is not used, the REGRESSION command will always give the user a list of the order in which the variables entered the regression, and will indicate if a variable was not put in the regression because of the EFIN and FOUT values. By use of relatively high EFIN and FOUT values and the STEPWISE option, the user can select a model with only significant t values. While there are some philosophical problems with such "fishing" operations (Leamer 1978), such exercises may be useful.

The REGRESSION command checks all prospective variables for multicollinearity, with variables presently in the regression via inspection of the reduced diagonal element. This procedure involves running a regression of the prospective variable against all the presently included variables on the right-hand side and recording the R^2. If $(1 - R^2) <$ TOLL on the REGRESSION sentence, the prospective variable will not be allowed into the regression. The default on TOLL is .00001. This indicates that if the R^2 of a regression of the prospective variable against already-included variables is $> .99999$, that variable will not enter the regression.

As a final check for multicollinearity, the REGRESSION command uses the Faddeeva(1959, 99-120) algorithm to form an estimate of the error in the calculation of the regression coefficients. At the end of each subproblem, an estimate is made of the numerical error in the regression coefficients resulting from a rounding error in inverting the cross-product matrix. These estimates are based on the second round of an iterative matrix inversion algorithm, the first round of which gives the computed matrix $(X'X)^{-1}$ used to compute the regression coefficients. The importance of this error check is not the absolute estimate, but the relative estimate of error for the different coefficients. If there is more than two-way multicollinearity in the regression, short of a tolerance check using TOLL mentioned above, verification is impossible, since the correlation matrix of the data vectors measures only two-way relationships. The estimate of computational error in the coefficients will determine which coefficients are being affected and will give the researcher a chance to experiment with alternative functional forms.

2.7 Overview of Options Involving Computed Residuals

The B34S REGRESSION command provides four basic categories of tests involving the OLS computed residuals. These are summarized below and discussed in detail in the following sections.

(a) Residuals from the data used in the regressions may be computed, plotted, characterized with respect to their autocorrelation properties , tested for normality, and tested for heteroskedasticity. Residuals are tested if the RESIDUALA option is specified. Plots are also given if the RESIDUALP option is used in place of the RESIDUALA option. For further detail on these tests, see section 2.8 below.

(b) The computed residuals may be used to provide an estimate of the disturbance covariance matrix, which is then used to give asymptotically efficient estimators for the regression coefficients under the assumption that the true disturbances follow an

autoregressive scheme (see section 2.5). The GLS options are
controlled by the parameter MAXGLS, which sets the maximum order of
GLS, and the GLSGRID, PHO and PHI parameters, which control other
GLS options. For further detail, see section 2.5.

(c) BLUS (Best Linear Unbiased Scaler) residuals (Theil 1971,
chap. 5) can be calculated and tested using both in-core and out-
of-core BLUS procedures to provide alternative tests on the
appropriateness of the equation specification. For further detail,
see section 2.9.

(d) Extensive functional form specification tests can be
performed using the RA sentence on both BLUS and OLS residuals. For
further detail, see section 2.10.

2.8 Residual Summary Statistics

This section outlines the exact specification of the residual
tests that are available if the keyword RESIDUALA is added to the
REGRESSION sentence. Four measures of autocorrelation are provided.
The Durbin-Watson test statistic d

$$d. \quad = \Sigma_{t=2}^{T}(u_t - u_{t-1})^2/\Sigma_{t=1}^{T}u_t^2 \qquad (2.8-1)$$

provides a test of the hypothesis of no first-order serial
correlation in the true disturbances. See Goldberger (1964, 243-
244) for instructions in its use. The modified von Neumann ratio
(displayed in B34S as von Neumann ratio #1) is defined as

$$Q' \quad = \quad (N\Sigma_{t=2}^{T}(u_t - u_{t-1})^2/(N-1))/\Sigma_{t=1}^{T}u_t^2, \qquad (2.8-2)$$

where N is the effective sample size. The von Neumann ratio
(displayed in B34S as von Neumann ratio #2) is defined as

$$Q \quad = \quad (N \Sigma_{t=2}^{N}(u_t - u_{t-1})^2/(N-1)) /\Sigma_{t=1}^{N}(u_t - \bar{u})^2. \qquad (2.8-3)$$

Discussion of the use of Q and Q' is given in Theil (1971, 219).
For OLS regressions Q=Q' since Σu_t = 0. For BLUS residuals, Q'
will not be equal to Q since, in this case, $\Sigma u_t \neq 0$. For OLS
residuals, a very common test for autocorrelation is the Durbin-
Watson test statistic d, although such a test only checks for
first-order serial correlation. When using BLUS residuals, the
modified von Neumann test statistic (Q') should be used. Tables
for the former statistic can be found in most econometrics books,
while tables for the latter are found in Theil (1971).[3]

The adjusted residual is equivalent to the unit normal deviate
form of the residual and is defined as the residual divided by the
standard error of estimate of the regression (see equation 2.1-10),
each element being u_t/s. Since 95% of these adjusted residuals
must lie in the range -1.96 to 1.96 for large samples, inspection

of their values gives both a test for normality and a means by which to judge the probability that one residual could arise by chance.   If the error term of the OLS equation is not normal, the estimates of β and σ^2 are no longer efficient or asymptotically efficient. The result is that F and t tests on the coefficients are not necessarily valid in finite samples, although such tests have an asymptotic justification. (For further discussion, see Judge, Griffiths, Hill, and Lee 1980, 298-301.)

While many tests, such as the Kolmogorov-Smirnov and the Shapiro-Wilk tests, give a summary measure, whether or not the residuals could be independent drawings from a normal distribution, these tests do not give a visual interpretation of what has caused the lack of normality.   In addition, the above tests are computationally burdensome. An inexpensive alternative, suggested by Draper and Smith (1966), is to test the adjusted residuals directly.   B34S uses a chi-square test on the adjusted residual and reports results for grids of 5 and 10 points.   Since the cell size of a chi-square test must be at least 5, the smaller grid should be used if the number of residuals is less than 50.   The statistic

$$ C \quad = \quad \Sigma_{i=1}^{KK}(E_i - A_i)^2 \, / \, E_i \qquad\qquad (2.8\text{-}4) $$

is distributed as chi-square with KK-2 degrees of freedom, given KK is the number of cells, E_i is the expected number of adjusted residuals expected to lie in cell i, and A_i is the actual number of observations in cell i.   Since a chi-square statistic with KK-2 degrees of freedom = $F((KK-2),\infty) * (KK-2)$, an F test could just as easily have been performed. The chi-square test procedure assumes drawing from an infinite population. An argument can be made that since the sample OLS residual has degrees of freedom (T-K), the appropriate degrees of freedom for the F statistic is not $F((KK-2),\infty)$ but $F((KK-2), (T-K))$.   Such a statistic is given in the output and will show a slightly higher probability of rejecting normality.[4]

If the BRTEST option is supplied in the REGRESSION sentence, the sum of the adjusted residuals, the mean adjusted residual, the sum of the residuals and the mean residual will be printed. In OLS and GLS regressions, these values should be close to machine 0.0 and thus provide a check on the program, while in BLUS analysis, these values will not be 0.0. Depending on the basis selected for BLUS analysis (see section 2.9), the values of these means and sums can vary quite substantially.   Their inspection gives another measure of the sensitivity of the BLUS residuals to the base selected.

The autocorrelation function

$$ \hat{p}_k = (\Sigma_{t=k+1}^{T}\hat{u}_t \, \hat{u}_{t-k}/\Sigma_{t=1}^{T} \, \hat{u}_t^2)(T/(T-k)) \quad \text{for } k=1,\ldots r \qquad (2.8\text{-}5) $$

as a function of the lag, k, provides a measure of autocorrelation among disturbances up to r periods apart. Although all attempts at basing an exact finite sample test on equation (2.8-5) have so far failed (Thornber 1965, 2-3, 9), these autocorrelations retain an intuitive appeal and are thus presented as a heuristic summary statistic only. The number of terms, r, of the autocorrelation function may be specified by the NTAC parameter on the REGRESSION sentence. If NTAC is omitted, 4 or more p values will be calculated, depending on the length of the longest lag in the data and the maximum order of the autoregressive equation, if any, assumed for the disturbances. The exact value is NTAC = MIN(MAX(4,(MAXGLS+1)),30). Many econometricians only test for first-order serial correlation with the Durbin-Watson statistic. This is often a serious mistake since higher orders of serial correlation may be present in the data. Routine use of the NTAC parameter to calculate higher-order autocorrelations of the residuals will protect against accepting results that are unknowingly contaminated with higher-order serial correlation.

An F test for heteroskedasticity

$$F(j,j) \quad = \quad (\hat{u}_1^2 + \ldots + \hat{u}_j^2)/(\hat{u}_{2j+1}^2 + \ldots + \hat{u}_T^2) \qquad (2.8-6)$$

is given for intuitive appeal only. The difficulty is that since the OLS (GLS) residuals are correlated (see section 2.9), the numerator and denominator of $F(j,j)$ are not independent. The middle third of the observations $(t=j+1,2j)$ have been removed to partially reduce this problem. The F test for heteroskedasticity is an appropriate procedure to use with BLUS residuals (see section 2.9-2.10), which by their construction are not correlated if the population residual is not correlated. The final statistics given are the sum of squared residuals and the mean squared residual. These statistics have been calculated from the residual directly and thus provide an independent check of the program code. Because the sum of squares of the (T-K) BLUS residuals is equal to the sum of squares on the T OLS residuals, inspection of the sum of squares statistic is a very important test of whether the BLUS residual option is functioning correctly.

2.9 BLUS Specification Test Options

B34S contains rather extensive BLUS residual testing procedures. These include the BLUS-out-of-core procedures, which are called from the REGRESSION sentence by use of the BLUS parameter, and the BLUS-in-core procedures, which are called with the RESID parameter on the RA sentence of the REGRESSION paragraph. As a general rule, the BLUS-in-core procedures should be used, if possible, since they have additional capability, especially for cross-section data. The BLUS-out-of-core procedures can be used when the data cannot fit into the workspace. All BLUS procedures have a current limit of 20 variables on the right-hand side of the regression. This restriction may be removed later. Prior to a detailed discussion of how the BLUS procedures are called, the specification of the tests available is given.   The B34S BLUS capability was developed to implement the tests suggested by Theil (1971, chapter 5). The BLUS-out-of-core procedures were originally developed by Thornber (1968) and were extended by the author. The BLUS-in-core procedures were developed completely by the author. An outline of the BLUS procedure follows.

The population error e is related to the sample error u by

$$u \quad = Me, \hspace{4cm} (2.9-1)$$

where

$$M \quad = I - X(X'X)^{-1}X'. \hspace{3cm} (2.9-2)$$

The implication of equations (2.9-1) and (2.9-2) is that even if the population residual e is free from problems of serial correlation and heteroskedasticity, the sample residual u will not be because of the term M.

Although from equation (2.3-2) the covariance matrix of the elements of e is $\sigma^2 I$, the covariance matrix of the elements of u is $\sigma^2(I-X(X'X)^{-1}X')$.   This renders any test of the null hypothesis, e. g., equation (2.3-2), inexact in finite samples if it is based on the OLS estimates, u.

The next step will be to sketch the proof of equation (2.9-1) and show how a BLUS estimate of the population residual can be calculated and used. We will redefine ε as the BLUS residual.

The sample residual u is defined as

$$u \quad = Y - X\hat{\beta}. \hspace{4cm} (2.9-3)$$

From equations (2.1-1) and (2.1-8) we obtain

$$u \quad = X\beta + e - X((X'X)^{-1}X'(X\beta+e)) \hspace{2cm} (2.9-4)$$

$$\quad = e - X(X'X)^{-1}X'e \hspace{3cm} (2.9-5)$$

$$\quad = (I - X(X'X)^{-1}X')e \hspace{3cm} (2.9-6)$$

$$\quad = Me. \hspace{5cm} (2.9-7)$$

The sum of squared sample residuals u'u = e'MMe = e'Me since M is a symmetric idempotent matrix. Theil (1971, chapter 5) has shown that it is possible to define a vector of (T-K) BLUS residuals ε_1, which is related to the vector of OLS residuals u_1 and u_0

$$\varepsilon_1 \quad = u_1 - X_1 X_0^{-1}(\Sigma_{h=1}^K (d_h / (1+d_h))Q_h Q_h')u_0, \hspace{1cm} (2.9-8)$$

where X_0 is a K by K matrix of the K excluded observations, X_1 is a (T-K) by K matrix of the (T-K) included observations, $d_1, \ldots, d_K$ are the square roots (eigenvalues) of the matrix $X_0(X'X)^{-1}X_0'$, $Q_1, \ldots, Q_K$ define the characteristic vectors (eigenvectors) of the matrix $X_0(X'X)^{-1}X_0'$ and u_0 and u_1 are the OLS residuals corresponding to X_0 and X_1, respectively. Theil has shown that within the class of linear unbiased residual vectors with a scaler covariance matrix, the BLUS residual vector ε_1 has a minimum expected squared length of the error vector given by

$$E((\varepsilon_1 - e_1)'(\varepsilon_1 - e_1)) = 2\sigma^2 \Sigma_{h=1}^K (1-d_h). \qquad (2.9-9)$$

Theil (1971, lemma 1, 209) has proved that the roots (eigenvalues) of $X_0(X'X)^{-1}X_0'$ are positive and, at most, equal to one. The greater the sum of the square root of these roots, the more appropriate that particular set of BLUS residuals. This criterion is particularly important where there are multiple possible bases for BLUS tests.[5]

The sum of squares of the (T-K) BLUS residuals is equal to the sum of squares of the T OLS residuals or

$$\varepsilon_1' \varepsilon_1 = (T-K)s.^2 \qquad (2.9-10)$$

B34S lists the sum of squares of BLUS residuals, which should be checked against the sum of squares of OLS residuals (or GLS residuals if BLUS analysis is performed after GLS) to verify that the BLUS residuals have been calculated correctly.

For every set of (T-K) BLUS residuals, there exists a BLUS implied coefficient vector defined as

$$\beta + X_0^{-1}(\Sigma_{h=1}^K (d_h/(1+d_h))Q_hQ_h')u_0, \qquad (2.9-11)$$

where β is the OLS coefficient vector. Theil (1971, 232) has developed a measure of BLUS efficiency defined as

$$\Sigma_{h=1}^K (1-d_h^2)/(2\Sigma_{h=1}^K (1 - d_h)). \qquad (2.9-12)$$

Equation (2.9-12) indicates that as T increases relative to K, the relative performance of BLUS residuals to OLS residuals as approximations of the population disturbances declines. This is not really a serious problem since as T gets larger, both the OLS and the BLUS errors themselves get smaller. Given that b_0 is the OLS coefficient vector for the base observations and b_1 is the OLS coefficient vector for the other (T-K) observations, the OLS coefficient vector β is a weighted sum of b_0 and b_1

$$\beta = W^2 b_0 + (I-W^2)b_1, \qquad (2.9-13)$$

where

$$W^2 \quad = \quad (X'X)^{-1}X_0'X_0 \tag{2.9-14}$$

$$b_0 \quad = \quad (X_0'X_0)^{-1}X_0'Y_0 = X_0^{-1}Y_0 \tag{2.9-15}$$

$$b_1 \quad = \quad (X_1'X_1)^{-1}X_1'Y_1 \tag{2.9-16}$$

and Y_0 and Y_1 are the left-hand variable vectors corresponding to X_0 and X_1. The BLUS implied coefficient vector (from equation 2.9-11) can be written in terms of b_0 and b_1 as

$$Wb_0 \quad + \quad (I-W)b_1. \tag{2.9-17}$$

For further discussion of these results and others, see Theil (1971, 234-235). The power of the BLUS residual test procedure is increased if the appropriate BLUS base is selected. B34S supports a number of base selection options that will be discussed later.

To test for serial correlation, Theil suggests that the original ordering of the data be preserved and that the BLUS base be selected via the criterion of maximizing the sum of the square roots of the eigenvalues from the following K+1 choices: first K observations, first K-1 and last observation, first K-2 and last two observations and ,..., last K observations. Equation (2.9-9) provides the motivation for this procedure. The serial correlation test uses the modified von Neumann statistic, defined in equation (2.8-2), for which tables are given in Theil (1971). Unlike the Durbin-Watson test statistic, the modified von Neumann ratio test does not have an indeterminate zone. The BLUS serial correlation procedure is relatively computer-intense in view of the many bases that have to be considered; however, it is easy to use since B34S will automatically search over the bases under consideration. The in-core BLUS procedure, discussed later, uses the most efficient computer routines available and is relatively cheaper than the out-of-core BLUS procedure. Its disadvantage is that it requires internal data storage.

If the original data vector is reordered with respect to an included or excluded variable prior to the selection of the appropriate BLUS base for the modified von Neumann test, a general test for nonlinearity in the functional form of the model can be performed. The above testing procedure works for both cross-section and time-series data. If the data vector has been reordered against an included variable and serial correlation is found, the implication is that the appropriate functional form will have a nonlinear term containing the variable that was used to reorder the data. If the data vector was reordered against an excluded variable, a finding of serial correlation indicates a missing variable difficulty. This procedure would fail only if X_0 was not full rank for some BLUS base. This might occur if there were dummy variables in the X matrix, or if some variables in the X matrix were unchanged for a number of observations. If B34S finds rank deficiency in X_0, a message is given and the decision on the appropriate base will be made from the other alternatives.

A specific test for convexity (Theil, 1971, 226, problem 5.2) can be performed if the coefficient G of the parabola

$$\varepsilon_i = G[(x_{ij} - m_j)^2 - v_j] + a_j \qquad (2.9\text{-}18)$$

is tested for significance. In equation (2.9-18), m_j and v_j are the mean and variance, respectively, of the (T-K) values of the j column of X (which was used to resort the X data matrix), ε_i is the BLUS residual vector and a_i is the disturbance term. Theil proves that if the null hypothesis of the standard linear model is true, with the additional specification of normality, the coefficient G will vanish. A t ratio to test the significance of G is

$$t_G = (A_j (T\text{-}K\text{-}1)^{.5}) / ((T\text{-}K)s^2D_j - A_j^2)^{.5}, \qquad (2.9\text{-}19)$$

where

$$A_j = \Sigma_i(x_{ij} - m_j)^2\varepsilon_i - v_j\Sigma_i\varepsilon_i \qquad (2.9\text{-}20)$$

$$D_j = \Sigma_i(x_{ij} - m_j)^4 - (T\text{-}K)v_j^2. \qquad (2.9\text{-}21)$$

The appropriate base for the BLUS heteroskedasticity test, shown in equation (2.8-6), is the middle K observations. If (T-K) is even, this base is unique. If (T-K) is odd, there are two possible bases. The B34S in-core BLUS option will select, on the basis of the maximum sum of the square roots of the eigenvalues, $d_1...d_K$ of the best of the two possible bases. The motivation for this selection criterion is equation (2.9-9).

The selection of the appropriate base for the BLUS convexity test, shown in equation (2.9-19), involves first ranking the data vector against column j. BLUS residuals are selected for the first (T-K)/4 observations in the new ranking, (T-K)/2 observations in the middle of the new ranking, and the last (T-K)/4 observations in the ranking. If there is no one unique BLUS base, B34S will use the sum of the square roots of the eigenvalues criterion to select the most appropriate BLUS base.

The BLUS-residual-equation testing procedure, as we have seen, involves carefully tailoring the BLUS base selection criteria to the specific test desired. For example, it is important to ignore the convexity test statistic when the base for the serial correlation test is being used. B34S allows the user to select a battery of tests to effectively rule out certain types of equation misspecification problems. Such tests, although easy to set up, involve substantial computation. The in-core BLUS procedure, discussed later, is the fastest and least expensive way to proceed. To obtain an idea of the computational difficulties, assume an equation with 20 right-hand variables in which eight variables are to be tested for convexity, heteroskedasticity, and serial

correlation (general nonlinearity). For each of eight orderings of
the data, the serial correlation test involves looking at 21 BLUS
bases, the heteroskedasticity test involves looking at one or two
bases, and the convexity test involves looking at one or two bases.
In this example, 200 BLUS bases (25 * 8) must be inspected in order
to test this regression. The B34S BLUS procedures use LINPACK and
EISPACK code to keep computer costs down and to insure that
accuracy problems do not arise. Nevertheless, the user should be
aware of the complexity of the task. Private research has shown
the value of carefully testing a regression. In many cases, the
OLS results indicated insignificant variables that later BLUS
analysis showed were functionally misspecified. When the proper
functional form was substituted, the formerly insignificant
variables became significant.[6] The next section contains further
detail on the B34S BLUS residuals available.

2.10   BLUS In-Core and Out-of-Core Options

     As was mentioned in the prior section, the B34S program has
two distinct sets of BLUS routines. The original out-of-core BLUS
routines do not load the residual vector into core at one time.
These BLUS routines are controlled by setting keywords for the BLUS
parameter on the REGRESSION sentence to select the appropriate BLUS
residual base. It should be noted that the out-of-core BLUS
procedures do not provide <u>reordering of the data vector prior to
BLUS residual calculation</u>. This limitation is removed in the in-
core BLUS options, which are called from the RA sentence of the
REGRESSION paragraph. If reordering of the data is desired with the
out-of-core BLUS procedures, the data must be sorted <u>prior</u> to being
loaded in B34S. The base selection options in the out-of-core BLUS
procedure include the following:

-BLUS=FIRST	BLUS base is first K observations.
-BLUS=MIDDLE	BLUS base is middle K observations.
-BLUS=LAST	BLUS base is last K observations.
-BLUS=$(n_1, \ldots, n_K)$	BLUS base is specified by the user.
-BLUS=BEST	BLUS base is selected from the K+1 possible adjacent bases via the criterion of maximizing the sum of the square root of the eigenvalues of $X_0(X'X)^{-1}X'$.
-BLUS=HET	BLUS base is selected by choosing K observations at equal intervals from the middle third of the sample.

-BLUS=BOTH   BLUS residuals are calculated
                              first using option BLUS=BEST, and
                              next using option BLUS=HET.

If the user wants a heteroskedasticity test only, set
BLUS=HET. If an exact serial correlation test is required, set
BLUS=BEST. If the user wants both heteroskedasticity tests and
serial correlation tests, set BLUS=BOTH. This is the usual setting.
The B34S out-of-core BLUS tests can be run on OLS and GLS models.
For example, to test for heteroskedasticity on up to second-order
GLS, in the REGRESSION sentence set switches MAXGLS=2, BLUS=BOTH,
and RESIDUALA. If the option RESIDUALP was supplied in place of
RESIDUALA, a substantial amount of output will result, especially
when there are many time periods. The options NOBLUSPLOT and
NOGLSPLOT can be selectively used to turn off plotting for BLUS,
GLS, and GLS-BLUS as necessary to save paper. The use of BLUS bases
is discussed further in Theil (1971, chapter 5).

The residuals generated by the BLUS out-of-core procedure can
be passed to the RA procedure, which is discussed in section 2.11.
This is not usually done because the RA procedure itself can
generate BLUS residuals with more specialized bases and sorting
options. It is important to note that unless the options
BLUS=FIRST, BLUS=BEST, or BLUS=LAST are requested, out-of-core BLUS
residuals contain gaps. If BLUS residuals with gaps are passed to
the RA procedure and cross correlation analysis is requested, the
results would be meaningless.

The in-core BLUS residual option is called from the RA
sentence of the REGRESSION command. The key parameters are VARS,
which sets a maximum of eight variables to sort against, and RESID,
which sets the appropriate set of residuals to use for the tests.
Options for the RESID parameter include the following:

-RESID=CONVEX   Calculate in-core BLUS residuals with a
                              base suitable for a convexity test and
                              perform tests.

-RESID=HET   Calculate in-core BLUS residuals with a
                              base suitable for heteroskedasticity
                              tests and perform tests.

-RESID=PARAB   Calculate in-core BLUS residuals with a
                              base usable for parabola convexity test
                              and perform test.

-RESID=ALLBLUS   Perform CONVEX, HET, and PARAB options.

-RESID=OUTBLUS   Analyze BLUS residuals from the
                              out-of-core BLUS procedures.

   -RESID=OLS   Analyze OLS residuals. This option is
                             used if BLUS tests are not wanted and is
                             the default.

   -RESID=ALL   Analyze both OLS and OUTBLUS residuals.

   All RA sentences require that variables to test against be
specified with the VARS parameter. Assume the following commands:

```
B34SEXEC REGRESSION RESIDUALA$
   MODEL Y=X1 X2 X5 X6 X7 X8$
   RA VARS=(X1 X2) RESID=ALLBLUS$ B34SEEND$
```

The B34S REGRESSION command will first run Y as a function of X1,
X2, X5, X6, X7, and X8 and report basic tests on the OLS residuals.
Next, the RA procedures will be called and the data will be
reordered against X1; three sets of BLUS residuals will be
calculated   and   used   to   perform   tests   for   convexity,
heteroskedasticity and parabolic convexity as discussed in Theil
(1971, chapter 5). Third, the data will be sorted against X2 and
three more sets of BLUS residuals will be calculated and used to
perform tests. If, for example, the convexity test indicates
problems when the data have been sorted against X1, then the
problem is nonlinearity with respect to X1. This example shows how
the RA sentence can assist in substantially narrowing down the
problems of a regression. The in-core and out-of-core BLUS
procedures have an upper limit of 20 variables on the right of any
OLS equation. In addition, only eight variables can be mentioned in
any one VARS parameter. If more than eight variables are desired,
two or more REGRESSION paragraphs should be used. The RA sentence
output for the aforementioned problems will be compact since the
options LIST, LISTA, and GRAPH have not been supplied. Detail on
the tests calculated will be given in section 2.11.

   The in-core BLUS output includes the modified von Neumann
ratio given in equation (2.8-2), a measure of BLUS efficiency given
in equation (2.9-12), the BLUS implied coefficient vector given in
equation (2.9-11), and an estimate of 1/condition of the BLUS
residual base X_0. The heteroskedasticity and convexity tests, which
are defined in equations (2.8-6) and (2.9-19), respectively, the
Durbin-Watson test statistic, defined in equation (2.8-1), and the
correlation between the residual and the variable used to make the
sort are also given. Although all statistics are calculated for
every BLUS base, it is important to report only the test statistic
for the most appropriate BLUS base for that test.

2.11 The Residual Analysis (RA) Option

   The previous section discussed use of the RA card to calculate
in-core BLUS residuals. The RA card may also be used in analysis
of OLS residuals to test for other types of functional form
problems. For example, the correct dynamic specification of an
equation is often difficult to determine. Assuming a model of the

form

$$Y = \beta_0 + \beta_1 X_{1t} + \beta_2 X_{2t} + \ldots + \beta_k X_{kt} + u_t, \qquad (2.11-1)$$

theory often will not determine whether any or all of the right-hand variables should be lagged, or whether, in fact, X_{jt} is an exogenous variable. While specialized and more complex dynamic specification tests can be performed if prewhitened series are cross-correlated (see chaps. 7 and 8 in which Box-Jenkins tests for Granger causality are discussed), in a multi-input model, such a procedure is difficult, owing to possible effects of other variables. The RA sentence supports the calculation of cross correlations between the variables listed with the VARS parameter and the residual, using the formula

$$r_{jk} = ((T-k) (\sum_t X_{jt-k} u_t) - (\sum_t X_{jt-k})(\sum_t u_t)) \; / \; A_{jk}^{.5} \; B_k^{.5} \qquad (2.11-2)$$

where

$$A_{jk} = (T-k)\sum_t X_{jt-k}^2 - (\sum_t X_{jt-k})^2 \qquad (2.11-3)$$

$$B_k = (T-k)\sum_t u_t^2 - (\sum_t u_t)^2 . \qquad (2.11-4)$$

If significant cross correlations ($|r_k| \geq 2(T-k)^{-.5}$) are found between the jth X variable (lagged k times) and the residual, the appropriate change in the functional form of equation (2.11-1) is to lag the jth X variable k times and enter it in the equation.[7] If significant cross correlations are observed for negative values of k for the jth variable, then the jth variable does not belong on the right-hand side of the equation since it is not exogenous.

Because cross correlations between autocorrelated series can produce spurious results (Box and Jenkins, 1976, 377), a simple filtering procedure via differencing can be performed. The parameter DIF on the RA sentence controls the level of differencing and the parameter PERIOD controls the number of periods for cross correlation or autocorrelation analysis. Inspection of the autocorrelations will indicate in a heuristic fashion how much autocorrelation is left in the series after the simple differencing filter has been applied. Since the 0th order correlation of the residual and any variable on the right-hand side of an OLS equation is constrained to zero, inspection of this correlation checks the program. If the residual is being sorted against a variable not in the OLS regression, the 0th order correlation provides information concerning whether that variable would enter significantly into the regression with a zero-order lag. Before autocorrelation tests are performed, B34S will put the data vector back in the original order. As was mentioned earlier, if BLUS residuals are being autocorrelated, it is imperative that the base used does not allow for gaps in the data. Clearly, the autocorrelation and cross correlation tests are not for cross-section data. A further discussion of the problems of cross correlating autocorrelated data is contained in Stokes and Neuburger (1979).

To hold down cost, nonlinearity, heteroskedasticity, or convexity tests are sometimes performed on OLS, not BLUS residuals. For OLS residuals, the Durbin-Watson test statistic, rather than the modified von Neumann ratio test statistic, should be used. The F test and the convexity test will still be useful, although their power will not be as great as when BLUS residuals were calculated. Experience has shown that if these tests appear "significant" with OLS residuals, the functional form should be adjusted. The final form of the equation can be tested by the more computationally expensive BLUS procedure.

The RA procedure has been especially useful for cross-section equations with many right-hand-side variables. In these models, there are many possible interaction effects, which, owing to multicollinearity, may not all be possible to estimate. The best procedure is to estimate the equation first without any interaction effects and build the interaction terms as they are indicated by the tests. Further specification tests can be made with the recursive residual approach (see chap. 9).

As mentioned earlier, the BLUS procedures have two limits: the number of exogenous variables in the equation must not exceed 20 and the sum of the number of variables analyzed against outside the equation plus the number of variables in the equation must be ≤ 20. If the number of observations exceeds the internal default work array, the size of B34S can be increased via MAXSIZ, being set on the EXEC card (see the OPTIONS section of the B34S manual). If the equation contains more than 20 variables on the right-hand side, all tests must be made on OLS, rather than BLUS, residuals.

2.12   BAYES Option in B34S

B34S contains a Bayesian option that is controlled from the REGRESSION sentence with the BAYES parameter. Options include computing the marginal posterior distributions for the regression coefficients, the autoregressive coefficient, and an estimate of the population R^2 (P^2).

The output produced by the BAYES option is discussed in more detail in Zellner (1971).[8] There are severe limits to the maximum number of observations handled (100) and the code is not very efficient. When the BAYES option is used, the number of variables in the data set should remain small and, if the grid sizes are small, the user must prepare to increase the time limits. The B34S timer will give an indication of the relative costs of this option. Calculation of the "Bayes R^2" is particularly expensive.

The Bayes posterior distribution of the population value, P^2, of the sample statistic R^2 has been worked out under an "uninformative" prior density by Press and Zellner (1967). This posterior density can be listed and plotted. The mean and higher central moments for P^2 are printed beneath the density plot. The plotting and listing of the posterior R^2 is controlled by the parameter BAYES in the REGRESSION sentence. The number of points in the grid for R^2 is set by the parameter NRS. The larger NRS, the more expensive the option. The output plots the distribution of the population P^2 statistic and is useful in interpreting the significance of the findings.

The regression model without a constant and with autoregressive disturbances has been analyzed from the Bayesian view by Zellner and Tiao (1964). Given the model

$$Y_t = X_t \beta + u_t \qquad\qquad (2.12\text{-}1)$$

$$u_t = p \, u_{t-1} + \sigma e_t, \qquad\qquad (2.12\text{-}2)$$

the marginal posterior distributions for the elements of β and p, under the "uninformative" prior density, can be listed and plotted. The parameter NBE controls the number of points in the plotting grid. As is the case with NRS, the larger NBE, the more expensive the calculation. If the user desires only the distribution of some coefficients, the DM sentence allows suppression of the marginals of the other coefficients.

The BAYES option can be run after OLS or after GLS. In principle, the posterior plots of the β coefficients should be the same after OLS or after GLS; however, since the limits of integration are a function of the OLS or GLS standard errors, the horizontal scales will differ and the higher moments of the density functions will differ. If the model contained serial correlation, the OLS standard errors are biased. As a consequence, the posterior plots after GLS are preferred over the posterior plots after OLS. The time required for BAYES analysis of β_i and p increases with the square of the sample size. This, together with the fact that its output seems to be well approximated by the generalized least squares, indicate that the BAYES option is only efficient for relatively small samples.

2.13 Examples

The commands in Table 2.1 will perform OLS estimation and BLUS analysis of the Theil (1971) data on textiles. B34S produces a LOG file and an output file. Except for this one case, to save space, the B34S log file will not be listed in this book. The B34S LOG shows if the B34S commands were parsed without errors and shows the time taken for each command. As noted earlier, if each B34S paragraph ends with the sentence B34SEEND\$, all the B34S commands will be parsed prior to any commands being run.[9] If any B34S paragraph ends with the B34SRUN\$ sentence, execution is forced so that the paragraph will run before any other paragraphs are parsed.

The advantage of delayed execution of the B34S command stream is
that many errors are caught before substantial time is wasted
running an incomplete job.

The sample job listed in Table 2.1 is in the form of a named
MACRO. If this file is placed in the input stream on unit 3, the
MACRO commands that begin with the delimiter == are stripped out
automatically. On the other hand, if there are a number of B34S
MACROS of the form:

```
==NAME1
.....  commands here
==
==NAME2
......  commands here
==
```

in a file on a unit other than 3, say 55, the B34S command

```
B34SEXEC OPTIONS  INCLUDE(55) MACRO(NAME2) $ B34SEEND$
```

will select the NAME2 macro from the list of macros and run only
this MACRO. The only restriction on this feature is that the B34S
MACRO must not call another B34S MACRO.

Table 2.1 BLUS Specification Tests on Data From Theil (1971)

```
==THEIL
B34SEXEC DATA NOOB=17 NOHEAD CORR$
 INPUT TIME CT RI RPT $
 BUILD LOG10CT LOG10RI LOG10RPT$
*                        $
GEN LOG10CT  =  LOG10(CT)  $
GEN LOG10RI  =  LOG10(RI)  $
GEN LOG10RPT =  LOG10(RPT) $
*                        $
 COMMENT=('TEXTILE DATA FROM THEIL(1971) PAGE 102')$
 DATACARDS$
  1923  99.2   96.7  101
  1924  99     98.1  100.1
  1925  100    100   100
  1926  111.6  104.9  90.6
  1927  122.2  104.9  86.5
  1928  117.6  109.5  89.7
  1929  121.1  110.8  90.6
  1930  136    112.3  82.8
  1931  154.2  109.3  70.1
  1932  153.6  105.3  65.4
  1933  158.5  101.7  61.3
  1934  140.6   95.4  62.5
  1935  136.2   96.4  63.6
  1936  168     97.6  52.6
  1937  154.3  102.4  59.7
  1938  149    101.6  59.5
  1939  165.5  103.8  61.3
B34SRETURN$
B34SEEND$
B34SEXEC LIST $ VAR LOG10CT LOG10RI LOG10RPT$
B34SEEND$
B34SEXEC REGRESSION RESIDUALA BLUS=BOTH$
   COMMENT=('THEIL(1971) TEST RAW DATA')$
   MODEL CT = RI RPT$
   B34SEEND$
B34SEXEC REGRESSION RESIDUALA STEPWISE$
   COMMENT=('ILLUSTRATE CONTROLLED STEPWISE') $
   MODEL LOG10CT = LOG10RI LOG10RPT$
   ORDER CONSTANT LOG10RI$
   B34SEEND$
B34SEXEC REGRESSION RESIDUALP BLUS=BOTH$
   COMMENT=('THEIL(1971) PAGE 220 COL 1, 3, 2 RESIDUALS')$
   MODEL LOG10CT = LOG10RI LOG10RPT$
   B34SEEND$
==
```

An edited version of the B34S LOG output from running the program listed in Table 2.1 follows. After parsing each command in the input stream, it is listed.[10] After all parsing, the job runs.

```
B34S II LOG         DATE (D:M:Y) 15/11/88, TIME (H:M:S) 13.04.36, PAGE    1

WORKING STORAGE SET AS      70000 REAL*4 WORDS.

                     September 1988

To obtain the B34S on line manual, give command

     B34SEXEC HELP=MANUAL NEWPAGE$  B34SEEND$

Note:  The correct region for B34S is R=2048
```

```
B34S PARSER ENTERED.

B34SEXEC DATA NOOB=17 NOHEAD CORR$
 INPUT TIME CT RI RPT $
 BUILD LOG10CT LOG10RI LOG10RPT$
*                              $
GEN LOG10CT  =  LOG10(CT)  $
GEN LOG10RI  =  LOG10(RI)  $
GEN LOG10RPT =  LOG10(RPT) $
*                              $
 COMMENT=('TEXTILE DATA FROM THEIL(1971) PAGE 102')$
  DATACARDS$
B34SRETURN$
B34SEEND$

B34SEXEC LIST $ VAR LOG10CT LOG10RI LOG10RPT$
B34SEEND$

B34SEXEC REGRESSION RESIDUALA BLUS=BOTH$
   COMMENT=('THEIL(1971) TEST RAW DATA')$
   MODEL CT = RI RPT$
   B34SEEND$

B34SEXEC REGRESSION RESIDUALA STEPWISE$
   COMMENT=('ILLUSTRATE CONTROLLED STEPWISE') $
   MODEL LOG10CT = LOG10RI LOG10RPT$
   ORDER CONSTANT LOG10RI$
   B34SEEND$

B34SEXEC REGRESSION RESIDUALP BLUS=BOTH$
   COMMENT=('THEIL(1971) PAGE 220 COL 1, 3, 2 RESIDUALS')$
   MODEL LOG10CT = LOG10RI LOG10RPT$
   B34SEEND$

STEP ENDING. SECONDS USED  1.5199986   . TOTAL JOB SECONDS    1.5233326   .

B34S DATA STEP ENTERED.

STEP ENDING. SECONDS USED  0.36666870E-01. TOTAL JOB SECONDS   1.5699997   .

LISTING (L) OPTION CALLED.
STEP ENDING. SECONDS USED  0.26666641E-01. TOTAL JOB SECONDS   1.5966663   .
```

The THEIL MACRO first loads the data and builds LOG10 transforms of CT, RI, and RPT as suggested by Theil. CT is the consumption of textiles in the Netherlands per capita in the period 1923-1939, while RI and RPT are the real income per capita and relative price of textiles, respectively. The CORR option on the DATA paragraph outputs the correlation matrix of the data, while the NOHEAD option reduces output by deleting the B34S header. The correlation matrix listed below shows that the log to the base 10 of the relative price of textiles (LOG10RPT) is significantly negatively correlated with LOG10CT (-.93596) but that log to the base 10 of the relative income (LOG10RI) is only weakly positively correlated with the LOG10CT (.097862). Given that T=17, only the first correlation is significant, since the standard error for the correlation coefficient is $(1/16)^{.5}$ = .25. Based just on correlation analysis, the researcher might be led to give up on attempting to model the effect of RI and conclude that only LOG10RPT matters. The B34S output follows.

```
UIC  B34S DATA ANALYSIS PROGRAM 21 NOV  86                                                      PAGE   1
 VARIABLE            MEAN              STANDARD DEVIATION        VARIANCE              MAXIMUM            MINIMUM

 TIME        1    1931.0000              5.0497525            25.500000             1939.0000          1923.0000

 CT          2    134.50589             23.577332            555.89059              168.00000          99.000000

 RI          3    102.98235              5.3009711           28.100294              112.30000          95.400000

 RPT         4    76.311768             16.866234            284.46985              101.00000          52.600000

 LOG10CT     5    2.1221352             0.79113140E-01       0.62588890E-02           2.2253093          1.9956352

 LOG10RI     6    2.0122242             0.22258719E-01       0.49545059E-03           2.0503798          1.9795484

 LOG10RPT    7    1.8725815             0.96157121E-01       0.92461919E-02           2.0043214          1.7209857

 CONSTANT    8    1.0000000             0.00000000E+00       0.00000000E+00           1.0000000          1.0000000

 CURRENT B34S DATA FILE CONSISTS OF        17.  OBSERVATIONS ON  8  VARIABLES
 UIC  B34S DATA ANALYSIS PROGRAM 21 NOV  86                                                      PAGE   2
  CORRELATION MATRIX
                           1
 CT        VAR  2   0.89535
                           1                  2
 RI        VAR  3  -0.98763E-01       0.61769E-01
                           1                  2                  3
 RPT       VAR  4  -0.94135           -0.94664           0.17885
                           1                  2                  3                  4
 LOG10CT   VAR  5   0.89914            0.99744           0.93936E-01   -0.94836
                           1                  2                  3                  4                  5
 LOG10RI   VAR  6  -0.95011E-01       0.66213E-01        0.99973            0.17511            0.97862E-01
                           1                  2                  3                  4                  5                  6
 LOG10RPT  VAR  7  -0.93807           -0.93820           0.22599            0.99750           -0.93596           0.22212
                           1                  2                  3                  4                  5                  6                  7
 CONSTANT  VAR  8   0.00000E+00       0.00000E+00        0.00000E+00    0.00000E+00        0.00000E+00        0.00000E+00        0.00000E+00
 STEP ENDING. SECONDS USED  0.36666870E-01. TOTAL JOB SECONDS     1.5699997   .
```

The LIST command displays the transformed data. This output is not shown. The first REGRESSION command performs OLS estimation, using the raw data. BLUS residuals are calculated for heteroskedasticity and serial correlation tests but since the RESIDUALA option was selected, the BLUS RESIDUALS were not listed. The second REGRESSION command illustrates controlled stepwise estimation. The ORDER command forces in the variables CONSTANT and LOG10RI first. Output for this paragraph, which has not been listed to save space, indicates that the t for LOG10RI is .3808 when only CONSTANT and LOG10RI are in the regression but that for the complete model the t scores for CONSTANT, LOG10RI and LOG10RPT become 4.489, 7.328, and -22.95, respectively.

The final REGRESSION command, whose output is listed below, illustrates the out-of-core BLUS option and replicates BLUS residual output given on page 220 of Theil (1971). The OLS results indicate CONSTANT, LOG10RI, and LOG10RPT and all significant predictors of LOG10CT when all variables are in the regression. The adjusted R^2 of the regression is .9707. Computational error estimates of .000, .3324E-11, and .5314E-13 indicate that multicollinearity is not a problem in this model. The number of observations in this problem is too small, even for the small sample normality test, which requires a cell size of 5 or greater. Nevertheless, there is no indication of a lack of normality of the residuals since the probability of the F test for the small sample test is only .6174. Readers are encouraged to verify that the residuals listed are the same as given in Theil (1971). Since the

BLUS=BOTH option was specified, BLUS analysis is performed for the best BLUS base for serial correlation (see output for option 5) and the best base for heteroskedasticity (see output for option 2).

The BLUS serial correlation test searches over the three admissible bases. The sum of the eigenvalues for the 1, 2, 3 base was .99; the 1, 2, 17 base 1.138; the 1, 16, 17 base 1.116 and for the 15, 16, 17 base .6784. B34S automatically selected the 1, 2, 17 base since the sum (1.138) was greatest. Theil (1971, 221) lists these results, which the reader is invited to verify. The modified von Neumann ratio statistic (von Neumann ratio 1) 1.04733 is a one-tailed test against positive autocorrelation. It is significant at the 1% level but not significant at the 5% level. For further details see Theil (1971, 221).

The BLUS heteroskedasticity test selects a base from the center of the observations. In this case, the base is unique and consists of 8, 9, 10. The F statistic for heteroskedasticity is 1.398 (this is actually 1/F since F < 1.0), which is not significant. BLUS analysis of the Theil problem shows no evidence of heteroskedasticity but some evidence of serial correlation. Although the number of observations is small, it is useful as an example for the B34S REGRESSION command since the residuals can be listed. For larger problems, the RESIDUALA option is usually used to save paper. The B34S REGRESSION command output follows.

```
UIC  B34S DATA ANALYSIS PROGRAM 21 NOV  86                                              PAGE   7

COMMENT     THEIL(1971) PAGE 220 COL 1, 3, 2 RESIDUALS

***************
  PROBLEM NUMBER                  1
  SUBPROBLEM NUMBER               3

  F TO ENTER                      0.10000002E-01
  F TO REMOVE                     0.49999990E-02
  TOLERANCE                       0.99999998E-05
  MAXIMUM NO OF STEPS             3
  DEPENDENT VARIABLE X( 5).  VARIABLE NAME  LOG10CT

  THE FOLLOWING VARIABLES ARE DELETED IN THIS SUBPROBLEM

  1   2   3   4

  THE FOLLOWING VARIABLES ARE FORCED INTO THE REGRESSION EQUATION AS CONTROL VARIABLES (COVARIATES)

  6   7   8

STANDARD ERROR OF Y =   0.79113126E-01   FOR DEGREES OF FREEDOM =        16.


.............
STEP NUMBER  3                            ANALYSIS OF VARIANCE FOR REDUCTION IN SS DUE TO VARIABLE ENTERING
   VARIABLE ENTERING      6              SOURCE          DF      SS           MS              F          F SIG.
   MULTIPLE R          0.98710          DUE REGRESSION    2   0.97582E-01   0.48791E-01     266.04      1.000000
   STD ERROR OF Y.X    0.01354          DEV. FROM REG.   14   0.25676E-02   0.18340E-03
   R SQUARE            0.97436          TOTAL            16   0.10015       0.62593E-02

   MULTIPLE REGRESSION EQUATION
   VARIABLE    COEFFICIENT    STD. ERROR     T VAL.    T SIG. P. COR. ELASTICITY    PARTIAL COR. FOR VAR. NOT IN EQUATION
LOG10CT  =                                                                          VARIABLE    COEFFICIENT   F FOR SELECTION
LOG10RI   X- 6  1.143156    0.1560002       7.328     1.00000  0.8906    1.084
LOG10RPT  X- 7 -0.8288375   0.3611135E-01  -22.95     1.00000 -0.9870   -0.7314
CONSTANT  X- 8  1.373914    0.3060903       4.489     0.99949

ADJUSTED R SQUARE FOR K=  3, N=      17 IS    0.97069794

-2  *  LN(MAXIMUM OF THE LIKELIHOOD FUNCTION)  -101.32217

AKAIKE  INFORMATION CRITERION (AIC) BASED ON JOINT LIKELIHOOD OF SIGMA AND BETA   -93.322167

SCHWARZ INFORMATION CRITERION (SIC) BASED ON JOINT LIKELIHOOD OF SIGMA AND BETA   -89.989314

NOTE: MODELS WITH LOWER AIC OR SIC ARE BETTER.

AIC = (N * LN(2*PI) ) + ( N * LN((SUM RES SQ)/N)) + N + (2*(K+1))
```

```
SIC = AIC - (2*(K+1))  +  ((K+1) * LN(N))


 RESIDUAL VARIANCE =   0.18339862E-03

 ORDER OF ENTRANCE (OR DELETION) OF THE VARIABLES =   8   7   6

 ESTIMATE OF COMPUTATIONAL ERROR IN COEFFICIENTS =
    1  0.3324E-11     2  0.5314E-13     3  0.0000E+00

 COVARIANCE MATRIX OF REGRESSION COEFFICIENTS

 ROW  1    VARIABLE X- 6    LOG10RI
      0.24336056E-01

 ROW  2    VARIABLE X- 7    LOG10RPT
     -0.12513115E-02  0.13040301E-02

 ROW  3    VARIABLE X- 8    CONSTANT
     -0.46626424E-01  0.76017246E-04  0.93691270E-01

 === PROGRAM TERMINATED - ALL VARIABLES PUT IN

                    TABLE OF RESIDUALS

 OBSERVATION Y VALUE    Y ESTIMATE    RESIDUAL      ADJRES
     1       1.9965       1.9823      0.14202E-01   1.05                              I       .
     2       1.9956       1.9927      0.29672E-02   0.219                             I .
     3       2.0000       2.0026     -0.25514E-02  -0.188                           . I
     4       2.0477       2.0618     -0.14171E-01  -1.05                        .    I
     5       2.0871       2.0785      0.85668E-02   0.633                             I    .
     6       2.0704       2.0867     -0.16328E-01  -1.21                       .      I
     7       2.0831       2.0890     -0.58569E-02  -0.432                          .  I
     8       2.1335       2.1281      0.54561E-02   0.403                             I  .
     9       2.1881       2.1746      0.13509E-01   0.998                             I     .
    10       2.1864       2.1810      0.53446E-02   0.395                             I  .
    11       2.2000       2.1871      0.12948E-01   0.956                             I     .
    12       2.1480       2.1484     -0.36894E-03  -0.272E-01                         .
    13       2.1342       2.1473     -0.13074E-01  -0.965                      .      I
    14       2.2253       2.2217      0.35609E-02   0.263                             I  .
    15       2.1884       2.2000     -0.11641E-01  -0.860                     .       I
    16       2.1732       2.1973     -0.24134E-01  -1.78                   .         I
    17       2.2188       2.1972      0.21570E-01   1.59                             I        .

 VON NEUMANN RATIO 1 ...              2.04710         DURBIN-WATSON TEST.....   1.92669
 VON NEUMANN RATIO 2 ...              2.04710

 FOR D. F.   14 T(.9999)=  5.3626, T(.999)= 4.1407, T(.99)= 2.9774, T(.95)= 2.1453, T(.90)= 1.7617, T(.80)= 1.3452

 SKEWNESS TEST (ALPHA 3) = -.159503      , PEAKEDNESS TEST (ALPHA 4)=  1.44345

                          NORMALITY TEST-- EXTENDED GRID, CELL SIZE =   1.70
 T STAT         INFIN   1.762   1.345   1.076   0.868   0.692   0.536   0.393   0.258   0.128
 CELL NO.       1.000   1.000   1.000   5.000   1.000   1.000   3.000   1.000   2.000   1.000
 INTERVAL       1.000   0.900   0.800   0.700   0.600   0.500   0.400   0.300   0.200   0.100
 ACT PER        1.000   0.941   0.882   0.824   0.529   0.471   0.412   0.235   0.176   0.059

                          NORMALITY TEST -- SMALL SAMPLE GRID              CELL SIZE =   3.40
 CELL NO.       2.000           6.000           2.000           4.000           3.000
 INTERVAL       1.000           0.800           0.600           0.400           0.200
 ACT PER        1.000           0.882           0.529           0.412           0.176

 EXTENDED GRID NORMALITY TEST - PROB OF REJECTING NORMALITY ASSUMPTION
 CHI=   9.471    CHI PROB=  0.6958     F(8,  14)=  1.18382     F PROB =0.626481

 SMALL SAMPLE NORMALITY TEST - LARGE GRID
 CHI=   3.294    CHI PROB=  0.6515     F(3,  14)=  1.09804     F PROB =0.617396

 AUTOCORRELATION FUNCTION OF RESIDUALS

    1) -0.0990     2) -0.1061     3)  0.0862     4) -0.3157

 F-RATIO FOR HETEROSKEDASTICITY =  0.5544     1/F =   1.804      D.F.(  6,  6)  HETEROSKEDASTICITY AT    0.7544  LEVEL

 SUM OF SQUARED RESIDUALS =  0.2568E-02       MEAN SQUARED RESIDUAL =  0.1510E-03

 BLUS OPTION 7 SELECTED, BLUS 5 DONE FIRST THEN BLUS 2

 UIC  B34S DATA ANALYSIS PROGRAM 21 NOV 86                                        PAGE   8

 RESIDUAL ESTIMATES USING BLUS TRANSFORMATION.  OPTION      5



 BLUS  1     0.9900           1    2    3

 BLUS  2     1.138            1    2   17

 BLUS  3     1.116            1   16   17

 BLUS  4     0.6784          15   16   17
       EIGVAL 1 =   0.7756
       EIGVAL 2 =   0.3271
       EIGVAL 3 =   0.3534E-01       RECIPROCAL OF COND OF X0 MATRIX   0.28746459E-03

 BLUS....SUM EIG. =    1.138       OBS. DELETED =    1    2   17

                    TABLE OF RESIDUALS

 OBSERVATION Y VALUE    Y ESTIMATE    RESIDUAL      ADJRES
     3       2.0000       2.0050     -0.49588E-02  -0.366                      .    I
     4       2.0477       2.0632     -0.15502E-01  -1.14                     .      I
     5       2.0871       2.0802      0.68482E-02   0.506                           I   .
     6       2.0704       2.0864     -0.16039E-01  -1.18                    .       I
     7       2.0831       2.0882     -0.50158E-02  -0.370                      .    I
```

```
 8     2.1335     2.1275     0.60795E-02   0.449                                    I
 9     2.1881     2.1764     0.11667E-01   0.862                                    I.       .
10     2.1864     2.1849     0.14426E-02   0.107                                    I.
11     2.2000     2.1929     0.71242E-02   0.526                                    I  .
12     2.1480     2.1566    -0.85705E-02  -0.633                              .      I
13     2.1342     2.1549    -0.20716E-01  -1.53                                     I
14     2.2253     2.2305    -0.51751E-02  -0.382                             .     I
15     2.1884     2.2058    -0.17413E-01  -1.29                              .      I
16     2.1732     2.2034    -0.30246E-01  -2.23                         .           I

VON NEUMANN RATIO 1 ...              1.04733          DURBIN-WATSON TEST.....     0.97252
VON NEUMANN RATIO 2 ...              1.35615

SKEWNESS TEST (ALPHA 3) = -1.38648    , PEAKEDNESS TEST (ALPHA 4)=   2.69489

                          NORMALITY TEST-- EXTENDED GRID, CELL SIZE =    1.40
T STAT        INFIN   1.762   1.345   1.076   0.868   0.692   0.536   0.393   0.258   0.128
CELL NO.      1.000   1.000   3.000   0.000   1.000   1.000   3.000   0.000   1.000   1.000
INTERVAL      1.000   0.900   0.800   0.700   0.600   0.500   0.400   0.300   0.200   0.100
ACT PER       1.000   0.929   0.857   0.643   0.643   0.571   0.500   0.286   0.071   0.071
                          NORMALITY TEST -- SMALL SAMPLE GRID              CELL SIZE =    2.80
CELL NO.      2.000           3.000           2.000           6.000           1.000
INTERVAL      1.000           0.800           0.600           0.400           0.200
ACT PER       1.000           0.857           0.643           0.500           0.071

EXTENDED GRID NORMALITY TEST - PROB OF REJECTING NORMALITY ASSUMPTION
CHI=  8.857    CHI PROB=  0.6455      F(8,  14)=  1.10714      F PROB =0.585901

SMALL SAMPLE NORMALITY TEST - LARGE GRID
CHI=  5.286    CHI PROB=  0.8480      F(3,  14)=  1.76190      F PROB =0.799490

AUTOCORRELATION FUNCTION OF RESIDUALS

  1)  0.3562    2)  0.2353    3)  0.3256    4) -0.1169

F-RATIO FOR HETEROSKEDASTICITY =  0.4071     1/F =   2.457      D.F.(  4,  5)  HETEROSKEDASTICITY AT    0.7977 LEVEL

SUM OF SQUARED RESIDUALS =  0.2568E-02       MEAN SQUARED RESIDUAL =  0.1834E-03

UIC B34S DATA ANALYSIS PROGRAM 21 NOV 86                                                   PAGE   9

RESIDUAL ESTIMATES USING BLUS TRANSFORMATION. OPTION    2


      EIGVAL 1 =   0.6773
      EIGVAL 2 =   0.2292
      EIGVAL 3 =   0.3820E-01    RECIPROCAL OF COND OF X0 MATRIX  0.57985517E-03

BLUS....SUM EIG. =  0.9448     OBS. DELETED =     8   9  10

               TABLE OF RESIDUALS
OBSERVATION Y VALUE    Y ESTIMATE   RESIDUAL      ADJRES
      1      1.9965     1.9777     0.18815E-01   1.39                              I           .
      2      1.9956     1.9887     0.68914E-02   0.509                             I  .
      3      2.0000     1.9995     0.54473E-03   0.402E-01                         .I
      4      2.0477     2.0616    -0.13944E-01  -1.03                        .     I
      5      2.0871     2.0787     0.84066E-02   0.621                             I  .
      6      2.0704     2.0884    -0.18013E-01  -1.33                       .      I
      7      2.0831     2.0911    -0.79685E-02  -0.588                        .    I
     11      2.2000     2.1888     0.11234E-01   0.830                             I   .
     12      2.1480     2.1472     0.81170E-03   0.599E-01                         I.
     13      2.1342     2.1464    -0.12193E-01  -0.900                      .      I
     14      2.2253     2.2230     0.23261E-02   0.172                             I .
     15      2.1884     2.2022    -0.13869E-01  -1.02                        .     I
     16      2.1732     2.1992    -0.26056E-01  -1.92                   .          I
     17      2.2188     2.1998     0.18982E-01   1.40                              I           .

VON NEUMANN RATIO 1 ...              2.09200          DURBIN-WATSON TEST.....     1.94257
VON NEUMANN RATIO 2 ...              2.12617

SKEWNESS TEST (ALPHA 3) = -.442431    , PEAKEDNESS TEST (ALPHA 4)=   2.00814

                          NORMALITY TEST-- EXTENDED GRID, CELL SIZE =    1.40
T STAT        INFIN   1.762   1.345   1.076   0.868   0.692   0.536   0.393   0.258   0.128
CELL NO.      1.000   2.000   1.000   3.000   1.000   2.000   1.000   0.000   1.000   2.000
INTERVAL      1.000   0.900   0.800   0.700   0.600   0.500   0.400   0.300   0.200   0.100
ACT PER       1.000   0.929   0.786   0.714   0.500   0.429   0.286   0.214   0.214   0.143
                          NORMALITY TEST -- SMALL SAMPLE GRID              CELL SIZE =    2.80
CELL NO.      3.000           4.000           3.000           1.000           3.000
INTERVAL      1.000           0.800           0.600           0.400           0.200
ACT PER       1.000           0.786           0.500           0.286           0.214

EXTENDED GRID NORMALITY TEST - PROB OF REJECTING NORMALITY ASSUMPTION
CHI=  4.571    CHI PROB=  0.1978      F(8,  14)= 0.571428      F PROB =0.215209

SMALL SAMPLE NORMALITY TEST - LARGE GRID
CHI=  1.714    CHI PROB=  0.3662      F(3,  14)= 0.571428      F PROB =0.356985

AUTOCORRELATION FUNCTION OF RESIDUALS

  1) -0.1189    2) -0.1798    3)  0.2233    4) -0.1785

F-RATIO FOR HETEROSKEDASTICITY =  0.7153     1/F =   1.398      D.F.(  6,  6)  HETEROSKEDASTICITY AT    0.6528 LEVEL

SUM OF SQUARED RESIDUALS =  0.2568E-02       MEAN SQUARED RESIDUAL =  0.1834E-03

STEP ENDING. SECONDS USED 0.22000027  . TOTAL JOB SECONDS    2.0699997  .
```

The next example is based on the Sinai and Stokes (1972)

analysis of the effect of real money balances on real output in a Cobb-Douglas production function. Sinai and Stokes (1972) used the Christensen and Jorgenson (1969, 1970) production data for the United States in the period 1929 through 1967. These data are later used in chapter 9 to illustrate equation dynamic stability tests, using recursive residuals, and in chapter 11 to illustrate nonlinear estimation options. The control setup for this problem is listed in Table 2.2.

The data are first loaded and OLS and up to second-order GLS results are given for production function models. Data on real output (Q), labor (L), capital (K), nominal money defined as M1, and nominal money defined as M2 were collected for the period 1929 through 1967. The money series were deflated by an index of factor prices (P) to form real balances, which we will call m1 and m2, respectively. The Cobb-Douglas production function is defined as

$$Q = Ae^{\mu T}L^{\alpha}K^{\beta}m1^{\delta}u,\qquad\qquad\qquad (2.13-1)$$

where T is a time trend. Equation (2.13-1) is usually estimated in log linear form as

$$\ln Q = \ln A + \mu\,T + \alpha\,\ln L + \beta\,\ln K + \delta\,\ln m1 + \ln u.\qquad (2.13-2)$$

When equation (2.13-2) is estimated for time-series data, it is important to test for serial correlation, heteroskedasticity, multicollinearity, and normality of the residuals.[11] The sample job listed in Table 2.2 first builds real money balances for M1 and M2. Next, all data are logged. Two regressions are run. The first contains ln L, ln K, and ln m1, while the second contains ln L, ln K, ln m1, and T. If real balances are significant in an equation not containing time, the question becomes do real balances just proxy for time. To save space, only the second of the two equations has been listed. Since MAXGLS=2, the job will run zero-order GLS (OLS), first-order GLS, and second-order GLS if needed. The parameter TOLL=.1E-12 was set to control for the multicollinearity in the data. The TOLL option must be used with caution and the estimated error of the coefficients must be checked closely.

Table 2.2 Real Money Balances in the Production Function

```
==SSRES
B34SEXEC DATA NOOB=39 NOHEAD$
COMMENT=('Data on Q, L, K, M1 and M2 from Stokes and Sinai (1972)')$
INPUT TIME P K L M1 M2 Q  $
BUILD M1DP M2DP LNK LNL LNQ LNRM1 LNRM2$
GEN M1DP=DIV(M1,P)$
GEN M2DP=DIV(M2,P)$
GEN LNK=LOG(K)$
GEN LNL=LOG(L)$
GEN LNQ=LOG(Q)$
GEN LNRM1=LOG(M1DP)$
GEN LNRM2=LOG(M2DP)$
DATACARDS$
   1929  .394   87.8  173.3   26.65   46.57  189.8
   1930  .355   87.8  165.4   25.71   45.66  172.1
   1931  .318   84    158.2   24.04   42.43  159.1
   1932  .262   78.3  141.7   21.05   35.93  135.6
   1933  .254   76.6  141.6   19.89   32.09  132
   1934  .269   76    148     21.99   34.53  141.8
   1935  .3     77.7  154.4   26.07   39.28  153.9
   1936  .318   79.1  163.5   29.96   43.67  171.5
   1937  .342   80    172     30.84   45.66  183
   1938  .328   77.6  161.5   30.63   45.62  173.2
   1939  .344   81.4  168.6   34.33   49.47  188.5
   1940  .358   87    176.5   39.91   55.48  205.5
   1941  .405   96.2  192.4   46.78   62.77  236
   1942  .466  104.4  205.1   55.96   71.78  257.8
   1943  .53   110    210.1   72.95   90.75  277.5
   1944  .563  107.8  208.8   85.78  107.47  291.1
   1945  .581  102.1  202.1   99.73  127.37  284.5
   1946  .624   97.2  213.4  109.19  139.1   274
   1947  .672  105.9  223.6  111.8   146     279.9
   1948  .71   113    228.2  112.38  148.13  297.6
   1949  .707  114.9  221.3  111.15  147.5   297.7
   1950  .767  124.1  228.8  114.13  150.8   328.9
   1951  .827  134.5  239    119.2   156.45  351.4
   1952  .85   139.7  241.7  125.23  164.93  360.4
   1953  .869  147.4  245.2  128.35  171.18  378.9
   1954  .889  148.9  237.4  130.33  177.18  375.8
   1955  .927  158.6  245.9  134.45  183.73  406.7
   1956  .946  167.1  251.6  136     186.88  416.3
   1957  .98   171.9  251.5  136.7   191.83  422.8
   1958 1      173.1  245.1  138.33  201.15  418.4
   1959 1.036  182.5  254.9  142.78  209.65  445.7
   1960 1.052  189    259.6  140.9   209.93  457.3
   1961 1.078  194.1  258.1  143.13  220.63  466.3
   1962 1.122  202.3  264.6  146.18  233.1   495.3
   1963 1.15   205.4  268.5  150.63  248.48  515.5
   1964 1.18   215.9  275.4  156.35  263.93  544.1
   1965 1.234  225    285.3  162.58  284.73  579.2
   1966 1.285  236.2  297.4  169.85  306.83  615.6
   1967 1.292  247.9  305    176.43  330.4   631.1
B34SRETURN$ B34SEEND$
B34SEXEC REGRESSION RESIDUALA MAXGLS=2 TOLL=.1E-12$
   COMMENT=('OLS, GLS1, GLS2 VERSIONS OF SINAI - STOKES(1972) ')$
   MODEL LNQ = LNK LNL LNRM1 $  B34SEEND$
B34SEXEC REGRESSION RESIDUALA MAXGLS=2 TOLL=.1E-12$
   COMMENT=('OLS, GLS1, GLS2 VERSIONS OF SINAI - STOKES(1972) WITH T')$
   MODEL LNQ = LNK LNL LNRM1 TIME$  B34SEEND$
==
```

The results of estimating equation (2.13-2) are given below. The OLS results initially indicated that only LNK and LNL were significant (t scores of 3.65 and 7.96, respectively), but these significance tests are suspect since the Durbin-Watson test statistic was .76, which indicates substantial serial correlation. Since the MAXGLS option was selected, B34S automatically tries first-order GLS. The Durbin-Watson test statistic now improves to 1.0655, Φ from equation (2.5-2) is .5951 and t scores for all variables except TIME are above 2.2 in absolute value. The problem with this equation is that the Durbin-Watson test statistic is inside the 1% bounds of 1.07 -1.52 for n=38 and K=5.

The second-order GLS output, which was reported in Table 1 of Sinai and Stokes (1972) and which is listed below, has a Durbin-Watson test statistic of 1.45, and t scores for LNK, LNL, LNRM1, and TIME of 3.68, 7.83, 2.46 and 1.47, respectively. The tentative conclusion is that the log of real money balances, defined as m1, is not a proxy for the TIME variable and should be considered as a possible input in the production function.[12] Since the TOLL parameter was passed, there is a danger that multicollinearity might be a problem in this equation. Inspection of the estimate of the computational error of the coefficients shows -.1560E-4, .1835E-08, -.6326E-09, .4537E-09, and .5038E-08 for TIME, LNK, LNL, LNRM1, and the CONSTANT and indicates that the TIME coefficient is most affected by the multicollinearity.

The small-sample normality test shows F(3,32)=1.67567, which is not significant (.8081), indicating normality is not a problem. The BLUS test is the preferred way to test for heteroskedasticity. To save space, a less powerful test is performed on the OLS residual. This F(12,12) was found to be 1.929 for the reported second-order model, which is not significant (.8653). This brief discussion of a time series example only highlights some of the B34S REGRESSION command options. Sinai and Stokes (1989) discuss some of the literature on this problem since their earlier work (1972).

```
UIC  B34S DATA ANALYSIS PROGRAM 21 NOV 86                                    PAGE  12

COMMENT      OLS, GLS1, GLS2 VERSIONS OF SINAI - STOKES(1972) WITH T

***************
  PROBLEM NUMBER                 2
  SUBPROBLEM NUMBER              2

  F TO ENTER              0.10000002E-01
  F TO REMOVE             0.49999990E-02
  TOLERANCE               0.99999978E-13
  MAXIMUM NO OF STEPS           5
  DEPENDENT VARIABLE X(12).  VARIABLE NAME  LNQ

  THE FOLLOWING VARIABLES ARE DELETED IN THIS SUBPROBLEM

  2   3   4   5   6   7   8   9  14

THE FOLLOWING VARIABLES ARE FORCED INTO THE REGRESSION EQUATION AS CONTROL VARIABLES (COVARIATES)

  1  10  11  13  15

STANDARD ERROR OF Y =   0.46095902      FOR DEGREES OF FREEDOM =      38.


.............
STEP NUMBER  5                        ANALYSIS OF VARIANCE FOR REDUCTION IN SS DUE TO VARIABLE ENTERING
  VARIABLE ENTERING   15                  SOURCE        DF      SS              MS              F          F SIG.
  MULTIPLE R          0.99777        DUE REGRESSION      4    8.0386          2.0096         1899.0      1.000000
  STD ERROR OF Y.X    0.03253        DEV. FROM REG.     34    0.35981E-01     0.10583E-02
  R SQUARE            0.99554        TOTAL              38    8.0745          0.21249

    MULTIPLE REGRESSION EQUATION
  VARIABLE     COEFFICIENT    STD. ERROR    T VAL.     T SIG. P. COR. ELASTICITY    PARTIAL COR. FOR VAR. NOT IN EQUATION
LNQ      =                                                                          VARIABLE    COEFFICIENT    F FOR SELECTION
TIME     X- 1  0.3042050E-02  0.2852789E-02  1.066    0.70622  0.1799   1.042
LNK      X-10  0.4058444      0.1112006      3.650    0.99913  0.5306   0.3439
LNL      X-11  1.196714       0.1503472      7.960    1.00000  0.8067   1.128
LNRM1    X-13  0.7133661E-01  0.5908095E-01  1.207    0.76440  0.2028   0.6019E-01
```

```
CONSTANT   X-15  -8.950424        5.167751      -1.732     0.90766

ADJUSTED R SQUARE FOR K=   5,  N=      39  IS    0.99501932

-2  *  LN(MAXIMUM OF THE LIKELIHOOD FUNCTION)   -161.86698

AKAIKE  INFORMATION CRITERION (AIC) BASED ON JOINT LIKELIHOOD OF SIGMA AND BETA    -149.86698

SCHWARZ INFORMATION CRITERION (SIC) BASED ON JOINT LIKELIHOOD OF SIGMA AND BETA    -139.88561

NOTE: MODELS WITH LOWER AIC OR SIC ARE BETTER.

AIC = (N * LN(2*PI) ) + ( N * LN((SUM RES SQ)/N)) + N + (2*(K+1))

SIC = AIC - (2*(K+1))   +  ((K+1) * LN(N))


RESIDUAL VARIANCE =   0.10582789E-02

ORDER OF ENTRANCE (OR DELETION) OF THE VARIABLES =  10  13   1  11  15

ESTIMATE OF COMPUTATIONAL ERROR IN COEFFICIENTS =
    1 -0.1560E-04     2  0.1835E-08     3 -0.6326E-09     4  0.4537E-09     5  0.5038E-08

  COVARIANCE MATRIX OF REGRESSION COEFFICIENTS

ROW   1    VARIABLE X- 1    TIME
      0.81384052E-05

ROW   2    VARIABLE X-10    LNK
     -0.25498943E-03  0.12365577E-01

ROW   3    VARIABLE X-11    LNL
      0.11238050E-03 -0.12792876E-01  0.22604267E-01

ROW   4    VARIABLE X-13    LNRM1
     -0.10618865E-03  0.55519079E-02 -0.70797531E-02  0.34905587E-02

ROW   5    VARIABLE X-15    CONSTANT
     -0.14717615E-01  0.47905504    -0.24444731      0.20129630   26.705646

=== PROGRAM TERMINATED - ALL VARIABLES PUT IN

           RESIDUAL STATISTICS FOR...

              ORIGINAL DATA

VON NEUMANN RATIO 1 ...        0.78202        DURBIN-WATSON TEST.....   0.76197
VON NEUMANN RATIO 2 ...        0.78202

FOR D. F.  34 T(.9999)=   4.4052, T(.999)= 3.6010, T(.99)= 2.7289, T(.95)= 2.0327, T(.90)= 1.6913, T(.80)= 1.3071

SKEWNESS TEST (ALPHA 3) = 0.281855   ,  PEAKEDNESS TEST (ALPHA 4)=   2.80789

                    NORMALITY TEST-- EXTENDED GRID,  CELL SIZE =   3.90
T STAT       INFIN  1.691  1.307  1.052  0.852  0.681  0.529  0.388  0.255  0.126
CELL NO.     4.000  1.000  4.000  4.000  2.000  6.000  3.000  4.000  5.000  6.000
INTERVAL     1.000  0.900  0.800  0.700  0.600  0.500  0.400  0.300  0.200  0.100
ACT PER      1.000  0.897  0.872  0.769  0.667  0.615  0.462  0.385  0.282  0.154

                    NORMALITY TEST -- SMALL SAMPLE GRID               CELL SIZE =   7.80
CELL NO.     5.000         8.000         8.000         7.000        11.000
INTERVAL     1.000         0.800         0.600         0.400         0.200
ACT PER      1.000         0.872         0.667         0.462         0.282

EXTENDED GRID NORMALITY TEST - PROB OF REJECTING NORMALITY ASSUMPTION
CHI=   5.872   CHI PROB=  0.3384    F(8,  34)= 0.733973   F PROB =0.339024

SMALL SAMPLE NORMALITY TEST - LARGE GRID
CHI=   2.410   CHI PROB=  0.5083    F(3,  34)= 0.803418   F PROB =0.499307

AUTOCORRELATION FUNCTION OF RESIDUALS

   1)  0.6042    2)  0.0464    3) -0.1711    4)  -0.0633

F-RATIO FOR HETEROSKEDASTICITY =  3.883    1/F =  0.2575     D.F.( 13, 13)  HETEROSKEDASTICITY AT    0.9898  LEVEL

SUM OF SQUARED RESIDUALS =  0.3598E-01     MEAN SQUARED RESIDUAL =  0.9226E-03

DOING GEN. LEAST SQUARES USING RESIDUAL DIF. EQ. OF ORDER   1.  LAG COEFFICIENTS =

   1) 0.5951

STANDARD ERROR OF Y =   0.49172741      FOR DEGREES OF FREEDOM =       37.
```

```
............
STEP NUMBER  5                       ANALYSIS OF VARIANCE FOR REDUCTION IN SS DUE TO VARIABLE ENTERING
  VARIABLE ENTERING     1           SOURCE            DF      SS          MS           F         F SIG.
  MULTIPLE R            0.99394     DUE REGRESSION     4    8.8384      2.2096      674.81      1.000000
  STD ERROR OF Y.X      0.05722     DEV. FROM REG.    33    0.10806     0.32744E-02
  R SQUARE              0.98792     TOTAL             37    8.9464      0.24180

   MULTIPLE REGRESSION EQUATION
  VARIABLE      COEFFICIENT     STD. ERROR     T VAL.    T SIG. P. COR. ELASTICITY   PARTIAL COR. FOR VAR. NOT IN EQUATION
LNQ                                                                                   VARIABLE     COEFFICIENT   F FOR SELECTION
  TIME    X- 1  0.7645990E-02  0.4200708E-02   1.820    0.92219  0.3021   2.619
  LNK     X-10  0.4110616      0.1278802       3.214    0.99708  0.4883   0.3483
  LNL     X-11  0.9084591      0.1414818       6.421    1.00000  0.7453   0.8561
  LNRM1   X-13  0.1789398      0.6537314E-01   2.737    0.99010  0.4302   0.1510
  CONSTANT X-15 -16.92504      7.576805       -2.234    0.96761

ADJUSTED R SQUARE FOR K=   5,  N=      38  IS    0.98645759
```

-2 * LN(MAXIMUM OF THE LIKELIHOOD FUNCTION) -114.94301

AKAIKE INFORMATION CRITERION (AIC) BASED ON JOINT LIKELIHOOD OF SIGMA AND BETA   -102.94301

SCHWARZ INFORMATION CRITERION (SIC) BASED ON JOINT LIKELIHOOD OF SIGMA AND BETA   -93.117493

NOTE: MODELS WITH LOWER AIC OR SIC ARE BETTER.

AIC = (N * LN(2*PI)) + (N * LN((SUM RES SQ)/N)) + N + (2*(K+1))

SIC = AIC - (2*(K+1)) + ((K+1) * LN(N))

RESIDUAL VARIANCE =   0.32744200E-02

ORDER OF ENTRANCE (OR DELETION) OF THE VARIABLES =   10 13 15 11   1

COVARIANCE MATRIX OF REGRESSION COEFFICIENTS

ROW 1   VARIABLE X- 1   TIME
        0.17645959E-04

ROW 2   VARIABLE X-10   LNK
       -0.44610245E-03 0.16353348E-01

ROW 3   VARIABLE X-11   LNL
        0.20322181E-04 -0.98716413E-02 0.20017127E-01

ROW 4   VARIABLE X-13   LNRM1
       -0.11287074E-03 0.48718226E-02 -0.56731474E-02 0.42736501E-02

ROW 5   VARIABLE X-15   CONSTANT
       -0.31800506E-01 0.81987013   -0.71936862E-01 0.20624857   57.408015

=== PROGRAM TERMINATED - ALL VARIABLES PUT IN

              RESIDUAL STATISTICS FOR...

                    SMOOTHED

                 ORIGINAL DATA
FOR GLS Y AND Y ESTIMATE SCALED BY   0.404934

VON NEUMANN RATIO 1 ...   1.09439   DURBIN-WATSON TEST.....   1.06559
VON NEUMANN RATIO 2 ...   1.09439

FOR D. F.   33 T(.9999)= 4.4225, T(.999)= 3.6112, T(.99)= 2.7338, T(.95)= 2.0350, T(.90)= 1.6927, T(.80)= 1.3079

SKEWNESS TEST (ALPHA 3) -.639379   , PEAKEDNESS TEST (ALPHA 4)= 3.00665

                          NORMALITY TEST-- EXTENDED GRID, CELL SIZE =   3.80
T STAT   INFIN 1.693 1.308 1.053 0.852 0.682 0.529 0.388 0.255 0.126
CELL NO.   3.000 1.000 3.000 6.000 3.000 5.000 4.000 4.000 5.000 4.000
INTERVAL   1.000 0.900 0.800 0.700 0.600 0.500 0.400 0.300 0.200 0.100
ACT PER   1.000 0.921 0.895 0.816 0.658 0.579 0.447 0.342 0.237 0.105

                          NORMALITY TEST -- SMALL SAMPLE GRID   CELL SIZE =   7.60
CELL NO.   4.000   9.000   8.000   8.000   9.000
INTERVAL   1.000   0.800   0.600   0.400   0.200
ACT PER   1.000   0.895   0.658   0.447   0.237

EXTENDED GRID NORMALITY TEST - PROB OF REJECTING NORMALITY ASSUMPTION
CHI=   4.632   CHI PROB= 0.2039   F(8, 33)= 0.578946   F PROB =0.212404

SMALL SAMPLE NORMALITY TEST - LARGE GRID
CHI=   2.263   CHI PROB= 0.4804   F(3, 33)= 0.754386   F PROB =0.472273

AUTOCORRELATION FUNCTION OF RESIDUALS

  1) 0.4570   2) -0.0542   3) -0.1735   4) -0.0780

F-RATIO FOR HETEROSKEDASTICITY =   2.555   1/F = 0.3915   D.F.(13, 13) HETEROSKEDASTICITY AT   0.9485 LEVEL

SUM OF SQUARED RESIDUALS =   0.1081   MEAN SQUARED RESIDUAL = 0.2844E-02

DOING GEN. LEAST SQUARES USING RESIDUAL DIF. EQ. OF ORDER   2. LAG COEFFICIENTS =

  1) 0.9039   2)-0.5003

STANDARD ERROR OF Y = 0.45159656   FOR DEGREES OF FREEDOM =   36.

. . . .
STEP NUMBER 5   ANALYSIS OF VARIANCE FOR REDUCTION IN SS DUE TO VARIABLE ENTERING
   VARIABLE ENTERING   1   SOURCE   DF   SS   MS   F   F SIG.
   MULTIPLE R   0.99763   DUE REGRESSION   4   7.3071   1.8268   1683.4   1.000000
   STD ERROR OF Y.X 0.03294   DEV. FROM REG.   32   0.34725E-01   0.10852E-02
   R SQUARE   0.99527   TOTAL   36   7.3418   0.20394

   MULTIPLE REGRESSION EQUATION
VARIABLE   COEFFICIENT   STD. ERROR   T VAL.   T SIG. P. COR. ELASTICITY   PARTIAL COR. FOR VAR. NOT IN EQUATION
LNQ   =   VARIABLE   COEFFICIENT   F FOR SELECTION
TIME   X- 1 0.5815846E-02 0.3948920E-02 1.473   0.84942 0.2520   1.992
LNK   X-10 0.4277840   0.1161821   3.682   0.99915 0.5455   0.3624
LNL   X-11 0.9661780   0.1234269   7.828   1.00000 0.8105   0.9105
LNRM1   X-13 0.1266514   0.5148589E-01 2.460   0.98052 0.3988   0.1069
CONSTANT X-15 -13.49131   7.081692   -1.905   0.93421

ADJUSTED R SQUARE FOR K= 5, N=   37 IS   0.99467897

-2 * LN(MAXIMUM OF THE LIKELIHOOD FUNCTION) -152.93307

AKAIKE INFORMATION CRITERION (AIC) BASED ON JOINT LIKELIHOOD OF SIGMA AND BETA   -140.93307

```
SCHWARZ INFORMATION CRITERION (SIC) BASED ON JOINT LIKELIHOOD OF SIGMA AND BETA    -131.26757

NOTE: MODELS WITH LOWER AIC OR SIC ARE BETTER.

AIC = (N * LN(2*PI) ) + ( N * LN((SUM RES SQ)/N)) + N + (2*(K+1))

SIC = AIC - (2*(K+1))  +  ((K+1) * LN(N))


RESIDUAL VARIANCE =   0.10851670E-02

ORDER OF ENTRANCE (OR DELETION) OF THE VARIABLES =  10  13  15  11   1

  COVARIANCE MATRIX OF REGRESSION COEFFICIENTS

ROW  1   VARIABLE X- 1   TIME
    0.15593975E-04

ROW  2   VARIABLE X-10   LNK
   -0.39902681E-03  0.13498287E-01

ROW  3   VARIABLE X-11   LNL
   -0.24064070E-05 -0.66683681E-02  0.15234192E-01

ROW  4   VARIABLE X-13   LNRM1
   -0.10465020E-03  0.42362966E-02 -0.41975709E-02  0.26507977E-02

ROW  5   VARIABLE X-15   CONSTANT
   -0.27946243E-01  0.72776449    -0.24644159E-01  0.19208293     50.150362

=== PROGRAM TERMINATED - ALL VARIABLES PUT IN

            RESIDUAL STATISTICS FOR...

                 SMOOTHED

                 ORIGINAL DATA
    FOR GLS  Y AND Y ESTIMATE SCALED  BY        0.596447

VON NEUMANN RATIO 1 ...            1.48757        DURBIN-WATSON TEST.....    1.44737
VON NEUMANN RATIO 2 ...            1.48757

FOR D. F.   32 T(.9999)=   4.4411, T(.999)= 3.6221, T(.99)= 2.7390, T(.95)= 2.0374, T(.90)= 1.6943, T(.80)= 1.3088

SKEWNESS TEST (ALPHA 3) = 0.379679E-01,  PEAKEDNESS TEST (ALPHA 4)=   2.43894

                    NORMALITY TEST-- EXTENDED GRID,  CELL SIZE =    3.70
T STAT       INFIN  1.694  1.309  1.054  0.853  0.682  0.529  0.388  0.255  0.126
CELL NO.     2.000  3.000  5.000  5.000  2.000  2.000  3.000  8.000  2.000  5.000
INTERVAL     1.000  0.900  0.800  0.700  0.600  0.500  0.400  0.300  0.200  0.100
ACT PER      1.000  0.946  0.865  0.730  0.595  0.541  0.486  0.405  0.189  0.135

                    NORMALITY TEST -- SMALL SAMPLE GRID              CELL SIZE =    7.40
CELL NO.     5.000         10.000        4.000        11.000        7.000
INTERVAL     1.000          0.800        0.600         0.400        0.200
ACT PER      1.000          0.865        0.595         0.486        0.189

EXTENDED GRID NORMALITY TEST - PROB OF REJECTING NORMALITY ASSUMPTION
CHI=  9.757   CHI PROB=  0.7175     F(8,  32)= 1.21959    F PROB =0.680581

SMALL SAMPLE NORMALITY TEST - LARGE GRID
CHI=  5.027     CHI PROB=  0.8302     F(3,  32)= 1.67567    F PROB =0.808170

AUTOCORRELATION FUNCTION OF RESIDUALS

  1)  0.2600    2) -0.0286    3)  0.0244    4)  0.0437

F-RATIO FOR HETEROSKEDASTICITY =  1.929    1/F =  0.5185    D.F.( 12,  12)  HETEROSKEDASTICITY AT    0.8653  LEVEL

SUM OF SQUARED RESIDUALS =  0.3473E-01        MEAN SQUARED RESIDUAL =  0.9385E-03

GEN. LEAST SQUARES ENDED BY MAX. ORDER REACHED.

STEP ENDING. SECONDS USED  0.15666676   .  TOTAL JOB SECONDS    2.4399996   .
```

The next problem uses generated data to illustrate equation specification testing, using the in-core BLUS options.[13] Assume that the correct underlying model is

$$Y = \beta_0 + \beta_1 X1 + \beta_2 X2 + \beta_3 X3 + \varepsilon, \qquad (2.13\text{-}3)$$

where $X3 = (X2)^2$, $\beta_0 = \beta_1 = \beta_2 = 1$, $\beta_3 = .5$ and X1, X2, and ε are independent, standardized normal variables. Instead of estimating equation (2.14-3), the model estimated was

$$Y = \beta_0 + \beta_1 X1 + \beta_2 X2 + \varepsilon, \qquad (2.13\text{-}4)$$

which has left off the squared X2 term. Not only is equation (2.13-4) incorrect and the coefficients biased, it is also highly misleading. The coefficient β_2 in equation (2.13-4) will be shown to be not significant, leading to the reasonable next step of dropping X2 from consideration. The BLUS tests will be seen to point to the correct model.

The code in Table 2.3 will load the data, list the data, and run the incorrect model (2.13-4), which ignores the second-order term (X3), and the correct model (2.13-3).

Table 2.3 Simulated Test Data for BLUS Analysis

```
==THEILRB1
B34SEXEC DATA NOOB=25$
COMMENT=('SAMPLE DATASET OF 25 OBSERVATIONS')$
COMMENT=('TRUE MODEL Y = 1   + 1   X1 + 1   X2 + .5 X3')$
COMMENT=('X1, X2 ARE RANDOM NORMAL VARIABLES. X3 = X2 * X2 ') $
COMMENT=('PROBLEM DEVELOPED FOR THEIL(1971) REVISIONS BY STOKES')$
INPUT Y X1 X2 X3$
DATACARDS$
    1.4602      0       .02   4E-4
   -2.5556   -2.1      -.33   .1089
    3.6521    2.27     -.21   .0441
    4.8045     .27     1.83   3.3489
    3.0712    1.22      .32   .1024
    1.1142    -.37    -1.22   1.4884
    1.1322     .43      .38   .1444
     .7038    -.52     -.74   .5476
    1.8702    1.02      .02   4E-4
    2.3402    -.59     1.02   1.0404
    1.0112    -.89      .68   .4624
    1.5065    -.79      .23   .0529
    1.8525     .26    -2.07   4.2849
    -.0452    -.74      .64   .4096
    1.565    -1.46      .9    .81
   -1.0642    -.9      -.54   .2916
    1.7492    -.74    -2.28   5.1984
    3.1362    -.23     -.82   .6724
    1.7813     .04      .65   .4225
    1.9982     .62     -.58   .3364
   -1.22       .48      -.4   .16
    -.87755  -1.06    -1.43   2.0449
    1.8282    -.35    -1.58   2.4964
     .2662    -.78      .18   .0324
    3.145     1.97      -.7   .49
B34SRETURN $
B34SEEND$
B34SEXEC LIST$ VAR X1 X2 X3 Y$ B34SEEND$
B34SEXEC REGRESSION RESIDUALA$
    COMMENT=('MODEL KNOWN NOT TO BE CORRECT - BLUS TESTS DONE')$
    MODEL Y = X1 X2$
    RA RESID=ALLBLUS VARS=(X1,X2)$
    B34SEEND$
B34SEXEC REGRESSION RESIDUALA$
    COMMENT=('MODEL KNOWN TO BE CORRECT - BLUS TESTS DONE')$
    MODEL Y = X1 X2 X3$
    RA RESID=ALLBLUS VARS=(X1,X2,X3)$
    B34SEEND$
==
```

In contrast to the Theil textile example discussed earlier, which utilized the out-of-core BLUS procedure, Table 2.3 illustrates how to use the more powerful in-core BLUS tests which are called from the RA sentence of the REGRESSION command. To save paper, the listing of the data has been deleted. The purpose of this example is to determine whether it is possible to detect the omitted quadratic term, β_3, from the battery of BLUS tests. OLS results for equation (2.13-4), which are listed below, show β_2 was not significant (t=1.318).

```
F TO ENTER                    0.10000002E-01
F TO REMOVE                   0.49999990E-02
TOLERANCE                     0.99999998E-05
MAXIMUM NO OF STEPS                    3
DEPENDENT VARIABLE X( 1).   VARIABLE NAME  Y

THE FOLLOWING VARIABLES ARE DELETED IN THIS SUBPROBLEM

 4

THE FOLLOWING VARIABLES ARE FORCED INTO THE REGRESSION EQUATION AS CONTROL VARIABLES (COVARIATES)

 2   3   5

STANDARD ERROR OF Y =    1.6530962        FOR DEGREES OF FREEDOM =        24.
```

```
..............
STEP NUMBER  3                                ANALYSIS OF VARIANCE FOR REDUCTION IN SS DUE TO VARIABLE ENTERING
   VARIABLE ENTERING        3                      SOURCE        DF       SS              MS              F            F SIG.
   MULTIPLE R           0.65752                DUE REGRESSION      2     28.355          14.177         8.3777        0.998028
   STD ERROR OF Y.X     1.30088                DEV. FROM REG.     22     37.231          1.6923
   R SQUARE            0.43234                 TOTAL              24     65.585          2.7327

       MULTIPLE REGRESSION EQUATION
   VARIABLE       COEFFICIENT      STD. ERROR      T VAL.     T SIG. P. COR. ELASTICITY      PARTIAL COR. FOR VAR. NOT IN EQUATION
   Y      =                                                                                 VARIABLE      COEFFICIENT    F FOR SELECTION
   X1     X- 2   1.013484        0.2618357        3.871     0.99917  0.6365 -0.8706E-01
   X2     X- 3   0.3534934       0.2681463        1.318     0.79903  0.2706 -0.6228E-01
   CONSTANT  X- 5  1.573470      0.2698321        5.831     0.99999

ADJUSTED R SQUARE FOR K=  3,  N=      25 IS    0.38072991
```

BLUS tests were run on data sorted against X1 and X2 in turn. For the data sorted against X1, the modified von Neumann ratio statistic was 1.61 and the estimated t for the parabola was -1.07696. These results indicate that there is no nonlinearity problem with respect to X1. The heteroskedasticity test result was 1.62551, which is not significant (.7834). For the data sorted with respect to X2, the modified von Neumann ratio statistic was .8493, which is substantially lower, the heteroskedasticity significance was now .9123 and the result of the t test for the parabola was 3.40939, which is <u>highly</u> significant. These results, which suggest the inclusion of the squared X2 term X3, follow.

```
SPECIFICATION TEST OPTION SELECTED


RECIPROCAL OF MATRIX CONDITION FOR XPX FOR COMPLETE SAMPLE    0.56151989


BLUS OBS . DEL     1    2    3
BLUS....SUM EIGENVALUES =    1.0369792

BLUS OBS . DEL     1    2   25
BLUS....SUM EIGENVALUES =    1.2291649

BLUS OBS . DEL     1   24   25
BLUS....SUM EIGENVALUES =    1.1573897

BLUS OBS . DEL    23   24   25
BLUS....SUM EIGENVALUES =    0.97557429

FOR MVN ANALYSIS ON DATA SORTED AGAINST X1      THE OPTIMUM BASE SELECTED FROM AMONG   4 CHOICES LISTED ABOVE IS:

BLUS OBS . DEL     1    2   25
    1  EIGENVALUE =    0.1748
    2  EIGENVALUE =    0.3647
    3  EIGENVALUE =    0.6897
BLUS....SUM EIGENVALUES =    1.2291649       SUM OF SQUARED BLUS RESIDUALS =    37.23      BLUS EFFICIENCY   0.745935

BLUS IMPLIED COEFFICIENT VECTOR

NAME          OLS COEF          OLS SE          BLUS COEF        OLS - BLUS        1/CONDITION XO  0.18600735
```

```
X1        X- 2        1.013484            0.2618357           1.100858        -0.8737401E-01
X2        X- 3        0.3534934           0.2681463           0.6915909       -0.3380975
CONSTANT  X- 5        1.573470            0.2698321           1.513667         0.5980299E-01

FOR RESIDUAL SORTED AGAINST X1        MOD VON NEUMANN    1.6144836    DURBIN WATSON   1.5410955    CORRELATION  -0.15993652

TEST AGAINST CONVEXITY, T STATISTIC FOR PARABOLA ESTIMATED USING RESIDUAL AND X1        = -0.85459272

F(   7,   7) = 0.767810    1/F =  1.30241    FOR RESIDUAL SORTED AGAINST X1        , HETEROSKEDASTICITY AT  0.631876768 LEVEL
**************************************************************************************************************

FOR DATA SORTED AGAINST X1        THE OPTIMUM BASE FOR  HETEROSKEDASTICITY TEST IS :

BLUS OBS . DEL     12    13    14
        1  EIGENVALUE =   0.1246E-01
        2  EIGENVALUE =   0.7777E-01
        3  EIGENVALUE =   0.5000
BLUS....SUM EIGENVALUES =  0.59022406          SUM OF SQUARED BLUS RESIDUALS =   37.23      BLUS EFFICIENCY  0.631937

BLUS IMPLIED COEFFICIENT VECTOR

NAME             OLS COEF         OLS SE           BLUS COEF        OLS - BLUS           1/CONDITION X0   0.22241235E-01
X1        X- 2   1.013484         0.2618357        1.191471         -0.1779875
X2        X- 3   0.3534934        0.2681463        0.2636757         0.8981773E-01
CONSTANT  X- 5   1.573470         0.2698321        1.895983         -0.3225126

FOR RESIDUAL SORTED AGAINST X1        MOD VON NEUMANN    1.7022590    DURBIN WATSON   1.6248810    CORRELATION  -0.13283875

TEST AGAINST CONVEXITY, T STATISTIC FOR PARABOLA ESTIMATED USING RESIDUAL AND X1        = -0.85540286

F(   11,   11) = 0.615192    1/F =  1.62551    FOR RESIDUAL SORTED AGAINST X1        , HETEROSKEDASTICITY AT  0.783430459 LEVEL
**************************************************************************************************************

BLUS OBS . DEL      7    18    19
BLUS....SUM EIGENVALUES =  0.88634206

BLUS OBS . DEL      7     8    19
BLUS....SUM EIGENVALUES =  0.67435111

FOR DATA SORTED AGAINST X1        THE OPTIMUM BASE FOR CONVEXITY TEST USING A PARABOLA IS :

BLUS OBS . DEL      7    18    19
        1  EIGENVALUE =   0.1322
        2  EIGENVALUE =   0.2036
        3  EIGENVALUE =   0.5505
BLUS....SUM EIGENVALUES =  0.88634206          SUM OF SQUARED BLUS RESIDUALS =   37.23      BLUS EFFICIENCY  0.714378

BLUS IMPLIED COEFFICIENT VECTOR

NAME             OLS COEF         OLS SE           BLUS COEF        OLS - BLUS           1/CONDITION X0   0.18628713
X1        X- 2   1.013484         0.2618357        0.9949487         0.1853510E-01
X2        X- 3   0.3534934        0.2681463        0.7306955        -0.3772021
CONSTANT  X- 5   1.573470         0.2698321        1.458628          0.1148424

FOR RESIDUAL SORTED AGAINST X1        MOD VON NEUMANN    2.1851585    DURBIN WATSON   2.0858298    CORRELATION   0.51696949E-03

TEST AGAINST CONVEXITY, T STATISTIC FOR PARABOLA ESTIMATED USING RESIDUAL AND X1        = -1.0769554

F(   7,   7) = 0.625139    1/F =  1.59964    FOR RESIDUAL SORTED AGAINST X1        , HETEROSKEDASTICITY AT  0.724782945 LEVEL
**************************************************************************************************************

BLUS OBS . DEL      1     2     3
BLUS....SUM EIGENVALUES =  0.91038395

BLUS OBS . DEL      1     2    25
BLUS....SUM EIGENVALUES =   1.1875325

BLUS OBS . DEL      1    24    25
BLUS....SUM EIGENVALUES =   1.1147241

BLUS OBS . DEL     23    24    25
BLUS....SUM EIGENVALUES =  0.96444088

FOR MVN ANALYSIS ON DATA SORTED AGAINST X2        THE OPTIMUM BASE SELECTED FROM AMONG  4 CHOICES LISTED ABOVE IS:

BLUS OBS . DEL      1     2    25
        1  EIGENVALUE =   0.1357
        2  EIGENVALUE =   0.3302
        3  EIGENVALUE =   0.7216
BLUS....SUM EIGENVALUES =   1.1875325          SUM OF SQUARED BLUS RESIDUALS =   37.23      BLUS EFFICIENCY  0.733475

BLUS IMPLIED COEFFICIENT VECTOR

NAME             OLS COEF         OLS SE           BLUS COEF        OLS - BLUS           1/CONDITION X0   0.14580979
X1        X- 2   1.013484         0.2618357        0.9227729         0.9071094E-01
X2        X- 3   0.3534934        0.2681463        0.4151396        -0.6164623E-01
CONSTANT  X- 5   1.573470         0.2698321        2.020678         -0.4472078

FOR RESIDUAL SORTED AGAINST X2        MOD VON NEUMANN    0.84932440    DURBIN WATSON   0.81071744    CORRELATION  -0.18436051E-01

TEST AGAINST CONVEXITY, T STATISTIC FOR PARABOLA ESTIMATED USING RESIDUAL AND X2        =   1.9721658
```

```
F(   7,   7) = 0.983960    1/F = 1.01630    FOR RESIDUAL SORTED AGAINST X2    , HETEROSKEDASTICITY AT  0.508234681 LEVEL
***********************************************************************************************************************


FOR DATA SORTED AGAINST X2       THE OPTIMUM BASE FOR  HETEROSKEDASTICITY TEST IS :


BLUS OBS . DEL    12   13   14
      1  EIGENVALUE =    0.4907E-01
      2  EIGENVALUE =    0.3448
      3  EIGENVALUE =    0.6266
BLUS....SUM EIGENVALUES =   1.0204365          SUM OF SQUARED BLUS RESIDUALS =     37.23          BLUS EFFICIENCY  0.697647

BLUS IMPLIED COEFFICIENT VECTOR

NAME            OLS COEF          OLS SE          BLUS COEF          OLS - BLUS         1/CONDITION X0   0.70111487E-01
X1      X- 2    1.013484         0.2618357        1.152705          -0.1392214
X2      X- 3    0.3534934        0.2681463        0.4941380         -0.1406446
CONSTANT X- 5   1.573470         0.2698321        1.417654           0.1558166

FOR RESIDUAL SORTED AGAINST X2       MOD VON NEUMANN  0.87768559   DURBIN WATSON  0.83778944     CORRELATION -0.11780989

TEST AGAINST CONVEXITY, T STATISTIC FOR PARABOLA ESTIMATED USING RESIDUAL AND X2    =   3.6794894

F(  11,  11) = 2.33463   1/F = 0.428333    FOR RESIDUAL SORTED AGAINST X2    , HETEROSKEDASTICITY AT  0.912311734 LEVEL
***********************************************************************************************************************



BLUS OBS . DEL     7   18   19
BLUS....SUM EIGENVALUES =  0.74858718

BLUS OBS . DEL     7    8   19
BLUS....SUM EIGENVALUES =  0.93613741

FOR DATA SORTED AGAINST X2       THE OPTIMUM BASE FOR CONVEXITY TEST USING A PARABOLA IS :


BLUS OBS . DEL     7    8   19
      1  EIGENVALUE =    0.1832
      2  EIGENVALUE =    0.2456
      3  EIGENVALUE =    0.5074
BLUS....SUM EIGENVALUES =  0.93613741          SUM OF SQUARED BLUS RESIDUALS =     37.23          BLUS EFFICIENCY  0.730386

BLUS IMPLIED COEFFICIENT VECTOR

NAME            OLS COEF          OLS SE          BLUS COEF          OLS - BLUS         1/CONDITION X0   0.26076352
X1      X- 2    1.013484         0.2618357        0.9848518          0.2863208E-01
X2      X- 3    0.3534934        0.2681463        0.2334411          0.1200523
CONSTANT X- 5   1.573470         0.2698321        1.430985           0.1424854

FOR RESIDUAL SORTED AGAINST X2       MOD VON NEUMANN  0.91584700   DURBIN WATSON  0.87421618     CORRELATION  0.11191804

TEST AGAINST CONVEXITY, T STATISTIC FOR PARABOLA ESTIMATED USING RESIDUAL AND X2    =   3.4093910

F(   7,   7) = 0.827049   1/F = 1.20912    FOR RESIDUAL SORTED AGAINST X2    , HETEROSKEDASTICITY AT  0.595704199 LEVEL
***********************************************************************************************************************
```

The next step is to try the power term in the model. Edited output
from this step is given next.

```
    F TO ENTER              0.10000002E-01
    F TO REMOVE             0.49999990E-02
    TOLERANCE               0.99999998E-05
    MAXIMUM NO OF STEPS             4
    DEPENDENT VARIABLE X( 1).  VARIABLE NAME   Y

    THE FOLLOWING VARIABLES ARE FORCED INTO THE REGRESSION EQUATION AS CONTROL VARIABLES (COVARIATES)

      2   3   4   5

    STANDARD ERROR OF Y =    1.6530962      FOR DEGREES OF FREEDOM =      24.


..............
STEP NUMBER  4                            ANALYSIS OF VARIANCE FOR REDUCTION IN SS DUE TO VARIABLE ENTERING
    VARIABLE ENTERING    3                    SOURCE          DF       SS          MS            F        F SIG.
    MULTIPLE R       0.81262               DUE REGRESSION    3       43.310      14.437       13.610     0.999963
    STD ERROR OF Y.X 1.02993               DEV. FROM REG.   21       22.276       1.0607
    R SQUARE         0.66036               TOTAL            24       65.585       2.7327

    MULTIPLE REGRESSION EQUATION
VARIABLE       COEFFICIENT    STD. ERROR    T VAL.    T SIG. P. COR. ELASTICITY    PARTIAL COR. FOR VAR. NOT IN EQUATION
Y      =                                                                          VARIABLE     COEFFICIENT   F FOR SELECTION
X1      X- 2    1.128127       0.2095353     5.384    0.99998  0.7615  -0.9691E-01
X2      X- 3    0.7997628      0.2433011     3.287    0.99649  0.5829  -0.1409
X3      X- 4    0.6463765      0.1721477     3.755    0.99883  0.6338   0.4720
CONSTANT X- 5   1.048456       0.2553211     4.106    0.99950

ADJUSTED R SQUARE FOR K=   4,  N=      25 IS    0.61183536
```

Now β_1, β_2 and β_3 are significant (t's = 5.384, 3.287 and 3.755, respectively). Diagnostic tests on the correct model have not been listed to save space. The residuals were sorted against X1, X2 and X3 in turn. The t scores for the parabola test were found to be -.337, .766, and -.777, respectively, which are all not significant. Corresponding modified von Neumann ratio statistics were 1.386, 1.399 and 1.374. When interpreting the B34S BLUS output, it is imperative that the correct base is used for each test. For example, even though the t for the parabola test is always calculated, it should only be used if the correct base for that test is selected. The B34S RA output gives many other BLUS base diagnostic tests, including the sum of the eigenvalues, a listing of the actual base selected, the BLUS efficiency, 1/condition of X_0 and the BLUS implied coefficient vector. Since the sum of the T-K BLUS residuals must equal the T OLS residuals, the sum of squared BLUS residuals will always be the same and provides a check on program accuracy.

The code in Table 2.4 illustrates how the Theil example given in Table 2.3 was generated with the B34S random number facilities. If this code is run, there will be very minor differences from the output from the above data, which was rounded. The LISTA option has been selected to illustrate listing of the BLUS residuals and the corresponding X1, X2, and X3 values. Clearly, if larger data sets are generated, the GRAPH option should be used to save paper. The rounded data are presented since these data will be used in the revised edition of Theil (1971). The reader is encouraged to modify this code to construct other examples for experimentation with the BLUS procedures. It would be a good idea to test how sensitive the results are to the sample size.

Table 2.4 Generating BLUS Test Data

```
==THEILRB2
  B34SEXEC DATA NOOB=25 NOHEAD
          HEADING=('EXACT REV THEIL(1971) DATA')$
COMMENT=('DATA BUILT BY H H STOKES FOR THEIL(1971) REVISIONS')$
COMMENT=('MINOR DIFFERENCES FROM USING THE THEIL ROUNDED DATA')$
    INPUT TIME$ BUILD X1 X2 Y X3 NOISE ABSX1 ABSX2 $
    GEN BACKSPACE() $
    GEN TIME=KOUNT()$
    GEN X1 = RN()    $
    GEN X2 = RN()    $
    GEN Y  = ADD(X1,1.0)    $
    GEN Y  = ADD(Y,X2)      $
    GEN X3 = MULT(X2,X2)    $
    GEN NOISE = MULT(X3,.5) $
    GEN Y = ADD(Y,NOISE)    $
    GEN NOISE = RN()        $
    GEN Y = ADD(Y,NOISE)    $
    GEN ABSX1 = MULT(X1,X1) $
    GEN ABSX1 = SQRT(ABSX1) $
    GEN ABSX2 = MULT(X2,X2) $
    GEN ABSX2 = SQRT(ABSX2) $
 DATACARDS$
 1.0
  B34SRETURN$ B34SEEND$
 B34SEXEC LIST $ VAR TIME X1 X2 X3 Y NOISE ABSX1 ABSX2$ B34SEEND$
 B34SEXEC REGRESSION RESIDUALP$
    COMMENT=('MODEL KNOWN NOT TO BE CORRECT - BLUS TESTS DONE')$
    MODEL Y = X1 X2$
    RA RESID=ALLBLUS VARS=(X1,X2) LISTA$
    B34SEEND$
 B34SEXEC REGRESSION RESIDUALP$
    COMMENT=('MODEL KNOWN TO BE CORRECT - BLUS TESTS DONE')$
    MODEL Y = X1 X2 X3$
    RA RESID=ALLBLUS VARS=(X1,X2,X3) LISTA$
    B34SEEND$
 ==
```

2.14 Conclusion

The B34S REGRESSION command performs OLS and GLS estimation of
linear single-equation models. A variety of specification tests,
based on the BLUS residuals, and dynamic specification tests,
utilizing cross correlation analysis, are optionally available and
are illustrated. Due to space considerations, RA sentence dynamic
specifications tests involving cross correlations have only been
discussed and have not been shown. More powerful dynamic
specification tests, using VAR models, are covered in chapter 8.
Further tests for time-series equation stability or cross-section
equation specification are covered in chapter 9, which documents
the recursive residual (RR) procedure. OLS is a special case of
more general estimation techniques, such as ARIMA and VARMA models,
which are covered in chapters 7 and 8. Prior to moving on to
discuss these more advanced topics, an outline of the B34S options
available when there are restrictions on the range of the dependent
variable will be given. These options are covered in chapter 3.

NOTES

1. A brief discussion of how to enter data into B34S using the DATA paragraph is contained in Stokes (1988b).

2. Sections of this chapter have been taken directly (with permission) from the original B34T manual (with addendums) by Hodson Thornber (1966, 1967, 1968).

3. Caution must be exercised in using Q and Q'. If the BLUS residuals (see section 2.9) are not adjacent or have not been resorted if cross-section data is used, Q' is meaningless. In contrast to T OLS residuals, there are T-K BLUS residuals. Q' should only be used for BLUS residuals; it is not valid for serial-correlation tests for OLS residuals.

4. A chi-square test with KK cells would have KK-J degrees of freedom, where J is the number of quantities determined from the data. Since the data mean, the data standard deviation, and the frequency of each cell are required, J is usually equal to 3. However, because the mean of the OLS residual is equal to zero, by assumption, in this case J=2. The chi-square probability statistics and F probability statistics are conservative because the probability of rejecting normality is lower than would be the case if the degrees of freedom were KK-3. I am in debt to Professor Gilbert Bassett for this point.

5. A complete discussion of the BLUS tests available follows. The eigenvalues listed in the BLUS in-core and out-of-core BLUS outputs have already been raised to the power 1/2.

6. An example was prepared by Stokes for Theil to be used in the revision of chapter 5 of his 1971 econometrics book. The estimated model was

$$Y = \beta_0 + \beta_1 X_1 + \beta_2 X_2 + u_t,$$

while the correct model was

$$Y = \beta_0 + \beta_1 X_1 + \beta_2 X_2 + \beta_3 (X_2)^2 + u_t.$$

In the first estimation run, β_2 was found to be insignificant. BLUS residual analysis indicated convexity that went away when $(X_2)^2$ was added to the equation. In contrast to the first equation, the coefficients (β_i, i=0,2) were all significant. This example is discussed later in this chapter.

7. Equation (2.11-2) is the usual cross-correlation formula. It is not the same as the Box-Jenkins cross correlation formula (given in chapter 7 of this book), which does not adjust the mean and the degrees of freedom as k increases. For a further discussion of the differences in the two formulas, see Box and Jenkins (1976, chap.

11), and Jenkins and Watts (1968, 182).

8. With the exception of increasing precision, improving the inversion routines and converting to FORTRAN 77, the code to implement the BAYES option in B34S has not been changed since it was built by Thornber in 1967. Changes have been unnecessary, because Zellner has produced a vastly improved program, BRAP, that supersedes the B34S BAYES option. B34S will branch to BRAP, if desired. For a discussion of this branch, see section C.19.1 of native command manual or the PGMCALL option in the on-line help file. The BRAP program has the same data-input structure as TSP. The BRAP program was built under Zellner's direction by John Abowd (The Bayesian Analysis Package--BRAP User's Manual, H. G. B. Alexander Research Foundation, Graduate School of Business, University of Chicago, September 1967). The actual calculations made by the B34S BAYES option are discussed in detail in Zellner (1971, chaps. 1-4, especially p. 95).

9. The B34S HELP and OPTIONS commands run at once.

10. The complete B34S example input code is given in the text. Only selected output is shown to save space. Readers are encouraged to run the complete example. Complete listings of these example input files, together with numerous other examples, are distributed with the B34S program.

11. Another problem to consider is whether, in fact, L, K, and ml are exogenous. This problem was discussed in Sinai and Stokes (1972, 1975, 1981, and 1989) and will not be addressed here.

12. Sinai and Stokes (1972, 1975, 1981) address a number of questions that are not discussed here. These references should be consulted for further research in this area.

13. This example was developed with the help of Theil for inclusion in a revision of Theil (1971).

3. Logit, Tobit, Probit

3.0 Introduction

The options discussed in this chapter concern models with restrictions on the range of the dependent variable. The B34S commands discussed in this chapter include the following:

- PROBIT: Runs a single-equation probit model for a 0-1 dependent variable.

- MPROBIT: Runs a single-equation probit model for a dependent variable with up to ten ordered states.

- LOGLIN: Runs up to a four-equation logit model for 0-1 dependent variables.

- MLOGLIN: Runs up to a 69-equation logit model with each dependent variable having up to 20 states.

- TOBIT: Runs a single-equation tobit model in which the dependent variable is bounded from above or below.

The B34S MPROBIT command includes the PROBIT command as a special case. Likewise, the LOGLIN command is a special case of the MLOGLIN command. If only the PROBIT or LOGLIN command is needed, substantial time will be saved by using these commands in place of the more general MPROBIT and MLOGLIN commands. These commands will be discussed in turn. Good general references for this chapter are Maddala(1983) and Daganzo(1979).

3.1 Probit Models

The B34S PROBIT command is based on heavily modified code originally obtained from Mathematica Policy Research. The discussion of its use is based on undated manuals, which were obtained with the original code.[1] Probit analysis is used in estimating models of the form

$$y_t = \beta_0 + \beta_1 x_{t1} + \beta_2 x_{t2} + \ldots + \beta_n x_{tn} \quad t=1,\ldots,T, \qquad (3.1-1)$$

where y_t takes the value 0-1 and $(x_{ti}, i=1,n)$ can be a continuous or discrete variable. If equation (3.1-1) is estimated with OLS, some of the estimated values of y_t will lie outside the range 0-1 and the residuals will be heteroskedastic. A better way to think of the problem would be to consider a probit model that specifies a random process for the determination of the dependent variable. Whether or not the response is observed depends on the relationship between the stimulus S_t and a random critical level of the stimulus S^*. In terms of the model

$$y_t = \begin{cases} 0 & \text{if } S_t < S^* \\ 1 & \text{if } S_t \geq S^*, \end{cases} \qquad (3.1\text{-}2)$$

where $S_t = \hat{\beta}X$ and it is assumed that $S^* \sim N(0,1)$. The assumption of zero mean is handled by estimating a constant in equation (3.1-1), while the assumption of a unit variance obviates the necessity of estimating a variance for S^*.

S^* takes the place of the random residual in the OLS model. The distribution of y in the probit model is as follows:

$$P(y_t = 0 \mid S_t) = P(S_t < S^* \mid S_t) = 1 - F(S_t) \qquad (3.1\text{-}3)$$

$$P(y_t = 1 \mid S_t) = P(S_t > S^* \mid S_t) = F(S_t), \qquad (3.1\text{-}4)$$

where F( ) is the cumulative normal density. We can define f( ) as the standard normal density and Q( ) as $1 = F( )$.

$$f(x) = (1/\sqrt{(2\pi)}) \, e^{-.5 x^2} \qquad (3.1\text{-}5)$$

$$F(x) = \int_{-\infty}^{x} (1/\sqrt{(2\pi)}) \, e^{-.5\Theta^2} \, d\Theta \qquad (3.1\text{-}6)$$

Equations (3.1-3) and (3.1-4) can be thought of as conditional probabilities. The expected value of the dependent variable is obtained by weighting the outcomes by their respective probabilities. This is shown in equations (3.1-7) and (3.1-8).

$$E(y_t \mid S_t) = P(y_t = 0) \, (0) + P(y_t = 1) \, (1) \qquad (3.1\text{-}7)$$

$$= P(y_t = 1 \mid S_t) = F(S_t) \qquad \varepsilon[0,1]. \qquad (3.1\text{-}8)$$

For each observation, equation (3.1-8) gives the expected probability (on the unit interval) that $y_t = 1$. This probability is the value of the cumulative normal at S_t.

In OLS models, the partial derivative of E(y) with respect to one of the independent variables x_k is the estimated coefficient. In probit models, this partial derivative changes, depending on the levels of the independent variables, and is equal to the estimated coefficient β_k weighted by the normal density evaluated at S, where the subscript t has been dropped for notational simplicity.

$$\partial E(y_t) / \partial x_k = f(S) \, \beta_k. \qquad (3.1\text{-}9)$$

As S runs from large negative values to large positive values,

$E(y|S)$ runs from zero to one. The partial derivative of $E(y)$ with respect to x_k converges to zero for very large or small values of S and will be maximum ($.398 \beta_k$) when S is near zero.

The PROBIT command prints out:

- Independent variable summations and means.

- The log of the likelihood function after each iteration (IITLK option).

- The estimates of the parameters after each iteration (IIEST option).

- The second-derivatives matrix after each iteration (ISECD option).

After the final iteration, the following output is available:

- The negative inverse of the second derivatives matrix (variance-covariance matrix of the estimated coefficients).

- The final maximum likelihood estimates of the parameters, their standard errors and the ratio of the coefficients to their standard errors.

- The partial derivatives of $E(y)$, with respect to each x_i, for the mean and the maximum value of each x_i.

- The number of limit and nonlimit observations.

- Minus two times the log likelihood ratio ($(-2)\log_e \mathcal{L}$).

The statistic $(-2)\log_e \mathcal{L}$ for a model with q right-hand-side variables is distributed as chi-square with q degrees of freedom, where

$$\mathcal{L} = \frac{\text{maximum likelihood with q constraints}}{\text{maximum likelihood without constraints.}} \qquad (3.1\text{-}10)$$

$\mathcal{L}$ is bounded at 1 for a situation in which the constraints do not matter. A larger $(-2)\log_e \mathcal{L}$ value indicates a more significant regression result since the imposition of the constraints has significantly reduced the likelihood of the sample.

By use of the NSTRT and NSTOP parameters, the user can output the actual and calculated values for y as well as the density of the normal distribution, $f(S)$, at that point. Although many users run probit models with 1-0 right-hand-side variables, such as sex and race dummies, it makes little sense to evaluate the partial

derivatives at the means of these 0-1 variables because it is very
hard to interpret the results. The B34S PROBIT NADJ option allows
the user to input up to 20 values of the explanatory variables and
calculate the partial derivatives for these specific values. These
partial derivatives are much easier to interpret since they give an
indication of the change in the probability of y=1 as the
explanatory variables change. A sample setup for the PROBIT command
is given below.

```
B34SEXEC PROBIT $
    MODEL Y= X Q H $
    B34SEEND$
B34SEXEC PROBIT NADJ=3 $
    MODEL Y= X Q H $
    MEANS X(.5, .88, 1.03)  H(1.0,2.0,1.0)$ B34SEEND$
```

In the first example, the model y = f(X, Q, H) is given. The second
case shows the use of the optional MEANS sentence, in which three
sets of Z scores and their associated partial derivatives are
calculated. In calculating the Z scores, the sample mean values are
used for Q; the X values used are .5, .88, and 1.3; and the H
values used are 1.0, 2.0, and 1.0 and a constant is included. The
following calculations are made:

$$Z(1) = \beta_0 + \beta_1 * .5 \quad + \beta_2 * 1.0 \quad + \beta_3 * (\text{mean } Q)$$

$$Z(2) = \beta_0 + \beta_1 * .88 \quad + \beta_2 * 2.0 \quad + \beta_3 * (\text{mean } Q)$$

$$Z(3) = \beta_0 + \beta_1 * 1.03 + \beta_2 * 1.0 \quad + \beta_3 * (\text{mean } Q).$$

The MEANS sentence outputs the values $(f(Z(i)), i=1,3)$.

The PROBIT command supports up to 48 variables on the right and has
no limit on the number of observations other than disk size
available. This command has routinely been run with 35 variables
on the right-hand side and 250,000 observations.

3.2 Multinomial Probit Models

The MPROBIT command is based on code initially obtained from
McKelvey and Zavoina (1971, 1975) and will perform multinomial
probit analysis with up to ten ordered categories on the left-hand-
side variable and up to 39 variables on the right-hand side. If the
left-hand variable has only two categories (0-1), the MPROBIT
command gives the same results as the PROBIT command. MPROBIT
estimates a model of the form

$$P(j,k) \quad = F(\mu(k) - X_j\beta) - F(\mu(k-1) - X_j\beta), \qquad (3.2-1)$$

where $P(j,k)$ is the probability that for the jth observation, the
dependent variable is in the kth category. $X_j\beta$ is the product of the
j^{th} observation vector X and the estimated coefficient vector β.
F( ) calculates the probabilities of the normal distribution

function and the μ's are estimates of the threshold parameters and have associated significance values similar to the estimated standard errors of the estimated coefficient vector β. μ_1 is assumed to equal 0.0. Thus, when there are only two categories, $P(y=1|S_t) = F(X_t\beta)$. After MPROBIT has been run, it is often desirable to be able to calculate the probability of being in each category. If we assume a five-category problem and the fact that an estimate of $X_j\beta$ is available as an observation in a SAS data set, and the estimated μ's are available from the B34S MPROBIT step, the SAS code listed below will calculate the MPROBIT of being in the five categories (PZ1, ..., PZ5).

```
DATA TEST;
       INPUT XB;
       MU1=0.0;
       MU2=1.9561290;
       MU3=5.5418716;
       MU4=8.6592352;
       PZ1     =PROBNORM(MU1 - XB);
       PZ2     =PROBNORM(MU2 - XB) - PROBNORM(MU1 - XB);
       PZ3     =PROBNORM(MU3 - XB) - PROBNORM(MU2 - XB);
       PZ4     =PROBNORM(MU4 - XB) - PROBNORM(MU3 - XB);
       PZ5     = 1.0 - Z1 - Z2 - Z3 - Z4;
       DROP MU1 MU2 MU3 MU4 ;
CARDS;
   (XB values here)
PROC PRINT DATA=TEST;
ENDSAS;
```

The MPROBIT command calculates and outputs $(-2) \log_e \mathcal{L}$, a table showing how the log likelihood changes at each iteration and estimates of the following:

- the explained sum of squares

- the residual sum of squares

- the total sum of squares

- the R^2,

following the approach outlined in McKelvey and Zavoina (1975). Since the multinomial probit model is quite different from the OLS model, the assumptions used to get these estimates follow.

We first assume that the dependent variable on its underlying interval scale satisfies a regression model. Because there is no way to know its variance, we normalize it so that its variance around the regression line, σ^2, is unity. We next define the residual sum of squares (RSS) to be

$$RSS = T \sigma^2 = T. \tag{3.2-2}$$

The total sum of squares (TSS) becomes

$$TSS = \Sigma (\hat{y}_i)^2 + T \qquad\qquad\qquad (3.2-3)$$

and the explained sum of squares (ESS).

$$ESS = TSS - RSS \qquad\qquad\qquad (3.2-4)$$

from which it is possible to calculate the R^2 as ESS / TSS. McKelvey and Zavoina (1975) caution that these values are only estimates. Unlike OLS models, we cannot observe the residuals about the regression plane or the deviations of the dependent variable about its mean. In addition, equation (3.2-3) assumes that the estimated β's are OLS estimates, not probit estimates. This latter problem is minimized in large samples.

Additional diagnostic output includes the following:

- the percent predicted correctly.

- the rank-order correlation, i. e., the predicted vs. the actual.

The purpose of these statistics is to give the user some comparison with what an OLS model would show, if y were a continuous variable.

In survey work, the researcher often wants to ask questions with more than two possible choices. If the choices are known to be ordered, but the degree of difference between the choices is not known, then the B34S MPROBIT command provides an alternative to forcing the problem into a standard 0-1 probit model. A study of the significance values for the μ's will determine whether there really are significant differences between the choices. Use of the VVALUES sentence, which will be discussed, facilitates this study. As an example of the MPROBIT command, consider a problem in which the dependent variable y is coded 1, 2, 3, 4, 5. The commands

```
B34SEXEC MPROBIT$
        VVALUES=(1.0,2.0,3.0,4.0,5.0)$
        MODEL Y =X1 X2 X3 X4 $
        B34SEEND$
```

will test if X1, X2, X3, and X4 significantly predict Y and if there really is a distinction between the cases. If μ_3 was found not to be significantly different from μ_2, this would suggest that category 2 and category 3 are, in fact, the same category.

Next, assume that the researcher wishes only to look at the first, third and fourth categories. The VVALUES sentence is used to define the problem so that only these categories are valid values for y. Observations coded y=2 and y=5 are dropped from the problem.

```
B34SEXEC MPROBIT$
       VVALUES=(1.0,3.0,4.0)$
       MODEL Y =X1 X2 X3 X4 $
       B34SEEND$
```

The above discussion of the MPROBIT command indicates that it is a superset of the PROBIT command. In problems in which there are only two categories, the PROBIT command will be faster than the MPROBIT command.

3.3 Logit Models

The B34S LOGLIN command is based on code developed by Nerlove and Press (1973). This command allows estimation of single-equation logit models. It can estimate more general multivariate models in which there are up to four jointly polytomous variables. The LOGLIN command is a subset of the more general MLOGLIN command, which is discussed next. While the LOGLIN command handles up to four 0-1 problems, the MLOGLIN command handles up to 69 jointly determined variables with up to 20 states. The advantage of the LOGLIN command is that it does not load the data into core and thus can work with substantially larger data sets than the MLOGLIN command. The binomial logit model estimated with the LOGLIN command assumes

$$P(y=1|S_i) = F(Z_i) = F(X\beta) = 1/(1 + e^{-2X\beta}), \qquad (3.3-1)$$

and because of the scaler 2 will produce estimates that are one-half the usual formulation, which does not use such a scaler. Estimated asymptotic t scores are not affected by the scaling. The logistic function, in contrast to the probit function, has slightly fatter tails. If we define P_i as the probability that y=1, then equation (3.3-1) can be transformed to

$$\log(P_i /(1 - P_i) = Z_i = 2(X\beta), \qquad (3.3-2)$$

where the dependent variable is the log of the odds that y=1. The slope of the cumulative logistic distribution is largest at P_i = .5. In an OLS model, the effect of a change in any independent variable on the dependent variable is always the estimated coefficient. In the probit and logit models, the effect varies, depending on the value of Z_i. Since the LOGIT procedure is a special case of the more general MLOGIT procedure, a detailed discussion of the econometric theory is left to the next section in which the MLOGIT command is discussed.

Output available from the LOGIT command includes the following:

- OLS starting values for the coefficients.

- Estimated coefficients, their asymptotic standard errors, t-ratios and significance and the gradient associated with each coefficient. The gradient is the first partial derivative of

F( ) with respect to each coefficient and should be small for the final values of the coefficients.

- The log of the likelihood function.

Optional output includes the following:

- Routines to test the data (KTEST option).

- Output at each iteration (KCHCK option).

- Options to suppress bivariate interaction terms (IALLB option), suppress trivariate interactions (IALLT option), and options to suppress all four-way interaction terms (IALL4 option). These options are only useful if there is more than one dependent variable in the problem.

- Options to control the tolerance for convergency of the likelihood function (ITOL1 parameter), and the tolerance for the coefficients (ITOL2 parameter), and limits on the iterations (LIMIT parameter).

The setup for a simple LOGIT run of one equation would be

```
B34SEXEC LOGLIN$
     MODEL Y1 = X1 X2 X3 $ B34SEEND$
```

A simple multiple dependent variable setup would be

```
B34SEXEC LOGLIN$
     MODEL Y1 Y2 Y3 Y4 = X1 X2 X3 X4 X5$ B34SEEND$
```

The LOGLIN command has options whereby selective bivariate interactions can be suppressed (BSUPP sentence), selective trivariate interaction terms are suppressed (TSUPP sentence), and exogenous variables can be selectively suppressed from some equations (SSUPP sentence). The following setup illustrates these options.

```
B34SEXEC LOGLIN$
     MODEL Y1 Y2 Y3 Y4 = X1 X2 X3 X4 X5 X6$
     BSUPP Y1 Y2$
     TSUPP Y1 Y2 Y4$
     SSUPP Y2 X1 Y3 X5$
     B34SEEND$
```

Here the bivariate interaction Y1 Y2 is suppressed, the trivariate interaction Y1 Y2 Y4 is suppressed, the exogenous variable X1 is suppressed from the equation for Y2, and the exogenous variable X5 is suppressed from the equation for Y3.

3.4 Multinomial Logit Models

The multinomial LOGIT code, called with the MLOGLIN command,

was developed by Kawasaki (1978, 1979) as an extension of the work
of Nerlove and Press (1973, 1976). The code was subsequently
extended by Lehrer and Stokes (1985) and further refined by Klein
and Klein (1988) and Klein (1988). Subsequent improvements were
made to the Klein code by Stokes. Currently, both versions of
MLOGLIN are in B34S. If VER=OLD is specified, the older code is
used. If VER=NEW is specified, the newer Klein version is run. It
is recommended that VER=NEW be used. The function used with the
MLOGLIN command is

$$P(y=1|S_i) = F(-Z_i) = F(-X\beta) = 1/(1 + e^{X\beta}), \qquad (3.4-1)$$

which implies that the estimated coefficients for the same problem
run with the LOGLIN and MLOGLIN command will differ by sign and
magnitude, with the MLOGLIN coefficients being twice the LOGLIN
coefficients. LIMDEP (Greene 1985) uses the formulation
$F(Z_i) = (1/(1 + e^{-X\beta})$ and produces coefficients that are the same
absolute value as MLOGLIN but differing in sign. LIMDEP's
coefficients are the same sign as those of LOGLIN, but twice the
value. The absolute value of the asymptotic t scores are the same
for all three programs.[2]

Assume a problem in which A is a trichotomous endogenous
variable and B is a dichotomous, endogenous variable. We define
indexes for A and B: i_A = 1,2,3; i_B = 1,2. If we assume for the sake
of this example that A and B are jointly dependent on one
continuous variable, x, the log-linear probability model may be
written as follows:

$$\log P[i_A = 1, i_B = 1] = \mu + c_1 + a_1x + d_1 + b_1x + \beta_{AB}(1,1)$$

$$\log P[i_A = 2, i_B = 1] = \mu + c_2 + a_2x + d_1 + b_1x + \beta_{AB}(2,1)$$

$$\log P[i_A = 3, i_B = 1] = \mu + c_3 + a_3x + d_1 + b_1x + \beta_{AB}(3,1)$$

$$\log P[i_A = 1, i_B = 2] = \mu + c_1 + a_1x + d_2 + b_2x + \beta_{AB}(1,2)$$

$$\log P[i_A = 2, i_B = 2] = \mu + c_2 + a_2x + d_2 + b_2x + \beta_{AB}(2,2)$$

$$\log P[i_A = 3, i_B = 2] = \mu + c_3 + a_3x + d_2 + b_2x + \beta_{AB}(3,2).$$

$$(3.4-2)$$

Identification restrictions are necessary. Nerlove and Press
(1973, 1976) impose the constraints that if any one of the effects
is summed over all the values of one of the indexes on which it
depends, the sum should equal zero. Because it facilitates the
interpretation of the results, we make the following alternative
assumptions:

$a_3 = b_2 = c_3 = d_2 = \beta_{AB}(3,2) = \beta_{AB}(2,2) = \beta_{AB}(1,2) = \beta_{AB}(3,1)=0.$

$$(3.4-3)$$

The justification for these alternative assumptions follows. Assume an alternative model with one trichotomous variable, A, as a function of one continuous variable, x. The log-linear probability model may be written as follows:

$\log P[i_A = 1] = \varepsilon + e_1 + f_1 \, x$

$\log P[i_A = 2] = \varepsilon + e_2 + f_2 \, x$

$\log P[i_A = 3] = \varepsilon + e_3 + f_3 \, x.$ $\qquad\qquad (3.4-4)$

If we impose the constraint that $e_1 + e_2 + e_3 = 0$, and $f_1 + f_2 + f_3 = 0$, we may write

$\log \{P[i_A = 1] \,/\, ((P[i_A{=}1]P[i_A{=}2]P[i_A{=}3])^{(1/3)})\} = e_1 + f_1 \, x$

$\log \{P[i_A = 2] \,/\, ((P[i_A{=}1]P[i_A{=}2]P[i_A{=}3])^{(1/3)})\} = e_2 + f_2 \, x$

$\log \{P[i_A = 3] \,/\, ((P[i_A{=}1]P[i_A{=}2]P[i_A{=}3])^{(1/3)})\} = e_3 + f_3 \, x.$ $\quad (3.4-5)$

Differentiation of the first equation in (3.4-5) with respect to x indicates that f_1 represents the change in the log odds that A will take the value 1, relative to the geometric average of the probabilities associated with a unit change in x. Similar statements may be made about f_2 and f_3.

If the constraints that $e_3 = 0$ and $f_3 = 0$ are imposed instead, from equation (3.4-4) we obtain

$\log\{P[i_A {=}1] \,/\, P[i_A = 3]\} = e_1 + f_1 \, x$

$\log\{P[i_A {=}2] \,/\, P[i_A = 3]\} = e_2 + f_2 \, x.$ $\qquad\qquad (3.4-6)$

In this case, f_1 represents the change in the log odds that A will take the value 1 rather than 3 associated with a unit change in x and f_2 may be interpreted analogously.

In general, one approach is to impose the restriction that if any one of the effects is summed over all the values of one of the indexes on which it depends, the sum should equal 0; this leads to comparisons between the probability of being in a particular category and the geometric average probability. This assumption is specified by setting BASIS = DCBASIS. An alternative strategy is to constrain the last effects to be zero; this leads to comparisons between the probability of being in the last category. This latter strategy is the default and is set by BASIS = ZBASIS.

Returning to the problem specified in equation (3.4-2), we note that analogous to the familiar ANOVA models, the log probabilities are decomposed into main effects ($c_j + a_j x$, j=1, 2, 3), and ($d_k + b_k x$, k=1,2), interaction effects (β_{AB}), and the grand mean, μ. μ is defined so as to ensure that

$$\Sigma_{i_A} \Sigma_{i_B} P[i_A, i_B] = 1. \qquad\qquad (3.4\text{-}7)$$

Algebraic manipulation of equation (3.4-2) yields the following interpretations for the parameters:

$$a_1 = \frac{\partial}{\partial x}\{ \log (P[i_A=1, i_B=2]/P[i_A=3, i_B=2]) \}$$

$$= \frac{\partial}{\partial x}\{ \log (P[i_A=1, i_B=1]/P[i_A=3, i_B=1]) \}$$

$$a_2 = \frac{\partial}{\partial x}\{ \log (P[i_A=2, i_B=2]/P[i_A=3, i_B=2]) \}$$

$$= \frac{\partial}{\partial x}\{ \log (P[i_A=2, i_B=1]/P[i_A=3, i_B=1]) \}$$

$$b_1 = \frac{\partial}{\partial x}\{ \log (P[i_A=3, i_B=1]/P[i_A=3, i_B=2]) \}$$

$$= \frac{\partial}{\partial x}\{ \log (P[i_A=2, i_B=1]/P[i_A=2, i_B=2]) \}$$

$$= \frac{\partial}{\partial x}\{ \log (P[i_A=1, i_B=1]/P[i_A=1, i_B=2]) \}$$

$$\beta_{AB}(1,1) = \log \left[\frac{P[i_A = 1, \ i_B = 1] \ / \ P[i_A = 1, \ i_B = 2]}{P(i_A = 3, \ i_B = 1] \ / \ P[i_A = 3, \ i_B = 2]} \right]$$

$$\beta_{AB}(2,1) = \log \left[\frac{P[i_A = 2, \ i_B = 1] \ / \ P[i_A = 2, \ i_B = 2]}{P(i_A = 3, \ i_B = 1] \ / \ P[i_A = 3, \ i_B = 2]} \right]. \quad (3.4\text{-}8)$$

Thus, a_1 in equation (3.4-8) represents the change in the log odds that A will take the value 1 rather than 3, variable B held constant, associated with a unit change in x, i. e., a_1 indicates the direct impact of x on the likelihood that A will equal 1 as opposed to 3.[3] If another exogenous variable, y, were introduced, a_1 would indicate the change in the log odds, B and y held constant. A similar interpretation applies to a_2 and b_1. The interaction term $\beta_{AB}(1,1)$ measures the relationship between levels

1 and 3 of variable A on the one hand and levels 1 and 2 of variable B on the other, net of exogenous effects. For instance, the odds that i_B will equal 1, given $i_A = 1$, are $P[i_A = 1, i_B = 1] / P[i_A = 1, i_B = 2]$. If A and B are not associated, the odds that i_B will equal 1, given $i_A = 3$, should be the same. Thus, if $\beta_{AB}(1,1) = 0$, this means that the value of B is not associated with whether variable A takes the value 1 or 3. Departures from 0 indicate lack of independence. $\beta_{AB}(2,1)$ may be interpreted in an analogous manner.

The likelihood function is

$$\mathcal{L} = \prod_{t=1}^{T}\prod_{j=1}^{3}\prod_{k=1}^{2}(p_{tjk})^{m_{tjk}},\qquad(3.4\text{-}9)$$

where T is the number of observations, m_{tjk} equals 1 if for the tth observation $i_A = j$, and $i_B = k$; m_{tjk} equals 0 otherwise. p_{tjk} is the probability that for the tth observation $i_A = j$ and $i_B = k$. These probabilities may be obtained from exponentiation of (3.4-2). Maximizing the log of $\mathcal{L}$ from equation (3.4-9) (using a numerical maximization program) yields maximum-likelihood estimates of a_1, a_2, b_1, $\beta_{AB}(1,1)$, and $\beta_{AB}(2,1)$.

Two other parameters of interest are

$$\frac{\partial}{\partial x} \log \{P[i_A=1,\ i_B=2] / P[i_A=2,\ i_B = 2]\}$$

$$\frac{\partial}{\partial x} \log \{P[i_A=1,\ i_B=1] / P[i_A=2,\ i_B = 1]\}\qquad(3.4\text{-}10)$$

and

$$\log \left[\frac{P[i_A = 1,\ i_B = 1] / P[i_A = 1,\ i_B = 2]}{P(i_A = 2,\ i_B = 1] / P[i_A = 2,\ i_B = 2]} \right].$$

$$(3.4\text{-}11)$$

Equations (3.4-10) and (3.4-11) are automatically determined from the equations in (3.4-2). Once parameter estimates are obtained, predicted probabilities may be computed. For instance, one can compute the probability that A equals 1, setting x first at m and then at n, where m and n are constants. The two probabilities will differ because (a) x affects A, (b) x affects B, and (c) A and B interact. Comparison of these probabilities thus provides a quantitative measure of the total impact of x on A.[3]

The MLOGLIN command defaults to loading the data into core. If the problem is so large that it will not fit into core, the OUTOFCORE option can be used. This option results in a substantial increase in computer resources used and should not be used unless

needed. The VER=NEW version of MLOGLIN saves substantial space over
the older VER=OLD version and should be used. The MLOGLIN command
contains a number of options that will be discussed briefly. For
further detail, see the B34S help file for MLOGLIN.

The MLOGLIN command proceeds first by estimating basis
vectors. Next, the negative log-likelihood function is minimized,
using the Davidon-Fletcher-Powell approach. To speed up
convergence, analytical evaluation of the initial Hessian matrix is
done if the starting values of all the parameters are initially
zero. If the parameter COV=DPF is set, then final-stage analytical
calculation of the Hessian matrix, from which standard errors are
obtained, is <u>not</u> performed. Final-stage analytical calculation of
the standard errors <u>is</u> performed when COV=ANAL, which is the
default setting. The setting COV=ANAL is more expensive, but
usually will result in better standard errors. The DPF method is
not appropriate in cases in which there are no exogenous variables.
If the ANAL method is too expensive, the NUMERIC method can be
used. This method was found by Kawasaki (1978) to be better than
the DPF method but less expensive than the ANAL method. In their
rewrite of the code, Klein and Klein (1988a, 1988b) made changes in
the updating procedure, which substantially reduced the computer
time needed for the NUMERIC method.   Using their revised code
(available with VER=NEW), Klein and Klein (1988a) found the ANAL
method to be 12 times more expensive than the NUMERIC method and
that there was a substantial speed up in their code of 96% to 198%
over the original Kawasaki (1978) code. For additional detail on
the calculation of H, see Klein and Klein (1988a). The final method
available for calculating the asymptotic covariance matrix is by
summation of individually estimated information matrices
(COV=INFORMATION). To be on the safe side, the user is encouraged
to use the default (COV=ANAL) method, and, as a second choice, move
to the COV=NUMERIC method, if computer time becomes a major
factor.[4]

The next job runs MLOGLIN in a situation in which the
endogenous variables Y1 and Y2 are coded 1, 2 and 1, 2, 3,
respectively. The covariance matrix has been optionally printed.

```
B34SEXEC MLOGIT VER=NEW IP=0 ICOV=PRINT$
        MODEL Y1 Y2 = X1 X2 X3 X4 $
        LEVEL Y1(FEMALE) Y2(LOWY,MIDDLEY)$ B34SEEND$
```

The next example uses the   VALUES sentences to calculate the
expected values of Y1 and Y2 for the case in which X1=10 and X3=8
and in which X1=12 and X4=66. In the first VALUES sentence since X2
and X4 are not mentioned, their mean values are used. In the second
VALUES sentence, the mean values of X2 and X3 are used. In
addition, elasticities are calculated for the values supplied for
the first VALUES sentence.

```
B34SEXEC MLOGIT VER=NEW IP=0 ICOV=PRINT$
       MODEL Y1 Y2 = X1 X2 X3 X4 $
       VALUES X1(10.0) X3(8.0)$
       VALUES X1(12.0) X4(66.0)$
       ELAST VALUES(1) EVARS(X1, X3)$
       LEVEL Y1(FEMALE) Y2(LOWY,MIDDLEY)$ B34SEEND$
```

The MLOGIT command has other options, which include the
following:

- Selectively suppressing basis-vector groups with the
  BASISSUP sentence.

- Selectively suppressing groups with the GSUPP sentence.

- Selectively suppressing exogenous effects.

- Selectively turning off output.

For further detail on these and other options, see the B34S on-line
help file for the MLOGLIN command.

3.5 Tobit Models

A lower-bound tobit model, first proposed by Tobin (1958),
involves estimation of a model in which

$$
\begin{aligned}
y_i &= X\beta + u_i & \text{if } X\beta + u_i > c \\
y_i &= c & \text{otherwise,}
\end{aligned}
$$
(3.5-1)

where c is the lower bound. The tobit model can alternatively be
estimated for problems with an upper bound.[5] The problem of
predicting grades for good students is an example of an upper bound
since the grade can never get larger than a certain value, no
matter how much the student studies. The problem of prediction of
housing expenses is an example of a lower bound since a person will
never spend a negative amount on housing. If OLS is used, instead
of a tobit model, predictions will lie outside the admissible range
for the y variable and, in addition, the OLS estimates will be
biased. The bias arises from the fact that in equation (3.5-1) y_i
is observed only when $X\beta + u_i$ is greater than zero. The
assumptions of OLS require that u_i be $\sim IN(0, \sigma^2)$ and that u_i be
uncorrelated with the explanatory variables. Assume c is the limit
value of a lower-limit tobit model.

$$
P(y_i = c) = P(X\beta - u_i < c)
$$
(3.5-2)

$$
P(y_i > c) = P(X\beta - u_i \geq c).
$$
(3.5-3)

In this model, $E(u_i \mid u_i > c - X\beta)$ is not equal to zero but a
function of X. The OLS estimates of β are downwardly biased and
inconsistent as a consequence of $E(u_i \mid u_i > c - X\beta)$ increasing as
X values increase, where we assume β values are plus (Maddala 1983

2). This can be visualized in an X - Y plot of the data of a model with an intercept and one explanatory variable. An OLS line to estimate the β associated with the X value will be lower than its true value because of the zero values for the Y variable. The tobit model avoids these problems. In the tobit model for <u>limit observations</u>

$$P(Y_i = c) = P[\ (u_i\ /\ \sigma) > ((X\beta - c)/\sigma)] = Q[(X\beta - c)/\sigma], \qquad (3.5\text{-}4)$$

while for <u>non-limit observations</u> $y_i - X\beta$ has a normal distribution.

$$P(Y_t\ |\ X_t\beta) \qquad = (1/\sigma)\ f[(X\beta - Y_t)/\sigma), \qquad\qquad (3.5\text{-}5)$$

where f( ) is the standard normal density defined in (3.1-5). The expected value of Y_t for any observation X_t is derived by summing the products of the possible outcomes for Y_t and their probabilities

$$E(Y_t\ |\ X_t\beta) = c\ Q[(X\beta - c)/\sigma] + \int_c^\infty Y\ (1/\sigma)f[(X_t\beta - Y)/\sigma]dy, \qquad (3.5\text{-}6)$$

which can be reduced to

$$E(Y_t\ |\ X_t\ \beta) \qquad = c\ Q(Z)\ + X_t\ \beta\ F(Z) + \sigma\ f(Z), \qquad\qquad (3.5\text{-}7)$$

where Z is the number of standard deviations from the limit c

$$Z \qquad = (X_t\beta - c)/\sigma, \qquad\qquad\qquad\qquad (3.5\text{-}8)$$

F( ) is the cumulative normal density defined in equation 3.1-6 and Q( ) = 1-F( ). The expected value of Y for a lower-limit problem becomes

$$E(Y_t\ |\ X_t\beta) \qquad = c\ + \sigma\ Z\ F(Z)\ + \ \sigma\ f(Z), \qquad\qquad (3.5\text{-}9)$$

which, when c=0, quickly reduces to

$$E(Y_t\ |\ X_t\beta) \qquad = X_t\beta\ F(Z) + \sigma f(Z). \qquad\qquad (3.5\text{-}10)$$

For an upper limit c, dropping the t subscript on X

$$Y_i \qquad = c \qquad\quad \text{if } X\beta - u_i > c$$

$$\qquad = X\beta - u_i \ \text{if } X\beta - u_i \le c \qquad\qquad\qquad (3.5\text{-}11)$$

$$P[Y=c\ |X\beta] \qquad = F[(XB-c)/\sigma] \qquad\qquad\qquad (3.5\text{-}12)$$

$$P[Y\ |X\beta] \qquad = (1/\sigma)\ f[(X\beta - Y)/\sigma]. \qquad\qquad (3.5\text{-}13)$$

Here the nonlimit values are integrated over the interval $(-\infty,\ c)$

$$E(Y_t \mid X_t\beta) = c \ F[(X\beta - c)/\sigma] + \int_{-\infty}^{c} Y \ (1/\sigma)f[(X_t\beta-Y)/\sigma]dy, \quad (3.5-14)$$

which can be reduced to

$$E(Y_i \mid X\beta) \qquad = c + \sigma Z \ Q(Z) \ - \sigma \ f(Z). \qquad\qquad (3.5-15)$$

Equation (3.5-15) for an upper limit should be compared with equation (3.5-9) for a lower limit.

McDonald and Moffitt (1980) have proposed important decompositions of this model, which have been incorporated in the B34S TOBIT command. If we define $E(Y^*)$ as the expected value of Y for observations above the limit and assume that c = 0, then

$$E(Y^* \mid X_t\beta) \quad = E(Y_t \mid Y_t > 0)$$

$$= E(Y_t \mid u_t > - X_t\beta)$$

$$= X_t \ \beta + [\sigma \ f(Z)]/ \ F(Z). \qquad\qquad (3.5-16)$$

The first term in equation (3.5-16) is the usual quantity $X_t\beta$, while the second expression is the value of the truncated normal error term, which must be taken into account since it <u>does not have a zero expectation</u>. Since $f(Z) / F(Z)$ converges to zero, the larger Z, $E(Y^* \mid X_t\beta)$ converges to $X_t \ \beta$ the farther one gets from the lower limit. Equation (3.5-10) can be rewritten as

$$E(Y_t \mid X_t\beta) \qquad = F(Z) \ E(Y^* \mid X_t\beta) \qquad\qquad (3.5-17)$$

if we multiply equation (3.5-16) by $F(Z)$. If we differentiate equation (3.5-17) by the i^{it} variable of X, x_i, ignoring t subscripts, we obtain

$$\delta \ E(Y) \ / \ \delta x_i \quad = F(Z)(\delta E(Y^*)/\delta x_i) + E(Y^*) \ (\delta F(Z)/\delta x_i). \qquad (3.5-18)$$

McDonald and Moffitt (1980, 318) interpret equation (3.5-18) as expressing the partial of the expected value of Y, given a change in x_i as being the sum of " (1) the change in Y of those being above the limit, weighted by the probability of being above the limit and (2) the change in the probability of being above the limit, weighted by the expected value of Y if above." It is important to note that equation (3.5-18) only holds for a zero lower limit. The usual error is to think that $\delta \ E(Y)/\delta x_i = \beta_i$.

Using equation (3.5-16) and the fact that

$$\delta \ F(Z) \ / \ \delta x_i \quad = f(Z) \ \beta_i \ / \ \sigma \qquad\qquad (3.5-19)$$

$$\delta \ f(Z) \ / \ \delta x_i \quad = -zf(Z) \ \beta_i \ / \ \sigma \qquad\qquad (3.5-20)$$

$F'(Z)= f(Z)$ and $f'(Z) = -zf(Z)$, equation (3.5-18) becomes

$$\delta\ E(Y^*)\ /\ \delta x_i\ =\ \beta_i\ +\ \quad [\sigma/F(Z)]\delta f(Z)/\delta x_i\ -$$
$$[\sigma f(Z)/(F(Z)^2]\delta F(Z)/\delta x_i$$

$$=\ \beta_i[1\ -\ zf(Z)/F(Z)\ -\ f(Z)^2/F(Z)^2].\qquad (3.5\text{-}21)$$

The importance of equation (3.5-21) is that it indicates that unless one is an infinite distance from the lower limit, where $f(Z)$ converges to zero and $F(Z)$ converges to 1, the effect on Y of a change in x_i is not β_i. As noted by McDonald and Moffitt (1980), if equations (3.5-21) and (3.5-19) are substituted into equation (3.5-18), the total effect $\delta E(Y)\ /\ \delta(x_i)\ =\ F(Z)\ \beta_i$. If equation (3.5-18) is divided by $F(Z)\beta_i$, the fraction of the total effect due to being above the limit becomes $[1-zf(Z)/F(Z)-[f(Z)]^2/[F(Z)]^2]$, which is the fraction that the coefficients must be adjusted to obtain the correct regression effects for observations above the limit.[6] For upper-limit problems, the basic setup is similar, except for the fact that Z is the number of standard deviations from the upper limit.[7]

The TOBIT command has relatively few options. The setup that follows will run a lower-limit model, where y = f(X1 X2 X3).

```
B34SEXEC TOBIT LOWER=1.2 $
    MODEL Y=X1 X2 X3$ B34SEEND$
```

Other options available include restricting of the model to not contain an intercept (NOINT), giving a summary table for each observation (ISUMM), which is very paper-intensive for large data sets, and weighting the model with the WEIGHT parameter. The WEIGHT option is used to attempt to correct for heteroskedasticity. Since the heteroskedasticity tests are not available, the best thing to do is run the REGRESSION heteroskedasticity tests and once a potential weight variable is selected, run the same variable with the WEIGHT option of the TOBIT command. Although it is rarely needed, if the TOBIT command runs out of iterations without convergence, the NIT command can be used to specify a larger number. The default of 25 iterations is usually sufficient for all but highly multicollinear problems.

The TOBIT command output includes a matrix of second moments for limit and nonlimit observations, and first and second derivatives of the likelihood function evaluated at the maximum. The first derivatives give an indication of how close the algorithm has gotten to the maximum. These values are usually very small, typically in the range of .1 E-13 and smaller. Since we are looking for a maximum of the likelihood function, the inverse of the second derivatives matrix times -1 is the variance-covariance matrix. Interpretation of this matrix is similar to that of OLS models. Finally, after the coefficient table, the log of the likelihood function, the total number of limit and nonlimit observations, and an estimate of σ are listed. The table of coefficients includes

B(i)   = estimated coefficient;
F(Z)   = probability for given Z value;
f(Z)   = density of cumulative normal distribution for Z.
SIGMA   = standard error of regression;
B(i)/SIGMA   = normalized coefficient;
PARTIAL1   = f(Z) * (B(i) / SIGMA)
PARTIAL2   = B(i) * (1.0 - (Z*f(Z)/F(Z)) - (f(Z)**2/F(Z) **2))
B(i)*F(Z)   = the total effect [d(Ey) / d(X(i))]
F(y)   = XB * F(Z)   +   (SIGMA * f(Z))
F(ystar)   = F(y) / F(Z)
Z   = XB / SIGMA .

In the coefficient table, Z and XB are calculated for mean X(i) in
the output. Often other X(i) values are of interest. If we assume
a model of the form Y = 10 + 1.2X1 + 2.2X2, where SIGMA = .9, the
SAS program given in Table 3.1 will calculate the desired values.
It makes use of the fact that

f(Z)   = EXP(-(Z*Z)/2.0) / SQRT(2 * π)
TTi   = B(i) * F(Z)
PARTIAL1i   = f(Z) * (B(i) / SIGMA)
PARTIAL2i   = B(i) * (1.0 - (Z*f(Z) / F(Z)) -(f(Z)**2 /F(Z)**2)).

Table 3.1 SAS Program to Calculate TOBIT Values

```
DATA TEST;
    INPUT X1 X2;
    B1 = 10.0 ;
    B2 = 1.2  ;
    B3 = 2.2  ;
    SIGMA = .9  ;
    XB = B1 + (B2 * X1)  + (B3 * X2) ;
    Z=XB / SIGMA;
    FZ = PROBNORM(Z) ;
    DENSITY = EXP(-1.0 * (Z*Z)/2.0) * .3989423  ;
    TT1 = B1 * FZ ;
    TT2 = B2 * FZ ;
    TT3 = B3 * FZ ;
    PART11 = DENSITY * (B1 / SIGMA);
    PART12 = DENSITY * (B2 / SIGMA);
    PART13 = DENSITY * (B3 / SIGMA);
    PART21 = B1 * (1.0 - (Z * DENSITY / FZ) - ((DENSITY
        *DENSITY) / (FZ * FZ)))  ;
    PART22 = (B2 / B1) * PARTIAL21 ;
    PART23 = (B3 / B1) * PARTIAL21 ;
    EYSTAR = XB + (SIGMA * DENSITY/FZ);
    EY     = EYSTAR * FZ;
CARDS;
    X1  X2 values here
;
PROC PRINT DATA=TEST;
```

3.6 Examples

The B34S MACRO MURDER, listed in Table 3.2, loads data from
McManus (1985) and illustrates output of some options from the
REGRESSION, LOGLIN, MLOGLIN, PROBIT, and MPROBIT commands.

Table 3.2 Examples Using McManus Data

```
==MURDER
B34SEXEC DATA NOOB=44 NOHEAD HEADING=('MCMANUS JPE 1985 ')$
* DATA ON DETERRENCE OF CAPITAL PUNISHMENT  $
* FOR DISCUSSION SEE MADDALA (1988) PAGE 279 -283 $
INPUT N M PC PX D1 T Y LF NW D2 $
*  N = OBSERVATION NUMBER$
*  M = MURDER RATE PER 100000  FBI ESTIMATE 1950$
*  PC = NUMBER OF CONVICTIONS / NUMBER OF MURDERS IN 1950 $
*  PX = AVERAGE NUMBER OF EXECUTIONS 46-50 / NUMBER OF CONVICTIONS $
*  Y  = MEDIAN FAMILY INCOME IN 1949 THOUSANDS OF DOLLARS  $
*  LF = LABOR FORCE PARTICIPATION RATE 1950 EXPRESSED AS A PERCENTAGE $
*  NW = PROPORTION OF POPULATION THAT IS NONWHITE IN 1950 $
*  D2 = DUMMY VARIABLE, 1 FOR SOUTHERN STATES, 0 FOR OTHERS  $
*  D1 = 1 IF STATE HAS CAPITAL PUNISHMENT, 0 OTHERWISE  $
*  T = MEDIAN TIME SERVED IN MONTHS OF CONVICTED MURDERERS RELEASES IN 1951$
*  D3 = 0 IF D1 = 0, D3 = 1 if D1 = 1 & PX LT .1, D3 = 2 IF PX GE .1  $
BUILD D3                                                  $
GEN D3 = GE(PX,0.100)$
GEN D3 = ADD(D1,D3)$
*  D1 =  F(       )  LOGIT/PROBIT , PX = F(        )  TOBIT  $
DATACARDS$
1  19.25  0.204  0.035  1   47 1.10  51.2  0.321  1
2   7.53  0.327  0.081  1   58  .92  48.5  0.224  1
3   5.66  0.401  0.012  1   82 1.72  50.8  0.127  0
4   3.21  0.318  0.070  1  100 2.18  54.4  0.063  0
5   2.80  0.350  0.062  1  222 1.75  52.4  0.021  0
6   1.41  0.283  0.100  1  164 2.26  56.7  0.027  0
7   6.18  0.204  0.050  1  161 2.07  54.6  0.139  1
8  12.15  0.232  0.054  1   70 1.43  52.7  0.218  1
9   1.34  0.199  0.086  1  219 1.92  52.3  0.008  0
10  3.71  0.138  0.0    0   81 1.82  53.0  0.012  0
11  5.35  0.142  0.018  1  209 2.34  55.4  0.076  0
12  4.72  0.118  0.045  1  182 2.12  53.5  0.299  0
13  3.81  0.207  0.040  1  185 1.81  51.6  0.040  0
14 10.44  0.189  0.045  1  104 1.35  48.5  0.069  1
15  9.58  0.124  0.125  1  126 1.26  49.3  0.330  1
16  1.02  0.210  0.060  1  192 2.07  53.9  0.017  0
17  7.52  0.227  0.055  1   95 2.04  55.7  0.166  1
18  1.31  0.167  0.0    0  245 1.55  51.2  0.003  0
19  1.67  0.120  0.0    0   97 1.89  54.0  0.010  0
20  7.07  0.139  0.041  1  177 1.68  52.2  0.076  0
21 11.79  0.272  0.063  1  125 0.76  51.1  0.454  1
22  2.71  0.125  0.0    0   56 1.96  54.0  0.032  0
23 13.21  0.235  0.086  1   85 1.29  55.0  0.266  1
24  3.48  0.108  0.040  1  199 1.81  52.9  0.018  0
25  0.81  0.672  0.0    0  298 1.72  53.7  0.038  0
26  2.32  0.357  0.030  1  145 2.39  55.8  0.067  0
27  3.47  0.592  0.029  1   78 1.68  50.4  0.075  0
28  8.31  0.225  0.400  1  144 2.29  58.8  0.064  0
29  1.57  0.267  0.126  1  178 2.34  54.5  0.065  0
30  4.13  0.164  0.122  1  146 2.21  53.5  0.065  0
31  3.84  0.128  0.091  1  132 1.42  48.8  0.090  1
32  1.83  0.287  0.075  1   98 1.97  54.5  0.016  0
33  3.54  0.210  0.069  1  120 2.12  52.1  0.061  0
34  1.11  0.342  0.0    0  148 1.90  56.0  0.019  0
35  8.90  0.133  0.216  1  123 1.15  56.2  0.389  1
36  1.27  0.241  0.100  1  282 1.70  53.3  0.037  0
37 15.26  0.167  0.038  1   79 1.24  50.9  0.161  1
38 11.15  0.252  0.040  1   34 1.55  53.2  0.127  1
39  1.74  0.418  0.0    0  104 2.04  51.7  0.017  0
40 11.98  0.282  0.032  1   91 1.59  54.3  0.222  1
41  3.04  0.194  0.086  1  199 2.07  53.7  0.026  0
42  .85   0.378  0.0    0  101 2.00  54.7  0.012  0
43  2.83  0.757  0.033  1  109 1.84  47.0  0.057  1
44  2.89  0.357  0.0    0  117 2.04  56.9  0.022  0
B34SRETURN$
B34SEEND$
```

```
B34SEXEC LIST $ VAR M PC PX D1 T Y LF NW D2 D3$ B34SEEND$
B34SEXEC REGRESSION RESIDUALA$
       MODEL M = PC PX D1 T Y LF NW D2$ B34SEEND$
B34SEXEC REGRESSION RESIDUALA$
       MODEL D1 = T Y LF NW D2$ B34SEEND$
B34SEXEC REGRESSION RESIDUALA$
       COMMENT=('REMOVES D2 ')$
       MODEL M = PC PX D1 T Y LF NW $ B34SEEND$
B34SEXEC REGRESSION RESIDUALA$
       COMMENT=('REMOVES D2 ')$
       MODEL D1 = T Y LF NW $ B34SEEND$
B34SEXEC PROBIT $ MODEL D1 = T Y LF NW D2$ B34SEEND$
B34SEXEC PROBIT $ MODEL D1 = T Y LF NW    $ B34SEEND$
B34SEXEC LOGLIN $ MODEL D1 = T Y LF NW    $ B34SEEND$
B34SEXEC MPROBIT $ MODEL D1 = T Y LF NW  $  VVALUES=(0.0,1.0)$ B34SEEND$
B34SEXEC MPROBIT $ MODEL D3 = T Y LF NW  $  VVALUES=(0.0,1.0,2.0)$
       B34SEEND$
B34SEXEC TOBIT LOWER  LIMIT=0.0$ MODEL PX = T Y LF NW D2$ B34SEEND$
B34SEXEC TOBIT LOWER  LIMIT=0.0$ MODEL PX = T Y LF NW  $ B34SEEND$
B34SEXEC MLOGLIN IP=1 VER=OLD$ MODEL D1= T Y LF NW $
  LEVEL D1(NOLAW)$         B34SEEND$
B34SEXEC MLOGLIN IP=1 VER=NEW$ MODEL D1= T Y LF NW $
  LEVEL D1(NOLAW)$         B34SEEND$
B34SEXEC MLOGLIN IP=1 VER=OLD$ MODEL D1= T Y LF NW D2$
  LEVEL D1(NOLAW)$         B34SEEND$
B34SEXEC MLOGLIN IP=1 VER=NEW$ MODEL D1= T Y LF NW D2$
  LEVEL D1(NOLAW)$         B34SEEND$
==
```

Because of space considerations, output from some of the commands in Table 3.2 has not been listed. Variable names and descriptions are given in Table 3.2 and will not be repeated. After loading the data, the dummy variable D3 was built. This is coded = 0 if the state does not have a capital punishment law. It is coded = 1 if the state has a capital punishment law and = 2 if $PX \geq .1$. M is a continuous variable and can be estimated by OLS. D1 is a 0-1 variable and should be estimated by probit or logit models. D3 is an ordered 0-1-2 variable and should be estimated by multinomial probit (MPROBIT) or multinomial logit (MLOGLIN). PX is bounded at the lower end and should be estimated by tobit models.

The first REGRESSION command estimates an OLS model for the continuous variable M on a vector of explanatory variables. The output from this command, which duplicates results reported in Maddala (1988, 281), has not been shown. The next REGRESSION command estimates the 0-1 variable D1 with OLS, which is not the most appropriate procedure. These results follow and duplicate the results in Maddala (1988, 281). All variables except for T (median time served in months for murderers released in 1951) are significant. The next two REGRESSION commands estimate subset models for M and D1, respectively, and are not shown.

```
.............
STEP NUMBER  6                         ANALYSIS OF VARIANCE FOR REDUCTION IN SS DUE TO VARIABLE ENTERING
  VARIABLE ENTERING        6               SOURCE           DF        SS            MS          F         F SIG.
  MULTIPLE R          0.58100              DUE REGRESSION    5       2.4166       0.48332     3.8727     0.993800
  STD ERROR OF Y.X    0.35327              DEV. FROM REG.   38       4.7425       0.12480
  R SQUARE            0.33756              TOTAL            43       7.1591       0.16649

     MULTIPLE REGRESSION EQUATION
  VARIABLE       COEFFICIENT     STD. ERROR     T VAL.    T SIG. P. COR. ELASTICITY    PARTIAL COR. FOR VAR. NOT IN EQUATION
D1       =                                                                            VARIABLE    COEFFICIENT   F FOR SELECTION
  T        X- 6   0.1461530E-02  0.9978231E-03   1.465    0.84878  0.2312   0.2508
  Y        X- 7   0.6577319      0.2404255       2.736    0.99059  0.4056   1.473
  LF       X- 8  -0.5456195E-01  0.2825693E-01  -1.931    0.93902 -0.2989  -3.640
  NW       X- 9   1.988241       0.7595480       2.618    0.98736  0.3909   0.2639
  D2       X-10   0.3433565      0.1892451       1.814    0.92247  0.2824   0.1472
  CONSTANT  X-12   1.992948       1.326070        1.503    0.85887

ADJUSTED R SQUARE FOR K=   6,  N=      44 IS     0.25039446

-2 * LN(MAXIMUM OF THE LIKELIHOOD FUNCTION)   26.850923
```

The preceding OLS model indicates that D2 was significant at the .92247 level (t=1.814). The PROBIT command was next used to estimate this model with a procedure that takes into account the 0-1 structure of the dependent variable D1. D2 was found to have a t of .0947, which indicates that it is not significant.[8] The next PROBIT command removes D2 and reruns the model. Unlike OLS, where the estimated coefficients can be interpreted as partial derivatives, probit coefficients can only be interpreted at a certain value. The B34S output lists these partial derivatives at the means of the data and at the maximums of each independent variable. While this calculation is usually done, in this case it does not make too much sense to use the mean of D2, which is itself a 0-1 variable. To further interpret the coefficients, the user might have supplied alternate exogenous variable values with the MEANS sentence.

The next example uses the LOGLIN command to run the corrected model with the D2 variable removed. The reported results have the same t scores as are reported in Maddala (1988, 283) but the coefficients are exactly half those reported in Maddala. The reason for the difference was discussed in sections 3.3 and 3.4 and is the result of the functional form of the estimated model used by both programs. The same problem is next estimated by the MLOGLIN command and here the results are the same as reported in Maddala (1988), except for the sign change. For further detail, see section 3.4.

```
MULTIVARIATE PROBIT ANALYSIS              EQUATION # 1

EQUATION ESTIMATED, INDEX # OF LEFT HAND THEN RIGHT HAND VARIABLES
  5 12  6  7  8  9 10

OPTION CARD - NADJ NSTRT       NSTOP
               0    1            5

DEPENDENT VARIABLE IS X- 5       D1

INDEPENDENT VARIABLE SUMMATIONS                MEANS

X-12  CONSTANT    0.44000000E+02          0.100000000000E+01
X- 6  T           0.60070000E+04          0.136522727273E+03
X- 7  Y           0.78360000E+02          0.178090909091E+01
X- 8  LF          0.23349000E+04          0.530659090909E+02
X- 9  NW          0.46460000E+01          0.105590909091E+00
X-10  D2          0.15000000E+02          0.340909090909E+00

THE ITERATION HAS CONVERGED
```

```
NEGATIVE INVERSE - VARIANCE COVARIANCE OF COEF         1/COND  0.15480461E-08
              CONSTANT         T              Y              LF             NW             D2
CONSTANT    0.128196E+03   -0.627157E-02   0.529172E+01   -0.255292E+01  -0.189363E+02  -0.943827E+01
T          -0.627157E-02    0.319874E-04   0.996877E-02   -0.339268E-03   0.103080E-01   0.524239E-02
Y           0.529172E+01    0.996877E-02   0.991195E+01   -0.486765E+00   0.143937E+02   0.290631E+01
LF         -0.255292E+01   -0.339268E-03  -0.486765E+00    0.661582E-01  -0.390837E+00   0.613380E-01
NW         -0.189363E+02    0.103080E-01   0.143937E+02   -0.390837E+00   0.430546E+03  -0.126032E+02
D2         -0.943827E+01    0.524239E-02   0.290631E+01    0.613380E-01  -0.126032E+02   0.214589E+04

ITERATION NUMBER    11 LOG OF LIKELIHOOD FUNCTION  -0.86404125D+01
```

SUMMARY OF RESULTS

```
                                                                              PARTIAL DERIVATIVES
VARIABLE          MAX LIKELIHOOD EST    STANDARD ERROR    ESTIMATE/STANDARD ERR    EVAL AT MAX      EVAL AT MEAN
X-12  CONSTANT      0.69154055E+01     0.11322386E+02        0.61077279E+00      0.27588319E+01    0.35711365E-03
X- 6  T             0.11312245E-01     0.56557361E-02        0.20001366E+01      0.45129070E-02    0.58416778E-06
X- 7  Y             0.64610744E+01     0.31483250E+01        0.20522260E+01      0.25775810E+01    0.33365185E-03
X- 8  LF           -0.40928369E+00     0.25721235E+00       -0.15912288E+01     -0.16327964E+00   -0.21135535E-04
X- 9  NW            0.42498076E+02     0.20749605E+02        0.20481390E+01      0.16954182E+02    0.21946136E-02
X-10  D2            0.43900449E+01     0.46323737E+02        0.94768800E-01      0.17513645E+01    0.22670326E-03
```

CALCULATED VALUE OF DEPENDENT VARIABLE = 1.0000 AT POINT OF MEANS

```
OBSERVATIONS      44

  LIMITS           9

  NONLIMITS       35
```

(-2.0) TIMES THE LOG LIKELIHOOD RATIO= 27.303456 , DISTRIBUTED AS CHI SQUARED WITH   5 DEGREES OF FREEDOM

THE CHI SQUARE SIGNIFICANCE FOR   5 DEGREES OF FREEDOM = 0.9999502300 FOR LOG LIKELIHOOD RATIO

CALCULATED PROBABILITIES FOR SELECTED OBS. NSTRT= 1 NSTOP=   5

```
         CALCULATED   ACTUAL
 OBS      VALUE      D1      DENSITY OF NORMAL DISTRIBUTION FOR OBSERVATION
  1       1.000     1.000      0.000
  2       1.000     1.000      0.000
  3       1.000     1.000      0.001
  4       0.995     1.000      0.016
  5       0.571     1.000      0.393
```

STEP ENDING. SECONDS USED 0.29234886 . TOTAL JOB SECONDS   1.8690348 .

MULTIVARIATE PROBIT ANALYSIS   EQUATION # 1

EQUATION ESTIMATED, INDEX # OF LEFT HAND THEN RIGHT HAND VARIABLES
  5 12 6 7 8 9

```
OPTION CARD - NADJ NSTRT    NSTOP
               0     1        5
```

DEPENDENT VARIABLE IS X- 5   D1

INDEPENDENT VARIABLE SUMMATIONS   MEANS

```
X-12  CONSTANT     0.44000000E+02              0.100000000000E+01
X- 6  T            0.60070000E+04              0.136522727273E+03
X- 7  Y            0.78360000E+02              0.178090909091E+01
X- 8  LF           0.23349000E+04              0.530659090909E+02
X- 9  NW           0.46460000E+01              0.105590909091E+00
```

THE ITERATION HAS CONVERGED

```
NEGATIVE INVERSE - VARIANCE COVARIANCE OF COEF         1/COND  0.81596376E-08
              CONSTANT         T              Y              LF             NW
CONSTANT    0.110192E+03    0.121080E-02   0.112725E+02   -0.245707E+01  -0.926051E+01
T           0.121080E-02    0.257087E-04   0.623940E-02   -0.332532E-03   0.234330E-01
Y           0.112725E+02    0.623940E-02   0.790803E+01   -0.519663E+00   0.234153E+02
LF         -0.245707E+01   -0.332532E-03  -0.519663E+00    0.657519E-01  -0.917490E+00
NW         -0.926051E+01    0.234330E-01   0.234153E+02   -0.917490E+00   0.403564E+03

ITERATION NUMBER     8 LOG OF LIKELIHOOD FUNCTION  -0.90166578D+01
```

SUMMARY OF RESULTS

					PARTIAL DERIVATIVES	
VARIABLE		MAX LIKELIHOOD EST	STANDARD ERROR	ESTIMATE/STANDARD ERR	EVAL AT MAX	EVAL AT MEAN
X-12	CONSTANT	0.10267272E+02	0.10497241E+02	0.97809244E+00	0.40960256E+01	0.67557503E-02
X- 6	T	0.94213373E-02	0.50703706E-02	0.18581161E+01	0.37585483E-02	0.61991345E-05
X- 7	Y	0.55510568E+01	0.28121218E+01	0.19739746E+01	0.22145386E+01	0.36525333E-02
X- 8	LF	-0.43654090E+00	0.25642135E+00	-0.17024359E+01	-0.17415363E+00	-0.28723903E-03
X- 9	NW	0.50248507E+02	0.20088909E+02	0.25013060E+01	0.20046139E+02	0.33062955E-01

CALCULATED VALUE OF DEPENDENT VARIABLE = 0.9998 AT POINT OF MEANS

OBSERVATIONS	44
LIMITS	9
NONLIMITS	35

(-2.0) TIMES THE LOG LIKELIHOOD RATIO=   26.550966   , DISTRIBUTED AS CHI SQUARED WITH   4 DEGREES OF FREEDOM

THE CHI SQUARE SIGNIFICANCE FOR   4 DEGREES OF FREEDOM = 0.9999755020 FOR LOG LIKELIHOOD RATIO

CALCULATED PROBABILITIES FOR SELECTED OBS. NSTRT=   1 NSTOP=   5

	CALCULATED	ACTUAL	
OBS	VALUE	D1	DENSITY OF NORMAL DISTRIBUTION FOR OBSERVATION
1	1.000	1.000	0.000
2	1.000	1.000	0.000
3	1.000	1.000	0.000
4	0.997	1.000	0.010
5	0.600	1.000	0.386

STEP ENDING. SECONDS USED 0.22088623   . TOTAL JOB SECONDS   2.1371059   .

The problem is next solved with the LOGLIN command, whose output has been edited to save space.

LEAST SQUARES COEFFICIENT AND STARTING VALUES FOR D1   -   CONDITIONAL ESTIMATION

		INVERSE TAYLOR SERIES
EXPLANATORY VARIABLE	OLS COEFFICIENT	STARTING VALUE

1/CONDITION OF XPX   0.68593665E-07

T	0.83418E-03	0.512690526582128E-02
Y	0.53533	3.29014622380234
LF	-0.61771E-01	-0.379647929081117
NW	2.5831	15.8759420889625
CONSTANT	2.7334	13.2687404077268

CONDITIONAL ESTIMATION OF EQUATION FOR D1

LOG OF LIKELIHOOD FUNCTION -9.10756709   AFTER 10 ITERATIONS

EXPLANATORY VARIABLE $$$$$$$$$$$$$$$	COEFFICIENT $$$$$$$$$$$$$$$	GRADIENT $$$$$$$$$$$$$$$	ASYMPTOTIC STANDARD ERROR $$$$$$$$$$$$$$$	ASYMPTOTIC T-RATIO $$$$$$$$$$$$$$$	ASYMPTOTIC SIGNIFICANCE $$$$$$$$$$$$$$$
CONSTANT	8.28347788	-0.114468226E-05	9.81961745	0.843564214	0.398912957
T	0.825822583E-02	-0.115808996E-03	0.480557814E-02	1.71846666	0.857115225E-01
Y	4.56577324	-0.256649477E-05	2.52657370	1.80710076	0.707465638E-01
LF	-0.357694302	-0.655771493E-04	0.239633529	-1.49267218	0.135523011
NW	42.6807639	0.753540879E-08	17.9272189	2.38077998	0.172760245E-01

The next example runs the preceding problem with the MPROBIT command, which gives results that are the same as those found with the PROBIT command. The reader is invited to verify by inspection of the printouts that the coefficients are the same . The MPROBIT command, unlike the PROBIT command, calculates estimated analysis of variance data. In the sample problem, the estimated R^2 was .95, and the percent predicted correctly was .9318. The history of the

computation shows that the problem converged in eight iterations
and tracks the change in the log likelihood function.

MPROBIT OPTION

WRITTEN BY RICHARD MCKELVEY BASED ON MODEL FOR CHOTOMOUS MULTIVARIATE PROBIT DEVELOPED BY WILLIAM ZAVOINA AND R. MCKELVEY

ROUTINES HEAVILY MODIFIED BY H. H. STOKES JANUARY 1985 FOR B34S.

FOR 0-1 CASE, MPROBIT ROUTINES PRODUCE SAME RESULTS AS B34S PB OPTION.

REFERENCES BY MCKELVEY AND ZAVOINA

- AN IBM FORTRAN IV PROGRAM TO PERFORM N-CHOTOMOUS MULTIVARIATE PROBIT ANALYSIS (BEHAVIORAL SCIENCE V 16, 1971 PP. 186-7)

- A STATISTICAL MODEL FOR THE ANALYSIS OF ORDINAL DEPENDENT VARIABLES (JOURNAL OF MATH. SOCIOLOGY V 4, 1975 PP. 103-120)

------ VERSION DATE 1 MARCH 1985 ------

TITLE CARDS (#1 - #2) READ:

MP CARD #3

NRESP (# OF CATEGORIES OF DEPENDENT VARIABLE) =   2
NCASE (# OF ITERATIONS ALLOWED (DEFAULT = 50)) =   50
NQRT (=1 RESIDUAL ANALYSIS, =0 NO RESIDUAL ANALYSIS) =   0
NORD (# OF SUBPROBLEMS (MUST BE IN RANGE 1-50), DEFAULT=1) =   1
INPUT (=0 USUAL CASE, =1 GROUPED DATA) =   5
NDUMP (=0 USUAL CASE, =1 FOR PRINT OF CHANGE IN COEF DURING EACH ITERATION) =   0
TOLA (CONVERGENCE TOLERANCE (DEFAULT = .000001)) =   0.10000000E-05

VALID RESPONSES CARD (# 4)   0. 1.

****
N-CHOTOMOUS PROBIT ANALYSIS:
****

                              DESCRIPTION OF VARIABLES INCLUDED
                                       IN ANALYSIS

                SAMPLE STATISTICS FOR ALL VARIABLES   I   BREAKDOWN OF DEPENDENT VARIABLE
                           IN ANALYSIS   I   (VARIABLE # 1)   B34S VAR # 5. B34S NAME = D1
                                                         I---
        VARIABLE   SAMPLE   SAMPLE   I CODE VALUE
NAME NUMBER B34S #   MEAN   VARIANCE   I OF RESPONSE   FREQUENCY   TOTALS
D1   1   5   0.79545455   0.16649049   I R(1)= 0.0   9
T   2   6   136.52273   3795.0925   I R(2)= 1.0   35   44 VALID RESPONSES
Y   3   7   1.7809091   0.15687822   I
LF   4   8   53.065909   6.1506712   I OTHER   0   0 MISSING DATA CASES
NW   5   9   0.10559091   0.12994387E-01   I
                                                         I   44 TOTAL CASES

                    A TOTAL OF 1 RUNS FOLLOW, USING A TOTAL OF 5 VARIABLES.
                    FOR ALL THESE RUNS, DEPENDENT VARIABLE IS VARIABLE # 1 ,
                    NUMBER OF ALLOWABLE ITERATIONS IS 50, AND TOLA= 0.10D-05

****
N-CHOTOMOUS PROBIT ANALYSIS:
****

                              BEGINNING EXECUTION OF RUN # 1.

                                 HISTORY OF COMPUTATION

                           CHANGE IN   LOG LIKELIHOOD
              ITERATION   ESTIMATE   1 / COND   FUNCTION
                 0   0.75090D+02   0.68597D-07   -0.30498D+02
                 1   0.93538D+02   0.53006D-07   -0.16590D+02
                 2   0.97379D+02   0.37543D-07   -0.12487D+02
                 3   0.12514D+03   0.24861D-07   -0.10502D+02
                 4   0.85704D+02   0.15885D-07   -0.94280D+01
                 5   0.18140D+02   0.11156D-07   -0.90698D+01
                 6   0.10904D+01   0.87671D-08   -0.90189D+01
                 7   0.30775D-02   0.81901D-08   -0.90167D+01
                 8   0.22053D-07   0.81598D-08   -0.90167D+01

****
N-CHOTOMOUS PROBIT ANALYSIS:
****

          THE ITERATION HAS CONVERGED ON THE 8TH ITERATION. MAXIMUM LIKELIHOOD ESTIMATES FOLLOW

-------------------------- BETAS --------------------------   -------------------------- MU'S --------------------------

                          MAXIMUM   MAXIMUM
            REPRESENTS   LIKELIHOOD   STANDARD   LIKELIHOOD   STANDARD
COEFFICIENT EFFECT OF   ESTIMATE   ERROR   MLE/SE   COEFFICIENT   ESTIMATE   ERROR   MLE/SE

BETA(0)   CONSTANT   10.267388   10.50   0.9781   MU(1)   0.00000
BETA(1)   T   0.94214572E-02 0.5070E-02 1.858
BETA(2)   Y   5.5510991   2.812   1.974
BETA(3)   LF   -0.43654497   0.2564   -1.702
BETA(4)   NW   50.248741   20.09   2.501

LOG OF THE LIKELIHOOD FUNCTION= -9.0166541

-2.0 TIMES LOG LIKELIHOOD RATIO =   26.550973
 (THIS IS CHI SQUARED WITH   4 DEGREES OF FREEDOM)   CHI SQUARE SIGNIFICANCE =   0.99997555

****
N-CHOTOMOUS PROBIT ANALYSIS:
****

ESTIMATED ANALYSIS OF VARIANCE

EXPLAINED SUM OF SQUARES =   863.14915
RESIDUAL SUM OF SQUARES =   44.000000
TOTAL SUM OF SQUARES =   907.14915
ESTIMATED R SQUARED =   0.95149640

OTHER SUMMARY STATISTICS

PERCENT PREDICTED CORRECTLY =   0.93181818
RANK ORDER CORRELATION- PREDICTED VERSUS ACTUAL =   0.78353876

MPROBIT PROGRAM ENDING

The D3 variable has the values 0, 1, and 2 and is not suitable for probit analysis. Since the MPROBIT command allows estimation of ordered probit models, it was used to predict D3 as a function of T, Y, LF, and NW in the second MPROBIT example, which is given next. In this example, the breakdown of the dependent variable D3 indicates that of 44 valid observations, 9 were D3=0, 28 were D3=1 and 7 were D3=2. The problem converged in four iterations and $\mu(2)$ was found to be 2.26 and highly significant (t=6.052). From equation (3.2-1) we can easily predict the expected value of D3, given $X\beta$, using FORTRAN or the sample SAS program given in Table 3.1.

MPROBIT OPTION

WRITTEN BY RICHARD MCKELVEY BASED ON MODEL FOR CHOTOMOUS MULTIVARIATE PROBIT DEVELOPED BY WILLIAM ZAVOINA AND R. MCKELVEY

ROUTINES HEAVILY MODIFIED BY H. H. STOKES JANUARY 1985 FOR B34S.

FOR 0-1 CASE, MPROBIT ROUTINES PRODUCE SAME RESULTS AS B34S PB OPTION.

REFERENCES BY MCKELVEY AND ZAVOINA

- AN IBM FORTRAN IV PROGRAM TO PERFORM N-CHOTOMOUS MULTIVARIATE PROBIT ANALYSIS (BEHAVIORAL SCIENCE V 16, 1971 PP. 186-7)

- A STATISTICAL MODEL FOR THE ANALYSIS OF ORDINAL DEPENDENT VARIABLES (JOURNAL OF MATH. SOCIOLOGY V 4, 1975 PP. 103-120)

------ VERSION DATE 1 MARCH 1985 ------

TITLE CARDS (#1 - #2) READ:

MP CARD #3

NRESP (# OF CATEGORIES OF DEPENDENT VARIABLE) =   3
NCASE (# OF ITERATIONS ALLOWED (DEFAULT = 50)) =   50
NQRT (=1 RESIDUAL ANALYSIS, =0 NO RESIDUAL ANALYSIS) =   0
NORD (# OF SUBPROBLEMS (MUST BE IN RANGE 1-50), DEFAULT=1) =   1
INPUT (=0 USUAL CASE, =1 GROUPED DATA) =   5
NDUMP (=0 USUAL CASE, =1 FOR PRINT OF CHANGE IN COEF DURING EACH ITERATION) =   0
TOLA (CONVERGENCE TOLERANCE (DEFAULT = .000001)) =   0.10000000E-05

VALID RESPONSES CARD (# 4)   0.   1.   2.

****
N-CHOTOMOUS PROBIT ANALYSIS:
****

DESCRIPTION OF VARIABLES INCLUDED
IN ANALYSIS

		SAMPLE STATISTICS FOR ALL VARIABLES IN ANALYSIS		I I I	BREAKDOWN OF DEPENDENT VARIABLE (VARIABLE # 1) B34S VAR # 11. B34S NAME = D3		
NAME	VARIABLE NUMBER B34S #	SAMPLE MEAN	SAMPLE VARIANCE	I I	CODE VALUE OF RESPONSE	FREQUENCY	TOTALS
D3	1 11	0.95454545	0.36997886	I	R(1)= 0.0	9	
T	2 6	136.52273	3795.0925	I	R(2)= 1.0	28	
Y	3 7	1.7809091	0.15687822	I	R(3)= 2.0	7	44 VALID RESPONSES
LF	4 8	53.065909	6.1506712	I			
NW	5 9	0.10559091	0.12994387E-01	I	OTHER	0	0 MISSING DATA CASES
				I			44 TOTAL CASES

A TOTAL OF 1 RUNS FOLLOW, USING A TOTAL OF 5 VARIABLES.
FOR ALL THESE RUNS, DEPENDENT VARIABLE IS VARIABLE # 1 ,

NUMBER OF ALLOWABLE ITERATIONS IS 50, AND TOLA= 0.10D-05

****
N-CHOTOMOUS PROBIT ANALYSIS:
****

BEGINNING EXECUTION OF RUN # 1.

HISTORY OF COMPUTATION

ITERATION	CHANGE IN ESTIMATE	1 / COND	LOG LIKELIHOOD FUNCTION
0	0.36001D+02	0.68512D-07	-0.49222D+02
1	0.39835D+01	0.66734D-07	-0.35532D+02
2	0.61563D+00	0.67273D-07	-0.33498D+02
3	0.75590D-02	0.67647D-07	-0.33344D+02
4	0.64630D-06	0.67694D-07	-0.33343D+02

****
N-CHOTOMOUS PROBIT ANALYSIS:
****

THE ITERATION HAS CONVERGED ON THE 4TH ITERATION. MAXIMUM LIKELIHOOD ESTIMATES FOLLOW

------------------------ BETAS ------------------------   ----------------------- MU'S ------------------------

COEFFICIENT	REPRESENTS EFFECT OF	MAXIMUM LIKELIHOOD ESTIMATE	STANDARD ERROR	MLE/SE	COEFFICIENT	MAXIMUM LIKELIHOOD ESTIMATE	STANDARD ERROR	MLE/SE
BETA(0)	CONSTANT	0.16841293	4.324	0.3894E-01	MU(1)	0.00000		
BETA(1)	T	0.53336696E-02	0.3202E-02	1.666	MU(2)	2.2638103	0.3740	6.052
BETA(2)	Y	1.5862470	0.8080	1.963				
BETA(3)	LF	-0.67820125E-01	0.9538E-01	-0.7111				
BETA(4)	NW	8.5618875	2.587	3.309				

LOG OF THE LIKELIHOOD FUNCTION= -33.342504

-2.0 TIMES LOG LIKELIHOOD RATIO = 12.927443
   (THIS IS CHI SQUARED WITH 4 DEGREES OF FREEDOM)   CHI SQUARE SIGNIFICANCE = 0.98836421

****
N-CHOTOMOUS PROBIT ANALYSIS:
****

ESTIMATED ANALYSIS OF VARIANCE

EXPLAINED SUM OF SQUARES =   21.400148
RESIDUAL SUM OF SQUARES =   44.000000
TOTAL SUM OF SQUARES =   65.400148
ESTIMATED R SQUARED =   0.32721864

OTHER SUMMARY STATISTICS

PERCENT PREDICTED CORRECTLY =   0.63636364
RANK ORDER CORRELATION- PREDICTED VERSUS ACTUAL =   0.26513959

MPROBIT PROGRAM ENDING

Since PX is bounded at zero, OLS is not an appropriate procedure to use. The next sample problem illustrates a tobit model that predicts PX as a function of T, Y, LF, NW, and D2. The TOBIT procedure output has been edited to save space. The results indicate that none of the coefficients are significant. Multicollinearity is suspected between the variable NW (proportion of the population that is nonwhite in 1950) and D2 (a dummy for southern states).

MULTIPLE TOBIT ANALYSIS

BASIC CONTROL CARD NX NB NIT IMX ALIM IWGHT NA NEQU IDEP

  6   0   0   0 0.00000000E+00 0   0   0   4

VARIABLE MEANS

X-12	CONSTANT	1.00000000000
X- 6	T	136.522727273
X- 7	Y	1.78090909091
X- 8	LF	53.0659090909
X- 9	NW	0.105590909091

```
X-10    D2        0.340909090909
X- 4    PX        0.603409090909E-01
```

SECOND MOMENTS ABOUT THE ORIGIN (LIMIT OBSERVATIONS)

CONSTANT	9.0000000					
T	1247.0000	224545.00				
Y	16.920000	2266.8600	32.020200			
LF	485.20000	66948.400	913.42800	26184.720		
NW	0.16500000	24.159000	0.31313000	8.9493000	0.39990000E-02	
D2	0.00000000E+00	0.00000000E+00	0.00000000E+00	0.00000000E+00	0.00000000E+00	0.00000000E+00
PX	0.00000000E+00	0.00000000E+00	0.00000000E+00	0.00000000E+00	0.00000000E+00	0.00000000E+00	0.00000000E+00

SECOND MOMENTS ABOUT THE ORIGIN (NON-LIMIT OBSERVATIONS)

CONSTANT	35.000000					
T	4760.0000	758736.00				
Y	61.440000	8749.5600	114.27760			
LF	1849.7000	252836.30	3268.3820	97983.350		
NW	4.4810000	508.67600	6.6784000	235.76230	1.0453350	
D2	15.000000	1439.0000	21.010000	777.00000	3.2330000	15.000000
PX	2.6550000	376.93100	4.7725400	143.05820	0.35461400	1.0440000	0.36273300

DEPENDENT VARIABLE FOR EQUATION #   1 IS X- 4 PX

INDEPENDENT VARIABLES SELECTED ARE

```
        CONSTANT    X-12
        T           X- 6
        Y           X- 7
        LF          X- 8
        NW          X- 9
        D2          X-10
```

WEIGHT SELECTED =1.000

VALUE INPUTED AS LIMIT =   0.00000000E+00

SECOND DERIVATIVES OF LOG OF LIKELIHOOD FUNCTION, EVALUATED AT MAXIMUM

CONSTANT	-41.232966					
T	-5646.2985	-922194.86				
Y	-73.152518	-10359.503	-136.43354			
LF	-2186.1451	-300474.66	-3901.4989	-116163.14		
NW	-4.5978233	-526.49641	-6.8995598	-242.10454	-1.0482196	
D2	-15.000000	-1439.0000	-21.010000	-777.00000	-3.2330000	-15.000000
PX	2.6550000	376.93100	4.7725400	143.05820	0.35461400	1.0440000	-0.54678100

FIRST DERIVATIVES OF LOG OF LIKELIHOOD FUNCTION, EVALUATED AT MAXIMUM

PX	0.75495166E-14	0.12256862E-11	0.10436096E-13	0.36948222E-12	0.77802348E-15	0.22898350E-14	-0.33382585E-15

THE NUMBER OF ITERATIONS IS   4

INVERSE OF MATRIX OF SECOND DERIVATIVES
(VAR-COV MATRIX OF NORMALIZED COEFFICIENTS TIMES (-1))

CONSTANT	-15.429852						
T	0.17566905E-02	-0.92542485E-05					
Y	-0.66229257	-0.87769714E-04	-0.48957726				
LF	0.30929637	-0.21675265E-05	0.31396900E-01	-0.70103965E-02			
NW	-1.8144305	-0.26671120E-03	-0.75057768	0.66610919E-01	-4.8607719		
D2	0.66450072	-0.61279731E-03	-0.11040933	-0.62706507E-02	0.46146452	-0.29712043	
PX	1.5230477	-0.52581690E-03	-0.32637650E-01	-0.28553099E-01	-0.38899886	-0.68191466E-01	-2.9338270

SUMMARY OF RESULTS

DEPENDENT VARIABLE IS PX

VARIABLE	B(I)	B(I)*F(Z)	B(I)/SIGMA	SE	T-STATISTIC	PARTIAL1	PARTIAL2
CONSTANT	-0.45751407	-0.34506767	-6.3091801	3.9280851	-1.6061720	-1.9867615	-0.24636984
T	0.29565657E-03	0.22299101E-03	0.40771436E-02	0.30420796E-02	1.3402488	0.12838929E-02	0.15921010E-03
Y	0.54637361E-01	0.41208759E-01	0.75345651	0.69969798	1.0768311	0.23726353	0.29422042E-01
LF	0.61362407E-02	0.46280944E-02	0.84619579E-01	0.83728111E-01	1.0106472	0.26646714E-01	0.33043457E-02
NW	0.26534054	0.20012596	3.6590814	2.2047158	1.6596613	1.1522451	0.14288502
D2	0.47175020E-01	0.35580490E-01	0.65054983	0.54508755	1.1934777	0.20485821	0.25403595E-01

NOTE: PARTIAL1 = DENSITY * (B(I) / SIGMA)
       PARTIAL2 = B(I)*(1.0 -(Z * DENSITY / F(Z)) -((DENSITY**2)/(F(Z)**2)))

AT POINT OF MEANS DENSITY = 0.31490010
                    F(Z)   = 0.75422309
                    Z   = 0.68783915
                    F(Y)   = 0.60455126E-01
                    F(YSTAR)= 0.80155496E-01

FOR FURTHER DETAIL SEE MCDONALD-MOFFITT (THE USES OF TOBIT ANALYSIS) RES MAY 1980

NUMBER OF OBSERVATIONS= 44

    9 LIMITS   35 NONLIMITS

STANDARD ERROR OF REGRESSION (SIGMA) =   0.072516
THE LOG OF THE MAXIMUM VALUE OF THE LIKELIHOOD FUNCTION IS   34.871612
STEP ENDING. SECONDS USED 0.31130123   . TOTAL JOB SECONDS   4.0353212

The next output shows PX as a function of T, Y, LF, and NW. D2 has been removed because it is likely to be correlated with NW. The TOBIT output has been heavily edited to save space.

SUMMARY OF RESULTS

DEPENDENT VARIABLE IS PX

VARIABLE	B(I)	B(I)*F(Z)	B(I)/SIGMA	SE	T-STATISTIC	PARTIAL1	PARTIAL2
CONSTANT	-0.35580035	-0.26803526	-4.8531010	3.7296328	-1.3012276	-1.5312154	-0.19130998
T	0.20102704E-03	0.15143980E-03	0.27419999E-02	0.28192166E-02	0.97261061	0.86513604E-03	0.10809005E-03
Y	0.37546624E-01	0.28285018E-01	0.51213430	0.66917182	0.76532556	0.16158492	0.20188412E-01
LF	0.51922028E-02	0.39114448E-02	0.70821417E-01	0.82799963E-01	0.85533150	0.22345063E-01	0.27917910E-02
NW	0.34264454	0.25812459	4.6736565	2.0308854	2.3012901	1.4745984	0.18423625

NOTE: PARTIAL1 = DENSITY * (B(I) / SIGMA)
       PARTIAL2 = B(I)*(1.0 -(Z * DENSITY / F(Z)) -((DENSITY**2)/(F(Z)**2)))

AT POINT OF MEANS DENSITY = 0.31551279
                    F(Z)   = 0.75333051
                    Z   = 0.68500742
                    F(Y)   = 0.60964257E-01
                    F(YSTAR)= 0.80926308E-01

FOR FURTHER DETAIL SEE MCDONALD-MOFFITT (THE USES OF TOBIT ANALYSIS) RES MAY 1980

NUMBER OF OBSERVATIONS= 44

9 LIMITS   35 NONLIMITS

STANDARD ERROR OF REGRESSION (SIGMA) =   0.073314
THE LOG OF THE MAXIMUM VALUE OF THE LIKELIHOOD FUNCTION IS   34.158702

The output now shows that NW is a significant (t=2.3) predictor of PX (the average number of executions in 1949-50 divided by convictions in 1950). These two tobit equations illustrate the problems of multicollinearity between NW and D2. The values PARTIAL1 and PARTIAL2 report equations (3.5-19) and (3.5-21) at the point of the means. For NW, PARTIAL2 is .1842 and is substantially below the estimated β_i value of .3426. The PARTIAL2 value gives a sense of how sensitive PX is to a one-unit change of NX at the point of the means. Only when all variables are very large, and F(Z) converges to 1, as f(Z) converges to 0, does PARTIAL2 converge to β_i. The change in F(Z), for a one-unit change in NW, is measured by PARTIAL1.

When the preceding equation is estimated by OLS (output not shown) the results are as follows:

PX = -.4298 + .1478E-3 T + .1233 Y + .8016E-2 LF +.2143 NW
     (-1.84)   (.85)   (.29)   (1.55)   (1.69)

where the adjusted R^2 = .1777 and σ = .06535. These coefficients are larger in absolute value than the tobit PARTIAL2 values, which was expected. Because PX is truncated on the left at zero, use of OLS gives biased results. The degree of bias will increase the more PX values are at the lower limit. In the preceding problem, 9 of 44 cases occurred when PX=0.

The final set of sample problems involves running the OLD and NEW versions of the MLOGLIN command on the same data that were run through the PROBIT and LOGLIN command. The model estimated was D1 = f(T, Y, LF, NW) and was estimated with the MLOGLIN command, where VER=NEW. The output, which is given next, agrees with the sample output given on page 283 of Maddala (1988), except for the sign, which is expected. Recall from sections 3.3 and 3.4 that the LOGLIN command estimates

$$P(y=1|S) \quad = F(Z_i) \quad = F(X\beta) \quad = 1/(1 + e^{-2X\beta}). \qquad (3.3-1)$$

The MLOGLIN command estimates

$$P(y=1|S) \quad = F(-Z_i) \quad = F(-X\beta) \quad = 1/(1 + e^{X\beta}), \qquad (3.4-1)$$

while Maddala (1988) reports results estimated with

$$P(y=1|S) \quad = F(-Z_i) \quad = F(-X\beta) \quad = 1/(1 + e^{-X\beta}). \qquad (3.6-1)$$

Inspection of equations (3.4-1) and (3.6-1) indicates why the
estimated coefficients differ only by sign. Equation (3.3-1) shows
why the LOGLIN results have the same sign as the Maddala (1988)
results but are one-half the value. The absolute value of the
estimated t scores are the same with all three equations.

```
SP CARD FOUND - IOPT =    4  ICOPY =     0

NSERIE, IBEGIN, IEND SET AS      5     1     0  RESPECTIVELY

    DATA IN ARRAY X FOR                        B34S #           NAME
                                               X- 5             D1
                                               X- 6             T
                                               X- 7             Y
                                               X- 8             LF
                                               X- 9             NW


    MAXIMUM LIKELIHOOD ESTIMATION OF MULTIVARIATE LOG-LINEAR
    PROBABILITY MODEL DEVELOPED BY M.NERLOVE AND S.J.PRESS
    WRITTEN BY S.KAWASAKI IN 1977, EVANSTON
    REVISED BY S.KAWASAKI IN 1982, BERLIN
    REVISED AND EXTENDED BY H. H. STOKES (WITH ASSISTANCE FROM E. LEHRER) APRIL 1983
    EXTENDED BY T.S.KLEIN AND R. KLEIN NOVEMBER 1987
    REVISED AND IMPROVED SEPTEMBER 1988 BY H. H. STOKES


INCORE VERSION OF XLOGLIN SELECTED.


MAIN CONTROL CARD M1 (FORMAT(8I5)  )
NEXO = N. OF VAR.S ON THE INPUT DATA FILE (NOT INCLUDING CONSTANT) - USUALLY NEXO = L + NEXR
L    = N. OF ENDOGENOUS VAR.S -
NEXR = N. OF EXOGENOUS VAR.S -
ID7  = 0 FOR DEVIATION-CONTRAST BASIS:= 1 FOR 0-1 BASIS
IH   = 0 FOR D-P-F COVARIANCE APPROXIMATION
     = 1 FOR ANALYTICAL COVARIANCE CALCULATION
     = 2 FOR NUMERICAL COVARIANCE CALCULATION
     = 3 FOR INFORMATION MATRIX COVARIANCE CALCULATION
LIMIT= MAXIMUM N. OF ITERATIONS
     = 0 FOR 25 ITERATIONS
ITAPE=  INPUT TAPE FOR DATA  (DEFAULT = 5 )

IBRI =  0 FOR SUPPRESS ITERATION OUTPUT
     =  1 TO GIVE ITERATION OUTPUT


MAIN CONTROL CARD M2 -  FORMAT (8I5)
IP   = 0 FOR CODE (1,2,...) OF END. VAR.
     = 1 FOR CODE (0,1,...) OF END. VAR.
INITB= N. OF INITIAL PARA. VALUES TO BE SUPPLIED
ICOV = 0 TO SUPPRESS PRINTING COVARIANCE MATRIX
     = 1 TO STORE THE COVARIANCE ON TAPE 9
     = 2 TO READ AND STORE THE COVARIANCE MATRIX ON TAPE 9
     = 3 TO READ AND STORE THE COVARIANCE MATRIX AND THE PARAMETERS  ON TAPE 9
     = 4 TO PRINT THE COVARIANCE MATRIX ON TAPE 6

IELAS= 1 TO CALCULATE ELASTICITIES
IPROB= N. OF SETS OF PROBABILITIES TO CALCULATED
ISKIP= 1 TO SUSPEND THE ITERATION TERMINATING DEVICE
       BY CONVERGENCE CRITERION
IZER = 0 COMPUTES INITIAL HESSIAN MATRIX DOING ANALYTICAL EVALUATION, PROVIDED INITB=0.
IZER = 1 SETS INITIAL HESSIAN MATRIX TO THE IDENTITY MATRIX
IZER = 2 COMPUTES INITIAL HESSIAN MATRIX DOING NUMERICAL DIFFERENTIATION, PROVIDED INITB NE 0
ICOEF = 0 FOR NO SCALING OF DATA, NE 0 MEANS ICOEF SERIES WILL BE SCALED.


MAIN CONTROL CARD M3 - DESIGN CARD - # OF LEVELS FOR EACH END. VAR (ARRAY KD(1) .. KD(L)) FORMAT 16I5

    2

MAIN CONTROL CARD M6 - SUPPRESSION CARD - FORMAT (4I5)  IS1, IS2, IS3, NT =      0    0    0    0

    IS1 = N. OF BASIS-VECTOR GROUPS TO BE SUPPRESSED
    IS2 = 0 TO SUPPRESS ALL EXOG. EFFECTS ON INTERACTIONS
        = 1 TO SUPPRESS ALL EXOG. EFFECTS ON INTERACTIONS
        EXCEPT SOME LOWER-ORDER INTERACTIONS
        = 2 FOR NO SYSTEMATIC SUPPRESSION
    IS3 = N. OF PARAMETER GROUPS TO BE SUPPRESSED
    NT  = SIZE OF EXTRA INTERACTIONS TO BE ESTIMATED
        WHEN IS2 = 1


SUMMARY OF PARAMETERS FOR CARD M1, M2, M6

    NEXO   =    5
    L      =    1
    NEXR   =    4
    ID7    =    1
    IH     =    1
    LIMIT  =    0
    ITAPE  =    5
    IBRI   =    0
    IP     =    1
    INITB  =    0
```

```
ICOV   =    0
IELAS  =    0
IPROB  =    0
ISKIP  =    0
IZER   =    0
IS1    =    0
IS2    =    0
IS3    =    0
NT     =    0
ICOEF  =    0
```

DESIGN PARAMETERS ENTERED (KD(1)..KD(L)) FROM CARD M3 --- # OF CATEGORIES FOR EACH ENDOGENOUS VARIABLE :

    2

INDEX OF ENDOGENOUS VARIABLES   1

INDEX OF EXOGENOUS VARIABLES   2   3   4   5

MAIN CONTROL CARD M10 -- NAME OF LEVEL FOR EACH ENDOGENOUS VARIABLE (EXCEPT THE LAST CATEGORY)

ENDOGENOUS VARIABLE   1   HAS   2   LEVELS

LEVEL   1 = NOLAW

ENDOGENOUS VARIABLES LOADED FROM B34S	XLOGLIN #		NAME	B34S #
	1		D1	X-(5)
EXOGENOUS VARIABLES LOADED FROM B34S	XLOGLIN #		NAME	B34S #
	1		CONSTANT	
	2		T	X-(6)
	3		Y	X-(7)
	4		LF	X-(8)
	5		NW	X-(9)

   THE NUMBER OF OBSERVATIONS IN THE DATA SET IS   44

GIVEN A MODEL WITH ONE TRICHOTOMOUS DEPENDENT VARIABLE AND ONE CONTINUOUS EXOGENOUS VARIABLE X. THEN:

1. LN P(Y=1) = A(1) + (B(1) * X) + MU

2. LN P(Y=2) = A(2) + (B(2) * X) + MU

3. LN P(Y=3) = A(3) + (B(3) * X) + MU

THE DEVIATION CONTRAST BASIS (ID7=0) IMPOSES THE CONSTRAINTS THAT A(1) + A(2) + A(3) = 0 AND B(1) + B(2) + B(3) = 0.

THE ESTIMATED B(1) COEFFICIENT REPRESENTS THE CHANGE IN THE LOG OF THE ODDS THAT Y=1, RELATIVE TO THE GEOMETRIC AVERAGE OF

THE PROBABILITIES, ASSOCIATED WITH A UNIT CHANGE IN X. THERE ARE SIMILAR INTERPRETATIONS FOR B(2) AND B(3) .

THE 0-1 BASIS (ID7=1) IMPOSES THE CONSTRAINTS THAT A(3) = 0 AND   B(3) = 0. THE ESTIMATED B(1) COEFFICIENT REPRESENTS THE CHANGE

IN THE LOG OF THE ODDS THAT Y = 1 RATHER THAT Y = 3 , ASSOCIATED WITH A UNIT CHANGE IN X.

A SIMILAR INTERPRETATION APPLIES TO THE OTHER PARAMETERS. FOR THE TRICHOTOMOUS CASE ONLY, A SIMILAR COMPARISON IS MADE BETWEEN

Y = 1 AND Y = 2 .

BASIS MATRIX USED

   1   1. 0.

INTERPRETATION OF BASIS MATRIX

       INDICATOR   INDEXES FOR GENERALIZED PARAMETER
                       1 2 3 4 5 6 7 8 9 10 11 12 13 14 15

   1   1   NOLAW   1.

   IF INDICATOR=0, THAT BASIS VECTOR IS NOT USED.

   THIS INDICATOR CORRESPONDS TO BOTH THE INDEX OF
   THE BASIS VECTOR ABOVE,AND ALSO TO THE INDICATOR
   OF END.VAR. IN THE FINAL PARAMETER-ESTIMATES TABLE.

         NUMBER OF PARAMETERS IB =   5

INITIAL VALUES OF PARAMETERS ARE ALL SET TO ZERO

   REQUIRED REAL*4 SPACE: 734 SPACE AVAILABLE: 70000

INITIAL VALUE OF LOG LIKELIHOOD FUNCTION -30.498476

GRADIENT=

   13.000000   1756.5000   22.260000   682.25000   2.1580000

```
XXXXX IT CONVERGED AT ITERATION  15 XXXXX

FINAL VALUE OF LOG-LIKELIHOOD FUNCTION=   -9.107567

PARAMETER ESTIMATES

           INDICATOR        ESTIMATED      STANDARD      T RATIO      GRADIENT        CORRECTION
       EXO.VAR.  END.VAR.   PARAMETER      ERROR
                 EFFECT

  1       1         1       -16.567        19.639       -0.84357     0.61727E-07     -0.22101E-04
       CONSTANT  NOLAW

  2       2         1       -0.16516E-01   0.96112E-02  -1.7185      -0.24252E-05     0.11369E-07
          T       NOLAW

  3       3         1       -9.1315        5.0531       -1.8071      0.13659E-06      0.13830E-04
          Y       NOLAW

  4       4         1        0.71539       0.47927       1.4927      0.36101E-05     -0.14034E-06
          LF      NOLAW

  5       5         1       -85.362        35.854       -2.3808      0.15260E-08      0.11583E-04
          NW      NOLAW


   CORRECTION IS THE CHANGE IN THE VALUE OF A PARAMETER FROM PREVIOUS POINT TO PRESENT POINT.

   FOR INTERPRETATION OF INTERACTIONS OF END.VAR., SEE CORRESPONDING INDICATORS
      IN INTERPRETATION OF BASIS-MATRIX TABLE ABOVE.


CONTINGENCY TABLE

         OBSERVED     ESTIMATED       OBSERVED     ESTIMATED      INDEXES OF
         FREQUENCIES  FREQUENCIES     PROPORTIONS  PROPORTIONS    ENDOGENOUS VARIABLES
                                                                  1  2  3  4  5  6  7  8  9 10 11 12 13 14 15

  1          9          0.10           0.2045       0.0022           1
  2         35         43.90           0.7955       0.9978           2
         ESTIMATED VALUES ARE EVALUATED AT THE MEANS OF EXOGENOUS VARIABLES.

                        MEAN VALUES OF EXO. VAR.S

                        INDEX OF   NAME         MEAN
                        EXO.VAR.

                            1      CONSTANT     1.0000000
                            2      T            136.52273
                            3      Y            1.7809091
                            4      LF           53.065909
                            5      NW           0.10559091

LIKELIHOOD RATIO STATISTIC  -2(LOG(L(0))-LOG(L(*)))=   42.781818       D.F.= 5

            L(*)=VALUE OF LIKELIHOOD FUNCTION OPTIMIZED HERE.
            L(0)=VALUE OF LIKELIHOOD FUNCTION WHOSE PARAMETERS ARE ALL ZEROS.
STEP ENDING. SECONDS USED  0.44159794   . TOTAL JOB SECONDS     5.6834259   .
```

The MLOGLIN output shows all option and switch settings. These settings are of interest to users who call for more specialized options and/or run the MLOGLIN command as a subroutine and have to set each switch with the low-level B34S command language. The only variable with a t score > 2 in absolute value was NW, which was found to be positively related to having a capital punishment law. The overall fit of the model is rather low. Contingency table analysis of the predictive ability of the equation reports that while 9 of 44 states (20.45%) have no capital punishment laws (D1=0), the model predicts they will be .22% of the cases. On the other side, while 35 states (79.55%) have capital punishment laws (D1=1), the equation predicts that 99.78% of the states will have capital punishment laws.

3.7 Conclusion

This chapter has been concerned with problems of truncation of the left-hand variable.   In such cases, OLS will give biased results. If the left-hand variable is 0-1, the most appropriate procedure to use is PROBIT.   If the left-hand variable is ordered with less than 11 categories, the procedure to use is MPROBIT. If multinomial logit is desired, where there are up to 4 equations with each left-hand variable of the 0-1 type, the LOGLIN command should be used. For bigger problems with up to 69 equations and up to 20 states on each left-hand variable, the MLOGLIN command should be used.   The MPROBIT command is a superset of the PROBIT command and the MLOGLIN command is a superset of the LOGLIN command. The TOBIT command should be used when there is a upper or lower bound on the left-hand variable, which is otherwise continuous. There is no observation limit for the TOBIT, LOGLIN, PROBIT, and MPROBIT commands. The number of observations for the MLOGLIN command is limited by available memory on the mainframe.

NOTES

1. The author of B34S was fortunate to be able to obtain the original PROBIT and TOBIT code from Mathematica Policy Research. There was no mention of the authors of these programs. My guess is that the PROBIT program was developed by John Cregg and the TOBIT code is the original Tobin (1958) program. Both programs have been almost totally rewritten for B34S. Their prior authors should have no blame for any problems but should share credit for the correct functioning of these programs. The discussion of the function of these programs is based on the undated manuals for the programs, which were obtained in the early 1970s by the author of B34S.

2. This section has been taken largely from Lehrer and Stokes (1985).

3. It should be emphasized that the parameter estimates and the predicted probabilities provide different types of information. For example, the first equation in the system (3.4-8) shows that a_1 reflects the impact of x on the odds that A will equal 1 rather than 3, <u>variable B held constant</u>; thus a_1 represents a direct effect. On the other hand, if we were to compute the predicted probability that A will equal 1, setting x first at say x=m, and then x=n, comparison of these two probabilities would provide information regarding the total impact of x on A, i. e., the direct impact of x on A plus the indirect impact of x on A through its influence on B.   The predicted probabilities that A will equal 1 are computed by adding the estimated values of $P[i_A = 1, i_B = 1]$ and $P[i_A = 1, i_B = 2]$, using equation (3.4-2), setting x first at x=m and then at x=n. This distinction between direct and total effects has been used by Lehrer and Nerlove (1984) and Lehrer (1985).

4. For further detail on the computations in the program, see Kawasaki (1978).

5. Maddala (1983, 5) makes a distinction between what he calls a "truncated regression model" and a "censored regression model." While both models involve truncated normal distributions, he argues that there are important distinctions between the models. In the truncated regression model, the experimenter does not have observations on the y or x variable if y is above or below a threshold. This would occur in a consumption function problem if all individuals spending more than $100,000 were excluded from the sample. In the censored regression model, which has been commonly called the tobit model, we have x values for all observations. The y values are limited downward or upward, depending in whether there is a lower or upper bound. Such a problem would occur if we were predicting consumption of a particular item. If the dependent variable of a lower-limit problem is multiplied by -1.0, and the resulting model is estimated as an upper-limit problem, the results will be identical to the original lower-limit problem, except all coefficients will be multiplied by -1.0. In this section only the lower-limit problem will be discussed.

6. This section is heavily influenced by McDonald and Moffitt's (1980) excellent treatment of the tobit model.

7. The B34S TOBIT command has been tested against the LIMDEP (Greene 1985) TOBIT command for both upper and lower limits. All coefficients agree. The SE of the coefficients differs slightly. B34S uses the Newton method of obtaining the SEs of the coefficients from the second derivatives of the log-likelihood, while LIMDEP uses the summed outer products of the first derivatives of the log-likelihood (Green 1985, 147). B34S calculated the t as the normalized coefficient divided by the SE, while LIMDEP calculates the t as the raw coefficient divided by the standard error.

8. This probit equation was reported in Maddala (1988, 282). The coefficients and t's that are listed inside parentheses, reported in B34S for CONSTANT, T, Y, LF NW D2 are 6.91 (.61), .0113 (2.00), 6.46 (2.05), -.4092 (-1.59), 42.498 (2.048), and 4.39 (.0947). The results reported in Maddala (1988) were 6.92 (.61), .0113 (2.00), 6.46 (2.05), -.409 (-1.59), 42.5 (2.05), and 4.63(.04), respectively, and agree with B34S, except for the insignificant D2 variable. The difference appears to be due to the way LIMDEP calculates the SE of the coefficients from the summed outer products. For more detail, see footnote 7.

9. As was discussed in the text, the MLOGLIN command has more capability than the LOGLIN command. Rather than run a more complex problem, in this test output a problem that can be run by both procedures was selected to facilitate comparison between the two commands. A more complex MLOGLIN test problem is distributed with the B34S system.

4. Simultaneous Equations Systems

4.0 Introduction

The SIMEQ command performs estimation of systems of equations by the methods of OLS, LIML, 2SLS, 3SLS, I3SLS, and FIML, using code developed by Les Jennings (1973, 1980). The Jennings code is unique in that it implements the QR approach to estimate systems of equations, which results in both substantial savings in time and increased accuracy.[1] The estimation methods are well known and covered in detail in such books as Johnston (1963, 1972, 1984), Kmenta (1971, 1986), and Pindyck and Rubinfeld (1976, 1981) and will only be sketched here. What will be discussed are the contributions of Jennings and others. The discussion of these techniques follows closely material in Jennings (1980) and Strang (1976).

4.1 Estimation of Structural Models

Assume a system of G equations with K exogenous variables[2]

$$
\begin{aligned}
b_{11}y_{1i} + \cdots + b_{1G}y_{Gi} + \delta_{11}x_{1i} + \cdots + \delta_{1K}x_{Ki} &= u_{1i} \\
b_{21}y_{1i} + \cdots + b_{2G}y_{Gi} + \delta_{21}x_{1i} + \cdots + \delta_{2K}x_{Ki} &= u_{2i} \\
&\cdots \\
b_{G1}y_{1i} + \cdots + b_{GG}y_{Gi} + \delta_{G1}x_{1i} + \cdots + \delta_{GK}x_{Ki} &= u_{Gi},
\end{aligned}
\qquad (4.1\text{-}1)
$$

where x_{ji} is the jth exogenous variable for the ith period, y_{ji} is the jth endogenous variable for the ith period, and u_{ji} is the jth equation error term for the ith period. If we define

$$
B = \begin{bmatrix}
b_{11} & b_{12} & \cdots & b_{1G} \\
b_{21} & b_{22} & \cdots & b_{2G} \\
& & \cdots & \\
b_{G1} & b_{G2} & \cdots & b_{GG}
\end{bmatrix}
$$

$$
\Gamma = \begin{bmatrix}
\delta_{11} & \delta_{12} & \cdots & \delta_{1G} \\
\delta_{21} & \delta_{22} & \cdots & \delta_{2G} \\
& & \cdots & \\
\delta_{G1} & \delta_{G2} & \cdots & \delta_{GG}
\end{bmatrix}
$$

$$
\mathbf{y}_i = \begin{bmatrix} Y_{1i} \\ Y_{2i} \\ \cdot \\ Y_{Gi} \end{bmatrix} \qquad \mathbf{x}_i = \begin{bmatrix} x_{1i} \\ x_{2i} \\ \cdot \\ x_{Ki} \end{bmatrix} \qquad \mathbf{u}_i = \begin{bmatrix} u_{1i} \\ u_{2i} \\ \cdot \\ u_{Gi} \end{bmatrix},
$$

equation (4.1-1) can be written as

$$ \mathbf{B}\mathbf{y}_i + \mathbf{\Gamma}\mathbf{x}_i = \mathbf{u}_i. \qquad (4.1\text{-}2) $$

If all observations in $\mathbf{y}_i$, $\mathbf{x}_i$ and $\mathbf{u}_i$ are included, then

$$
\mathbf{X} = \begin{bmatrix} x_{11} & x_{12} & \cdots & x_{1N} \\ x_{21} & x_{22} & \cdots & x_{2N} \\ \hdotsfor{4} \\ x_{K1} & xK_{2} & \cdots & x_{kN} \end{bmatrix}
$$

$$
\mathbf{Y} = \begin{bmatrix} Y_{11} & Y_{12} & \cdots & Y_{1N} \\ Y_{21} & Y_{22} & \cdots & Y_{2N} \\ \hdotsfor{4} \\ Y_{G1} & Y_{G2} & \cdots & Y_{GN} \end{bmatrix}
$$

$$
\mathbf{U} = \begin{bmatrix} u_{11} & u_{12} & \cdots & u_{1N} \\ u_{21} & u_{22} & \cdots & u_{2N} \\ \hdotsfor{4} \\ u_{G1} & u_{G2} & \cdots & u_{GN} \end{bmatrix}
$$

and equation (4.1-2) can be written as

$$ \mathbf{B}\mathbf{Y} + \mathbf{\Gamma}\mathbf{X} = \mathbf{U}. \qquad (4.1\text{-}3) $$

From equation (4.1-3), the constrained reduced form can be calculated as

$$ \mathbf{Y} = -\mathbf{B}^{-1}\mathbf{\Gamma}\mathbf{X} + \mathbf{B}^{-1}\mathbf{U} = \pi\mathbf{X} + \mathbf{V}, \qquad (4.1\text{-}4) $$

where $\pi = -\mathbf{B}^{-1}\mathbf{\Gamma}$. If π is estimated directly with OLS, then it is called the unconstrained reduced form. The B34S SIMEQ command estimates $\mathbf{B}$, using either OLS, 2SLS, LIML, 3SLS, I3SLS, or FIML. For each estimated vector $\mathbf{B}$, the associated reduced form coefficient vector π can optionally be calculated. If $\mathbf{B}$ is estimated by OLS, the coefficients will be biased since the key OLS assumption that the right-hand-side variables are orthogonal with the error term is violated. Model (4.1-3) can be normalized such that the coefficients $b_{ij} = 1$ for $i=j$. The necessary condition for identification of each equation is that the number of endogenous variables - 1 be less than or equal to the number of excluded exogenous variables. If the excluded exogenous variables of the ith equation are not significant in any other equation, then the ith equation will not be identified, even if it is correctly specified. There are several common mistakes made in setting up simultaneous equations systems. These include the following:

- Not fully checking for multicollinearity in the equations system.

- Attempting to interpret the estimated B and Γ coefficients as partial derivatives, rather than looking at the reduced form G by K matrix π.

- Not effectively testing whether excluded exogenous variables are significant in at least one other equation in the system.

- Not building into the solution procedure provisions for taking into account the number of significant digits in the data.

The B34S SIMEQ code has unique design characteristics that allow solutions for some of these problems. In the next sections, we will briefly outline some of these features.

Assume for a moment that X is a T by K matrix of observations of the exogenous variables, Y is a T by 1 vector of observations of the endogenous variable, and β is a K element array of OLS coefficients, the OLS solution for the estimated β from equation (2.1-8) is $(X'X)^{-1}X'Y$. The problem with this approach is that some accuracy is lost by forming the matrix X'X. The QR approach[3] proceeds by operating directly on the matrix X to express it in terms of the upper triangular K by K matrix R and the T by T orthogonal matrix Q. X is factored as

$$X \quad = Q \begin{bmatrix} R \\ 0 \end{bmatrix} = [Q_1 \mid Q_2] \begin{bmatrix} R \\ 0 \end{bmatrix} = Q_1 R. \qquad (4.1-5)$$

Since $Q'Q = I$, then

$$(X'X)^{-1}X'Y \quad = (R'Q_1'Q_1R)^{-1} \quad R'Q_1'Y \quad = (R'R)^{-1} R'Q_1'Y$$

$$= R^{-1}Q_1'Y. \qquad (4.1-6)$$

Following Jennings (1980), we define the condition number of matrix X (C(X)) as the ratio of the square root of the largest eigenvalue of X'X $[E_{max}(X'X)]$ to the smallest eigenvalue of X'X

$[E_{min}(X'X)]$

$C(X) = \{E_{max}(X'X) / E_{min}(X'X)\}^{.5}$.   (4.1-7)

If $||X|| = \{E_{max}(X'X)\}^{.5}$, and X is square and nonsingular, then

$C(X) = ||X||\;||X^{-1}||$.   (4.1-8)

Throughout B34S, $1/C(X)$ is checked to test for rank problems. Jennings (1980) notes that $C(X)$ can also be used as a measure of relative error. If μ is a measure of round-off error, then $\mu[C(X)]^2$ is the bound for the relative error of the calculated solution. In an IBM 370 running double precision, μ is approximately .1E-16. If $C(X)$ is > .1E+8 (1 /$C(X)$ is < .1E-8), then $\mu[C(X)]^2$ is 1.0, meaning that <u>no</u> digits in the reported solution are significant. Jennings (1980) looks at the problem from another perspective. If matrix X has a round-off error of τX such that the actual X used is $X+\tau X$, then $||\tau X|| / ||X||$ <u>must be less than</u> $1/C(X)$ for a solution to exist. If

$||\tau X|| / ||X||\qquad = 1 / C(X),$ (4.1-9)

then there exists a τX such that $X + \tau X$ is singular.[4] The user can inspect the estimate of the condition and determine the degree of multicollinearity. Most programs only report problems when the matrix is singular. Inspection of $C(X)$ gives warning of the degree of the problem. The SIMEQ command contains the IPR parameter option with which the user can inform the program of the number of significant digits in X. This information is used to terminate the iterative three-stage (ILS3) iterations when the relative change in the solution is within what would be expected, given the number of significant digits in the data.

Jennings (1980) notes that the relative error of the QR solution to the OLS problem given in equation (4.1-6) has the form

$n_1 C(X) + n_2 C(X)^2(||\hat{e}|| / ||\hat{\beta}||),$ (4.1-10)

where n_1 and n_2 are of the order of machine precision and $||\hat{e}||$ and $||\hat{\beta}||$ are the lengths of the estimated residual and estimated coefficients, respectively. (The length or L2NORM of a vector e_i is defined as $[\Sigma e_i^2]^{.5}$). Equation (4.1-10) indicates that as the relative error of the computer solution improves, the closer the model fits. An estimate of this relative error is made for OLS, LIML and 2SLS estimators reported by SIMEQ.

4.2 Estimation of OLS, LIML, LS2, LS3, and ILS3

For OLS estimation of a system of equations, SIMEQ uses the QR approach discussed earlier. If the REDUCED option is used, once the structural coefficients B and Γ in equation (4.1-3) are known, the constrained reduced form coefficients π from equation (4.1-4) are displayed. If B and Γ are estimated using OLS, and all structural equations are <u>exactly</u> identified, then the constraints on π imposed from the structural coefficients B and Γ are not binding and π could be estimated directly with OLS or indirectly via (4.1-4). However, if one or more of the equations in the structural equations system (4.1-2) are over identified, π must be estimated as -BΓ.

Although the reduced-form coefficients π exist and may be calculated from any set of structural estimates B and Γ, in practice it is not desirable to report those derived from OLS estimation because in the presence of endogenous variables on the right-hand side of an equation, the OLS assumption that the error term is orthogonal with the explanatory variables is violated. Since OLS imposes this constraint as a part of the estimation process, the resulting estimated B and Γ are biased.

The reason that OLS is often used as a benchmark is because from among the class of all linear estimators, OLS produces minimum variance. The loss in predictive power of LIML and LS2 has to be weighed against the fact that OLS produces biased estimates. If reduced-form coefficients are desired, identities in the system must be entered. The number of identities plus the number of estimated equations must equal the number of endogenous variables in the model. The SIMEQ command requires that the number of MODEL sentences and IDENTITY sentences is equal to the number of variables listed in the ENDOGENOUS sentence.

The LS2 estimator (2SLS) first estimates all endogenous variables as a function of all exogenous variables. This is equivalent to estimating an unconstrained form of the reduced-form equation (4.1-4). Next, in stage 2 the estimated values of the endogenous variables on the right in the jth equation Y_j^* are used in place of the actual values of the endogenous variables Y_j on the right to estimate equation (4.1-2). Since the estimated values of the endogenous variables on the right are <u>only</u> a function of exogenous variables, the theory suggests they can be assumed to be orthogonal with the population error, and OLS can be safely used for the second stage. In terms of our prior notation, the two-stage estimator for the first equations is

$$
\begin{bmatrix} b_{11} \\ \cdot \\ b_{1g} \\ \delta_{11} \\ \cdot \\ \delta_{1k} \end{bmatrix} = \{(Y_1^* \; X_1)'(Y_1^* \; X_1)\}^{-1} (Y_1^* \; X_1)'y_1, \qquad (4.2\text{-}1)
$$

where Y_1^* is the matrix of predicted endogenous variables in the first equation and X_1 is the matrix of exogenous variables in the first equation. For further details on this traditional estimation approach, see Pindyck and Rubinfeld (1981, 345-347).

The QR approach used by Jennings (1980) involves estimating equation (4.2-1) as the solution of

$$Z_j'(XX^+)Z_j\alpha_j = Z_j'(XX^+)Y_j \qquad (4.2-2)$$

for α_j where $\alpha_j' = \{(b_{11}, \ldots b_{ig})', (\delta_{11}, \ldots, \delta_{1k})'\}$, $Z_j = [X_j|Y_j]$ and X^+ is the pseudoinverse[5] of X. Z_j consists of the X and Y variables in the jth equation. XX^+ is not calculated directly but is expressed in terms of the QR factorization of X. By working directly on X, and not forming $X'X$, substantial accuracy is obtained. Jennings proceeds by writing

$$XX^+ = Q\begin{bmatrix} I_r & 0 \\ 0 & 0 \end{bmatrix}Q' \qquad (4.2-3)$$

where I_r is the r by r identity matrix and r is the rank of X. Using equation (4.2-3), equation (4.2-2) becomes

$$Z_j^*\begin{bmatrix} I_r & 0 \\ 0 & 0 \end{bmatrix}Z_j^* \alpha_j = Z_j^*\begin{bmatrix} I_r & 0 \\ 0 & 0 \end{bmatrix}y_j^* \qquad (4.2-4)$$

where $Z_j^* = Q'Z_j$ and $y_j^* = Q'y_j$.

The 2SLS covariance matrix can be estimated as

$$(||e_j||^2 d_f)(Z_j'XX^+Z_j)^{-1}, \qquad (4.2-5)$$

where d_f is the degrees of freedom and $||e_j||^2$ is the residual sum of squares (or the square of the L2NORM of the residual). There is a substantial controversy in the literature about the appropriate value for d_f. Since the SEs of the estimated 2SLS coefficients are known only asymptotically, Theil (1971) suggests that d_f be set equal to T, the number of observations used to estimate the model. Others suggest that d_f be set to T-K, similar to what is being used in OLS. If Theil's suggestion is used, the estimated SEs of the coefficients are larger. The T-K option is more conservative. The B34S SIMEQ command produces both estimates of the coefficient standard errors to facilitate comparison with other programs and researcher preferences..

Two-stage least squares estimation of an equation with

endogenous variables on the right, in contrast with OLS estimation, in theory produces unbiased coefficients at the cost of some loss of efficiency. If a large system is estimated, it is often impossible to use all exogenous variables in the system because of loss of degrees of freedom. The usual practice is to select a subset of the exogenous variables. The greater the number of exogenous variables relative to the degrees of freedom, the closer the predicted Y variables on the right are to the raw Y variables on the right. In this situation, the 2SLS estimator sum of squares of residuals will approach the OLS estimator sum of squares of residuals. Such an estimator will lose the unbiased property of the 2SLS estimator. Usual econometric practice is to use OLS and 2SLS and compare the results to see how sensitive the OLS results are to simultaneity problems.

While 2SLS results are sensitive to the variable that is used to normalize the system, limited information maximum likelihood (LIML) estimation, which can be used in place of 2SLS, is not so sensitive. The LIML estimator,[6] which is hard to explain in simple terms, involves selecting values for b and δ for each equation such that $\mathcal{L}$ is minimized where $\mathcal{L} = SSE_1 / SSE$. We define SSE_1 as the residual variance of estimating a weighted average of the y variables in the equation on all exogenous variables in the equation, while SSE is the residual variance of estimating a weighted average of the y variables on all the exogenous variables in the system. Since $SSE \leq SSE_1$, $\mathcal{L}$ is bounded at 1. The difficulty in LIML estimation is selecting the weights for combining the y variables in the equation. Assume equation 1 of (4.1-1)

$$b_{11}y_{1i} + \ldots + b_{1G}y_{Gi} + \delta_{11}x_{1i} + \ldots + \delta_{1K}x_{Ki} = u_{1i}. \qquad (4.2-6)$$

Ignoring time subscripts, we can define

$$y_1^* = y_1 - [b_{12}y_2 + \ldots b_{1G}y_G]. \qquad (4.2-7)$$

If we define $Y_{1*} = [y_{1i}, \ldots, y_{1G}]$ and we knew the vector $B_{1*} = [1, -b_{12}, \ldots, -b_{1G}]'$ we would know y_1^* since $y_1^* \equiv Y_{1*}B_{1*}$ and could regress y_1^* on all x variables on the right and call the residual variance SSE_1 and next regress y_1^* on <u>all</u> x variables in the system and call the residual variance SSE. If we define X_1 as a matrix consisting of the columns of the x variables on the right $X_1 = [x_{1i}, \ldots, x_{1K}]$, and we knew B_{1*}, then we could estimate $\Gamma_1 = [\delta_{11}, \ldots, \delta_{1K}]$ as

$$\Gamma_1 = (X_1'X_1)^{-1}X_1'y_1^* = (X_1'X_1)^{-1}X_1'Y_{1*}B_{1*}. \qquad (4.2-8)$$

However, we do not know B_{1*}. If we define

$$W_{1*} = Y_{1*}'Y_{1*} - (Y_{1*}'X_1)(X_1'X_1)^{-1}X_1'Y_{1*}, \qquad (4.2-9)$$

$$W_1 = Y_{1*}'Y_{1*} - (Y_{1*}'X)(X'X)^{-1}X'Y_{1*}, \qquad (4.2-10)$$

where **X** is the matrix of all X variables in the system, then $\mathscr{L}$ can be written as

$$\mathscr{L} = [B'_{1*}W_1B_{1*}] \; / \; B'_{1*}W_1B_{1*} \; . \tag{4.2-11}$$

Minimizing $\mathscr{L}$ implies that

$$(W_{1*} - \mathscr{L}W_1)B_{1*} = 0. \tag{4.2-12}$$

The LIML estimator uses eigenvalue analysis to select the vector B_{1*} such that $\mathscr{L}$ is minimized. This calculation involves solving the system

$$\det(W_{1*} - \mathscr{L}W_1) \; = 0 \tag{4.2-13}$$

for the smallest root $\mathscr{L}$. This root can be substituted back into equation (4.2-12) to get B_{1*} and into equation (4.2-8) to get Γ_1.

Jennings shows that equation (4.2-13) can be rewritten as

$$\det|Y_{1*}'\{(I \; -X_1X_1^+)-E_{min}(I-XX^+)\}Y_{1*}| \; = 0, \tag{4.2-14}$$

where E_{min} is the minimum eigenvalue. Further factorizations lead to accuracy improvements and speed over the traditional methods of solution outlined in Johnston (1984), Kmenta (1971), and other books. Jennings (1973, 1980) briefly discusses tests made for computational accuracy, given the number of significant digits in the data and various tests for nonunique solutions. One of the main objectives of the SIMEQ code was to be able to inform the user if there were problems in identification in theory and in practice. Since the LIML standard errors are known only asymptotically and are, in fact, equal to the 2SLS estimated standard errors, these are used for both the 2SLS and LIML estimators.

In the first stage of 2SLS, π is the unconstrained, reduced form.

$$Y = \pi X + V \tag{4.2-15}$$

and is estimated to obtain the Y^* predicted variables. 2SLS, OLS, and LIML are all special cases of the Theil (1971) k class estimators. The general formula for the k class estimator for the first equation (Kmenta 1971, 565) is

$$\begin{bmatrix} B_1^{(k)} \\ \Gamma_1^{(k)} \end{bmatrix} = \begin{bmatrix} Y_1'Y_1-kV_{1*}'V_{1*} & Y_1'X_1 \\ X_1'Y_1 & X_1'X_1 \end{bmatrix}^{-1} \begin{bmatrix} Y_1'y_1 - kV_{1*}'y_1 \\ X_1' \end{bmatrix}, \tag{4.2-16}$$

where V_{1*} is the predicted residual from estimating all but the 1st

y variable in equation (4.2-15), $Y_1 - V_{1*} = Y_{1*}$, and X_1 is the X variables on the right-hand side of the first equation. If k=0, equation (4.2-15) is the formula for OLS estimation of the first equation.   If k=1, equation (4.2-16) is the formula for 2SLS estimation of the first equation and can be transformed to equation (4.2-5). If k = the minimum root $\mathcal{L}$ of equation (4.2-13), equation (4.2-16) is the formula for the LIML estimator (Theil 1971, 504). Hence, OLS, 2SLS, and LIML are all members of the k class of estimators.

Three-stage least squares utilizes the covariance of the residuals across equations from the estimated 2SLS model to improve the estimated coefficients B and Γ. If the model has only exogenous variables on the right-hand side (B = 0), the OLS estimates can be used to calculate the covariance of the residuals across equations. The resulting estimator is the seemingly unrelated regression model (SUR). In this discussion, we will look at the 3SLS model only, since the SUR model is a special case. From (4.2-2) we rewrite the 2SLS estimator for the ith equation as

$$\alpha_i = [Z_i'X(X'X)^{-1}X'Z_i]^{-1}Z_i'X(X'X)^{-1}X'y_i, \qquad (4.2\text{-}17)$$

which estimates the ith 2SLS equation

$$y_i = Z_i\alpha_i + u_i . \qquad (4.2\text{-}18)$$

If we define[7] $(X'X)^{-1} = PP'$ and multiply equation (4.2-18) by $P'X'$, we obtain

$$P'X'y_i = P'X'Z_i\alpha_i + P'X'u_i, \qquad (4.2\text{-}19)$$

which can be written

$$w_i = W_i\alpha_i + \varepsilon_i, \qquad (4.2\text{-}20)$$

where $w_i = P'X'y_i$, $W_i = P'X'Z_i$, and $\varepsilon_i = P'X'u_i$. If all G 2SLS equations are written as

$$\begin{bmatrix} w_1 \\ w_2 \\ \cdot \\ w_G \end{bmatrix} = \begin{bmatrix} W_1 & 0 & & 0 \\ 0 & W_2 & & 0 \\ & \cdots\cdots\cdots \\ 0 & 0 & \cdots & W_G \end{bmatrix} \begin{bmatrix} \alpha_1 \\ \alpha_2 \\ \cdot \\ \alpha_G \end{bmatrix} + \begin{bmatrix} \varepsilon_1 \\ \varepsilon_2 \\ \cdot \\ \varepsilon_G \end{bmatrix},$$

$$\qquad (4.2\text{-}21)$$

then the system can be written as

$$w = W\alpha + \varepsilon . \qquad (4.2\text{-}22)$$

For each equation, i=j and

$$E[\varepsilon_i(\varepsilon_j)'] = E[P'X(\varepsilon_i(\varepsilon_j)'XP] = \sigma_{ij}P'X'XP = \sigma_{ij}I, \qquad (4.2\text{-}23)$$

while the covariance of the error term for the system becomes

$$
G = \begin{bmatrix} \sigma_{11}I & \sigma_{12}I & \cdots & & \sigma_{1G}I \\ \sigma_{21}I & \sigma_{22}I & \cdots & & \sigma_{2G}I \\ \cdots\cdots\cdots\cdots\cdots\cdots\cdots\cdots\cdots\cdots \\ \sigma_{G1}I & \sigma_{G2}I & \cdots & & \sigma_{GG}I \end{bmatrix} = \Sigma \otimes I \qquad (4.2\text{-}24)
$$

Equation (4.2-24) indicates that for each equation there is no heteroskedasticity, but that there is contemporaneous correlation of the residuals across equations. Equation (4.2-24) can be estimated from the 2SLS estimates of the residuals of each equation for 3SLS or the OLS estimates of the residuals of each equation for SUR models. Let

$$
\hat{V} = \hat{\sigma} \otimes I \qquad (4.2\text{-}25)
$$

be such an estimate. The 3SLS estimator of the system δ, where δ' = [B Γ] becomes

$$
\delta = (W'\hat{V}^{-1}W)^{-1} W'\hat{V}^{-1}w. \qquad (4.2\text{-}26)
$$

In a model with G equations, if the equation of interest is the jth equation, then assuming the exogenous variables in the system are selected correctly and the jth equation is specified correctly, 2SLS estimates are invariant to any other equation. 3SLS of the jth equation, in contrast, is sensitive to the specification of other equations in the system since changes in other equation specifications will alter the estimate of V and thus the 3SLS estimator of δ from equation (4.2-26). Because of this fact, it is imperative that users first inspect the 2SLS estimates closely. The constrained reduced form estimates, π, should be calculated from the OLS and 2SLS models and compared. The differences show the effects of correcting for simultaneity. Next 3SLS should be performed. A study of the resulting changes in δ and π will show the gain of moving to a system-wide estimation procedure. Since changes in the functional form of one equation i can possibly impact the estimates of another equation j, in this step of model building, sensitivity analysis should be attempted. In a multiequation system, the movement from 2SLS to 3SLS often produces changes in the estimate of δ_i for one equation but not for another equation. In a model in which <u>all</u> equations are over identified, in general the 3SLS estimators will differ from the 2SLS estimators. If all equations are exactly identified, then V is a diagonal matrix (Theil 1971, 511) and there is no gain for any equation from using 3SLS. In the test problem from Kmenta (1971, 565), which is discussed in the next section, one equation is over identified and one equation is exactly identified. In this case, only the exactly identified equation will be changed by 3SLS. This is because the exactly identified equation gains from information in the over identified equation but the reverse in not true. The over identified equation does not gain from information from the exactly identified equation.

In SUR models, if all equations contain the same variables, there is no gain over OLS from going to SUR, since **V** is again a diagonal matrix. Just as the LIML method of estimation is an alternative to 2SLS, the full information maximum likelihood method (FIML) is a more costly alternative to 3SLS and I3SLS.

Full information maximum likelihood[8] is a generalization of LIML for systems of models. Like LIML, it is invariant to the variable used to normalize the model. FIML, in contrast to 3SLS, is highly nonlinear and, as a consequence, much more costly. Because FIML is asymptotically equivalent to 3SLS (Theil 1971, 525) and the SIMEQ code does not contain any major advantages over other programs, the discussion of FIML is left to Theil (1971), Kmenta (1971) and Johnston(1984). In the next section, an annotated output is presented.

Iterative 3SLS is an alternative final step, in which the estimate of **V** is updated from the information from the 3SLS estimates. The problem now becomes where do you stop iterating on the estimates of **V**? The SIMEQ command uses the information on the number of significant digits (see IPR parameter) in the raw data and equation (4.1-8) to terminate the I3SLS iterations if the relative change is within what would be expected, given the number of significant digits in the raw data. If IPR is not set, the SIMEQ command assumes ten digits.

4.3 Examples

Using data on supply and demand from Kmenta (1971, 565), Table 4.1 shows B34S code to estimate models for OLS, limited information maximum likelihood estimation (LIML), two-stage least squares (LS2), and three-stage least squares (LS3). The reduced-form estimates for each model are listed. Not all output is shown below to save space. The results are the same, digit for digit, as reported in Kmenta (1971, 582).

Table 4.1 B34S SIMEQ Setup for OLS, LIML, LS2, LS3, and ILS3

```
==KMENTA1
B34SEXEC DATA NOOB=20 NOHEAD CORR$
 INPUT Q P D F A $
 COMMENT=('KMENTA(1971) PAGE 565 ANSWERS PAGE 582')$
 DATACARDS$
   98.485  100.323  87.4   98.0   1
   99.187  104.264  97.6   99.1   2
  102.163  103.435  96.7   99.1   3
  101.504  104.506  98.2   98.1   4
  104.240   98.001  99.8  110.8   5
  103.243   99.456 100.5  108.2   6
  103.993  101.066 103.2  105.6   7
   99.900  104.763 107.8  109.8   8
  100.350   96.446  96.6  108.7   9
  102.820   91.228  88.9  100.6  10
   95.435   93.085  75.1   81.0  11
   92.424   98.801  76.9   68.6  12
   94.535  102.908  84.6   70.9  13
   98.757   98.756  90.6   81.4  14
  105.797   95.119 103.1  102.3  15
  100.225   98.451 105.1  105.0  16
  103.522   86.498  96.4  110.5  17
   99.929  104.016 104.4   92.5  18
  105.223  105.769 110.7   89.3  19
  106.232  113.490 127.1   93.0  20
B34SRETURN$
B34SEEND$
B34SEXEC SIMEQ PRINTSYS REDUCED OLS LIML LS2 LS3 KCOV=DIAG$
 HEADING=('TEST CASE FROM KMENTA (1971) PAGES 565 - 582 ' ) $
 EXOGENOUS CONSTANT D F A $
 ENDOGENOUS P Q $
 MODEL LVAR=Q RVAR=(CONSTANT P D)    NAME=('DEMAND EQUATION')$
 MODEL LVAR=Q RVAR=(CONSTANT P F A) NAME=('SUPPLY EQUATION')$
 B34SEEND$
==
```

The OLS results are as follows:

SYSTEMS DESCRIBED BY THE FOLLOWING COLUMNS OF DATA (VARIABLES)

NAME OF THE SYSTEM	LHS		NO. X		NO. Y
DEMAND EQUATION	2 Q	1	2 CONSTANT	1	1 P
		2	D		

* *

SUPPLY EQUATION	2 Q	1	3 CONSTANT	1	1 P
		3	F		
		4	A		

* *

TEST CASE FROM KMENTA (1971) PAGES 565 - 582
****

LEAST SQUARES SOLUTION FOR SYSTEM NUMBER   1   DEMAND EQUATION

CONDITION NUMBER OF MATRIX IS GREATER THAN   21.049
RELATIVE NUMERICAL ERROR IN THE SOLUTION   0.13020E-10

LHS ENDOGENOUS VARIABLE NO.   2   Q

EXOGENOUS VARIABLES (PREDETERMINED)		STD. ERROR	T
1 CONSTANT	99.895	7.5194	13.285
2 D	0.33464	0.45422E-01	7.3673

ENDOGENOUS VARIABLES (JOINTLY DEPENDENT)		STD. ERROR	T
3 P	-0.31630	0.90677E-01	-3.4882

RESIDUAL VARIANCE (FOR STRUCTURAL DISTURBANCES)   3.7254

RATIO OF NORM RESIDUAL TO NORM LHS   0.17625E-01

COVARIANCE MATRIX IS

		CONSTANT 1	D 2	P 3
CONSTANT	1	56.54		
D	2	0.3216E-01	0.2063E-02	
P	3	-0.5948	-0.2333E-02	0.8222E-02

CORRELATION MATRIX IS

		CONSTANT 1	D 2	P 3
CONSTANT	1	1.000		
D	2	0.9931	1.000	
P	3	0.9983	0.9953	1.000

TEST CASE FROM KMENTA (1971) PAGES 565 - 582
****

LEAST SQUARES SOLUTION FOR SYSTEM NUMBER   2   SUPPLY EQUATION

CONDITION NUMBER OF MATRIX IS GREATER THAN   17.676
RELATIVE NUMERICAL ERROR IN THE SOLUTION   0.13187E-10

LHS ENDOGENOUS VARIABLE NO.   2   Q

EXOGENOUS VARIABLES (PREDETERMINED)

			STD. ERROR	T
1	CONSTANT	58.275	11.463	5.0838
2	F	0.24813	0.46188E-01	5.3723
3	A	0.24830	0.97518E-01	2.5462

ENDOGENOUS VARIABLES (JOINTLY DEPENDENT)

			STD. ERROR	T
4	P	0.16037	0.94884E-01	1.6901

RESIDUAL VARIANCE (FOR STRUCTURAL DISTURBANCES)   5.7844

RATIO OF NORM RESIDUAL TO NORM LHS   0.21306E-01

COVARIANCE MATRIX IS

		CONSTANT 1	F 2	A 3	P 4
CONSTANT	1	131.4			
F	2	-0.3044	0.2133E-02		
A	3	-0.2792	0.1316E-02	0.9510E-02	
P	4	-0.9875	0.8440E-03	0.5220E-03	0.9003E-02

CORRELATION MATRIX IS

		CONSTANT 1	F 2	A 3	P 4
CONSTANT	1	1.000			
F	2	0.9919	1.000		
A	3	0.8765	0.8518	1.000	
P	4	0.9983	0.9889	0.8751	1.000

TEST CASE FROM KMENTA (1971) PAGES 565 - 582
****
CONTEMPORANEOUS COVARIANCE OF RESIDUALS (STRUCTURAL DISTURBANCES)
FOR LEAST SQUARES SOLUTION.

CONDITION NUMBER OF RESIDUAL COLUMNS,   2.6648

		DEMAND E 1	SUPPLY E 2
DEMAND E	1	3.167	
SUPPLY E	2	3.411	4.628

TEST CASE FROM KMENTA (1971) PAGES 565 - 582
****
COEFFICIENTS OF THE REDUCED FORM EQUATIONS.

LEAST SQUARES SOLUTION.

CONDITION NUMBER OF THE MATRIX USED TO FIND THE REDUCED FORM COEFFICIENTS IS NO SMALLER THAN,   4.1958

		P 1	Q 2
CONSTANT	1	87.31	72.28
D	2	0.7020	0.1126
F	3	-0.5206	0.1647
A	4	-0.5209	0.1648

MEAN SUM OF SQUARES OF RESIDUALS FOR THE REDUCED FORM EQUATIONS.

    1   P   0.42748D+01

    2   Q   0.39192D+01

For each estimated equation, the condition number of the matrix, equation (4.1-7), and the relative numerical errors in the solution, equation (4.1-8), are given. The relative numerical errors for the supply and demand equations were .1302E-10 and .13187E-10, respectively. Estimated coefficients agree with Kmenta (1971, 582). From the estimated **B** and **Γ** coefficients, the constrained reduced form *π* coefficients are calculated. The condition number of the exogenous columns, .11845E+2, shows little multicollinearity among the exogenous variables. The next outputs show the corresponding estimates for LIML, 2SLS, and 3LSL. As was discussed earlier, since the asymptotic SEs for LIML are the same as for 2SLS, the SIMEQ command does not print these values.

CONDITION NUMBER OF COLUMNS OF EXOGENOUS VARIABLES,   0.11845E+02

                    TEST CASE FROM KMENTA (1971) PAGES 565 - 582
        ****

LIMITED INFORMATION - MAXIMUM LIKELIHOOD SOLUTION FOR   1   DEMAND EQUATION

RANK AND CONDITION NUMBER OF EXOGENOUS COLUMNS,   2   0.8517E+01
RANK AND CONDITION NUMBER OF ENDOGENOUS VARIABLES,ORTHOGONAL TO X(K),   2   6.559
RANK AND CONDITION NUMBER OF ENDOGENOUS VARIABLES ORTHOGONAL TO X,   2   2.301

VALUE OF LIMLE PARAMETER IS,   1.1739

CONDITION NUMBER OF MATRIX IS GREATER THAN   8.5175
RELATIVE NUMERICAL ERROR IN THE SOLUTION   0.44879E-11

LHS ENDOGENOUS VARIABLE NO.   2   Q

  STANDARD DEVIATION EQUALS 2SLSQ STANDARD DEVIATION.

EXOGENOUS VARIABLES (PREDETERMINED)
          1   CONSTANT   93.619
          2   D   0.31001

ENDOGENOUS VARIABLES (JOINTLY DEPENDENT)
          3   P   -0.22954

RESIDUAL VARIANCE (FOR STRUCTURAL DISTURBANCES)   3.9260

RATIO OF NORM RESIDUAL TO NORM LHS   0.18093E-01

                    TEST CASE FROM KMENTA (1971) PAGES 565 - 582
        ****

LIMITED INFORMATION - MAXIMUM LIKELIHOOD SOLUTION FOR   2   SUPPLY EQUATION

RANK AND CONDITION NUMBER OF EXOGENOUS COLUMNS,   3   0.8210E+01
RANK AND CONDITION NUMBER OF ENDOGENOUS VARIABLES,ORTHOGONAL TO X(K),   1   1.000
RANK AND CONDITION NUMBER OF ENDOGENOUS VARIABLES ORTHOGONAL TO X,   2   1.000

VALUE OF LIMLE PARAMETER IS,   1.0000

CONDITION NUMBER OF MATRIX IS GREATER THAN   8.2098
RELATIVE NUMERICAL ERROR IN THE SOLUTION   0.49430E-11

LHS ENDOGENOUS VARIABLE NO.   2   Q

  STANDARD DEVIATION EQUALS 2SLSQ STANDARD DEVIATION.

EXOGENOUS VARIABLES (PREDETERMINED)
          1   CONSTANT   49.532
          2   F   0.25561
          3   A   0.25292

ENDOGENOUS VARIABLES (JOINTLY DEPENDENT)
          4   P   0.24008

RESIDUAL VARIANCE (FOR STRUCTURAL DISTURBANCES)   6.0396

RATIO OF NORM RESIDUAL TO NORM LHS   0.21771E-01

                    TEST CASE FROM KMENTA (1971) PAGES 565 - 582
        ****

CONTEMPORANEOUS COVARIANCE OF RESIDUALS (STRUCTURAL DISTURBANCES)
FOR LIMLE SOLUTION.

CONDITION NUMBER OF RESIDUAL COLUMNS,   2.8116

              DEMAND E   SUPPLY E
                1   2

DEMAND E 1   3.337

SUPPLY E 2   3.629   4.832

TEST CASE FROM KMENTA (1971) PAGES 565 - 582
****

COEFFICIENTS OF THE REDUCED FORM EQUATIONS.

LIMLE SOLUTION.

CONDITION NUMBER OF THE MATRIX USED TO FIND THE REDUCED FORM COEFFICIENTS IS NO SMALLER THAN,   4.2588

		P 1	Q 2
CONSTANT	1	93.88	72.07
D	2	0.6601	0.1585
F	3	-0.5443	0.1249
A	4	-0.5386	0.1236

MEAN SUM OF SQUARES OF RESIDUALS FOR THE REDUCED FORM EQUATIONS.

1	P	0.41286D+01
2	Q	0.38401D+01

TEST CASE FROM KMENTA (1971) PAGES 565 - 582
****

TWO STAGE LEAST SQUARES SOLUTION FOR SYSTEM NUMBER   1   DEMAND EQUATION

CONDITION NUMBER OF MATRIX IS GREATER THAN   21.985
RELATIVE NUMERICAL ERROR IN THE SOLUTION   0.14114E-10

LHS ENDOGENOUS VARIABLE NO.   2   Q

EXOGENOUS VARIABLES (PREDETERMINED)			STD. ERROR	T	THEIL SE	THEIL T
1	CONSTANT	94.633	7.9208	11.947	7.3027	12.959
2	D	0.31399	0.46944E-01	6.6887	0.43280E-01	7.2549
ENDOGENOUS VARIABLES (JOINTLY DEPENDENT)			STD. ERROR	T	THEIL SE	THEIL T
3	P	-0.24356	0.96484E-01	-2.5243	0.88954E-01	-2.7380

RESIDUAL VARIANCE (FOR STRUCTURAL DISTURBANCES)   3.8664

RATIO OF NORM RESIDUAL TO NORM LHS   0.17955E-01

COVARIANCE MATRIX IS

		CONSTANT 1	D 2	P 3
CONSTANT	1	62.74		
D	2	0.4930E-01	0.2204E-02	
P	3	-0.6734	-0.2642E-02	0.9309E-02

CORRELATION MATRIX IS

		CONSTANT 1	D 2	P 3
CONSTANT	1	1.000		
D	2	0.9931	1.000	
P	3	0.9983	0.9953	0.9998

TEST CASE FROM KMENTA (1971) PAGES 565 - 582
****

TWO STAGE LEAST SQUARES SOLUTION FOR SYSTEM NUMBER   2   SUPPLY EQUATION

CONDITION NUMBER OF MATRIX IS GREATER THAN   18.219
RELATIVE NUMERICAL ERROR IN THE SOLUTION   0.14314E-10

LHS ENDOGENOUS VARIABLE NO.   2   Q

EXOGENOUS VARIABLES (PREDETERMINED)			STD. ERROR	T	THEIL SE	THEIL T
1	CONSTANT	49.532	12.011	4.1241	10.743	4.6109
2	F	0.25561	0.47250E-01	5.4096	0.42262E-01	6.0482
3	A	0.25292	0.99655E-01	2.5380	0.89134E-01	2.8376
ENDOGENOUS VARIABLES (JOINTLY DEPENDENT)			STD. ERROR	T	THEIL SE	THEIL T
4	P	0.24008	0.99934E-01	2.4023	0.89384E-01	2.6859

RESIDUAL VARIANCE (FOR STRUCTURAL DISTURBANCES)   6.0396

RATIO OF NORM RESIDUAL TO NORM LHS   0.21771E-01

COVARIANCE MATRIX IS

		CONSTANT 1	F 2	A 3	P 4
CONSTANT	1	144.3			
F	2	-0.3238	0.2233E-02		

```
A       3   -0.2952   0.1377E-02  0.9931E-02
P       4   -1.095     0.9362E-03  0.5791E-03  0.9987E-02
```

CORRELATION MATRIX IS

		CONSTANT 1	F 2	A 3	P 4
CONSTANT	1	1.000			
F	2	0.9919	1.000		
A	3	0.8765	0.8518	1.000	
P	4	0.9983	0.9889	0.8751	0.9998

```
                        TEST CASE FROM KMENTA (1971) PAGES 565 - 582
          **********************************************************************************
```

CONTEMPORANEOUS COVARIANCE OF RESIDUALS (STRUCTURAL DISTURBANCES)
FOR TWO STAGE LEAST SQUARES SOLUTION.

CONDITION NUMBER OF RESIDUAL COLUMNS,   2.8047

		DEMAND E 1	SUPPLY E 2
DEMAND E	1	3.286	
SUPPLY E	2	3.593	4.832

```
                        TEST CASE FROM KMENTA (1971) PAGES 565 - 582
          **********************************************************************************
```

COEFFICIENTS OF THE REDUCED FORM EQUATIONS.

TWO STAGE LEAST SQUARES SOLUTION.

CONDITION NUMBER OF THE MATRIX USED TO FIND THE REDUCED FORM COEFFICIENTS IS NO SMALLER THAN,   4.1354

		P 1	Q 2
CONSTANT	1	93.25	71.92
D	2	0.6492	0.1559
F	3	-0.5285	0.1287
A	4	-0.5230	0.1274

MEAN SUM OF SQUARES OF RESIDUALS FOR THE REDUCED FORM EQUATIONS.

```
    1   P                          0.39831D+01
    2   Q                          0.38317D+01
```

CONDITION NUMBER OF THE LARGE MATRIX IN THREE STAGE LEAST SQUARES   0.60702E+02

```
                        TEST CASE FROM KMENTA (1971) PAGES 565 - 582
          **********************************************************************************
**************************************************************************************************
```

THREE STAGE LEAST SQUARES SOLUTION FOR SYSTEM NUMBER   1   DEMAND EQUATION

LHS ENDOGENOUS VARIABLE NO.   2   Q

EXOGENOUS VARIABLES (PREDETERMINED)			STD. ERROR	T	THEIL SE	THEIL T
1	CONSTANT	94.633	7.9208	11.947	7.3027	12.959
2	D	0.31399	0.46944E-01	6.6887	0.43280E-01	7.2549
ENDOGENOUS VARIABLES (JOINTLY DEPENDENT).			STD. ERROR	T	THEIL SE	THEIL T
3	P	-0.24356	0.96484E-01	-2.5243	0.88954E-01	-2.7380

RESIDUAL VARIANCE (FOR STRUCTURAL DISTURBANCES)   3.2865

THREE STAGE LEAST SQUARES COVARIANCE FOR SYSTEM   DEMAND EQUATION

		CONSTANT 1	D 2	P 3
CONSTANT	1	62.74		
D	2	0.4930E-01	0.2204E-02	
P	3	-0.6734	-0.2642E-02	0.9309E-02

```
**************************************************************************************************
**************************************************************************************************
```

THREE STAGE LEAST SQUARES SOLUTION FOR SYSTEM NUMBER   2   SUPPLY EQUATION

LHS ENDOGENOUS VARIABLE NO.   2   Q

EXOGENOUS VARIABLES (PREDETERMINED)			STD. ERROR	T	THEIL SE	THEIL T
1	CONSTANT	52.118	11.893	4.3821	10.638	4.8993
2	F	0.22898	0.43994E-01	5.2048	0.39349E-01	5.8191
3	A	0.35791	0.72889E-01	4.9103	0.65194E-01	5.4899
ENDOGENOUS VARIABLES (JOINTLY DEPENDENT).			STD. ERROR	T	THEIL SE	THEIL T
4	P	0.22893	0.99673E-01	2.2968	0.89150E-01	2.5679

```
RESIDUAL VARIANCE (FOR STRUCTURAL DISTURBANCES)                  5.3608
THREE STAGE LEAST SQUARES COVARIANCE FOR SYSTEM      SUPPLY EQUATION

                  CONSTANT    F           A           P
                     1        2           3           4

CONSTANT   1       141.5

F          2      -0.2950    0.1935E-02

A          3      -0.4090    0.2548E-02  0.5313E-02

P          4      -1.083     0.8119E-03  0.1069E-02  0.9935E-02
```

****
```
                       TEST CASE FROM KMENTA (1971) PAGES 565 - 582
```
****
```
CONTEMPORANEOUS COVARIANCE OF RESIDUALS (STRUCTURAL DISTURBANCES)
FOR THREE STAGE LEAST SQUARES SOLUTION.

CONDITION NUMBER OF RESIDUAL COLUMNS,        6.3215

                 DEMAND E    SUPPLY E
                    1           2

DEMAND E   1       3.286

SUPPLY E   2       4.111       5.361
```
```
                     TEST CASE FROM KMENTA (1971) PAGES 565 - 582
```
****
```
                 COEFFICIENTS OF THE REDUCED FORM EQUATIONS.

                 THREE STAGE LEAST SQUARES SOLUTION.

CONDITION NUMBER OF THE MATRIX USED TO FIND THE REDUCED FORM COEFFICIENTS IS NO SMALLER THAN,     4.2329

                   P          Q
                   1          2

CONSTANT   1      89.98      72.72

D          2      0.6645     0.1521

F          3     -0.4846     0.1180

A          4     -0.7575     0.1845

MEAN SUM OF SQUARES OF RESIDUALS FOR THE REDUCED FORM EQUATIONS.
     1     P                       0.19065D+01

     2     Q                       0.42494D+01

STEP ENDING. SECONDS USED  0.12000001    . TOTAL JOB SECONDS    0.94333333   .
```

In the Kmenta test problem, one equation (demand) was over-identified and one equation (supply) was exactly identified. As was mentioned earlier, the 2SLS and 3SLS results for the over identified equation are the same because the other equation was exactly identified. However, the 3SLS results for the exactly identified equation (supply) differ from the 2SLS results because the other equation (demand) is over identified. Close inspection of the results for 3SLS for the demand equation shows that the results are the same as those of Kmenta (1971, 582) and Kmenta (1986, 712). The supply-equation results are the same as those of Kmenta (1971) but differ slightly from those of Kmenta (1986), which appear to be in error.

As noted earlier, the 2SLS and 3SLS results for the over-identified equation (demand) are the same. However, the printout shows that the residual variance for the 2SLS result is 3.8664, while the residual variance for the 3SLS result is 3.2865. The reason for this apparent error is that the 2SLS residual variance equals the sum of squared residuals divided by T-K, while the 3SLS calculation uses T; hence, 3.8664 = 3.2865 *(20/17).

4.4 Conclusion

The SIMEQ command should be used when either there are endogenous variables on the right-hand side of a regression model or when the seemingly unrelated regression model is desired. In the former case, if OLS is attempted, the results would be biased estimates. Jennings (1973, 1980), the original developer of the SIMEQ code, made a major contribution in developing fast and accurate code that was designed to alert the user to problems in the structure of the model. These include rank tests on all the key matrices as well as rank tests on the matrix of exogenous variables in the system.

NOTES

1. The B34S QR command is designed to provide up to 16 digits of accuracy. This command, which also allows estimation of the principle component (PC) regression, uses LINPACK code and is documented in chapter 10. The QR command also allows branches to be made to the Leamer (1978) SEARCH program. The QR command is distinct from the code in the SIMEQ command.

2. For further discussion see Pindyck and Rubinfeld (1981, 339-349).

3. A good discussion of the QR factorization is contained in Strang (1976). Other references include Jennings (1980) and Dongarra, Bunch, Moler, and Stewart (1979).

4. For more detail on techniques used in SIMEQ to avoid numerical error in the calculations arising from differences in the means of the data, see Jennings (1980).

5. If we define X^+ as the pseudoinverse of the T by K matrix X, then it can be shown (Strang 1976, 138, exercise 3.4.5) that the following four conditions hold: 1. $XX^+X=X$; 2. $X^+XX^+=X^+$; 3. $(XX^+)'=XX^+$; and 4. $(X^+X)'=X^+X$. The pseudoinverse can be obtained from the singular value decomposition or the QR factorization of X.

6. Kmenta (1971, 565-572) has one of the clearest descriptions. The discussion here complements that material.

7. This discussion is based on material contained in Johnston (1984, 486).

8. The FIML section of the SIMEQ command is the weakest link. Apart from possibly a scaler error in the FIML standard errors, there often are convergence problems that appear to be data related. In view of this and the fact that 3SLS is an inexpensive substitute, users are encouraged to employ 3SLS and I3SLS in place of FIML. Future releases of B34S will endeavor to improve the FIML code.

5. Error-Components Analysis

5.0 Introduction

The B34S ECOMP command implements the Freiden (1973) error-components program, which was heavily modified by Henry, McDonald and Stokes (1976). The error-components model provides a way in which a data set containing pooled-time-series and cross-section data can be modeled without having to assume the error structure is the same across time and across regions. The ECOMP command will estimate a model that is the same as a pooled-cross-section time-series model with a cross-section-specific dummy variable. The ECOMP procedure can also be used on a purely time-series model, if correction with seasonal dummies is desired, but the specific seasonal dummy coefficients are not needed. The ECOMP procedure also allows seasonal harmonic analysis. An example showing these more novel uses of the ECOMP procedure will be presented later.

5.1 Error-Component Model Specification

The ECOMP command[1] implements a model suggested by Nerlove (1971a) to capture the effects of pooled-time-series and cross-section data. Assume a model of the form

$$Y_{it} = \Sigma_k \beta_k x_{kit} + u_{it}, \qquad (5.1-1)$$

where $(i=1,\ldots,N)$, $(t=1,\ldots,T)$, and $(k=1,\ldots,K)$. There are N individuals and T time periods and K right-hand side independent variables in the model. The sample size = T * N. Let u_{it} be the total error term for the ith individual[2] at time t. The Nerlove (1971a) model assumes

$$u_{it} = \mu_i + v_{it}, \qquad (5.1-2)$$

where μ_i is an individual effect that is invariant over time and v_{it} is an effect that varies over time and individuals. We define τ as the interclass correlation coefficient, where

$$\tau = \sigma_\mu^2 / (\sigma_\mu^2 + \sigma_v^2) = \sigma_\mu^2 / \sigma_u^2, \qquad (5.1-3)$$

σ_u^2 is the variance of the error term u_{it}, σ_μ^2 is the variance of the individual effect μ_i, and σ_v^2 is the variance of the effect that varies over time and individuals v_{it}. If $\tau=0$, then the total effect $u_{it} = v_{it}$ and there is no individual specific effect.[3] An error-components model would not be appropriate and, as we show later, the error-components model is the OLS model for the complete data set.

In terms of our notation

$E\mu_i = Ev_{it} = 0$ for all i and t. $E\mu_i\mu_i' = \sigma_\mu^2$ for i=i',
$E\mu_i\mu_{i'} = 0$ for i $\neq$ i', $Ev_{it}v_{i't'} = \sigma_v^2$ for i=i' and, $Ev_{it}v_{i't'} = 0$ for
i $\neq$ i'. The variance-covariance matrix of the error terms is

$$Euu' = (\sigma_u)^2 \begin{bmatrix} A & 0 & \cdots & 0 \\ 0 & A & \cdots & 0 \\ \cdot & \cdot & & \cdot \\ \cdot & \cdot & & \cdot \\ 0 & 0 & \cdots & A \end{bmatrix},$$ (5.1-4)

where

$$A = \begin{bmatrix} 1 & \tau & \cdots & \tau \\ \tau & 1 & \cdots & \tau \\ \cdot & \cdot & & \cdot \\ \cdot & \cdot & & \cdot \\ \tau & \tau & \cdots & 1 \end{bmatrix}.$$ (5.1-5)

As noted in Freiden (1973), Nerlove (1971a, 1971b) conducted Monte Carlo experiments concerning five alternative ways to estimate the intraclass correlation coefficient τ. He selected a two-stage procedure, which he concluded "compares favorably with all the other techniques investigated." Once we discuss this estimation procedure, we will show how this method cannot be used in a situation in which any independent variable is constant over time for all members of a cross section. Finally, we show how the Henry-McDonald-Stokes (1976) procedure provides an alternative method for obtaining an estimate of τ for cases in which the Nerlove two-step procedure is not appropriate.

The Nerlove (1971a) two-step procedure first involves estimation of the β_k in a regression of deviations of the dependent variable from the individual means on deviations of the independent variable from the individual means. Assume

$$\bar{y}_i = (1/T) \Sigma_{t=1}^T Y_{it}$$ (5.1-6)

$$\bar{y} = (1/NT)\Sigma_{i=1}^N \Sigma_{t=1}^T Y_{it}$$ (5.1-7)

$$\bar{x}_i(k) = (1/T) \Sigma_{t=1}^T x_{kit}$$ (5.1-8)

$$\bar{x}(k) = (1/NT)\Sigma_{i=1}^N \Sigma_{t=1}^T x_{kit}.$$ (5.1-9)

We obtain the b_k, the coefficients of the "within" estimator (LSDV least-squares, dummy-variables model), by estimating the equation

$$(\overline{y}_{it} - y_i) = \qquad \Sigma_{k=2}^{K} b_k(x_{kit} - \overline{x}_i(k)) + \overline{u}_t. \qquad (5.1\text{-}10)$$

If we define $(s^*)^2$ as the sum of squares from estimating equation (5.1-10), Nerlove (1971a, 1971b) suggests estimating τ as

$$\hat{\tau} = \hat{\sigma}_\mu^2 / (\hat{\sigma}_\mu^2 + ((s^*)^2/NT)), \qquad (5.1\text{-}11)$$

where

$$\hat{\sigma}_\mu^2 = (1/N)\Sigma_{i=1}^{N} \{(\overline{y}_i - \overline{y}) - \Sigma_{k=1}^{K} b_k[\overline{x}_i(k) - \overline{x}(k)]\}^2. \qquad (5.1\text{-}12)$$

$\hat{\tau}$ is then used to form the weights Θ_1 and Θ_2

$$\Theta_1 = (1 - \hat{\tau}) + \qquad T\tau \qquad (5.1\text{-}13)$$

$$\Theta_2 = (1 - \hat{\tau}). \qquad (5.1\text{-}14)$$

It can be shown that Θ_1 and Θ_2 are the characteristic roots of the matrix Euu'/σ_u^2. These weights can be used to transform the variables y_{it} and $x_{it}(k)$

$$y_{it}^* \qquad = (y_{it} - \overline{y}_i)/\sqrt{(\Theta_2)} \qquad + \qquad \overline{y}_i/\sqrt{(\Theta_1)} \qquad (5.1\text{-}15)$$

$$x_{it}^*(k) \qquad = (x_{kit} - \overline{x}_i(k))/\sqrt{(\Theta_2)} \qquad + \qquad \overline{x}_i(k)/\sqrt{(\Theta_1)}. \qquad (5.1\text{-}16)$$

The third round provides estimates of the original equation, using the transformed data.

$$y_{it}^* \qquad = \qquad \Sigma_k\beta_k x_{kit}^* + u_{it} \qquad (5.1\text{-}17)$$

which can be thought of as the GLS error-components model. If $\tau = 0$, then $\Theta_1 = \Theta_2 = 1$ and $y_{it}^* = y_{it}$ and $x^{*k}_{it} = x_{kit}$ and the error-components results are the same as the OLS results on the complete sample.

The Nerlove (1971a, 1971b) equation to estimate τ (5.1-11) requires an estimate of $(s^*)^2$ from equation (5.1-10). Equation (5.1-10) is not possible to estimate when there are independent variables that are constant over time for all members of the cross section. For example, consider a model with N individuals in which there are data for T time periods. If we want to control for sex, then the sex dummy will be constant for each individual for all time periods, making equation (5.1-10) impossible to estimate.

Henry, McDonald and Stokes (1976) provide an alternative way to estimate τ that is possible even when there is no variation of an independent variable for all time periods for one individual (region).

The Henry-McDonald-Stokes (1976) approach uses equation (5.1-3) to estimate τ. First, OLS estimates of equation (5.1-1) will provide an estimate of σ_u^2. Next, the estimate of σ_μ^2 is computed by finding the mean residual for each of the N individuals (regions) and computing the variance of these mean residuals, weighting each mean residual by T. This is illustrated in equation (5.1-18)

$$(TN)\hat{\sigma}_\mu^2 \quad = \quad \Sigma_i \; T(y_i - \bar{x}_i'\hat{\beta})^2, \qquad\qquad (5.1\text{-}18)$$

where

$$\bar{x}_i'\beta \quad = \quad \Sigma_{k=1}^K \; (\bar{x}_i(k)\hat{\beta}_k). \qquad\qquad (5.1\text{-}19)$$

Now we have alternative estimates σ_u^2 and σ_μ^2 and equation (5.1-3) can be used to obtain an estimate of τ. Once we have an alternative estimate of τ, equations (5.1-15) and (5.1-16) are used in a manner similar to the Nerlove (1971a) approach to transform the variables, and equation (5.1-17) is used to form the error-components estimate of β_k. This discussion shows how the Henry-McDonald-Stokes (1976) approach provides a way to obtain an estimate of τ when the Nerlove (1971a) approach is impossible.

When analyzing panel data, the researcher is faced by three choices:

1. Handle the model as if it were one sample and make no adjustments in the data.

2. Run the LSDV estimator, using equation (5.1-10).

3. Select the appropriate way to estimate τ and run the error-components model, using equation (5.1-17).

The LSDV estimator[4] has been characterized as a "fixed effect" method of estimation, while the error-components model has been characterized as a "random-effect" model. As T goes to ∞, the GLS error-components model becomes the same as the LSDV estimator. Assume a model in which we have N individuals for T time periods and wish to predict consumption. If the method of estimation used is the error-components model, we save on the number of parameters to estimate and thus gain in efficiency. If the individual specific effect is correlated with the right-hand- side variables, the estimated coefficients are biased and inconsistent. By implicitly including a dummy for each individual, the LSDV estimator does not have this problem, although it is less efficient because of the increased number of parameters that were actually implicitly estimated. As was discussed earlier, the LSDV estimator is not possible when some of the right-hand-side variables are constant for individuals. In view of the following discussion, it appears that the best approach is to calculate all three estimates, wherever possible, and see how sensitive the major findings of the study are to the three approaches. Since the B34S can test for either time-specific or individual-specific effects, in effect there would be five models to inspect: the OLS model, the LSDV model for time or individual effects, and the error-components model for time or individual effects.

5.2 ECOMP-Command Options

The B34S ECOMP procedure in default mode (REGFIRST) assumes that the data are stored in the form:

Period 1	Region 1
Period 2	Region 1
.	.
Period T-1	Region N
Period T	Region N.

The alternative setup (PERFIRST) is as follows:

Period 1	Region 1
Period 1	Region 2
.	.
Period T	Region N-1
Period T	Region N

The user must specify NREG and NPER, which are set to N and T, respectively. It is not clear whether the error-components correction should be by individuals (regions) or by periods. The ECOMP option ISWITH allows the program to test the error-components model in the other direction. Setting ISWITH is equivalent to switching the NREG and NPER values and interchanging PERFIRST with REGFIRST or REGFIRST with PERFIRST. Inspection of the estimated value of τ will indicate which way to run the model.

The default (BOTHP option) way to run the ECOMP command is to use the Nerlove (1971a) method of obtaining an estimate of τ but, in addition, to print the Henry-McDonald-Stokes (1976) estimate of τ. The latter estimate of τ can be turned off by selecting the STAGE2P option. If the OLSP option is selected, the Henry-McDonald-Stokes (1976) estimate of τ is used. This option must be selected if there is no variation for some independent variable for the cross section for one individual or region. This problem can often arise with control variables for individual data, such as sex or race, since these variables will not change for one individual over time.

The B34S ECOMP command allows the user to sort the data once and use it in multiple ECOMP commands if the ISTORE and IRECALL options are specified. These must be used carefully and are most valuable for very large data sets. Several output options are available, such as the PRINT and PRINTALL commands. The PRINTALL command should be used cautiously since it generates a great deal of output.

5.3 Further Detail on Estimating τ

The Henry-McDonald-Stokes (1976) approach to obtaining an estimate of τ makes use of equations (5.1-4) and (5.1-5). If we define

$$
H \;=\; \begin{bmatrix} A & 0 & \cdots & 0 \\ 0 & A & \cdots & 0 \\ \cdot & \cdot & & \cdot \\ \cdot & \cdot & & \cdot \\ 0 & 0 & \cdots & A \end{bmatrix}, \tag{5.3-1}
$$

we can write the covariance matrix of u_{it} as $\sigma_u^2 H$. From equation (5.3-1) we note that H is block diagonal. From equation (5.1.5) we see that the ith block H_i is of order T, with ones on its main diagonal and τ everywhere else. Once τ is known, GLS would provide a minimum variance, unbiased estimator of the βs in equation (5.1-1). The GLS estimator of β is

$$
\tilde{\beta} \;=\; (X'\hat{H}^{-1}X)^{-1}\, X'\hat{H}^{-1}Y, \tag{5.3-2}
$$

where X consists of the elements x_{kit} and Y consists of the elements y_{it}. The variance / covariance matrix of β is

$$
\tilde{\sigma}_u^2 (X'\hat{H}^{-1}X)^{-1}. \tag{5.3-3}
$$

The inverse of $\hat{H}$ is block diagonal, where the ith block is the inverse of $\hat{H}_i$.

$$
\hat{H}_i^{-1} = I/(1-\hat{\tau}) \; - ee'\; \hat{\tau}/(1-\hat{\tau})(1-\hat{\tau} + \hat{\tau}\, T_i), \tag{5.3-4}
$$

where e is a column vector of the T_i ones.

$$
\tilde{\sigma}_u^2 \;=\; (Y'\hat{H}^{-1}Y - \tilde{\beta}'X'\hat{H}^{-1}Y)/(NT) \tag{5.3-5}
$$

and $T_i \equiv T$.

The difference in the Nerlove (1971a) approach and the Henry-McDonald-Stokes (1976) approach lies only in how H is estimated. When $\tau=0$, H becomes an identity matrix and the GLS and OLS estimate of β will be the same. The Henry-McDonald-Stokes (1976) approach to obtaining an estimate of τ is comparable, but much simpler computationally, to an alternative suggested by Nerlove (1971a) that involved including a dummy variable for each individual in an OLS regression and computing the variance of the estimated N dummies.

5.4 Examples

Some of the capabilities of the B34S ECOMP command can be illustrated by the SAS/B34S job listed in Table 5.1, which generates two simulated panel data sets of 200 observations. Data has been listed in both SAS and B34S, although this is not necessary. The sample program generates two models. The first left-hand variable YTIME has a quarter-specific, fixed effect (seasonal). The model is:

$$YTIME_t = \beta_1 + \beta_2 X1_t + \beta_3 X2_t + \beta_4 QT_t + e_t, \qquad (5.4-1)$$

where $X1_t$ and $X2_t$ are normally distributed, QT_t takes the values (1, 2, 3, 4, 1, ...), and $\beta_1 = \beta_2 = \beta_3 = \beta_4 = 5$. The variables Q1 - Q4 that are built in SAS are used in the B34S REGRESSION step to validate that the ECOMP command

```
B34SEXEC ECOMP NREG=4 NPER=50 PERFIRST BOTHP$
   MODEL YTIME = X1 X2$ B34SEEND$
```

will give the same estimated coefficients as the B34S REGRESSION commands

```
B34SEXEC REGRESSION$
   MODEL YTIME = X1 X2 Q1 Q2 Q3$ B34SEEND$
```

for the second-stage LSDV output. Note that to avoid falling in the dummy variable trap, Q4 is <u>not</u> on the right-hand side of equation (5.4-1). In this example, we have a time series for 200 observations. This is alternatively viewed as a "pooled cross-section time-series model " in which there are 4 observations in the cross section (NREG=4) and 50 observations (NPER=50) in the time series.

Table 5.1 B34S ECOMP Setup

```
/*JOBPARM R=2048,T=1,L=10,WTP
// EXEC SASB34S
//SAS.SYSIN DD *
DATA CH5;
DO I=1 TO 200;
X1= RANNOR(1234);
X2= RANNOR(1234);
QT=MOD(I,4);
Q1=0; IF QT EQ 1 THEN Q1 = 1;
Q2=0; IF QT EQ 2 THEN Q2 = 1;
Q3=0; IF QT EQ 3 THEN Q3 = 1;
Q4=0; IF QT EQ 0 THEN Q4 = 1;
YTIME = 5  + 5 *X1 +  5*X2 + 5*QT + 10*RANNOR(12345);
ADJ= MOD(I,10) *(ABS(X1));
YREG = YTIME - 5*QT + 5*ADJ;
OUTPUT;
END;
PROC MEANS DATA=CH5;
PROC PRINT DATA=CH5;
PROC CB34S NOHEAD DATA=CH5;
VAR YTIME YREG X1 X2   Q1 Q2 Q3 Q4 ;
PARMCARDS;
B34SEXEC LIST$          VAR YTIME YREG X1 X2 Q1 Q2 Q3 Q4$
B34SEXEC REGRESSION$
   MODEL YTIME=X1 X2 Q1 Q2 Q3$ B34SEEND$
B34SEXEC ECOMP NREG=4 NPER=50 PERFIRST BOTHP$
   MODEL YTIME = X1 X2$  B34SEEND$
B34SEXEC ECOMP NREG=10 NPER=20 PERFIRST BOTHP$ * OK SETUP      $
   MODEL YREG = X1 X2$  B34SEEND$
B34SEXEC ECOMP NREG=10 NPER=20 REGFIRST BOTHP$ * NOT OK SETUP $
   MODEL YREG = X1 X2$  B34SEEND$
B34SEXEC ECOMP NREG=20 NPER=10 PERFIRST BOTHP$ * 2 X OK SETUP $
   MODEL YREG = X1 X2$  B34SEEND$
B34SEXEC ECOMP NREG=20 NPER=10 REGFIRST BOTHP$ * NOT OK SETUP $
   MODEL YREG = X1 X2$  B34SEEND$
B34SEXEC ECOMP NREG=4 NPER=50 PERFIRST OLSP$
   MODEL YTIME = X1 X2$  B34SEEND$
B34SEXEC ECOMP NREG=10 NPER=20 PERFIRST OLSP$  * OK SETUP      $
   MODEL YREG = X1 X2$  B34SEEND$
B34SEXEC ECOMP NREG=10 NPER=20 REGFIRST OLSP$  * NOT OK SETUP $
   MODEL YREG = X1 X2$  B34SEEND$
B34SEXEC ECOMP NREG=20 NPER=10 PERFIRST OLSP$  * 2 X OK SETUP $
   MODEL YREG = X1 X2$  B34SEEND$
B34SEXEC ECOMP NREG=20 NPER=10 REGFIRST OLSP$  * NOT OK SETUP $
   MODEL YREG = X1 X2$  B34SEEND$
;
```

The output from running the job in Table 5.1 follows.[5]

```
UIC  B34S DATA ANALYSIS PROGRAM 21 NOV  86                B34S RUNNING UNDER SAS              PAGE   2

**************
PROBLEM NUMBER                     1
SUBPROBLEM NUMBER                  1

F TO ENTER                   0.10000002E-01
F TO REMOVE                  0.49999990E-02
TOLERANCE                    0.99999998E-05
MAXIMUM NO OF STEPS                6
DEPENDENT VARIABLE X( 1).  VARIABLE NAME  YTIME

THE FOLLOWING VARIABLES ARE DELETED IN THIS SUBPROBLEM

  2   8

THE FOLLOWING VARIABLES ARE FORCED INTO THE REGRESSION EQUATION AS CONTROL VARIABLES (COVARIATES)

  3   4   5   6   7   9

STANDARD ERROR OF Y =   13.663384      FOR DEGREES OF FREEDOM  =       199.
```

```
...............
STEP NUMBER  6                         ANALYSIS OF VARIANCE FOR REDUCTION IN SS DUE TO VARIABLE ENTERING
   VARIABLE ENTERING      5               SOURCE          DF        SS            MS           F         F SIG.
   MULTIPLE R          0.63516            DUE REGRESSION   5       14988.       2997.5      26.238    1.000000
   STD ERROR OF Y.X   10.68849            DEV. FROM REG.  194      22163.       114.24
   R SQUARE           0.40343             TOTAL          199       37151.       186.69
```

```
   MULTIPLE REGRESSION EQUATION
VARIABLE          COEFFICIENT    STD. ERROR    T VAL.    T SIG. P. COR. ELASTICITY    PARTIAL COR. FOR VAR. NOT IN EQUATION
YTIME    =                                                                           VARIABLE    COEFFICIENT   F FOR SELECTION
X1      X- 3     5.677010       0.8347968     6.800    1.00000  0.4387   0.7894E-01
X2      X- 4     5.051204       0.7289028     6.930    1.00000  0.4454  -0.5811E-02
Q1      X- 5     9.153202       2.139492      4.278    0.99997  0.2936   0.1716
Q2      X- 6    12.27023        2.152444      5.701    1.00000  0.3788   0.2300
Q3      X- 7    13.69484        2.148492      6.374    1.00000  0.4161   0.2567
CONSTANT X- 9    3.580830       1.524527      2.349    0.98016
```

```
ADJUSTED R SQUARE FOR K=   6,  N=      200  IS    0.38804984

-2  *  LN(MAXIMUM OF THE LIKELIHOOD FUNCTION)   1509.1505

AKAIKE  INFORMATION CRITERION (AIC) BASED ON JOINT LIKELIHOOD OF SIGMA AND BETA    1523.1505

SCHWARZ INFORMATION CRITERION (SIC) BASED ON JOINT LIKELIHOOD OF SIGMA AND BETA    1546.2387

NOTE: MODELS WITH LOWER AIC OR SIC ARE BETTER.

AIC = (N * LN(2*PI) ) + ( N * LN((SUM RES SQ)/N)) + N + (2*(K+1))

SIC = AIC - (2*(K+1))  +  ((K+1) * LN(N))
```

```
   RESIDUAL VARIANCE =    114.24379

   ORDER OF ENTRANCE (OR DELETION) OF THE VARIABLES =    9   3   4   7   6   5

ESTIMATE OF COMPUTATIONAL ERROR IN COEFFICIENTS =
     1  0.1059E-13    2   0.3032E-14    3  0.8346E-14    4  0.5769E-14    5  0.1034E-13    6  0.1812E-13

   COVARIANCE MATRIX OF REGRESSION COEFFICIENTS

ROW  1    VARIABLE X- 3    X1
   0.69688587

ROW  2    VARIABLE X- 4    X2
   0.21620508E-01  0.53129937

ROW  3    VARIABLE X- 5    Q1
   0.23732011E-02  0.63855177E-01   4.5774263

ROW  4    VARIABLE X- 6    Q2
   0.57553929E-01  0.17799155       2.3062518     4.6330176

ROW  5    VARIABLE X- 7    Q3
  -0.54704354E-01  0.14754042       2.3026279     2.3299153     4.6160185

ROW  6    VARIABLE X- 9    CONSTANT
  -0.13019371    -0.93204390E-01  -2.2960369    -2.3252373    -2.2997333    2.3241819

=== PROGRAM TERMINATED - ALL VARIABLES PUT IN

EC ANALYSIS, IREAD SET TO     1 ON EC CARD
```

```
THE NUMBER OF INDIVIDUALS OR REGIONS IN THE CROSS SECTION IS    4

THE NUMBER OF PERIODS IN THE TIME SERIES IS   50

THE NUMBER OF INDEPENDENT VARIABLES (EXCLUDING THE CONSTANT) IS    2

    894 WORDS OF  70000 AVAILABLE USED.
```

```
OLS REGRESSION OF YTIME     ON LEVELS:


COEFFICIENT OF DETERMINATION, R**2 = 0.2526
SUM OF SQUARED RESIDUALS =    27765.
STANDARD ERROR OF ESTIMATE =    11.872
1/COND OF MATRIX XPX   0.65801972


VARIABLE COEFFICIENT             STANDARD ERROR                  T-RATIO

X1        5.707047              0.9253844                       6.1672
X2        4.460953              0.8031323                       5.5544
CONSTANT 12.34577               0.8568211                      14.4088

RHOHAT CALCULATED FROM OLS EQUATION  0.1990

RHOHAT CALCULATED FROM OLS EQUATION NOT USED THIRD STAGE
```

```
OLS REGRESSION OF YTIME     ON DEVIATIONS FROM REGIONAL MEANS:


COEFFICIENT OF DETERMINATION, R**2 = 0.3194
SUM OF SQUARED RESIDUALS =    22163.
STANDARD ERROR OF ESTIMATE =    10.580
1/COND OF MATRIX XPX   0.79607859


VARIABLE_COEFFICIENT_____STANDARD_ERROR_____T-RATIO__


X1          5.677010              0.8263216                    6.8702
X2          5.051204              0.7215026                    7.0009

    RHOHAT CALCULATED FROM SECOND STAGE EQUATION      0.2039



OLS REGRESSION OF YTIME     ON TRANSFORMED VARIABLES:


COEFFICIENT OF DETERMINATION, R**2 = 0.3138
SUM OF SQUARED RESIDUALS =    28358.
STANDARD ERROR OF ESTIMATE =    11.998
1/COND OF MATRIX XPX   0.72954482


VARIABLE_COEFFICIENT_____STANDARD_ERROR_____T-RATIO__


X1          5.679140              0.8359378                    6.7937
X2          5.007825              0.7295768                    6.8640
CONSTANT    3.727583              0.8496590                    4.3872

STEP ENDING. SECONDS USED  0.21097583    . TOTAL JOB SECONDS    1.1019468    .
```

The estimated coefficients for β_2 and β_3 were found to be 5.677010 and 5.051204, respectively, in the B34S REGRESSION command output in which dummies were used and in the ECOMP output in the section "OLS REGRESSION OF YTIME ON DEVIATIONS FROM THE REGIONAL MEANS," which is the LSDV model. Although in this case only three dummy variables were needed, in a situation with more "regions," the use of dummies would not be practical. The ECOMP least-squares dummy variables model (LSDV) provides a useful way to proceed. The third-stage output, which uses the second-stage estimate of τ (called rho on the printout) of .2039 from equation (5.1-11), estimates a model on the transformed variables and obtains values for β_2 and β_3 of 5.6791 and 5.0078, respectively. In the OLS stage without the dummies, these coefficients were 5.70705 and 4.46095, respectively . If τ is estimated from the OLS stage via equation (5.1-18), it would have been .1990, and the results would not equal the third-stage results. The output illustrates the advantage of the ECOMP procedure. In the sample illustration, there are so few "regions" that OLS with dummies is a viable alternative to running the ECOMP command. However, in a case with many "regions" it is not feasible to have many dummies in the regression. Hence, OLS with dummies is not a viable alternative.

Inspection of the LSDV output indicates that the sum of squared residuals for the REGRESSION command and the ECOMP command are the same (22163.0), yet the standard error of estimate and the t scores and the R^2 are different. The variance of the YTIME variable is 186.68809. From equation (2.1-10) the estimated residual variance is u'u / (T-K-1). In the REGRESSION command, we get 114.24379 = 22163 / 194. The standard error of estimate becomes $\sqrt{114.24379}$ = 10.68849, which is exactly what was reported with the REGRESSION command. The ECOMP command reports a standard error of estimate of 10.580, which is $\sqrt{(22163 / 198)}$. The R^2 in the regression command is calculated from equation (2.1-15) and becomes $(1-(22163/(186.68809 * 199)))$, which reduces to .40343. The R^2 for the ECOMP output on "DEVIATIONS FROM THE REGIONAL MEANS" of .3194 arises from the fact that the variance of the transformed right-hand-side variable (deviations from the regional means YTIME) is used instead of the variance of YTIME. Users wanting the OLS equivalent R^2 can easily make the calculation by hand since the sum of squares of the residuals is given.

The standard errors of β_2 and β_3 were .8347968 and .7289028, respectively, with the REGRESSION command and .8263216 and .7215026 with the ECOMP command. The value $\sqrt{(198/194)} = 1.01025668$ can be used to adjust the ECOMP standard error values if that is desired. For example, .834768 = $\sqrt{(198/194)}$ * .8263216.

In the above example, the ECOMP command was run with the BOTHP option. τ was calculated from the OLS stage (.1990) and the second-stage (.2039). The second-stage τ was used in the third-stage "OLS REGRESSION OF YTIME ON TRANSFORMED VARIABLES." If the OLSP option is used, the first-stage τ of .1990 will be used to transform the data. As was discussed in the previous section, the OLSP option is used when there is the possibility that any independent variable is constant over one cross section. While the YTIME problem does not have this difficulty, this model was run with the OLSP option for illustration purposes. Sample output from this model is given next and shows the values for β_1, β_2, and β_3 were 3.7691, 5.6792, and 5.0066, respectively, which are very close to the values obtained from the three-stage Nerlove (1971a) procedure discussed earlier.

```
EC ANALYSIS, IREAD SET TO    1 ON EC CARD



THE NUMBER OF INDIVIDUALS OR REGIONS IN THE CROSS SECTION IS    4

THE NUMBER OF PERIODS IN THE TIME SERIES IS  50

THE NUMBER OF INDEPENDENT VARIABLES (EXCLUDING THE CONSTANT) IS    2

    894 WORDS OF  70000 AVAILABLE USED.


OLS REGRESSION OF YTIME    ON LEVELS:

COEFFICIENT OF DETERMINATION, R**2 = 0.2526
SUM OF SQUARED RESIDUALS =    27765.
STANDARD ERROR OF ESTIMATE =    11.872
1/COND OF MATRIX XPX   0.65801972

VARIABLE COEFFICIENT            STANDARD ERROR                    T-RATIO

X1          5.707047                0.9253844                          6.1672
X2          4.460953                0.8031323                          5.5544
CONSTANT   12.34577                 0.8568211                         14.4088
    RHOHAT CALCULATED FROM OLS EQUATION  0.1990
```

```
OLS REGRESSION OF YTIME    ON TRANSFORMED VARIABLES:


COEFFICIENT OF DETERMINATION, R**2 = 0.3136
SUM OF SQUARED RESIDUALS =    28198.
STANDARD ERROR OF ESTIMATE =    11.964
1/COND OF MATRIX XPX   0.73091390

VARIABLE_COEFFICIENT_____STANDARD_ERROR_____T-RATIO__

X1           5.679201              0.8361523                       6.7921
X2           5.006582              0.7297548                       6.8606
CONSTANT     3.769058              0.8473075                       4.4483

STEP ENDING. SECONDS USED 0.21985245   . TOTAL JOB SECONDS    3.0693312   .
```

In the first sample problem, the "seasonal" component was linear and deterministic. A seasonal time variable could have been used with an OLS model in place of the QT dummies (Q1, Q2, Q3). In general, the seasonal component is not linear and deterministic and a time variable will not capture the seasonal component. Hence, the ECOMP procedure is useful.

The variable YREG has been built to have a stochastic or random-effect "seasonal" component. For purposes of the example, the number of periods is 50 and the number of regions is 10. Four problems are run for each of the options BOTHP and OLSP. The output will not be listed to save space, but some of the implications of the results and the output of the various models follows. Not all problems have been set up correctly to illustrate the effect on the estimated τ as the researcher investigates alternative error-components effects. An overview of the models estimated is given in Table 5.2.

Table 5.2 Models Investigated for Stochastic Error-Components Model

MODEL #	NREQ	NPER	SORT	Comment
1	10	20	PERFIRST	Correct setup
2	10	20	REGFIRST	Not correct setup
3	20	10	PERFIRST	Correct harmonic setup
4	20	10	REGFIRST	Not correct setup

Output from these models is listed in Table 5.3. All models were estimated, using both methods, to obtain an estimate of τ. In every case, the OLS model estimated values are

YREG =   21.55534   +   8.454931 X1 +   1.631363 X2
          (15.89)   (5.77)   (1.28)

R^2 = .1490   e'e = 69593,

where the population values for $\beta_1 = \beta_3 = 5$. Table 5.3 gives the values for various options of the ECOMP command.

Table 5.3 Output for the Stochastic Error-Components Model

Model	1	2	3	4
OLS τ	.3420	.0110	.4267	.0506
2nd-stage τ	.3711	.0110	.4582	.0511
LSDV β_2	8.2038	8.4614	8.5628	8.4450
t	6.81	5.75	7.54	5.71
LSDV β_3	4.0534	1.5953	4.2745	1.3351
t	3.85	1.23	4.29	1.02
LSDV R^2	.234	.147	.270	.145
LSDV e'e	44588.	68828.	38531.	66055.
3rd-stage β_1	7.6238	19.602	9.5303	17.8390
t	5.55	14.44	6.78	13.01
3rd-stage β_2	8.2290	8.4561	8.5521	8.4493
t	6.68	5.76	7.23	5.74
3rd-stage β_3	3.85023	1.6250	3.9668	1.5347
t	3.57	1.27	3.83	1.20
3rd-stage R^2	.223	.149	.249	.1476
3rd-stage e'e	74149.	70227.	77445.	72041.
2nd-stage β_1	7.8990	19.6040	9.8059	17.8671
t	5.86	14.44	7.14	13.03
2nd-stage β_2	8.2320	8.4561	8.5508	8.4493
t	6.66	5.76	7.20	5.74
2nd-stage β_3	3.8254	1.6250	3.9303	1.5354
t	3.54	1.27	3.78	1.20
2nd-stage R^2	.2222	.1486	.247	.1476
2nd-stage e'e	71258.	70226.	73896.	72011.

The 3rd-stage results arise from using the 2nd-stage τ estimate (the BOTHP option). The 2nd-stage results use the OLS stage τ estimate (the OLSP option). Models 2 and 4 are clearly incorrectly specified as can be seen by the low values of τ for both the OLS τ (.0110 and .0506, respectively) and the 2nd stage τ (.0110 and .0511, respectively). Since the estimated τ was so low, from equation (5.1-11) we find the 3rd-stage and 2nd-stage results are close to the OLS results. The LSDV results for these incorrect setups are not influenced by the estimated τ. However, since the numbers of regions and periods are not correctly specified, the estimated value for the coefficient β_3 is close to the OLS result.

Model 1 is correctly specified, based on how the data set was

built. In comparison with the OLS results, the LSDV coefficient for
β_3, 4.05334, is closer to the population value of 5. Model 3 is
correctly specified but tests harmonic effects. In contrast with
model 1 in which we assumed that NREG=10 and NPER=20, here we
assumed that NREG=20 and NPER=10. This implicitly assumes that the
"regions-specific" error-component extends over 20 observations,
not just 10. The estimated OLS-stage τ and 2nd-stage τ are larger
(.4267 vs. .3420 and .4582 vs. .3711), indicating this assumption
is warranted.

Many people mistakenly believe that error-components models
are appropriate only for situations in which cross-section and
time- series data are pooled. While this is the usual case, the
preceding example shows how error-components analysis could be used
with just time-series data. Additional examples include the
following:

- Having monthly data for 96 years and using the setup
NREG=12, NPER= 96 to control for a seasonal effect, and NREG=48,
NPER=48, NPER= 24 to control for a four-year "political cycle." In
this situation, the LSDV model is particularly appropriate.

5.5 Conclusion

The ECOMP option of the B34S system allows various error-
components models to be estimated. While these models are usually
used with panel data consisting of time series and cross sections,
it was shown that the error-components procedure can be used with
purely time-series models if it is desired to control for seasonal
effects without explicitly introducing dummy variables. By
selectively setting input options, harmonics of the seasonal models
can be investigated. Such an approach could be used with monthly
data to investigate whether, in fact, there was a four-year
political cycle.

NOTES

1. The discussion of the models estimated in this chapter has
benefited from Freiden (1973), Henry, McDonald and Stokes (1976)
and unpublished notes prepared by Henry that were condensed for
Henry, McDonald and Stokes (1976).

2. The terms "individual" and "region" can be used interchangeably.

3. Nerlove (1971b) proposed a more complex model in which there is
a period-specific effect Φ_t. In this setup, $u_{it} = \mu_i + \Phi_t + v_{it}$. This
model has not been implemented in B34S yet. However, the ECOMP
ISWITH option allows the researcher to easily switch the data such
that individuals (regions) become "periods" and periods become
"individuals." Running the altered model will test whether there is
a period-specific error that is invariant across regions. In terms

of Nerlove's (1971b) notation, this is equivalent to assuming u_{it} = Φ_t + v_{it}. In addition to the basic references, Kmenta (1986, 625–635) provides a concise summary of some of the relevant issues.

4. Kmenta (1986, 622–635), from which some of this discussion has been based, has an excellent discussion of some of these issues.

5. The SAS output and B34S listing of the data have been removed to save space.

6. Markov Probability Analysis

6.0 Introduction

The B34S TRANSPROB command estimates and decomposes a Markov probability model. The basic code for estimation of the Markov model was adapted from Lee, Judge and Zellner (1970). The decomposition of the Markov model was developed by the author of B34S from suggestions contained in Theil (1972, chap. 5). A good discussion of the theory of Markov chains is contained in Isaacson and Madsen (1976). Recent economic applications are contained in Stokey and Lucas (1989, chaps. 8, 11, and 12).[1] After an initial overview of the model, the Theil (1972) decompositions are discussed. The Kosobud and Stokes (1979) model of OPEC behavior is used to illustrate an economics application of Markov model building.

6.1 Overview of the Markov Model

First, assume that at equidistant time points there are a finite number of possible outcomes that a discrete random variable x_t {t=0,1,2,..., T} may take. Second, assume that the probability distribution for an outcome of a given trial depends only on the outcome of the immediate preceding trial.[2] These assumptions can be summarized by

$$Pr(x_t \mid x_{t-1}, x_{t-2}, \ldots) = Pr(x_t \mid x_{t-1}). \qquad (6.1-1)$$

The probability distribution of the process $(x_0, x_1, \ldots, x_T)$ becomes

$$Pr(x_0, x_1, \ldots, x_T) = Pr(x_0) \prod_{t=1}^{T} Pr(x_t \mid x_{t-1}). \qquad (6.1-2)$$

If we assume that there are r states, the probability that x_t takes on state j (S_j), given that x_{t-1} was in state i (S_i), can be represented as $p_{ij}(t)$ or p_{ij}, if we drop the t for notational simplicity.

$$Pr(x_t = S_j \mid x_{t-1} = S_i) = p_{ij}. \qquad (6.1-3)$$

We define P as the r by r <u>transition probability matrix</u> consisting of elements $[p_{ij}]$. P has the important properties that

$$0 \leq p_{ij} \leq 1 \qquad (6.1-4)$$

and

$$\sum_j p_{ij} = 1 \text{ for } i=1,2, \ldots, r. \qquad (6.1-5)$$

Given that $q_j(t)$ is the unconditional probability that x_t takes on state j in period t, then

$$q_j(t) = Pr(x_t = s_j). \tag{6.1-6}$$

It follows quickly from the definition of P that

$$q_j(t) = \sum_i q_i(t-1)p_{ij}. \tag{6.1-7}$$

In the limit

$$q_j(\infty) = \sum_i q_i(0)p_{ij}^*, \tag{6.1-8}$$

where p_{ij}^* is an element of the matrix P^t as t approaches ∞. If we define $Q(t)$ as an r element row vector, where

$$Q(t) = \{q_1(t),\ldots,q_r(t)\}, \tag{6.1-9}$$

then

$$Q(t) = Q(t-1) \ P \tag{6.1-10}$$

and

$$Q(t) = Q(0) \quad P^t. \tag{6.1-11}$$

As t approaches ∞, the problem is to calculate P^t. As P converges to P^t, each element of P, $[p_{ij}]$, converges to $[p_{ij}^*]$.

Strang (1976, chap. 5) shows how any n by n matrix A that possesses n linearly independent eigenvectors can be diagonalized

$$A = S\ D\ S^{-1}, \tag{6.1-12}$$

where S is an r by r matrix of the eigenvectors of A and D is a diagonal matrix with the corresponding eigenvalues of A, d_i, along the diagonal. Repeated application of equation (6.1-12) leads to the relationship

$$A^t = S\ D^t\ S^{-1}. \tag{6.1-13}$$

Strang (1976, 193) proves that the difference equation

$$Q(t) = Q(t-1) \ A \tag{6.1-14}$$

is _stable_ if $|d_i| < 0$, is _neutrally stable_ if $|d_i| \le 1$, and is _unstable_ if at least one eigenvalue of A has the property $|d_i| > 1$. Assume that A=P, where P is defined in equations (6.1-4) and (6.1-5). It follows that

$P^t = S D^t S^{-1}.$ (6.1-15)

Theil (1972, 263) proves that the largest eigenvalue of P cannot exceed 1 in absolute value. Assume that $|d_i| = 1$. Since D is a diagonal matrix with elements d_i along the diagonal, D^t approaches the null matrix, except for the value 1.0 in the position ii on the diagonal since in the limit, $d_j = 0$ for $j \neq i$. Once D^t is formed, equation (6.1-15) can be used to calculate P^t.

Stokey and Lucas (1989, chap. 11) contains an elegant discussion of five examples that treat all possible types of limiting behavior of finite Markov chains. The main point is that the structure of the elements of P determines the long-run pattern of Q(t) as t approaches ∞. Theil (1972, 256) proves that if P has no 0.0 elements, then P^t converges to a matrix whose rows are all identical with the asymptotic, or limit, distribution, $\{\pi_1, \pi_2, \ldots, \pi_r\}$

$$\lim_{t \to \infty} P^t = \begin{bmatrix} \pi_1 & \pi_2 & . & . & . & \pi_r \\ \pi_1 & \pi_2 & . & . & . & \pi_r \\ . & . & . & . & . & . \\ . & . & . & . & . & . \\ \pi_1 & \pi_2 & . & . & . & \pi_r \end{bmatrix},$$ (6.1-16)

where each element $\pi_i > 0$. Such a Markov matrix is called regular and has the property $p_{ij}^* = \pi_j$ for i=1, r where $0 < \pi_j < 1$.

If, on the other hand, we have a situation with some elements 0.0, such as the matrix

$$P = \begin{bmatrix} .5 & .5 \\ 0.0 & 1.0 \end{bmatrix},$$ (6.1-17)

then

$$\lim_{t \to \infty} P^t = \begin{bmatrix} 0.0 & 1.0 \\ 0.0 & 1.0 \end{bmatrix}$$ (6.1-18)

and the system is absorbing since in the limit, as t -> ∞, state 1 disappears.

The limit distribution reproduces itself since

$$(\pi_1, \pi_2, \ldots, \pi_r) = (\pi_1, \pi_2, \ldots, \pi_r)P. \qquad (6.1\text{-}19)$$

Since all Markov models imply convergence to a limit distribution $(\pi_1, \pi_2, \ldots, \pi_r)$, Theil (1972, 258) suggests a measure I_t, defined as

$$I_t = \Sigma_{i=1}^n \pi_i \log [\pi_i / q_i(t)], \qquad (6.1\text{-}20)$$

that measures the distance from the limit distribution. At the limit, or asymptotic distribution, $I_\infty = 0$ and

$$Q(a) = (q_1(a), q_2(a), \ldots, q_r(a)) = (\pi_1, \pi_2, \ldots, \pi_r). \qquad (6.1\text{-}21)$$

The absolute value[3] of the second and third largest eigenvalues, $(d_1, d_2, \ldots, d_r)$, of P characterize the path to the limit distribution $(\pi_1, \pi_2, \ldots, \pi_r)$. If the second largest root is complex, the path will be damped oscillatory. Theil (1972, 264) defines the rate of convergence as I_t / I_{t-1}, which can be approximated as the square of the absolute value of the second largest eigenvalue. The accuracy of this approximation is the ratio of the absolute value of the third and the second largest eigenvalue. The B34S TRANSPROB command outputs both these measures. If the absolute values of the second and third largest eigenvalues are the same, which would be the case if they were a complex pair, the accuracy of the convergence measure would be 1.

6.2 Decomposing the Transition Probability Matrix

The B34S TRANSPROB command provides summary measures of the dynamic path to the asymptotic distribution implicit in the P matrix. These measures, which were discussed in Theil (1972, chap. 5), and their uses will be discussed next. The <u>fundamental matrix</u>, Z, is defined as

$$Z = (I - P + P^a)^{-1}, \qquad (6.2\text{-}1)$$

where $P^a = P^t$ for $t=\infty$. Z is a summary measure proportional to how far the current transition matrix P is from the asymptotic, or limit, transition matrix P^a. From the fundamental matrix Z, containing elements z_{ij}, and the asymptotic shares $Q(a)$, from equation (6.1-21), the <u>mean first passage matrix M</u>, containing elements m_{ij}, is defined as

$$m_{ij} = 1/q_i(a) = 1 / \pi_i \qquad \text{for } i=j \qquad (6.2\text{-}2)$$

and

$$m_{ij} \quad = \quad (z_{jj} - z_{ij})/q_i(a)$$

$$= \quad (z_{jj} - z_{ij})/\pi_i \qquad \text{for } i \neq j. \qquad (6.2\text{-}3)$$

An element of the mean first passage matrix m_{ij} (for $i \neq j$) measures the number of periods before x_t in the ith state will be transferred to the jth state. If $i = j$, the mean passage matrix is called the mean recurrence matrix. Equations (6.2-2) and (6.2-3) show how m_{ij} is related to the distance that P is from P^a (summarized in the fundamental matrix Z) and the limit or asymptotic shares $q_i(a)$. The mean first passage matrix can be decomposed into the waiting-time vector, W, consisting of elements $(w_1, w_2, \ldots, w_r)$, and the travel-time matrix, T, consisting of elements $[\tau_{ij}]$. The waiting-time vector elements w_i are defined as

$$w_i = 1/\pi_i. \qquad (6.2\text{-}4)$$

The term w_i can be regarded as a lower limit on the expected number of time periods to enter the ith category. If $\pi_j = 0$, it means that in the limit there is nothing in the jth state. In this case, $w_j = \infty$, which indicates that it is impossible to get to the jth state in a finite number of periods. When $\pi_j = 1$, $w_j = 1$, meaning that since x_t is already in state j, in the next period x_t will also be in state j. The mean first passage matrix is related to the waiting-time vector and the travel-time matrix by

$$m_{ij} \quad = \quad \tau_{ij} + w_i, \qquad (6.2\text{-}5)$$

which leads to the following formulas for the travel-time matrix elements τ_{ij}:

$$\tau_{ij} \quad = \quad 0 \qquad\qquad\qquad \text{if } i=j \qquad (6.2\text{-}6)$$

and

$$\tau_{ij} \quad = \quad (z_{jj} - z_{ij} - 1)/\pi_j \qquad \text{if } i \neq j. \qquad (6.2\text{-}7)$$

Element τ_{ij} of the travel-time matrix measures the number of periods to go from the ith state to the jth state.

The exchange matrix, B, consisting of elements $[b_{ij}]$, is defined as

$$B \quad = \quad \Theta P, \qquad (6.2\text{-}8)$$

where Θ is an r by r diagonal matrix with $(\pi_1, \pi_2, \ldots, \pi_r)$ along the diagonal and P is the r by r transition probability matrix. B has the property that its rows and columns sum to the limit distribution. An element b_{ij} of the exchange matrix B measures the probability of exchange between the ith and j^{th} states in successive steps, once equilibrium has been attained.

$$\pi_j = \Sigma_{i=1}^{r} b_{ij} \qquad\qquad \text{for } j=1,r \qquad\qquad (6.2\text{-}9)$$

and

$$\pi_i = \Sigma_{j=1}^{r} b_{ij} \qquad\qquad \text{for } i=1,r. \qquad\qquad (6.2\text{-}10)$$

The exchange matrix has the property that the estimated transition probability matrix can be recovered by dividing each element of the exchange matrix by the row (column) sum,

$$\hat{p}_{ij} = b_{ij} / \pi_j. \qquad\qquad (6.2\text{-}11)$$

If the exchange matrix B is symmetric or almost symmetric, the Markov chain is said to be reversible. In this situation, the travel-time matrix consisting of elements τ_{ij} can be broken into a distance effect, s_{ij}, and a destination effect, which is defined as $(z_{jj}-1)/\pi_j$:

$$\tau_{ij} = s_{ij} + (z_{jj} - 1)\pi_j. \qquad\qquad (6.2\text{-}12)$$

The decomposition in equation (6.2-12) is only meaningful when $\tau_{ij} \neq 0$. From equation (6.2-5), it quickly follows that

$$m_{ij} = s_{ij} + (z_{jj}-1)/\pi_j + w_j. \qquad\qquad (6.2\text{-}13)$$

Theil (1972) shows that waiting time, w_j, is the only nonzero component of m_{ij} if there is perfect mobility and the system has reached its asymptotic state. Here $P = P^a$, which implies from equation (6.2-1) that the exchange matrix Z is equal to the identity matrix. It is easy to show that the destination effect is equal to zero since $z_{jj} - 1 = 0$. From equation (6.2-12), we note that

$$s_{ij} = \tau_{ij} - ((z_{jj} - 1)/\pi_j) \quad = -z_{ij}/\pi_j \qquad\qquad \text{if } i \neq j$$

$$= -((z_{jj} - 1)/\pi_j) \quad \text{if } i=j, \qquad (6.2\text{-}14)$$

which proves that $s_{ij} = 0$ since $z_{ij} = 0$ and $(z_{jj}-1)=0$ in this case.

The above discussion has outlined how to characterize the dynamic path $\{Q(0), Q(1), \ldots ,Q(t)\}$, once the transition probability matrix, P, has been estimated. The matrices already discussed are automatically printed when the transition probability matrix, P, is estimated. The next section outlines some of the options available in the TRANSPROB command to estimate P.

6.3 Estimating the Transition Probability Matrix

Miller (1952) proposed estimating the transition probability matrix, P, with unrestricted OLS methods on the first pass.[4] The unconditional expected probability vector, $Q(t)$, is defined in equation (6.1-10). Let $Y(t)$ be the r element vector $\{y_1(t), y_2(t),$

..., $y_r(t)$} of actual proportions. The prediction error vector, $U(t)$, for period t consists of elements {$u_1(t)$, $u_2(t)$, ..., $u_r(t)$}, and is defined as

$$U(t) = Y(t) - Q(t).$$ (6.3-1)

The preceding discussion motivates Miller's (1952) suggestion of estimating the jth column of P with OLS as

$$y_j(t) = \Sigma_{i=1}^{r} y_i(t-1) p_{ij} + u_j(t).$$ (6.3-2)

Define y_j as a T element column vector {$y_j(1)$, $y_j(2)$,..., $y_j(T)$} , p_j as an r x 1 vector of the jth column of P, and X_j as a T x r matrix of observed proportions, whose rows consist of Y(t), where t goes from 0 to T-1. X_j can be written as

$$X_j = \begin{bmatrix} y_1(0) & y_2(0) & \cdots & y_r(0) \\ \cdot & \cdot & \cdots & \\ \cdot & \cdot & \cdots & \\ y_1(t-1) & y_2(t-1) & \cdots & y_r(t-1) \\ \cdot & \cdot & \cdots & \cdot \\ \cdot & \cdot & \cdots & \cdot \\ y_1(T-1) & y_2(T-1) & \cdots & y_r(T-1) \end{bmatrix}.$$ (6.3-3)

Equation (6.3-2) can now be written in compact notation as

$$y_j = X_j p_j + u_j.$$ (6.3-4)

The system of equations becomes

$$\begin{bmatrix} y_1 \\ y_2 \\ \cdot \\ \cdot \\ y_r \end{bmatrix} = \begin{bmatrix} X_1 & 0 & \cdots & 0 \\ 0 & X_2 & \cdots & 0 \\ \cdot & \cdot & \cdots & \cdot \\ \cdot & \cdot & \cdots & \cdot \\ \cdot & \cdot & \cdots & X_r \end{bmatrix} \begin{bmatrix} p_1 \\ p_2 \\ \cdot \\ \cdot \\ p_r \end{bmatrix} + \begin{bmatrix} u_1 \\ u_2 \\ \cdot \\ \cdot \\ u_r \end{bmatrix}$$ (6.3-5)

or

$$Y = X\Phi + U,$$ (6.3-6)

where Y is made up of the subvectors y_j, j=1,2,...,r, and X is a diagonal matrix made up of X_1, ... , X_r along the diagonal, where $X_1 = X_2 = \ldots = X_r$. Φ is a column vector consisting of r^2 elements from which P can be recovered. OLS can be used to obtain an estimate of Φ from

$$\hat{\Phi} = (X'X)^{-1}X'Y. \qquad (6.3-7)$$

OLS estimation of Φ in equation (6.3-6) provides a way to estimate P since p_j' is the jth row of estimated value of P. Lee, Judge and Zellner (1970) prove that although the row-sum condition in equation (6.1-5) is always met by the OLS estimator, the nonnegativity condition in equation (6.1-4) may not be met by the OLS model. If this occurs, a restricted estimator must be used. Lee, Judge and Zellner (1970), who provide sampling results, propose use of quadratic programming as one solution to provide an estimate that would lie on the boundary of the restricted parameter subset.

A problem with equation (6.3-7) is that since the model involves proportions, the OLS estimator of Φ is inefficient due to heteroskedasticity in the errors U. The correct approach is to use the generalized least squares estimator of Φ

$$\hat{\Phi}^* = (X'\Omega^{-1} X)^{-1} X'\Omega^{-1}Y, \qquad (6.3-8)$$

where Ω is the variance-covariance matrix of the disturbances U. As was discussed in chapter 2, equation (6.3-8) is the result of multiplying equation (6.3-6) by a suitably selected weighting matrix H, as is shown in equation (6.3-9), and estimating Φ with OLS, using the transformed data, where $H'H = \Omega^{-1}$

$$HY = HX\Phi + HU. \qquad (6.3-9)$$

However, for a Markov model, because of the adding-up constraint of equation (6.1-5), Ω is singular and Ω^{-1} cannot be calculated. The B34S TRANSPROB command provides a number of ways to introduce a Tr by Tr alternative matrix to Ω. Lee, Judge and Zellner (1970) provide sampling experiments for these alternatives, which can be selected by the user with the TRANSPROB control language. If none of the built-in alternatives are desired, the WEIGHT sentence of the TRANSPROB command allows the user to supply the weight matrix, Ω, used in equation (6.3-8) directly. The weight-matrix choices include using different weights among the equations and the same weights within equations, or different weights among and within equations. Following Lee, Judge and Zellner (1970, 65), we define H as

$$H = \begin{bmatrix} a_1 d_1 & & & \\ & a_2 d_2 & & \\ & & \cdots & \\ & & & a_r d_r \end{bmatrix}, \qquad (6.3-10)$$

where a_i is a scaler to be defined later and d_i is a block diagonal T by T matrix. H'H becomes an rT by rT matrix unless a column has

to be dropped to avoid multicollinearity resulting in **H'H** being
$(r-1)T$ by $(r-1)T$.

$$\mathbf{H'H} = \begin{bmatrix} a_1^2 d_1' d_1 & & & \\ & a_2^2 d_2' d_2 & & \\ & & \cdots & \\ & & & a_r^2 d_r' d_r \end{bmatrix} \tag{6.3-11}$$

The B34S TRANSPROB keyword KW controls the assignment of
weights during the estimation of P. If the keyword KEY2=PRINT, the
weight matrix used will be printed.[5] We define $N(t)$ as the sample
size in the tth period. If the keyword SS is set to an integer, $N(t)$
$= N(t-k)$ for all k. If SS is set to the name of a variable
containing the sample for that time period, the sample can vary
across time periods and, in general, $N(t) \neq N(t-k)$ for $k \neq 0$.
Built-in weighting options include the following:

- If KW=CLASSICAL, the default unweighted OLS method is
chosen. In this case **H** is an identity matrix.

- If KW=ML, the maximum likelihood function is used to derive
the weight matrix. Following Lee, Judge and Zellner (1970, 78),
since we have to drop a column to avoid multicollinearity, we
define **H** in this situation as an $(r-1)T$ by $(r-1)T$ matrix consisting
of elements H_{ij} that are themselves T by T matrices.

$$H_{ij} = N(i) / q_r(i) \text{ for } i \neq j \tag{6.3-12}$$

$$H_{ij} = N(i) /(q_r(i)) + (N(i)/q_i(i)) \text{ for } i=j \tag{6.3-13}$$

- If KW=WEIGHTEDSS, the H matrix is diagonal with elements
consisting of T by T diagonal matrices H_{ij}, where

$$\begin{aligned} H_{ij} &= N(i) / q_j(i) & \text{for } i = j \\ &= 0 & \text{for } i \neq j. \end{aligned} \tag{6.3-14}$$

It can easily be seen that $a_j = H_{jj}$.

- If KW=USER, the user supplies the weights with the WEIGHT
sentence.

- If KW=MEANW, mean proportions weights are used to form a_i
and hence H from equation (6.3-10), where a_i is defined as

$$a_i = T / \sum_t y_i(t). \tag{6.3-15}$$

- If KW= MEANPROD, the products of the mean proportions are used to form H from equation (6.3-10), where a_i is defined as

$$a_i = 1 \ /([\textstyle\sum_t y_i(t) \ / \ T] \ [(1 - \textstyle\sum_t y_i(t))/T] \ ). \tag{6.3-16}$$

- If KW=DERIV, derived weights from the generalized inverse method of obtaining an estimate of the P transition matrix are used to form H. Lee, Judge and Zellner (1970, app. A) outline the construction of this weighting matrix, which is also used in the minimum chi-square approach. This reference shows that the unique solution of the generalized inverse estimator is Aitken's generalized least squares estimator with the redundant parameters deleted. The topic is very complex and will not be discussed further here.

- If KW=MSS, the weighting matrix H is calculated as

$$
\begin{aligned}
H_{ij} &= N(i) \ / \ ((q_j(i))(1.0 - q_j(i))) &\quad \text{for } i = j \\
&= 0 &\quad \text{for } i \neq j,
\end{aligned} \tag{6.3-17}
$$

where we note that $a_j = H_{jj}$.

- If KW=TWOSTAGEW, a two-stage scheme is used whereby the weights are derived from the estimated disturbance in the first stage. Specifically, an estimate of the ith equation disturbance variance is used to form a_i as

$$a_i = (T - r)/ \ [(y_i - X\hat{\Phi}_i)'(y_i - X\hat{\Phi}_i)] \tag{6.3-18}$$

and hence H from equation (6.3-10).

Lee, Judge and Zellner (1970) compare the TWOSTAGEW, MEANW and MEANPROD methods and find that all are superior to the CLASSICAL unweighted case. Of the three studied, the TWOSTAGEW method seems to be inferior.

There are a number of methods to use to calculate a solution to the model. These will be briefly discussed later. Monte Carlo results in Lee, Judge and Zellner (1970) showed that weighted estimators were superior to unweighted classical estimators, using the criterion of minimum sum of squares. A proposed minimum chi-square (MCS) estimator was shown to be identical to the GLS estimator when there was a known disturbance vector. The maximum likelihood (ML) estimator was found to have the same form as the GLS and MCS estimators. ML estimation and MCS estimation were shown to be looking for the same saddle point, one from above and one from below. An iterative scheme to improve estimates of the parameters of the disturbance matrix was shown to be a recursive quadratic programming problem. As an alternative, a Bayesian approach was suggested whereby it was possible to incorporate prior knowledge on the distribution of the covariance matrix. The difficulty of this approach is that this information is rarely known.

The QP and classical estimators minimize the sum of squares of the errors. In contrast, the linear programming (LP) estimator minimizes the sum of the absolute deviations. Using the MCS criterion, this estimator will be inferior; however, the estimates obtained are normally distributed and converge to the true parameter values (Lee, Judge and Zellner 1970, 159). The LP estimator has been found to be computationally stable and is not as sensitive to residual outliers as estimators that minimize the sum of squares of the residuals. The implementation of the LP estimator will now be discussed briefly.

Recall equation (6.3-6), which outlines the estimation of Φ. The LP approach minimizes

$$\alpha'\mu_{rT}, \tag{6.3-19}$$

subject to the constraints of equation (6.3-6)

$$G\Phi = \mu_r \tag{6.3-20}$$

and

$$\Phi \geq 0, \tag{6.3-21}$$

where α' is a 1 by rT vector of elements

$$\alpha'=(|u_1(1)|,|u_1(2)|,\ldots,|u_1(T)|,\ldots,|u_r(1)|,\ldots,|u_r(T)|) \tag{6.3-22}$$

and μ_{rT} and μ_r are unit vectors with dimensions rT and r, respectively. From the definition of α', it can be seen that equation (6.3-19) is the sum of the absolute values of the errors. Lee, Judge and Zellner (1970, 132) show that if we assume that U_1 contains the positive elements of U and U_2 contains the absolute value of the negative elements of U, then the unweighted LP problem is to minimize

$$(U_1 + U_2)'\mu_{rt}, \tag{6.3-23}$$

subject to equations (6.3-20), (6.3-21) and (6.1-4)

$$Y = X\Phi + U_1 + U_2 \tag{6.3-24}$$

and

$$U_1, U_2 \geq 0, \tag{6.3-25}$$

while the weighted LP problem is to minimize

$$(U_1 + U_2)'H'\mu_{rt}, \tag{6.3-26}$$

subject to equations (6.3-24), (6.3-20), (6.1-4) and (6.3-21), where H is defined by equation (6.3-10).

The keyword KEY8 controls the iteration method used for the solution. The options available are as follows:

- If KEY8 = LPSQRT, the problem is solved by linear programming weighted by the square roots of the column sum of H.

- If KEY8 = LPSUM, the problem is solved by linear programming weighted by the column sum of M.

- If KEY8 = QP, the problem is solved by quadratic programming.

- If KEY8 = QPBAYES, the problem will be solved by QP for the Bayesian estimator. If this option is selected, the PRIOR sentence must be used to input the prior knowledge. For detail on this option, see Lee, Judge and Zellner (1970, chap. 9).

The RECURSIVE sentence allows calculation of the exact numerical solution of the ML and Bayesian estimators. This sentence allows specification of the number of iterations allowed and the tolerance limit to use.

After each estimation, the TRANSPROB command provides several of the usual diagnostic tests. These include the sum of squared errors, the mean squared error, and chi-square and modified chi-square test for goodness of fit. The goodness-of-fit test is distributed as chi-square with $(r-1)T$ degrees of freedom and is defined as

$$\sum_{t=1}^{T} \sum_{i=1}^{r} N(t) \ (y_i(t) - \hat{y}_i(t))^2 \ / \ \hat{y}_i(t). \qquad (6.3-27)$$

If $\hat{y}_i(t) = 0$, $y_i(t)$ is used. The modified chi-square test is the same as equation (6.3-23), except $y_i(t)$ is used in the denominator. If in calculating the modified chi-square test, $y_i(t)=0$, then $y_i(t)$ is used. A significant chi-square test statistic indicates that the data are not well described by a first-order Markov model and that other lags and/or variables should be considered. The next section illustrates the use of the TRANSPROB command, using an example from the world oil market.

6.4 Examples

Kosobud and Stokes (1978, 1979, 1980) and Neuburger and Stokes (1979a) illustrate applications of the Markov model to the world oil market research and to economic history research. The data in Kosobud and Stokes (1979) is used in this chapter to illustrate the use of the TRANSPROB command. The model chosen assumes a world of two producers (Iran and Saudi Arabia) and two consumers (United States and Japan). The data consisted of quarterly shares of OPEC production and sales between the first quarter of 1974 and the first quarter of 1977 for these two producer and consumer countries. The data and the B34S loading commands are listed in Table 6.1. For 1974 (quarter 1), the value for USSA of .0154 represents the share of the world oil volume of 2,931 thousand barrels per day that went from Saudi Arabia to the United States. In terms of the notation in equation (6.1-6), $\{q_1(1), q_2(1), q_3(1), q_4(1)\}$ are the values of {USSA, USIRAN, JAPANSA, JAPANIR}, respectively, for the period 1974 (quarter 1) listed in Table 6.1. USSA represents the United States /Saudi Arabia share, USIRAN represents the United States / Iran share, JAPANSA represents the Japan / Saudi Arabia share, and JAPANIR represents the Japan / Iran share. The example uses a Markov model to predict changes in the trading relationships over time by estimating a transition probability matrix, P. Since the keyword SS was set to the variable VOL and the keyword KEY8 was set to LPSQRT, the problem will be solved by the LP method weighted by the square roots of the column sum of H. However, since the KW option was not supplied, the H matrix is an identity matrix.

Table 6.1 A Markov Model for the International Oil Market

```
==OIL1979
B34SEXEC DATA NOOB=13 NOHEAD$
* Data from Kosobud and Stokes "Oil Market Share Dynamics:
  A Markov Chain Analysis of Consumer and Producer Adjustments"
  The Journal of Empirical Economics Vol. 3, No. 4., pp 253-275 1979 $
* USSA =    U. S. - S. A. $
* USIRAN=   U. S. - Iran. $
* JAPANSA   Japan - Saudi Arabia $
* JAPANIR   Japan - Iran $
INPUT YEAR QT USSA USIRAN JAPANSA JAPANIR VOL$
DATACARDS$
74 1  .0154 .1344 .4456 .4046 2931.
74 2  .1199 .1647 .3826 .3328 3486.
74 3  .1540 .1375 .3711 .3374 3577.
74 4  .1966 .1053 .3376 .3605 3703.
75 1  .2044 .0780 .3390 .3786 3679.
75 2  .1291 .0883 .4230 .3596 3137.
75 3  .2049 .0707 .4162 .3082 3280.
75 4  .2544 .0832 .3859 .2765 3833.
76 1  .3000 .0826 .4008 .2166 3703.
76 2  .2821 .0696 .3991 .2492 3953.
76 3  .3233 .0777 .4066 .1924 4043.
76 4  .3086 .0678 .3613 .2623 4376.
77 1  .2954 .1044 .3954 .2048 4670.
B34SRETURN$  B34SEEND$
B34SEXEC TRANSPROB SS=VOL KDROP=JAPANIR KP=PREDICT KEY8=LPSQRT $
    VAR USSA USIRAN JAPANSA JAPANIR$
    HEADING=('DATA FROM KOSOBUD-STOKES 1979')$
    FINISH $
B34SEEND$
B34SEXEC DATA NOOB=6 NOHEAD$
* Data on Pre OPEC Period $
* Data from Kosobud and Stokes "Oil Market Share Dynamics:
  A Markov Chain Analysis of Consumer and Producer Adjustments"
  The Journal of Empirical Economics Vol. 3, No. 4., pp 253-275 1979 $
* USSA =    U. S. - S. A. $
* USIRAN=   U. S. - Iran. $
* JAPANSA   Japan - Saudi Arabia $
* JAPANIR   Japan - Iran $
INPUT YEAR  USSA USIRAN JAPANSA JAPANIR VOL$
DATACARDS$
68 .0373 .0416 .3604 .5607 1429.
69 .0214 .0259 .3301 .6226 1663.
70 .0092 .0182 .3050 .6676 1944.
71 .0431 .0396 .2883 .6290 2741.
72 .0700 .0536 .2488 .6276 2622.
73 .1447 .0666 .2836 .5051 3364.
B34SRETURN$
B34SEEND$
==
```

The output from the B34S MACRO OIL1979 is given next. The data are first listed. Note that the LP option takes 19313 REAL*8 words of storage out of 35000 available. If user problems are bigger than the available storage, the B34S work space can be increased a number of ways.[6]

```
TRANSFER PROBABILITY (MARKOV PROBABILITY MODEL) OPTION SELECTED
FOR DISCUSSION OF PROCEDURES USED SEE LEE, JUDGE AND ZELLNER (1970)
ON MAIN CONTROL CARD
NT1, NS, SS, TOL, KDROP, KW, KV, KP, KEY(1)- (9), IKILL, ISMP, ITIT
   13  4    0. 0.10000000E-05   4 0 0 1   0 0 0 0 0 0 2 0 0   0 7 1
```

```
VARIABLES INPUTED FROM B34S

  B34S #            NAME           COL # ON INPUT

     3              USSA               1
     4              USIRAN             2
     5              JAPANSA            3
     6              JAPANIR            4

OF     35000 SPACE AVAILABLE     19313 REQUIRED   (NOTE: SPACE GIVEN IN REAL*8)

SAMPLE SIZE READ FROM B34S X- 7   NAME = VOL


DATA FROM KOSOBUD-STOKES 1979

THE OBSERVED UNITS AND SAMPLE SIZES

        1 USSA      2 USIRAN      3 JAPANSA    4 JAPANIR      5 VOL
  1   0.154000E-01  0.134400     0.445600     0.404600     0.859076E+07
  2   0.119900      0.164700     0.382600     0.332800     0.121522E+08
  3   0.154000      0.137500     0.371100     0.337400     0.127949E+08
  4   0.196600      0.105300     0.337600     0.360500     0.137122E+08
  5   0.204400      0.780000E-01  0.339000    0.378600     0.135350E+08
  6   0.129100      0.883000E-01  0.423000    0.359600     0.984077E+07
  7   0.204900      0.707000E-01  0.416200    0.308200     0.107584E+08
  8   0.254400      0.832000E-01  0.385900    0.276500     0.146919E+08
  9   0.300000      0.826000E-01  0.400800    0.216600     0.137122E+08
 10   0.282100      0.696000E-01  0.399100    0.249200     0.156262E+08
 11   0.323300      0.777000E-01  0.406600    0.192400     0.163458E+08
 12   0.308600      0.678000E-01  0.361300    0.262300     0.191494E+08
 13   0.295400      0.104400     0.395400     0.204800     0.218089E+08


YOU HAVE INDICATED THAT THIS PROBLEM WILL BE SOLVED BY LINEAR PROGRAMMING

AS DESIRED,COLUMN 4 IS DROPPED IN FORMING THE SYSTEM.

READ THE FOLLOWING MATRICES IN THE SEQUENCE

 1 USSA     2 USIRAN    3 JAPANSA   4 JAPANIR

THE WEIGHT MATRIX IS AN IDENTITY MATRIX (UNWEIGHTED).

NUMBER OF CYCLES =     60  ORIGINAL VALUE FOR LP OR ROUNDING ERROR FOR QP=  0.6149896

THE MINIMUM ABSOLUTE DEVIATION ESTIMATOR OF THE TRANSITION MATRIX

          1               2              3               4
  1    0.669281      0.000000E+00    0.330719      0.000000E+00


          1               2              3               4
  2    0.000000E+00  0.609360        0.000000E+00  0.390640


          1               2              3               4
  3    0.245945      0.153705E-01    0.562743      0.175941


          1               2              3               4
  4    0.000000E+00  0.939231E-01    0.343199      0.562878
```

The estimated transition probability matrix, $\hat{P}$, agrees with what was reported in Kosobud and Stokes (1979, Table 2). The eigenvalue vector is next calculated and the largest eigenvalue was found to be d_1, which was equal to 1 as was expected following Theil (1972). Using the eigenvectors $\{d_1,...,d_4\}$ and the eigenvector matrix S, equation (6.1-15) is used to form P^a and hence the asymptotic prediction vector Q(a) from equation (6.1-11). Q(a)={.300535, .0700649, .404125, .225275}, which agree with Kosobud and Stokes (1979, Table 2). Slight differences in the last digits arise due to the fact that LINPACK matrix routines have been added to the TRANSPROB command since publication of the paper. From the second and third largest eigenvalues (d_4 and d_3), the Theil measure of convergence (I_t / I_{t-1}) and the accuracy of this measure of convergence are calculated as .5563 and .62263, respectively.

The estimated transition probability matrix, $\hat{P}$, is used to calculate predictions for 20 periods ahead, using equation (6.1-

10). These are shown to be quite close to the asymptotic prediction vector, Q(a), discussed earlier.

PREDICTIONS USING TRANSFER PROBABILITY MATRIX 20 PERIODS AHEAD

	1 USSA	2 USIRAN	3 JAPANSA	4 JAPANIR
1	0.294952	0.889302E-01	0.390490	0.225627
2	0.293445	0.813842E-01	0.394727	0.230444
3	0.293478	0.773035E-01	0.398266	0.230953
4	0.294371	0.749190E-01	0.400443	0.230267
5	0.295504	0.734351E-01	0.401728	0.229333
6	0.296578	0.724629E-01	0.402505	0.228454
7	0.297488	0.717998E-01	0.402996	0.227716
8	0.298218	0.713340E-01	0.403320	0.227128
9	0.298786	0.709999E-01	0.403542	0.226672
10	0.299221	0.707569E-01	0.403698	0.226324
11	0.299550	0.705786E-01	0.403811	0.226060
12	0.299799	0.704469E-01	0.403892	0.225862
13	0.299985	0.703492E-01	0.403952	0.225714
14	0.300124	0.702767E-01	0.403997	0.225602
15	0.300228	0.702228E-01	0.404030	0.225519
16	0.300306	0.701826E-01	0.404054	0.225457
17	0.300364	0.701527E-01	0.404072	0.225411
18	0.300408	0.701303E-01	0.404086	0.225376
19	0.300440	0.701137E-01	0.404096	0.225351
20	0.300464	0.701013E-01	0.404103	0.225331

EIGENVALUES FOR TRANSITION MATRIX

1	1.0000000	+ , -	0.00000000E+00 IMAGINARY
2	0.19402549	+ , -	0.00000000E+00 IMAGINARY
3	0.46439000	+ , -	0.00000000E+00 IMAGINARY
4	0.74584710	+ , -	0.00000000E+00 IMAGINARY

THEIL MEASURE OF CONVERGENCE RATE = 0.55628790   , ACCURACY OF CONVERGENCE MEASURE =   0.62263432

ESTIMATE OF RECIPROCAL CONDITION OF POSSIBLY COMPLEX EIGENVECTOR MATRIX   0.29726391

EIGENVECTOR MATRIX

	1	2	3	4
1	-0.500000	0.335899	-0.308517	0.445620
2	-0.500000	-0.555451	-1.14335	-1.18042
3	-0.500000	-0.482699	0.191136	0.103167
4	-0.500000	0.590564	0.424308	-0.412432

ASYMPTOTIC PREDICTION - CALCULATED USING EIGENVALUE DECOMPOSITION OF TRANSITION MATRIX

	1 USSA	2 USIRAN	3 JAPANSA	4 JAPANIR
1	0.300535	0.700649E-01	0.404125	0.225275

The next group of calculations decompose the estimated transition probability matrix, $\hat{P}$, into the fundamental matrix from equation (6.2-1), Z, the exchange matrix from equation (6.2-8), B, the mean first-passage matrix from equation (6.2-2), M, from equation (6.2-3), the travel-time matrix from equations (6.2-6) and (6.2-7), T, and the waiting-time vector, W, from equation (6.2-4). Inspection of the values indicates that the adding-up conditions from equations (6.2-11), (6.2-12) and (6.2-13) hold. Kosobud and Stokes (1979) argued that in this problem, economic insight could be obtained by partitioning the estimated transition matrix, $\hat{P}$, as

$$
\hat{P} = \begin{bmatrix} H_1 & H_2 \\ H_3 & H_4 \end{bmatrix}, \tag{6.4-1}
$$

where each H_i is a 2 by 2 submatrix.[7]

Since each row of $\hat{P}$ must sum to one from equation (6.1-5),
the larger the elements of H_3 relative to H_2, the more the United
States will gain in its share at the expense of Japan. The
implication is that if, in fact, the United States is gaining in a
competition for oil shares through time, the elements of H_3 should
increase relative to the elements of H_2. The reasoning for this
assertion is illustrated by noting that $\hat{p}_{42}$ measures the
probability that oil formerly being shipped by Iran to Japan will
be shipped by Iran to the United States. Similar arguments can be
made to show that for every element of H_3, an increase means that
the United States will gain at the expense of Japan, and that,
conversely, for every element in H_2, an increase means that the
Japanese will gain oil shares at the expense of the United States.
The United States and Japan can be considered to be indifferent, in
an economic sense, between any changes in matrices H_1 and H_4 as long
as such changes do not affect any elements in H_2 and H_3. Inspection
of the transition matrix, P, which has been decomposed into
$\{H_1,...,H_4\}$ indicates that for each submatrix H_i, any increase in
the lower-left-hand element (p_{21}, p_{23}, p_{41}, p_{43}) of H_i will signify a
supplier's share gain for Saudi Arabia over Iran. Conversely, any
increase in the upper-right-hand element of each matrix H_i (p_{12}, p_{14},
p_{32}, p_{34}) will signify a gain for Iran over Saudi Arabia. For all
elements in the upper-left-hand position, where $i \neq j$, Saudi Arabia
is transferring sales from one country to another (see elements p_{13}
and p_{31}), while Iran is doing the same for all elements in the
lower-right-hand position (p_{24}, p_{42}). For elements in which $i=j$ and
i is even, Iran gains (p_{22}, p_{44}), whereas when i is odd, Saudi Arabia
gains (p_{11}, p_{33}). Since all elements in each row must sum to 1.0,
from equation (6.1-5), it is impossible for just one element to
change. Thus, a complete determination of the relative probability
of gains and losses must look at _all_ elements that are changing.

In addition to the post-OPEC quarterly data given earlier,
Kosobud and Stokes (1979) estimated the same model for yearly data
from 1968 through 1973. These data are given in Table 6.1 but not
analyzed in this book. It was difficult to compare the adjustment
dynamics in the two periods. The mean passage matrix, M, was used
to test whether there had been any changes in the dynamics of
adjustment in the pre- and post-OPEC periods, both with respect to
producers and consumers. Define submatrices R and A as

$$R = \begin{bmatrix} m_{12} & m_{14} \\ m_{32} & m_{34} \end{bmatrix} \qquad (6.4-2)$$

$$A = \begin{bmatrix} m_{21} & m_{23} \\ m_{41} & m_{43} \end{bmatrix}. \qquad (6.4-3)$$

The sum of the elements in submatrix R is proportional to the time required to transfer an average barrel of oil from Saudi Arabian sales to Iranian sales, while the sum of the elements of the submatrix A is proportional to the time required to transfer an average barrel of oil from Iranian sales to Saudi Arabian sales. Iran (Saudi Arabia) would prefer R/A to fall (increase). Although individual elements of the two matrices cannot be compared across the two samples because the 1968 – 1973 data used a period of years, while the 1973 – 1977 data used a period of quarters, it is possible to compare the ratios of the sums of the elements of R and A for the two samples. Kosobud and Stokes (1979) report that in the 1968 – 1973 period, the ratio of the sum of the elements of R divided by the sum of the elements of A was .5496, while in the 1974/1 – 1977/1 period, the ratio was 3.132.[8] The implication of this finding is that Saudi Arabia has gained relative to Iran since in the latter period, it could more quickly take oil markets from Iran. Because Saudi Arabia was able to increase her share of the world market, as we have defined it, these findings appear plausible.

If we redefine our submatrices to investigate the speed of adjustment (dynamics of market sharing) between the United States and Japan, we find that the sum of the elements of the submatrix R^* is proportional to the time required to transfer an average barrel of oil from Japanese markets to United States markets and that the sum of the elements of submatrix A^* is proportional to the time required to transfer an average barrel of oil from United States markets to Japanese markets.

$$R^* = \begin{bmatrix} m_{31} & m_{32} \\ m_{41} & m_{42} \end{bmatrix} \qquad (6.4-4)$$

$$A^* = \begin{bmatrix} m_{13} & m_{14} \\ m_{23} & m_{24} \end{bmatrix}. \qquad (6.4-5)$$

Kosobud and Stokes (1979) found that the sum of the elements in R^*

divided by the sum of the elements in A^* was 4.0774 in the earlier period; in the latter period, the ratio had fallen slightly to 3.8183. The results suggested that the United States had made only marginal gains with respect to Japan, assuming the 2 by 2 subsample of the world oil market.

The mean passage matrix, M, measures the speed of adjustment of shares <u>before</u> equilibrium is reached; the exchange matrix, B, measures for a given element, b_{ij}, the probability of finding, in equilibrium, a tanker of oil in trading relationship i at the beginning of the period that will be in relationship j at the end of the period. Kosobud and Stokes (1979) argued that the exchange matrix was more symmetric in the latter period than in the former period and that such a finding indicates <u>less</u> potential for conflict at the equilibrium state since displacements of sellers and buyers in one trading relationship would be matched in probability by the opposite displacement in another. In a manner similar to what was discussed earlier for the mean passage matrix, the R, A, R^*, and A^* submatrices can be calculated. Since the exchange matrix represents equilibrium, an implicit assumption is that the sum of elements of R (ΣR) equals the sum of the elements of A (ΣA) and the sum of the elements of R^* (ΣR^*) equals the sum of the elements of A^* (ΣA^*). In the 1968-1973 period $\Sigma R = \Sigma A = .13839$, while in the 1974-1977 period, both matrices were nearly symmetric and $\Sigma R = \Sigma A = .07731$. Such a change represents a relative reduction (of .558639) in the probability of movement of one tanker of oil from Saudi Arabia to Iran or visa versa and is consistent with the increased share stability suggested by the optimal market shares model after the formation of a cartel. Similar analysis finds $\Sigma R^* = \Sigma A^* = .05183$ in the former period, while in the latter period, the sum was .12676. The relative increase was 2.4456, which suggests that at equilibrium in the post-OPEC period, there appears to be more probability of consumer competition (conflict) than in the equilibrium suggested by the pre-OPEC period. This discussion shows only some of the analysis possible with the Theil (1972) decomposition of the Markov model. Only the results of the latter period are given in this book. The data for the former period are given in Table 6.1 and can be loaded and run by interested readers.

To attempt to validate whether the simplifications implicit in the first-order Markov model were appropriate, predicted proportions within the sample were given and the sum of squared errors, the mean squared errors, the chi-square, and the modified chi-square values were listed. The fact that the chi-square and modified chi-square statistics are highly significant suggests that a less-restrictive model should be investigated. Since there are so few observations, especially in the earlier period, in the present case such a course of action would be difficult.

STATISTICAL DECOMPOSITION OF ASYMPTOTIC TRANSITION MATRIX - FOR A DETAILED DISCUSSION SEE THEIL(1972)

FUNDAMENTAL MATRIX Z   1 / CONDITION   0.17719899

	1 USSA	2 USIRAN	3 JAPANSA	4 JAPANIR
1	2.15460	-0.377028	0.532771E-01	-0.830852
2	-1.81595	2.66270	-1.21993	1.37318
3	0.396204E-01	-0.165172	1.27524	-0.149685
4	-1.04661	0.282159	-0.185407	1.94986

EXCHANGE MATRIX (BIG PI) - PROB OF EXCHANGE BETWEEN TWO STATES IN SUCCESSIVE STEPS AFTER EQUILIBRIUM

	1 USSA	2 USIRAN	3 JAPANSA	4 JAPANIR
1	0.201142	0.000000E+00	0.993926E-01	0.000000E+00
2	0.000000E+00	0.426948E-01	0.000000E+00	0.273701E-01
3	0.993926E-01	0.621163E-02	0.227419	0.711024E-01
4	0.000000E+00	0.211585E-01	0.773140E-01	0.126802

MEAN FIRST PASSAGE (MEAN RECURRENCE WHEN I=J) TIME (MATRIX M)

	1 USSA	2 USIRAN	3 JAPANSA	4 JAPANIR
1	3.32740	43.3845	3.02371	12.3437
2	13.2116	14.2725	6.17424	2.55990
3	7.03740	40.3608	2.47448	9.31994
4	10.6517	33.9763	3.61433	4.43902

DECOMPOSITION OF MEAN PASSAGE MATRIX INTO TRAVEL TIME (TAU) AND WAITING TIME (OMEGA)

TRAVEL TIME (TAU) MATRIX

	1 USSA	2 USIRAN	3 JAPANSA	4 JAPANIR
1	0.000000E+00	29.1120	0.549235	7.90463
2	9.88423	0.000000E+00	3.69976	-1.87912
3	3.70999	26.0883	0.000000E+00	4.88091
4	7.32433	19.7038	1.13985	0.000000E+00

WAITING TIME (OMEGA)

	1 USSA	2 USIRAN	3 JAPANSA	4 JAPANIR
1	3.32740	14.2725	2.47448	4.43902

CAN FURTHER BREAK DOWN TRAVEL TIME MATRIX (TAU) INTO DISTANCE MATRIX (S) AND DESTINATION EFFECT

DISTANCE MATRIX WILL ONLY BE MEANINGFUL IF EXCHANGE MATRIX (BIG PHI) IS SYMMETRIC OR ALMOST SYMMETRIC

FURTHER DECOMPOSITION IS POSSIBLE IF STATES CAN BE RANK ORDERED - FOR FURTHER RESULTS SEE THEIL(1972)

DISTANCE MATRIX (S)

	1 USSA	2 USIRAN	3 JAPANSA	4 JAPANIR
1	-3.84183	5.38113	-0.131833	3.68817
2	6.04240	-23.7309	3.01869	-6.09558
3	-0.131833	2.35741	-0.681068	0.664457
4	3.48250	-4.02710	0.458787	-4.21646

DESTINATION EFFECT MATRIX (IN ROW FORM)

	1 USSA	2 USIRAN	3 JAPANSA	4 JAPANIR
1	3.84183	23.7309	0.681068	4.21646

LEAVING DECOMPOSITION SECTION OF B34S TRAPB - THE ABOVE LISTED MATRIXES MUST BE INTERPRETED GIVEN ASSUMPTIONS IN THEIL(1972)

PREDICTED PROPORTIONS WITHIN SAMPLE

	1 USSA	2 USIRAN	3 JAPANSA	4 JAPANIR
2	0.119900	0.126748	0.394710	0.356642
3	0.174345	0.137500	0.369175	0.318979
4	0.194339	0.121181	0.375560	0.308920
5	0.214612	0.103214	0.378725	0.303450
6	0.220176	0.883000E-01	0.388304	0.303220
7	0.190439	0.940830E-01	0.404150	0.311328
8	0.239498	0.784261E-01	0.407752	0.274324
9	0.265175	0.826000E-01	0.396192	0.256033
10	0.299359	0.768374E-01	0.399100	0.224704
11	0.286961	0.719515E-01	0.403412	0.237676
12	0.316380	0.716678E-01	0.401764	0.210188
13	0.295400	0.715040E-01	0.395400	0.237696
14	0.294952	0.889302E-01	0.390490	0.225627

```
SUM OF SQUARED ERROR =    0.43397230E-01
MEAN SQUARED ERROR =    0.90410896E-03
CHI SQUARE VALUE =      2626735.3
MODIFIED CHI SQUARE STATISTIC =    2741671.1


STEP ENDING. SECONDS USED  0.13600636   . TOTAL JOB SECONDS    2.5894880   .
```

6.5 Conclusion

The B34S TRANSPROB command allows estimation of a Markov probability model, using a number of alternative estimators and weighting schemes.   Once the transition probability matrix is estimated by OLS, quadratic program, ML, or linear programming, it can be decomposed to study the dynamic path that is implicit in the structure of the matrix. Such matrices as the mean first-passage matrix, the waiting-time matrix, the travel-time matrix, and the exchange matrix can be used to characterize the dynamic path. The asymptotic vector and two measures of the rate of convergence are also given. Inspection of the eigenvalues of the transition matrix will determine whether the path to the asymptotic vector will be damped oscillatory, and summary measures are provided for the rate of convergence. A chi-square goodness-of-fit statistic will determine whether the underlying data structure can be explained by a first-order Markov scheme or whether more general methods of analysis are needed. Since the first-order Markov model is a special case of the more general vector autoregressive moving-average (VARMA) model estimated with the B34S BTEST command, if a model chi-square goodness-of-fit statistic is significant, a possible future research route is to move to a VARMA model. One advantage of the Markov probability model is that the data requirements are substantially less than are required with the VARMA model.[9]

NOTES

1. Because of the availability of the Lee, Judge and Zellner (1970) reference, this chapter will not contain a detailed discussion of the Markov model theory or a detailed discussion of what the TRANSPROB code calculates. The extensions to the original Lee-Judge-Zellner (1970) FORTRAN IV code included modifying the code for increased accuracy by converting all REAL*4 variables to REAL*8 variables, modifying the code to allow for bigger problems by removing all fixed dimensions and going to variable dimensions set at run time, conversion to FORTRAN 77, and the addition of the Theil (1972) decomposition extensions. Most of the keywords of the TRANSPROB command have been taken from internal variable names in the original code to facilitate understanding the command.

2. This discussion is heavily influenced by the material in Lee, Judge and Zellner (1970), Theil (1972, chap. 5), and Stokey and Lucas (1989).

3. The absolute value of a complex root a $\pm$ bi is defined as $\sqrt{(a^2 + b^2)}$.

4. More detail on other approaches to estimate P is contained in Lee, Judge and Zellner (1970), from which much of this discussion is based.

5. For more detail on the complexity of the weighting options, see Lee, Judge and Zellner (1970), which lists the basic code that was modified to build the B34S TRANSPROB command.

6. The B34S OPTIONS command help document discusses the ways this can be done. The B34S work space size is limited to what the IBM operating system will allow your account. Currently, B34S runs below the 16-megabite line. In the future, an XA release of B34S is planned.

7. Sections discussing the decomposition of $\hat{P}$ and the mean first passage matrix, M, with respect to the oil example have been taken directly from Kosobud and Stokes (1979).

8. Kosobud and Stokes (1979) gave the ratios as 1.809936 and .319252, respectively, and erroneously reported that they were the sum of the elements of R divided by the sum of the elements of A, when, in fact, it was the reverse.

9. The VARMA model is discussed in chapter 8.

7. Time Series Analysis Part I: Identification of ARIMA and Transfer Function Models

7.0 Introduction

The B34S commands BJIDEN and BJEST control identification and estimation of Box-Jenkins (1976) models. The basic code was originally developed by David Pack (1977) and was extensively modified by the author.[1] The basic reference for these commands is the classic work of Box and Jenkins (1976). Nelson (1973) provides a simplified treatment of univariate models. Since these excellent references are available, only a brief discussion of the identification and estimation steps will be given here. Zellner and Palm (1974) outline how the Box-Jenkins univariate and transfer function models are special cases of the more general vector autoregressive moving-average models. The simultaneous equations model is shown to be another special case. The BTIDEN and BTEST commands to estimate these more complex models are discussed in chapter 8, while the simultaneous equations command SIMEQ is discussed in chapter 4. A frequency interpretation of the VAR model is discussed in chapter 12.

7.1 Identifying and Estimating an ARIMA Model

Assume two jointly distributed, discrete random variables $\{x_1,\ldots,x_T\}$ and $\{y_1,\ldots,y_T\}$.[2] Define $p(x^*,y^*)$ as the <u>joint distribution</u> of x and y or the probability at the point $x = x^*$ and $y = y^*$. The <u>marginal distribution</u> of x (y) is the probability distribution of x (y) without regard to y (x) and is defined as $p(x) = \Sigma_y\, p(x,y)$ $(p(y) = \Sigma_x\, p(x,y))$. The <u>conditional distribution</u> of x, given that $y = y^*$, is $p(x|y^*)$, where

$$p(x|y^*) = p(x,y^*)\ /\ \Sigma_x\, p(x,y^*). \tag{7.1-1}$$

The conditional distribution is the joint distribution divided by the marginal distribution. A series x_t is said to have the property of <u>strict stationarity</u> if

$$p(x_t,\ldots,x_{t+k}) = p(x_{t+n},\ldots,x_{t+k+n}), \tag{7.1-2}$$

which implies that the marginal distribution of each observation is the same $(p(x_t) = p(x_{t+n})$ for $n \neq 0)$, the expected value of each observation is the same $(E(x_t) = E(x_{t+n})$ for $n \neq 0)$, the variances of each observation are the same $(V(x_t) = V(x_{t+n})$ for $n \neq 0)$ and the covariances $C(x_t,x_{t+j})$ are invariant of any offset in time

$$C(x_t,x_{t+j}) = C(x_{t+m},x_{t+m+j}) = \gamma_j \quad \text{for } m \neq 0. \tag{7.1-3}$$

Define B as the backshift operator such that $B^k x_t = x_{t-k}$. A correctly specified, autoregressive integrated moving-average (ARIMA) model

will filter a series $\{x_1, \ldots, x_t\}$ such that the estimated
covariances vanish ($\hat{\gamma}_i = 0$ for all $i > 0$). The general form of the
ARIMA model is

$$(1-\Phi_1 B-\Phi_2 B^2-,\ldots,-\Phi_p B^p)(1-\Gamma_1 B^s -\Gamma_2 B^{2s}-,\ldots,-\Gamma_P B^{Ps})(1-B)^d(1-B^s)^D x_t =$$

$$(1-\Theta_1 B-\Theta_2 B^2-,\ldots,-\Theta_q B^q)(1-\Delta_1 B^s -\Delta_2 B^{2s}-,\ldots,-\Delta_Q B^{Qs})e_{xt}, \qquad (7.1-4)$$

where Φ_i is a regular autoregressive coefficient, Γ_i is a seasonal
autoregressive coefficient, d is the order of regular differencing,
D is the order of seasonal differencing, s is the seasonal period,
Θ_i is a moving-average coefficient, Δ_i is a seasonal moving-average
coefficient and e_t is a white-noise error process having the
following three properties:

$$E(e_{xt}) \qquad = 0 \qquad \text{for all t} \qquad\qquad (7.1-5)$$

$$E(e_{xt}^2) \qquad = \sigma_{xe}^2 \qquad \text{for all t} \qquad\qquad (7-1-6)$$

$$E(e_{xt}\,e_{xt-s}) \qquad = 0 \qquad \text{for all t and } s \neq 0. \qquad (7.1-7)$$

It is possible to write equation (7.1-4) in more compact notation
as

$$\Phi_x(B)\Gamma_x(B)x_t = \Theta_x(B)\Delta_x(B)e_{xt} \qquad\qquad (7.1-8)$$

or

$$H_x(B)x_t = F_x(B)e_{xt}, \qquad\qquad (7.1-9)$$

where $H_x(B) \equiv \Phi_x(B)\Gamma_x(B)$ and $F_x(B) \equiv \Theta_x(B)\Delta_x(B)$ and we assume for
simplicity that x_t has been suitably differenced to make it
stationary. If $F_x(B)$ is invertible[3], equation (7.1-9) can be written
in the <u>inverted</u> form as an autoregressive model

$$A_x(B)x_t = e_{xt}, \qquad\qquad (7.1-10)$$

while if $H_x(B)$ is invertible, equation (7.1-9) can be written in
the <u>random shock</u> form as a moving average model

$$x_t = C_x(B)e_{xt}, \qquad\qquad (7.1-11)$$

where

$$A_x(B) \equiv [F_x(B)]^{-1}H_x(B) \qquad\qquad (7.1-12)$$

and

$$C_x(B) \equiv [H_x(B)]^{-1}F_x(B). \qquad\qquad (7.1-13)$$

Assume that the model that prewhitens the x_t series is applied to the series y_t. In general, the error

$$e_{yt}^* = A_x(B)y_t \qquad\qquad (7.1-14)$$

will <u>not</u> be white noise since the appropriate model for prewhitening y_t is

$$e_{yt} = A_y(B)y_t \qquad\qquad (7.1-15)$$

and, in general, $A_y(B) \neq A_x(B)$. Problems concerning the one-filter and two-filter identification technique will be discussed in sections 7.2 and 7.3.

To aid in the selection of the appropriate ARIMA model, Box and Jenkins (1976) recommend calculation of the autocorrelation function (ACF) and the partial autocorrelation function (PACF). The ACF and the PACF are used in a four-step procedure to identify an ARIMA model. The steps include the following:

a. Make the x_t series stationary so the ACF and PACF can be calculated.

b. Use the ACF and PACF to determine a preliminary ARIMA model.

c. Obtain an estimate of the preliminary model, using ML estimation.

d. Diagnostically check the preliminary model to see if the residual is white noise. If the residual <u>is</u> white noise, the model is complete. If the residual <u>is not</u> white noise, then adjust the model based on the ACF and PACF of the residual and repeat steps c through d as many times as necessary to obtain white noise in the residual.

e. Optionally, use the ARIMA model identified in step d to forecast.

Define μ as the estimated mean of the series $\{x_1, \ldots, x_T\}$. An estimate of the autocorrelation at lag j, $\hat{\rho}_j$, is defined as

$$\hat{\rho}_j = \hat{\gamma}_j / \hat{\gamma}_0, \qquad\qquad (7.1-16)$$

where the estimated covariance is

$$\hat{\gamma}_j = (1/T)\Sigma_{t=1}^{T-j} [(x_t - \mu)(x_{t+j} - \mu)] \text{ for } j=0,\ldots \qquad (7.1-17)$$

Equation (7.1-17) uses T in the denominator in contrast with the usual covariance formula, which uses the small sample approximation, T-j. Equation (7.1-16) will make the estimated autocorrelation smaller than the formula with the small sample

approximation. A series is deemed white noise if there are no
significant spikes in the ACF.[4] The Bartlett (1946) formula for
the estimated standard error of $\hat{\rho}_j$, $\hat{s}_j$ is

$$\hat{s}_j \approx [(1/T) \{1 + 2 \Sigma_{i=1}^{q} \rho_i^2 \}]^{.5} \text{ for } j > q. \qquad (7.1-18)$$

Equation (7.1-18) reduces to the large sample approximation $(1/T)^{.5}$
if $\rho_i = 0$ for $i < j$. The Bartlett-corrected standard error will be
greater than or equal to the large sample approximation. An
estimated autocorrelation coefficient for lag k will be deemed
significant at approximately the 95% confidence interval if
$2\hat{s}_j \leq |\hat{\rho}_k|$. The first k estimated autocorrelations $\{\hat{\rho}_1,...,\hat{\rho}_k\}$ can
be tested with the Box-Pierce (1970) Q_k statistic

$$Q_k = T \Sigma_{j=1}^{k} \hat{\rho}_j^2, \qquad (7.1-19)$$

which is distributed as chi-square with k-p-q degrees of freedom
where p and q are the number of AR and MA coefficients in the
multiplied out ARIMA model given in equation (7.1-9), or the Ljung-
Box (1978) modified Q statistic

$$Q_k^* = [T(T+2)] \Sigma_{i=1}^{k} \{\hat{\rho}_i^2 /(T-i)\}, \qquad (7.1-20)$$

which is thought to be closer to chi-square with k-p-q degrees of
freedom in moderate-sized samples. The B34S autocorrelation
function in the BJIDEN and BJEST paragraphs provides an estimate of
the modified Q for each estimated autocorrelation coefficient, and
the Q and the modified Q and the levels of significance for the
first NCHI estimated autocorrelation coefficients. If NCHI is not
set, it defaults to MIN(24,NAC), where NAC is the number of
autocorrelation coefficients.

    The estimated partial autocorrelation coefficients $\{\Phi_1,...,\Phi_k\}$,
where k is specified by the user with the NPAC parameter, are
calculated as the successive solutions to the Yule-Walker equations
for Φ_i, given the estimated autocorrelations ρ_i [5]

$$
\begin{aligned}
\rho_1 &= \Phi_1 \\
\rho_2 &= \Phi_1 \rho_1 + \Phi_2 \\
&\cdots\cdots\cdots\cdots\cdots\cdots\cdots\cdots\cdots\cdots\cdots\cdots\cdots\cdots \qquad (7.1-21)\\
\rho_p &= \Phi_1 \rho_{p-1} + \Phi_2 \rho_{p-2} + ,..., + \Phi_p.
\end{aligned}
$$

Inspection of the PACF indicates the maximum order of the pure AR
model given in equation (7.1-10). Table 7.1, which was taken from
Box and Jenkins (1976, 79), illustrates how the ACF and the PACF
are used to determine the appropriate orders p and q of the AR and
MA parts of an ARIMA model.

Table 7.1 Use of the ACF and PACF to Identify an ARIMA Model

Model	ACF Pattern	PACF Pattern
Pure MA (7.1-11)	Spikes at lags 1 - q then cut off	Tail off
Pure AR (7.1-10)	Tail off according to (7.1-21)	Spikes at lags 1-p then cut off
ARIMA (7.1-9)	Irregular pattern 1-q then tail off according to (7.1-21)	Tail off

For the purposes of the table, q is the maximum MA term in $F_x(B)$ for an ARIMA model and p is the maximum AR term in $H_x(B)$ in equation (7.1-9).

    If a series is not stationary, the ACF and PACF are not defined although they can be calculated. The usual procedure to check for stationarity is to calculate the ACF and see if the coefficients die out. If the coefficients do not die out, more differencing is used. The following B34S commands will perform estimation of the ACF and PACF for a series, MONEY and PRICE, which are assumed to be active B34S variables.

```
B34SEXEC BJIDEN LIST=(MONEY,PRICE) PLOT=(MONEY,PRICE)
      NAC=48 IWTPA $
      VAR MONEY PRICE$
      SERIESN VAR=MONEY NAME=('MONEY SUPPLY M2')$
      SERIESN VAR=PRICE NAME=('CPI ALL ITEMS')$
      RTRANS DIF=(2,1)(1,12)$
      RAUTO MONEY PRICE$
      B34SEEND$
```

    There will be six sets of autocorrelations calculated. These are MONEY, $(1-B)$MONEY, $(1-B)^2$MONEY, $(1-B^{12})$MONEY, $(1-B)(1-B^{12})$MONEY and $(1-B)^2(1-B^{12})$MONEY and the corresponding transformations for PRICE. Both series have been optionally listed and plotted (LIST and PLOT parameters) and the autocorrelations have been plotted (IWTPA option). The number of autocorrelations and partial autocorrelations has been set at 48. Assume that $(1-B)$MONEY is stationary. The ACF of $(1-B)^2$MONEY would show added spikes due to the over differencing. Once the series is deemed stationary, Table 7.1 is used to select the model. Assume a preliminary guess for the correct model is an ARIMA model of the form

$$(1-B)(1-\Gamma_1 B^{12})MONEY_t = (1-\Theta_1 B)e_t, \qquad (7.1-22)$$

where, if there is no confusion, we assume $e_t \equiv e_{moneyt}$.

The following BJEST commands will estimate the model listed in equation (7.1-22) and forecast for 12 periods ahead, starting from the 200th observation.

```
B34SEXEC BJEST $
    MODEL MONEY $
    MODELN P=12 Q=1$
    FORECAST NF=12 NT=200 $
    B34SEEND $
```

The BJEST command uses a variant of the Meeter (1964a, 1964b) nonlinear routine, GAUSHAUS, to minimize the sum of squares of the residual of the general ARIMA model listed in equation (7.1-9). Since the shocks of the system before observation one are not known, the procedure sets them to their expected value of zero. If the IWBF option is set, the model is run backward through time to generate estimates of the errors prior to the first observation. The developer of B34S suggests that this option not be used because of convergence problems. The SAS PROC ARIMA attempts to get around the problem of obtaining values for the error terms prior to observation 1 by optionally removing them from the calculated residual sum of squares. This approach has not been implemented in B34S at this time because it appears to be arbitrary.

A major problem in ARIMA model estimation is high parameter correlation. Consider the following alternative models for series x_t.

$$(1-\Phi_1 B)(1-\Phi_2 B^{12}) \ x_t = e_{xt} \tag{7.1-23}$$

$$(1-\Phi_1 B - \Phi_2 B^{12} - \Phi_3 B^{13}) \ x_t = e_{xt}. \tag{7.1-24}$$

Equation (7.1-23), which is specified as P=(1)(12), implies a model of the form of equation (7.1-24), where

$$\Phi_3 \equiv \Phi_1 \Phi_2. \tag{7.1-25}$$

Model (7.1-24) can be estimated directly as P=(1,12,13) without constraining Φ_3 by equation (7.1-25). If model (7.1-24) is estimated in error, when model (7.1-23) is the correct model, the correlation between Φ_3 and the other two parameters, Φ_1 and Φ_2, will be high. The BJEST command displays a correlation matrix of the parameters to test for this problem. The reciprocal of the condition of the correlation matrix of the parameters is given as a further measure to detect problems of parameter redundancy.

The B34S BJEST command provides a rank condition on the covariance matrix. If there is extreme parameter collinearity, a message is given and the SEs of the coefficients are not calculated. If the user still wants to proceed, the IRISK option can be specified to force inversion. If IRISK is set, the B34S may generate a traceback. SEs calculated with IRISK set should be used with caution. Rather than proceeding with IRISK, the correct procedure is to try and determine whether it is possible to simplify a model of the form of equation (7.1-24) to a form like equation (7.1-23). The covariance of the parameters will indicate which parameters are related. If this is not available due to extreme rank problems, the best strategy is to simplify the model and attempt to "walk" in the parameters one at a time to determine what is causing the problem.

Define $x_{t+j|t}$ as the forecast for x in period t+j, given information in period t. From equation (7.1-11), we can write

$$x_{t+j} = \mu + \psi_{x0}e_{xt+j} + \psi_{x1}e_{xt+j-1} + \psi_{x2}e_{xt+j-2} + \dots, \qquad (7.1-26)$$

where, by notational convention, $-c_{xi}(B) \equiv \psi_{xi}$ and μ is the mean of the process. Since $E(e_{xk}) = 0$ for $k \geq t$, then

$$x_{t+j|t} = \mu + \psi_{xj}e_{xt} + \psi_{xj+1}e_{xt-1} + \dots \qquad (7.1-27)$$

and

$$\lim_{j \to \infty} [x_{t+j}|t] = \mu \qquad (7.1-28)$$

since the sum $\Sigma_{i=0}^{\infty} \psi_i$ converges where $\psi_{x0} \equiv 1$. The BJEST command lists the psi weights if forecasting is requested. Inspection of these weights will indicate how soon the forecast will converge to the mean. The standard deviation of the error in the forecast j periods in the future, $e_{xt}(j) \equiv [x_{t+j} - (x_{t+j}|t)]$, is defined in terms of psi weights as

$$SD[e_{xt}(j)] = \sigma_e \, \Sigma_{i=0}^{j} (\psi_{xi})^2. \qquad (7.1-29)$$

The nonlinear estimation of the model uses a variant of the GAUSHAUS program developed by Meeter (1964a, 1964b). Further discussion of this program is contained in chapter 11, which discusses nonlinear estimation with the NONLIN command. Using this command, the user specifies the model with a FORTRAN subroutine to which B34S dynamically links. The BJEST command contains a number of parameters to assist the user in estimating the model. The parameter MIT sets the maximum allowable iterations. The default is 20 and is rarely exceeded. The parameter ESP1 sets the maximum change in the sum of squares before iteration stops. If this parameter is not given, this stopping rule is not used. The parameter ESP2 allows the user to set the maximum allowable change in any parameter before iteration stops. The default for ESP2 is .004. The user is cautioned against raising ESP2. In the next section, ARIMA filters are used to identify transfer functions.

7.2 Identifying and Estimating a Transfer Function Model

Assume a multiple-input transfer function model of the form

$$Y_t = c + \Sigma_{i=1}^{k} \ [\omega_i(B) \ / \ \delta_i(B)] \ X_{i,t} + [\Theta(B)/\Phi(B)]e_t, \qquad (7.2\text{-}1)$$

where $\omega_i(B)$, $\delta_i(B)$, $\Theta(B)$ and $\Phi(B)$ are all polynomials in the lag operator B, and there are k input series, where $X_{i,t}$ is the tth observation of the ith input series, e_t is the error term for the tth observation and y_t is the dependent variable. If we assume that $[\omega_i(B) \ / \ \delta_i(B)] \equiv 0$, then equation (7.2-1) converges to an ARIMA model such as equation (7.1-4). If we assume that $[(\Theta(B) \ / \ \Phi(B)] \equiv 1$, equation (7.2-1) is a <u>rational distributed lag</u> model. If, in addition, we simplify $[\omega_i(B) \ / \ \delta_i(B)]$, then equation (7.2-1) converges to a multiple-input OLS model, such as equation (2.1-7). Thus, the transfer function model is a more general case of the OLS and the ARIMA models. The difficulty of estimating equation (7.2-1) lies in specifying the orders of $[\omega_i(B) \ / \ \delta_i(B)]$ and $[\Theta(B)/\Phi(B)]$. These difficulties magnify as k increases, <u>except</u> in the case in which the series $X_{i,t}$ are all orthogonal. A number of proposed methods for identification of such a transfer function model have been suggested in the literature. These include the original one-filter identification procedure, suggested by Box and Jenkins (1970, 1976); the two-filter identification procedure, suggested by Haugh (1976), Pierce and Haugh (1977), Haugh and Box (1977) and others; and a least-squares method involving estimation of a linear transfer function (LTF) , suggested by Liu and Hanssens (1982) and modified by Liu and Hudak (1986a). In practice, problems often arise in detecting whether it was the input rational polynomial $[\omega_i(B)/\delta_i(B)]$ or the noise rational polynomial $[\Theta(B)/\Phi(B)]$ that was not correctly specified, since either (or both problems) could result in spikes in the cross correlations between the residual and the input series. Section 7.3 discusses an additional diagnostic test on the cross correlations to pinpoint the nature of any specification problems. First, the alternative identification approaches and problems are outlined.

Assume there is only one input series in equation (7.2-1) or that k=1. Following Box and Jenkins (1976, 379), equation (7.2-1) can be written in impulse-response form[6] as

$$Y_t \quad = \quad V(B) \ x_t + [\Theta(B)/\Phi(B)] \ e_t$$

$$= \quad v_0 \ x_t + v_1 \ x_{t-1} + \ldots + v_k \ x_{t-k} + [\Theta(B)/\Phi(B)] \ e_t. \qquad (7.2\text{-}2)$$

The steps to identify a transfer function with the one-filter method include the following:

    a. Difference y_t and x_t to achieve stationarity so that the ACF is defined.

    b. Estimate an ARIMA filter for x_t from equation (7.1-9) such that e_{xt} is white noise.

c. Apply the filter estimated for the x_t series to the Y_t series, using equation (7.1-14) to form the nonwhite noise series e_{yt}^*.

d. Cross correlate α_t and β_t, where $\alpha_t \equiv e_{xt}$ and $\beta_t \equiv e_{yt}^*$, to form the cross correlation function $r_{\alpha\beta}(k)$ at lag k for $k = -maxk, \ldots, 0, \ldots, maxk$. The value of maxk is set so that the cross correlations die out.

e. Using the estimated cross correlations contained in $r_{\alpha\beta}(k)$, obtain an estimate of the impulse response weights, $\hat{V}(B)$, in equation (7.2-2).

It can be shown that

$$\hat{v}_k = r_{\alpha\beta}(k) \ \sigma_\beta \ / \ \sigma_\alpha \qquad\qquad (7.2-3)$$

since if we multiply equation (7.2-2) by $A_x(B)$, we obtain

$$\beta_t = V(B) \ \alpha_t + [H_x(B)/F_x(B)][\Theta(B)/\Phi(B)]e_t. \qquad (7.2-4)$$

Equations (7.2-3) and (7.2-4) show that the cross correlations $r_{\alpha\beta}(k)$ weighted by their standard errors σ_α and σ_β are directly proportional to the impulse-response function $V(B)$ in equation (7.2-1). Inspection of $\hat{v}_k$ from equation (7.2-3) provides a guide to select the model for $[\omega_i(B)/\delta_i(B)]$ in equation (7.2-1) prior to estimation with ML methods. An estimate of the noise series can be obtained by noting that

$$\hat{e}_t = y_t - \Sigma_{k=0}^{K} \ \hat{v}_k B^k x_t, \qquad\qquad (7.2-5)$$

where $K \equiv maxk$. The ACF of $\hat{e}_t$ is used to obtain a preliminary guess on the appropriate form of $[\Theta(B)/\Phi(B)]$. Problems arise if the initial guess for the form of $[\Theta(B)/\Phi(B)]$ and/or $[\omega_i(B)/\delta_i(B)]$ is not correct. A proposed diagnostic test for this problem is discussed in section 7.3. Before discussing this test, a brief examination of the two-filter identification approach, the more complex Liu and Hanssens (1982) LTF identification method and the simplified Liu and Hudak (1986a) LTF identification method are in order.

The two-filter approach estimates a separate prewhitening model for x_t and y_t and cross correlates the two prewhitened series e_{yt} and e_{xt}, which can be thought of as being related by the model

$$e_{yt} = \tilde{V}(B) \ e_{xt} + e_t'. \qquad\qquad (7.2-6)$$

An estimate of $[\omega_i(B)/\delta_i(B)]$ can be obtained if we multiply equation (7.2-6) by the y_t prewhitening model and substitute for the x_t prewhitening model to form

$$Y_t = [F_y(B)/H_y(B)][H_x(B)/F_x(B)] \, \tilde{V}(B)x_t + [\Theta_y(B)/\Phi_y(B)]e_t' \qquad (7.2\text{-}7)$$

from which we can obtain an estimate of V(B) by noting that

$$\hat{V}(B) = [F_y(B)/H_y(B)][H_x(B)/F_x(B)] \, \tilde{V}(B). \qquad (7.2\text{-}8)$$

There are a number of problems with the two-filter method of analysis that are discussed in Stokes and Neuburger (1979) and briefly below. The Liu and Hanssens (1982) approach, which was modified in Liu and Hudak (1986a), estimates $\hat{V}(B)$ by running a transfer function with many lags. This method shows promise, but suffers from multicollinearity problems. Its most important advantage is the fact that it works best in multiple-input models, when the one- and two-filter approaches break down. The B34S BJIDEN command allows all three methods to be used. Details of the command setup are found in the B34S On-Line Manual.

The cross correlation vector $r_{\alpha\beta}(k)$ can be tested with the Haugh (1976, 382) S statistic defined as

$$S = T \, \Sigma_{k=-M}^{M} \, (r_{ij}(k)), \qquad (7.2\text{-}9)$$

which is distributed as chi-square with degrees of freedom equal to the number of lags incorporated (2M+1) or the more accurate Haugh (1976, 383) modified S statistic MS, which is distributed as chi-square with 2M+1 degrees of freedom.

$$MS = T^2 \, \Sigma_{k=-M}^{M} \, (r_{ij}(k))^2 \, / \, (T - |k|), \qquad (7.2\text{-}10)$$

where T is the number of observations used to form the cross correlations and M is the number of lags in each cross-correlation vector and $r_{ij}(k)$ is the cross correlation between the ith and the jth series lagged k periods. Haugh (1976) initially proposed to use the MS statistic to test for independence. Pierce (1977) proposed using the Haugh test on one side only. This approach was criticized because the distribution of $r_{ij}(k)$ depends on nonzero population cross correlations, even when such nonzero population cross correlations occur at lags different from the sample cross correlations used in the calculation of MS in equation (7.2-10), thus inflating the standard errors. For further discussions of these problems, see Pierce and Haugh (1977) and Stokes and Neuburger (1979).

After the transfer function model listed in equation (7.2-1) is estimated, B34S calculates the impulse response function

$$V_{0i}(B) = [\omega_i(B)/ \, \delta_i(B)] \qquad (7.2\text{-}11)$$

for each input series i. Summing the terms in $V_{0i}(B)$ gives an estimate on how fast y_t adjusts to a one-unit change in $X_{i,t}$. If the model is correctly specified, then

$$V_{0i}(B) \sim V_i(B) \qquad \text{for } i=1,k. \qquad (7.2\text{-}12)$$

If the model is not correctly specified, then, in general,

$$V_{0i}(B) \neq V_i(B) \qquad \text{for } i=1,k. \qquad (7.2\text{-}13)$$

Box and Jenkins (1976, 392-393) suggest a number of diagnostic tests for model specification. Assuming c =0, equation (7.2-1) can be rewritten as

$$Y_t = \Sigma_{i=1}^k V_i(B)X_{i,t} + \psi(B)e_t. \qquad (7.2\text{-}14)$$

If we assume only one input, the estimated model becomes

$$Y_t = V_{01}(B)X_{1,t} + \psi_0(B)a_{0t}. \qquad (7.2\text{-}15)$$

Rewriting equation (7.2-15) in terms of a_{0t} and substituting for y_t from the true model in equation (7.2-14) gives

$$a_{0t} = [\psi_0(B)]^{-1}\{V_1(B) - V_{01}(B)\}X_{1,t} + [\psi_0(B)]^{-1}\psi(B)e_t. \qquad (7.2\text{-}16)$$

Equation (7.2-16) indicates that the error of the incorrect model, a_{0t}, will be correlated with $X_{1,t}$ because of the first term and autocorrelated because of the second term. Two cases are worth mentioning. If the input model is correct, equation (7.2-12) holds and equation (7.2-16) can be written

$$a_{0t} = [\psi_0(B)]^{-1}\psi(B)e_t. \qquad (7.2\text{-}17)$$

In this case the series a_{0t} is not cross correlated with $X_{1,t}$ but is autocorrelated. The next section discusses the possibility of spurious cross correlations being observed. If the input model was not correct but the noise model was correct, then from equation (7.2-16)

$$\psi_0(B) = \psi(B) \qquad (7.2\text{-}18)$$

and

$$a_{0t} = [\psi_0(B)]^{-1}\{V_1(B) - V_{01}(B)\}X_{1,t} + e_t, \qquad (7.2\text{-}19)$$

which implies that a_{0t} is not autocorrelated but is cross correlated with $X_{1,t}$, and hence α_t. If $X_{1,t}$ is autocorrelated, a_{0t} will be autocorrelated although this will not indicate problems with the noise model. A further complication arises if the orders of the input (noise) model are correct, but due to problems in the noise (input) model, equation (7.2-12) (equation [7.2-18]) does not hold due to the correlation between the estimated parameters. If both the noise model and the input model are not correct, equation

(7.2-16) holds. The above discussion suggests that the estimated impulse response function $V_{0i}(B)$ from equation (7.2-11) should be corrected to form $V_{ci}(B)$, which contains elements v_{cki} defined as

$$v_{cki} = v_{0ki} + [\rho_{\alpha\varepsilon}(k)\sigma_\varepsilon/\sigma_\alpha], \qquad (7.2\text{-}20)$$

where

$$\varepsilon_{0t} = \beta_t - V_{0i}(B)\alpha_t. \qquad (7.2\text{-}21)$$

The corrected impulse response weights are used two ways: First, their sum provides a way to measure the effect of a one-unit change in X_{it} on y_t, given the specified model. Second, the degree to which equation (7.2-12) holds determines how well the model captures the dynamic relationship. In short, $V_i(B)$ measures the modeled impulse response function, while $V_{ci}(B)$ measures the correct impulse response function.

If forecasts are available beyond period t, a transfer function model can be used to forecast. These forecasts are usually obtained from an ARIMA forecasting model such as equation (7.1-27). The noise model $[\Theta(B)/\Phi(B)]$ is used to form psi weights $\{\psi_0, \psi_1, \ldots\}$. The variance of the conditional forecast of y_{t+j} given information at period t, $[y_{t+j}|t]$, is

$$V[y_{t+j}|t] = \sigma_e^2[\Sigma_{k=0}^{j-1}((v_k)^2 + (\psi_k)^2)]. \qquad (7.2\text{-}22)$$

One problem in transfer function model building is that the rational polynomial $[\omega_i(B)/\delta_i(B)]$ is not unique. Most of the time, initial guesses on the parameters are not needed. If initial guesses are needed or the user desires to experiment with alternative models, the BJIDEN command has a STARTVALUE option that implements suggestions contained in Box and Jenkins (1976, 383, 512-513). Assume that equation (7.2-3) is used to obtain an initial estimate of the impulse response vector, $\hat{V}(B)$. Given user-specified orders for $\omega_i(B)$ and $\delta_i(B)$, the STARTVALUE option will generate an initial guess on the parameters. The STARTVALUE option will also optionally output the "A matrix" and "H vector" as defined in Box and Jenkins (1976, 512). By supplying alternative orders and numbers of parameters in $\omega_i(B)$ and $\delta_i(B)$, the user can study the changes in the coefficients prior to attempting estimation of the transfer function model. The commands listed below show preliminary identification of the Box and Jenkins (1976) gas furnace data model. The user is investigating the effect of changing the numerator orders from 1, 2, 3 to 1, 2, 3, 4, 5, given the denominator orders. The IRWCNT parameter on the first BJIDEN call is all that is needed to save the $\hat{V}(B)$ vector for the subsequent BJIDEN TYPE=STARTVALUE steps. The default of 24 cross correlations and 24 terms in $\hat{V}(B)$ is used. The data set used in this example is discussed further in the next section and used in chapter 8.

```
B34SEXEC BJIDEN TYPE=TRANSI NCC=50 IRWCNT=5$
      VAR GASIN GASOUT$
      SERIESN VAR=GASIN  NAME=('Series J X from BJ 1976 gas input ')$
      SERIESN VAR=GASOUT NAME=('Series J Y from BJ 1976 gas output')$
      MODELP VAR=GASIN P=(1,2,3) AR=(1.97494,-1.3732,.3424) AVEPA=-.061$
      OUTPUT VAR=GASOUT AVEPA=53.507996 $
      PCROSS=(GASIN,GASOUT)$
      B34SEEND$
B34SEXEC BJIDEN TYPE=STARTVALUE$
      STARTVALUE NTERMS=(1,2,3)      DTERMS=(1,2,3) RUFILE=SDATA5
      PRINT=(HA,RW)$ B34SEEND$
B34SEXEC BJIDEN TYPE=STARTVALUE$
      STARTVALUE NTERMS=(1,2,3,4,5) DTERMS=(1,2,3) RUFILE=SDATA5
      PRINT=(HA,RW)$ B34SEEND$
```

Before discussing the examples, the effects of autocorrelation in a series on the structure of the estimated cross correlation function will be examined.

7.3 Diagnostic Tests on the Autocorrelations of the Cross Correlations

This section describes a diagnostic procedure that will distinguish between spikes in the cross correlations of the residual and the prewhitened input series that arise from inadequacies in the noise model from those that arise due to problems in the specification of the input model.[7] The proposed procedure simplifies the second-round iterations of transfer function model building discussed in section 7.2.

Assume a multiple-input transfer function model of the form of equation (7.2-1). Problems often arise in detecting whether it was the input rational polynomial $[\omega_i(B)/\delta_i(B)]$ or the noise rational polynomial $[\Theta(B)/\Phi(B)]$ that was not correctly specified in the first pass since either (or both problems) could result in spikes in the cross correlations between the residual and the input series. An additional diagnostic test on the cross correlations to help pinpoint the nature of the problem is proposed. First, the theory behind the proposed diagnostic test will be developed and outlined. Finally, an example will be given.

While the original one-filter procedure showed promise in identifying one-input models, there were problems in identifying more-than-one-input models, unless the inputs were orthogonal with each other. The one-filter procedure had a major weakness, even in a one-input model, since the x_t series prewhitening model usually would not prewhiten the y_t series. If this was the case, there was the distinct possibility that the observed cross correlation between the two filtered series was due to the y_t series not being completely prewhitened rather than to the series being related. The reasons for these spurious cross correlations occurring are outlined below. Further information can be found in Bartlett (1955), Box and Jenkins (1976, 376-377) and Stokes and Neuburger (1979). Often, no matter what method of identification has been selected, in the second-round identification process,[8] when the preliminary specification of the model had been estimated by maximum likelihood techniques and the model was being fine tuned, the noise would show some autocorrelation and the cross correlation between the prewhitened x_t series and the noise would show some spikes. In this situation, it was difficult to determine whether it was best to try to clean up the input model or the noise model first. The proposed new diagnostic test is always appropriate in the second-round identification step, no matter which of the procedures is used in the first stage. If the one-filter procedure is used in the first stage of the identification of a one-input transfer function, the proposed diagnostic procedure can also be used to reject spurious cross correlations as was done in Stokes and Neuburger (1979) and Neuburger and Stokes (1979b).

The two-filter procedure does not suffer from the problem of spurious correlations being observed in the first-round identification stage when the one-filter procedure is used, and initially showed promise. However, Sims (1977) and others have shown that the two-filter procedure produces downwardly biased estimates of the cross correlations because the two prewhitening filters are not estimated jointly with the cross correlations. The major drawback of this proposed method is that a relationship between the two series, y_t and x_t, can be hidden from the researcher.[9] A secondary drawback is that, as Liu and Hanssens (1982) and others have noted, it often results in very complex models being attempted. The search for common factors to delete often resulted in difficult judgment calls having to be made on how to initially set up the model. The second-stage identification process, using the two-filter procedure for the first stage, often was more difficult than when the one-filter procedure was used for the first-stage since the model tended to be overly complex initially. The proposed diagnostic procedure is most helpful in assisting the researcher on just what terms to add or change in the second-stage.

The original Liu and Hanssens (1982) LTF identification procedure, which involves the use of an OLS equation to identify the impulse response function so that an initial model can be selected for $[\omega_i(B) / \delta_i(B)]$, is clearly superior to both the other two proposed methods in the multiple-input case when the one-filter technique breaks down. Liu and Hanssens (1982, 306-307) outline five steps.[10] The proposed diagnostic procedure would be applied after step 5 in the fine-tuning, second- stage identification stage and would be similar to what would be done had another identification procedure, such as the one-filter or two-filter procedure, been used initially. The problem to be solved is what to do next if after an initial input model and noise model is selected and estimated, using a maximum likelihood, the researcher is confronted with a situation when it appears that one or more parts of the model are not correct. For example, often there are still spikes in the correlation between one of the prewhitened inputs and the noise, indicating a possible change in the appropriate input model, $[\omega_i(B)/\delta_i(B)]$, and autocorrelation in the noise model, indicating possible changes in $[\Theta(B)/\Phi(B)]$. Deciding the correct course to follow is complicated by the possibility that the spikes in the cross correlations <u>may</u> have been spurious, having arisen because of the autocorrelation in the noise, <u>not</u> because of something wrong with the input model. The proposed second-round identification procedure, outlined below, provides a means by which the researcher will be able to choose whether to change the noise model or the input model first. As was mentioned earlier, it can be used no matter which initial identification procedure is selected. Use of any of the identification procedures <u>assumes</u> that there is no feedback from the y_t series to any of the $X_{i,t}$ series. While most software that implements the one-filter and two-filter procedures calculates the cross correlations in both directions and thus gave some indication of feedback signifying that a transfer function was not appropriate, in the usual implementation of the Liu-Hanssens (1982) method, this feedback check is usually not done. Because of the potentially serious problems of feedback, it has been my practice to estimate a VAR model to check for feedback <u>prior</u> to attempting the Liu-Hanssens (1982) transfer function identification procedure. In private discussion, Liu agrees with this approach. Liu stresses that the revised three-step LTF identification method should be used in place of the more complex original approach

In the sections below, the distribution of cross correlations is discussed first. Next, the causality diagnostic testing procedure suggested by Stokes and Neuburger (1979) is discussed in the context of transfer function model building. Finally, an example using the Box-Jenkins (1976) gas furnace data is presented.

Box and Jenkins (1976, 377), utilizing a special case of the Bartlett (1955) general formula on the general distribution of the cross correlation function, prove that if one series, a_t, is white noise and the other series, x_t, is not white noise (lower case x is being used for ease of notation) and if a_t and x_t are <u>not</u> related, an autocorrelation of the sample cross correlation function of x_t and a_t at lag k $[r_{xa}(k)]$ "can be expected to vary about zero with standard deviation $(n-k)^{-.5}$ <u>in a systematic pattern</u> typical of the behavior of the autocorrelation function of x_t" $\rho_{xx}(j)$. Their formula,

$$\rho[r_{xa}(k),r_{xa}(k+j)] = \rho_{xx}(j), \hspace{2cm} (7.3-1)$$

implies the following four propositions (Stokes and Neuburger 1979).

1. If series x_t and a_t <u>are</u> cross correlated, and both x_t and a_t are white noise, the sample cross correlations of x_t and a_t will indicate the true relationship between the two series.

2. If series x_t and a_t <u>are</u> <u>not</u> cross correlated and if one series, e. g., a_t, is white noise and the other series, e. g., x_t,

is not white noise, then "in this case the cross correlations have the same autocorrelation function as the process generating" (Box and Jenkins 1976, 377) the nonwhite noise series x_t. Equation (7.3-1) describes the distribution of the autocorrelation function of the cross correlations for this case.

3. If series a_t and x_t are both white noise and "are not cross correlated, then the covariance between the cross correlations will be zero" (Box and Jenkins 1976, 377).

4. If neither series a_t or x_t is white noise and the two series are not cross correlated, then from inspection of the sample cross correlations, it is impossible to distinguish between true cross correlations and spurious results arising from the autocorrelations left in the two series.

Stokes and Neuburger (1979) and Neuburger and Stokes (1979b) suggested that these four propositions could be used to assist in using the one-filter identification procedure to determine causality between x_t and y_t. The suggested procedure was to first filter one series, e. g., x_t. Next, the x_t filter was applied to y_t and the two filtered series were cross correlated. The autocorrelations of the cross correlations were calculated and, using proposition 2 above, compared with the autocorrelations remaining in filtered y_t (e^*_{yt}) that were caused from using the filter identified for x_t. By using the one-filter procedure with the suggested diagnostic test for spurious cross correlations, causality tests can be made without having to resort to using the two-filter procedure and having the potential problem of the downward bias of the estimated cross correlation coefficients discussed earlier. Although causality tests can now be more effectively performed, using vector autoregressive model procedures, the diagnostic procedures suggested by Stokes and Neuburger (1979) can be effectively used in second-round transfer function model building identification. The use of these tests in this application is covered below. Prior to that, a few observations on how to determine whether two autocorrelation functions are the same are in order.

Stokes and Neuburger (1979) suggested a preliminary test statistic, in conjunction with visual inspection, to determine if the two autocorrelation functions are the same. The best visual procedure is to compare the locations of the significant spikes in the two autocorrelations. A more formal, but still preliminary, procedure is to calculate the test statistic h(i), distributed as a chi-square statistic with degrees of freedom 1, which is defined as

$$h(i) = (\alpha_i - \mu_i) / (v_\alpha + v_\mu), \qquad (7.3-2)$$

where α_i and μ_i are corresponding elements of two autocorrelation functions for lag i, and v_α and v_μ are the corresponding variances of α_i and μ_i, respectively. Since the sum of two chi-square statistics with degrees of freedom f_1 and f_2 is a chi-square statistic with degrees of freedom $f_1 + f_2$, from the h(i) statistics we can form an estimate H(k) defined as

$$H(k) = \Sigma_{i=1}^k \ h(i), \qquad\qquad\qquad (7.3-3)$$

which is distributed as chi-square with degrees of freedom k. This statistic can be used to test whether the first k autocorrelation terms for the two autocorrelation functions are significantly different. If H(k) is not significant, it suggests that the cross correlations found are spurious, since from proposition 2 above, the autocorrelation of the cross correlations is not significantly different from the autocorrelation remaining in one of the series that was cross correlated.

The above sections have shown when two series are cross correlated, and when one of the series is known to be white noise, the autocorrelations remaining in the other series can have influences on the sample-estimated cross correlations. If there is a relationship between the two series in question, this influence is added to the influence of the autocorrelation remaining in one of the series. When estimating a transfer function, a situation such as this frequently arises in the second stage of the identification process. In discussing the proposed second-round identification diagnostic procedure, the Liu-Hanssens (1982) first-round identification technique is assumed, although, as was discussed earlier, any of the appropriate first-round identification procedures can be used.

Assume that the Liu-Hanssens (1982) procedure was used to get an initial estimate for the impulse response function of up to k $X_{i,t}$ series mapping to the y_t series. After inspection of the preliminary estimate of the impulse response function, an initial model is selected and estimated, using a suitable maximum likelihood estimation program as outlined in steps 1 through 5 in Liu and Hanssens (1982) or the simpler three-step procedure in Liu and Hudak (1986a). The next task is to determine whether the appropriate input model, $[\omega_i (B) \ / \ \delta_i (B)]$, and/or noise model, $[\Theta(B)/\Phi(B)]$, was selected. The following steps, added after Liu-Hanssens (1982) step 5, will facilitate a solution to this problem.

6. Cross correlate the noise series with each input series that has been filtered with its ARIMA model, which was developed in step 1 of the Liu-Hanssens (1982) procedure. If a common filter has been used for all input series, the test will increasingly break down if this filter does not prewhiten the input series.

7. Autocorrelate the cross correlations calculated in step 6 above and compare these autocorrelations with those of the noise series. Assuming there appear to be spikes in the cross correlations and the noise model autocorrelations, there are two

possibilities: If the autocorrelations of the cross correlations
are similar to the autocorrelations of the noise series, the
proposed identification procedure suggests that it would be unwise
to attempt a change in the input model, $[\omega_i (B) / \delta_i (B)]$, for the
respective input i, since the estimated cross correlations are
spurious, having apparently arisen from the autocorrelation
remaining in the noise model, $[\Theta(B)/\Phi(B)]$. In this case, a change
in the noise model should be attempted first. On the other hand, if
the autocorrelations of the residuals were not similar to the
autocorrelations of the cross correlations, a change in the input
model for that input should be attempted prior to any change in the
noise model.[11]

Step 7 should be repeated for all input series in the model.
In practice, the autocorrelations of the cross correlations in the
negative direction (testing for feedback, which would invalidate
the use of a transfer function model) are tested separately from
the cross correlations in the positive direction (testing for the
appropriate specification of the input model). Often, the negative
cross correlations are found to be spurious and the positive cross
correlations are found to be valid. This suggests a change in the
input model but the initial indication of feedback was not
substantiated after further diagnostic testing.

The proposed procedure will be illustrated, using the Box-Jenkins
(1976, 386) model of the gas furnace data

$$y_t=[\omega(B)/\delta(B)]X_{t-3} + [1/(1-\Phi_1 B-\Phi_2 B^2)]e_t, \qquad (7.3-4)$$

where y_t = CO_2 outlet gas, x_t = input gas rate and where
$\omega(B)$ = $(w_0 - w_1 B - w_2 B^2)$ and $\delta(B)$ = $(1 - d_1 B - d_2 B^2)$. Assume that
case 1 is the original model. Case 2 is the same as case 1, except
that the input model has been modified such that $w_1 = w_2 = 0$. Case
3 is the same as case 1, except that the noise model has been
modified such that $[\Theta(B)/\Phi(B)]$ = $(1-\Theta_1 B)$. Case 4 combines the
incorrect noise polynomial from case 2 with the incorrect input
polynomial from case 3 to illustrate a situation in which both the
input and the noise models are not correct.

Table 7.2   B34S Setup to Illustrate CCF Diagnostic Tests

```
==GASDATA
/$              DATA FROM BJ (1976) PAGE 532-533 *************
/$              SETUP FOR PAPER
/$      "CLUES IN THE ERROR PROCESS; A SECOND ROUND DIAGNOSTIC
/$      PROCEDURE FOR TRANSFER FUNCTION MODELING"
/$
B34SEXEC OPTIONS MAXSIZ=200 $ B34SEEND$
B34SEXEC DATA NOOB=296 NOHEAD$
   INPUT TIME GASIN GASOUT$
* DATA COMES FROM B-J TIME SERIES BOOK $
DATACARDS$
   1 -0.109 53.8
   2  0.000 53.6
 .   .   .   .   .
295 -0.182 57.3
296 -0.262 57.0
B34SRETURN$
B34SEEND $

B34SEXEC BJEST$ * CHECK INPUT FILTER HERE $
    MODEL GASIN$
    MODELN P=(1,2,3) AR=(.97,-.94,.5) AVEPA=.5$
    FORECAST NF=24 NT=(296) $ B34SEEND$

B34SEXEC BJEST IAUTCR NCC=54 NAC=36 $ * TABLE 7.3 $
    * INPUT AND NOISE  MODELS ARE CORRECT - CASE 1 $
    MODEL GASOUT=GASIN$
    MODELN P=(1,2) AR=(.8,.76) AVEPA=53.509 $
    MODELI VAR=GASIN LAG=3 NUM=(0,1,2) DENOM=(1,2)
           NUMC=(-.53, .4 .6) DENOMC=(.6,.2)$
    MODELPRE VAR=GASIN P=(1,2,3) AR=(1.97494,-1.3732,.3424)
           AVEPA=-.061 $
    B34SEEND$

B34SEXEC BJEST IAUTCR NCC=54 NAC=36 $ * TABLE  7.4 $
    * INPUT NOT OK ------- NOISE OK - CASE 2     $
    MODEL GASOUT=GASIN$
    MODELN P=(1,2) AR=(.8,.76) AVEPA=53.509 $
    MODELI VAR=GASIN LAG=3 NUM=(0) DENOM=(1,2)
           NUMC=(-.53) DENOMC=(.6,.2)$
    MODELPRE VAR=GASIN P=(1,2,3) AR=(1.97494,-1.3732,.3424)
           AVEPA=-.061 $
    B34SEEND$

B34SEXEC BJEST IAUTCR NCC=54 NAC=36 $ * TABLE  7.5 $
    * INPUT OK, NOISE NOT OK  - CASE 3          $
    MODEL GASOUT=GASIN$
    MODELN Q=(1) MA=(-.8) AVEPA=53.509 $
    MODELI VAR=GASIN LAG=3 NUM=(0,1,2) DENOM=(1,2)
           NUMC=(-.53, .4 .6) DENOMC=(.6,.2)$
    MODELPRE VAR=GASIN P=(1,2,3) AR=(1.97494,-1.3732,.3424)
           AVEPA=-.061 $
    B34SEEND$

B34SEXEC BJEST IAUTCR NCC=54 NAC=36 $ * TABLE  7.6 $
    * INPUT AND NOISE  MODELS NOT OK - CASE 4     $
    MODEL GASOUT=GASIN$
    MODELN Q=(1) MA=(-.8) AVEPA=53.509 $
    MODELI VAR=GASIN LAG=3 NUM=(0) DENOM=(1,2)
           NUMC=(-.53) DENOMC=(.6,.2)$
    MODELPRE VAR=GASIN P=(1,2,3) AR=(1.97494,-1.3732,.3424)
           AVEPA=-.061 $
    B34SEEND$
==
```

The B34S setup to run this problem is given in Table 7.2. The

Box-Jenkins (1976, 532-533) gas furnace data have not been listed to save space. Other problems using this data are used in chapter 8. The first call to BJEST estimated the prewhitening model for GASIN suggested by Box and Jenkins. The model used was

$$(1- \Phi_1 B- \Phi_2 B^2 - \Phi_3 B^3)GASIN + \mu = e_t. \qquad (7.3-5)$$

The autocorrelation function (ACF) of the residuals and the ACF of the left-hand[12] cross correlations for cases 1 through 4 are given in Tables 7.3 through 7.6.

The results for case 1, listed in Table 7.3, show white noise for the ACF of the residuals and white noise for the ACF of the cross correlations. H(2) = 5.401 and is not significant. The cross correlations, which are not shown, show that the input model is correct. These results illustrate a correct model. The results for case 2, which has a defective input model, are shown in Table 7.4. In this case the noise model is correct and the ACF of the residuals is white noise. There is nothing to reflect into the cross correlations and they can be interpreted directly. This illustrates proposition 1. Information on how to correct the input model is contained in the cross correlations of the residual and the prewhitened input series. The fact that the two ACFs are different is shown by H(2)=6.77 being significant at the 5% level in Table 7.4. Visual inspection of the two AFCs shows that they are both quite clean, as would be expected.

The results for case 3, which contains a correct input model and an incorrect noise model, are shown in Table 7.5. This is an example of proposition 2. Here there is marked autocorrelation in the noise ACF. We note a similar pattern in the ACF of the cross correlations as the theory predicts. H(6) = 9.76 and is not significant. In this situation the correct action is to fix the noise model. As in the preceding case, since there was only one thing wrong with the model, the usual tests would indicate how to correct it. The additional proposed test just confirms this decision.

Case 4 has problems in both the noise model and the input model. The ACF of the residuals listed in Table 7.6 is not clean and is visually the same as that of the cross correlations. H(4) = 5.55 and is not significant, suggesting that some of the information contained in the ACF of the cross correlations is coming from the noise side. In this situation it is usually best to attempt to clean up the noise ACF and get to case 2 before working on the input model. In multiple-input models, it is most important to work on cleaning up the noise before working on adjusting the input model since many of the spikes in the cross correlations are due to the cross correlations being influenced by the incorrect noise rather than by specific terms having to be added to the input model.

Table 7.3   ACF of Residuals and Cross Correlations for Case 1

ACF Residuals (Case 1)

1- 12	0.02	0.06	-0.07	-0.06	-0.05	0.12	0.03	0.03	-0.08	0.05	0.02	0.10
ST.E.	0.06	0.06	0.06	0.06	0.06	0.06	0.06	0.06	0.06	0.06	0.06	0.06
MOD. Q	0.2	1.1	2.7	3.6	4.4	8.9	9.2	9.5	11.6	12.4	12.5	15.5
13- 24	-0.04	0.05	-0.09	-0.01	-0.08	0.00	-0.12	0.00	-0.01	0.08	0.02	-0.01
ST.E.	0.06	0.06	0.06	0.06	0.06	0.06	0.06	0.06	0.06	0.06	0.06	0.06
MOD. Q	16.0	16.8	19.4	19.4	21.3	21.3	25.6	25.6	25.6	27.4	27.5	27.6
25- 36	0.04	-0.02	0.02	0.09	-0.12	0.06	-0.02	-0.05	0.11	0.02	0.03	0.06
ST.E.	0.06	0.06	0.06	0.06	0.07	0.07	0.07	0.07	0.07	0.07	0.07	0.07
MOD. Q	28.0	28.1	28.2	31.0	35.7	37.0	37.2	38.1	42.3	42.4	42.7	43.9

ACF Left-Hand Cross Correlations (Case 1)

1- 12	0.11	-0.08	-0.03	-0.40	-0.06	0.21	-0.08	-0.01	0.02	-0.01	0.25	0.06
ST.E.	0.13	0.14	0.14	0.14	0.16	0.16	0.16	0.16	0.16	0.16	0.16	0.17
MOD. Q	0.7	1.2	1.2	10.8	11.0	13.8	14.2	14.2	14.2	14.2	18.5	18.7
13- 24	-0.09	-0.05	-0.27	-0.10	0.09	-0.24	-0.07	0.06	-0.11	0.22	0.15	-0.08
ST.E.	0.17	0.17	0.17	0.18	0.18	0.18	0.19	0.19	0.19	0.19	0.19	0.19
MOD. Q	19.3	19.5	25.2	26.0	26.7	31.5	32.0	32.3	33.3	38.0	40.3	41.0
25- 27	-0.03	-0.16	-0.07									
ST.E.	0.20	0.20	0.20									
MOD. Q	41.1	43.8	44.3									

H(2) = 5.401

Both input and noise models are correct. Q is the Ljung and Box (1978) statistic. The input series GASIN was filtered by the AR(3) model suggested by Box and Jenkins (1976, 381). Fifty-four cross correlations were calculated between the prewhitened input series and the residuals. These have not been listed to save space. Only the ACF of the left-hand cross correlations have been reported, since feedback in the model is not at issue. H(i) is a chi-square statistic with i degrees of freedom and tests whether or not the significant (2 SEs in absolute value) autocorrelation coefficients are significantly different. The B34S printout gives the H( ) statistic for all terms, those elements greater in absolute value than 2 * SE (either or both terms) and those greater in value than 1 * SE (either or both terms).

Table 7.4   ACF of Residuals and Cross Correlations for   Case 2

ACF Residuals (Case 2)

1- 12	0.04	0.05	-0.09	-0.08	-0.04	0.14	0.04	0.05	-0.10	0.03	0.03	0.09
ST.E.	0.06	0.06	0.06	0.06	0.06	0.06	0.06	0.06	0.06	0.06	0.06	0.06
MOD. Q	0.5	1.2	3.6	5.6	6.0	12.1	12.7	13.4	16.3	16.5	16.8	19.4
13- 24	-0.03	0.06	-0.11	0.00	-0.06	-0.01	-0.12	-0.01	-0.01	0.09	0.01	-0.03
ST.E.	0.06	0.06	0.06	0.06	0.06	0.06	0.06	0.06	0.06	0.06	0.06	0.06
MOD. Q	19.7	20.9	24.5	24.5	25.5	25.6	29.8	29.8	29.8	32.4	32.5	32.8
25- 36	0.04	-0.05	0.02	0.11	-0.09	0.08	-0.05	-0.08	0.11	0.04	0.05	0.08
ST.E.	0.06	0.06	0.06	0.06	0.07	0.07	0.07	0.07	0.07	0.07	0.07	0.07
MOD. Q	33.4	34.1	34.2	38.4	40.9	42.8	43.5	45.7	49.6	50.2	51.1	53.3

ACF Left-Hand Cross Correlations (Case 2)

1- 12	0.10	-0.09	-0.07	-0.46	0.05	0.27	0.02	0.11	-0.06	-0.13	0.14	-0.03
ST.E.	0.13	0.14	0.14	0.14	0.16	0.16	0.17	0.17	0.17	0.17	0.17	0.18
MOD. Q	0.6	1.1	1.3	14.2	14.3	19.0	19.0	19.9	20.1	21.3	22.8	22.9
13- 24	-0.06	0.06	-0.26	-0.05	0.10	-0.24	-0.03	-0.01	-0.14	0.20	0.06	-0.09
ST.E.	0.18	0.18	0.18	0.18	0.19	0.19	0.19	0.19	0.19	0.19	0.20	0.20
MOD. Q	23.2	23.5	28.9	29.0	29.9	35.0	35.1	35.1	37.0	40.9	41.2	42.1
25- 27	0.05	-0.25	-0.06									
ST.E.	0.20	0.20	0.20									
MOD. Q	42.3	49.1	49.6									

H(2)=6.77

Noise model is correct and input model is not correct.

Table 7.5   ACF of Residuals and Cross Correlations for   Case 3

ACF Residuals (Case 3)

1- 12	0.69	0.72	0.37	0.36	0.09	0.14	-0.05	0.04	-0.10	0.02	-0.07	0.03
ST.E.	0.06	0.08	0.10	0.11	0.11	0.11	0.11	0.11	0.11	0.11	0.11	0.11
MOD. Q	141.0	292.6	332.3	370.0	372.5	378.6	379.3	379.7	382.5	382.6	384.0	384.4
13- 24	-0.09	-0.03	-0.16	-0.11	-0.21	-0.14	-0.18	-0.06	-0.06	0.06	0.06	0.13
ST.E.	0.11	0.11	0.11	0.11	0.11	0.11	0.11	0.12	0.12	0.12	0.12	0.12
MOD. Q	386.7	386.9	394.9	398.6	411.9	417.7	427.8	429.1	430.0	431.1	432.3	437.7
25- 36	0.11	0.15	0.10	0.11	0.02	0.00	-0.04	-0.01	0.03	0.07	0.07	0.07
ST.E.	0.12	0.12	0.12	0.12	0.12	0.12	0.12	0.12	0.12	0.12	0.12	0.12
MOD. Q	441.6	448.4	451.9	455.5	455.6	455.6	456.2	456.3	456.5	458.1	459.6	461.1

ACF Left-Hand Cross Correlations (Case 3)

1- 12	0.70	0.42	0.10	-0.03	-0.05	0.01	-0.07	-0.09	-0.11	-0.02	0.07	0.04
ST.E.	0.13	0.19	0.21	0.21	0.21	0.21	0.21	0.21	0.21	0.21	0.21	0.21
MOD. Q	28.7	39.2	39.8	39.8	40.0	40.0	40.3	40.8	41.6	41.6	41.9	42.1
13- 24	-0.11	-0.29	-0.47	-0.47	-0.40	-0.33	-0.20	-0.06	0.06	0.20	0.19	0.10
ST.E.	0.21	0.21	0.22	0.24	0.25	0.26	0.27	0.27	0.27	0.27	0.28	0.28
MOD. Q	42.9	49.3	66.4	84.4	97.6	106.9	110.5	110.9	111.3	115.3	118.6	119.7
25- 27	0.01	-0.01	0.01									
ST.E.	0.28	0.28	0.28									
MOD. Q	119.7	119.7	119.8									

H(6)=9.76

Input model is correct and noise model is not correct

Table 7.6   ACF of Residuals and Cross Correlations for   Case 4

ACF Residuals (Case 4)

1- 12	0.69	0.71	0.36	0.35	0.10	0.15	-0.04	0.04	-0.10	0.01	-0.07	0.03
ST.E.	0.06	0.08	0.10	0.11	0.11	0.11	0.11	0.11	0.11	0.11	0.11	0.11
MOD. Q	142.6	293.3	332.7	370.1	372.9	379.7	380.2	380.7	383.5	383.6	385.1	385.4
13- 24	-0.09	-0.03	-0.16	-0.11	-0.20	-0.13	-0.18	-0.07	-0.06	0.05	0.05	0.12
ST.E.	0.11	0.11	0.11	0.11	0.11	0.11	0.11	0.11	0.11	0.12	0.12	0.12
MOD. Q	387.8	388.0	395.7	399.2	412.0	417.7	427.7	429.2	430.4	431.2	432.0	436.6
25- 36	0.11	0.14	0.11	0.11	0.03	0.01	-0.04	-0.02	0.03	0.08	0.08	0.08
ST.E.	0.12	0.12	0.12	0.12	0.12	0.12	0.12	0.12	0.12	0.12	0.12	0.12
MOD. Q	440.2	446.8	450.6	454.9	455.2	455.2	455.8	455.9	456.2	458.2	460.3	462.7

ACF Left Hand Cross Correlations (Case 4)

1- 12	0.70	0.42	0.11	0.01	0.05	0.12	0.03	-0.03	-0.13	-0.10	-0.03	-0.04
ST.E.	0.13	0.19	0.21	0.21	0.21	0.21	0.21	0.21	0.21	0.21	0.21	0.21
MOD. Q	28.2	38.6	39.4	39.4	39.5	40.5	40.5	40.6	41.7	42.3	42.4	42.6
13- 24	-0.15	-0.27	-0.43	-0.42	-0.37	-0.34	-0.25	-0.15	-0.04	0.10	0.09	0.04
ST.E.	0.21	0.21	0.22	0.23	0.25	0.26	0.26	0.27	0.27	0.27	0.27	0.27
MOD. Q	44.3	49.7	63.9	77.8	89.1	98.8	104.0	105.9	106.1	107.0	107.8	107.9
25- 27	-0.01	0.00	0.05									
ST.E.	0.27	0.27	0.27									
MOD. Q	107.9	107.9	108.1									

H(4)=5.44

Both input and noise models are not correct.

The preceding examples illustrate that in practice, after first-round estimation of a transfer function it is often difficult to determine whether to change the input model or the noise model when the usual autocorrelation and cross correlation tests suggest the possibility of problems in both models. A second-round diagnostic test procedure can be easily incorporated into a time series computer program and will provide an additional test to help detect spurious cross correlations and avoid false signals for inadequacies in the input model. Its use will significantly speed up fine tuning of a transfer function model, once the first-round identification has been done, using the Liu-Hanssens (1982) or another appropriate procedure.

7.4 Spectral Analysis

The BJIDEN and BJEST spectral options are based on a heavily modified version of the IMSL FORTRAN routine FTFREQ, which was available in the now obsolete IMSL version 8. For complex spectral analysis it is suggested that the user transfer data to SAS and use the SAS/ETS PROC SPECTRA.[13] The SPECTRAL sentence, supported in the BJIDEN and BJEST commands, facilitates the display of the information in the cross correlation function in the frequency domain. The user inputs the number of frequencies calculated (NFREQ option), which defaults to the number of cross correlations, whether to detrend the series (DETREND option), the time interval (XINDSP1 option), and whether to prewhiten all the series with an AR1 model having a coefficient set by the XINDSP2 option. If the SPECTRAL sentence is <u>not</u> present, but the SPECTRAL option is given on the BJEST sentence or the RCROSS or PCROSS sentences of the BJIDEN command, the default options are used.

Frequency is defined as f_i, where

$$f_i = (i-1) / (2.0 * XINDSP1 * NFREQ) \text{ for } i=1,\ldots,NFREQ+1. \quad (7.4-1)$$

The unsmoothed power spectrum of the input series X at frequency f_i, $PS_x(i)$, is defined as

$$PS_x(i) = [2.0*XINDSP1/\pi]*[[\gamma_x(0)/2]+[\Sigma_{j=1}^m(\gamma_x(j) \, COS((I-1)*j\pi/(m+1)))]]$$

$$+ \gamma_x(m+1) \, COS((i-1)*\pi)/2.0], \quad (7.4-2)$$

where $\gamma_x(k)$ is the covariance of series x_t at lag k and m=NFREQ −1. The power spectrum is smoothed by a Hamming window. Similarly, the power spectrum of y_t, $PS_y(i)$, the cospectrum between x_t and y_t at frequency f_i $CS_{xy}(i)$ (real part of the cross spectrum) and the quadrature spectrum $QS_{xy}(i)$ (imaginary part of the cross spectrum) can be calculated from the cross covariance function for x_t and y_t (Jenkins and Watts 1968, 344). The amplitude at frequency f_i of x_t and y_t $A_{xy}(i)$ is defined as

$$A_{xy}(i) = \sqrt{[(CS_{xy}(i))^2 + (QS_{xy}(i))^2]}, \quad (7.4-3)$$

while the phase $PH_{xy}(i)$ is

$$PH_{xy}(i) = [ARCTAN\ (QS_{xy}(i)\ /\ CS_{xy}(i))]/\pi^2 \qquad (7.4-4)$$

if $CS_{xy}(i)$ is > 0.0 and

$$PH_{xy}(i) = [[ARCTAN\ (QS_{xy}(i)\ /\ CS_{xy}(i))] + \pi]/\pi^2 \qquad (7.4-5)$$

if $CS_{xy}(i) < 0.0$. If $CS_{xy}(i) = 0.0$ and $QS_{xy}(i) > 0$, then $PH_{xy}(i)$ is set to .25, while if $CS_{xy}(i)$ and $QS_{xy}(i) < 0$, $PH_{xy}(i)$ is set to .75. If $PH_{xy}(i)$ is found to be < 0.0, then 1.0 is added to the reported value. The coherence squared at frequency f_i, $K_{xy}(i)$, becomes

$$K_{xy}(i) = [A_{xy}(i)]^2\ /[PS_x(i)\ PS_y(i)]. \qquad (7.4-6)$$

An estimate of the transfer function amplitude from x_t to y_t at frequency f_i, $T_{xy}(i)$, is

$$T_{xy}(i) = A_{xy}(i)\ /\ PS_x(i), \qquad (7.4-7)$$

while an estimate of the transfer function amplitude from y to x at frequency f_i is

$$T_{yx}(i) = A_{xy}(i)\ /\ PS_y(i). \qquad (7.4-8)$$

The values given in equations (7.4-1) through (7.4-8) are listed and can be optionally plotted. They are especially useful in detecting the effects of prewhitening on the information in the cross correlation. The coherence squared, $K_{xy}(i)$, can be interpreted as a correlation coefficient <u>at each frequency</u> f_i. The transfer function amplitude, $T_{xy}(i)$, measures the amplitude of the mapping of x_t to y_t at frequency i <u>implicit</u> in the impulse-response function, $V(B)$.

7.5 Examples

Table 7.7 lists the data loading and BJIDEN and BJEST commands to produce output that will replicate the Stokes and Neuburger (1979) study of the effect of money on interest rates. The B34S DATA command loads and builds real and nominal M1 and M2 and a variety of interest rates. The data set RES79 is distributed with the B34S system to facilitate replication of the basic paper and investigation of ARIMA and transfer function model building. Due to space limitations, the data are <u>not</u> listed in Table 7.7, although the specific series studied in the example are listed in compressed form in Tables 7.8 and 7.9. The BJIDEN and BJEST commands produce voluminous output, only a fraction of which is shown in this book.

Table 7.7 Program to Estimate the Effect of M2 on Interest Rates


```
==RES79
B34SEXEC DATA NOOB=373  MAXLAG=1
 HEADING=('STOKES/NEUBURGER RES 79')  $
* DATA FROM NBER DATA BANK. USED IN STOKES / NEUBURGER RES 79 $
DATACARDS$
 1.095E+02 1.428E+02 2.540E+00 1.000E+00 6.440E+01 3.800E-01 3.750E-01
        .        .        .        .        .        .
        .        .        .        .        .        .
 3.374E+02 8.883E+02 8.700E+00 6.790E+00 1.869E+02 6.440E+00 6.448E+00
B34SRETURN$
*  END OF 373 OBS ON STOKES / NEUBURGER RES79 DSN    $
INPUT FMS FMSCOM FYAAC FYCP PC FYGM3 FYGN3 $
*  NOW BUILD DATA AND GIVE VARIABLE DESCRIPTIONS $
*  RAW DATA FROM JAN 1947 - JAN 1978 $
* FMS    = MONEY STOCK M1 : FRIEDMAN $
* FMSCOM = MONEY STOCK M2 : FRIEDMAN $
* FYAAC  = MONETARY RATES : AA NEW CORPORATE BOND $
* FYCP   = MONETARY RATES : COMMERCIAL PAPER $
* PC     = CONSUMER PRICE INDEX : ALL ITEMS $
* FYGM3  = MARKET YIELD ON 3 MONTH TREASURY $
* FYGN3  = NEW ISSUE RATE ON 3 MONTH TR $
* M1DP   = M1 / PC $
* M2DP   = M2 / PC $
* PCM1   = PERCENT CHANGE M1 $
* PCM2   = PERCENT CHANGE M2 $
* PCRM1  = PERCENT CHANGE REAL M1 $
* PCRM2  = PERCENT CHANGE REAL M2 $
* PCAA   = PERCENT CHANGE AA CORP RATE $
* PCCPIN = PERCENT CHANGE COMMERCIAL PAPER $
* PCCMYTB= PERCENT CHANGE THREE MONTH TREASURY $
* PCCNYTB= PERCENT CHANGE THREE MONTH NEW ISSUES $
BUILD M1DP M2DP PCM1 PCM2 PCRM1 PCRM2 PCAA PCCPIN PCCMYTB PCCNYTB $
GEN M1DP=DIV(FMS,PC)$
GEN M2DP=DIV(FMSCOM,PC)$
GEN PCM1=LAG(FMS)$ GEN PCM1=DIV(FMS,PCM1)$
        GEN PCM1=ADD(PCM1,-1.0)$
GEN PCM2=LAG(FMSCOM)$ GEN PCM2=DIV(FMSCOM,PCM2)$
        GEN PCM2=ADD(PCM2,-1.0)$
GEN PCRM1=LAG(M1DP)$ GEN PCRM1=DIV(M1DP,PCRM1)$
        GEN PCRM1=ADD(PCRM1,-1.0)$
GEN PCRM2=LAG(M2DP)$ GEN PCRM2=DIV(M2DP,PCRM2)$
        GEN PCRM2=ADD(PCRM2,-1.0)$
GEN PCAA=LAG(FYAAC)$ GEN PCAA=DIV(FYAAC,PCAA)$
        GEN PCAA=ADD(PCAA,-1.0)$
GEN PCCPIN=LAG(FYCP)$ GEN PCCPIN=DIV(FYCP,PCCPIN)$
        GEN PCCPIN=ADD(PCCPIN,-1.0)$
GEN PCCMYTB=LAG(FYGM3)$ GEN PCCMYTB=DIV(FYGM3,PCCMYTB)$
        GEN PCCMYTB=ADD(PCCMYTB,-1.0)$
GEN PCCNYTB=LAG(FYGN3)$ GEN PCCNYTB=DIV(FYGN3,PCCNYTB)$
        GEN PCCNYTB=ADD(PCCNYTB,-1.0)$
B34SEEND$

/$    RUNNING THE CHANGES IN NOMINAL M2 ON COMMERCIAL PAPER
/$    RES TABLE 5 AND PREWHITENING MODELS TABLE 1
/$    FIRST LOOK AT ACF'S OF BOTH SERIES OF INTEREST

B34SEXEC BJIDEN LIST=(FMSCOM,FYCP) NAC=24$
VAR FMSCOM FYCP$
TITLE=('IDENTIFY RES79 TABLE 1 MODELS: DATES FEB 1947 - JAN 1978')$
SERIESN VAR=FMSCOM NAME=('MONEY STOCK M2 FRIEDMAN')$
SERIESN VAR=FYCP NAME=('COMMERCIAL PAPER INTEREST RATE')$
RTRANS VAR=FMSCOM DIF=(2,1)(1,12)$
RAUTO FMSCOM FYCP$
B34SEEND$
```

```
/$ NOW WE ESTIMATE THE M2 MODEL PREWHITENING FILTER

B34SEXEC BJEST  NAC=24 $
MODEL FMSCOM $
TITLE=('IDENTIFY RES79 TABLE 1 MODELS: DATES FEB 1947 - JAN 1978')$
SERIESN VAR=FMSCOM NAME=('MONEY STOCK M2 FRIEDMAN')$
MODELN P=(1,2) Q=(3,4,7) DIF=(2,1)$
* TRY A FEW FORECASTS $ FORECAST NF=10 NT=372$ B34SEEND$

/$ NOW WE DO THE CROSS CORRELATIONS

B34SEXEC BJIDEN TYPE=TRANSI NIRW=24 IAUTCR $
VAR FMSCOM FYCP$
TITLE=('IDENTIFY RES79 TABLE 1 MODELS: DATES FEB 1947 - JAN 1978')$
SERIESN VAR=FMSCOM NAME=('MONEY STOCK M2 FRIEDMAN')$
SERIESN VAR=FYCP NAME=('COMMERCIAL PAPER INTEREST RATE')$
PCROSS=(FMSCOM FYCP) SPECTRAL$
MODELPRE VAR=FMSCOM DIF=(2,1) P=(1,2) AR=(-.46005,-.45503)
  Q=(3,4,7) MA=(.16193,.13687,.29612) $
OUTPUT DIF=(1,1)$
B34SEEND$

/$ NOW WE ESTIMATE THE FINAL MODEL REPORTED IN TABLE 5
/$ DEFAULT STARTING VALUES

B34SEXEC BJEST $
MODEL FYCP= FMSCOM$
TITLE=('IDENTIFY RES79 TABLE 1 MODELS: DATES FEB 1947 - JAN 1978')$
SERIESN VAR=FMSCOM NAME=('MONEY STOCK M2 FRIEDMAN')$
SERIESN VAR=FYCP NAME=('COMMERCIAL PAPER INTEREST RATE')$
MODELN P=(1)(12) Q=(2,6,14,20) $
MODELI VAR=FMSCOM NUM=(0,3,4,9,16,23) DENOM=(1)(12) DIF=(2,1)$
MODELPRE VAR=FMSCOM DIF=(2,1) P=(1,2) AR=(-.46005,-.45503)
  Q=(3,4,7) MA=(.16193,.13687,.29612) $
OUTPUT DIF=(1,1) $
B34SEEND$

/$ NOW WE ESTIMATE THE FINAL MODEL REPORTED IN TABLE 5
/$ USE RES79 STARTING VALUES TO SEE EFFECT

B34SEXEC BJEST $
MODEL  FYCP= FMSCOM$
TITLE=('IDENTIFY RES79 TABLE 1 MODELS: DATES FEB 1947 - JAN 1978')$
SERIESN VAR=FMSCOM NAME=('MONEY STOCK M2 FRIEDMAN')$
SERIESN VAR=FYCP NAME=('COMMERCIAL PAPER INTEREST RATE')$
MODELN P=(1)(12) Q=(2,6,14,20) AR=(.5)(.23) MA=(.1,.2,.3,-.2)$
MODELI VAR=FMSCOM NUM=(0,3,4,9,16,23) DENOM=(1)(12) DIF=(2,1)
  DENOMC=(.54)(.68) NUMC=(-.03,.01,.02,.01,-.01,-.05)$
MODELPRE VAR=FMSCOM DIF=(2,1) P=(1,2) AR=(-.46005,-.45503)
  Q=(3,4,7) MA=(.16193,.13687,.29612) $
OUTPUT DIF=(1,1) $
B34SEEND$
==
```

Table 7.8 Data on M2

VAR=FMSCOM   MONEY STOCK M2 FRIEDMAN

LISTING OF OBSERVED SERIES

Index	1	2	3	4	5	6	7	8
1– 8	0.14320E+03	0.14390E+03	0.14480E+03	0.14550E+03	0.14600E+03	0.14620E+03	0.14700E+03	0.14770E+03
9– 16	0.14790E+03	0.14850E+03	0.14850E+03	0.14890E+03	0.14890E+03	0.14830E+03	0.14800E+03	0.14780E+03
17– 24	0.14780E+03	0.14800E+03	0.14820E+03	0.14810E+03	0.14800E+03	0.14780E+03	0.14750E+03	0.14730E+03
25– 32	0.14730E+03	0.14730E+03	0.14750E+03	0.14780E+03	0.14770E+03	0.14760E+03	0.14740E+03	0.14730E+03
33– 40	0.14730E+03	0.14740E+03	0.14760E+03	0.14790E+03	0.14870E+03	0.14910E+03	0.14990E+03	0.15060E+03
41– 48	0.15100E+03	0.15140E+03	0.15170E+03	0.15180E+03	0.15220E+03	0.15250E+03	0.15290E+03	0.15340E+03
49– 56	0.15370E+03	0.15420E+03	0.15450E+03	0.15500E+03	0.15550E+03	0.15630E+03	0.15700E+03	0.15810E+03
57– 64	0.15880E+03	0.16000E+03	0.16090E+03	0.16150E+03	0.16230E+03	0.16270E+03	0.16320E+03	0.16380E+03
65– 72	0.16450E+03	0.16500E+03	0.16570E+03	0.16670E+03	0.16720E+03	0.16800E+03	0.16850E+03	0.16870E+03
73– 80	0.16900E+03	0.16990E+03	0.17040E+03	0.17090E+03	0.17110E+03	0.17150E+03	0.17190E+03	0.17210E+03
81– 88	0.17260E+03	0.17290E+03	0.17330E+03	0.17380E+03	0.17430E+03	0.17480E+03	0.17470E+03	0.17620E+03
89– 96	0.17670E+03	0.17760E+03	0.17850E+03	0.17880E+03	0.17960E+03	0.18030E+03	0.18060E+03	0.18150E+03
97– 104	0.18260E+03	0.18240E+03	0.18290E+03	0.18360E+03	0.18360E+03	0.18410E+03	0.18410E+03	0.18460E+03
105– 112	0.18490E+03	0.18480E+03	0.18520E+03	0.18540E+03	0.18540E+03	0.18580E+03	0.18630E+03	0.18620E+03
113– 120	0.18670E+03	0.18690E+03	0.18690E+03	0.18770E+03	0.18790E+03	0.18840E+03	0.18880E+03	0.18950E+03
121– 128	0.18990E+03	0.19060E+03	0.19090E+03	0.19150E+03	0.19170E+03	0.19230E+03	0.19280E+03	0.19290E+03
129– 136	0.19310E+03	0.19330E+03	0.19330E+03	0.19310E+03	0.19540E+03	0.19700E+03	0.19850E+03	0.19980E+03
137– 144	0.20160E+03	0.20240E+03	0.20370E+03	0.20430E+03	0.20500E+03	0.20610E+03	0.20650E+03	0.20850E+03
145– 152	0.20860E+03	0.20920E+03	0.20990E+03	0.21060E+03	0.21070E+03	0.20970E+03	0.21030E+03	0.21010E+03
153– 160	0.21100E+03	0.21120E+03	0.21090E+03	0.21070E+03	0.21470E+03	0.21560E+03	0.21650E+03	0.21710E+03
161– 168	0.21060E+03	0.21210E+03	0.21350E+03	0.22180E+03	0.22340E+03	0.22450E+03	0.22560E+03	0.22670E+03
169– 176	0.21970E+03	0.22050E+03	0.22180E+03	0.22340E+03	0.23490E+03	0.23690E+03	0.23870E+03	0.23940E+03
177– 184	0.22920E+03	0.23070E+03	0.23140E+03	0.23320E+03	0.23490E+03	0.24690E+03	0.24850E+03	0.25070E+03
185– 192	0.24060E+03	0.24150E+03	0.24210E+03	0.24310E+03	0.24500E+03	0.24690E+03	0.26180E+03	0.26340E+03
193– 200	0.25200E+03	0.25360E+03	0.25540E+03	0.26850E+03	0.27030E+03	0.27190E+03	0.27430E+03	0.27650E+03
201– 208	0.26550E+03	0.26820E+03	0.27030E+03	0.27190E+03	0.28450E+03	0.28640E+03	0.28990E+03	0.29290E+03
209– 216	0.27840E+03	0.28030E+03	0.28210E+03	0.28450E+03	0.30030E+03	0.30290E+03	0.30710E+03	0.31010E+03
217– 224	0.29520E+03	0.29700E+03	0.29870E+03	0.30030E+03	0.32050E+03	0.32200E+03	0.32730E+03	0.33290E+03
225– 232	0.31340E+03	0.31570E+03	0.31770E+03	0.32050E+03	0.33330E+03	0.33250E+03	0.33360E+03	0.33690E+03
233– 240	0.33000E+03	0.33100E+03	0.33180E+03	0.33330E+03	0.35540E+03	0.35800E+03	0.36120E+03	0.36410E+03
241– 248	0.34140E+03	0.34490E+03	0.34640E+03	0.35040E+03	0.37240E+03	0.37500E+03	0.37850E+03	0.38120E+03
249– 256	0.36650E+03	0.36860E+03	0.37050E+03	0.37240E+03	0.39470E+03	0.39840E+03	0.40280E+03	0.40660E+03
257– 264	0.38380E+03	0.38680E+03	0.39090E+03	0.39470E+03	0.40800E+03	0.40810E+03	0.40280E+03	0.40260E+03
265– 272	0.40680E+03	0.40710E+03	0.40780E+03	0.40800E+03	0.40350E+03	0.43540E+03	0.41100E+03	0.41350E+03
273– 280	0.40240E+03	0.40330E+03	0.40330E+03	0.47340E+03	0.40350E+03	0.43950E+03	0.44380E+03	0.45480E+03
281– 288	0.41580E+03	0.42250E+03	0.42930E+03	0.43540E+03	0.47900E+03	0.48380E+03	0.48710E+03	0.49270E+03
289– 296	0.46240E+03	0.46920E+03	0.47340E+03	0.47340E+03	0.51040E+03	0.51630E+03	0.52490E+03	0.52960E+03
297– 304	0.49700E+03	0.50080E+03	0.50500E+03	0.51040E+03	0.55170E+03	0.55670E+03	0.56880E+03	0.57500E+03
305– 312	0.53460E+03	0.53990E+03	0.54610E+03	0.59580E+03	0.60320E+03	0.60840E+03	0.62090E+03	0.62350E+03
313– 320	0.58200E+03	0.58940E+03	0.63030E+03	0.63440E+03	0.64150E+03	0.64860E+03	0.66180E+03	0.66880E+03
321– 328	0.62610E+03	0.63030E+03	0.63440E+03	0.68590E+03	0.68830E+03	0.69340E+03	0.70140E+03	0.70660E+03
329– 336	0.67500E+03	0.68100E+03	0.68590E+03	0.71310E+03	0.71460E+03	0.71190E+03	0.72990E+03	0.73280E+03
337– 344	0.71040E+03	0.71310E+03	0.71460E+03	0.74410E+03	0.74650E+03	0.74870E+03	0.76180E+03	0.76430E+03
345– 352	0.73710E+03	0.74410E+03	0.77410E+03	0.77540E+03	0.77940E+03	0.78820E+03	0.80350E+03	0.80930E+03
353– 360	0.76840E+03	0.77410E+03	0.81820E+03	0.82620E+03	0.82990E+03	0.83680E+03	0.84630E+03	0.85090E+03
361– 368	0.81400E+03	0.81820E+03	0.82620E+03	0.82990E+03	0.83680E+03	0.84630E+03	0.85090E+03	0.85620E+03
369– 372	0.86590E+03	0.87350E+03	0.88120E+03	0.88830E+03				

Table 7.9 Data on the Commercial Paper Interest Rates

VAR=FYCP   COMMERCIAL PAPER INTEREST RATE

LISTING OF OBSERVED SERIES

1- 8	0.10000E+01	0.10000E+01	0.10000E+01	0.10000E+01	0.10000E+01	0.10000E+01	0.10000E+01	0.10200E+01
9- 16	0.10600E+01	0.11000E+01	0.12200E+01	0.13000E+01	0.13800E+01	0.13800E+01	0.13800E+01	0.13800E+01
17- 24	0.13800E+01	0.13800E+01	0.14700E+01	0.15400E+01	0.15600E+01	0.15600E+01	0.15600E+01	0.15600E+01
25- 32	0.15600E+01	0.15600E+01	0.15600E+01	0.15600E+01	0.15600E+01	0.15600E+01	0.14300E+01	0.13800E+01
33- 40	0.13800E+01	0.13800E+01	0.13300E+01	0.13100E+01	0.13100E+01	0.13100E+01	0.13100E+01	0.13100E+01
41- 48	0.13100E+01	0.13100E+01	0.14200E+01	0.16500E+01	0.17200E+01	0.16900E+01	0.17200E+01	0.18600E+01
49- 56	0.19600E+01	0.20400E+01	0.21100E+01	0.21600E+01	0.23100E+01	0.23100E+01	0.22600E+01	0.21900E+01
57- 64	0.22200E+01	0.22500E+01	0.23000E+01	0.23800E+01	0.23800E+01	0.23800E+01	0.23500E+01	0.23100E+01
65- 72	0.23100E+01	0.23100E+01	0.23100E+01	0.23100E+01	0.23100E+01	0.23100E+01	0.23100E+01	0.23100E+01
73- 80	0.23100E+01	0.23600E+01	0.24400E+01	0.26700E+01	0.27500E+01	0.27500E+01	0.27500E+01	0.27400E+01
81- 88	0.25500E+01	0.23100E+01	0.22500E+01	0.21100E+01	0.20000E+01	0.20000E+01	0.17600E+01	0.15800E+01
89- 96	0.15600E+01	0.14500E+01	0.13300E+01	0.13100E+01	0.13100E+01	0.13100E+01	0.13100E+01	0.14700E+01
97- 104	0.16800E+01	0.16900E+01	0.19000E+01	0.20000E+01	0.20000E+01	0.21100E+01	0.23300E+01	0.25400E+01
105- 112	0.27000E+01	0.28100E+01	0.29900E+01	0.30000E+01	0.30000E+01	0.30000E+01	0.31400E+01	0.32700E+01
113- 120	0.33800E+01	0.32700E+01	0.32800E+01	0.35000E+01	0.36300E+01	0.36300E+01	0.36300E+01	0.36300E+01
121- 128	0.36300E+01	0.36300E+01	0.36300E+01	0.36300E+01	0.37900E+01	0.38800E+01	0.39800E+01	0.40000E+01
129- 136	0.41000E+01	0.40700E+01	0.38100E+01	0.34900E+01	0.26300E+01	0.23300E+01	0.19000E+01	0.17100E+01
137- 144	0.15400E+01	0.15000E+01	0.19600E+01	0.29300E+01	0.32300E+01	0.30800E+01	0.33300E+01	0.33000E+01
145- 152	0.32600E+01	0.33500E+01	0.34200E+01	0.35600E+01	0.38300E+01	0.39800E+01	0.39700E+01	0.46300E+01
153- 160	0.47300E+01	0.46700E+01	0.48800E+01	0.49100E+01	0.46600E+01	0.44900E+01	0.41600E+01	0.42500E+01
161- 168	0.38100E+01	0.33900E+01	0.33400E+01	0.33900E+01	0.33000E+01	0.32800E+01	0.32300E+01	0.29800E+01
169- 176	0.30300E+01	0.30300E+01	0.29100E+01	0.27600E+01	0.29100E+01	0.27200E+01	0.29200E+01	0.30500E+01
177- 184	0.30000E+01	0.29800E+01	0.31900E+01	0.32600E+01	0.32200E+01	0.32500E+01	0.32000E+01	0.31600E+01
185- 192	0.32500E+01	0.33600E+01	0.33000E+01	0.33400E+01	0.32700E+01	0.32300E+01	0.32900E+01	0.33400E+01
193- 200	0.32500E+01	0.33400E+01	0.33200E+01	0.32500E+01	0.33800E+01	0.34900E+01	0.37200E+01	0.38800E+01
201- 208	0.38800E+01	0.38800E+01	0.39600E+01	0.39700E+01	0.38800E+01	0.40000E+01	0.39100E+01	0.38900E+01
209- 216	0.40000E+01	0.39600E+01	0.38800E+01	0.38900E+01	0.40000E+01	0.40200E+01	0.41700E+01	0.42500E+01
217- 224	0.42700E+01	0.43800E+01	0.43800E+01	0.43800E+01	0.43800E+01	0.43800E+01	0.43800E+01	0.43800E+01
225- 232	0.43800E+01	0.43800E+01	0.46500E+01	0.48200E+01	0.48800E+01	0.52100E+01	0.53800E+01	0.53900E+01
233- 240	0.55100E+01	0.56300E+01	0.58500E+01	0.58900E+01	0.60000E+01	0.60000E+01	0.60000E+01	0.57300E+01
241- 248	0.53800E+01	0.52400E+01	0.48300E+01	0.46700E+01	0.46500E+01	0.49200E+01	0.50000E+01	0.50000E+01
249- 256	0.50700E+01	0.52800E+01	0.55600E+01	0.56000E+01	0.55000E+01	0.56400E+01	0.58100E+01	0.61800E+01
257- 264	0.62500E+01	0.61900E+01	0.58800E+01	0.58200E+01	0.58000E+01	0.59200E+01	0.61700E+01	0.65300E+01
265- 272	0.66200E+01	0.68200E+01	0.70400E+01	0.73500E+01	0.82300E+01	0.86500E+01	0.83300E+01	0.84800E+01
273- 280	0.85600E+01	0.84600E+01	0.88400E+01	0.87800E+01	0.85500E+01	0.83300E+01	0.80600E+01	0.82300E+01
281- 288	0.82100E+01	0.82900E+01	0.79000E+01	0.73200E+01	0.68500E+01	0.63000E+01	0.57300E+01	0.51100E+01
289- 296	0.44700E+01	0.41900E+01	0.45700E+01	0.51000E+01	0.54500E+01	0.57500E+01	0.57300E+01	0.57500E+01
297- 304	0.55400E+01	0.49200E+01	0.47400E+01	0.40800E+01	0.39300E+01	0.41700E+01	0.45800E+01	0.45100E+01
305- 312	0.46400E+01	0.48500E+01	0.48200E+01	0.51400E+01	0.53000E+01	0.52500E+01	0.54500E+01	0.57800E+01
313- 320	0.62200E+01	0.68500E+01	0.71400E+01	0.72700E+01	0.79900E+01	0.91800E+01	0.10210E+02	0.10230E+02
321- 328	0.89200E+01	0.89400E+01	0.90800E+01	0.86600E+01	0.78300E+01	0.84200E+01	0.97900E+01	0.10620E+02
329- 336	0.10960E+02	0.11720E+02	0.11650E+02	0.11230E+02	0.93600E+01	0.88100E+01	0.89800E+01	0.73000E+01
337- 344	0.63300E+01	0.60600E+01	0.61500E+01	0.58200E+01	0.57900E+01	0.64400E+01	0.67000E+01	0.68600E+01
345- 352	0.64800E+01	0.59100E+01	0.59700E+01	0.52700E+01	0.52300E+01	0.53700E+01	0.52300E+01	0.55400E+01
353- 360	0.59400E+01	0.56700E+01	0.54700E+01	0.54500E+01	0.52200E+01	0.50500E+01	0.47000E+01	0.47400E+01
361- 368	0.48200E+01	0.48700E+01	0.48700E+01	0.53500E+01	0.54900E+01	0.54100E+01	0.58400E+01	0.61700E+01
369- 372	0.65500E+01	0.65900E+01	0.66400E+01	0.67900E+01				

The first call to BJIDEN calculates the ACF and PACF for various transformations of M2 and FYCP. To save space, only the ACF and PACF of M2, (1-B)M2 and (1-B)^{2}M2 are shown. It is clear that second differencing is required since the ACF of (1-B)M2 <u>does not</u> die out. The ACF of (1-B)^{2}FYCP, which is not shown, does show some seasonality at lag 12 (correlation is .32), but because it does not occur at lag 24, seasonal differencing will over difference the series. This is shown in the ACF of (1-B)^2(1-B^{12})FYCP, which was <u>not</u> shown to save space. The model selected was

$$1+.46735B+.45992B^2)(1-B)^2M2 = (1-.16668B^3-.14210B^4-.29737B^7)e_t$$
$$\quad(-9.03)\ (-8.51) \qquad\qquad\qquad (2.86)\quad (2.71)\quad (5.68)$$

RSS = 429.33   RSE = 1.0874   MQ(24) = 24.04,   (7.5-1)

which agrees with the results in Stokes and Neuburger (1979).[14] The output illustrating these results is given next. Output showing forecasting of M2, which is <u>not</u> required in the identification of a transfer function, has not been listed to save space. Note that the ACF of the residuals of the model show white noise, indicating that the ARIMA model listed in equation (7.5-1) is adequate.

AUTOCORRELATION FUNCTION

DATA - VAR=FMSCOM   MONEY STOCK M2 FRIEDMAN   372 OBSERVATIONS

DIFFERENCING - ORIGINAL SERIES IS YOUR DATA.

                DIFFERENCES BELOW ARE OF ORDER   1

ORIGINAL SERIES
MEAN OF THE SERIES =0.33436E+03
ST. DEV. OF SERIES =0.20420E+03
NUMBER OF OBSERVATIONS =   372
S. E. OF MEAN = 0.10601E+02
T VALUE OF MEAN (AGAINST ZERO) = 0.31539E+02

1- 12	0.99	0.98	0.97	0.96	0.95	0.93	0.92	0.91	0.90	0.89	0.88	0.87
ST.E.	0.05	0.09	0.11	0.13	0.15	0.17	0.18	0.19	0.20	0.21	0.22	0.23
MOD. Q	366.7	726.1	1078.5	1423.8	1762.4	2094.2	2419.3	2737.9	3050.1	3355.9	3655.5	3948.9

13- 24	0.86	0.85	0.84	0.83	0.82	0.81	0.80	0.79	0.78	0.77	0.76	0.75
ST.E.	0.24	0.25	0.26	0.26	0.27	0.28	0.28	0.29	0.30	0.30	0.31	0.31
MOD. Q	4236.1	4517.3	4792.5	5062.0	5325.8	5584.0	5836.6	6083.6	6325.2	6561.2	6791.9	7017.2

MEAN DIVIDED BY ST. ERROR (USING N IN S. D.) = 0.31581E+02

TO TEST WHETHER THIS SERIES IS WHITE NOISE, THE VALUE 0.67639E+04
SHOULD BE COMPARED WITH A CHI-SQUARE VARIABLE WITH 24 DEGREES OF FREEDOM   CHI SQUARE PROB 1.000000

MODIFIED Q STATISTIC 0.70172E+04 FOR D. F.   24   CHI SQUARE PROB 1.000000

NOTE: IN SOME CASES DEGREES OF FREEDOM FOR Q AND MODIFIED Q STATISTICS MAY HAVE TO BE ADJUSTED.

DIFFERENCE 1
MEAN OF THE SERIES =0.20084E+01
ST. DEV. OF SERIES =0.22527E+01
NUMBER OF OBSERVATIONS =   371
S. E. OF MEAN = 0.11711E+00
T VALUE OF MEAN (AGAINST ZERO) = 0.17149E+02

1- 12	0.83	0.77	0.77	0.72	0.72	0.70	0.61	0.62	0.60	0.58	0.58	0.57
ST.E.	0.05	0.08	0.10	0.11	0.12	0.14	0.14	0.15	0.16	0.16	0.17	0.17
MOD. Q	257.3	476.8	700.9	895.2	1088.5	1272.6	1415.7	1560.7	1699.2	1827.9	1955.5	2080.0

13- 24	0.55	0.52	0.50	0.50	0.52	0.50	0.48	0.48	0.49	0.50	0.48	0.48
ST.E.	0.18	0.18	0.19	0.19	0.19	0.20	0.20	0.21	0.21	0.21	0.21	0.22
MOD. Q	2194.9	2298.5	2396.9	2495.3	2599.2	2698.5	2790.5	2881.2	2977.2	3074.9	3167.2	3257.8

MEAN DIVIDED BY ST. ERROR (USING N IN S. D.) = 0.17172E+02

TO TEST WHETHER THIS SERIES IS WHITE NOISE, THE VALUE 0.31508E+04
SHOULD BE COMPARED WITH A CHI-SQUARE VARIABLE WITH 24 DEGREES OF FREEDOM   CHI SQUARE PROB 1.000000

MODIFIED Q STATISTIC 0.32578E+04 FOR D. F.   24   CHI SQUARE PROB 1.000000

NOTE: IN SOME CASES DEGREES OF FREEDOM FOR Q AND MODIFIED Q STATISTICS MAY HAVE TO BE ADJUSTED.

DIFFERENCE 2
MEAN OF THE SERIES =0.17298E-01
ST. DEV. OF SERIES =0.12891E+01
NUMBER OF OBSERVATIONS =   370
S. E. OF MEAN = 0.67105E-01
T VALUE OF MEAN (AGAINST ZERO) = 0.25777E+00

1- 12	-0.33	-0.22	0.17	-0.12	0.05	0.16	-0.24	0.08	-0.01	-0.03	0.01	0.04
ST.E.	0.05	0.06	0.06	0.06	0.06	0.06	0.07	0.07	0.07	0.07	0.07	0.07
MOD. Q	40.8	58.5	69.2	74.8	76.0	85.4	107.8	110.3	110.3	110.6	110.7	111.2

13- 24	-0.01	-0.03	-0.06	0.00	0.10	-0.02	-0.03	-0.04	0.00	0.09	-0.05	0.03
ST.E.	0.07	0.07	0.07	0.07	0.07	0.07	0.07	0.07	0.07	0.07	0.07	0.07
MOD. Q	111.2	111.4	112.7	112.7	116.7	116.8	117.2	117.9	117.9	120.8	121.8	122.1

MEAN DIVIDED BY ST. ERROR (USING N IN S. D.) = 0.25812E+00

TO TEST WHETHER THIS SERIES IS WHITE NOISE, THE VALUE 0.11987E+03
SHOULD BE COMPARED WITH A CHI-SQUARE VARIABLE WITH 24 DEGREES OF FREEDOM   CHI SQUARE PROB 1.000000

MODIFIED Q STATISTIC 0.12211E+03 FOR D. F.   24   CHI SQUARE PROB 1.000000

NOTE: IN SOME CASES DEGREES OF FREEDOM FOR Q AND MODIFIED Q STATISTICS MAY HAVE TO BE ADJUSTED.

PARTIAL AUTOCORRELATIONS

DATA - VAR=FMSCOM   MONEY STOCK M2 FRIEDMAN   372 OBSERVATIONS

DIFFERENCING - ORIGINAL SERIES IS YOUR DATA.

                DIFFERENCES BELOW ARE OF ORDER   1

ORIGINAL SERIES
MEAN OF THE SERIES =0.33436E+03
ST. DEV. OF SERIES =0.20420E+03
NUMBER OF OBSERVATIONS =   372
S. E. OF MEAN = 0.10601E+02
T VALUE OF MEAN (AGAINST ZERO) = 0.31539E+02

1- 12	0.99	0.00	0.00	0.00	0.00	0.00	-0.01	0.00	0.00	-0.01	0.00	-0.01
13- 24	0.00	0.00	0.00	0.00	0.00	-0.01	-0.01	0.00	-0.01	-0.01	0.00	-0.01

```
DIFFERENCE  1
MEAN OF THE SERIES =0.20084E+01
ST. DEV. OF SERIES =0.22527E+01
NUMBER OF OBSERVATIONS =    371
S. E. OF MEAN = 0.11711E+00
T VALUE OF MEAN (AGAINST ZERO) = 0.17149E+02

  1- 12     0.83    0.25    0.30   -0.01    0.17    0.01   -0.17    0.10    0.00    0.08    0.02    0.09

 13- 24     0.00   -0.10    0.02    0.03    0.13   -0.01    0.02    0.01    0.06    0.03   -0.05    0.05


DIFFERENCE  2
MEAN OF THE SERIES =0.17298E-01
ST. DEV. OF SERIES =0.12891E+01
NUMBER OF OBSERVATIONS =    370
S. E. OF MEAN = 0.67105E-01
T VALUE OF MEAN (AGAINST ZERO) = 0.25777E+00

  1- 12    -0.33   -0.37   -0.07   -0.20   -0.03    0.13   -0.11    0.01   -0.12   -0.03   -0.12    0.00

 13- 24     0.03   -0.03   -0.08   -0.14    0.03   -0.02    0.02   -0.07   -0.05    0.02   -0.08    0.05
```

Note that the output has been edited to save space.

```
SUMMARY OF MODEL  1

*******************************************************************************************************

DATA -   Z = VAR=FMSCOM    MONEY STOCK M2 FRIEDMAN                                        372 OBSERVATIONS

DIFFERENCING ON   Z - 1) 2 OF ORDER  1

*******************************************************************************************************

UNIVARIATE MODEL PARAMETERS

*******************************************************************************************************
```

PARAMETER NUMBER	PARAMETER TYPE	PARAMETER ORDER	ESTIMATED VALUE	LOWER LIMIT	95 PER CENT T	UPPER LIMIT
1	AUTOREGRESSIVE 1	1	-.46735E+00	-.57082E+00	-9.033	-.36388E+00
2	AUTOREGRESSIVE 1	2	-.45992E+00	-.56805E+00	-8.507	-.35179E+00
3	MOVING AVERAGE 1	3	0.16668E+00	0.50295E-01	2.864	0.28307E+00
4	MOVING AVERAGE 1	4	0.14210E+00	0.37321E-01	2.712	0.24689E+00
5	MOVING AVERAGE 1	7	0.29737E+00	0.19272E+00	5.683	0.40202E+00

```
*******************************************************************************************************

OTHER INFORMATION AND RESULTS

*******************************************************************************************************

RESIDUAL SUM OF SQUARES     0.42923E+03    363 D.F.        RESIDUAL MEAN SQUARE            0.11824E+01

NUMBER OF RESIDUALS              368                       RESIDUAL STANDARD ERROR         0.10874E+01

BACKFORECASTING WAS SUPPRESSED IN PARAMETER ESTIMATION

AUTOCORRELATION FUNCTION

DATA - THE ESTIMATED RESIDUALS - MODEL 1                                               368 OBSERVATIONS


ORIGINAL SERIES
MEAN OF THE SERIES =0.74638E-01
ST. DEV. OF SERIES =0.10774E+01
NUMBER OF OBSERVATIONS =    368
S. E. OF MEAN = 0.56241E-01
T VALUE OF MEAN (AGAINST ZERO) = 0.13271E+01

  1- 12    -0.01   -0.02   -0.02    0.01    0.07    0.08    0.02   -0.01   -0.10    0.02    0.00    0.02
 ST.E.      0.05    0.05    0.05    0.05    0.05    0.05    0.05    0.05    0.05    0.05    0.05    0.05
 MOD. Q     0.1     0.3     0.4     0.5     2.5     4.7     4.8     4.8     8.7     8.9     8.9     9.0

 13- 24    -0.03   -0.08   -0.06   -0.04    0.10   -0.01   -0.07   -0.07   -0.02    0.07   -0.03   -0.01
 ST.E.      0.05    0.05    0.05    0.05    0.05    0.05    0.05    0.05    0.06    0.06    0.06    0.06
 MOD. Q     9.4    12.1    13.4    14.2    17.8    17.9    19.9    21.9    22.0    23.7    24.0    24.0

MEAN DIVIDED BY ST. ERROR (USING N IN S. D.  ) = 0.13289E+01

TO TEST WHETHER THIS SERIES IS WHITE NOISE, THE VALUE  0.23028E+02
SHOULD BE COMPARED WITH A CHI-SQUARE VARIABLE WITH  19 DEGREES OF FREEDOM      CHI SQUARE PROB 0.763909

MODIFIED Q STATISTIC  0.24043E+02 FOR D. F.     19                             CHI SQUARE PROB 0.805499

NOTE: IN SOME CASES DEGREES OF FREEDOM FOR Q AND MODIFIED Q STATISTICS MAY HAVE TO BE ADJUSTED.
```

The next step in the identification of the transfer function model is to use the prewhitening model for M2, given in equation (7.5-1), to calculate the cross correlations between prewhitened M2, called α_t, and filtered FYCP, called β_t in equation (7.2-3), to attempt to identify a model of the income effect.[15] Because theory suggests that changes in money influence the level of interest rates, M2 was differenced twice and FYCP was differenced once. The cross correlations suggest an effect of a change in money on interest rates 16 periods later (see cross correlation value of .137). The Haugh modified S statistics suggest feedback, which was noted in the original paper. Spectral analysis of the information in the cross correlations indicates that there is high-frequency feedback from interest rates to prices indicated in the column A TRANS Y-X, while the mapping of (1-B)M2 to FYCP appears to be at lower frequency.

There are problems with the above analysis. The highly significant modified Q of 1018.2 for the ACF of the FYCP series indicates it is <u>not white noise</u>. The H statistic is used to test whether the cross correlations are spurious. The h statistics (equation 7.3-2) for the "left-hand" cross correlations, which measure the income effect, are <u>substantially</u> lower than the h statistics for the "right-hand" cross correlations, which are testing for feedback. For the first 12 ACF values on the left, H(12) was 3.95, which is not significant, while H(12) was 23.02 for the right-hand side, which is significant. This pattern carries through if we look at only elements ≥ the SE or elements ≥ 2 times the SE. Although the ACF of the cross correlation function only used 24 observations in this example, and a more appropriate approach might be to calculate more cross correlations prior to performing the diagnostic tests, the tentative finding is that the indicated feedback at lag 1 and 2 is probably not spurious. This problem was noted in Stokes and Neuburger (1979), who qualified their work in this regard. A better estimation method for the problem would be a VAR or VARMA model, whose estimation is discussed in chapter 8. The estimated cross correlations on the left are next used to form an estimate of response weights from equation (7.2-3). These, together with the ACF of the generated noise series from equation (7.2-5), are used to specify a tentative estimate of the transfer function model.

CROSS CORRELATIONS

SERIES 1 - PREWHITENED VAR=FMSCOM   MONEY STOCK M2 FRIEDMAN
SERIES 2 - PREWHITENED VAR=FYCP   COMMERCIAL PAPER INTEREST RATE

MEAN OF SERIES 1   = 0.72924E-01
ST. DEV. OF SERIES 1 = 0.10776E+01
MEAN OF SERIES 2   = 0.65250E-01
ST. DEV. OF SERIES 2 = 0.48055E+00

NUMBER OF LAGS ON SERIES 1	CROSS CORRELATION	NUMBER OF LAGS ON SERIES 2	CROSS CORRELATION	S LEFT	S RIGHT	MOD S LEFT	MOD S RIGHT
0	-0.169	0	-0.169	10.5	10.5	10.5	10.5
1	-0.094	1	-0.127	13.8	16.5	13.8	16.5
2	-0.073	2	-0.126	15.7	22.3	15.8	22.4
3	-0.014	3	-0.088	15.8	25.1	15.8	25.2
4	0.022	4	-0.033	16.0	25.5	16.0	25.6

5	-0.010	5	0.034	16.0	26.0	16.0	26.0
6	-0.013	6	0.031	16.1	26.3	16.1	26.4
7	-0.021	7	0.028	16.2	26.6	16.3	26.7
8	-0.005	8	-0.044	16.3	27.3	16.3	27.4
9	-0.063	9	0.019	17.7	27.5	17.8	27.6
10	-0.067	10	0.012	19.4	27.5	19.5	27.6
11	-0.018	11	-0.051	19.5	28.5	19.6	28.6
12	0.005	12	-0.052	19.5	29.5	19.6	29.7
13	0.045	13	-0.043	20.2	30.2	20.4	30.4
14	0.048	14	0.025	21.1	30.4	21.3	30.6
15	0.071	15	-0.054	23.0	31.5	23.2	31.7
16	0.137	16	-0.021	29.9	31.6	30.5	31.9
17	0.071	17	-0.048	31.7	32.5	32.4	32.8
18	0.080	18	-0.074	34.1	34.5	34.8	34.9
19	0.086	19	-0.063	36.8	36.0	37.7	36.5
20	0.084	20	-0.118	39.4	41.1	40.5	41.9
21	0.036	21	-0.035	39.9	41.6	41.0	42.4
22	0.003	22	0.015	39.9	41.6	41.0	42.5
23	0.077	23	-0.075	42.1	43.7	43.3	44.6
24	0.021	24	-0.083	42.2	46.2	43.5	47.3

SUM OF CROSS CORRELATIONS SQUARED FOR   25 TERMS

        0.11474144E+00   0.12559325E+00

HAUGH S STATISTIC - SEE JASA JUNE 76 PAGE 382

S FOR LEFT   SIDE 0.42225E+02 DF   25 CHI PROB 0.983002

S FOR RIGHT SIDE   0.35698E+02 DF   24 CHI PROB 0.941303

S FOR BOTH SIDES   0.77923E+02 DF   49 CHI PROB 0.994659

TEST FOR FEEDBACK PLUS INSTANTANEOUS CAUSALITY

S FOR RIGHT SIDE   0.46218E+02 DF   25 CHI PROB 0.993946

HAUGH MODIFIED S STATISTIC - SEE JASA JUNE 76 PAGE 383

S FOR LEFT   SIDE 0.43487E+02 DF   25 CHI PROB 0.987631

S FOR RIGHT SIDE   0.36828E+02 DF   24 CHI PROB 0.954485

S FOR BOTH SIDES   0.80316E+02 DF   49 CHI PROB 0.996828

TEST FOR FEEDBACK PLUS INSTANTANEOUS CAUSALITY

S FOR RIGHT SIDE   0.47348E+02 DF   25 CHI PROB 0.995540

NOTE: CROSS CORRELATIONS ON LEFT ARE FOR SERIES 2 ON LAGS OF SERIES 1

     CROSS CORRELATIONS ON RIGHT ARE FOR SERIES 1 ON LAGS OF SERIES 2

NOTE: DEGREES OF FREEDOM OF HAUGH STATISTICS HAVE TO BE ADJUSTED WHEN TRANSFER FUNCTION CHECKING IS PERFORMED

SPECTRAL ANALYSIS OF

X SERIES - PREWHITENED VAR=FMSCOM   MONEY STOCK M2 FRIEDMAN

Y SERIES - PREWHITENED VAR=FYCP   COMMERCIAL PAPER INTEREST RATE

X MEAN = 0.72923839E-01 X VAR =   1.1612148   Y MEAN = 0.65249860E-01 Y VAR =   0.23093236   INTERVAL   1.

FREQUENCY	COSPECTRUM	QUAD SP	AMPLITUDE	PHASE	A TRANS X-Y	A TRANS Y-X	COHERENCE SQ	X POW SPEC	Y POW SPEC
0.00000E+00	-0.12327	0.59659E-01	0.13694	0.42826	0.42159	0.25830	0.10890	0.32483	0.53018
0.20833E-01	-0.11982	0.30718E-01	0.12370	0.46006	0.30370	0.22868	0.69452E-01	0.40730	0.54092
0.41667E-01	-0.88686E-01	-0.40747E-01	0.97598E-01	0.56855	0.23965	0.34134	0.81801E-01	0.40725	0.28593
0.62500E-01	-0.64051E-01	0.22534E-01	0.67899E-01	0.44616	0.23768	0.42126	0.10013	0.28568	0.16118
0.83333E-01	-0.93564E-01	0.55041E-01	0.10855	0.41537	0.45253	0.58729	0.26577	0.23988	0.18484
0.10417	-0.89835E-01	0.35060E-01	0.96434E-01	0.44078	0.36451	1.0033	0.36570	0.26455	0.96120E-01
0.12500	-0.35287E-01	0.21327E-01	0.41232E-01	0.41348	0.13824	1.1110	0.15358	0.29827	0.37112E-01
0.14583	-0.10992E-01	0.11031E-01	0.15572E-01	0.37472	0.43469E-01	0.81021	0.35219E-01	0.35824	0.19220E-01
0.16667	-0.99673E-02	0.15964E-01	0.18820E-01	0.33883	0.33979E-01	1.0170	0.34558E-01	0.55386	0.18504E-01
0.18750	0.15019E-02	0.97935E-02	0.99080E-02	0.22578	0.18473E-01	0.56197	0.10381E-01	0.53635	0.17631E-01
0.20833	0.49047E-02	-0.14519E-01	0.15325E-01	0.80185	0.45466E-01	1.4033	0.63803E-01	0.33707	0.10921E-01
0.22917	0.27444E-02	-0.36611E-01	0.36714E-01	0.76191	0.10252	2.2103	0.22660	0.35812	0.16610E-01
0.25000	-0.52523E-02	-0.20230E-01	0.20900E-01	0.70957	0.62049E-01	0.72269	0.44843E-01	0.33684	0.28920E-01
0.27083	-0.61282E-02	0.21330E-01	0.22193E-01	0.29453	0.61997E-01	0.92166	0.57140E-01	0.35797	0.24080E-01
0.29167	-0.11947E-02	0.11596E-01	0.11657E-01	0.26634	0.29297E-01	1.2639	0.37030E-01	0.39789	0.92228E-02
0.31250	0.23732E-02	0.51079E-02	0.56323E-02	0.18078	0.15774E-01	1.5039	0.23722E-01	0.35706	0.37451E-02
0.33333	-0.13919E-01	-0.55138E-02	0.14971E-01	0.56003	0.43655E-01	3.4087	0.14881	0.34295	0.43920E-02
0.35417	-0.12517E-01	-0.18407E-02	0.12652E-01	0.52324	0.33436E-01	4.2278	0.14136	0.37839	0.29925E-02
0.37500	-0.77914E-02	0.21312E-03	0.77943E-02	0.49565	0.19382E-01	2.3740	0.46013E-01	0.40214	0.32832E-02
0.39583	-0.18346E-01	0.20428E-01	0.27457E-01	0.36646	0.61147E-01	3.5692	0.21825	0.44903	0.76927E-02
0.41667	-0.75687E-02	0.90297E-02	0.11782E-01	0.36103	0.28705E-01	1.2123	0.34800E-01	0.41047	0.97185E-02
0.43750	0.88933E-03	-0.15273E-01	0.15299E-01	0.75926	0.53660E-01	2.2731	0.12197	0.28511	0.67305E-02
0.45833	-0.15724E-01	-0.15076E-01	0.21784E-01	0.62166	0.65208E-01	5.0133	0.32691	0.33406	0.43451E-02
0.47917	-0.15005E-01	-0.62161E-02	0.16242E-01	0.56251	0.40399E-01	4.4394	0.17934	0.40204	0.36586E-02
0.50000	-0.80048E-02	-0.23017E-02	0.83291E-02	0.54456	0.20014E-01	3.1313	0.62670E-01	0.41617	0.26599E-02

AUTOCORRELATION FUNCTION

DATA - CROSS CORRELATIONS SERIES # 1   25 OBSERVATIONS

ORIGINAL SERIES
MEAN OF THE SERIES =0.95050E-02
ST. DEV. OF SERIES =0.67077E-01
NUMBER OF OBSERVATIONS =   25
S. E. OF MEAN = 0.13692E-01
T VALUE OF MEAN (AGAINST ZERO) = 0.69420E+00

1- 12	0.67	0.49	0.34	0.22	0.15	0.03	0.07	0.05	0.06	0.00	-0.11	-0.14
ST.E.	0.20	0.28	0.31	0.32	0.33	0.33	0.33	0.33	0.33	0.33	0.33	0.33
MOD. Q	12.8	19.7	23.2	24.8	25.6	25.6	25.8	25.9	26.0	26.0	26.6	27.6

MEAN DIVIDED BY ST. ERROR (USING N IN S. D.) = 0.70852E+00

TO TEST WHETHER THIS SERIES IS WHITE NOISE, THE VALUE 0.22969E+02
SHOULD BE COMPARED WITH A CHI-SQUARE VARIABLE WITH 12 DEGREES OF FREEDOM   CHI SQUARE PROB 0.972011

MODIFIED Q STATISTIC 0.27560E+02 FOR D. F.   12   CHI SQUARE PROB 0.993587

NOTE: IN SOME CASES DEGREES OF FREEDOM FOR Q AND MODIFIED Q STATISTICS MAY HAVE TO BE ADJUSTED.

AUTOCORRELATION FUNCTION

DATA - CROSS CORRELATIONS SERIES # 2   25 OBSERVATIONS

ORIGINAL SERIES
MEAN OF THE SERIES =-.45614E-01
ST. DEV. OF SERIES =0.54251E-01
NUMBER OF OBSERVATIONS =   25
S. E. OF MEAN = 0.11074E-01
T VALUE OF MEAN (AGAINST ZERO) = -.41190E+01

1- 12	0.49	0.21	0.06	-0.08	-0.17	-0.27	-0.15	-0.03	-0.13	-0.17	-0.09	-0.05
ST.E.	0.20	0.24	0.25	0.25	0.25	0.26	0.27	0.27	0.27	0.27	0.28	0.28
MOD. Q	6.8	8.2	8.3	8.5	9.5	12.1	12.9	13.0	13.6	15.0	15.4	15.5

MEAN DIVIDED BY ST. ERROR (USING N IN S. D.) = 0.42040E+01

TO TEST WHETHER THIS SERIES IS WHITE NOISE, THE VALUE 0.12045E+02
SHOULD BE COMPARED WITH A CHI-SQUARE VARIABLE WITH 12 DEGREES OF FREEDOM   CHI SQUARE PROB 0.557906

MODIFIED Q STATISTIC 0.15533E+02 FOR D. F.   12   CHI SQUARE PROB 0.786428

NOTE: IN SOME CASES DEGREES OF FREEDOM FOR Q AND MODIFIED Q STATISTICS MAY HAVE TO BE ADJUSTED.

AUTOCORRELATION FUNCTION

DATA - PREWHITENED VAR=FMSCOM   MONEY STOCK M2 FRIEDMAN   368 OBSERVATIONS

ORIGINAL SERIES
MEAN OF THE SERIES =0.72924E-01
ST. DEV. OF SERIES =0.10776E+01
NUMBER OF OBSERVATIONS =   368
S. E. OF MEAN = 0.56250E-01
T VALUE OF MEAN (AGAINST ZERO) = 0.12964E+01

1- 12	-0.02	-0.03	-0.02	0.00	0.07	0.08	0.02	-0.01	-0.10	0.02	0.00	0.02
ST.E.	0.05	0.05	0.05	0.05	0.05	0.05	0.05	0.05	0.05	0.05	0.05	0.05
MOD. Q	0.2	0.4	0.6	0.6	2.6	4.7	4.8	4.9	8.7	8.9	8.9	9.0
13- 24	-0.03	-0.08	-0.06	-0.04	0.10	-0.02	-0.07	-0.07	-0.02	0.07	-0.03	-0.01
ST.E.	0.05	0.05	0.05	0.05	0.05	0.05	0.05	0.05	0.06	0.06	0.06	0.06
MOD. Q	9.4	12.1	13.4	14.1	17.8	17.9	19.8	21.7	21.8	23.6	23.9	23.9

MEAN DIVIDED BY ST. ERROR (USING N IN S. D.) = 0.12982E+01

TO TEST WHETHER THIS SERIES IS WHITE NOISE, THE VALUE 0.22918E+02
SHOULD BE COMPARED WITH A CHI-SQUARE VARIABLE WITH 24 DEGREES OF FREEDOM   CHI SQUARE PROB 0.475328

MODIFIED Q STATISTIC 0.23924E+02 FOR D. F.   24   CHI SQUARE PROB 0.534070

NOTE: IN SOME CASES DEGREES OF FREEDOM FOR Q AND MODIFIED Q STATISTICS MAY HAVE TO BE ADJUSTED.

AUTOCORRELATION FUNCTION

DATA - PREWHITENED VAR=FYCP   COMMERCIAL PAPER INTEREST RATE   368 OBSERVATIONS

ORIGINAL SERIES
MEAN OF THE SERIES =0.65250E-01
ST. DEV. OF SERIES =0.48055E+00
NUMBER OF OBSERVATIONS =   368
S. E. OF MEAN = 0.25085E-01
T VALUE OF MEAN (AGAINST ZERO) = 0.26012E+01

1- 12	0.84	0.67	0.54	0.42	0.28	0.17	0.18	0.17	0.16	0.16	0.18	0.16
ST.E.	0.05	0.08	0.09	0.10	0.11	0.11	0.11	0.11	0.11	0.11	0.11	0.11
MOD. Q	261.2	427.9	535.2	600.4	630.1	640.8	652.3	663.4	672.7	682.8	695.4	705.7
13- 24	0.06	-0.02	-0.08	-0.17	-0.25	-0.32	-0.36	-0.36	-0.34	-0.30	-0.26	-0.24
ST.E.	0.11	0.11	0.11	0.11	0.11	0.12	0.12	0.12	0.12	0.13	0.13	0.13
MOD. Q	707.2	707.3	709.5	720.1	744.7	785.6	835.0	886.9	932.1	968.0	994.5	1018.2

MEAN DIVIDED BY ST. ERROR (USING N IN S. D.) = 0.26047E+01

TO TEST WHETHER THIS SERIES IS WHITE NOISE, THE VALUE 0.99032E+03
SHOULD BE COMPARED WITH A CHI-SQUARE VARIABLE WITH 24 DEGREES OF FREEDOM   CHI SQUARE PROB 1.000000

MODIFIED Q STATISTIC 0.10182E+04 FOR D. F.   24   CHI SQUARE PROB 1.000000

NOTE: IN SOME CASES DEGREES OF FREEDOM FOR Q AND MODIFIED Q STATISTICS MAY HAVE TO BE ADJUSTED.

TEST TO DETERMINE WHETHER AUTOCORRELATIONS OF SERIES # 2 ARE SIMILAR TO AUTOCORRELATIONS OF CROSS CORRELATIONS

CHI SQUARE TO TEST FOR SPURIOUS LEFT HAND CROSS CORRELATIONS - FOR   12 TERMS

1-12   0.642   1.043   1.422   1.758   1.901   2.060   2.149   2.267   2.342   2.549   3.222   3.953

CHI SQUARE TO TEST FOR SPURIOUS RIGHT HAND CROSS CORRELATIONS - FOR   12 TERMS

1-12   2.807   5.977   9.130   12.545   15.294   17.740   18.988   19.482   20.402   21.702   22.525   23.023

TEST USING CHI SQUARE ONLY FOR ELEMENTS GE 2 SE IN ABSOLUTE VALUE (EITHER OR BOTH ELEMENTS) -- SERIES # 2 ONLY

FOR LEFT HAND CROSS CORRELATIONS, # ELEMENTS =   5, CHI SQUARE=   1.90070   , ONLY SERIES #2 SIG, #=   5, CHI=   1.90070
FOR RIGHT HAND CROSS CORRELATIONS, # ELEMENTS =   5, CHI SQUARE=   15.2935   , ONLY SERIES #2 SIG, #=   5, CHI=   15.2935

TEST USING CHI SQUARE ONLY FOR ELEMENTS GE SE IN ABSOLUTE VALUE (EITHER OR BOTH ELEMENTS) -- SERIES # 2 ONLY

FOR LEFT HAND CROSS CORRELATIONS, # ELEMENTS =   12, CHI SQUARE=   3.95341   , ONLY SERIES #2 SIG, #=   12, CHI=   3.95341
FOR RIGHT HAND CROSS CORRELATIONS, # ELEMENTS =   12, CHI SQUARE=   23.0228   , ONLY SERIES #2 SIG, #=   12, CHI=   23.0228

ESTIMATED IMPULSE RESPONSE WEIGHTS V(K)   REVERSE RESPONSE WEIGHTS

K	V(K)		K	
0	-0.75399876E-01		0	-0.37913895
1	-0.42083874E-01		1	-0.28480101
2	-0.32356646E-01		2	-0.28279454
3	-0.63690841E-02		3	-0.19679892
4	0.97164735E-02		4	-0.74311495E-01
5	-0.46044812E-02		5	0.75345695E-01
6	-0.58904700E-02		6	0.69818795E-01
7	-0.92371143E-02		7	0.63662469E-01
8	-0.24335368E-02		8	-0.98336697E-01
9	-0.27999457E-01		9	0.42967070E-01
10	-0.29988278E-01		10	0.27335383E-01
11	-0.80440827E-02		11	-0.11525118
12	0.22991416E-02		12	-0.11742854
13	0.19933198E-01		13	-0.97103119E-01
14	0.21391090E-01		14	0.55737287E-01
15	0.31809960E-01		15	-0.12082279
16	0.61238293E-01		16	-0.47129024E-01
17	0.31507790E-01		17	-0.10833710
18	0.35539683E-01		18	-0.16597372
19	0.38411994E-01		19	-0.14216226
20	0.37489936E-01		20	-0.26419473
21	0.16122118E-01		21	-0.78373253E-01
22	0.12750344E-02		22	0.34188904E-01
23	0.34326326E-01		23	-0.16736019
24	0.93152337E-02		24	-0.18585223

AUTOCORRELATION FUNCTION

DATA - THE GENERATED NOISE SERIES   346 OBSERVATIONS

ORIGINAL SERIES
MEAN OF THE SERIES =0.15681E-01
ST. DEV. OF SERIES =0.29323E+00
NUMBER OF OBSERVATIONS =   346
S. E. OF MEAN = 0.15787E-01
T VALUE OF MEAN (AGAINST ZERO) = 0.99330E+00

1- 12	0.47	0.13	0.14	0.11	-0.03	-0.22	-0.18	-0.05	-0.04	0.00	0.12	0.22
ST.E.	0.05	0.06	0.07	0.07	0.07	0.07	0.07	0.07	0.07	0.07	0.07	0.07
MOD. Q	77.6	83.2	89.9	94.5	94.7	112.3	124.1	124.9	125.3	125.3	130.2	147.3
13- 24	0.06	-0.03	0.02	0.00	-0.14	-0.25	-0.23	-0.22	-0.15	-0.10	0.01	0.04
ST.E.	0.07	0.07	0.07	0.07	0.07	0.07	0.08	0.08	0.08	0.08	0.08	0.08
MOD. Q	148.4	148.7	148.9	148.9	155.9	178.7	197.9	215.0	223.4	227.1	227.1	227.6

MEAN DIVIDED BY ST. ERROR (USING N IN S. D.) = 0.99474E+00

TO TEST WHETHER THIS SERIES IS WHITE NOISE, THE VALUE 0.22020E+03
SHOULD BE COMPARED WITH A CHI-SQUARE VARIABLE WITH 24 DEGREES OF FREEDOM   CHI SQUARE PROB 1.000000

MODIFIED Q STATISTIC 0.22758E+03 FOR D. F.   24   CHI SQUARE PROB 1.000000

NOTE: IN SOME CASES DEGREES OF FREEDOM FOR Q AND MODIFIED Q STATISTICS MAY HAVE TO BE ADJUSTED.

PARTIAL AUTOCORRELATIONS

DATA - THE GENERATED NOISE SERIES   346 OBSERVATIONS

ORIGINAL SERIES
MEAN OF THE SERIES =0.15681E-01
ST. DEV. OF SERIES =0.29323E+00
NUMBER OF OBSERVATIONS =   346
S. E. OF MEAN = 0.15787E-01
T VALUE OF MEAN (AGAINST ZERO) = 0.99330E+00

1- 12	0.47	-0.12	0.17	-0.02	-0.10	-0.23	0.02	0.05	0.01	0.08	0.12	0.09
13- 24	-0.19	0.00	-0.01	-0.02	-0.10	-0.08	-0.10	-0.14	0.06	-0.03	0.08	-0.08

The above transfer function identification suggests, after some iterations, a model of the form of

$$(1-B)FYCP=(\omega_0-\omega_1 B^3-\omega_2 B^4-\omega_3 B^9-\omega_4 B^{16}-\omega_5 B^{23})(1-\delta_1 B)^{-1}(1-\delta_2 B^{12})^{-1}(1-B)^2 M2 +$$

$$(1-\Theta_1 B^2-\Theta_2 B^6-\Theta_3 B^{14}-\Theta_4 B^{20})(1-\Phi_1 B)^{-1}(1-\Phi_2 B^{12})^{-1}e_t. \qquad (7.5-2)$$

The implied impulse-response function, $V(B)$, is calculated from equation (7.2-11). The sum of the $V(B)$ weights measures the cumulative effect of a change in M2 on the level of interest rates. After starting off negative, which economic theory suggests is due to the liquidity effect, the sum turns positive at lag 4, .0405477, reaching a peak of .208599 at lag 20. This positive sum confirms the income effect.[16] Diagnostic tests on the residual indicate that the form of the noise model $[\Theta(B)/\Phi(B)]$ is correct. Since there are no spikes in the cross correlations, the input model $[\omega_1(B)/\delta_1(B)]$ is appropriate. The second transfer function setup in Table 7.7 differs from the first in that the default starting values are not used. The output from this example is not shown to save space. Slight differences in the estimated coefficients can be seen by an interested reader who runs the problem.

SUMMARY OF MODEL 1

****

DATA -   Y = VAR=FYCP   COMMERCIAL PAPER INTEREST RATE   372 OBSERVATIONS

DIFFERENCING ON Y - 1) 1 OF ORDER 1

****

****

NOISE SERIES

DIFFERENCING ON NOISE - NONE

NOISE MODEL PARAMETERS

****

PARAMETER NUMBER	PARAMETER TYPE	PARAMETER ORDER	ESTIMATED VALUE	95 PER CENT LOWER LIMIT	T	UPPER LIMIT
1	AUTOREGRESSIVE 1	1	0.59390E+00	0.49251E+00	11.71	0.69530E+00
2	AUTOREGRESSIVE 2	12	0.14200E+00	0.24980E-01	2.427	0.25903E+00
3	MOVING AVERAGE 1	2	0.22550E+00	0.11970E+00	4.263	0.33130E+00
4	MOVING AVERAGE 1	6	0.26314E+00	0.15441E+00	4.840	0.37188E+00
5	MOVING AVERAGE 1	14	0.22579E+00	0.11473E+00	4.066	0.33685E+00
6	MOVING AVERAGE 1	20	0.15461E+00	0.43078E-01	2.772	0.26615E+00

****

****

INPUT SERIES 1

DATA -   X1 = VAR=FMSCOM   MONEY STOCK M2 FRIEDMAN

DIFFERENCING ON X1 - 1) 2 OF ORDER 1

VALUE OF LAG PARAMETER IS 0

****

TRANSFER FUNCTION PARAMETERS

****

| 7 | OUTPUT LAG 1 | 1 | 0.58945E+00 | 0.35913E+00 | 5.119 | 0.81977E+00 |
| 8 | OUTPUT LAG 2 | 12 | 0.81441E+00 | 0.71005E+00 | 15.61 | 0.91878E+00 |

9	INPUT LAG 1	0	-.29054E-01	-.42753E-01 -4.242	-.15355E-01
10	INPUT LAG 1	3	-.41199E-01	-.60785E-01 -4.207	-.21613E-01
11	INPUT LAG 1	4	-.40797E-01	-.61421E-01 -3.956	-.20173E-01
12	INPUT LAG 1	9	0.34491E-01	0.13664E-01 3.312	0.55318E-01
13	INPUT LAG 1	16	-.29701E-01	-.56452E-01 -2.221	-.29514E-02
14	INPUT LAG 1	23	-.11401E-01	-.29258E-01 -1.277	0.64560E-02

****

OTHER INFORMATION AND RESULTS

****

RESIDUAL SUM OF SQUARES   0.17325E+02   320 D.F.   RESIDUAL MEAN SQUARE   0.54140E-01

NUMBER OF RESIDUALS   334   RESIDUAL STANDARD ERROR   0.23268E+00

BACKFORECASTING WAS SUPPRESSED IN PARAMETER ESTIMATION

AUTOCORRELATION FUNCTION

DATA - THE ESTIMATED RESIDUALS - MODEL 1

                                                                      334 OBSERVATIONS

ORIGINAL SERIES
MEAN OF THE SERIES =0.20310E-01
ST. DEV. OF SERIES =0.22685E+00
NUMBER OF OBSERVATIONS =   334
S. E. OF MEAN = 0.12431E-01
T VALUE OF MEAN (AGAINST ZERO) = 0.16338E+01

1- 12	-0.05	-0.02	0.08	0.06	0.08	0.01	-0.11	0.04	-0.05	-0.04	0.05	0.00
ST.E.	0.05	0.05	0.05	0.06	0.06	0.06	0.06	0.06	0.06	0.06	0.06	0.06
MOD. Q	0.9	1.0	3.0	4.2	6.3	6.3	10.5	11.1	11.9	12.3	13.1	13.1

13- 24	-0.10	-0.01	0.06	0.06	0.02	-0.09	-0.03	0.01	-0.01	-0.09	0.08	-0.06
ST.E.	0.06	0.06	0.06	0.06	0.06	0.06	0.06	0.06	0.06	0.06	0.06	0.06
MOD. Q	16.6	16.6	17.8	19.0	19.1	22.0	22.4	22.4	22.5	25.4	27.5	28.7

MEAN DIVIDED BY ST. ERROR (USING N IN S. D.) = 0.16363E+01

TO TEST WHETHER THIS SERIES IS WHITE NOISE, THE VALUE 0.27451E+02
SHOULD BE COMPARED WITH A CHI-SQUARE VARIABLE WITH 18 DEGREES OF FREEDOM   CHI SQUARE PROB 0.929090

MODIFIED Q STATISTIC 0.28705E+02 FOR D. F.   18   CHI SQUARE PROB 0.947900

NOTE: IN SOME CASES DEGREES OF FREEDOM FOR Q AND MODIFIED Q STATISTICS MAY HAVE TO BE ADJUSTED.

PARTIAL AUTOCORRELATIONS

DATA - THE ESTIMATED RESIDUALS - MODEL 1

                                                                      334 OBSERVATIONS

ORIGINAL SERIES
MEAN OF THE SERIES =0.20310E-01
ST. DEV. OF SERIES =0.22685E+00
NUMBER OF OBSERVATIONS =   334
S. E. OF MEAN = 0.12431E-01
T VALUE OF MEAN (AGAINST ZERO) = 0.16338E+01

| 1- 12 | -0.05 | -0.02 | 0.07 | 0.07 | 0.09 | 0.02 | -0.12 | 0.01 | -0.06 | -0.03 | 0.05 | 0.03 |

| 13- 24 | -0.09 | -0.03 | 0.06 | 0.06 | 0.04 | -0.07 | -0.07 | -0.04 | -0.01 | -0.08 | 0.10 | -0.02 |

CROSS CORRELATIONS

SERIES 1 - PREWHITENED VAR=FMSCOM   MONEY STOCK M2 FRIEDMAN
SERIES 2 - THE ESTIMATED RESIDUALS - MODEL 1

MEAN OF SERIES 1   = 0.87970E-01
ST. DEV. OF SERIES 1 = 0.11264E+01
MEAN OF SERIES 2   = 0.20310E-01
ST. DEV. OF SERIES 2 = 0.22685E+00

NUMBER OF LAGS ON SERIES 1	CROSS CORRELATION	NUMBER OF LAGS ON SERIES 2	CROSS CORRELATION	S LEFT	S RIGHT	MOD S LEFT	MOD S RIGHT
0	-0.012	0	-0.012	0.475E-01	0.475E-01	0.475E-01	0.475E-01
1	0.057	1	-0.050	1.14	0.889	1.15	0.891
2	-0.072	2	-0.139	2.87	7.35	2.88	7.39
3	-0.026	3	-0.086	3.09	9.81	3.11	9.88
4	0.004	4	-0.142	3.10	16.6	3.12	16.7
5	-0.041	5	0.032	3.66	16.9	3.68	17.1
6	0.027	6	-0.004	3.89	16.9	3.92	17.1
7	0.067	7	0.013	5.40	17.0	5.46	17.1
8	-0.005	8	0.019	5.41	17.1	5.47	17.3
9	0.005	9	0.010	5.41	17.1	5.47	17.3
10	-0.035	10	0.078	5.82	19.2	5.89	19.4
11	0.019	11	0.038	5.94	19.7	6.02	19.9
12	0.116	12	-0.020	10.5	19.8	10.7	20.0
13	0.060	13	-0.093	11.7	22.7	12.0	23.0
14	0.008	14	0.127	11.7	28.1	12.0	28.7
15	0.002	15	-0.123	11.7	33.2	12.0	34.0
16	-0.012	16	0.037	11.7	33.6	12.0	34.5
17	0.006	17	0.053	11.7	34.6	12.0	35.5
18	0.037	18	-0.013	12.2	34.6	12.5	35.5

19	0.058	19	0.046	13.3	35.4	13.7	36.3
20	-0.002	20	-0.199	13.3	48.5	13.7	50.3
21	-0.031	21	-0.065	13.7	50.0	14.1	51.9
22	0.000	22	0.144	13.7	56.9	14.1	59.2
23	0.101	23	0.032	17.1	57.2	17.8	59.6
24	-0.085	24	0.007	19.5	57.2	20.4	59.6

SUM OF CROSS CORRELATIONS SQUARED FOR   25 TERMS

0.58426660E-01   0.17132777E+00

HAUGH S STATISTIC - SEE JASA JUNE 76 PAGE 382

S FOR LEFT SIDE   0.19514E+02 DF   25 CHI PROB 0.228193

S FOR RIGHT SIDE 0.57176E+02 DF   24 CHI PROB 0.999842

S FOR BOTH SIDES 0.76690E+02 DF   49 CHI PROB 0.993066

TEST FOR FEEDBACK PLUS INSTANTANEOUS CAUSALITY

S FOR RIGHT SIDE 0.57223E+02 DF   25 CHI PROB 0.999750

HAUGH MODIFIED S STATISTIC - SEE JASA JUNE 76 PAGE 383

S FOR LEFT SIDE 0.20371E+02 DF   25 CHI PROB 0.272895

S FOR RIGHT SIDE 0.59578E+02 DF   24 CHI PROB 0.999927

S FOR BOTH SIDES 0.79949E+02 DF   49 CHI PROB 0.996560

TEST FOR FEEDBACK PLUS INSTANTANEOUS CAUSALITY

S FOR RIGHT SIDE 0.59625E+02 DF   25 CHI PROB 0.999882

NOTE: CROSS CORRELATIONS ON LEFT ARE FOR SERIES 2 ON LAGS OF SERIES 1

      CROSS CORRELATIONS ON RIGHT ARE FOR SERIES 1 ON LAGS OF SERIES 2

NOTE: DEGREES OF FREEDOM OF HAUGH STATISTICS HAVE TO BE ADJUSTED WHEN TRANSFER FUNCTION CHECKING IS PERFORMED

INPUT SERIES 1
****

LAG	MODEL IMPLIED IMPULSE RESPONSE WEIGHTS	ESTIMATED CORRECT IMPULSE RESPONSE WEIGHTS	DIFFERENCE	SUM IMPLIED WGT	SUM CORR WGT
0	-0.29054128E-01	-0.83111227E-01	-0.54057106E-01	-0.290541E-01	-0.831112E-01
1	-0.17126009E-01	-0.41025460E-01	-0.23899451E-01	-0.461801E-01	-0.124137
2	-0.10094956E-01	-0.23368556E-01	-0.13273601E-01	-0.562751E-01	-0.147505
3	0.35248298E-01	0.13008874E-01	-0.22239424E-01	-0.210268E-01	-0.134496
4	0.61574448E-01	0.36373004E-01	-0.25201444E-01	0.405477E-01	-0.981233E-01
5	0.36295172E-01	0.83938539E-02	-0.27901318E-01	0.768428E-01	-0.897294E-01
6	0.21394253E-01	-0.64594299E-03	-0.22040196E-01	0.982370E-01	-0.903754E-01
7	0.12610879E-01	0.52246042E-02	-0.73862746E-02	0.110848	-0.851507E-01
8	0.74335039E-02	0.41681081E-02	-0.32653932E-02	0.118281	-0.809826E-01
9	-0.30109227E-01	-0.34892838E-01	-0.47836117E-02	0.881721E-01	-0.115875
10	-0.17747939E-01	-0.41505851E-01	-0.23757912E-01	0.704242E-01	-0.157381
11	-0.10461554E-01	-0.20562913E-01	-0.10101359E-01	0.599626E-01	-0.177944
12	-0.29828664E-01	-0.99834129E-02	0.19845251E-01	0.301340E-01	-0.187927
13	-0.17582558E-01	0.19064680E-01	0.36647238E-01	0.125514E-01	-0.168863
14	-0.10364067E-01	0.26473913E-01	0.36837980E-01	0.218736E-02	-0.142389
15	0.27443748E-01	0.50315980E-01	0.22872232E-01	0.296311E-01	-0.920727E-01
16	0.79104066E-01	0.94687283E-01	0.15583273E-01	0.108735	0.261456E-02
17	0.46628021E-01	0.56493439E-01	0.98654181E-02	0.155363	0.591080E-01
18	0.27484968E-01	0.47161851E-01	0.19676883E-01	0.182848	0.106270
19	0.16201060E-01	0.53125978E-01	0.36924917E-01	0.199049	0.159396
20	0.95497444E-02	0.42648364E-01	0.33098619E-01	0.208599	0.202044
21	-0.22460766E-01	-0.15048645E-02	0.20955902E-01	0.186138	0.200539
22	-0.13239536E-01	-0.53700283E-02	0.78695081E-02	0.172898	0.195169
23	0.35969354E-02	0.35394803E-01	0.31797867E-01	0.176495	0.230564
24	-0.17150503E-01	0.21533296E-03	0.17365836E-01	0.159345	0.230779

The above example shows a marked difference in the model-implied impulse response weights, $V_i(B)$, and the corrected impulse response weights, $V_{ci}(B)$, although what to correct in the model is not that obvious since the ACF of the residuals is clean and the cross correlations between α_t and the estimated residual does not show obvious spikes. The problem may be feedback, which needs the VARMA technique, or the fact that nominal instead of real M2 was used. This is the subject of chapter 8.

7.6 Conclusions

The OLS and ARIMA models were shown to be special cases of the more general transfer function model. The identification procedure for ARIMA and transfer function models was discussed and illustrated with the gas furnace data and a macroeconomics problem suggested by Stokes and Neuburger (1979), involving the relationship between interest rates and M2. A major problem in time series analysis is detecting spurious cross correlations that arise from the autocorrelation remaining in one or both of the series cross correlated. A detailed diagnostic test involving autocorrelating the cross correlations was discussed and illustrated, using the above two data sets.

NOTES

1. David Reilly of Automatic Forecasting Systems, P. O. Box 563 Hatboro, PA 19040, has made a number of enhancements to the Pack program, which have been incorporated and extensively modified before being placed in B34S. David Reilly is currently maintaining the original Pack program.

2. The discussion on identification draws heavily on material in Box and Jenkins (1976), Nelson (1973) and Stokes, Jones, and Neuburger (1975, chap. 5).

3. For further discussion of invertibility, see Granger and Newbold (1986) and Sargent (1987, 291). Note that $F_x(B) = \Sigma_{j=0}^{n} f_{xj}B^j$, where f_{xj} is a coefficient in the model filtering x_t and B is the backshift operator. $F_x(B)$ will have one-sided inverse if the roots, μ, of the equation $F_x(B) = \Sigma_{j=0}^{n} f_{xj}\mu^j$ all have absolute values > 1.0 or, in other words, are outside the unit circle.

4. For the purposes of this chapter, this definition of white noise will be used. Since only the second-order cumulant (ACF) is tested, a better term might be second-order white instead of white noise. The Hinich test (1982) for third-order whiteness is outlined in chapter 8 and is available as an option in the BTIDEN and BTEST paragraphs. Hinich is developing a fourth-order whiteness test.

5. To reduce notational clutter, the hats (^) have been left off where the meaning is clear. The ρ_i values are assumed to be the estimated autocorrelation values.

6. Since there is only one input, for notational simplicity we assume $X_{1t} \equiv x_t$, where X_{1t} was defined in equation (7.2-1) and x_t was defined in the previous section.

7. This section has been adapted from Stokes (1990).

8. The first-round identification process occurs <u>prior</u> to actual estimation of the model with maximum likelihood techniques. The second-round identification process takes place after the initial specification of the model has been estimated, using maximum likelihood techniques as the model is being refined.

9. The use of this method of detecting Granger (1969) causality resulted in findings of causality or lack of causality in the same series, depending on the method of analysis. For further details on this and other points, see Stokes and Neuburger (1979).

10. The five steps of the Liu-Hanssens (1982, 306-307) procedure include: (1) building ARIMA models for all input series and choosing a common filter for all input and output series from these models; (2) using OLS to estimate the transfer function weights on the filtered series; (3) building an ARIMA model for the residuals of the model in step 2; (4) using the ARIMA model of the noise to estimate the transfer function model weights with OLS; and (5) computing the noise of the original series by using the transfer function weights from steps 2 or 4 to identify a rational polynomial of the form $[\omega_i(B)/\delta_i(B)]$ for the ith input series and to identify a final noise model $[\Theta(B)/\Phi(B)]$. The simplified three-step procedure suggested by Liu and Hudak (1986a) involved: (1) asserting a simple noise model, such as AR(1), and estimating a linear transfer function with OLS to obtain a preliminary estimate of the impulse response weights; (2) building an ARIMA model for the residuals of the model estimated in step 1.; (3) computing the noise of the original series by using the transfer function weights from steps 1 or 2 to identify a rational polynomial of the form $[\omega_i(B)/\delta_i(B)]$ for the ith input series and to identify a final noise model, $[\Theta(B)/\Phi(B)]$. In the five-step and the three-step approaches the final step had to be repeated many times to get the most appropriate form of the noise and input models. This paper outlines an additional step after steps 5 or 3 that will simplify the process of the final determination of the most appropriate input and noise models. This additional step will be discussed and illustrated later.

11. The B34S command BJIDEN and BJEST have been modified to perform the Stokes and Neuburger (1979) identification diagnostic test automatically. Assuming k autocorrelations have been calculated, H(j), j=1,k is calculated for the cross correlations going <u>both</u> directions.

12. The left-hand cross correlations correlate the residuals with lags of the prewhitened input series. In this problem, the input series, GASIN, has been prewhitened by means of the AR(3) model suggested by Box and Jenkins (1976, 381). The estimated cross correlations and the estimated coefficients of each model are not given to save space.

13. B34S provides a number of ways to transfer data to SAS. One

option is to save the data in an SCA FSAVE file with the B34S command SCAINPUT and read this file into SAS with the SAS PROC LINKSCA, which is supplied with B34S. Another option is to use the B34S PGMCALL option to call SAS under B34S. Another option is to make a data file with the B34S LIST command or other output commands.

14. Slight differences between the results reported here and in Stokes and Neuburger (1979) are due to differences in the starting values and the fact that more accurate LINPACK inverters are now used in the BJEST command. The last two BJEST problems listed in Table 7.7 illustrate the effect of changes in the starting values on the estimated coefficients in a transfer function model. The important thing to note is that the ACF of the residuals is white noise for the prewhitening model for M2.

15. The cross correlations exactly replicate Table 3 in Stokes and Neuburger (1979). The autocorrelations of the cross correlations <u>do not</u> exactly replicate the original paper since in the original paper, 55 cross correlations were estimated and used in the calculation of the autocorrelations, while in the output given in this book, only 24 were used.

16. The V(B) vector reported in Stokes and Neuburger (1979) was scaled by 117.386 to make it comparable with the V(B) calculated for real M2. Once this calculation is made, the two vectors agree in magnitude.

8. Time Series Analysis Part II: VAR, VARMA and VMA Models

8.0 Introduction

The B34S commands BTIDEN and BTEST control the identification and estimation of VAR and VARMA models. The basic code for this section was obtained from the Department of Statistics, University of Wisconsin, and is documented in Tiao et al (1979)[1] and Tiao and Box (1981). After first discussing how VAR and VARMA models relate to structural models and the concept of Granger (1969) causality, VAR and VARMA model identification is reviewed. These models are used to test for Granger (1969) causality. The Hinich (1982) nonlinearity test is shown to be an added diagnostic tool to determine whether the model is correctly specified. The VAR and VARMA models are illustrated, using the gas furnace data, which is also used in chapter 12 to illustrate the frequency approach to the VAR model estimation proposed by Geweke (1982a, 1982b, 1982c, 1984).

8.1 The Relationship Between VAR, VARMA and Structural Models

Quenouille (1957) argued that a dynamic system of simultaneous equations could be written and estimated in the form

$$G(B)Z_t = D(B)e_t, \qquad\qquad (8.1-1)$$

where Z_t' is a row vector of the tth observation on k series $\{x_{1t}, \ldots x_{kt}\}$, and $G(B)$ and $D(B)$ are k by k polynomial matrices in which each element, $G_{ij}(B)$ and $D_{ij}(B)$, is itself a polynomial vector in the lag operator B. We assume that Z_t has been suitably differenced to achieve stationarity. Assuming k=3, then (8.1-1) can be written in expanded form as

$$\begin{bmatrix} G_{11}(B) & G_{12}(B) & G_{13}(B) \\ G_{21}(B) & G_{22}(B) & G_{23}(B) \\ G_{31}(B) & G_{32}(B) & G_{33}(B) \end{bmatrix} \begin{bmatrix} x_{1t} \\ x_{2t} \\ x_{3t} \end{bmatrix} = \begin{bmatrix} D_{11}(B) & D_{12}(B) & D_{13}(B) \\ D_{21}(B) & D_{22}(B) & D_{23}(B) \\ D_{31}(B) & D_{32}(B) & D_{33}(B) \end{bmatrix} \begin{bmatrix} e_{1t} \\ e_{2t} \\ e_{3t} \end{bmatrix}.$$

$$(8.1-2)$$

If

$$G_{ij}(B)=D_{ij}(B) = 0 \quad \text{for } i \neq j, \qquad\qquad (8.1-3)$$

then equation (8.1-2) reduces to three ARIMA models of the form of equation (7.1-9), where

$$G_{ii}(B) \equiv H_i(B) \qquad\qquad (8.1-4)$$

and

$$D_{ii}(B) \equiv F_i(B) \qquad\qquad\qquad\qquad\qquad\qquad (8.1\text{-}5)$$

and where $H_i(B)$ and $F_i(B)$ are the AR and MA polynomials of the ith vector of Z_t, x_{it}. In this case, the three series $,\{x_{1t}, x_{2t}, x_{3t}\}$, are independent. If

$$G_{ij}(B) = D_{ij}(B) = 0 \qquad \text{for } j > i, \qquad\qquad (8.1\text{-}6)$$

then we can say that the series $x_{1t}(B)$ is exogenous with respect to x_{2t} and x_{3t} and that x_{2t} is exogenous with respect to x_{3t}. In such a situation, a transfer function of the form of equation (7.2-1) can be estimated. If, on the other hand,

$$G_{ij}(B) \neq 0 \qquad \text{for } j > i \qquad\qquad\qquad (8.1\text{-}7)$$

and/or

$$D_{ij}(B) \neq 0 \qquad \text{for } j > i, \qquad\qquad\qquad (8.1\text{-}8)$$

then there is feedback in the system and a transfer function model of the form of equation (7.2-1) is not the appropriate way to proceed. The above discussion has highlighted the fact that the VARMA model of the form of equation (8.1-1) is a very general functional form of which the transfer function and the ARIMA model are increasingly more special cases. If we assume that $D_{ij}(B) = 0$ for $i \neq j$ and $D_{ij}(B) = 1$ for $i = j$ or that $D(B)$ is a matrix of degree 0 in B, then equation (8.1-1) reduces to the VAR form of the model

$$Q(B) \ Z_t = e_t, \qquad\qquad\qquad\qquad\qquad\qquad (8.1\text{-}9)$$

where $Q(B) \equiv G(B)$. In the more general case, a VARMA model, such as equation (8.1-1), can be written as a VAR model, provided that $D(B)$ is invertible. Here

$$Q(B) \equiv [D(B)]^{-1}G(B). \qquad\qquad\qquad\qquad (8.1\text{-}10)$$

In a like manner, equation (8.1-1) can be written in VMA form as

$$Z_t = R(B)e_t, \qquad\qquad\qquad\qquad\qquad\qquad (8.1\text{-}11)$$

where $R(B) \equiv D(B)$ if $G_{ij}(B) = 0$ for $i \neq j$ and $G_{ij}(B) = 1$ for $i = j$ or that $G(B)$ is a matrix of degree zero in B. In general,

$$R(B) \equiv [G(B)]^{-1}D(B) \qquad\qquad\qquad\qquad (8.1\text{-}12)$$

if $G(B)$ is invertible.[2] It is to be stressed that provided invertibility conditions are satisfied, equations (8.1-1), (8.1-9) and (8.1-11) are alternative forms. Usually, equation (8.1-1), the VARMA form, is the most parsimonious representation. Equation (8.1-9), the VAR form, is usually estimated first as a way to

identify the order of the VARMA model. Sims (1980) advocated
estimating the model in the form of equation (8.1-9) and
calculating R(B) in equation (8.1-11) as $[Q(B)]^{-1}$. The pattern in
the elements of the polynomials in R(B), element by element, would
trace the effects of "shocks" on the variables in Z_t. For example,
the term $R_{21}(B)$ measures the effect of an unexplained shock
"innovation" in the first series on the second series. The concept
of Granger (1969) causality is related to the econometric concept
of exogeneity. A series x_{1t} is said to Granger cause a series x_{2t} if,
and only if, a model that predicts x_{2t} as a function of only its
past has a greater sum of squares of the error term than a model
that predicts x_{2t} as a function of its own past and the past of x_{1t}.
Thus, in equation (8.1-2) if $G_{21}(B) \neq 0$ and x_{1t} is exogenous, then
we can say that x_{1t} Granger (1969) causes x_{2t}. The assumptions
needed to estimate equation (8.1-9) include the following:

   - What variables to place in Z_t.

   - The orders of the differencing in Z_t to make the series
     stationary.

   - The maximum degree of any element in the matrix Q(B).

These assumptions are substantially less that those needed to
estimate a simultaneous equations model of the form of equation
(4.1-1). Zellner and Palm (1974) recommend rewriting equation (8.1-
1) as

$$Z_t = [G(B)]^{-1}D(B)e_t$$

$$= [G^*(B)/|G(B)|]D(B)e_t, \qquad\qquad (8.1\text{-}13)$$

where $G^*(B)$ and $|G(B)|$ are the adjoint and determinant of G(B).
Equation (8.1-13) quickly reduces to

$$|G(B)|Z_t = [G^*(B)]D(B)e_t, \qquad\qquad (8.1\text{-}14)$$

which expresses the VARMA model in the form of a restricted,
seemingly unrelated, autoregressive model with correlated moving
average errors. This can be seen if we rewrite the ith equation of
(8.1-14) as

$$|G(B)|x_{it} = \alpha_t' e_t, \qquad\qquad (8.1\text{-}15)$$

where α_t' is the ith row of $[G^*(B)]D(B)$. Following Zellner and Palm's
(1974) classic paper showing the relationship between VARMA models
and structural equations models, we next can partition Z_t into the
k_1 endogenous (y_t) and k_2 exogenous (x_t) variables ($k \equiv k_1 + k_2$) and
rewrite equation (8.1-1) as

$$\begin{bmatrix} G_{11}(B) & G_{12}(B) \\ G_{21}(B) & G_{22}(B) \end{bmatrix} \begin{bmatrix} y_t \\ x_t \end{bmatrix} = \begin{bmatrix} D_{11}(B) & D_{12}(B) \\ D_{21}(B) & D_{22}(B) \end{bmatrix} \begin{bmatrix} e_{1t} \\ e_{2t} \end{bmatrix},$$

(8.1-16)

where $G_{11}(B)$, $G_{21}(B)$, $D_{11}(B)$ and $D_{21}(B)$ are <u>now</u> k_1 by k_1 matrices and $G_{12}(B)$, $G_{22}(B)$, $D_{12}(B)$ and $D_{22}(B)$ are <u>now</u> k_2 by k_2 matrices. The assumptions of structural equation modeling that k_1 variables in vector y_t are endogenous and the k_2 variables in the x_t vector are exogenous imply that

$$G_{21}(B) \equiv D_{12}(B) \equiv D_{21}(B) \equiv 0.$$

(8.1-17)

A major contribution of VARMA model building is that such maintained assumptions are now subject to formal testing. Sims (1980) makes this point forcefully. From equations (8.1-16) and (8.1-17) we obtain the implied structural equations

$$G_{11}(B)y_t + G_{12}(B)x_t = D_{11}(B)e_{1t}$$

(8.1-18)

and

$$G_{22}(B)x_t = D_{22}(B)e_{2t}.$$

(8.1-19)

Assuming that $G_{11}(B)$ is invertible, equation (8.1-18) can be transformed to the <u>final form</u> set of k_1 equations, where all endogenous variables are functions of the exogenous variables

$$y_t = -[G_{11}(B)]^{-1}G_{12}(B)x_t + [G_{11}(B)]^{-1}D_{11}(B)e_{1t}$$

(8.1-20)

or the <u>reduced form</u> set of k_1 equations, where the endogenous variables are a function of the exogenous variables and the lagged endogenous variables

$$y_t = -\Sigma_{m=1}^{r}[G_{110}]^{-1}G_{11m}B^m y_t - \Sigma_{m=0}^{r}[G_{110}]^{-1}G_{12m}B^m x_t + \Sigma_{m=0}^{q}[G_{110}]^{-1}D_{11m}B^m e_{1t},$$

(8.1-21)

where

$$G_{ij}(B) \equiv \Sigma_{m=0}^{r}G_{ijm}B^m$$

(8.1-22)

and

$$D_{ij}(B) \equiv \Sigma_{m=0}^{q}D_{ijm}B^m.$$

(8.1-23)

The above discussion shows that the structural equations assumptions place testable restrictions on the form of G(B) and D(B). The revealed structure of G(B) and D(B) will impose restrictions on the reduced form model given in equation (8.1-21) and final form model given in equation (8.1-20). Rather than seeing time series and structural equations modeling as distinct approaches, Zellner and Palm (1974) showed how these econometric techniques were related. Econometric practice has not been the same since. The steps to identify a VARMA model will be discussed in the next section.

Equation (8.1-1) writes the series in Z_t <u>only</u> in terms of their lags and the lags of the other series. Contemporaneous effects are captured in the error process since, in general, the covariance matrix Σ_e is not diagonal. Granger and Newbold (1977, 223) discuss the possible transformations. Equation (8.1-1) assumes the off diagonal elements of order 0 in G(B) and D(B) are zero but that the covariance of the error terms was not necessarily zero. The covariance between the error process will be zero <u>if there is no instantaneous causality</u> in the system. Granger and Newbold (1977, 223) argue that this form of the model, which they call model A, can be transformed into a model in which the off diagonal elements in G(B) <u>are not zero</u>, yet the covariance matrix, Σ_u, is diagonal. This transformation requires calculation of a k by k P matrix defined such that

$$P\Sigma_e P' = \Sigma_u, \qquad\qquad (8.1\text{-}24)$$

where off diagonal elements in P measure the contemporaneous relationship between the variables in the Z_t vector. The B34S BTIDEN command, which is used to estimate the VAR model, and the BTEST command, which is used to estimate the VMA and VARMA model, automatically print P, P^{-1} and the diagonal elements of Σ_u as well as Σ_e. These values can be used to transform the estimated model to what Granger and Newbold (1977, 224) call model C:

$$PG(B)\ Z_t = PD(B)e_t = D(B)u_t, \qquad\qquad (8.1\text{-}25)$$

since $Pe_t = u_t$.[3]

8.2 Identification of VAR and VARMA Models

The first step of VARMA model building is to make all series stationary so that the calculated ACF and CCF can be interpreted. Assume two series, GASIN and GASOUT, from the gas furnace data discussed in chapter 7. The B34S BTIDEN command

```
B34SEXEC BTIDEN NSTDER=3.0$
        TITLE=('CALCULATION OF ACF AND CCF ON GAS DATA')$
        SERIESN VAR=GASIN  TITLE=('INPUT GAS FROM B-J BOOK')$
        SERIESN VAR=GASOUT TITLE=('OUTPUT GAS FROM B-J BOOK')$
        IDEN LAGRHO=36 ISACF ISCCF IVALUE$ B34SEEND$
```

will list and plot 36 autocorrelations and cross correlations. If the IVALUE parameter is left off, these are only plotted in terms of + or - for significant and . for not significant terms. The NSTDER parameter on the BTIDEN sentence allows specification of a value different from the usual ± 2 SE convention. The ACF and CCF plots are useful to test for stationarity. "Line up" plots can optionally be made for the raw, transformed or differenced data to assist in spotting lead lag relationships visually. Hinich (1982) tests for Gaussianity and nonlinearity, which are discussed in section 8.3, are also possible options.[4] Once the series are deemed stationary, the ESTVAR sentence is used to estimate VAR models of the form of equation (8.1-9) for increasingly longer lags. The setup listed below will run a VAR model of up to order 6 on the gas furnace data.

```
B34SEXEC BTIDEN $
     TITLE=('CALCULATION OF VAR MODEL ON GAS DATA')$
     SERIESN VAR=GASIN  TITLE=('INPUT GAS FROM B-J BOOK')$
     SERIESB VAR=GASOUT TITLE=('OUTPUT GAS FROM B-J BOOK')$
     ESTVAR P=6 OUTPUT=NORMAL LAGRHO=36$ B34SEEND$
```

If the keyword ILARF is set on the ESTVAR sentence, only the last VAR fit is printed. If OUTPUT=BRIEF is set, the estimated coefficients are not given and only a summary table is printed.

Inspection of the cross correlations and autocorrelations of the residuals determine whether the order of the VAR model, k, is sufficient to summarize all the information in the series. Assume that P=12, yet after the 6th-order VAR is estimated, there are no spikes in the cross correlations of the residuals. The researcher next should set P=6 and rerun the command. The answers for the 6th-order VAR model will not be exactly the same as were found the first time. This surprising result is due to the BTIDEN command deleting observations based on the maximum lag of the final VAR model estimated. Using this data set for all VAR estimations allows comparisons of the effects of adding another lag. Hence, once the maximum lag is determined, it is a good plan to rerun the model with that lag specified as the maximum. The ILARF option is especially useful on this second run to save paper.

The next step in estimating a VARMA model is to delete the nonsignificant VAR coefficients and rerun the model in constrained VAR form with the BTEST command. Inspection of the cross correlations of the residuals indicates how to specify the MA part of the model. As a general rule, the same principles used in the transfer function identification should be used.

Before we proceed, it is important to discuss some of the diagnostic aids available in the ESTVAR sentence of the BTIDEN command. As each order of the VAR model is estimated, output includes the residual covariance matrix S(J), the residual correlation matrix RS(J) and the eigenvalues and eigenvectors of S(J) and the determinant and reciprocal of S(J). Zero eigenvalues in S(J) indicate that, rather than having k independent series, we actually have a process driven by less than k innovation series. Tiao and Box (1981) recommend calculating M(l), for l ε {1,..,P}, which is distributed as chi-square with k^2 degrees of freedom, where

$$M(l) = -(T-.5-1)\ln(|S(l)|/|S(l-1)|).$$ 　　　　　(8.2-1)

If j is the correct maximum order of the VAR process, M(j+1) will not be significant since $\ln(|S(j+1)|/|S(j)|)$ approaches zero. Inspection of the diagonal elements of S(J) will show how the residual variance is decreasing as additional lags of the VAR model are added. The ICANON option of the ESTVAR sentence provides output associated with canonical analysis. This option will not be discussed here. Interested readers are referred to Box and Tiao (1977).

If the OUTPUT=BRIEF option is used, the output includes only

- $M(1),\ldots,M(P)$.
- The significance of the M( )'s.
- The diagonal elements of S(J) at each lag.
- The t scores of the last VAR matrix estimated for that lag.
- The t scores displayed in +, -, . form in two plots.

The BTEST command estimates VARMA models of the form of equation (8.1-1) with conditional nonlinear least squares, or optionally exact nonlinear least squares. For further details on this complex subject, see Tiao and Box (1981) and Hillmer and Tiao (1979). Assume p is the maximum order of G(B). The conditional method assumes that the value of all error terms for observations 1-p are zero, while the exact method attempts to compute estimates of these values. The exact method corrects for possible bias in the MA coefficients in D(B) in equation (8.1-1) that arise when some of the roots of D(B) are close to the unit circle. Most VARMA estimation is done with the default conditional method because of cost. The exact method can be speeded up if the conditional estimates are used as starting values. The diagnostic checking of the VARMA model consists of adding and removing coefficients to remove all significant cross correlations and significant autocorrelations. If these spikes are removed, the linear VARMA model is correctly specified and there is no information in the residuals to model with a linear model. The Hinich (1982) nonlinearity tests discussed next let us relax the assumption of linearity that is implicit in testing only the cross correlations and autocorrelations of the residuals. If the Hinich (1982) test indicates nonlinearity, we are led to question the appropriateness of our linear specification inherent in the VARMA model.

If forecasting is requested, and the NFMAT=n parameter is supplied on the OUTPUT sentence, psi matrices up to order n will be printed. These matrices write the model in the form of equation (8.1-11) but reverse the reported signs, as is the customary practice with ARIMA model building. For further detail, see equations (7.1-26) and (7.1-27). For all nonzero-order elements of R(B) and $\Psi(B)$,

$$R_{ijm}(B) = -\Psi_{ijm}(B) \text{ for m>0.} \tag{8.2-2}$$

For example, a 2 by 2 VMA model of the form

$$\begin{bmatrix} x_t \\ y_t \end{bmatrix} = \begin{bmatrix} (1-.7B-.8B^2) & (-.8B) \\ (\quad.9B\quad) & (1+.3B) \end{bmatrix} \begin{bmatrix} e_{1t} \\ e_{2t} \end{bmatrix}$$

(8.2-3)

can be expanded to

$$x_t = e_{1t} - .7e_{1t-1} - .8e_{1t-2} - .8e_{2t-1}$$ (8.2-4)

$$y_t = .9e_{1t-1} + e_{2t} + .3e_{2t-1}$$ (8.2-5)

or written in terms of $\Psi(B)$ as

$$\Psi_1 = \begin{bmatrix} -.7 & -.8 \\ .9 & .3 \end{bmatrix}$$

(8.2-6)

$$\Psi_2 = \begin{bmatrix} -.8 & 0 \\ 0 & 0 \end{bmatrix}.$$

(8.2-7)

8.3 Testing Series for Nonlinearity With Hinich Tests

In this section, the Hinich (1982) tests for nonlinearity and Gaussianity are briefly discussed and illustrated with the Box and Jenkins (1976) gas furnace data, which are used in section 8.4 to illustrate the BTIDEN and BTEST commands.[5]

Let $\{x(t)\}$ denote a third-order stationary random process with zero mean, $\mu_x = E[x(t)]$, where t is a continuous time index. The covariance $c_{xx}(m) = E[x(t+m)x(t)] - [\mu_x]^2$, and the general third-order moments $c_{xxx}(s,r) = E[x(t+r)x(t+s)x(t)]$ are independent of t. If $c_{xx}(m) = 0$ for all m not zero, the series is white noise. Priestley (1981) and Hinich and Patterson (1985) stress that although a series may be white noise, if it is not Gaussian, x(n) and x(m) may not be independent. If the distribution of $\{x(n_1),\ldots,x(n_T)\}$ is multivariate normal for all $n_1,\ldots,n_T$, then in addition to being white noise, the series is Gaussian. If the process is not Gaussian, then the expected value of the triple product $x(t)x(t+r)x(t+s)$ is, in general, not zero. The notation $c_{xxx}(s,r)$, defined above, is called the bicovariance of the signal. The bispectrum of this signal is defined as the two-dimensional Fourier transform of the bicovariance function (see equation [8.3-3]).

Now let us define a third-order linear random process. Suppose that x(t) can be represented as

$$x(t) = \Sigma_{i=-\infty}^{\infty} a(s)\, e(t-i)$$ (8.3-1)

for a discrete time series with index t, where a(t) is a deterministic function that is absolutely integrable, and {e(t)} is a third-order stationary zero mean random process whose covariance $c_{xx}(r)=0$ for all $r \neq 0$ (i. e., it is white noise), and, in addition, {e(t)} has the bicovariance structure $c_{xxx}(s,r)=0$, unless r=s=0. This bicovariance structure is a third-order analogy to the covariance structure of white noise. If a process has this property, we call it <u>third-order white noise</u>. If a process {e(t)} is a time-reversible martingale difference, that is, if it has the following conditional expectation structure:

$$E[e(t)|e(s)] = 0 \qquad \text{if } s<t, \qquad (8.3-2)$$

and {e(-t)} has the same probabilistic structure as {e(t)}, then it follows that {e(t)} is third-order white noise (Hinich and Patterson 1985). Actually, the process is n^{th}-order white noise, where the definition of nth-order whiteness is an obvious generalization of the third order case. The proof of this follows in a direct manner from the type of conditioning argument given in Hinich and Patterson (1985).

Hinich and Patterson (1985, 70) fault Box and Jenkins (1976, 8 vs. 46) and Jenkins and Watts (1968, 149 vs. 157) for blurring the definitions of whiteness and independence. Many researchers implicitly assume the errors of their models are Gaussian and test for white noise using the covariance $c_{xx}(m)$, ignoring the information regarding possible nonlinear relationships that are found in the third-order moments, $c_{xxx}(s,r)$. In this section, the third-order moments are used to test the residuals of the Tiao-Box (1981) model for the possibility of nonlinearities. We define a pure white noise series as one in which $x(n_1),\ldots, x(n_T)$ are <u>independent and identically distributed random</u> variables for all values of $n_1,\ldots,n_T$. All pure white noise series are white. All white noise series are <u>not</u> pure white noise, unless, in addition, they are Gaussian. The above discussion suggests the need to test a linear model for both nonlinearity and Gaussianity to see if the assumption of linearity is warranted.

Hinich and Patterson (1985) argue that the bispectrum is easier to interpret than the multiplicity of third-order cumulants $\{c_{xxx}(r,s): s \leq r, r=0,1,\ldots\}$. The bispectrum is defined for frequencies f_1 and f_2 in the domain $\Omega = \{0 < f_1 < .5, f_2 < f_1, 2f_1 + f_2 < 1\}$ as $B_{xxx}(f_1,f_2)$, where

$$B_{xxx}(f_1,f_2) = \Sigma_{r=-\infty}^{\infty} \Sigma_{s=-\infty}^{\infty} c_{xxx}(r,s)\exp[-i2\pi(f_1 r + f_2 s)]. \qquad (8.3-3)$$

Equation (8.3-3) expresses the bispectrum as a double Fourier transformation of the third-order cumulant function. The statistical tests based on the sample bispectrum that are briefly discussed were applied with success to the study of acoustic signals and noise by Brockett, Hinich, and Wilson (1987) and to stock prices and exchange rates by Hinich and Patterson (1985) and

Brockett, Hinich, and Patterson (1988).

The <u>skewness function</u>, $\Gamma(f_1, f_2)$, is defined in terms of the bispectrum as follows:

$$\Gamma^2(f_1, f_2) = |(B_{xxx}(f_1, f_2))|^2 / S_x(f_1)S_x(f_2)S_x(f_1+f_2), \qquad (8.3-4)$$

where $S_x(f)$ is the spectrum of x(t) at frequency f. Brillinger (1965) proves that the skewness function, $\Gamma(f_1, f_2)$, is constant over all frequencies f_1, f_2 in Ω if {x(t)} is linear and zero over all frequencies if {x(t)} is Gaussian. This key proof suggests that once a consistent estimator of the bispectrum is calculated, nonlinearity and Gaussianity tests can be performed, using a sample estimator of the skewness function, $\Gamma(f_1, f_2)$. The next section outlines the procedure to obtain the bispectrum.

For the sample {x(0),x(1),...,x(T-1)}, define $F_{xxx}(j,k)$ as an estimate of the bispectrum of {x(t)} at the frequency pair (f_j, f_k), where $f_k = k/T$ for each integer k, as follows:

$$F_{xxx}(j,k) = X(f_j)X(f_k)X^*(f_{j+k})/T , \qquad (8.3-5)$$

where $X(f_j) = \Sigma_{t=0}^{T-1} x(t) \exp(-i2\pi f_j t)$. $F_{xxx}(j,k)$ must be smoothed to form a consistent estimator. Let $<B_{xxx}(m,n)>$ denote an estimator of $B_{xxx}(m,n)$, which is obtained by averaging over adjacent frequency pairs of $F_{xxx}(j,k)$:

$$<B_{xxx}(m,n)> = M^{-2} \Sigma_{j=(m-1)}^{mM-1} \Sigma_{k=(n-1)M}^{nM-1} F_{xxx}(j,k) . \qquad (8.3-6)$$

This estimator, $<B_{xxx}(f_m, f_n)>$, is the average value of the $F_{xxx}(j,k)$ over a square of M^2 points. It is a consistent and asymptotically complex normal estimator of the bispectrum $B_{xxx}(f_1, f_2)$, if the sequence (f_m, f_n) converges to (f_1, f_2) (see Hinich, 1982).

As discussed earlier, the estimated bispectrum will not be significantly different from zero under the null hypothesis of Gaussianity and linearity. As shown in Hinich (1982), $2|\delta(f_m, f_n)|^2$ is a normalized test statistic at frequency pair (f_m, f_n), which is approximately distributed as an independent, <u>noncentral chi-squared</u> variate with two degrees of freedom, where

$$\delta(f_m, f_n) = <B_{xxx}(f_m, f_n)>/[(N/M^2)<S_x(f_m)><S_x(f_n)><S_x(f_{m+n})>]^{1/2} \qquad (8.3-7)$$

$<S_x(.)>$ is a consistent and asymptotically normal estimator of the power spectrum $S_x(.)$, and $f_m = (2m-1)M/2T$ for each integer m.

The larger M, the less the finite sample variance and the larger the sample bias. Because of this trade-off, there is no one unique M that is appropriate to use for performing nonlinearity and Gaussianity tests, using the estimated statistics given by equation (8.3-7). An important innovation of this work is to

perform the tests over a range of values of M and see if the
results are robust. Hinich (1982) has suggested that a good value
for M is the square root of the number of observations. If a sixth-
order model is fit to the gas furnace data, T=296-6=290 and M would
be 17. The B34S implementation of the Hinich test does a grid
search over the admissible range of M values to test the
sensitivity of the results to the M value chosen. The grid search
reports M values from 9 to 18. When M is large, the bandwidth is
large, the variance is reduced and the resolution of the tests is
small since there are too few terms for the linearity test. If M is
small, there is a large number of terms to sort for the linearity
test, the variance may be too large and the chi-square
approximation used for the linearity test may not be good. Let P
denote the number of frequency pairs in the principal domain Ω.
Hinich (1982) shows that the P estimates of $2 \ |[\delta(f_m,f_n)]|^2$ are
approximately distributed as independent, noncentral, chi-square
variates with <u>noncentrality parameter</u> $\tau(f_m,f_n)$, where

$$\tau(f_m,f_n) \quad =[2 \ M^2/T]\,|B_{xxx}(f_m,f_n)|^2/[S_x(f_m)S_x(f_n)S_x(f_{m+n})]$$
$$=[2 \ M^2/T] \ \Gamma^2 \ (f_m,f_n) \qquad\qquad (8.3-8)$$

for all m and n such that the lattice square lies entirely within
the principal domain. Define the test statistic

$$\text{CHISUM}= 2 \ \Sigma_m \ \Sigma_n \ |\delta(f_m,f_n)|^2 \ . \qquad\qquad (8.3-9)$$

The distribution of CHISUM is approximately a noncentral chi-square
with 2P degrees of freedom with a noncentrality parameter that is
the sum of the $\tau(f_m,f_n)$ in Ω.

Under the null hypothesis that $\{x(t)\}$ is Gaussian and thus B_{xxx}
is identically zero, CHISUM is approximately a central chi-square
2P variate. Equation (8.3-9) gives us an asymptotic chi-square test
of the Gaussianity hypothesis. If the time series is linear, then
the skewness function is constant, which implies that the
noncentrality parameters are constant from equation (8.3-8). The
Hinich linearity test uses the empirical distribution function of
$\{2|\delta(f_m,f_n)|\}$ in the principal domain to test the hypothesis that
the $\tau(f_m,f_n)$'s are all the same. A robust single-test statistic
for this dispersion is the 80th quantile of these statistics. For
details of this test, see Hinich (1982) , Hinich and Patterson
(1985), and Ashley, Patterson, and Hinich (1986). In this chapter
we report normal approximations of the Gaussianity and linearity
tests (G and L) for a range of values of M. Mean values for G and
L are also reported.

Ashley, Patterson, and Hinich (1986, 174) presented an
equivalence theorem that proved that the Hinich bispectral
linearity test statistic is invariant to linear filtering of the
data. This important result proves that the linearity test can be
either applied to the raw series or the residuals of a linear

model. An additional important implication of the theorem is that if x(t) is found to be nonlinear, then the residuals of a linear model of the form y(t) = f(x(t)) will be nonlinear since the nonlinearity in x(t) will pass through any linear filter. Ashley, Patterson, and Hinich (1986) also reported tables on the power of the Hinich linearity test for detecting violations of the linearity assumption for a variety of common nonlinear models appearing in the literature and a table of the power of the linearity and Gaussianity tests for a number of sample sizes and M values. The table indicates substantial power for both tests, even when T is a small value such as 256, if the value of M used is between 12 and 17. For this sample size, as M increases, the power of the test falls off. This is later illustrated in test results for the gas furnace data reported in Stokes and Hinich (1989).

One of the examples in Tiao and Box (1981) was the gas furnace data discussed in Box and Jenkins (1976). Tiao and Box (1981) only tested the error terms for significant autocorrelations and cross correlations.   They first determined that an unconstrained VAR model of the form of equation (8.1-9) of order 6 would clean the residuals. Next, using conditional least squares, they removed what they felt were nonsignificant VAR coefficients and estimated a constrained VAR model. Their results are replicated and reported in Table 8.1. In Table 8.2 the Hinich bispectrum tests are performed on a grid of M values, going from 9 to 18, to test the residuals from the two equations implicit in equation (8.1-9). As was discussed earlier, Z score equivalents of the two tests have been reported to aid in interpretation.   While the distribution of the Hinich test statistics is only known asymptotically, it is worthwhile to use them to study the appropriateness of the proposed model for a well-known data set that had relatively few observations (T=290 after lags).

In many situations linear models are often considered a good approximation, even if the underlying data may be nonlinear and non-Gaussian. If no tests are made for linearity or Gaussianity, the researcher never knows the properties of the underlying data and is unable to systematically explore alternative models or determine whether such experimentation might be worthwhile to reduce the residual sum of squares. The results of the Hinich tests applied to the gas furnace data are listed in Table 8.2. Equation 1 (GASIN) and equation 2 (GASOUT) are tested in unconstrained and constrained form. The Z values of the G test are all above 4.98 for GASIN and 10.92 for GASOUT, indicating that both residual series (for both constrained and unconstrained models) reject the assumption of Gaussianity (G test) at a very high level of significance. For virtually all values of M, the assumption of linearity is rejected (L test). The lower Z scores were found only with the higher M scores (17 and 18), which have a large bandwidth. As was mentioned earlier, Ashley, Patterson, and Hinich (1986, Table I and II) investigated the size (number of observations) needed for the Hinich linearity and Gaussianity tests and the power of such tests for various values of M and number of observations. Their findings indicate that both tests give satisfactory convergence and that both tests detect nonlinearity with considerable frequency, even in cases in which T=256. These simulation results suggest that it is appropriate to use the Hinich tests in the present case, where T=290.

The finding of nonlinearity is invariant as to whether the estimated model is unconstrained or constrained. In results not reported, the lag length of the unconstrained VAR model was increased from 6 to 12. The results were similar. The conclusion is that even though the distribution of the Hinich tests is known only asymptotically, the magnitude of the Z scores indicates, at a high confidence level, that both the input series and the output series fail the null hypotheses of Gaussianity and linearity that were assumed by Tiao and Box (1981) for the gas furnace data[6]. If only the output series residuals were nonlinear, it might be possible to select a nonlinear model that was linearizable and would both improve the sum of squares of the residuals and reduce the measured nonlinearity in the output series residuals. In the present case, both input and output residuals are shown to fail the nonlinearity test. In this situation, it is impossible to identify a linearizable model that would transform the output series residuals so that they no longer fail the linearity tests because the nonlinearity in the input series residual will pass through any linear filter to the output series. This statement is based on the powerful equivalence theorem that was both proved and tested by simulations performed by Ashley, Patterson, and Hinich (1986). Their theorem proved that the Hinich linearity test could be applied to either the raw series or the residuals of a linear model since the nonlinearity would pass through any linear model.

In view of the above problems, two possible courses are possible. The first, which is beyond the scope of this chapter, would be to search for an appropriate nonlinear model that would clean the residuals of both the input and output series. The second course of action is to proceed to attempt to identify a linear model with nonlinear interaction terms and also log transformations that would improve the fit of the model in the sense of reducing the sum of squares of the output series, with the full realization that such a model will not reduce the measured nonlinearity in the residuals due to the equivalence theorem discussed earlier. If only the output series residuals had been nonlinear, it might have been possible to identify a model that would both reduce the sum of squares of the output series and remove the nonlinearity. In summary, testing has called into question the adequacy of the specification of a linear model for a famous data set.[7]

Table 8.1 Estimated Coefficients for Gas Furnace Data

lag	Unconstrained Model $A_{1,1}$	$A_{1,2}$	$A_{2,1}$	$A_{2,2}$	Constrained Model $A_{1,1}$	$A_{1,2}$	$A_{2,1}$	$A_{2,2}$
1	1.93	-.0508	.0632	1.55	1.982			1.522
	(.0581)	(.0457)	(.0743)	(.0585)	(.055)			(.0571)
2	-1.20	.0999	-.133	-.593	-1.387			-.568
	(.126)	(.0843)	(.161)	(.108)	(.0998)			(.1063)
3	.17	-.0796	-.441	-.171	.349		-.530	-.159
	(.144)	(.0881)	(.184)	(.113)	(.0551)		(.0741)	(.0997)
4	- .16	.0269	.152	.132			.1180	.1312
	(.145)	(.0877)	(.186)	(.112)			(.1631)	(.0431)
5	.38	-.0414	-.120	.0569			-.0451	
	(.137)	(.0771)	(.175)	(.0985)			(.1734)	
6	-.214	.0305	.249	-.0421			.2091	
	(.0839)	(.0328)	(.107)	(.0419)			(.1056)	
S	.03408				.03593			
	-.00229	.0557			-.00290	.056143		

Standard errors are listed parenthetically. Constants were estimated for the
constrained problem and were -.004138 and 3.9992, respectively, with standard
errors .01115 and .8335 for equations 1 and 2, respectively. The constrained
and unconstrained AR models were selected by Tiao and Box (1981). S = residual
error covariance matrix.

Table 8.2   Z Scores for Gaussianity and Linearity Tests

	Equation 1 Unconstrained G	L	Constrained G	L	Equation 2 Unconstrained G	L	Constrained G	L
M								
9	10.86	5.80	11.76	7.75	11.27	5.53	11.64	5.81
10	12.07	6.30	12.53	5.91	11.86	4.52	12.05	6.34
11	7.05	6.77	8.62	7.30	11.24	5.29	11.35	6.00
12	12.75	3.08	12.77	7.01	12.22	6.27	12.21	4.87
13	5.99	2.63	6.94	2.74	11.19	4.00	11.41	5.81
14	7.51	1.45	8.07	1.37	10.92	8.45	11.36	4.75
15	4.99	4.04	4.98	1.98	11.45	3.27	11.58	6.21
16	6.47	3.40	6.95	8.19	12.91	3.46	12.91	2.49
17	7.63	1.11	9.30	6.59	12.05	.17	12.39	.99
18	6.48	.60	6.90	.63	12.46	4.23	12.67	4.06
Mean	8.18	3.52	8.88	4.95	11.76	4.52	11.96	4.73

G = Z score for normal approximation for Gaussianity test.
L = Z score for linearity test.
M = Square root of the number of terms used to estimate the bispectrum
    at the center of the square.

The number of residuals was 290.

Equation 1 is for the gas furnace input data (Box-Jenkins (1970)).
Equation 2 is for the gas furnace output data (Box-Jenkins (1970)).

8.4 Examples

Table 8.3 lists a sample B34S setup to illustrate the

options in the BTIDEN and BTEST commands discussed in this
chapter. The data-loading step was shown in Table 7.2 and is not
duplicated here. The first BTIDEN step illustrates the
calculation of the ACF, the CCF and the Hinich (1982) tests for
GASIN and GASOUT from the gas furnace data. The GASIN data was
first differenced and "seasonally differenced" for illustrative
purposes only. Plots of the ACF and CCF are shown. The ACF of the
GASIN series clearly shows the effects of over differencing. The
plot of the CCF of the GASIN and GASOUT series shows clearly that
GASOUT is a function of lags of GASIN. The Hinich (1982) mean G
and mean L tests for GASOUT of 159.606 and 20.80, respectively,
suggest that GASOUT fails both the Gaussianity and linearity
tests, as is also true for the overdifferenced GASIN series.[8] The
output shows the +, -, . output convention for displaying the ACF
and CCF values. These are shown in matrix form at each position.
By convention, for element (i,j) series i is lagged. Hence, the
1,2 position for various lags shows the effect of lags of series
1 (GASIN) on series 2 (GASOUT). This convention is only for the
output of the correlation matrices.

Table 8.3   Estimating VAR Models for the Gas Furnace Data

```
B34SEXEC BTIDEN$
   TITLE=('IDENTIFICATION RUN WITH GAS DATA')  $
   SERIESN VAR=GASIN  NAME=('B-J GAS INPUT DATA')  DIF=(1 1)(1 12)  $
   SERIESN VAR=GASOUT NAME=('B-J GAS OUTPUT DATA') $
   IDEN LAGRHO=36 ISACF ISCCF $
   BISPEC  IAUTO ITURNO $
   B34SEEND $

B34SEXEC BTIDEN$
   TITLE=('IDENTIFICATION RUN WITH GAS DATA')  $
   SERIESN VAR=GASIN  NAME=('B-J GAS INPUT DATA')  $
   SERIESN VAR=GASOUT NAME=('B-J GAS OUTPUT DATA') $
   ESTVAR P=6 OUTPUT=NORMAL ILARF$
   BISPEC IAUTO ITURNO $
   B34SEEND$

B34SEXEC BTEST$
   TITLE=('ESTIMATION RUN WITH GAS DATA')  $
   SERIESN VAR=GASIN  NAME=('B-J GAS INPUT DATA')  $
   SERIESN VAR=GASOUT NAME=('B-J GAS OUTPUT DATA') $
   AR(1,1,1)=1.9    $
   AR(1,2,2)=1.5    $
   AR(2,1,1)=-1.2   $
   AR(2,2,2)=-.59   $
   AR(3,1,1)=.17    $
   AR(3,2,1)=-.44   $
   AR(3,2,2)=-.17   $
   AR(4,2,1)=.15    $
   AR(4,2,2)=.13    $
   AR(5,2,1)=-.12   $
   AR(6,2,1)=.11    $
   OUTPUT IPRINT  LAGRHO=24 $
   CONSTANT=(YES,YES) $
   COVARIANCE(1,1)=.3$
   COVARIANCE(2,1)=  -.1   $
   COVARIANCE(2,2)=  .06   $
   FORECAST NT=(296,250) NF=(24,20) SE ACTUAL OUTPUT=BOTH $
   BISPEC IAUTO ITURNO $
   B34SEEND$
==
```

Edited output for this problem follows. First, the ACF of GASIN
and GASOUT is given. Next, the CCF is displayed.

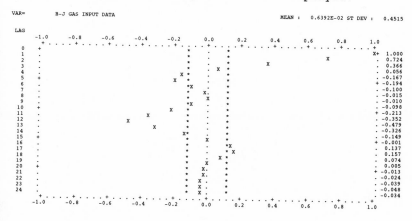

VAR=   B-J GAS OUTPUT DATA   MEAN :   53.54   ST DEV :   3.264

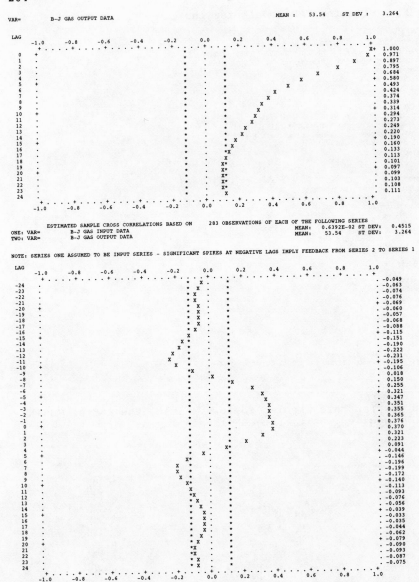

```
LAG
     -1.0    -0.8    -0.6    -0.4    -0.2     0.0     0.2     0.4     0.6     0.8     1.0
  0                                                                                   X+   1.000
  1                                                                               X    .   0.971
  2                                                                           X        .   0.897
  3                                                                     X               .   0.795
  4                                                               X                     +   0.684
  5                                                          X                          .   0.580
  6                                                     X                                .   0.493
  7                                                 X                                    .   0.424
  8                                               X                                      .   0.374
  9                                             X                                        +   0.339
 10                                           X                                          .   0.314
 11                                          X                                           .   0.294
 12                                         X                                            .   0.273
 13                                        X                                             .   0.249
 14                                       X                                              +   0.220
 15                                      X                                               .   0.190
 16                                     X                                                .   0.160
 17                                    X                                                 .   0.133
 18                                   X                                                  .   0.113
 19                                   X                                                  +   0.101
 20                                   X                                                  .   0.097
 21                                   X                                                  .   0.099
 22                                   X                                                  .   0.103
 23                                  X                                                   .   0.108
 24                                  X                                                   .   0.111
     -1.0    -0.8    -0.6    -0.4    -0.2     0.0     0.2     0.4     0.6     0.8     1.0
```

                 ESTIMATED SAMPLE CROSS CORRELATIONS BASED ON   283 OBSERVATIONS OF EACH OF THE FOLLOWING SERIES
                                                                 MEAN: 0.6392E-02 ST DEV: 0.4515
ONE: VAR=   B-J GAS INPUT DATA   MEAN: 53.54 ST DEV: 3.264
TWO: VAR=   B-J GAS OUTPUT DATA

NOTE: SERIES ONE ASSUMED TO BE INPUT SERIES - SIGNIFICANT SPIKES AT NEGATIVE LAGS IMPLY FEEDBACK FROM SERIES 2 TO SERIES 1

```
LAG
      -1.0    -0.8    -0.6    -0.4    -0.2     0.0     0.2     0.4     0.6     0.8     1.0
-24                                          X                                          .  -0.049
-23                                          X                                          .  -0.063
-22                                          X                                          .  -0.074
-21                                          X                                          .  -0.076
-20                                          X                                          +  -0.069
-19                                          X                                          .  -0.060
-18                                          X                                          .  -0.057
-17                                          X                                          .  -0.068
-16                                         X                                           .  -0.088
-15                                       X                                             +  -0.115
-14                                     X                                               .  -0.151
-13                                   X                                                 .  -0.190
-12                                 X                                                   .  -0.222
-11                                X                                                    .  -0.231
-10                                 X                                                   +  -0.195
 -9                                      X                                              .  -0.106
 -8                                            X                                        .   0.018
 -7                                               X                                     .   0.150
 -6                                                   X                                 +   0.255
 -5                                                       X                             .   0.321
 -4                                                        X                            .   0.347
 -3                                                        X                            .   0.351
 -2                                                        X                            .   0.355
 -1                                                        X                            +   0.365
  0                                                         X                           .   0.376
  1                                                         X                           .   0.370
  2                                                     X                               .   0.321
  3                                               X                                     .   0.223
  4                                          X                                          +   0.091
  5                                        X                                            .  -0.044
  6                                      X                                              .  -0.146
  7                                   X                                                 .  -0.196
  8                                   X                                                 .  -0.199
  9                                    X                                                +  -0.172
 10                                     X                                               .  -0.140
 11                                      X                                              .  -0.113
 12                                       X                                             .  -0.093
 13                                        X                                            .  -0.076
 14                                        X                                            +  -0.056
 15                                         X                                           .  -0.039
 16                                         X                                           .  -0.033
 17                                         X                                           .  -0.035
 18                                        X                                            .  -0.044
 19                                        X                                            +  -0.062
 20                                       X                                             .  -0.079
 21                                       X                                             .  -0.090
 22                                       X                                             .  -0.093
 23                                       X                                             .  -0.087
 24                                        X                                            .  -0.075
      -1.0    -0.8    -0.6    -0.4    -0.2     0.0     0.2     0.4     0.6     0.8     1.0
```

SUMMARIES OF CROSS CORRELATION MATRICES USING +,-,., WHERE
    + DENOTES A VALUE GREATER THAN G/SQRT(NOBE)
    - DENOTES A VALUE LESS THAN -G/SQRT(NOBE)
    . DENOTES A NON-SIGNIFICANT VALUE BASED ON THE ABOVE CRITERION, WHERE G =   2.000   .

BEHAVIOR OF VALUES IN (I,J)TH POSITION OF CROSS CORRELATION MATRIX OVER ALL OUTPUTTED LAGS

    ++.--....---   +++..------..
    --.++.......   ....
    ....++..   ....

    +++++++.----   ++++++++++++
    --..........   +++++.......
    ....

CROSS CORRELATION MATRICES IN TERMS OF +,-,.

NOTE: SERIES I IS LAGGED FOR EACH TERM P(I,J)

LAGS 1 THROUGH   6

    + +   + +   . +   - .   - .   . -
    + +   + +   + +   + +   + +   + +

LAGS 7 THROUGH 12

    . -   . -   . -   - -   - .   - .
    + +   . +   . +   - +   - +   - +

LAGS 13 THROUGH 18

    - .   - .   . .   + .   + .   . .
    - +   - +   . +   . +   . +   . .

LAGS 19 THROUGH 24

    . .   . .
    . .   . .

LAGS 25 THROUGH 30

    . .   . .
    . .   . .

LAGS 31 THROUGH 36

    . .   . .   + .   + ...
    . .   . .

The second BTIDEN call estimates a VAR model with six lags. The ILARF option has been specified to display only the last set of VAR matrices. The Hinich (1982) tests have been requested with the BISPEC sentence for a grid of M values going from 9 to 18, respectively. These lower and upper values of M default to $(T/3)^{.5}$ and $(T)^{.5}$, respectively, unless specified by the user.[9] The estimated VAR coefficients agree with what was reported in Table 8.1 for the unconstrained model and the Hinich values agree with what was reported in Table 8.2. The major finding is that both the input series, GASIN, and the output series, GASOUT, fail the Gaussianity and linearity tests since the mean G and L values were (8.18, 3.52) and (11.76, 4.52), respectively. The AFC and CCF plots show that the sixth-order VAR model is adequate from a linear perspective, even though the nonlinearity tests suggest that there are problems. Stokes and Hinich (1989) make the point that it is imperative to test models thought to be linear beyond just looking at the AFC and CCF. The gas furnace data were selected to illustrate this point since they were used by Tiao and Box (1981) to illustrate the VAR and VARMA techniques. The stepwise autoregression summary suggests that a model of order 5 or 6 is adequate since the chi-square test statistic has fallen from its initial value of 1678.12 to 12.85.[10] Edited output for this identification run follows. Series 1 is GASIN; series 2 is GASOUT.

```
        SERIES 1 HAS SAMPLE MEAN = -0.56834459E-01    AND SAMPLE STD. DEV. =  1.0709519

        SERIES 2 HAS SAMPLE MEAN =  53.509122         AND SAMPLE STD. DEV. =  3.1967072

OUTPUT CONTROL CARD (S8) READ    IBRIEF LAGRHO ICANON PHICOR NVALUE ISCAU SCAP ILARF IBISP IIRES IURES NSTDER
                                   0      0      0      0      0      0     0    1     1     0     0  0.0000E+00
```

```
*********** P = 6, PS = 0, S = 0, J = 6,   LAGS:  1   2   3   4   5   6

********** PHI( 1) **********              ******** STD. ERRORS ********         ** SIGNIFICANCE **
  0.193E+01-0.508E-01                        0.581E-01 0.457E-01                    +  .
  0.632E-01 0.155E+01                        0.743E-01 0.585E-01                    .  +
********** PHI( 2) **********              ******** STD. ERRORS ********         ** SIGNIFICANCE **
 -0.120E+01 0.999E-01                        0.126E+00 0.843E-01                    -  .
 -0.133E+00-0.593E+00                        0.161E+00 0.108E+00                    .  -
********** PHI( 3) **********              ******** STD. ERRORS ********         ** SIGNIFICANCE **
  0.170E+00-0.796E-01                        0.144E+00 0.881E-01                    .  .
 -0.441E+00-0.171E+00                        0.184E+00 0.113E+00                    -  .
********** PHI( 4) **********              ******** STD. ERRORS ********         ** SIGNIFICANCE **
 -0.160E+00 0.269E-01                        0.145E+00 0.877E-01                    .  .
  0.152E+00 0.132E+00                        0.186E+00 0.112E+00                    .  .
********** PHI( 5) **********              ******** STD. ERRORS ********         ** SIGNIFICANCE **
  0.380E+00-0.414E-01                        0.137E+00 0.771E-01                    +  .
 -0.120E+00 0.569E-01                        0.175E+00 0.985E-01                    .  .
********** PHI( 6) **********              ******** STD. ERRORS ********         ** SIGNIFICANCE **
 -0.214E+00 0.305E-01                        0.839E-01 0.328E-01                    -  .
  0.249E+00-0.421E-01                        0.107E+00 0.419E-01                    +  .
******** RESIDUAL COVARIANCE MATRIX S(J) ********        ******** RESIDUAL CORRELATION MATRIX RS(J) ********
  0.341E-01                                                 1.00
 -0.229E-02 0.557E-01                                      -0.05    1.00
```

```
*****************************************************************************************
NOTE: MODEL AS ESTIMATED IS IN THE FORM AR(0)=MA(0)=I AND SIGMA-N NOT A DIAGONAL MATRIX

      MODEL CAN BE WRITTEN IN FORM AR(0) NE I AND MA(0) = I WHERE SIGMA-U IS A DIAGONAL MATRIX

THE FORMER CASE BEING MODEL A AND THE LATTER BEING MODEL C ON PAGE 223 OF GRANGER AND NEWBOLD (1977)

WANT TO CALCULATE DIAGONAL ELEMENTS OF SIGMA-U AND CALCULATE LOWER TRIANGULAR MATRIX P SUCH THAT

                    P * SIGMA-N  *  P TRANSPOSE = SIGMA-U

IN MODEL C  NEW AR(0)=P * AR(0)......NEW AR(J)= P* AR(J)  --  NOTE: AR(0) WILL BE LOWER TRIANGULAR


DIAGONAL ELEMENTS OF DIAGONAL MATRIX SIGMA-U

  0.34085314E-01  0.55495793E-01

P INVERSE

   1.0000000

 -0.67324068E-01  1.0000000

P MATRIX

   1.0000000

  0.67324068E-01  1.0000000
*****************************************************************************************
******** EIGENVALUES AND EIGENVECTORS OF S(J) ********

   EIGENVALUES     EIGENVECTORS

   0.3384E-01       0.9945    0.1047

   0.5589E-01      -0.1047    0.9945


DETERMINANT OF S(J) =  0.1892E-02, 1/CONDITION =  0.65778949

LEADING TO A VALUE OF THE TEST STATISTIC M = -W*LN(U) =   12.85

          APPROXIMATELY DISTRIBUTED AS A CHI SQUARE WITH   4 DF AND PROB =  0.9880
          WHERE U = DET(S(J))/DET(S(J-1))
```

S(J) = RESIDUAL COVARIANCE MATRIX AFTER JTH FIT
W = (NOBE-MAXLAG-1)-J*K-.5, AND DF = K*K.

SUMMARIES OF CROSS CORRELATION MATRICES USING +,-,., WHERE
  + DENOTES A VALUE GREATER THAN G/SQRT(NOBE)
  - DENOTES A VALUE LESS THAN -G/SQRT(NOBE)
  . DENOTES A NON-SIGNIFICANT VALUE BASED ON THE ABOVE CRITERION, WHERE G =   2.000   .

BEHAVIOR OF VALUES IN (I,J)TH POSITION OF CROSS CORRELATION MATRIX OVER ALL OUTPUTTED LAGS

    ....-   ....

    ....

CROSS CORRELATION MATRICES IN TERMS OF +,-,.

NOTE: SERIES I IS LAGGED FOR EACH TERM P(I,J)

LAGS   1 THROUGH   6

    . .   . .
    . .   . .
LAGS   7 THROUGH 12

    . .   . .   - .
    . .   . .

SUMMARY TABLE FOR RESIDUALS FOR EQUATION   1
MEAN=   0.13304970E-14
VARIANCE=   0.34085314E-01
STANDARD DEVIATION=   0.18462209
SKEWNESS=   0.33264134E-01
KURTOSIS=   6.4218618
OF OBSERVATIONS=   290

HINICH BISPECTRUM SUMMARY TABLE

M	G	Z	BICOH	LAMDA
9	10.861086	5.8015164	2.1962023	0.21326145
10	12.066392	6.2986763	2.3970713	1.4411906
11	7.0446751	6.7687438	2.0293502	0.35584957E-01
12	12.750474	3.0802343	2.6610967	1.4805421
13	5.9925537	2.6303579	2.0221384	0.67583871
14	7.5115334	1.4465442	2.2496022	1.8271821
15	4.9896172	4.0394177	1.9894589	0.26802819
16	6.4668424	3.4031907	2.2431744	0.26659665
17	7.6306709	1.1089245	2.4460538	3.1206068
18	6.4782033	0.60189779	2.3418767	2.0447888

MEAN FOR G =   8.1792047
MEAN FOR Z =   3.5179504

FOR THE ABOVE TABLE NWD =   53
WT =   -1.3462879

M   = # OF TERMS AVERAGED TO ESTIMATE BISPECTRUM
G   = (Z) STATISTIC TO TEST FOR GAUSSIANITY
Z   = (Z) STATISTIC TO TEST FOR LINEARITY
BICOH = AVERAGE SKEWNESS (MEASURE OF NONLINEAR PREDICTABILITY)
LAMDA = ESTIMATE OF NON-CENTRALITY
WT   = WHITENESS STATISTIC

SMOOTHING HAS NOT BEEN DONE.

SUMMARY TABLE FOR RESIDUALS FOR EQUATION   2
MEAN=   0.22131722E-13
VARIANCE=   0.55650286E-01
STANDARD DEVIATION=   0.23590313
SKEWNESS=   1.0691018
KURTOSIS=   5.5911437
OF OBSERVATIONS=   290

HINICH BISPECTRUM SUMMARY TABLE

M	G	Z	BICOH	LAMDA
9	11.269996	5.5274581	2.2257128	0.83303883
10	11.857019	4.5153034	2.3799762	0.88937093
11	11.240068	5.2914111	2.3973104	0.10000000E-15
12	12.219749	6.2680419	2.6090549	1.0172540
13	11.185675	4.0006476	2.5521591	1.6430483
14	10.924630	8.4519941	2.6311980	0.66557286
15	11.448641	3.2659577	2.7403052	1.1481693
16	12.909613	3.4586398	3.0749325	1.9372543
17	12.047212	0.16760852	3.0470690	4.3164527
18	12.461484	4.2347047	3.2054889	2.7544375

MEAN FOR G =   11.756409
MEAN FOR Z =   4.5181767

FOR THE ABOVE TABLE NWD =   53
WT =   -0.66316780

```
M       = # OF TERMS AVERAGED TO ESTIMATE BISPECTRUM
G       = (Z) STATISTIC TO TEST FOR GAUSSIANITY
Z       = (Z) STATISTIC TO TEST FOR LINEARITY
BICOH   = AVERAGE SKEWNESS (MEASURE OF NONLINEAR PREDICTABILITY)
LAMDA   = ESTIMATE OF NON-CENTRALITY
WT      = WHITENESS STATISTIC

SMOOTHING HAS NOT BEEN DONE.

**********  STEPWISE AUTOREGRESSION SUMMARY  **********
```

LAG	STD. PARTIAL AR COEFFICIENTS		SIGNIF.	RESIDUAL VARIANCES	CHI-SQ TEST	PROB
1	50.35	4.46	+ +	0.101E+00	1678.12	1.0000
	-13.65	73.48	- +	0.341E+00		
2	-20.17	2.38	- +	0.365E-01	677.52	1.0000
	-9.88	-21.90	- -	0.679E-01		
3	2.86	-0.72	+ .	0.354E-01	32.50	1.0000
	-1.86	4.69	. +	0.622E-01		
4	1.24	0.54	. .	0.352E-01	22.96	0.9999
	2.71	3.92	+ +	0.578E-01		
5	1.15	0.33	. .	0.350E-01	5.77	0.7828
	2.00	-0.42	+ .	0.570E-01		
6	-2.55	0.93	. .	0.341E-01	12.85	0.9880
	2.32	-1.00	+ .	0.557E-01		

```
    NOTE: DEGREES OF FREEDOM FOR CHI-SQUARE STAT =   4

    NOTE: THE PARTIAL AUTOREGRESSION COEFFICIENT MATRIX FOR LAG L IS THE
          ESTIMATED PHI(L) FROM THE FIT WHERE THE MAXIMUM LAG USED IS L
          (IE THE LAST COEFFICIENT MATRIX). THE ELEMENTS ARE
          STANDARDIZED BY DIVIDING EACH BY ITS STANDARD ERROR.


*********  SIGNIFICANCE OF PARTIAL AUTOREGRESSION COEFFICIENTS BY LAG  *********
```

EQN	COEFF. OF	LAG L: 1 2 3 4 5 6
W(1,T)	W(1,T-L)	+ - + . . -
	W(2,T-L)	+ + ...
W(2,T)	W(1,T-L)	- - . + + +
	W(2,T-L)	+ - + + . .

The BTEST call estimates a constrained VAR model and replicates the constrained VAR coefficients reported in Table 8.1 and Hinich tests reported in Table 8.2. Forecasting is done for 24 periods out from observation 296 and 20 periods out from observation 250. Two styles of forecast output are shown and actual values are given when available. Box and Jenkins (1976) argued that the effect of GASIN on GASOUT occurred after a three-period lag. This is apparent when we note that the significant VAR coefficients occur in $Q_{ij}(B)$ in equation (8.1-9), where $i > j$ when the lag is $\geq$ 3. The OUTPUT sentence contains the option IPRINT to display both the values and the summarized cross correlation matrices. Inspection of these matrices indicate that the linear model is apparently adequate, although the Hinich summary tests for GASIN and GASOUT of (8.88, 4.95) and (11.96, 4.73), respectively, for G and L tell us otherwise.

The next section shows edited output for constrained VAR estimation.[11] Correlation matrix output and display of some of the forecast tables has been shortened to save space.

********** M U L T I V A R I A T E   T I M E   S E R I E S   E S T I M A T I O N **

FOR: ESTIMATION RUN WITH GAS DATA

    SERIES 1: VAR=   B-J GAS INPUT DATA
    SERIES 2: VAR=   B-J GAS OUTPUT DATA

    SPECIFIED MODEL = (6, 0)

    NUMBER OF OBSERVATIONS =   296 (EFFECTIVE NUMBER = NOBE =   290)

    ** CONDITIONAL LIKELIHOOD METHOD **

    FORECASTS REQUESTED:

        24 FORECASTS, BEGINNING AT ORIGIN = 296
        20 FORECASTS, BEGINNING AT ORIGIN = 250

***** FINAL MODEL SUMMARY WITH CONDITIONAL LIKELIHOOD PARAMETER ESTIMATES **

PARAMETER NUMBER	PARAMETER DESCRIPTION	FINAL ESTIMATE	ESTIMATED STD. ERROR	T STAT
**********	****************************	***********	***********	***********
1	CONSTANT(1)	-.413819E-02	0.111516E-01	-0.3711
2	CONSTANT(2)	3.99921	0.833512	4.798
3	REG AUTOREGRESSIVE (1, 1, 1)	1.98203	0.550517E-01	36.0030
4	REG AUTOREGRESSIVE (1, 2, 2)	1.52151	0.570689E-01	26.6609
5	REG AUTOREGRESSIVE (2, 1, 1)	-1.38669	0.997954E-01	-13.8954
6	REG AUTOREGRESSIVE (2, 2, 2)	-.568423	0.106336	-5.34554
7	REG AUTOREGRESSIVE (3, 1, 1)	0.349328	0.551084E-01	6.33893
8	REG AUTOREGRESSIVE (3, 2, 1)	-.530301	0.740718E-01	-7.15928
9	REG AUTOREGRESSIVE (3, 2, 2)	-.159244	0.997400E-01	-1.59659
10	REG AUTOREGRESSIVE (4, 2, 1)	0.118027	0.163055	0.723847
11	REG AUTOREGRESSIVE (4, 2, 2)	0.131277	0.431379E-01	3.04318
12	REG AUTOREGRESSIVE (5, 2, 1)	-.450575E-01	0.173376	-.259884
13	REG AUTOREGRESSIVE (6, 2, 1)	0.209106	0.105586	1.98044

****

ERROR COVARIANCE MATRIX,
****

  0.359287E-01

  -.290209E-02 0.561434E-01

****

ERROR CORRELATION MATRIX - SIGNIFICANT OFF DIAGONAL ELEMENTS SIGNIFY INSTANTANEOUS CAUSALITY
****

  1.00000

  -.646161E-01 1.00000

****

NOTE: MODEL AS ESTIMATED IS IN THE FORM AR(0)=MA(0)=I AND SIGMA-N NOT A DIAGONAL MATRIX

      MODEL CAN BE WRITTEN IN FORM AR(0) NE I AND MA(0) = I WHERE SIGMA-U IS A DIAGONAL MATRIX

THE FORMER CASE BEING MODEL A AND THE LATTER BEING MODEL C ON PAGE 223 OF GRANGER AND NEWBOLD (1977)

WANT TO CALCULATE DIAGONAL ELEMENTS OF SIGMA-U AND CALCULATE LOWER TRIANGULAR MATRIX P SUCH THAT

                   P * SIGMA-N * P TRANSPOSE = SIGMA-U

IN MODEL C NEW AR(0)=P * AR(0)......NEW AR(J)= P* AR(J) -- NOTE: AR(0) WILL BE LOWER TRIANGULAR

DIAGONAL ELEMENTS OF DIAGONAL MATRIX SIGMA-U

  0.35928675E-01 0.55908966E-01

P INVERSE

  1.0000000

 -0.80773653E-01 1.0000000

P MATRIX

  1.0000000

  0.80773653E-01 1.0000000

****

OBJECTIVE FUNCTION AT FINAL MAXIMUM LIKELIHOOD PARAMETER ESTIMATES = 580.00000

****

CORRELATION MATRIX, OF THE PARAMETERS
****

	1	2	3	4	5	6	7	8	9	10	11	12	13
1	1.0												
2	.	1.0											
3	.	.	1.0										
4	.	.	.	1.0									
5	.	.	-.9	.	1.0								
6	.	.	.	-.8	.	1.0							
7	.	.	.7	.	-.9	.	1.0						
8	.	.	.	.	.	.	.	1.0					
9	.	.	.	.	.	-.8	.	.	1.0				
10	.	.	.	.	.	.	.	-.8	.	1.0			
11	.	.	.	.	.5	.	.	.	-.9	.	1.0		
12	.	.	.	.	.	.	.	.5	.	-.8	.	1.0	
13	.	.	.	.	.	.	.	.	.	.	.	-.8	1.0

****

DIAGNOSTIC CHECKS ON RESIDUALS :

SUMMARY STATISTICS OF RESIDUAL SERIES

SERIES	MEAN	STANDARD DEVIATION	MEAN / (SE MEAN)
1	0.22360877E-05	0.18954861	0.20089412E-03
2	-0.46256811E-04	0.23694593	-0.33244930E-02

SUMMARY TABLE FOR RESIDUALS FROM EQUATION   1
MEAN=   0.22360877E-05
VARIANCE=   0.35928675E-01
STANDARD DEVIATION=   0.18954861
SKEWNESS=   0.14881109E-01
KURTOSIS=   6.3136774
OF OBSERVATIONS=   290

HINICH BISPECTRUM SUMMARY TABLE

M	G	Z	BICOH	LAMDA
9	11.756425	7.7540258	2.2608178	0.10788980
10	12.526883	5.9133029	2.4346702	0.77587950
11	8.6206191	7.3000778	2.1675696	0.10000000E-15
12	12.772764	7.0115886	2.6632825	0.80218458
13	6.9379230	2.7406422	2.1186247	0.50910935
14	8.0742639	1.3686043	2.3125174	0.80589617
15	4.9753058	1.9839356	1.9877953	0.69124883
16	6.9486852	8.1914093	2.3053801	0.10000000E-15
17	9.2967231	6.5935270	2.6727748	1.6245443
18	6.8958040	0.63477464	2.4021522	1.4301280

MEAN FOR G =   8.8805396
MEAN FOR Z =   4.9491888

FOR THE ABOVE TABLE NWD =   53
WT =   -1.2139964

M   = # OF TERMS AVERAGED TO ESTIMATE BISPECTRUM
G   = (Z) STATISTIC TO TEST FOR GAUSSIANITY
Z   = (Z) STATISTIC TO TEST FOR LINEARITY
BICOH = AVERAGE SKEWNESS (MEASURE OF NONLINEAR PREDICTABILITY)
LAMDA = ESTIMATE OF NON-CENTRALITY
WT   = WHITENESS STATISTIC

SMOOTHING HAS NOT BEEN DONE.

SUMMARY TABLE FOR RESIDUALS FROM EQUATION   2
MEAN=   -0.46256811E-04
VARIANCE=   0.56143376E-01
STANDARD DEVIATION=   0.23694593
SKEWNESS=   1.0350425
KURTOSIS=   5.5185977
OF OBSERVATIONS=   290

HINICH BISPECTRUM SUMMARY TABLE

M	G	Z	BICOH	LAMDA
9	11.637054	5.8056103	2.2522030	0.50544912
10	12.053151	6.3367069	2.3959903	0.63120262
11	11.349314	5.9995558	2.4068920	0.10000000E-15
12	12.206490	4.8712265	2.6077548	0.99330369
13	11.406849	5.8079097	2.5747325	1.1011931

14	11.357837	4.7478265	2.6796320	1.3810425
15	11.579359	6.2070784	2.7555009	0.52811939
16	12.912967	2.4918686	3.0753655	2.0831858
17	12.390240	0.98776262	3.0937491	3.9471472
18	12.670003	4.0564274	3.2355860	2.8345125

MEAN FOR G =   11.956326
MEAN FOR Z =   4.7311973

FOR THE ABOVE TABLE NWD =   53
WT =   -0.61390680

M   = # OF TERMS AVERAGED TO ESTIMATE BISPECTRUM
G   = (Z) STATISTIC TO TEST FOR GAUSSIANITY
Z   = (Z) STATISTIC TO TEST FOR LINEARITY
BICOH = AVERAGE SKEWNESS (MEASURE OF NONLINEAR PREDICTABILITY)
LAMDA = ESTIMATE OF NON-CENTRALITY
WT   = WHITENESS STATISTIC

SMOOTHING HAS NOT BEEN DONE.

SAMPLE CORRELATION MATRICES FOR 24 LAGS.

NOTE: SERIES I IS LAGGED FOR EACH TERM P(I,J).

P(I,J) IS INTERPRETED AS THE TRANSPOSE OF THE WAY VAR(I,J) AND VMA(I,J) TERMS ARE INTERPRETED.

************** LAG = 1 **************

  -0.0495 0.0477

  -0.0530 0.0265
************** LAG = 2 **************

   0.0684 -0.0082

   0.0252 0.0136
************** LAG = 3 **************

   0.0590 -0.0078

  -0.0526 0.0132

Note: Output edited to save space here.

************** LAG = 23 **************

   0.0391 0.0267

  -0.0740 0.0174
************** LAG = 24 **************

  -0.0029 -0.0016

  -0.0608 -0.0068

SUMMARIES OF CROSS CORRELATION MATRICES USING +,-,., WHERE
      + DENOTES A VALUE GREATER THAN G/SQRT(NOBE)
      - DENOTES A VALUE LESS THAN -G/SQRT(NOBE)
      . DENOTES A NON-SIGNIFICANT VALUE BASED ON THE ABOVE CRITERION, WHERE G =   2.000   .

BEHAVIOR OF VALUES IN (I,J)TH POSITION OF CROSS CORRELATION MATRIX OVER ALL OUTPUTTED LAGS

     ...-......+.   ....
     ....-.....

     ....
     ....-.....

CROSS CORRELATION MATRICES IN TERMS OF +,-,.

NOTE: SERIES I IS LAGGED FOR EACH TERM P(I,J)

LAGS 1 THROUGH 6

     . .   . .   . .   - .   . .   . .
     . .   . .
LAGS 7 THROUGH 12

```
  . .          . .         . .          . .         + .          . .
  . .          . .         . .          . .         . .          . .
```
LAGS 13 THROUGH 18

```
  . .          . .         . .          . .         . .          . .
  . .          . .         . .          . .         . .          . .
```
LAGS 19 THROUGH 24

```
  . -          . .         . .          . .         . .          . .
  . -          . .         . .          . .         . .          . .
```

****

    24 FORECASTS, BEGINNING AT ORIGIN = 296
    ****

T	K	FORECAST	STANDARD ERROR	ACTUAL VALUE (IF AVAILABLE)
297	1	-.265112	0.189549	
	2	56.6544	0.236946	
298	1	-.229862	0.420799	
	2	56.3959	0.431410	
299	1	-.183625	0.639677	
	2	56.1919	0.597814	
300	1	-.141951	0.811999	
	2	56.0214	0.722695	
301	1	-.111155	0.930531	
	2	55.8167	0.867252	

Note: Output edited to save space here.

    20 FORECASTS, BEGINNING AT ORIGIN = 250
    ****

T	K	FORECAST	STANDARD ERROR	ACTUAL VALUE (IF AVAILABLE)
251	1	0.354098E-01	0.189549	0.185000
	2	56.2299	0.236946	56.3000
252	1	0.307778	0.420799	0.662000
	2	56.1509	0.431410	56.4000
253	1	0.418799	0.639677	0.709000
	2	55.9102	0.597814	56.4000
254	1	0.411508	0.811999	0.605000
	2	55.3387	0.722695	56.0000
255	1	0.338252	0.930531	0.501000
	2	54.5326	0.867252	55.2000
256	1	0.241949	1.00344	0.603000
	2	53.7134	1.13272	54.0000
257	1	0.150110	1.04417	0.943000
	2	53.0792	1.52823	53.0000

8.5 Conclusion

This chapter has discussed VAR, VARMA and VMA models and shown their relationship to ARIMA models, transfer function models, single-equation OLS models and simultaneous equations models. The Tiao and Box (1981) model identification strategy was discussed and illustrated and additional tests for Gaussianity and nonlinearity proposed by Hinich (1982) were applied to the gas furnace data. An apparently well specified model was found to have nonlinear aspects that were not discernible with the usual AFC and CCF tests.

NOTES

1. The code in B34S was derived from WMTS-1, which was developed by Tiao and Box at the University of Wisconsin with grants from the U. S. Bureau of the Census and the Army Research Office. Changes made by the developer of B34S include adding the Hinich (1982) tests (over 4000 lines of code), adding a front end for input of commands, and adding a decomposition of the residuals suggested by Granger and Newbold (1977, 223) as well as many changes to improve accuracy and speed. The Hinich code was developed by Hinich and Patterson (1985, 1986) and has been further enhanced. This code is discussed further in section 8.3. The accuracy and speed changes involved adding LINPACK for matrix inversion and taking advantage of the fact that when the matrix is known to be positive definite, substantial speed can be obtained by using a Cholesky decomposition factorization approach. The developer of B34S is grateful for access to this code. The WMTS-1 program has been enhanced and incorporated in the SCA statistical system and is fully documented in Liu and Hudak (1986a). The B34S implementation is a complement to the SCA implementation in that while there is some overlap of function, each version has distinct capabilities. The B34S implementation allows the coefficients to be saved in a SCA format so that they can be later inputed into SCA or SAS via the SAS PROC LINKSCA.

2. The conditions for $G(B)$ and $D(B)$ being invertible are that the roots of $|G(B)| = 0$ and $|D(B)| = 0$ lie <u>outside</u> the unit circle.

3. For further detail on this point, see the appendix to Sargent (1978). What Sargent calls the F matrix is P^{-1} in the notation of Granger and Newbold (1977, 224). I am in debt to John Sfondouris for this reference.

4. In contrast to the BJIDEN and BJEST commands, which use the Bartlett (1946) formula to calculate the standard error, the BTIDEN and BTEST commands use the more simple equation $1/\sqrt{T}$, where T is the effective number of observations. Section 8.3 discusses the basic Hinich (1982) nonlinearity test. The BISPEC sentence also supports the Hinich and Patterson (1986) martingale test and the Hinich and Wolinsky (1888) test for aliasing. Since Hinich is

currently in the process of improving the power of these tests, they are not discussed in section 8.3. For further detail on these additional tests, see the <u>B34S On-Line Help Manual</u>.

5. This section has been adapted from Stokes and Hinich (1989).

6. These results were informally discussed with George Box. It was his impression that the finding that the gas furnace input series was nonlinear was highly plausible in view of the data source.

7. Alternative models were developed in Stokes and Hinich (1989) that reduce the residual sum of squares substantially. These have not been shown here due to space limitations.

8. Since neither series is white noise, a better option would have been to set the ISMOO option on the BISPEC sentence. If ISMOO <u>is</u> <u>not</u> set, each spectral estimate is set to the variance of the series that would be appropriate for a white-noise series that had the same variance at all frequencies. In this case it would be appropriate to smooth the estimated spectrum with a cosine bell in the frequency domain. The parameter NWD sets the width of the smoothing cosine. NWD will default to 3*M, where M^2 is used in equation (8.3-6) in the calculation of the bispectrum. The Hinich (1982) output for the raw series has not been shown to save space. The output also shows the use of the +, -, . conventions to display the ACF and CCF.

9. These values have been rounded up and down, respectively.

10. Stokes and Hinich (1989) suggest that a substantial reduction in the sum of squares is possible, even though nonlinearity problems remain, if the model is changed to a 5 by 5, sixth-order VAR model containing {GASIN, ln(GASOUT), (GASIN*GASIN), (ln(GASOUT)*GASIN(-1)), (ln(GASOUT)*GASIN(-2))}. Note that the suggested model uses ln(GASOUT) rather than GASOUT. The residual variance of the 2 by 2 unconstrained VAR model is .0557, while the suggested 5 by 5 model has a corrected residual variance of .176E-04, a substantial reduction. For further details on this model and others, see Stokes and Hinich (1989). The reader is encouraged to attempt this model.

11. Due to space limitations, examples using VARMA models have not been shown.

9. Testing the Specification of OLS Equations With Recursive Residuals

9.0 Introduction

In recent years, there has been increasing interest in the development of tests to determine the correct functional specification of linear and nonlinear models. Potential specification problems include the stability of the coefficients over time, the effect of omitted variables on the estimated coefficients, and the effect of misspecified included variables on the other coefficients in the regression. The recursive residual technique, outlined in the classic article by Brown, Durbin, and Evans (1975), devised tests for equation misspecification that do not make assumptions about the nature of the possible problem.[1] These techniques have been implemented in the RR procedure. The recursive residuals can be shown to be of the LUS class (linear unbiased scaler), of which the BLUS residual (see sec. 2.9) is a special case. Many of the BLUS tests can be applied to the recursive residual, with the advantage that the calculation of the RR is computationally simpler than the corresponding calculation of BLUS residuals. Because the RR procedure involves calculating updated coefficient vectors as additional observations are added to the regression, tests can be made for parameter stability. Analogous tests are not possible with the BLUS technique.

9.1 Overview of the RR Procedure

The RR technique involves calculation of the standardized k step-ahead forecast errors. If the underlying population generating the sample coefficients is stable, the recursive residuals will not be systematically on one side or the other of the zero line. However, if the population changes as new observations are added to the data matrix, the recursive residuals will be on one side or the other of the zero line, i.e., they will be systematically biased. A regression assumes that one must draw a representative sample from the population. If the order in which the sample is drawn influences the estimated coefficients, and the data have been sorted against a specific variable, it can be inferred that the population is shifting as a function of that variable.

For example, assume a consumption function estimated in the time domain. As new observations are added to the regression, the marginal propensity to consume may shift. As new observations are added, plots of updates of the coefficients, representing the marginal propensity to consume, will show a specific pattern, if a shift has occurred. Using cross-section data, it is assumed that the marginal propensity to consume in the consumption function is the same for high-income individuals as for low-income individuals.

If the data matrix is sorted so that observations containing low-income individuals are selected first, a plot of the updated estimate of the marginal propensity to consume will test whether the estimated marginal propensity to consume drifts down. It is also possible that, owing to an unspecified interaction effect, the variable with which the data set has been sorted (in this case income) will influence another coefficient. Inspection of the plots of coefficients for variables other than income will test for this problem.

9.2 Calculation of Recursive Residuals

The vector of recursive residuals, V, is of length (T-K). If the population residual vector, e, has a scaler covariance matrix, the recursive residual does also. The RR does not have the minimum variance property of the BLUS residual but, given a sorting of the data matrix, is unique and relatively easy to calculate.[2]

If the estimated residual vector, $\hat{u}$, is linear, it can be written Cy, where C is a matrix of P rows and T columns not involving y. If the residual vector is unbiased, CX=0, since Cy = C(XB+e) has zero expectation if, and only if, CX=0. The linear unbiased residual vector has the form Ce, its covariance matrix,

$$E(Cee'C') = \sigma^2 CC', \qquad (9.2-1)$$

is a scaler matrix if, and only if,

$$CC' = I. \qquad (9.2-2)$$

Following Theil (1971, 203), it can be shown that C is of order P x T and Cy represents P disturbances and CC' is a P x P matrix, where 1 < P < T. Since

$$CX = 0, \qquad (9.2-3)$$

the columns of C are subject to K linear dependencies. The rank of C <u>cannot</u> exceed (T-K). Since the ranks of C and CC' are equal and the identity matrix, I, in equation (9.2-2) has full rank, P ≤ (T-K). This result proves that there can only be, at most, (T-K) LUS residuals. From equations (2.9-1) and (2.9-2), the relationship between the population residual, e, and the sample OLS residual, u, is

$$u = Me = Cy = CM, \qquad (9.2-4)$$

where

$$M = I - X(X'X)^{-1}X'. \qquad (9.2-5)$$

It follows from equation (9.2-3) that

CM = C   (9.2-6)

and

MC' = C'.   (9.2-7)

Since M is a symmetric idempotent matrix,

C'C = MC'CM = MIM = MM = M.   (9.2-8)

The sum of squares of the (T-K) LUS residuals (Cy) is y'C'Cy. From equation (9.2-8), we have

y'C'Cy = y'My = u'u   (9.2-9)

or the result that the sum of squares of the (T-K) LUS residuals is equivalent to the sum of squares of the T OLS residuals.

Equation (9.2-9) holds only for (T-K) LUS residuals and not for more than one-step-ahead standardized residuals. Theil (1971, 208) proves that the rows of C are eigenvectors of M associated with the unit eigenvalues of M.[3] Depending on the ordering of the data in the X matrix, a large number of LUS vectors can be calculated. As is the case with BLUS residuals (a subset of LUS residuals), particular LUS vectors are used to make specific tests.

For the duration of this chapter, X_i is defined as the X matrix for the first i observations, β_i as the OLS coefficient vector for the first i observations, Y_i as the vector of the dependent variable for the first i observations, and V_i as the one-step-ahead forecast error vector as shown below:

$$\beta_i = (X_i'X_i)^{-1}X_i'Y_i \qquad i \; \varepsilon \; \{K, \; K+1,\ldots,T\} \qquad (9.2-10)$$

$$X_i' = (x_1 \; \ldots \; x_i) \qquad (9.2-11)$$

$$Y_i = (y_1 \; \ldots \; y_i)' \qquad (9.2-12)$$

$$V_i = (v_1 \; \ldots \; v_i)'. \qquad (9.2-13)$$

The one-step-ahead forecast error vector for observation i, v_i, uses the coefficient vector estimated for i-1 observations β_{i-1} to predict the dependent variable, y_i. Using the fact that x_i is a column vector consisting of the ith observation of the independent variables, v_i can be written as

$$v_i = y_i - x_i'\beta_{i-1} \qquad i \; \varepsilon \; \{K+1,\ldots,T\}. \qquad (9.2-14)$$

Brown, Durbin, and Evans (1975) show that under the assumption of constancy of regression parameters and homoskedasticity, V_i has mean zero and variance $\sigma^2 d_i^2$, where

$d_i = (1 + x_i' (X_{i-1}' X_{i-1})^{-1} x_i)^{.5}$ $i \; \varepsilon \; \{K+1,\ldots,T\}$.   (9.2-15)

Dividing v_i by d_i gives the standardized one-step-ahead prediction error w_i or the standardized recursive residual.

$w_i = v_i \; / \; d_i$ $i \; \varepsilon \; \{K+1,\ldots,T\}$.   (9.2-16)

Brown, Durbin, and Evans (1975) show that if the OLS assumption of homoskedasticity is met,

$E(w_j \; w_i) = 0$ for $i \neq j$.   (9.2-17)

If, in addition, the assumption of parameter stability is met, $w_{K+1}, \ldots, w_T$ will be independent normally distributed with mean zero and variance σ^2.   Equation (9.2-18) calculates $(X_i' X_i)^{-1}$ without having to invert a matrix as each observation is added, equation (9.2-20) updates the coefficient vector β_i and equation (9.2-21) updates the regression standard errors as the ith observation is added.[4] To simplify notation, we define the update formula for $(X_i' X_i)^{-1}$ as

$A_i \qquad = A_{i-1} - \quad (A_{i-1} \; x_i x_i' \; A_{i-1}) \; / \; d_i^2$,   (9.2-18)

where

$A_{i-1} \qquad = (X_{i-1}' X_{i-1})^{-1}$ (9.2-19)

$$\beta_i \qquad \begin{aligned} &= \beta_{i-1} + A_i \; x_i \; (y_i - x_i' \; \beta_{i-1}) \\ &= \beta_{i-1} + A_i \; x_i \; v_i. \end{aligned}$$ (9.2-20)

$S_i \qquad = S_{i-1} + \quad w_i^2$ (9.2-21)

Phillips and Harvey (1974) have shown the relationship between the recursive residuals and the C matrix. If we define

$W = (w_{K+1}, \; w_{K+2} \; \ldots, w_T \;)'$,   (9.2-22)

then

$W = Cy$ (9.2-23)

if

$$C = \begin{bmatrix} \alpha_{11} & \alpha_{12} & \cdots & \alpha_{1K} & 1/d_{K+1} & 0 & 0 & \cdots & 0 \\ \alpha_{21} & \alpha_{22} & \cdots & \alpha_{2K} & \alpha_{2k+1} & 1/d_{K+2} & 0 & \cdots & 0 \\ \cdot & & & \cdot & \cdot & & & \cdots & 0 \\ \alpha_{N1} & \alpha_{N2} & \cdots & \alpha_{NK} & \alpha_{NK+1} & \alpha_{NK+2} & \cdots & \cdots & 1/d_T \end{bmatrix},$$ (9.2-24)

where $N = T-K$ and

$$a_t \quad \equiv (\alpha_{t1},\ \alpha_{t2},\ \ldots,\ \alpha_{t\,K+t-1})$$

$$= -(1/d_{K+t})(x'_{K+t}(X'_{K+t-1}X_{K+t-1})^{-1}X'_{K+t-1}\quad t\ \varepsilon\ \{1,\ldots,N\}. \qquad (9.2\text{-}25)$$

It is left as an exercise for the reader to show that $CX = 0$ and $CC' = I_{T-K}$.[5] This discussion has shown that if the population residual vector e has mean zero and a constant and finite variance, the recursive residual vector W will have the same property. The relationship between the recursive residual and the standardized differences of the coefficients as additional observations are added will now be discussed.

9.3 Standardized Recursive Coefficients

The recursive residual procedure involves testing both the recursive residuals[6] and the recursive coefficients. From equation (9.2-20), the difference in the recursive coefficient vector $\beta_i - \beta_{i-1}$ is

$$\beta_i - \beta_{i-1} = (X'_i X_i)^{-1}x_i v_i = A_i x_i v_i, \qquad (9.3\text{-}1)$$

which can be written

$$\beta_i - \beta_{i-1} = d_i(X'_i X_i)^{-1}x_i w_i = d_i A_i x_i w_i. \qquad (9.3\text{-}2)$$

Dufour (1979) proves that the vectors of standardized differences of individual coefficients constitute K sets of LUS residuals, which have the same absolute values as the recursive residuals w_i. A sketch of Dufour's proof follows.

If the coefficient values are stable, the expected value of the difference of the recursive coefficients is

$$E(\beta_i - \beta_{i-1}) = 0 \qquad\qquad i\ \varepsilon\ \{K+1,\ldots,T\}, \qquad (9.3.\text{-}3)$$

with covariance

$$E((\beta_i-\beta_{i-1})(\beta_i-\beta_{i-1})') = \sigma^2 d_i^2 A_i x_i x'_i A_i \qquad i\ \varepsilon\ \{K+1,\ldots,T\}. \qquad (9.3\text{-}4)$$

If we define

$$\beta_i = (\beta_{i,j},\ \ldots,\ \beta_{K,i})' \qquad (9.3\text{-}5)$$

$$A_i = (\alpha_{1,i},\ldots,\alpha_{K,i}), \qquad (9.3\text{-}6)$$

the jth coefficient difference is

$$\beta_{j,i} - \beta_{j,i-1} = d_i(\alpha'_{j,i}\ x_i)w_i. \qquad (9.3\text{-}7)$$

From equation (9.3-4), the covariance of the differences of the jth coefficient is $\sigma^2 D_{j,i}^2$ and from equation (9.9-3), the mean of the differences is 0.0, where

$$D_{j,i} = d_i(\alpha'_{j,i} \, x_i). \tag{9.3-8}$$

If $D_{ji} \neq$ to 0.0, the differences in the coefficients can be standardized:

$$G_{j,i} = (\beta_{j,i} - \beta_{j,i-1}) \, / \, |D_{j,i}| \qquad i \, \varepsilon \, \{K+1,\ldots,T\}. \tag{9.3-9}$$

If the jth coefficient is stable, the resulting j^{th} standardized differences G_{ji} are independent $N(0, \sigma^2)$. The vector G_j

$$G_j = (G_{j,K+1} \, , \, \ldots \, , \, G_{j,T}) \qquad j \, \varepsilon \, \{1,\ldots,K\} \tag{9.3-10}$$

constitutes K sets of LUS residuals. From equations (9.3-7) and (9.3-8), we can simplify equation (9.3-9) as

$$G_{j,i} = D_{j,i} \, w_i \, / \, |D_{j,i}| \qquad i \, \varepsilon \, \{K+1,\ldots,T\} \tag{9.3-11}$$

to prove the standardized differences in the jth coefficient have the same absolute value as the recursive residuals. $G_{j,i}$ will, in general, not exhibit the same sign patterns as w_i. The importance of equation (9.3-11) is that the tests that can be performed on the recursive residual vectors can be performed on the standardized differences of the coefficient vectors. These tests will be discussed in detail in later sections.

9.4 More Than One-Step-Ahead Recursive Residuals

The jth step-ahead recursive residual,

$$v_{j,i} = y_i - x'_i \beta_{i-j} \qquad i \, \varepsilon \, \{K+j,\ldots,T\}, \tag{9.4-1}$$

can be standardized as

$$w_{j,i} = v_{j,i} \, / \, d_{j,i} \qquad i \, \varepsilon \, \{K+j,\ldots,T\}, \tag{9.4-2}$$

where

$$d_{j,i} = (1 + x'_i A_{i-j} x_i)^{.5} \qquad i \, \varepsilon \, \{K+j,\ldots,T\}. \tag{9.4-3}$$

If we assume $j = 2$,

$$v_{2,i} = y_i - x'_i \beta_{i-1} + x'_i(\beta_{i-1} - \beta_{i-2}), \tag{9.4-4}$$

and using equation (9.3-1), equation (9.4-4) can be written as

$$v_{2,i} = d_{1,i} w_{1,i} + d_{1,i-1} x'_i A_{i-1} x_{i-1} w_{1,i-1}. \tag{9.4-5}$$

Dufour proved that

$$E(v_{2,i} \; v_{2,k}) \qquad = \sigma^2 \; d_{2,i}^2 \qquad\qquad\qquad i = k \qquad\qquad (9.4\text{-}6)$$

$$= \sigma^2 \; d_i^2 \; x'_{i+1} \; A_i \; x_i \qquad i\text{-}k = 1 \qquad\qquad (9.4\text{-}7)$$

$$= 0 \qquad\qquad\qquad i\text{-}k > 1. \qquad\qquad (9.4\text{-}8)$$

Equations (9.4-6), (9.4-7) and (9.4-8) prove that for two-step-ahead recursive residuals, $v_{2,i}$ and $v_{2,k}$ will be independent, provided i-k $\geq$ 2. These results generalize to the jth-step-ahead recursive residual. Residuals $v_{j,i}$ and $v_{j,k}$ will be independent, provided that i-k $\geq$ j. These proofs are very important in later sections when tests on the recursive residual will be discussed.

9.5 Testing the Recursive Residual

Independence of the components of the recursive residual vector, w_i, is assured by the homoskedasticity condition, while nonconstancy of the regression parameters affects only the central tendency of W, where W is defined by equation (9.2-22). Assuming heteroskedasticity is not a problem, it is possible to obtain an unbiased estimate of σ^2, which is used as an important component of three summary tests for parameter stability: the CUSUM test, the CUSUMSQ test and the Harvey-Collier (1977) test. If we can show that serial correlation of the recursive residuals is not a problem, we can proceed with these tests with some confidence.

Brown, Durbin and Evans (1975) proposed the CUSUM test as a summary measure of whether there was parameter stability. The test consists of plotting the quantity

$$CUSUM_i = \Sigma_{j=K+1}^{i} \; w_j / \sigma. \qquad\qquad (9.5\text{-}1)$$

Approximate bounds are available for the CUSUM test and are given in this reference. The CUSUM test is particularly good at detecting systematic departure of the B coefficients, while the CUSUMSQ test is useful when the departure of the B coefficients from constancy is haphazard rather than systematic. The CUSUMSQ test involves a plot of CUSUMSQ defined as

$$CUSUMSQ_i = \Sigma_{j=K+1}^{i} \; w_j^2 \; / \; \Sigma_{j=K+1}^{T} \; w_j^2 \qquad i = K+1, \; \ldots, \; T. \qquad (9.5\text{-}2)$$

Assuming a rectangular plot, the upper-right-hand value is 1.0 and the lower-left-hand value is 0.0. A regression with stable B coefficients will generate a CUSUMSQ plot up the diagonal. If the plot lies above the diagonal, the implication is that the regression is tracking poorly in the early subsample in comparison with the total sample. A plot below the diagonal suggests the reverse, namely, that the regression is tracking better in the early subsample than in the complete sample. B34S will plot the CUSUM and CUSUMSQ against the original data order or against the X value, which was used to sort the data matrix. A measure of the maximum distance from the diagonal DMAX,

DMAX = MAX $|(\text{CUSUMSQ}_i - (i/T)|$,   (9.5-3)

is calculated.   If $T \le 500$, a table routine will provide the probability of rejecting the assumption of parameter stability.[7]

The Harvey-Collier (1977) test statistic is distributed as a t statistic and is defined as

$t_c = \overline{W} / S_{\overline{W}}$,   (9.5-4)

where

$\overline{W} = \Sigma^T_{i=K+1} w_i/(T-K)$ (9.5-5)

and

$S_{\overline{W}} = \Sigma^T_{i=K+1} (w_i - \overline{W})^2/(T-K-1)$.   (9.5-6)

The Harvey-Collier test can be performed on the recursive residuals w_i and the standardized differences in the regression coefficients G_{ji}, which were defined in equation 9.3-11.

Other tests provided include the Durbin-Watson test statistic, defined in equation (2.8-1); the modified Von Neumann ratio, defined in equation (2.8-2); and the Siegal-Sign test, which counts the number of plus signs.   The Wilcoxon, or signed rank, test can be applied to the recursive residual w_i directly, where it becomes a median test, or to the series $z_i = w_i * w_{i+k}$, where it becomes a nonparametric test for serial correlation.   Assume that the test will be performed on the series z_i. $U(z_i) = 1$ if $z_i > 0$, otherwise $U(z_i) = 0$. If R_t^+ is the rank of each observation, the signed rank statistic S_R is defined as

$S_R = \Sigma^{T-K-1}_{i=1} U(z_i)R_i^+$,   (9.5-7)

where w_i is defined for $i = 1, \ldots, (T-K)$ and $z_i = w_i * w_{i+1}$. If we assume that $N = T-K-1$, the Wilcoxon Z statistic becomes

$Z = (S_R - (N(N+1)/4))/(N(N+1)(2N+1)/24)^{.5}$,   (9.5-8)

which is distributed as a normal variable.   If the number of recursive residuals is < 50, tables from Wilcoxon, Katti, and Wilcox (1973) can be used.

When the Wilcoxon test is applied to a series z_i calculated from the first-step-ahead recursive residuals, there are no problems of interpretation since from equation (9.2-17) we have shown that if the homoskedasticity assumptions of the OLS equation are met, $E(w_{1,i} w_{1,i+k}) = 0$ for all k. On the other hand, a series z_i calculated for the jth-step-ahead recursive residual of an OLS equation meeting the homoskedasticity assumption will have $E(w_{1,i} w_{1,i+k}) = 0$ if, and only if, $k \ge j$. This result follows from equations (9.4-6), (9.4-7) and (9.4-8). The parameters IRB and IWN in the RR sentence set the maximum order of the recursive residuals and Wilcoxon tests, respectively.

If it is known where to break a series, the Chow test for homogeneity is a very powerful means by which to test for shifts in the parameter values. However, it is not always possible to make this determination from the theory of the model. The moving-regression procedure, the Quandt log-likelihood ratio procedure and the multisegment Chow test are means by which to test for parameter shifts when it is not certain where in the sample the changes are occurring.

The moving-regression procedure allows calculation of regressions of varying lengths to test for the optimum number of observations in the regression. It is a common mistake to attempt to fit a model for the longest period of available data when it is suspected that there have been shifts in the underlying structure of the model. One view of a regression is that it is primarily a procedure to summarize data. If that is the intent, long periods of data may be appropriate. On the other hand, if the purpose of the regression is to forecast or test the magnitude of relationships between variables, the additional degrees of freedom obtained by longer data series must be balanced against the possible bias in the estimated coefficients if there has been a change in the underlying population coefficients. If we define $\beta(m-n, m-1)$ as the vector of K coefficients estimated in the time segment $(m-n, m-1)$ and y_m and x_m are the dependent and independent variables for time period m, the moving regression means square error one period ahead M_1 is

$$M_1 = \sum_{m=n+1}^{T} (y_m - x_m' \beta(m-n, m-1))^2 / (T-n). \qquad (9.5-9)$$

If M_1 is calculated for a number of moving regressions of different lengths, its minimum value will give an indication of the optimum number of observations in the regression for prediction purposes. Also of interest is M_2, which is similar to M_1 except that the regression is passed in the reverse:

$$M_2 = \sum_{m=1}^{T-n} (y_m - x_m' \beta(m+1, m+n))^2 / (T-n). \qquad (9.5-10)$$

M is defined as the sum of M_1 and M_2. M_3 is defined as the same as M_1 except that all regressions are tested over the same period of record, i.e.,

$$M_3 = \sum_{m=n1+n}^{T} (y_m - x_m' \beta(m-n, m-1))^2 / (T-n1), \qquad (9.5-11)$$

where n1 is the maximum length of the regression considered.

The moving-regression option is controlled by the parameters IMORR, NBEGIN, MMRNOB, and INCR on the RR sentence. If

IMORR=MTEST, only M_1, M_2, M_3 and M are given for each set of moving
regressions.   Setting IMORR = LIST will list the moving
coefficients as well as the statistics listed with MTEST. This
option uses a great deal of paper, but will give an indication of
the movement of the coefficients.   A preferable approach would be
to set IMORR = LIST and set INCR to a number > 1 so that the
increment of the moving regressions is larger.   For example, a
moving regression from 30 to 60 observations will be calculated if
we set IMORR=LIST, NBEGIN = 30, and MMRNOB = 60.   If INCR = 1, this
implies 31 sets of moving regressions.   If INCR is set to 10, there
will be only four sets of moving regressions.[8]

The Quandt log-likelihood ratio test, controlled with the
parameter IQUANT, involves the calculation of the $\mathcal{L}_i$, defined as

$$\mathcal{L}_i = .5 \; i \; \ln(\sigma_1^2) \; + .5 \; (T-i) \; \ln(\sigma_2^2) \; - .5 \; T \; \ln(\sigma^2), \qquad (9.5\text{-}12)$$

where σ_1^2, σ_2^2 and σ^2 are the variances of regressions fitted to the
first i observations, the last T-i observations and the whole T
observations, respectively.   The minimum of the plot of $\mathcal{L}_i$ is can
be used to select the "break" in the sample.   Although no specific
tests are available for $\mathcal{L}_i$, the information suggested by the plot
can be tested with the multiperiod Chow test, which is discussed
next.

If structural change is suspected, a homogeneity test (Chow)
of equal segments n can be performed.   Given that S(r,i) is the
residual sum of squares from a regression calculated from
observations t=r to i, the appropriate statistic is distributed as
F(kp-k, T-kp) and defined as

$$(F_1 \; (T\text{-}kp)) \; / \; (F_2 \; (kp \; - \; k)), \qquad (9.5\text{-}13)$$

where

$$F_1 = (S(1,T) - (S(1,n) + S(n+1,2n) + .. + S(pn-2n+1,pn-n) + S(pn-n+1,T)))$$
$$\qquad (9.5\text{-}14)$$
and

$$F_2 = (S(1,n) + S(n+1,2n) + ... + S(pn-n+1,T)). \qquad (9.5\text{-}15)$$

The Chow test is controlled from the RR sentence by the ICHOW and
IOBSCH parameters. ICHOW controls printing options and IOBSCH
controls the number of observations per subsample. In terms of
equation (9.5-13), IOBSCH = n.   IOBSCH should go into T evenly.   If
some of the subsamples are rank deficient, B34S will not calculate
the F test but will give the results for the subsamples that are
rank sufficient.   The Chow test uses the Cholesky decomposition
routine DPOCO for all calculations so that the matrix condition of
each subsample can be inspected and printed.

The IMOVE parameter of the RR sentence controls whether

autocorrelations of the recursive residual sets are desired.   The
formula used consists of equations (2.11-2), (2.11-3) and (2.11-4).
If more than first-step-ahead recursive residuals are
autocorrelated, caution must be used in interpretation of the
results in view of equations (9.4-6), (9.4-7), and (9.4-8).

The recursive residual option allows data to be analyzed,
using its original order, for data resorted against included
variables (SORTF option) and for data that have been sorted in
reverse direction (SORTB option).   If data are analyzed with the
original order, plots of the coefficients will indicate whether
there have been shifts in the underlying population coefficients at
particular periods in time.   If the data matrix has been sorted
against one explanatory variable, plots of the coefficient of the
variable used to make the sort will indicate whether the
coefficient is stable for different values of that variable. Plots
of other coefficients will indicate whether there are unspecified
interaction effects.   For example, assume the estimated model was

$$Y = \beta_1 + \beta_2 X_1 + \beta_2 X_2 + u, \qquad\qquad (9.5-16)$$

where the true model was

$$Y = \beta_1 + \beta_2 X_1 + \beta_3 X_2 - \beta_3 (X_1 X_2) + u. \qquad\qquad (9.5-17)$$

Assuming that both X_1 and X_2 are positive, if equation (9.5-16) is
estimated and the data are resorted against X_1, a plot of the β_3
coefficient will show a negative slope.[9]

In summary, both the RR procedure discussed here and the BLUS
procedure discussed in chapter 2 are methods by which the
econometrician can test the assumptions of the estimated OLS model.
Phillips and Harvey (1974, 313) have compared the two procedures
and have concluded that for heteroskedasticity tests the BLUS
procedures are, on average, of higher power than the RR test.   They
conclude "the difference in power is so small that in our opinion,
it in no way compensates for the additional computations necessary
to obtain the BLUS residuals."   The RR procedure, in addition,
allows tests on the stability of the coefficients, something not
possible with the BLUS residuals.   The judgment of Phillips and
Harvey (1974) was made before the development of the additional RR
tests suggested by Dufour (1979, 1982).   B34S will calculate the
numerous BLUS tests virtually automatically, which makes the
additional computational burden of the BLUS procedure of little
consequence.   In my view, the best approach is to use both
procedures since they are targeted to answer somewhat different
questions.

9.6 Examples

Table 9.1 lists the code to run the RR equation specification
tests on the Christensen-Jorgenson (1969, 1970) data that was

studied by Sinai and Stokes (1972) and used to illustrate GLS
models in chapter 2. This data was also used in Maddala (1988, 415
- 416) to illustrate the recursive residual procedure. The data-
loading part of the code has not been shown since it is given in
Table 2.2.[10] Table 9.1 shows the setup for estimating production
functions with and without real balances and with and without time.
Because of space considerations and since Maddala (1988, 415 - 416)
only reported a simple production function containing labor and
capital, only output from this model is shown.

The options selected include the following: up to first-order
recursive residuals calculated (IRB=1), plotting and listing
recursive residuals (IRRPT=PLOTO IRRLS=LIST), plotting and listing
recursive coefficients (IBCPT=PLOTO IBCLS=LIST), calculating and
plotting the CUSUM and CUSUMSQ tests (ICUM=PLOTO ICUMSQ=PLOTO),
calculating and plotting the Quandt likelihood ratio test
(IQUANT=PLOT) and Chow tests for ten observations per sample
(ICHOW=CALPRINT IOBSCH=10).

Table 9.1 Program to Perform Recursive Residual Analysis

```
B34SEXEC RR NTEST=2 IRB=1 IRRPT=PLOTO IRRLS=LIST IBCPT=PLOTO
       IBCLS=LIST ICUM=PLOTO ICUMSQ=PLOTO ICHOW=CALPRINT IOBSCH=10
       IQUANT=PLOT$
       * Production Function Stability Test$
       MODEL LNQ = LNK LNL $ B34SEEND$

B34SEXEC RR NTEST=2 IRB=1 IRRPT=PLOTO IRRLS=LIST IBCPT=PLOTO
       IBCLS=LIST ICUM=PLOTO ICUMSQ=PLOTO ICHOW=CALPRINT IOBSCH=10
       IQUANT=PLOT$
       * Production Function Stability Test for model with Time$
       MODEL LNQ = LNK LNL TIME$ B34SEEND$

B34SEXEC RR NTEST=2 IRB=1 IRRPT=PLOTO IRRLS=LIST IBCPT=PLOTO
       IBCLS=LIST ICUM=PLOTO ICUMSQ=PLOTO ICHOW=CALPRINT IOBSCH=10
       IQUANT=PLOT$
       * Test of Sinai-Stokes (1972) without time $
       MODEL LNQ = LNK LNL LNRM1$ B34SEEND$

B34SEXEC RR NTEST=2 IRB=1 IRRPT=PLOTO IRRLS=LIST IBCPT=PLOTO
       IBCLS=LIST ICUM=PLOTO ICUMSQ=PLOTO ICHOW=CALPRINT IOBSCH=10
       IQUANT=PLOT$
       * Test of Sinai-Stokes (1972) with time $ COEF$
       MODEL LNQ = LNK LNL TIME LNRM1 $ B34SEEND$
```

Since the SORTF and SORTB options[11] were not supplied, NTEST
could have been set = 1. Output for the first problem follows.

RECURSIVE RESIDUAL (RR) OPTION CONTROL CARD

IBGIN,	IEND,	NOIN,	ISORT,	NTEST,	IRB,	IRRPT,	IRRLS,	IBCPT,	IBCLS,	INOPUL,	INOPLT,	ICUM,	ICUMSQ,	IMOVE,	ICHOW,	IOBSCH	IWN	ICARD
1	39	3	0	2	1	1	1	1	1	0	0	2	2	0	2	10	0	1

RR OPTION (ICARD=1) READ   IADD IQUANT IMORR NBEGIN MMRNOB INCR
                            1   1   0   0   0   0

VERSION DATE   1 DECEMBER 1988

OF   35000 DOUBLE PRECISION SLOTS IN SPACE,   2916 ARE BEING USED

ALL TESTS WILL BE PERFORMED USING ORIGINAL DATA ORDER

OLS RESULTS FOR COMPLETE DATA SET (39 OBS)

VARIABLE		COEFFICIENT	STD. ERROR	T
LNK	X-16	0.38380813	0.48017824E-01	7.9930345
LNL	X-17	1.4507860	0.83228446E-01	17.431372
CONSTANT	X-23	-3.9377145	0.23699929	-16.614879

Y = LNQ   X-18 ADJ RSQ= 0.9943 SEE= 0.3471E-01

SUM RES SQ   0.4338E-01 1/COND XPX   0.81009398E-05

****

PROBLEM #   1

****

B COEFFICIENT VECTOR FOR FIRST   3 OBSERVATIONS

             LNK   -0.33540532
             LNL   2.0981699
             CONSTANT   -4.0691864   RECIPROCAL MATRIX CONDITION   0.31858978E-06

LISTING OF OBSERVATION # AND RECURSIVE RESIDUALS UP TO ORDER   1 THEN DATA

DATA LISTED IN ORDER	LNK	LNL	CONSTANT	LNQ	
4.	0.1594E-01	4.361	4.954	1.000	4.910
5.	-0.1975E-01	4.339	4.953	1.000	4.883
6.	-0.8093E-02	4.331	4.997	1.000	4.954
7.	0.5118E-02	4.353	5.040	1.000	5.036
8.	0.1115E-01	4.371	5.097	1.000	5.145
9.	-0.1039E-01	4.382	5.147	1.000	5.209
10.	0.3825E-01	4.352	5.085	1.000	5.154
11.	0.4163E-01	4.399	5.128	1.000	5.239
12.	0.4182E-01	4.466	5.173	1.000	5.325
13.	0.1335E-01	4.566	5.260	1.000	5.464
14.	-0.1455E-01	4.648	5.323	1.000	5.552
15.	0.1608E-01	4.700	5.348	1.000	5.626
16.	0.6065E-01	4.680	5.341	1.000	5.674
17.	0.8487E-01	4.626	5.309	1.000	5.651
18.	-0.4812E-01	4.577	5.363	1.000	5.613
19.	-0.1032	4.662	5.410	1.000	5.634
20.	-0.7172E-01	4.727	5.430	1.000	5.696
21.	-0.1600E-01	4.744	5.400	1.000	5.696
22.	0.1342E-01	4.821	5.433	1.000	5.796
23.	-0.8823E-02	4.902	5.476	1.000	5.862
24.	-0.6650E-02	4.939	5.488	1.000	5.887
25.	0.8817E-02	4.993	5.502	1.000	5.937
26.	0.4138E-01	5.003	5.470	1.000	5.929
27.	0.3539E-01	5.066	5.505	1.000	6.008
28.	0.1877E-02	5.119	5.528	1.000	6.031
29.	0.7718E-02	5.147	5.527	1.000	6.047
30.	0.2918E-01	5.154	5.502	1.000	6.036
31.	0.1083E-01	5.207	5.541	1.000	6.100
32.	-0.3691E-02	5.242	5.559	1.000	6.125
33.	0.1401E-01	5.268	5.553	1.000	6.145
34.	0.1963E-01	5.310	5.578	1.000	6.205
35.	0.2864E-01	5.325	5.593	1.000	6.245
36.	0.2296E-01	5.375	5.618	1.000	6.299
37.	0.1562E-01	5.416	5.654	1.000	6.362
38.	-0.3289E-02	5.465	5.695	1.000	6.423
39.	-0.3160E-01	5.513	5.720	1.000	6.447

The output first gives the OLS coefficients for the complete sample, where the coefficients for Ln K, Ln L and the constant were found to be .38381, 1.45079 and -3.9377, respectively. Next, the recursive first-step-ahead forecast error and data are listed. The residuals agree with those of Maddala (1988, 416). The recursive residuals are next plotted and a number of tests are run. The Wilcoxon test shows a Z score of 2.473, with a probability of

.9933, which indicates a change in structure.

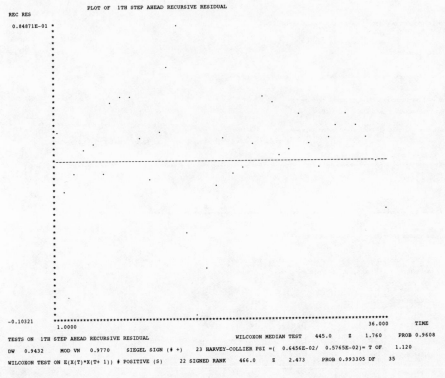

PLOT OF 1TH STEP AHEAD RECURSIVE RESIDUAL

REC RES

0.84871E-01

-0.10321
        1.0000   36.000   TIME

TESTS ON 1TH STEP AHEAD RECURSIVE RESIDUAL   WILCOXON MEDIAN TEST   445.0   Z   1.760   PROB 0.9608

DW   0.9432   MOD VN   0.9770   SIEGEL SIGN (# +)   23 HARVEY-COLLIER PSI =(0.6456E-02/ 0.5765E-02)= T OF   1.120

WILCOXON TEST ON E(X(T)*X(T+ 1)) # POSITIVE (S)   22 SIGNED RANK   466.0   Z   2.473   PROB 0.993305 DF   35

Next, the coefficients are listed in Table 9.2 and plotted. Note that the coefficients listed for the 39th observation agree with the OLS results for the complete sample and those reported in Maddala (1988, 132, eq. [4.25]). Both the LNK and LNL coefficients are moving as observations are added to the sample. This indicates changes in the structure or the effect on LNQ of an omitted variable. The coefficients are next plotted and plots of the CUSUM and CUSUMSQ tests are shown.

Table 9.2 Listing of β Coefficients

OBS #	LNK	LNL	CONSTANT
4.	-0.7242	2.086	-2.273
5.	-0.9296E-01	1.757	-3.406
6.	0.1574	1.592	-3.677
7.	0.9462E-01	1.638	-3.636
8.	-0.8501E-02	1.727	-3.630
9.	0.5537E-01	1.667	-3.604
10.	-0.8159E-01	1.755	-3.447
11.	-0.1308	1.832	-3.615
12.	-0.6423E-01	1.875	-4.121
13.	-0.1823E-01	1.879	-4.346
14.	-0.6335E-01	1.883	-4.168
15.	-0.2108E-01	1.870	-4.288
16.	0.5553E-01	1.860	-4.571
17.	0.7909E-01	1.893	-4.844
18.	0.1926	1.757	-4.654
19.	0.2607	1.626	-4.287
20.	0.2197	1.617	-4.058
21.	0.1968	1.629	-4.021
22.	0.2237	1.611	-4.047
23.	0.2060	1.624	-4.034
24.	0.1946	1.633	-4.028
25.	0.2086	1.621	-4.031
26.	0.2694	1.566	-4.017
27.	0.3118	1.527	-4.008
28.	0.3137	1.525	-4.007
29.	0.3206	1.519	-4.004
30.	0.3450	1.493	-3.980
31.	0.3522	1.485	-3.975
32.	0.3501	1.488	-3.976
33.	0.3579	1.479	-3.968
34.	0.3672	1.469	-3.959
35.	0.3783	1.458	-3.952
36.	0.3865	1.450	-3.947
37.	0.3909	1.446	-3.948
38.	0.3902	1.447	-3.947
39.	0.3838	1.451	-3.938

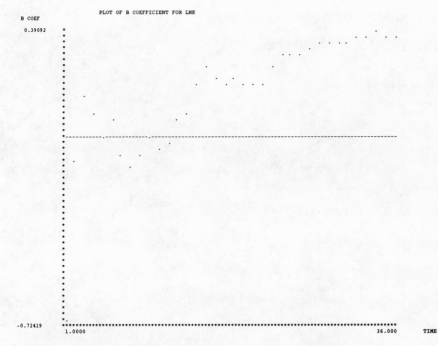

PLOT OF B COEFFICIENT FOR LNK

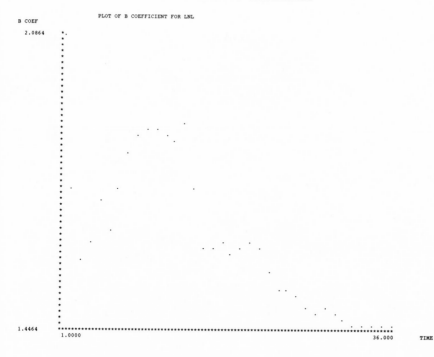

PLOT OF B COEFFICIENT FOR LNL

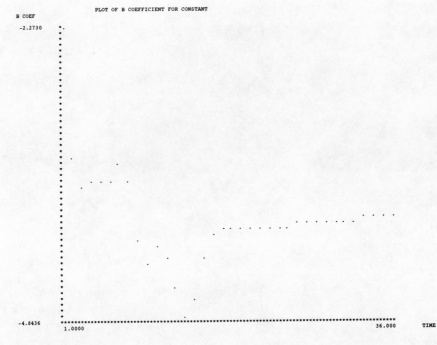

PLOT OF B COEFFICIENT FOR CONSTANT

B COEF

-2.2730

-4.8436

1.0000   36.000   TIME

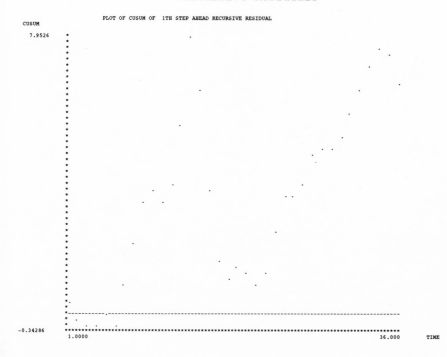

PLOT OF CUSUM OF 1TH STEP AHEAD RECURSIVE RESIDUAL

PLOT OF CUSUMSQ OF 1TH STEP AHEAD RECURSIVE RESIDUAL   C0(.95) = 0.28032 DF =   17

CUSUMSQ

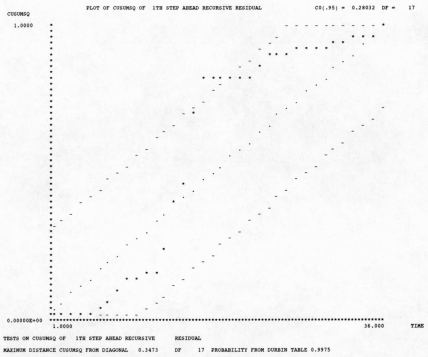

TESTS ON CUSUMSQ OF   1TH STEP AHEAD RECURSIVE   RESIDUAL

MAXIMUM DISTANCE CUSUMSQ FROM DIAGONAL   0.3473   DF   17   PROBABILITY FROM DURBIN TABLE 0.9975

DW   0.3769E-02 MOD VN   0.3535   SIEGEL SIGN (# +)   0 HARVEY-COLLIER PSI =(-3.956   / 0.6942E-01)= T OF   -56.99

```
*****************************************************************************************************
CHOW TEST OPTION SELECTED

*****************************************************************************************************

FOR EQUATION      1  (   10) OBS GO FROM     1  TO    10

VARIABLE          COEFFICIENT         STD. ERROR            T              Y = LNQ      X-18  ADJ RSQ= 0.9783  SEE=  0.1863E-01
LNK      X-16    -0.81594955E-01      0.15094190          -0.54057193
LNL      X-17     1.7550062           0.11171676          15.709426
CONSTANT X-23    -3.4467775           0.52150228          -6.6093240         SUM RES SQ  0.2431E-02 1/COND XPX   0.24449890E-05

---------------------------------------------------------------------------------------------------

FOR EQUATION      2  (   10) OBS GO FROM    11  TO    20

VARIABLE          COEFFICIENT         STD. ERROR            T              Y = LNQ      X-18  ADJ RSQ= 0.9003  SEE=  0.4915E-01
LNK      X-16     0.70386925          0.39188474           1.7961129
LNL      X-17     0.81333167          0.42522161           1.9127242
CONSTANT X-23    -2.0117042           0.93708946          -2.1467579         SUM RES SQ  0.1691E-01 1/COND XPX   0.45521860E-05

---------------------------------------------------------------------------------------------------

FOR EQUATION      3  (   19) OBS GO FROM    21  TO    39

VARIABLE          COEFFICIENT         STD. ERROR            T              Y = LNQ      X-18  ADJ RSQ= 0.9953  SEE=  0.1448E-01
LNK      X-16     0.57908661          0.55248190E-01       10.481549
LNL      X-17     1.0089902           0.14402970            7.0054318
CONSTANT X-23    -2.4980651           0.53121614          -4.7025399         SUM RES SQ  0.3357E-02 1/COND XPX   0.55900906E-06

F(   6,   30) =    4.55788    1/F =   0.219400    F PROBABILITY  0.99786866


    PLOT OF THE QUANDT LIKELIHOOD RATIO  ..  MINIMUM IS AN INDICATION OF A SHIFT IN STRUCTURE
LAMBDA
   -4.3079        *
                  *
                  *
                  *
                  *                                                                          .
                  *
                  *                                                                 .
                  *
                  *.                                                        .
                  *
                  *       .
                  *
                  *
                  *                                                  .
                  *
                  *                                           .
                  *                                                                .
                  *
                  *                                    .
                  *                             .
                  *                   .                                  .
                  *                       .
                  *             .
                  *                                                .
                  *                .
                  *                              .
                  *                                                    .
                  *
                  *             .
                  *
                  *                   .
                  *
                  *
                  *             .
                  *
                  *
  -18.792         ****************************************.***********************************
                  1.0000                                                         32.000      TIME
```

The CUSUM should sum to 0.0. The plot shows that the sum was
positive for most of the sample. The CUSUMSQ test plot indicates
that the maximum distance from the diagonal was .3473, which is
significant at the .9975 level from the Durbin Table. After
tracking well for the first third of the sample, there was an
abrupt shift. This shift can be seen if we inspect the three Chow

test subperiod regressions. Note that the coefficients for the model for the first ten observations (-3.447, -.08159, and 1.755 for the CONSTANT, LNK and LNL, respectively) <u>are</u> the same as those listed in the moving-coefficient table. The moving-coefficient table results for observation 20 <u>are not</u> the same as the Chow results for observations 11 through 20 since the moving-coefficient table for observation 20 includes data from observations 1 to 20, which the Chow Table result does not. The F test for the Chow test was found to be 4.55788, which is significant at the .99786 level. To save space, the RR sentence options for moving-regression tests (see IMORR, NBEGIN, MMRNOB and INCR keywords) have not been activated. These commands can be used to search for the most appropriate number of observations to use for a regression in a time-series or sorted cross-section data set. The Chow test is a very powerful way to test whether two samples come from the same underlying population. The problem is determining which samples to use for the Chow test. The moving-regression options can help in this decision.

The preceding discussion indicates that there was a significant shift in structure of the production function between 1929 and 1967. The plot of the Quandt likelihood ratio indicates that this occurred in 1944 (=1929+15), which is reasonable, given that this was near the end of World War II. If we compare results for LNK, LNL and the CONSTANT for the complete period (.3838, 1.4508, -3.938) with results for the last 19 observations of the data set, which includes the period 1949 through 1967, the corresponding coefficients are .5791, 1.009, and -2.498, respectively. An interesting conclusion is that the regression R^2 and coefficient standard errors have masked the true variation in the coefficients within the sample. Although the structure appeared to change, this was hidden since the serial correlation in the estimated residual biased the estimated SE of the coefficients. The serial correlation <u>did not</u> bias the estimated coefficients.[12]

9.7 Conclusion

The B34S RR command allows testing of whether parameters are shifting over time for time-series models, or whether there are equation specification problems in cross-section models. The RR command is based on procedures proposed by Brown, Durbin, and Evans (1975) and Dufour (1979, 1982). The RR procedure essentially involves sorting the data with respect to time or some variable of interest and estimating an OLS model for a small subset of the data. Additional observations are added, in turn, and the model reestimated. Inspection of the pattern of the coefficients and the 1,...,k step-ahead forecast error will reveal whether the probability density function underlying the coefficients is shifting in a predictable manner. The recursive residual is in the class of LUS residuals. The RR command equation specification tests supplement the BLUS residual equation specification tests discussed in chapter 2.

NOTES

1. Arnold Zellner suggested that I include the procedures proposed by Brown, Durbin, and Evans (1975) in the B34S program. At the time, Jean-Marie Dufour was working on a thesis in this area. The B34S recursive residual option implements all the procedures suggested by Brown, Durbin, and Evans (1975) and adds the enhancements proposed by Dufour (1979, 1982). The RR procedure uses the most advanced computational techniques and contains some of the most efficient code now in B34S.

2. The notation of this chapter has been modified somewhat from other sections of the book to simplify the exposition. The discussion in this chapter follows those of Brown, Durbin, and Evans (1975), Dufour (1979, 1982), and Theil (1971).

3. Since M is an idempotent matrix of rank T-K, it has T-K unit eigenvalues. This can be seen if equation (9.2-7) is written as $(M-I)C' = 0$. From equation (9.2-2), we know that these vectors have unit length and are pairwise orthogonal.

4. Formulas such as equations (9.2-18), (9.2-19), (9-2-20), and (9.2-21) make the calculation of recursive residuals possible. Define X_i as a matrix made up of the first i observations of X. The RR procedure first checks $X_i'X_i$ to see if it is of rank K, where i=K+1. In the early versions of the B34S RR option, the determinant was inspected. When LINPACK became available, DPOCO, a Cholesky decomposition routine that checks matrix condition, was employed to factor $X_i'X_i$, if possible. If this matrix is rank deficient, B34S will add one observation at a time until it obtains a base with rank K for the recursive residual calculation. Once a full-rank base is found, formulas (9.2-18), (9.2-19), (9.2-20) and (9.2-21) can be used, since after observations are added, it is impossible to "fall into" degeneracy. Later in this chapter, the problem of downdating the system will be discussed in the context of the Quandt likelihood ratio test and the moving-regression test. An alternative to equation (9.2-18) would be to use a Cholesky updating routine, such as DCHUD, which is available in the LINPACK library. The use of DCHUD for this calculation was rejected since it involves extra calculation. The recursive residual analysis requires that d_i, w_i and v_i be calculated. Inspection of equations (9.2-14), (9-2-15), (9.2-16), and (9.2-18) will convince the reader that once these values are calculated, a substantial amount of the calculations involved in updating the inverse are already complete.

5. Because C is a relatively large matrix (T-K, T-K), it is not computationally advisable to attempt to calculate W as Cy directly. The formulas (9.2-14), (9.2-15) and (9.2-16), together with the update formulas (9.2-18), (9.2-19) and (9.2-20), can be used recursively with the size of the arrays a function of K, not of T-K. Another advantage of the latter procedure is that more than

one-step-ahead recursive residuals can be calculated if the formula for d_i and v_i is slightly modified. For further discussion, see formulas (9.4-1), (9.4-2) and (9.4-3).

6. In section 9.4 the calculation and testing of the more-than-one-step-ahead recursive residual is discussed.

7. Durbin (1969, 4, Table 1) has provided significance values for DMAX. In implementing the RR option, I found great difficulty in developing a routine to calculate this probability. The routines finally used (DURBIN and BINCOE) were built by Ron Golland and will work if the number of observations is less than 500. Durbin suggests entering his table with degrees of freedom = .5(T-K) - 1 and .5 alpha. The lines plotted are not determined from the table routine but are approximations from the table. While it is possible to enter the routine with DMAX and obtain a probability, it requires a very expensive nonlinear search to determine the specific DMAX associated with the probability of 95%. For this reason, a plot of the approximate values of the 95% boundaries was selected. The DURBIN routine is the most costly part of the RR procedure. Since Durbin's (1969) table only allows degrees of freedom ≤ 100, the performance of DURBIN, which allows degrees of freedom up to 250, should be judged accordingly. Users wanting to experiment with this routine can enter DURBIN as CALL DURBIN (DMAX,M,A,P), where DMAX, M, A and P are REAL*8 variables. DMAX is defined from equation (9.5-3), M is the degrees of freedom, A is a work array of size M, and P is the calculated probability. The probability of rejecting the hypothesis of stable coefficients is (1 - (P/2)).

8. The moving regression section of the RR command uses the LINPACK routines, DCHUD and DCHDD, to update and downdate $(X'X)^{-1}$ as observations are added and taken away.

9. Plots of the coefficients must be inspected with caution. The plot scale will adjust so that the full height of the graph is used. A correctly specified model will show a shape of a level horn pointed to the left. The estimates of the coefficient for the first few observations will be poorer than when the complete sample is being used.

10. In chapter 2 TIME was coded as 1929 through 1967. In Sinai and Stokes (1972), TIME was coded 0 through 38.

11. The SORTF option sorts the data against each NTEST variable in the MODEL sentence. Unless SORTF is supplied, NTEST can be set to any number in the range 1 to the number of right-hand-side variables in the model sentence.

12. A common problem in time series research is to determine whether the data used in a study go back far enough. Experience

with the RR paragraph in B34S indicates that many time series models will fail the recursive residual equation specification test. If this occurs, either the equation must be respecified and / or the data set must be truncated so as to use only the later more consistent time period in the analysis. The RR sentence SORTB option can be used first to sort the data backward so that recursive residual calculations can be made, starting with the K latest observations. Inspection of the coefficient plots and the CUSUMSQ plots can usually pinpoint where to truncate the sample.

10. Special Topics in OLS Estimation

10.0 Introduction

The QR command in B34S allows calculation of a high accuracy solution to the OLS regression problem. In addition, the principal component regression can be calculated. Finally, a branch to the Leamer (1978) SEARCH program is provided.

10.1 The QR Approach

Interest in the QR approach to estimation was stimulated by Longley's (1967) seminal paper on computer accuracy.[1] Equation (4.1-6) indicated how the OLS solution $(X'X)^{-1}X'Y$ could be written as $R^{-1}Q_1'Y$, where the T by K matrix X was initially factored as a product of the T by T orthogonal matrix Q and the upper triangular K by K Cholesky matrix R:

$$Q'X = \begin{bmatrix} R \\ 0 \end{bmatrix}.$$ (10.1-1)

Matrix Q is usually partitioned as $Q = [Q_1 \quad Q_2]$ so that

$$X = Q_1 R,$$ (10.1-2)

where Q_1 is a T by K matrix that is usually kept in factored form as

$$Q_1 = H_1 H_2, \ldots, H_K,$$ (10.1-3)

where H_i is the Householder transformation (Strang 1976, 279). Q_2 is a T by (T-K) matrix. Dongarra et al (1979, sec. 9.1) show that given X is of rank K, then the matrix

$$P_X = Q_1 Q_1'$$ (10.1-4)

is the orthogonal projection onto the column space of X and

$$P_X^{\perp} = Q_2 Q_2'$$ (10.1-5)

is the projection onto the orthogonal complement of X in view of equation (10.1-1). The residuals of an OLS model are constrained to be orthogonal or have zero correlation with the right-hand sides of the equation. Omitting t subscripts to avoid notational clutter,

$$\hat{e} = y - X\hat{\beta}$$ (10.1-6)

and it follows from equation (10.1-2) that

$$\hat{e} \quad = P_x^\perp y = Q_2 Q_2' y \qquad\qquad (10.1\text{-}7)$$

and

$$X\hat{B} \quad = Q_1 Q_1' y. \qquad\qquad (10.1\text{-}8)$$

The QR command has a number of options that facilitate its use in cases in which rank may be a problem. The EPS option allows the user to specify a nonnegative number such that 1 ÷ the condition number of X'X must be < 1 ÷ ESP. If ESP is not supplied, it defaults to V * 1.0E-16, where V is the largest sum of absolute values in any row of X. The IFREZ option allows the user to require that certain variables be placed in any final model when all variables cannot be entered in the regression due to rank problems.

10.2 The Principal-Component Regression Model

The principal component regression model can easily be calculated from the data and provides a useful transformation, especially in cases in which there is collinearity.[2] Assume X is a T by K matrix. The singular value decomposition of X is

$$X = U\Theta V', \qquad\qquad (10.2\text{-}1)$$

where U is T by r, Θ is r by r, V is K by r, T ≥ K and r ≤ K. U and V have the property that

$$U'U = I \qquad\qquad (10.2\text{-}2)$$

and

$$V'V = I. \qquad\qquad (10.2\text{-}3)$$

$\Theta_{ij} = 0$ for i ≠ j and the elements Θ_{ii} are the square roots of the nonzero eigenvalues of X'X or XX'. The rows of V' are the eigenvectors of X'X, while the columns of U are the eigenvectors of XX'. If K = r, then X is of full rank. If we replace X in equation (2.1-7) by its singular value decomposition, we obtain

$$Y = X\beta + e = U\Theta V'\beta + e, \qquad\qquad (10.2\text{-}4)$$

which can be written

$$Y = U\alpha + e \qquad\qquad (10.2\text{-}5)$$

if we define

$$\alpha = \Theta V'\beta. \qquad\qquad (10.2\text{-}6)$$

An estimate of $\hat{\alpha}$ can be calculated from equation (2.1-8) as

$$\hat{\alpha} \quad = (U'U)^{-1}U'y \quad = U'y, \tag{10.2-7}$$

given equation (10.2-2). From equation (10.2-6) we can recover $\hat{\beta}$ as

$$\hat{\beta} \quad = (V')^{-1}\Theta^{-1}\hat{\alpha} \quad = V\Theta^{-1}\hat{\alpha}. \tag{10.2-8}$$

Mandel (1982) points out that the variance of each coefficient is

$$\text{var}(\hat{\beta}_j) \quad = \Sigma_{m=1}^{k}[v_{jm}^2 \ / \ \Theta_{mm}^2]\hat{\sigma}^2, \tag{10.2-9}$$

where $\hat{\sigma}^2$ is defined in equation (2.1-10), v_{ij} is an element of matrix V and

$$\text{var}(\hat{\alpha}_j) = \hat{\sigma}^2. \tag{10.2-10}$$

Equation (10.2-9) shows that it is possible to determine just what vectors in X are causing the increase in the variance since the elements of V are in the range 0 through 1. As the smallest Θ_{mm} approaches 0, the $\text{var}(\hat{\beta}_j)$ approaches ∞. The t test for each coefficient $\hat{\alpha}_j$, $t_{\alpha j}$ is

$$t_{\alpha j} \quad = \hat{\alpha}_j \ / \ \sigma \tag{10.2-11}$$

in view of equation (10.2-10). The singular value decomposition can be used to illustrate the problems of near collinearity. Following Mandel (1982), from equation (10.2-1) we write

$$U\Theta = XV \tag{10.2-12}$$

or

$$U\begin{bmatrix} \Phi_a & 0 \\ 0 & \Phi_b \end{bmatrix} \quad = \quad X[V_a \ \ V_b], \tag{10.2-13}$$

where Φ_a and Φ_b are square diagonal matrices that contain the k_a larger and k_b very small singular values ($k_a + k_b = K$) along the diagonals, respectively. V_a and V_b are K by k_a and K by k_b, respectively. In terms of our prior notation $r \equiv k_a$. If X is close to not being full rank, then

$$XV_b \quad \approx 0 \tag{10.2-14}$$

since $U[0 \ \Phi_b]' \approx 0$ as Φ_b approaches zero. Equation (10.2-14) is very important in understanding why predictions of OLS models with rank problems in X have high variance in cases of near collinearity and why there is no unique solution for $\hat{\beta}_i$ when there is exact collinearity ($r < K$). The perfect collinearity case will be discussed first. Assume the vector $\hat{\beta}$ is partitioned into $\hat{\beta}_a$ containing k_a elements and $\hat{\beta}_b$ containing k_b elements. Given a new vector x_{T+j} consisting of K elements, a forecast of y in period T+j can be calculated from

$$\hat{y}_{T+j} = x_{T+j}(\hat{\beta}_a \ \hat{\beta}_b)' = (x_{a \ T+j} \ x_{b \ T+j})(\hat{\beta}_a \ \hat{\beta}_b)', \tag{10.2-15}$$

where x_{T+j} is partitioned into $x_{a \ T+j}$ and $x_{b \ T+j}$. Following Mandel (1982), if $Z \equiv \Theta V'$, where Z is r by K, equation (10.2-8) becomes

$$Z\hat{\beta} = (Z_a \ Z_b)(\hat{\beta}_a \ \hat{\beta}_b)' = \hat{\alpha}, \tag{10.2-16}$$

where Z has been partitioned into Z_a, which is k_a by k_a, and Z_b, which is k_a by k_b. From equation (10.2-16) $\hat{\beta}_a$ is written as

$$\hat{\beta}_a = -Z_a^{-1}Z_b\hat{\beta}_b + Z_a^{-1}\hat{\alpha}. \tag{10.2-17}$$

Equation (10.2-17) shows that if a value for $\hat{\beta}_b$ is arbitrarily determined, $\hat{\beta}_a$ is uniquely determined. Using equation (10.2-17), we substitute for $\hat{\beta}_a$ in equation (10.2-15)

$$\hat{y}_{T+j} = x_{a \ T+j}(Z_a^{-1}\hat{\alpha}) + (x_{b \ T+j} - x_{a \ T+j}Z_a^{-1}Z_b)\beta_b. \tag{10.2-18}$$

Equation (10.2-18) suggests that the only way we can make $\hat{y}_{T+j}$ independent of any arbitrary value of $\hat{\beta}_b$ is to impose the constraint

$$x_{b \ T+j} = x_{a \ T+j} \ Z_a^{-1}Z_b, \tag{10.2-19}$$

which implies that

$$\hat{y}_{T+j} = x_{a \ T+j}(Z_a^{-1}\hat{\alpha}). \tag{10.2-20}$$

We note that

$$Z_a^{-1}Z_b \equiv (V_a')^{-1}V_b', \tag{10.2-21}$$

where V' has been partitioned as we did with Z. The above discussion repeats Mandel's (1982) important proof that if there is collinearity such that $r < K$, there is no unique solution of $\hat{y}_{T+j}$, given a vector x_{T+j}, except when the new x vector (x_{T+j}) fulfills equation (10.2-19). Next, near collinearity will be discussed.

Consider a new vector x_{T+j} from which we want to obtain a prediction $\hat{y}_{T+j}$. If x_{T+j} satisfies the <u>near collinearity</u> condition of the X matrix expressed in equation (10.2-14), then from equation (10.2-1) we can write

$$x_{T+j} = u_{T+j}\Theta V', \qquad\qquad (10.2\text{-}22)$$

which, since Θ^{-1} exists, can be written

$$u_{T+j} = x_{T+j}V\Theta^{-1}, \qquad\qquad (10.2\text{-}23)$$

where x_{T+j} and u_{T+j} are K element vectors.

From equation (10.2-7)

$$\hat{y}_{T+j} = u_{T+j}\,\hat{\alpha} \qquad\qquad (10.2\text{-}24)$$

and in view of equation (10.2-10),

$$var(\hat{y}_{T+j}) = \hat{\sigma}^2\, \Sigma_{i=1}^{K} u_i^2. \qquad\qquad (10.2\text{-}25)$$

From equation (10.2-13)

$$u_{T+j} = (x_{T+j}V_a \quad x_{T+j}V_b) \begin{bmatrix} \Theta_a^{-1} & 0 \\ 0 & \Theta_b^{-1} \end{bmatrix}. \qquad\qquad (10.2\text{-}26)$$

If the new vector x_{T+j} satisfies the near collinearity condition of the X matrix expressed in equation (10.2-14), $x_{T+j}V_b \approx 0$ and the variance of $\hat{y}_{T+j}$ will be small. However, if $x_{T+j} V_b \neq 0$, then the value $(x_{T+j}V_b)(\Theta_b^{-1})$ will be very large, because of having to invert Θ_b where there are small values along the diagonal. These small values will imply large values in u_{T+j} from equation (10.2-26) and a large variance in $\hat{y}_{T+j}$ from equation (10.2-25). This rather long discussion, which has benefited from Mandel's (1982) excellent paper, has stressed the problems of using an OLS regression model for prediction purposes when the original X matrix has collinearity problems. The singular value decomposition approach to OLS estimation has been shown to highlight the effect of collinearity, which potentially impacts OLS, ARIMA, VAR and VARMA models.

The B34S QR command provides easy access to the singular value decomposition procedure. Assume a model y = f(x1, x2, x3). The following command will estimate both the QR approach to the OLS model and the associated principal components regression.

B34SEXEC QR IPCC=PCREGLIST$ MODEL Y = X1 X2 X3$ B34SEEND$

Values printed include $\hat{\alpha}_j$, $t_{\alpha j}$ U, V, $\hat{Y}$,$\hat{e}$, $\hat{\beta}_j$ and $t_{\beta j}$. If IPCC=PCREG, U, V, $\hat{Y}$ and $\hat{e}$ are not printed.

10.3 Specification Searches

The QR command optionally allows a branch to the Leamer (1978) SEARCH program. This option is fully documented in the above reference and will not be discussed here. The SEARCH input language has been maintained and is documented in the B34S 'Native' Command Manual. A major point made by Leamer is that if a researcher makes many runs and finally selects a reportable model, then the estimated standard errors of the coefficients are <u>understated</u>.

10.4 Examples

Table 10.1 lists the commands to load the data from Wampler (1970).

Table 10.1 Wampler Test Problem

```
==WAMPLER
B34SEXEC DATA NOOB=21 HEADING=('DATA FROM WAMPLER JASA JUNE 1970')
     FILEF=@@$
* DATA FROM ROY WAMPLER JASA JUNE 1970 VOL 65, NO 330, PP. 549 -564 $
INPUT X1  DELTA$
BUILD Y1 Y2 Y3 Y4 Y5 X2 X3 X4 X5 AX1 AX2 AX3 AX4 AX5$
* Y1 = 1 + X + X**2  + X**3 + X**4 + X**5 $
* Y2 = 1 + .1X + .01X**2 + .001X**3 + .0001X**4 + .00001X**5 $
* Y3 = Y1 + DELTA $
* Y4 = Y1 + 100 DELTA $
* Y5 ' Y1 + 1000 DELTA$
GEN X2 = MULT(X1,X1)$
GEN X3 = MULT(X2,X1 )$
GEN X4 = MULT(X3,X1 )$
GEN X5 = MULT(X4,X1)$
GEN AX1= MULT(X1,.1 )$
GEN AX2= MULT(X2,.01)$
GEN AX3= MULT(X3,.001)$
GEN AX4= MULT(X4,.0001)$
GEN AX5= MULT(X5,.00001)$
GEN Y1 = ADD(X1,1.0)$      GEN Y1=ADD(Y1, X2)$  GEN Y1=ADD(Y1, X3)$
                           GEN Y1=ADD(Y1, X4)$  GEN Y1=ADD(Y1, X5)$
GEN Y2 = ADD(AX1,1.0)$     GEN Y2=ADD(Y2,AX2)$  GEN Y2=ADD(Y2,AX3)$
                           GEN Y2=ADD(Y2,AX4)$  GEN Y2=ADD(Y2,AX5)$
GEN Y3 = ADD(Y1,DELTA)$
GEN Y4 = MULT(DELTA,100.0) $ GEN Y4 = ADD(Y1,Y4)$
GEN Y5 = MULT(DELTA,10000.)$ GEN Y5 = ADD(Y1,Y5)$
DATACARDS$
0.    759. 1.   -2048. 2.    2048. 3.   -2048. 4.    2523. 5. -2048.
6.   2048. 7.   -2048. 8.    1838. 9.   -2048. 10.   2048. 11. -2048.
12.  1838. 13.  -2048. 14.   2048. 15.  -2048. 16.   2523. 17. -2048.
18.  2048. 19.  -2048. 20.    759.
B34SRETURN$
B34SEEND$
B34SEXEC LIST$ VAR  X1  X2  X3  X4  X5 Y1 Y2 Y3 Y4 DELTA$ B34SEEND$
B34SEXEC LIST$ VAR AX1 AX2 AX3 AX4 AX5                $ B34SEEND$
B34SEXEC QR $ MODEL Y1=X1 X2 X3 X4 X5       $ B34SEEND$
B34SEXEC QR $ MODEL Y2=AX1 AX2 AX3 AX4 AX5$ B34SEEND$
B34SEXEC QR $ MODEL Y3=X1 X2 X3 X4 X5       $ B34SEEND$
B34SEXEC QR $ MODEL Y4=X1 X2 X3 X4 X5       $ B34SEEND$
B34SEXEC QR $ MODEL Y5=X1 X2 X3 X4 X5       $ B34SEEND$
==
```

Five problems are run:

$$Y1 = 1 + x + x^2 + x^3 + x^4 + x^5 \qquad\qquad (10.4\text{-}1)$$

$$Y2 = 1 + .1x + .01x^2 + .001x^3 + .0001x^4 + .00001x^5 \qquad (10.4\text{-}2)$$

$$Y3 = Y1 + \delta \qquad\qquad (10.4\text{-}3)$$

$$Y4 = Y1 + 100\delta \qquad\qquad (10.4\text{-}4)$$

$$Y5 = Y1 + 10000\delta \qquad\qquad (10.4\text{-}5)$$

Equations (10.4-1) and (10.4.2) are perfect fits and all estimated coefficients should be 1.0 since the parameters {.1, .01, .001, .0001, .00001} have been built into the variables {AX1,...,AX5}. Equations (10.4-3) - (10.4-5) are not perfect fits and have increasing amounts of noise. X is defined as {0,1,...,20}. Edited output from running this test problem is given below.

```
OLS RESULTS USING QR DECOMPOSITION FOR      21 OBS

VARIABLE          COEFFICIENT           STANDARD ERROR            T VALUE                 Y = Y1    X- 3

X5       X-11    1.00000000000001688    0.73909565916003103 7E-14    135300483449801.199
X4       X-10    0.99999999999985450    0.37148381775683254 6E-12    2691907297705.14429
X3       X- 9    1.00000000002190959    0.66770713708600373 0E-11    149766258959.892609
X2       X- 8    0.99999999789353861    0.51280673139748891 7E-10    19500524048.5860472
CONSTANT X-17    0.99999999891929515 5  0.14162270591261681 7E-09    7061014633.74318695
X1       X- 1    1.00000000085805030    0.15552130757720358 3E-09    6429987095.89444637

ADJ RSQ   1.00000000000000000    STANDARD ERROR OF ESTIMATE  0.155297146571297289E-09 SUM SQ RESIDUALS   0.361758055997804885E-18

OLS RESULTS USING QR DECOMPOSITION FOR      21 OBS

VARIABLE          COEFFICIENT           STANDARD ERROR            T VALUE                 Y = Y2    X- 4

AX5      X-16    1.00000000000000133    0.43488365444737335 85E-14    229946559203319.066
CONSTANT X-17    0.99999999999998723    0.83330753718473363 8E-15    1200037147603900.12
AX3      X-14    1.00000000000003486    0.39287868758517515 2E-13    254531495751 65.9258
AX1      X-12    1.00000000000001399    0.91508664562964678 3E-14    109279269321206.254
AX4      X-15    0.99999999999986663    0.21858094617018229 7E-13    457496418387 0.4883
AX2      X-13    0.99999999999965083    0.30173526313792156 3E-13    33141635140698.5000

ADJ RSQ   1.00000000000000000    STANDARD ERROR OF ESTIMATE  0.913767901179539574E-15 SUM SQ RESIDUALS   0.125245766583909118E-28

OLS RESULTS USING QR DECOMPOSITION FOR      21 OBS

VARIABLE          COEFFICIENT           STANDARD ERROR            T VALUE                 Y = Y3    X- 5

X5       X-11    1.00000000000001843    0.11232485467931296 9        8.90274910975860689
X4       X-10    0.99999999998917422    5.64566512170757862          0.177127048530370326
X3       X- 9    1.00000000002273270    101.475507550351118          0.985459471120696609E-02
X2       X- 8    0.99999999788626887    779.343524331598132          0.128313121052269494E-02
CONSTANT X-17    0.99999999003698459    2152.32624678172698          0.464613578215176157E-03
X1       X- 1    1.00000000082829366    2363.55173469686281          0.423092072049164832E-03

ADJ RSQ   0.999994078701093192    STANDARD ERROR OF ESTIMATE  2360.14502379264667       SUM SQ RESIDUALS   83554267.9999978878

OLS RESULTS USING QR DECOMPOSITION FOR      21 OBS

VARIABLE          COEFFICIENT           STANDARD ERROR            T VALUE                 Y = Y4    X- 6

X5       X-11    1.00000000000019162    11.2324854679314305          0.890274910976004280E-01
X4       X-10    0.99999999990065391    564.566512170764611          0.177127048528800279E-02
X3       X- 9    1.00000000018348700    10147.5507550352331          0.985459471279101673E-04
X2       X- 8    0.99999999886561061934 77934.3524331607332          0.128313120894755289E-04
CONSTANT X-17    0.99999996964094709    215232.624678175256          0.464613577267543025E-05
X1       X- 1    1.00000000434190439    236355.173469689107          0.423092073535740635E-05

ADJ RSQ   0.943304587767549663    STANDARD ERROR OF ESTIMATE  236014.502379267476       SUM SQ RESIDUALS   835542679999.998779

OLS RESULTS USING QR DECOMPOSITION FOR      21 OBS

VARIABLE          COEFFICIENT           STANDARD ERROR            T VALUE                 Y = Y5    X- 7

X5       X-11    1.00000000001559752    1123.24854679314194          0.890274910989720652E-03
X4       X-10    0.99999999196972258    56456.6512170764045          0.177127048388322198E-04
X3       X- 9    1.00000001468951849    1014755.07550352228          0.985459485574208739E-06
X2       X- 8    0.99999887047164610    7793435.24331606599          0.128313106586059191E-06
CONSTANT X-17    0.99999981089 74866296 21523262.4678175040         0.464613490818470702E-07
X1       X- 1    1.00000032533961192    23635517.3469688855          0.423092209347326177E-07

ADJ RSQ  -0.330337747712329710    STANDARD ERROR OF ESTIMATE  23601450.2379267253       SUM SQ RESIDUALS   8355426799999971.00
```

Since they are exact fits, the models for Y1 and Y2 show 1.0 as the adjusted R^2. The model for Y1 shows approximately 11 to 12 correct digits, while the model for Y2 shows approximately 14 correct digits. This is because in the model for Y2, the higher power X terms are multiplied by smaller coefficients, making it easier to factor X. This problem shows the effects of matrix scaling when the answers are known. The models for Y3, Y4 and Y5 are <u>not</u> exact. As we gradually increase the error, the adjusted R^2 falls from .99 to .94 to -.33 and the round-off error increases <u>with the same X matrix</u>. Most people assume that only rank problems in X can cause problems. These examples show the effect of changes in the left-hand vector on the accuracy of the solution.

The second problem to be studied is the Longley (1967) data set, which is given in Table 10.2. Three types of problems are run. These are the QR command, which obtains $\hat{\beta}_i$ from equation (4.1-6), the usual REGRESSION command in which the constant is a vector of 1's in the data set and $\hat{\beta}_i$ is obtained from equation (2.1-3) and the deviations from the mean approach, which obtains $\hat{\beta}_i$ from equation (2.1-5) for all variables except the constant and equation (2.1-6) for the constant. The deviations-from-the-mean estimation strategy is implemented by rereading the data back into B34S from unit 8 (with the UNIT=8 option) and specifying the NOCONSTANT option on the second DATA command. In the subsequent REGRESSION command the NOINT option is used because the deviations-from-the-mean approach obtains an estimate of the constant from equation (2.1-6). The deviations-from-the-mean option is rarely used since the usual approach is quite accurate. Its use here is to study the effect of multicollinearity on estimation. Although Table 10.2 lists all the Longley data, only results for Y1 are given. The reader is encouraged to run the other problems.

Table 10.2 Longley Test Data

```
==LONGLEY
B34SEXEC DATA NOOB=16 NOHEAD HEADING=('LONGLEY DATA')$
INPUT Y1 X1 X2 X3 X4 X5 X6 Y2 Y3 Y4 Y5 Y6 Y7 Y8     $
*  DATA FROM LONGLEY JASA SEPTEMBER 1967$
*  ALL EQUATIONS CONTAIN VARIABLES X1-X7, Y1-Y8 ARE $
*          ALTERNATIVE LEFT HAND VARIABLES $
DATACARDS$
60323. 83.0 234289. 2356. 1590. 107608. 1947.
8256. 6045. 427. 1714. 38407. 1892. 3582.
61122. 88.5 259426. 2325. 1456. 108632. 1948.
7960. 6139. 401. 1731. 39241. 1863. 3787.
60171. 88.2 258054. 3682. 1616. 109773. 1949.
8017. 6208. 396. 1772. 37922. 1908. 3948.
61187. 89.5 284599. 3351. 1650. 110929. 1950.
7497. 6069. 404. 1995. 39196. 1928. 4098.
63221. 96.2 328975. 2099. 3099. 112075. 1951.
7048. 5869. 400. 2055. 41460. 2302. 4087.
63639. 98.1 346999. 1932. 3594. 113270. 1952.
6792. 5670. 431. 1922. 42216. 2420. 4188.
64989. 99.0 365385. 1870. 3547. 115094. 1953.
6555. 5794. 423. 1985. 43587. 2305. 4340.
63761 100.0 363112. 3578. 3350. 116219. 1954.
6495. 5880. 445. 1919. 42271. 2188. 4563.
66019 101.2 397469. 2904. 3048. 117388. 1955.
6718. 5886. 524. 2216. 43761. 2187. 4727.
67857 104.6 419180. 2822. 2857. 118734. 1956.
6572. 5936. 581. 2359. 45131. 2209. 5069.
68169 108.4 442769. 2936. 2798. 120445. 1957.
6222. 6089. 626. 2328. 45278. 2217. 5409.
66513 110.8 444546. 4681. 2637. 121950. 1958.
5844. 6185. 605. 2456. 43530. 2191. 5702.
68655 112.6 482704. 3813. 2552. 123366. 1959.
5836. 6298. 597. 2520. 45214. 2233. 5957.
69564 114.2 502601. 3931. 2514. 125368. 1960.
5723. 6367. 615. 2489. 45850. 2270. 6250.
69331 115.7 518173. 4806. 2572. 127852. 1961.
5463. 6388. 662. 2594. 45397. 2279. 6548.
70551 116.9 554894. 4007. 2827. 130081. 1962.
5190. 6271. 623. 2626. 46652. 2340. 6849.
B34SRETURN$ B34SEEND$

B34SEXEC QR IPCC=PCREG $ MODEL Y1 = X1 X2 X3 X4 X5 X6 $
   TITLE=('REGRESSION ON TOTAL')$ B34SEEND$

B34SEXEC REGRESSION MANYDIGITS TOLL=.1E-08$
  COMMENT=('REGRESSION ON TOTAL    ')$
  MODEL Y1=X1 X2 X3 X4 X5 X6 $     B34SEEND$


B34SEXEC DATA NOOB=16 NOHEAD NOCONSTANT UNIT=08 FILEF=DP$
       HEADING=('NO CONSTANT ON INPUT')$
     INPUT Y1 X1 X2 X3 X4 X5 X6 Y2 Y3 Y4 Y5 Y6 Y7 Y8 $
   B34SEEND$

B34SEXEC REGRESSION MANYDIGITS TOLL=.1E-08 NOINT$
  MODEL Y1=X1 X2 X3 X4 X5 X6 $
  COMMENT=('REGRESSION ON TOTAL - DEVIATION FROM MEANS   ')$
  MODEL Y1=X1 X2 X3 X4 X5 X6 $     B34SEEND$

==
```

Edited output from running the problem in Table 10.2 is given next. The MANYDIGITS option has been specified on the B34S REGRESSION command to write the coefficients with 16 digits of accuracy. In addition, the usual coefficient output is given.

```
QR OPTION CONTROL CARD                              VERSION DATE 1 JUNE 1982

IBEGIN, IEND, NOIN, IFREZ, IPLOT,      EPS, ICOM, IPCL, ISEAR
   1    16    7     0      1    .00E+00   1    1     0


COMMENTS

REGRESSION ON TOTAL




OF    35000 DOUBLE PRECISION SLOTS IN SPACE,      144 ARE BEING USED


GIVEN MAX SUM OF ABS VALUES OF ANY ROW =    693888.90     EPS HAS BEEN SET =   0.693888899999999980E-10

OLS RESULTS USING QR DECOMPOSITION FOR      16 OBS

VARIABLE         COEFFICIENT                 STANDARD ERROR              T VALUE              Y = Y1     X- 1

X2       X- 3    -0.358191792925927430E-01   0.334910077722500189E-01   -1.06951631722088081
X5       X- 6    -0.511041056536485324E-01   0.226073200069394423       -0.226051144664479661
X3       X- 4    -2.02022980381681849        0.488399681651787723       -4.13642735593995181
X4       X- 5    -1.03322686717366818        0.214274163161719239       -4.82198531044482648
X6       X- 7    1829.15146461368289         455.478499142339388         4.01588981270894974
X1       X- 2    15.0618722714175008         84.9149257747803006         0.17737602823049125
CONSTANT X-15    -3482258.63459606981        890420.383607620475        -3.91080291815353220

ADJ RSQ  0.992465007628824072     STANDARD ERROR OF ESTIMATE  304.854073562003975     SUM SQ RESIDUALS  836424.055506129458


COVARIANCE MATRIX OF REGRESSION COEFFICIENTS

X2          X- 3

  0.11216476016009112E-02

X5          X- 6

 -0.63085501354375115E-02  0.51109091789616439E-01

X3          X- 4

  0.15467297383493973E-01 -0.83722173237227054E-01  0.23853424903756759

X4          X- 5

  0.33628299081402744E-02 -0.91513289491012787E-02  0.64733776695698478E-01  0.45913416998655077E-01

X6          X- 7

 -12.229187935075037      39.969400260528435      -183.32591022848234    -53.616744037398508     207460.66318095806

X1          X- 2

 -1.8468727376279301      12.654240717598773      -23.017190824427043     -6.3467106462916523    7204.9126273941292
 7210.5446193364478

CONSTANT    X-15

 24337.496555432309      -82671.305069967944     363554.79859269453     104883.69233408640      -405441421.49396718
 -15495015.833218027    792848459543.94200

IN SVDQR CALCULATING SINGULAR VALUE DECOMPOSITION OF X.  OF     70000 SPACE AVAILABLE,     626  USED.

SINGULAR VALUE FACTORIZATION OF X

X= U * DIMATRIX(S) * TRANSPOSE(V)

DIAGONAL ELEMENTS OF S ARE THE UNORDERED SQUARE ROOTS OF EIGENVALUES OF TRANSPOSE(X) * X

COLUMNS OF U ARE EIGENVECTORS OF X * TRANSPOSE(X)

COLUMNS OF V ARE THE EIGENVECTORS OF TRANSPOSE(X) * X

A, THE PRINCIPAL COMPONENT REGRESSION COEFFICIENTS, SOLVES THE SYSTEM Y= U * A  +  R  WHERE R IS THE RESIDUAL

REF. USE OF SINGULAR VALUE DECOMPOSITION IN REGRESSION ANALYSIS. BY J. MANDEL, AMERICAN STATISTICIAN FEB 1982 VOL 36 NO. 1

SINGULAR VALUES OF X

    0.1663668227889468D+07   0.8389957794622066D+05   0.3407197376095863D+04   0.1582643681003794D+04   0.4169360109707004D+02
    0.3648093794782314D+01   0.3423709062092338D-03

PC REGRESSION COEF.

   -0.2574977072024466D+06  -0.4609311125516972D+05   0.2880890760850670D+04   0.1604488608619043D+04   0.1776626531885894D+04
   -0.2106907153946040D+03   0.1192224208618982D+04

T VAL. PC REG. COEF.

   -0.8446589025161061D+03  -0.1511972948781834D+03   0.9450064836560986D+01   0.5263136522572027D+01   0.5827793314772773D+01
   -0.6911198952759010D+00   0.3910802944794820D+01
```

STEP ENDING. SECONDS USED 0.11655808E-01. TOTAL JOB SECONDS   1.5339146   .

UIC B34S DATA ANALYSIS PROGRAM 21 NOV 86   LONGLEY DATA   PAGE   2

COMMENT   REGRESSION ON TOTAL

****
  PROBLEM NUMBER   1
  SUBPROBLEM NUMBER   1

  F TO ENTER   0.10000002E-01
  F TO REMOVE   0.49999990E-02
  TOLERANCE   0.10000001E-08
  MAXIMUM NO OF STEPS   7
  DEPENDENT VARIABLE X(1).   VARIABLE NAME Y1

  THE FOLLOWING VARIABLES ARE DELETED IN THIS SUBPROBLEM

  8   9 10 11 12 13 14

  THE FOLLOWING VARIABLES ARE FORCED INTO THE REGRESSION EQUATION AS CONTROL VARIABLES (COVARIATES)

  2   3   4   5   6   7 15

STANDARD ERROR OF Y =   3511.9678   FOR DEGREES OF FREEDOM =   15.

....
STEP NUMBER 7   ANALYSIS OF VARIANCE FOR REDUCTION IN SS DUE TO VARIABLE ENTERING
  VARIABLE ENTERING   3   SOURCE   DF   SS   MS   F   F SIG.
  MULTIPLE R   0.99774   DUE REGRESSION   6   0.18417E+09   0.30695E+08   330.29   1.000000
  STD ERROR OF Y.X 304.85376   DEV. FROM REG.   9   0.83642E+06   92936.
  R SQUARE   0.99548   TOTAL   15   0.18501E+09   0.12334E+08

       MULTIPLE REGRESSION EQUATION
  VARIABLE   COEFFICIENT   STD. ERROR   T VAL.   T SIG. P. COR. ELASTICITY   PARTIAL COR. FOR VAR. NOT IN EQUATION
  Y1   =   VARIABLE   COEFFICIENT   F FOR SELECTION

EXTENDED PRECISION VAR   COEF   SE

  X- 2   X1   15.06187281288034   84.91483838534519
  X- 3   X2   -0.3581917998584900E-01   0.3349097337316176E-01
  X- 4   X3   -2.020229814090662   0.4883991800464668
  X- 5   X4   -1.033226870110064   0.2142739428110601
  X- 6   X5   -0.5110410315999900E-01   0.2260729675050852
  X- 7   X6   1829.151475721324   455.4780317113570
  X-15   CONSTANT   -3482258.656344591   890419.4698297482

  X1   X- 2   15.06187   84.91484   0.1774   0.13686   0.0590   0.2345E-01
  X2   X- 3 -0.3581918E-01   0.3349097E-01   -1.070   0.68732 -0.3358   -0.2126
  X3   X- 4   -2.020230   0.4883992   -4.136   0.99746 -0.8095   -0.9877E-01
  X4   X- 5   -1.033227   0.2142739   -4.822   0.99906 -0.8491   -0.4123E-01
  X5   X- 6 -0.5110410E-01   0.2260730   -0.2261   0.17379 -0.0751   -0.9187E-01
  X6   X- 7   1829.151   455.4780   4.016   0.99696   0.8011   54.73
  CONSTANT   X-15   -3482259.   890419.5   -3.911   0.99644

ADJUSTED R SQUARE FOR K=   7, N=   16 IS   0.99246502

-2 * LN(MAXIMUM OF THE LIKELIHOOD FUNCTION)   219.23487

AKAIKE INFORMATION CRITERION (AIC) BASED ON JOINT LIKELIHOOD OF SIGMA AND BETA   235.23487

SCHWARZ INFORMATION CRITERION (SIC) BASED ON JOINT LIKELIHOOD OF SIGMA AND BETA   241.41558

NOTE: MODELS WITH LOWER AIC OR SIC ARE BETTER.

AIC = (N * LN(2*PI)) + (N * LN((SUM RES SQ)/N)) + N + (2*(K+1))

SIC = AIC - (2*(K+1)) + ((K+1) * LN(N))

  RESIDUAL VARIANCE =   92936.005

  ORDER OF ENTRANCE (OR DELETION) OF THE VARIABLES =   6   4   2   7 15   5   3

ESTIMATE OF COMPUTATIONAL ERROR IN COEFFICIENTS =
    1 -0.4144E-01   2   1619.   3   1.177   4 0.1705   5 -476.8   6 -355.0
    7 0.1557

  COVARIANCE MATRIX OF REGRESSION COEFFICIENTS

ROW 1   VARIABLE X- 2   X1
     7210.5445

ROW 2   VARIABLE X- 3   X2
     -1.8468727   0.11216476E-02

ROW 3   VARIABLE X- 4   X3
     -23.017191   0.15467297E-01   0.23853425

ROW 4   VARIABLE X- 5   X4
     -6.3467106   0.33628299E-02   0.64733776E-01   0.45913417E-01

ROW 5   VARIABLE X- 6   X5
     12.654241   -0.63085501E-02 -0.83722173E-01 -0.91513289E-02   0.51109091E-01

ROW 6   VARIABLE X- 7   X6
     7204.9126   -12.229188   -183.32591   -53.616744   39.969400   207460.66

ROW 7   VARIABLE X-15   CONSTANT
     -15495016.   24337.496   363554.80   104883.69   -82671.305   -0.40544142E+09 0.79284846E+12

```
=== PROGRAM TERMINATED - ALL VARIABLES PUT IN

UIC B34S DATA ANALYSIS PROGRAM 21 NOV 86                                              PAGE 11

COMMENT     REGRESSION ON TOTAL - DEVIATION FROM MEANS


***************
  PROBLEM NUMBER                   2
  SUBPROBLEM NUMBER                1

  F TO ENTER              0.10000002E-01
  F TO REMOVE             0.49999990E-02
  TOLERANCE               0.10000001E-08
  MAXIMUM NO OF STEPS             6
  DEPENDENT VARIABLE X( 1).  VARIABLE NAME  Y1

  THE FOLLOWING VARIABLES ARE DELETED IN THIS SUBPROBLEM

   8   9  10  11  12  13  14

  THE FOLLOWING VARIABLES ARE FORCED INTO THE REGRESSION EQUATION AS CONTROL VARIABLES (COVARIATES)

   2   3   4   5   6   7

STANDARD ERROR OF Y =    3511.9678      FOR DEGREES OF FREEDOM  =       15.


.............
STEP NUMBER  6                          ANALYSIS OF VARIANCE FOR REDUCTION IN SS DUE TO VARIABLE ENTERING
  VARIABLE ENTERING        2             SOURCE          DF        SS          MS         F         F SIG.
  MULTIPLE R          0.99774            DUE REGRESSION   6    0.18417E+09  0.30695E+08  330.29    1.000000
  STD ERROR OF Y.X  304.85376            DEV. FROM REG.   9    0.83642E+06  92936.
  R SQUARE            0.99548            TOTAL           15    0.18501E+09  0.12334E+08

    MULTIPLE REGRESSION EQUATION
  VARIABLE    COEFFICIENT    STD. ERROR    T VAL.   T SIG. P. COR. ELASTICITY    PARTIAL COR. FOR VAR. NOT IN EQUATION
Y1      =                                                                        VARIABLE    COEFFICIENT    F FOR SELECTION
CONST.     -3482259.       890420.5      -3.911   0.99644

EXTENDED PRECISION FOR CONSTANT AND SE     -3482258.634727585        890420.4793627653

EXTENDED PRECISION  VAR      COEF                     SE

X- 2         X1       15.06187235777704      84.91483837269987
X- 3         X2      -0.3581917931572967E-01  0.3349097330311414E-01
X- 4         X3      -2.020229804108214       0.4883991789806454
X- 5         X4      -1.033226867254283       0.2142739426124010
X- 6         X5      -0.5110410549935582E-01  0.2260729673785396
X- 7         X6       1829.151464719417       455.4780303242364


X1         X- 2   15.06187      84.91484     0.1774    0.13686  0.0590   0.2345E-01
X2         X- 3 -0.3581918E-01  0.3349097E-01 -1.070    0.68732 -0.3358  -0.2126
X3         X- 4  -2.020230      0.4883992    -4.136    0.99746 -0.8095  -0.9877E-01
X4         X- 5  -1.033227      0.2142739    -4.822    0.99906 -0.8491  -0.4123E-01
X5         X- 6 -0.5110411E-01  0.2260730    -0.2261    0.17379 -0.0751  -0.9187E-01
X6         X- 7   1829.151      455.4780      4.016    0.99696  0.8011   54.73

ADJUSTED R SQUARE FOR K=   7, N=      16  IS     0.99246502

-2  *  LN(MAXIMUM OF THE LIKELIHOOD FUNCTION)   219.23487

AKAIKE  INFORMATION CRITERION (AIC) BASED ON JOINT LIKELIHOOD OF SIGMA AND BETA    235.23487

SCHWARZ INFORMATION CRITERION (SIC) BASED ON JOINT LIKELIHOOD OF SIGMA AND BETA    241.41558

NOTE: MODELS WITH LOWER AIC OR SIC ARE BETTER.

AIC = (N * LN(2*PI) ) + ( N * LN((SUM RES SQ)/N)) + N + (2*(K+1))

SIC = AIC - (2*(K+1))  +  ((K+1) * LN(N))


  RESIDUAL VARIANCE =   92936.006

  ORDER OF ENTRANCE (OR DELETION) OF THE VARIABLES =   3   4   5   7   6   2

ESTIMATE OF COMPUTATIONAL ERROR IN COEFFICIENTS =
   1 -0.5321E-09    2  0.8714E-05    3  0.1280E-07    4  0.3817E-08    5 -0.6287E-06    6 -0.5206E-09

  COVARIANCE MATRIX OF REGRESSION COEFFICIENTS

ROW  1    VARIABLE X- 2   X1
          7210.5446

ROW  2    VARIABLE X- 3   X2
          -1.8468727    0.11216476E-02

ROW  3    VARIABLE X- 4   X3
          -23.017191    0.15467297E-01  0.23853425

ROW  4    VARIABLE X- 5   X4
          -6.3467106    0.33628299E-02  0.64733777E-01  0.45913417E-01

ROW  5    VARIABLE X- 6   X5
          12.654241    -0.63085501E-02 -0.83722173E-01 -0.91513290E-02  0.51109092E-01

ROW  6    VARIABLE X- 7   X6
          7204.9126    -12.229188     -183.32591     -53.616744      39.969400     207460.66

=== PROGRAM TERMINATED - ALL VARIABLES PUT IN
```

Table 10.3 lists the estimated coefficients for the three
approaches and also lists results obtained by Beaton, Rubin, and
Barone (1976), using DORTHO. This routine uses the classical Gram-
Schmidt approach, which they state "agree with Longley's hand
calculated solution in every published place."[3] The B34S QR results
on raw, unscaled data are very close to these results. The
deviations-from-the-means output is next best in accuracy, while
the levels output is least accurate. Unless the TOLL parameter is
set to a very low number, the B34S REGRESSION command will not
attempt the problem. The REGRESSION command's measure of accuracy,
based on the Faddeeva (1959) algorithm, shows values ranging from
.04144 to 1619. in absolute value for output using the level data.
These are orders of magnitude from what is usually found for
problems such as those reported in chapter 2. Nevertheless, about
eight digits are correct and, if the usual output is used, there
would be no way to tell any difference from the DORTHO results. The
REGRESSION results from the deviations-from-the-means approach are
more accurate and the error estimate values range from .5206E-09 to
.8714E-05 in absolute value. The PC regression output shows the
singular values of X. These range from .1664E+07 to .34237D-03,
which is a large spread. Equation (10.2-9) shows how this spread
magnifies the variance of the coefficients.

Table 10.3 Results From the Longley Total Equation

Variable	DORTHO	QR	LEVELS	DMEANS
Constant	-3482258.634597	-3482258.63459606981	-3482258.656344591	-3482258.634727585
X1	15.06187227176	15.0618722714175008	15.06187281288034	15.06187235777704
X2	-.035819179293	-.035819179292592743	-.0358191799858490	-.035819179315730
X3	-2.020229803818	-2.02022980381681849	-2.020229814090662	-2.02022980410821
X4	-1.033226867174	-1.03322686717366818	-1.033226870110064	-1.03322686725428
X5	-0.051104105653	-0.05110410565364853	-.0511041031599990	-.051104105499356
X6	1829.151464614112	1829.15146461368289	1829.151475721324	1829.15146471942

DORTHO reports results from Beaton, Rubin, and Barone (1976). QR reports results from the
B34S QR command. LEVELS reports the B34S REGRESSION command where data are levels.
DMEANS reports results from the REGRESSION command where the data are deviations from
the means.

10.5 Conclusions

This chapter has illustrated the QR approach to regression
analysis and the associated PC regression. Two examples were used
to illustrate various problems. The Wampler data set shows the
effects on accuracy of rank problems in the X matrix, given the y
vector, and changes in the y vector, given the X matrix. While most
researchers realize that problems can occur with X close to not
being full rank, only a few realize that the y vector can also
cause problems. The Longley data set was used to show the effects
on accuracy from estimating the coefficients with $(X'X)^{-1}X'Y$, with
the deviations-from-the-means approach, or with the QR approach.

The PC regression was shown to provide important information about the structure of the OLS problem, especially in the case of collinearity or near collinearity.

NOTES

1. The literature on the QR approach is vast. No attempt will be made to provide a summary in the limited space available in this book. Good references include Longley (1984), Dongarra et al (1979) and Strang (1976). Chapter 4 of this book provides a discussion of this approach applied to systems estimation. This chapter provides some examples and a brief intuitive discussion based in part on Dongarra et al (1979), which documents the LINPACK routines DQRDC and DQRSL. These routines are used for all QR calculations.

2. Mandel (1982) provides a good summary of the uses of the principal components regression and the discussion here has benefited from that treatment. The LINPACK FORTRAN routine DSVDC has been used to calculate the singular value decomposition. This routine has been found to be substantially more accurate than the singular value decomposition routines in versions 8 and 9 of the IMSL Library and substantially faster than the corresponding NAG routine to calculate the singular value decomposition. Stokes (1983, 1984) implemented LINPACK in SPEAKEASY ®. Subsequent testing of the SPEAKEASY LINKULE SVDCM, which uses DSVDC, against the LINKULE SVD, which uses the NAG routine, documented the speed advantage.

3. Since most economic data is only known to a few significant digits, reporting regression coefficients to 16 places makes no sense. However, the study of all 16 digits does makes sense when testing program calculation accuracy. When performing these tests, an implicit assumption is that we have at least 16 significant digits of accuracy for the input data. If we have n significant digits, where n < 16, reporting 16 digits of accuracy in the answer assumes implicitly that the last 16-n digits in the raw data were 0.

11. Nonlinear Estimation Options in B34S

11.0 Introduction

The B34S NONLIN command allows estimation of nonlinear models. Most software with nonlinear capability requires the user to input the model by means of a higher level programming language. While this may seem a reasonable approach, there are a number of problems. First, the higher level programming language is usually quite restrictive and inherently limiting in the models that can be considered. Even if this is not the case, this approach is quite slow because the nonlinear software has to parse the model specification at each iteration of the estimation process.[1]

An alternative way to specify the nonlinear model is with a FORTRAN subroutine and relink the program. This approach has the advantage of fast execution speed but the disadvantage of having to relink the program.[2] The B34S approach to nonlinear estimation involves first having the user specify the model in the form of a FORTRAN subroutine, which is compiled and placed in a library. At execution time, the B34S program will perform a dynamic link with the user subroutine. This approach provides a completely flexible way to input models and provides fast execution time.[3] This chapter will first discuss the basic nonlinear estimation theory. The Sinai-Stokes (1972) money in the production function data, which was discussed in chapter 2, is used to illustrate estimation of a constant elasticity of substitution (CES) production function model.

11.1 Nonlinear Estimation Theory

The basic code used in the NONLIN command was originally developed by Duane Meeter (1964a, 1964b).[4] Extensive modifications were made by the author to incorporate LINPACK and to add the dynamic call feature to B34S. The Meeter code implements the Marquardt (1963) approach to nonlinear estimation, which combines the Gauss-Newton method with the method of steepest descent. Define

$$\hat{y}_i = f(\Theta, X_i) \tag{11.1-1}$$

as a nonlinear function, where X_i is the ith row of the independent variable T by K matrix X, and Θ is a row vector of p parameters to be estimated. In general, $p \neq K$. An estimate of the parameters, $\hat{\Theta}$, is obtained by minimizing the sum of squares, $S(\Theta)$, where

$$S(\Theta) = \Sigma_{i=1}^{T} [y_i - f(\Theta, X_i)]^2. \tag{11.1-2}$$

If the errors from equation (11.1-2) are (a) independent random variables with the same variance, (b) have expected value of zero and (c) have a normal probability distribution, then the least squares estimates, $\hat{\Theta}$, have the property of being maximum likelihood estimates. Define Θ_{ij} as the jth iteration values for the ith parameter and Θ_j as the vector of parameters for the jth iteration, where we drop the ^ to reduce notational clutter. Assume an initial guess on the vector Θ, which we denote Θ_0. The object of each iteration is to minimize $S(\Theta)$ in equation (11.1-2). This is done by obtaining a correction vector, δ_j, of length p defined such that

$$\Theta_j = \delta_j + \Theta_{j-1} \qquad\qquad\qquad (11.1-3)$$

and

$$S(\Theta_j) < S(\Theta_{j-1}). \qquad\qquad\qquad (11.1-4)$$

The Marquardt (1963) method employed in the NONLIN command first linearizes the function f( ) about Θ_0, using a first-order Taylor series approximation. This can be written

$$f(\Theta_j, X_i) \approx f(\Theta_{j-1}, X_i) + z_i \delta_j, \qquad\qquad (11.1-5)$$

where z_i is a vector of length p defined as

$$z_i \equiv \partial\ f(\Theta, X_i)\ /\ \partial\Theta_{kj} \text{ for k=1, p.} \qquad (11.1-6)$$

Define Z as a T by p moment matrix consisting of rows $(z_1, \ldots, z_T)$. Equation (11.1-5) can be thought of as a linear approximation of the nonlinear model for a small change, δ_j, in the parameter vector Θ_{j-1}. Assuming $y \equiv (y_1, \ldots, y_T)$, and Φ_j is a column vector of length T containing values for $\hat{y}$ given Θ_j

$$\Phi_j \equiv [f(\Theta_j, X_1), \ldots, f(\Theta_j, X_T)], \qquad (11.1-7)$$

then a linear approximation for $S(\Theta)$ at iteration j can be written

$$S(\Theta_j) \approx (y - \Phi_{j-1} - Z\delta_j)'(y - \Phi_{j-1} - Z\delta_j). \qquad (11.1-8)$$

Given that $r_{j-1} \equiv y - \Phi_{j-1}$, we can solve for δ_j in equation (11.1-8) as

$$\hat{\delta}_j^* = (Z'Z)^{-1}Z'r_{j-1}. \qquad\qquad\qquad (11.1-9)$$

Equation (11.1-9) is called the Gauss-Newton approach and is a possible way to proceed. Problems can arise if the Taylor series approximation to $f(\Theta_j, X_i)$ in equation (11.1-5) is poor and, after the new parameter vector is updated from equation (11.1-3), equation (11.1-4) is violated. The Gauss-Newton approach, while useful in the final stages of the iterative search for the minimum sum of squares, often runs into problems in the early stages of the iteration process, especially when the initial guesses of the parameters are poor or when Z'Z is not full rank. Another approach called steepest decent defines

$$\hat{\delta}_j^{**} = Z'r_{j-1} \qquad (11.1\text{-}10)$$

and is useful in the initial phases of the iteration processes, but has the problem of approaching the minimum sum of squares slowly. The solution proposed by Marquardt (1963) was to limit the step size and hence improve the Taylor series approximation. Instead of using either equation (11.1-9) or (11.1-10), he proposed

$$\hat{\delta}_j = (Z'Z + \lambda_j\Lambda)^{-1} Z'r_{j-1}, \qquad (11.1\text{-}11)$$

where $\lambda_j > 0$ and Λ is positive definite. The B34S NONLIN command assumes $\Lambda \equiv I$. Note that as $\lambda_j \to 0$, $\hat{\delta}_j \to \hat{\delta}_j^*$, while as $\lambda_j \to \infty$, $\hat{\delta}_j \to \hat{\delta}_j^{**}$. Hence, we can think of the Marquardt method as a compromise between the Gauss-Newton approach and the steepest descent method.[5]

Since the steepest descent is not scale invariant, equation (11.1-11) is modified to incorporate a correction that is in the same units of the standard deviations of z_i that make up the matrix Z. Define D as a p by p diagonal matrix where $D_{ii} \equiv$ the ith diagonal element of Z'Z. Equation (11.1-11) becomes

$$\hat{\delta}_j = D^{-.5}(D^{-.5}Z'ZD^{-.5} + \lambda_j\Lambda)^{-1}D^{-.5}Z'r_{j-1}. \qquad (11.1\text{-}12)$$

Define γ_j as the angle in degrees between $\hat{\delta}_j$ in equation (11.1-12) and $\hat{\delta}_j^{**}$ in equation (11.1-10). $\gamma_j \to 0$ as $\lambda_j \to \infty$. Inspection of γ_j indicates how the solution is proceeding. The object of the iteration process is to start λ_j large and reduce it if satisfactory progress is being made toward reducing S(Θ). Define v > 1 and S(λ_j) as the value of S(Θ) obtained by using equation (11.1-12) to update Θ_{j-1} to Θ_j given λ_j. The rules used to change λ_j are:

(a) If $S(\lambda_{j-1}/v) \leq S(\Theta_{j-1})$, then $\lambda_j = \lambda_j / v$.
(b) If $S(\lambda_{j-1}/v) > S(\Theta_{j-1})$, and $S(\lambda_{j-1}) \leq S(\Theta_{i-1})$, then $\lambda_j=\lambda_{j-1}$.
(c) Otherwise increase λ_j by successive multiplication by v until, for some smallest w, if $S(\lambda_{j-1}v^w) \leq S(\Theta_{i-1})$, then $\lambda_j = \lambda_{j-1}v^w$.

Note that $S(\lambda_{j-1} / v) \equiv S(\Theta_j)$ where Θ_j is calculated from equations (11.1-12) and (11.1-3), using $\lambda_j = \lambda_{j-1} / v$. If the first condition holds, the iterative process is making steady progress and the method of estimation is becoming more like Gauss-Newton. If the second condition holds, progress is being made, but it is not warranted to change λ_j. If the last condition holds, the iterative process is going poorly and the step size must be reduced until an improvement in the sum of squares is obtained. The iterative process will stop if either the maximum relative change in any parameter falls below a user-specified tolerance, the maximum number of iterations is exceeded or the change in the sum of squares falls below the maximum. While there are program defaults, the NONLIN command allows the user to specify options to control the estimation. For further detail see the B34S on-line manual. A few options are discussed here to give the reader a feel for the solution process.

-FLAM: Optionally specifies λ_0. The default is .01.
-FLU: Optionally specifies v. The default is 10.
-MIT: Optionally specifies the maximum number of iterations. The default is 20.
-EPS1:   Optionally specifies the maximum relative change in the sum of squares. If $\{[S(\Theta_j)-S(\Theta_{j-1})]/S(\Theta_{j-1})\}<$ EPS1, iteration stops.
-EPS2:   Optionally specifies the maximum relative change in each parameter before iteration stops. The default is .004.   If $|(\Theta_{k\ j} - \Theta_{k\ j-1})/\Theta_{k\ j-1}| <$ EPS2 for $k=1,\ldots,p$, then iteration stops.

The SIGNS sentence optionally allows the user to restrict any parameter not to change sign, while the DIFF sentence optionally allows the user to control the calculation of z_i in equation (11.1-6) by setting the change in Θ_i used to approximate $\partial\Theta_i$. The default is that $\Delta\Theta_i \equiv .01\ \Theta_i$. If the solution will not converge, the user should try a DIFF value < .01. The user usually inputs starting values for the NP parameters with the IVALUES sentence, although if this sentence is not supplied, the default of .1 will be used. Although the usual situation is to use the NONLIN program to estimate a nonlinear least squares problem, if the dependent variable is specified as a vector of 0's, NONLIN can be used to solve NP nonlinear equations in NP unknowns. In this situation the user must specify each of the NP nonlinear equations in the FORTRAN subroutine that is used to describe the model. The form of the subroutine, which can be any name, is given in Table 11.1. By use of the DMODEL and B34SLB parameters, the user specifies the name of this routine and its location.

The NONLIN command optionally outputs a number of statistics. These include the following:

1. One over the condition of the scaled moment matrix $(D^{-.5}Z'ZD^{-.5} + \lambda_j I)$ from equation (11.1-12). If this is close to zero, it suggests that there are too many parameters in the model.

2. γ_j, λ_j, and $S(\Theta_j)$.

3. Lists and plots of the residuals.

The output will always include the following:

1. The estimated parameters, standard errors on the linear hypothesis and t scores.

2. The correlation matrix of the estimated parameters.

3. The variance of the residuals, the SEE and the adjusted R^2.

4. A Durbin-Watson test of the residuals.

5. The square root of the elements of the diagonal of $(Z'Z)^{-1}$. If $V \equiv (Z'Z)^{-1}$, the correlation matrix of the parameters, C_{ij}, is defined as $V_{ij} / (V_{ii}V_{jj})^{.5}$. Hence, knowledge of V_{ii} and C_{ij} allows calculation of V_{ij} for $i \neq j$.

The following section illustrates the NONLIN command, using two CES production function models.

11.2 Examples

Assuming the Sinai-Stokes (1972) real money balances data has been loaded (see Table 2.2), the FORTRAN subroutine listed in Table 11.1 and the control statements listed in Table 11.2 will estimate two CES models of the form of

$$Q = \alpha(\delta K^p + (1.0 - \delta)L^p)^{v/p} \tag{11.2-1}$$

and

$$Q = \alpha(\delta_1 K^p + \delta_2 L^p + (1.0 - \delta_1 - \delta_2)(M1/P)^p)^{v/p}, \tag{11.2-2}$$

where Q, K, L, M1 and P are real output capital, labor, M1 and prices, respectively. The subroutine CH11MOD has two paths. If NPROB=1, then equation (11.2-1) is estimated, while if NPROB=2, equation (11.2-2) is estimated. The two models were estimated as a consequence of a reply to Sinai and Stokes (1972) by Boyes and Kavanaugh (1979), who questioned the Cobb-Douglas form of the production function and argued for the CES. The Cobb-Douglas models were discussed in chapter 2, Table 2.2. Boyes and Kavanaugh (1979) estimated a model of the form of

$$Q^{p/v} = \delta_1 K + \delta_2 L + \delta_3(M1/P) + e, \tag{11.2-3}$$

using OLS with a grid search procedure for various values of p and v. The "advantage" of this approach was that OLS could be used. The disadvantage was that, by assumption, the correlation between v and p and the other parameters was assumed to be zero, and α was assumed to be = 1. Sinai-Stokes (1981) were able to relax these assumptions by use of the NONLIN procedure. A number of models, including equations (11.1-1) and (11.2-2) were tried.

Table 11.1 FORTRAN SUBROUTINE for CES Production Function

```
      SUBROUTINE CH11MOD(NPROB,TH,F,NOB,NP,X,NVAR,NOBS1)
      IMPLICIT REAL*8(A-H,O-Z)
      DIMENSION TH(*),F(*),X(NOB,*)
C
C     NPROB   - USER CONTROLLED SWITCH.
C     TH      - THE PARAMETERS TO BE ESTIMATED.
C     F       - THE YHAT VECTOR. F(1),...,F(NOB) SET IN SUBROUTINE.
C     NOB     - NUMBER OF OBSERVATIONS.
C     NP      - NUMBER OF PARAMETERS.
C     X       - DATA MATRIX (NOB BY NSERIE) WHERE NSERIE = # X + 1.
C             - X COLS. X1 ----- Xmax, Y
C     NVAR    - NUMBER OF X VARIABLES. OPTIONALLY SET TO A VALUE NE 0
C                 BY IXIND PARAMETER.
C     NOBS1   - USER CONTROLLED SWITCH.
C
C     SET UP FOR CES PRODUCTION FUNCTION - SEE SINAI-STOKES RES 1981
C     NPROB = 1  **** A 2 FACTOR MODEL WITHOUT TIME
C     NPROB=2 -- A 3 FACTOR MODEL
C
      IF(NPROB.EQ.2)GO TO 100
      TH222=1.0D+00 - TH(1)
      DO 10 I=1,NOB
   10 F(I)=((TH(1)*(X(I,1)**TH(4)))+(TH222*(X(I,2)**TH(4))))**(TH(3)/
     *TH(4))*TH(2)
      GO TO 999
C
  100 TH333=1.0D+00 - TH(1) - TH(2)
      DO 120 I=1,NOB
  120 F(I)=((TH(1)*(X(I,1)**TH(4)))+(TH(2)*(X(I,2)**TH(4))) +
     * (TH333*(X(I,3)**TH(4))))**(TH(5)/TH(4))*TH(3)
  999 RETURN
      END
```

Table 11.2 Program to Estimate CES Production Functions

```
B34SEXEC NONLIN  NPROB=1 MIT=50  DMODEL=CH11MOD$
 VAR Q = K L  $
 COMMENT=('BOYES KAVANAUGH  CES WITHOUT REAL BAL ')$
 COMMENT=('PARM # 1 = A1 (K), #2 = ALPHA,    #3 = V, # 4 =  P ')$
 COMMENT=('HERE WE ARE CONSTRAINING VALUES TO ADD UP')$
 IVALUES=(.3053   1.000   1.85    .03)$
 B34SEEND$

B34SEXEC NONLIN NPROB=2 MIT=50  DMODEL=CH11MOD$
 VAR Q =K L M1DP$
 COMMENT=(' BOYES KAVANAUGH CES WITH REAL M1')$
 COMMENT=('PARM #1 = A1(K), #2 =A2(L),  #3 =ALPHA, #4 =P, #5 = V')$
 COMMENT=('HERE WE ARE CONSTRAINING VALUES TO ADD UP')$
 IVALUES=(.27698,  .7754,  1.000 ,  -.05 ,  1.8)$
 B34SEEND$
```

Output from running equation (11.2-2), or NPROB=2, is given next.

PROGRAM NONLIN

BASIC SUBROUTINES FROM U WISCONSIN

PROGRAM MODIFIED BY HOUSTON H. STOKES

20 DECEMBER 1988

ON MAIN CONTROL CARD - IOPT, NSERIE, IBEGIN, IEND   SET =   0   4   1   39

DATA INPUTED FROM B34S

                   B34S #   NAME

                      3   K

                      4   L

                      8   M1DP

                      7   Q

NON LINEAR ESTIMATION USING SUBROUTINE DWHAUS WILL BE ATTEMPTED

SERIES IN X LISTED FIRST - # OBS =   39

SERIES #   B34S #   B34S NAME   MEAN   VARIANCE   STANDARD DEVIATION
   1   X- 3   K   133.03590   2727.4234   52.224739
   2   X- 4   L   217.55641   2102.2625   45.850436
   3   X- 8   M1DP   125.28391   887.65715   29.793576
   4   X- 7   Q   325.94359   20453.893   143.01711

CONTROL CARD N1 READ AS

NPROB DMODEL   B34SLB   ICOMM NP IDIFF ISIGN IXIND IJUMP IPLOT IRC IRSAVE ISPEC NOBS1
  2 CH11MOD   3   5   0   0   0   1   0   3   0   0   0

  COMMENTS

  BOYES KAVANAUGH CES WITH REAL M1
  PARM #1 = A1(K), #2 =A2(L), #3 =ALPHA, #4 =P, #5 = V
  HERE WE ARE CONSTRAINING VALUES TO ADD UP

  CARD N4 BEING READ (TH)

  OUTPUT AT EACH ITERATION HAS BEEN SUPPRESSED

  RESIDUAL OUTPUT HAS BEEN SUPPRESSED

  NON-LINEAR ESTIMATION, PROBLEM NUMBER   2

    39 OBSERVATIONS,   5   PARAMETERS   323   SCRATCH REQUIRED

  INITIAL PARAMETER VALUES (TH)

     1   2   3   4   5
  0.2770E+00 0.7754E+00 0.1000E+01 -0.5000E-01 0.1800E+01

  PROPORTIONS USED IN CALCULATING DIFFERENCE QUOTIENTS   (DIFF)

     1   2   3   4   5
  0.1000E-01 0.1000E-01 0.1000E-01 0.1000E-01 0.1000E-01

  SIGN RESTRICTION VECTOR (GT 0.0 MEANS PARAMETER RESTRICTED TO BE THE SAME SIGN AS INITIAL GUESS (TH) - (SIGNS)

     1   2   3   4   5
  0.0000E+00 0.0000E+00 0.0000E+00 0.0000E+00 0.0000E+00

MAX ITERATIONS   20 STARTING LAMBDA (FLAM)   0.10000000E-01 (FLU) (LAMBDA T+1 = LAMBDA T * (FLU**OMEGA))   10.000000

EPS1= 0.00000000E+00 EPS2= 0.40000000E-02 IJUMP =   1 NVAR =   3 IRC =   3

DYNAMIC CALL OPTION SELECTED, DDNAME B34SLIB   WILL BE SEARCHED FOR MEMBER CH11MOD

INITIAL SUM OF SQUARES =   0.86267930E+10

ITERATION STOPS - RELATIVE CHANGE IN EACH PARAMETER LESS THAN   0.40000000E-02

CORRELATION MATRIX OF ESTIMATED PARAMETERS   1/ CONDITION   0.31790551E-06

       1   2   3   4   5

  1 1.0000

  2 -0.9554   1.0000

  3 0.8404   -0.8279   1.0000

  4 0.6564   -0.5815   0.1935   1.0000

  5 -0.8157   0.7795   -0.9948   -0.1734   1.0000

NORMALIZING ELEMENTS

1	2	3	4	5
0.7145E-02	0.1049E-01	0.3359E-02	0.5551E-01	0.6171E-02

VARIANCE OF RESIDUALS   68.809843   DEGREES OF FREEDOM   34   SEE   8.2951699   ADJUSTED R SQUARE   0.99663586

PARAMETER #	COEFFICIENT	STANDARD ERROR	T VALUE
1	0.5201787490812586	0.5927013034094430E-01	8.776406363356936
2	0.3329709716629894	0.8703766093203333E-01	3.825596507275195
3	0.8424541105461282E-01	0.2785935757202650E-01	3.023953830837915
4	1.184767990376016	0.4604681283097873	2.572964158724455
5	1.618323955435729	0.5118689978202279E-01	31.61597913386612

NOTE: CONFIDENCE LIMITS FOR EACH PARAMETER ON LINEAR HYPOTHESIS

DURBIN WATSON   0.85890558

END OF PROBLEM NO.   2

PLOT OF RESIDUAL AGAINST TIME
  RESIDUAL

Results for equations (11.2-1) and (11.2-2) are summarized in Table 11.3, which replicates results reported in Sinai and Stokes (1981, Table 2).[6] The first model that Sinai and Stokes (1981) estimated was the Boyes and Kavanaugh (1979) "ideal form" $Q^{p/v} = \delta_1 K + \delta_2 L$. The results showed that δ_1, δ_2 and p were <u>not</u> significant, that δ_1 and δ_2 were correlated (.9963) and that p was correlated with δ_1 and δ_2 (-.9978) and (-.9998), respectively. The next model attempted was equation (11.1-1), which imposed an adding up constraint on the distribution parameters δ_1 and δ_2 in the Boyes and Kavanaugh "ideal form." The results in Table 11.3 show no significance on p (t=.42) and high serial correlation of the residual as is shown by the low Durbin-Watson test statistic of

.8615. The next model attempted was equation (11.2-2), which added real balances. The output for this problem has been shown above and the results are summarized in Table 11.3. Here all parameters were "significant," although the low Durbin-Watson test statistic (.8589) questions these values. In this model δ_1 and δ_2 were correlated (-.9554) and v and α were correlated (-.9948), calling into question the Boyes and Kavanaugh OLS grid search procedure, which imposes the constraint that these parameters are not related.

Table 11.3 Results of CES Model With and Without Real M1

Model (11.2-1)   SEE = 9.8039   DW = .8615

Correlation of Parameters				Coefficients	t Scores
δ	1.0000			.316770	2.65
α	.5050	1.0000		.035399	3.18
v	-.4021	-.9931 1.0000		1.735587	34.61
p	.9450	.2201 -.1096 1.0000		.466813	.42

Model (11.2-2)   SEE = 8.2952   DW = .8589

Correlation of Parameters				Coefficients	t Scores
δ_1	1.0000			.520179	8.78
δ_2	-.9554	1.0000		.332971	3.83
α	.8404	-.8279 1.0000		.084245	3.02
p	.6564	-.5815 .1935 1.0000		1.184768	2.57
v	-.8157	.7795 -.9948 -.1734 1.0000		1.618324	31.62

Since both equations have low Durbin-Watson test statistics, the next step is to attempt a GLS correction to remove the serial correlation. Another important test is to see how well the results stand up to the inclusion of time in equation (11.2-2), which is illustrated in

$$Q = \alpha e^{\gamma t}(\delta_1 K^p + \delta_2 L^p + (1.0 - \delta_1 - \delta_2)(M1/P)^p)^{v/p}, \qquad (11.2-4)$$

where Q, K, L, M1 and P are real output capital, labor, M1 and prices, respectively, and t is a time variable going from 1929 to 1967. A second-order GLS version of equations (11.2-1), (11.2-2) and (11.2-4) was run by Sinai and Stokes (1981). Given that the basic model was in the form

$$Q_t = F_t(L, K, \ldots\ldots), \qquad (11.2-5)$$

a GLS model of order r estimates the nonlinear model

$$Q_t - \lambda_1 Q_{t-1}-,\ldots,-\lambda_r Q_{t-r} = F_t(\ ) -\lambda_1 F_{t-1}(\ )-,\ldots,\lambda_{t-r}F_{t-r}\cdot(\ ). \qquad (11.2-6)$$

The FORTRAN SUBROUTINE CH11MOD, given in Table 11.1, has been modified to estimate equation (11.2-6) and is displayed in Table 11.4

Table 11.4 FORTRAN SUBROUTINE for GLS CES Models

```
      SUBROUTINE CH11MOD(NPROB,TH,F,NOB,NP,X,NVAR,NOBS1)
      IMPLICIT REAL*8(A-H,O-Z)
      DIMENSION TH(*),F(*),X(NOB,*)
C
C     SET UP FOR CES PRODUCTION FUNCTION - SEE SINAI-STOKES RES 1981
C     NPROB=1 -- A 2 FACTOR MODEL WITHOUT TIME
C     NPROB=2 -- A 3 FACTOR MODEL
C     NPROB=3 -- 3 FACTOR WITH TIME
C     NPROB=4 -- GLS 2 VERSION OF 2 FACTOR WITHOUT TIME
C     NPROB=5 -- GLS 2 VERSION OF 3 FACTOR
C     NPROB=6 -- GLS 2 VERSION OF 3 FACTOR WITH TIME
C
      GO TO(100,100,100,400,400,400),NPROB
C
  100 DO 110 I=1,NOB
  110 F(I)=CES(NPROB,X(I,1),NOB,TH,I)
      GO TO 990
C
C
  400 L1=NP-1
      L2=NP
      DO 410 I=1,NOBS1
  410 F(I)=(TH(L1)*X(I+1,NVAR+1))   + (TH(L2)*X(I,NVAR+1))
     *  +            CES(NPROB,X(I+2,1),NOB,TH,I+2)
     *  - (TH(L1)*CES(NPROB,X(I+1,1),NOB,TH,I+1))
     *  - (TH(L2)*CES(NPROB,X(I  ,1),NOB,TH,I  ))
      GO TO 990
C
  990 RETURN
      END
      DOUBLE PRECISION FUNCTION CES(NPROB,X,NOB,TH,I)
      IMPLICIT REAL*8(A-H,O-Z)
      DIMENSION X(NOB,*),TH(*)
C
C     FUNCTION TO CALCULATE A MODEL BASED ON CH11MOD SWITCH NPROB
C
      GO TO(100,200,300,100,200,300),NPROB
C
  100 THH=1.0D+00 - TH(1)
      CES=((TH(1)*(X(1,1)**TH(4)))+(THH*(X(1,2)**TH(4))))**(TH(3)/
     *TH(4))*TH(2)
      GO TO 990
C
  200 THH=1.0D+00 -TH(1)-TH(2)
      CES=((TH(1)*(X(1,1)**TH(4)))+(TH(2)*(X(1,2)**TH(4))) +
     * (THH*(X(1,3)**TH(4))))**(TH(5)/TH(4) )*TH(3)
      GO TO 990
C
  300 THH=1.0D+00 -TH(1)-TH(2)
      CES=((TH(1)*(X(1,1)**TH(4)))+(TH(2)*(X(1,2)**TH(4))) +
     * (THH*(X(1,3)**TH(4))))**(TH(5)/TH(4))*TH(3)*
     * DEXP(TH(6)*DFLOAT(I))
      GO TO 990
C
  990 RETURN
      END
```

The revised version of subroutine CH11MOD works the same as the one listed in Table 11.1 for NPROB=1 and NPROB=2, although the code is different. NPROB=3 estimates equation (11.2-2) with the addition of time. Second-order GLS versions of these models are run for NPROB=4,...,6. The revised CH11MOD subroutine makes use of the double precision function CES and the fact that when NOBS1 < NOB, less than the full number of observations are used, although the complete data set has been passed in the X array.

    The B34S NONLIN command uses the estimated Y vector F(*) from
the user subroutine and calculates the residual, using the
following FORTRAN loop:

```
          SSQ=0.0D+00
          DO 90 I=1,NOBS1
          R(I)=Y((NOB-NOBS1)+I) -F(I)
          SSQ=SSQ+R(I)*R(I)
    90    CONTINUE
```

When NOB=NOBS1, the residual and sum of squares (SSQ) are
calculated as would be expected. However, when NOBS1 < NOB, the
F( ) vector of length NOBS1 is matched against the last NOBS1
values of the Y( ) vector. All X values are passed to the CH11MOD
subroutine in the X array. The Y values are not part of the X array
but can be accessed as the $(NVAR+1)^{th}$ column of X due to the
storage convention in B34S. The DO 410 loop in CH11MOD in Table
11.4 makes use of these features. For example, the FORTRAN
expression $(TH(L1)*X(I+1,NVAR+1))$ is nothing more than $\lambda_1 Q_{t-1}$ in
equation (11.2-5). Note that because of alignment, the $(I+1)^{th}$ row
of X is accessed to obtain the $(t-1)^{th}$ data value. The function CES
is called three times in this loop, each time passing a different
row of X. The logic of the revised version of CH11MOD can be
extended to write an even more general user subroutine to estimate
GLS models of any order. The difference (NOB-NOBS1) can be used to
determine the order of the GLS model. Such revised code might be

```
    C     Code to illustrate a general GLS CES MODEL
    400   IGLS=NOB-NOBS1
          DO 410 I=1,NOBS1
          F(I)=CES(NPROB,X(IGLS+I,1),NOB,TH,IGLS+I)
          DO 410 II=1,IGLS
          J=NP-IGLS-II
          K=IGLS+I-II
          F(I)=F(I) +(TH(J)*X(K,NVAR+1))-(TH(J)*CES(NPROB,X(K,1),NOB,TH,K))
    410   CONTINUE
```

Table 11.5 GLS CES Estimation

```
B34SEXEC NONLIN  NPROB=4 MIT=500          DMODEL=CH11MOD NOBS1=37$
   VAR Q   = K L   $
   COMMENT=('BOYES KAVANAUGH  CES WITHOUT REAL BAL ')$
   COMMENT=('GLS ORDER 2  '  )$
   COMMENT=('PARM # 1 = A1 (K), #2 = ALPHA, #3 = V, # 4 =  P')$
   COMMENT=(' #5  = LAMBDA1,  #6 = LAMBDA2 ')$
   COMMENT=('HERE WE ARE CONSTRAINING VALUES TO ADD UP')$
   IVALUES=(.3053   .01      1.85     .03 .8 -.6)$
   B34SEEND$


B34SEXEC NONLIN NPROB=5 MIT=500 FLAM=.10  DMODEL=CH11MOD NOBS1=37$
   VAR Q   =K L M1DP$
   COMMENT=('BOYES KAVANAUGH CES WITH REAL M1')$
   COMMENT=('GLS ORDER 2 ')$
   COMMENT=('PARM #1 = A1(K), #2 =A2(L),  #3 =ALPHA, #4 =P, #5 = V')$
   COMMENT=(' #6  = LAMBDA1,  #7 = LAMBDA2 ')$
   COMMENT=('HERE WE ARE CONSTRAINING VALUES TO ADD UP')$
   IVALUES=(.27698,  .7754,   1.000 ,   .05 ,   1.8 .8 -.6)$
   B34SEEND$


B34SEXEC NONLIN NPROB=6 MIT=500 FLAM=.10  DMODEL=CH11MOD NOBS1=37$
   VAR Q   =K L M1DP$
   COMMENT=(' BOYES KAVANAUGH CES WITH REAL M1')$
   COMMENT=(' TIME IS IN THE MODEL')$
   COMMENT=('PARM #1 = A1(K), #2 =A2(L), #3 =ALPHA, #4 =P, #5 = V') $
   COMMENT=(' #6  =  TIME, #7  = LAMBDA2 ')$
   COMMENT=('HERE WE ARE CONSTRAINING VALUES TO ADD UP')$
   IVALUES=(.27698,  .7754,   1.000 ,   .05 ,   1.8 .0004 .8 -.6)$
   B34SEEND$


B34SEXEC NONLIN NPROB=5 MIT=500           DMODEL=CH11MOD NOBS1=37$
   VAR Q   =K L M1DP$
   COMMENT=('BOYES KAVANAUGH CES WITH REAL M1')$
   COMMENT=('GLS ORDER 2 ')$
   COMMENT=('PARM #1 = A1(K), #2 =A2(L), #3 =ALPHA, #4 =P, #5 = V')$
   COMMENT=(' #6  = LAMBDA1,  #7 = LAMBDA2 ')$
   COMMENT=('HERE WE ARE CONSTRAINING VALUES TO ADD UP')$
   IVALUES=(.27698,  .7754,   1.000 ,   .05 ,   1.8 .8 -.6)$
   B34SEEND$

B34SEXEC NONLIN NPROB=6 MIT=500           DMODEL=CH11MOD NOBS1=37$
   VAR Q   =K L M1DP$
   COMMENT=(' BOYES KAVANAUGH CES WITH REAL M1')$
   COMMENT=(' TIME IS IN THE MODEL')$
   COMMENT=('PARM #1 = A1(K),  #2 =A2(L), #3 = ALPHA, #4 =P, #5 = V')$
   COMMENT=(' #6  =  TIME, #7  = LAMBDA1,  #8 = LAMBDA2 ')$
   COMMENT=('HERE WE ARE CONSTRAINING VALUES TO ADD UP')$
   IVALUES=(.27698,  .7754,   1.000 ,   .05 ,   1.8 .0004 .8 -.6)$
   B34SEEND$
==
```

Table 11.5 illustrates calling the revised CH11MOD subroutine to perform GLS estimation for a number of models. Five models are listed. These include NPROB=4 and two versions of NPROB=5, one with the default FLAM setting (FLAM=.01) and one with FLAM=.1. The purpose of this experiment was to see how sensitive the results are to the iteration parameter adjustment correction. Edited output from the default setting of FLAM for NPROB=5 and NPROB=6 are shown next. Output from all models in Table 11.5 have been summarized in Table 11.6.

PROGRAM NONLIN

BASIC SUBROUTINES FROM U WISCONSIN

PROGRAM MODIFIED BY HOUSTON H. STOKES

20 DECEMBER 1988

ON MAIN CONTROL CARD - IOPT, NSERIE, IBEGIN, IEND   SET =   0   1   39

DATA INPUTED FROM B34S

	B34S #	NAME
	3	K
	4	L
	8	M1DP
	7	Q

NON LINEAR ESTIMATION USING SUBROUTINE DWHAUS WILL BE ATTEMPTED

SERIES IN X LISTED FIRST - # OBS =   39

SERIES #	B34S #	B34S NAME	MEAN	VARIANCE	STANDARD DEVIATION
1	X- 3	K	133.03590	2727.4234	52.224739
2	X- 4	L	217.55641	2102.2625	45.850436
3	X- 8	M1DP	125.28391	887.65715	29.793576
4	X- 7	Q	325.94359	20453.893	143.01711

CONTROL CARD N1 READ AS

NPROB	DMODEL	B34SLB	ICOMM	NP	IDIFF	ISIGN	IXIND	IJUMP	IPLOT	IRC	IRSAVE	ISPEC	NOBS1
5	CH11MOD		5	7	0	0	0	1	0	3	0	1	37

COMMENTS

BOYES KAVANAUGH CES WITH REAL M1
GLS ORDER 2
PARM #1 = A1(K), #2 =A2(L), #3 =ALPHA, #4 =P, #5 = V
#6 = LAMBDA1, #7 = LAMBDA2
HERE WE ARE CONSTRAINING VALUES TO ADD UP

CARD N4 BEING READ (TH)

CARD N5 BEING READ (ESTIMATION CONTROL CARD)

OUTPUT AT EACH ITERATION HAS BEEN SUPPRESSED

RESIDUAL OUTPUT HAS BEEN SUPPRESSED

NON-LINEAR ESTIMATION, PROBLEM NUMBER   5

     37   OBSERVATIONS,   7   PARAMETERS   435   SCRATCH REQUIRED

DATA IN MATRIX X CONTAINS   39 OBSERVATIONS, THE LAST   37 ARE USED IN ESTIMATION

INITIAL PARAMETER VALUES (TH)

1	2	3	4	5	6	7
0.2770E+00	0.7754E+00	0.1000E+01	0.5000E-01	0.1800E+01	0.8000E+00	-0.6000E+00

PROPORTIONS USED IN CALCULATING DIFFERENCE QUOTIENTS   (DIFF)

1	2	3	4	5	6	7
0.1000E-01	0.1000E-01	0.1000E-01	0.1000E-01	0.1000E-01	0.1000E-01	0.1000E-01

SIGN RESTRICTION VECTOR (GT 0.0 MEANS PARAMETER RESTRICTED TO BE THE SAME SIGN AS INITIAL GUESS (TH)   -   (SIGNS)

1	2	3	4	5	6	7
0.0000E+00	0.0000E+00	0.0000E+00	0.0000E+00	0.0000E+00	0.0000E+00	0.0000E+00

MAX ITERATIONS   500 STARTING LAMBDA (FLAM) 0.10000000E-01 (FLU) (LAMBDA T+1 = LAMBDA T * (FLU**OMEGA))   10.000000

EPS1= 0.00000000E+00 EPS2= 0.40000000E-02 IJUMP = 1 NVAR = 3 IRC = 3

DYNAMIC CALL OPTION SELECTED, DDNAME B34SLIB   WILL BE   SEARCHED FOR MEMBER CH11MOD

INITIAL SUM OF SQUARES =   0.52527896E+10

ITERATION STOPS - RELATIVE CHANGE IN EACH PARAMETER LESS THAN   0.40000000E-02

CORRELATION MATRIX OF ESTIMATED PARAMETERS   1/ CONDITION   0.18599062E-06

	1	2	3	4	5	6	7
1	1.0000						
2	-0.9586	1.0000					
3	0.6526	-0.5872	1.0000				
4	0.7737	-0.7408	0.0835	1.0000			
5	-0.5770	0.4840	-0.9901	-0.0155	1.0000		

```
6  -0.1242    0.1272     0.1894    -0.2799    -0.2174     1.0000
7   0.0005    0.0139     0.1244    -0.0883    -0.1353    -0.5358     1.0000
```

NORMALIZING ELEMENTS

```
       1          2          3          4          5          6          7
  0.1305E-01  0.1832E-01  0.4584E-02  0.1164E+00  0.9704E-02  0.2993E-01  0.2829E-01
```

VARIANCE OF RESIDUALS   37.072875   DEGREES OF FREEDOM   30   SEE   6.0887499   ADJUSTED R SQUARE   0.99817867

PARAMETER #	COEFFICIENT	STANDARD ERROR	T VALUE
1	0.4624709466307499	0.7943511739420621E-01	5.821996137245985
2	0.4209391221433659	0.1115718262207334	3.772808390808098
3	0.7609842416928998E-01	0.2791027082160620E-01	2.726538364879636
4	0.7676657700979502	0.7088791483461321	1.082928975819040
5	1.628338323393291	0.5908434981576832E-01	27.55955389998594
6	0.9888103766503662	0.1822294477536974	5.426183247763827
7	-0.5752815233879459	0.1722638016988587	-3.339538067281360

NOTE: CONFIDENCE LIMITS FOR EACH PARAMETER ON LINEAR HYPOTHESIS

DURBIN WATSON   1.7075821

END OF PROBLEM NO.   5

PLOT OF RESIDUAL AGAINST TIME
  RESIDUAL

```
NON LINEAR SUBPROBLEM COMPLETE
```

STEP ENDING. SECONDS USED 0.22004795   . TOTAL JOB SECONDS   2.0796928   .

PROGRAM NONLIN

BASIC SUBROUTINES FROM U WISCONSIN

PROGRAM MODIFIED BY HOUSTON H. STOKES

20 DECEMBER 1988

ON MAIN CONTROL CARD - IOPT, NSERIE, IBEGIN, IEND   SET =   0   4   1   39

DATA INPUTED FROM B34S

	B34S #	NAME
	3	K
	4	L
	8	M1DP
	7	Q

NON LINEAR ESTIMATION USING SUBROUTINE DWHAUS WILL BE ATTEMPTED

SERIES IN X LISTED FIRST - # OBS =   39

SERIES #	B34S #	B34S NAME	MEAN	VARIANCE	STANDARD DEVIATION
1	X- 3	K	133.03590	2727.4234	52.224739
2	X- 4	L	217.55641	2102.2625	45.850436
3	X- 8	M1DP	125.28391	887.65715	29.793576
4	X- 7	Q	325.94359	20453.893	143.01711

CONTROL CARD N1 READ AS

NPROB	DMODEL	B34SLB	ICOMM	NP	IDIFF	ISIGN	IXIND	IJUMP	IPLOT	IRC	IRSAVE	ISPEC	NOBS1
6	CH11MOD		5	8	0	0	0	1	0	3	0	1	37

COMMENTS

BOYES KAVANAUGH CES WITH REAL M1
TIME IS IN THE MODEL
PARM #1 = A1(K), #2 =A2(L), #3 = ALPHA, #4 =P, #5 = V
#6 = TIME, #7 = LAMBDA1, #8 = LAMBDA2
HERE WE ARE CONSTRAINING VALUES TO ADD UP

CARD N4 BEING READ (TH)

CARD N5 BEING READ (ESTIMATION CONTROL CARD)

OUTPUT AT EACH ITERATION HAS BEEN SUPPRESSED

RESIDUAL OUTPUT HAS BEEN SUPPRESSED

NON-LINEAR ESTIMATION, PROBLEM NUMBER   6

37 OBSERVATIONS,   8   PARAMETERS   494   SCRATCH REQUIRED

DATA IN MATRIX X CONTAINS   39 OBSERVATIONS, THE LAST   37 ARE USED IN ESTIMATION

INITIAL PARAMETER VALUES (TH)

1	2	3	4	5	6	7	8
0.2770E+00	0.7754E+00	0.1000E+01	0.5000E-01	0.1800E+01	0.4000E-03	0.8000E+00	-0.6000E+00

PROPORTIONS USED IN CALCULATING DIFFERENCE QUOTIENTS   (DIFF)

1	2	3	4	5	6	7	8
0.1000E-01	0.1000E-01	0.1000E-01	0.1000E-01	0.1000E-01	0.1000E-01	0.1000E-01	0.1000E-01

SIGN RESTRICTION VECTOR (GT 0.0 MEANS PARAMETER RESTRICTED TO BE THE SAME SIGN AS INITIAL GUESS (TH) - (SIGNS)

1	2	3	4	5	6	7	8
0.0000E+00	0.0000E+00	0.0000E+00	0.0000E+00	0.0000E+00	0.0000E+00	0.0000E+00	0.0000E+00

MAX ITERATIONS   500 STARTING LAMBDA (FLAM)   0.10000000E-01 (FLU) (LAMBDA T+1 = LAMBDA T * (FLU**OMEGA))   10.000000

EPS1= 0.00000000E+00 EPS2= 0.40000000E-02 IJUMP =   1 NVAR = 3 IRC = 3

DYNAMIC CALL OPTION SELECTED, DDNAME B34SLIB   WILL BE SEARCHED FOR MEMBER CH11MOD

INITIAL SUM OF SQUARES =   0.53783029E+10

ITERATION STOPS - RELATIVE CHANGE IN EACH PARAMETER LESS THAN   0.40000000E-02

CORRELATION MATRIX OF ESTIMATED PARAMETERS   1/ CONDITION   0.11848620E-07

	1	2	3	4	5	6	7	8
1	1.0000							
2	-0.9900	1.0000						
3	-0.4678	0.4667	1.0000					
4	0.8684	-0.8642	-0.3405	1.0000				
5	0.6035	-0.6021	-0.9838	0.4300	1.0000			
6	-0.7451	0.7255	0.8696	-0.4682	-0.9384	1.0000		
7	-0.1496	0.1593	0.0877	-0.2997	-0.0784	-0.0019	1.0000	
8	-0.2808	0.2781	0.3035	-0.2093	-0.3285	0.3449	-0.5499	1.0000

NORMALIZING ELEMENTS

1	2	3	4	5	6	7	8
0.3095E-01	0.4124E-01	0.2357E-01	0.2194E+00	0.2896E-01	0.9614E-03	0.3004E-01	0.2834E-01

VARIANCE OF RESIDUALS   36.066193   DEGREES OF FREEDOM   29   SEE   6.0055136   ADJUSTED R SQUARE   0.99822812

PARAMETER #	COEFFICIENT	STANDARD ERROR	T VALUE
1	0.3192597729349837	0.1858869221123359	1.717494535425399
2	0.6095839660884944	0.2476431206503789	2.461542095284373
3	0.188209360288073	0.1415623802373022	1.329515369639945
4	0.2133992633695341	1.317751776152251	0.1619419280865217
5	1.397975940974312	0.1739018510689465	8.038879013542298
6	0.7593876912275691E-02	0.5773414300502296E-02	1.315318201157851
7	1.037797469733132	0.1804248033901709	5.751966748656401
8	-0.5710312112391086	0.1701946012933662	-3.355166420671688

NOTE: CONFIDENCE LIMITS FOR EACH PARAMETER ON LINEAR HYPOTHESIS

DURBIN WATSON   1.7715770

END OF PROBLEM NO.   6

PLOT OF RESIDUAL AGAINST TIME
    RESIDUAL

    -10.705

STEP ENDING. SECONDS USED   0.35145187   . TOTAL JOB SECONDS   2.4414759   .

Output from estimating the models in Table 11.5 is summarized below in Table 11.6. Changing FLAM from .1 to the default of .01 was shown to produce some changes in the reported answers, <u>even with the same starting values</u>. Sinai and Stokes (1981) set FLAM = 1.0 in their estimation, and the reported results differ slightly for the GLS versions of equations (11.2-2) and (11.2-4). Equation (11.2-1) is _very_ difficult to estimate because of collinearity between the parameters. When this model was estimated by Sinai and Stokes (1981) with FLAM=1.0, after 22 iterations the message "THE SUM OF SQUARES CANNOT BE REDUCED TO THE SUM OF SQUARES AT THE END OF THE LAST ITERATION" was given. At this point the SEE was 6.7980. The setup in Table 11.5 calls for a 500 iteration limit and FLAM = .01 and results in an estimated model in which the SEE = 6.534 and some differences in the reported t scores. While Sinai and Stokes (1981) reported t scores for δ_1, α, v, p, λ_1 and λ_2 of 6.55, 2.691, 28.369, .45E-04, 6.002, -3.959, respectively, with FLAM=.01 these become 1.44, 1.44, 12.73, -.82, 6.67, -2.62, respectively, indicating that only v, λ_1 and λ_2 are significant. The problems with the "ideal form" relate to correlation between the parameters. Once the serial correlation is taken out with the second-order GLS model, the t scores of the coefficients are no longer biased and are found to be significant. These problems suggest that highly misleading results will be obtained with grid search estimation methods. The reader is encouraged to experiment with alternative values for FLAM and alternative starting values. Often the model will fail to estimate at all. This problem is a good test case for other nonlinear estimation programs. The author's current thinking is to change FLAM only when absolutely necessary and that increasing the iteration limit is preferred to adjusting FLAM and FLU.

Table 11.6 Second-Order GLS Models of the Production Function

Equation	(11.2-1)	(11.2-2)	(11.2-4)	(11.2-2)	(11.2-4)
δ_1	.2978245	.4626846	.3246788	.4624709	.3192598
	(1.44)	(5.83)	(1.78)	(5.82)	(1.72)
δ_2		.4205825	.6022017	.4209391	.6095840
		(3.77)	(2.48)	(3.77)	(2.46)
α	.1855837	.0762096	.1839853	.0760984	.1882094
	(1.44)	(2.72)	(1.33)	(2.73)	(1.33)
v	1.437421	1.628090	1.403820	1.628338	1.397976
	(12.73)	(27.50)	(8.10)	(27.56)	(8.04)
p	-1.46792	.7680312	.2455442	.7676658	.2133993
	(-.82)	(1.08)	(.19)	(1.08)	(.16)
γ			.0074135		.00759388
			(1.29)		(1.32)
λ_1	1.210025	.9888024	1.035511	.9888104	1.037797
	(6.67)	(5.42)	(5.74)	(5.43)	(5.75)
λ_2	-.448198	-.574617	-.571298	-.575282	-.571031
	(-2.62)	(-3.33)	(-3.35)	(-3.34)	(-3.6)
SEE	6.534	6.089	6.006	6.089	6.006
DW	1.693	1.708	1.770	1.708	1.77
FLAM	.01	.1	.1	.01	.01

The preceding shows how the B34S NONLIN command can be used to estimate a wide variety of models, the only restriction being that the user must be able to specify the model in a user- supplied FORTRAN subroutine. This approach provides great flexibility, with no loss in speed. Its availability suggests that when linear models reject the Hinich (1982) tests, as was shown in chapter 8, nonlinear models are a viable option.

11.3 Conclusion

It has been demonstrated that the NONLIN command is able to either estimate a user-supplied nonlinear model for T observations and NP parameters or solve a system of NP equations and NP parameters. A detailed discussion of the Marquardt approach indicates that it is a compromise between the method of steepest descent, which is useful in the initial stages of the iterative process, and the method of Gauss-Newton, which is useful in the final stages of the iterative process. The Sinai-Stokes (1981) CES production function data were used to illustrate this command.

NOTES

1. The author believes the SAS/ETS software is the only exception to this statement. The SAS parser on MVS and CMS translates the model statements to BAL code on the fly, which substantially increases execution speed.

2. The B34S currently has over 1500 subroutines. On MVS the load module is overlaid to save space. On an IBM 3081 just the link step takes almost one minute of CPU time. After the program is relinked, the load module must be stored. For these reasons, routine relinking of a program the size of B34S is not a viable option.

3. The B34S OPTCONTROL command also requires the input of a complex model. The dynamic link approach used in the NONLIN command is also used in the OPTCONTROL command.

4. The Meeter program, GAUSHAUS, has been widely used and represents a major contribution to nonlinear estimation. Variants are used in the BTEST command and the BJEST command. The technical discussion in this chapter has been adapted from Meeter (1964b). GAUSHAUS was initially adapted by Peter Wolfe for the University of Wisconsin Computing Center. It is a very stable program, is quite fast and allows the user wide flexibility in both specifying models and fine tuning the iteration progress. With the addition of LINPACK and other improvements, the basic subroutines have been successfully used on IBM equipment for over 20 years. Draper and Smith (1966, 263-273) provide a good introductory discussion of some of the issues involved in the linearization method, the steepest descent method and the Marquardt compromise. For a more modern summary, Gallant (1987) provides a good discussion of nonlinear estimation and should be consulted for further reading.

5. Judge et al (1980, chap. 17) provide an excellent discussion of various approaches for obtaining updates for δ_j.

6. If FLAM is set to 1.0, the results will exactly match. As discussed earlier, FLAM sets λ_0. Sinai and Stokes (1981) used FLAM=1.0, which sets a small step size and is appropriate with very ill conditioned problems. Using the default $\lambda_0 = .01$ results in substantially faster convergence but slightly different coefficients. The reader is encouraged to experiment with different values for λ_0 (FLAM) and v (FLU) to see how the convergence rate is changed. The above discussion suggests that it is not a good idea to just set FLAM=1.0 to "be safe" since there will be increased computer costs. Note that the FLU v is not the same as the v in the CES models.

12. Special Topics in Time Series Analysis

12.0 Introduction

The VARFREQ command allows decomposition of the VAR model into the frequency domain to provide additional insight into the dynamic structure implicit in the model, using techniques developed by Geweke (1982a, 1982b, 1982c, 1984).[1] In economics the concept of "short run" and "long run" usually mean short lag and long lag. For example, in the area of monetary policy, the income effect, which measures a positive correlation between changes in the monetary base and interest rates, is thought to take up to 16 months. The shorter term liquidity effect, or negative correlation between changes in the monetary variable and the interest rate, is thought to take only a few months (Stokes and Neuburger 1979). Clearly, in these cases the concept of long and short run can be appropriately thought of in terms of time lag. However, in other situations we might define "short run" to mean high frequency and "long run" to mean low frequency. As an example, consider the behavior of prices during the long deflation in the United States after the Civil War until nearly the turn of the century. It might be reasonable to suppose that a rational person might find the long run (low frequency) component of the price movements "expected price movements" while the short run (high frequency) movements "unexpected price movements." Both measures are present in a VAR model such as equation (8.1-9). The VARFREQ allows these effects to be measured.

The KFILTER command provides the capability to estimate a state space model with use of an identification strategy suggested by Aoki (1987).[2] A state space model can be written in VARMA form and vice versa. The Aoki approach uses the covariance matrices between the past data and future realizations of time series to build the Hankel matrix of covariance matrices. Aoki (1987) argues that the numerically determined rank of this Hankel matrix is the dimension of the state space model. The KFILTER command provides an automatic means by which a state space model can be estimated. It will provide a baseline forecast by which ARIMA and VARMA model forecasts can be tested.

12.1 The Frequency Decomposition of the VAR Model

Assuming x and y are two time series of length T, Geweke (1982b) shows that the linear dependence of x_t and y_t, $F_{x,y}$, is the sum of linear feedback from x to y, $F_{x \rightarrow y}$, linear feedback from y to x, $F_{y \rightarrow x}$, and instantaneous linear feedback, $F_{x \cdot y}$. These measures will be illustrated first in the time domain and, finally, in the frequency domain. The main concern is to be able to measure at what frequencies the effects are strongest and/or exist.[3]

Assume that vector w_t of length k contains k_1 series x_t and k_2 series y_t. Assume w_t can be written in finite VMA form as equation (8.1-11). This assumption assumes that the spectral-density matrix, $S_z(\lambda)$, exists at almost all frequencies, $\lambda \in [-\pi, \pi]$, and can be partitioned as

$$S_z(\lambda) \quad = \begin{bmatrix} S_x(\lambda) & S_{xy}(\lambda) \\ S_{yx}(\lambda) & S_y(\lambda) \end{bmatrix}. \tag{12.1-1}$$

The vector w_t can also be written in VAR form as shown in equation (8.1-9), provided that R(B) in equation (8.1-11) is invertible. If we assume that $Q_{ij}(B) = 0$ for $i \neq j$, equation (8.1-9) can be written as two AR models as

$$x_t = \Sigma_{i=1}^{\infty} E_{1i}x_{t-i} + u_{1t} \tag{12.1-2}$$

$$y_t = \Sigma_{i=1}^{\infty} G_{1i}y_{t-i} + v_{1t}, \tag{12.1-3}$$

where $var(u_{1t}) = \Upsilon_1$ and $var(v_{1t}) = \Lambda_1$. The sequence $\{E_{11},...,E_{1\infty}\} \equiv$ the coefficients in the polynomial $Q_{11}(B)$ and the sequence $\{G_{11},...,G_{1\infty}\}$ $\equiv$ the coefficients in the polynomial $Q_{22}(B)$. The vectors u_{1t} and v_{1t} are not autocorrelated but may be cross correlated. Relaxing the assumption that the off diagonal terms in Q(B) for orders greater than zero are zero, x_t and y_t can be written

$$x_t = \Sigma_{i=1}^{\infty} E_{2t-i}x_{t-i} + \Sigma_{i=1}^{\infty} F_{2i}y_{t-i} + u_{2t} \tag{12.1-4}$$

$$y_t = \Sigma_{i=1}^{\infty} G_{2t-i}y_{t-i} + \Sigma_{i=1}^{\infty} H_{2i}x_{t-i} + v_{2t}, \tag{12.1-5}$$

where $var(u_{2t}) = \Upsilon_2$ and $var(v_{2t}) = \Lambda_2$. The vectors u_{2t} and v_{2t} are the error terms of the VAR model from equation (8.1-9) and are not autocorrelated or cross correlated, except possibly contemporaneously. The variance-covariance matrix of the error vectors is

$$\begin{bmatrix} \Upsilon_2 & C \\ C' & \Lambda_2 \end{bmatrix}. \tag{12.1-6}$$

The P matrix from equation (8.1-24) is related to the above expression by

$$\begin{bmatrix} I & -C\Upsilon_2^{-1} \\ -C'\Sigma_2^{-1} & I \end{bmatrix} = P\Sigma P'. \tag{12.1-7}$$

Relaxing the assumption that the off-diagonal terms in Q(B) for any order are zero, x_t and y_t can be written

$$x_t = \Sigma_{i=1}^{\infty} E_{3t-i}x_{t-i} + \Sigma_{i=0}^{\infty} F_{3i}y_{t-i} + u_{3t} \qquad (12.1-8)$$

$$y_t = \Sigma_{i=1}^{\infty} G_{3t-i}y_{t-i} + \Sigma_{i=0}^{\infty} H_{3i}x_{t-i} + v_{3t}, \qquad (12.1-9)$$

where $\text{var}(u_{3t}) = \Upsilon_3$ and $\text{var}(v_{3t}) = \Lambda_3$. The vectors u_{3t} and v_{3t} are the error terms of a linear transfer function model of the form of equation (7.2-1) and are <u>not</u> autocorrelated or cross correlated. Equations (12.1-2) and (12.1-3) write x_t and y_t as a linear projection on lagged x and lagged y, respectively. Equation (12.1-4) writes x_t as a linear projection on lagged x and lagged y, while equation (12.1-5) writes y_t as a linear projection on lagged y and lagged x. Equation (12.1-8) writes x_t as a linear projection on lagged x and current and lagged y, while equation (12.1-9) writes y_t as a linear projection on lagged y and current and lagged x. Equations (12.1-10) and (12.1-11) write x_t and y_t as a linear projection of lagged x and all y values and lagged y and all x values, respectively. This is shown below:

$$x_t = \Sigma_{i=1}^{\infty} E_{4t-i}x_{t-i} + \Sigma_{i=-\infty}^{\infty} F_{4i}y_{t-i} + u_{4t} \qquad (12.1-10)$$

$$y_t = \Sigma_{i=1}^{\infty} G_{4t-i}y_{t-i} + \Sigma_{i=-\infty}^{\infty} H_{4i}x_{t-i} + v_{4t}, \qquad (12.1-11)$$

where $\text{var}(u_{4t}) = \Upsilon_4$ and $\text{var}(v_{4t}) = \Lambda_4$. Geweke (1982b) shows that this projection exists and all coefficients are square summable. Equations (12.1-2) through (12.1-5) and (12.1-8) through (12.1-11) imply that

$$|\Upsilon_4| \le |\Upsilon_3| \le |\Upsilon_2| \le |\Upsilon_1| \qquad (12.1-12)$$

and

$$|\Lambda_4| \le |\Lambda_3| \le |\Lambda_2| \le |\Lambda_1|. \qquad (12.1-13)$$

Equations (12.1-12) and (12.1-13) motivate Geweke's definitions:

$$F_{x \cdot y} = \ln(|\Upsilon_2|/|\Upsilon_3|) = \ln(|\Lambda_2|/|\Lambda_3|) \qquad (12.1-14)$$

$$F_{x \to y} = \ln(|\Upsilon_3|/|\Upsilon_4|) = \ln(|\Lambda_1|/|\Lambda_2|) \qquad (12.1-15)$$

$$F_{y \to x} = \ln(|\Upsilon_1|/|\Upsilon_2|) = \ln(|\Lambda_3|/|\Lambda_4|) \qquad (12.1-16)$$

$$F_{x,y} = \ln(|\Upsilon_1|/|\Upsilon_4|) = \ln(|\Lambda_1|/|\Lambda_4|), \qquad (12.1-17)$$

which are proved[4] in theorem 1 of Geweke (1982b), given

$$F_{x,y} = F_{y \to x} + F_{x \to y} + F_{x \cdot y}. \qquad (12.1-18)$$

Equations (12.1-14) through (12.1-18) can be expressed in the frequency domain. In theorem 2, Geweke proves that if we define

$f_{x \to y}(\lambda)$ $(f_{y \to x}(\lambda))$ as the measure of linear feedback from x to y (y to x), then

$$(1/2\pi)\int_{-\pi}^{\pi} f_{y \to x}(\lambda)d\lambda \leq F_{y \to x} \qquad (12.1-19)$$

$$(1/2\pi)\int_{-\pi}^{\pi} f_{x \to y}(\lambda)d\lambda \leq F_{x \to y}. \qquad (12.1-20)$$

If we define $E_j(B) \equiv I - \Sigma_{i=1}^{\infty} E_{ji}B^i$ and $G_j(B) \equiv I - \Sigma_{i=1}^{\infty} G_{ji}B$ for $j=\{1,..,4\}$, strict equalities hold for equations (12.1-19) and (12.1-20) if the roots of $|G_3(B)|$ and $|E_3(B)|$ lie outside the unit circle. Equations (12.1-19) and (12.1-20) show that measures of linear feedback from x to y (y to x) can be measured in the frequency domain. While space does not permit a detailed discussion of technicalities of this calculation, some of the major ideas will be sketched.

Consider the VAR systems

$$\begin{bmatrix} E_2(B) & F_2(B) \\ H_3(B) & G_3(B) \end{bmatrix} \begin{bmatrix} x_t \\ y_t \end{bmatrix} = \begin{bmatrix} u_{2t} \\ v_{3t} \end{bmatrix} \qquad (12.1-21)$$

$$\begin{bmatrix} E_3(B) & F_3(B) \\ H_2(B) & G_2(B) \end{bmatrix} \begin{bmatrix} x_t \\ y_t \end{bmatrix} = \begin{bmatrix} u_{3t} \\ v_{2t} \end{bmatrix}, \qquad (12.1-22)$$

which can be written in VMA form as

$$\begin{bmatrix} x_t \\ y_t \end{bmatrix} = \begin{bmatrix} E_2^*(B) & F_2^*(B) \\ H_3^*(B) & G_3^*(B) \end{bmatrix} \begin{bmatrix} u_{2t} \\ v_{3t} \end{bmatrix} \qquad (12.1-23)$$

$$\begin{bmatrix} x_t \\ y_t \end{bmatrix} = \begin{bmatrix} E_3^*(B) & F_3^*(B) \\ H_2^*(B) & G_2^*(B) \end{bmatrix} \begin{bmatrix} u_{3t} \\ v_{2t} \end{bmatrix}. \qquad (12.1-24)$$

Since x_t and y_t contain k_1 and k_2 variables each, then from the first k_1 rows of equation (12.1-23) we can obtain a decomposition of the spectral density of x_t, $S_x(\lambda)$,

$$S_x(\lambda) = \tilde{E}_2^*(\lambda)\Upsilon_2\tilde{E}_2^*(\lambda)' + \tilde{F}_2^*(\lambda)\Lambda_3\tilde{F}_2^*(\lambda)', \qquad (12.1-25)$$

where $\tilde{E}_2^*(\lambda)$ and $\tilde{F}_2^*(\lambda)$ are the Fourier transforms of the MA polynomials $E_2^*(B)$ and $F_2^*(B)$ and ' is the conjugate transposition of the complex matrix. Equation (12.1-25) shows that the spectral density of x can be decomposed into the spectral information coming from the innovations of the x series model plus the spectral information from the innovations from the y series model. Thus, Geweke's measure of $f_{y \to x}(\lambda)$ can be defined as

$$f_{y \to x}(\lambda) = \ln(\,|\tilde{S}_x(\lambda)|\ /\ |\tilde{E}_2^*(\lambda)\Upsilon_2\tilde{E}_2^*(\lambda)'|\,).\qquad(12.1\text{-}26)$$

If y adds nothing to the explanation of x <u>at frequency λ</u>, then from equation (12.1-25)

$$\tilde{F}_2^*(\lambda)\Lambda_3\tilde{F}_2^*(\lambda)' = 0,\qquad(12.1\text{-}27)$$

$$\tilde{S}_x(\lambda) = \tilde{E}_2^*(\lambda)\Upsilon_2\tilde{E}_2^*(\lambda)',\qquad(12.1\text{-}28)$$

and from equation (12.1-26) $f_{y \to x}(\lambda) = 0$. Using a similar decomposition of the last k_2 rows of equation (12.1-24),

$$\tilde{S}_y(\lambda) = \tilde{H}_2^*(\lambda)\Upsilon_3\tilde{H}_2^*(\lambda)' + \tilde{G}_2^*(\lambda)\Lambda_2\tilde{G}_2^*(\lambda)',\qquad(12.1\text{-}29)$$

which implies that

$$f_{x \to y}(\lambda) = \ln(\,|\tilde{S}_y(\lambda)|\ /\ |\tilde{G}_2^*(\lambda)\Lambda_2\tilde{G}_2^*(\lambda)'|\,).\qquad(12.1\text{-}30)$$

To implement this estimation strategy, the lengths of the polynomials in equations (12.1-2) through (12.1-5), (12.1-8) and (12.1-9) must be limited. While Geweke uses the Whittle (1963) approach, which estimates the coefficients from the covariance function, Stokes (1985) suggests that when determining the appropriate lag, a VAR model should be estimated by means of the methods suggested in chapter 8. Once the appropriate lag is determined, the faster Geweke procedure can be used. If a longer lag is specified, more frequencies, λ, can be calculated. If the lag length p is even, it must be $\geq 2\pi/|\lambda_0 - \lambda_1|$. If too few lags are specified, the estimated model really will not capture the relationship between x_t and y_t. The Geweke procedure displays the frequency information <u>implicit in the VAR model that was estimated</u>. Checks of the cross correlations determine if p is large enough. Putting more lags in the VAR model is equally questionable, even though more λ frequencies could be calculated and the difference $|\lambda_0 - \lambda_1|$ made smaller. In the VARFREQ command the user either specifies the λ's directly or specifies the periods that are transformed into the λ's by the relationship $2\pi\ /\ $FREQ = PERIOD.

Geweke (1984) proposed using a bootstrap to obtain confidence bounds on the frequency feedback estimates. The essential idea is to draw samples of data having asymptotic distribution equal to the original data and calculate the frequency measures. By inspection of the ranges of the frequency measures, 25% and 75% bounds on the frequency measures can be calculated. Geweke (1984) provides additional detail on this procedure, which will be now sketched.

The user selects the number of replications desired with the NREP parameter. Assume that $f_{0x \to y}(\lambda)$ is the vector of feedback measures at different frequencies calculated for the original data. Define $f_{ix \to y}(\lambda)$ as the corresponding measure for the NREP sets of artificial data that were generated with the same asymptotic covariance distribution as the original data. An adjustment factor a_j is calculated for each frequency λ_j, where

$$a_j = f_{0x \to y}(\lambda_j) / ((\Sigma_{j=1}^{NREP} f_{ix \to y}(\lambda_j))/ NREP). \qquad (12.1\text{-}31)$$

The adjusted feedback for the jth frequency λ_j is $a_j f_{ix \to y}(\lambda_j)$. The 25% and 75% adjusted values are calculated as the raw values times a_j^2. The importance of this procedure is that the user is able to obtain bounds on the estimated feedback measures.

Geweke (1984) extends the above definitions of unconditional feedback for the case of conditional feedback. Assume that vector w_t contains subvectors x_t, y_t and z_t containing k_1, k_2 and k_3 series, respectively, and write the model as

$$\begin{bmatrix} \beta_{11}(B) & \beta_{12}(B) & \beta_{13}(B) \\ \beta_{21}(B) & \beta_{22}(B) & \beta_{23}(B) \\ \beta_{31}(B) & \beta_{32}(B) & \beta_{33}(B) \end{bmatrix} \begin{bmatrix} x_t \\ y_t \\ z_t \end{bmatrix} = \begin{bmatrix} u_{1t} \\ u_{2t} \\ u_{3t} \end{bmatrix}. \qquad (12.1\text{-}32)$$

The notion $F_{y \to x \mid z-} = 0$ is the same as setting $\beta_{12}(B) = 0$. Another way to look at the problem is in terms of conditional variances. Define $var(x_t \mid x_{t-1}, z_{t-1})$ as the variance of a model predicting x_t as a function of lagged x's and lagged z's and $var(x_t \mid w_{t-1})$ as the variance of a model predicting x_t as a function of lagged x's, lagged y's and lagged z's. Geweke (1984) proves

$$F_{y \to x \mid z-} = F_{yz \to x} - F_{z \to x} \qquad (12.1\text{-}33)$$

$$F_{x \cdot y \cdot z} = \ln\{(\mid var(x_t \mid w_{t-1}) \mid \cdot \mid var(y_t \mid w_{t-1}) \mid \cdot \mid var(z_t \mid w_{t-1}) \mid)/ \mid var(w_t \mid w_{t-1}) \mid \} \qquad (12.1\text{-}34)$$

$$F_{x,y \mid z-} = F_{y \to x \mid z-} + F_{x \to y \mid z-} + F_{x \cdot y \mid z-} \qquad (12.1\text{-}35)$$

$$F_{x \cdot y \mid z-} = F_{x \cdot y \cdot z} - F_{z \cdot xy}. \qquad (12.1\text{-}36)$$

In section 12.3, the unconditional feedback measures will be illustrated with the gas furnace data and price expectations data.

12.2 The Kalman-Filter Approach to Time Series Analysis

The theory behind state space model building is very complex. Interested readers are referred to Aoki (1987) or Anderson and Moore (1979) for further detail. Only the outline of the approach is given in this section, which summarizes Aoki's (1987) pioneering efforts.[5] Assume a model

$$Z_{t+1} = AZ_t + Bu_t \qquad (12.2\text{-}1)$$

$$Y_t = CZ_t + u_t, \qquad (12.2\text{-}2)$$

where Z_t is the state vector of dimension s. u_t is the noise vector with mean zero and constant covariance matrix $Eu_t u_s' = \Delta \delta_{s,t}$. Equation (12.2-1) is the state transition equation, while equation (12.2-2) shows how the state vector is related to the data vector y_t. The matrices A, B and C are the system matrices that determine the dynamics of the system. To illustrate how the state space representation relates to a VAR model for two series, x_t and y_t, of order 2, consider the model

$$x_t = 1.6x_{t-1} + .4y_{t-1} - .33x_{t-2} - .66y_{t-2} + \varepsilon_{1,t} \qquad (12.2\text{-}3)$$

$$y_t = .2x_{t-1} + .5y_{t-1} - .11x_{t-2} - .15y_{t-2} + \varepsilon_{2,t}, \qquad (12.2\text{-}4)$$

where $\varepsilon_{1,t}$ and $\varepsilon_{2,t}$ are the usual error terms. If we define $x_{t+j|t}$ and $y_{t+j|t}$ as the forecast of x and y for period t+j, conditional on the information up to period t, then

$$x_{t+1|t} = 1.6x_t + .4y_t - .33x_{t-1} - .66y_{t-1} \qquad (12.2\text{-}5)$$

$$y_{t+1|t} = .2x_t + .5y_t - .11x_{t-1} - .15y_{t-1} \qquad (12.2\text{-}6)$$

$$x_{t+2|t} = 1.6x_{t+1|t} + .4y_{t+1|t} - .33x_t - .66y_t \qquad (12.2\text{-}7)$$

$$y_{t+2|t} = .2x_{t+1|t} + .5y_{t+1|t} - .11x_t - .15y_t \qquad (12.2\text{-}8)$$

since $E(\varepsilon_{j,i}) \equiv 0$ for i>t and j=1,2. From equations (12.2-7) and (12.2-8) we note that $x_{t+2|t}$ and $y_{t+2|t}$ are written in terms of x_t, y_t, $x_{t+1|t}$ and $y_{t+1|t}$; hence, the order of the state vector, Z_t, in equation (12.2-1) is 4 and

$$Z_t \equiv (x_t, y_t, x_{t+1|t}, y_{t+1|t})'. \qquad (12.2\text{-}9)$$

The state space form of equations (12.2-3) and (12.2-4) is

$$\begin{bmatrix} x_{t+1} \\ y_{t+1} \\ x_{t+2|t+1} \\ y_{t+2|t+1} \end{bmatrix} = \begin{bmatrix} 0 & 0 & 1 & 0 \\ 0 & 0 & 0 & 1 \\ -.33 & -.66 & 1.6 & .4 \\ -.11 & -.15 & .2 & .5 \end{bmatrix} \begin{bmatrix} x_t \\ y_t \\ x_{t+1|t} \\ y_{t+1|t} \end{bmatrix} + \begin{bmatrix} 1 & 0 \\ 0 & 1 \\ 1.6 & .4 \\ .2 & .5 \end{bmatrix} \begin{bmatrix} \varepsilon_{1,t+1} \\ \varepsilon_{2,t+1} \end{bmatrix},$$

$$(12.2\text{-}10)$$

which flows directly from substitution in equations (12.2-5) through (12.2-8) when we note that

$$x_{t+2|t+1} = 1.6x_{t+1} + .4y_{t+1} - .33x_t - .66y_t$$
$$= 1.6(x_{t+1|t} + \varepsilon_{1,t+1}) + .4(y_{t+1|t} + \varepsilon_{2,t+1}) - .33x_t - .66y_t$$

$$(12.2-11)$$

and

$$y_{t+2|t+1} = .2x_{t+1} + .5y_{t+1} - .11x_t - .15y_t$$
$$= .2(x_{t+1|t} + \varepsilon_{1,t+1}) + .5(y_{t+1|t} + \varepsilon_{2,t+1}) - .11x_t - .15y_t.$$

$$(12.2-12)$$

The next example writes a VARMA model in state space form. Assume

$$x_t = .45x_{t-1} + .33y_{t-1} + \varepsilon_{1,t} - .11\varepsilon_{1,t-1} - .36\varepsilon_{2,t-1} \qquad (12.2-13)$$

$$y_t = .44x_{t-1} + .6y_{t-1} + \varepsilon_{2,t}. \qquad (12.2-14)$$

Equations (12.2-13) and (12.2-14) imply that

$$x_{t+1|t} = .45 x_t + .33y_t - .11\varepsilon_{1,t} - .36\varepsilon_{2,t} \qquad (12.2-15)$$

$$y_{t+1|t} = .44x_t + .6y_t \qquad (12.2-16)$$

$$x_{t+2|t} = .45x_{t+1|t} + .33y_{t+1|t}$$
$$= .45x_{t+1|t} + .1452x_t + .1980y_t \qquad (12.2-17)$$

from which the state vector $Z_t \equiv (x_t , y_t, x_{t+1|t})'$. The state space form of the model is

$$\begin{bmatrix} x_{t+1} \\ y_{t+1} \\ x_{t+2|t+1} \end{bmatrix} = \begin{bmatrix} 0 & 0 & 1 \\ .44 & .6 & 0 \\ .1452 & .1980 & .45 \end{bmatrix} \begin{bmatrix} x_t \\ y_t \\ x_{t+1|t} \end{bmatrix} + \begin{bmatrix} 1 & 0 \\ 0 & 1 \\ .45 & .33 \end{bmatrix} \begin{bmatrix} \varepsilon_{1,t+1} \\ \varepsilon_{2,t+1} \end{bmatrix},$$

$$(12.2-18)$$

which follows directly from substitution in equations (12.2-15) through (12.2-17) if we note that

$$x_{t+2|t+1} = .45x_{t+1} + .33 y_{t+1}$$
$$= .45(x_{t+1|t} + \varepsilon_{1,t+1}) + .33(y_{t+1|t} + \varepsilon_{2,t+1})$$
$$= .45x_{t+1|t} + .45\varepsilon_{1,t+1} + .1452x_t + .1980y_t + .33\varepsilon_{2,t+1}.$$

$$(12.2-19)$$

The following is a sketch of how Aoki (1987) suggests obtaining the dimension s of the state vector Z_t and an estimate of

A and B in equation (12.2-1).[6] Define the <u>observability matrix</u>, O, of the system of equations (12.2-1) and (12.2-2) as

$$O = [C'A'C' \ A'^{2}C', \ldots, A'^{n-1}C', \ldots]' \tag{12.2-20}$$

and the <u>reachability matrix</u>, or <u>controllability matrix</u>, C, as

$$C = [B \ AB \ A^{2}B, \ldots, A^{n-1}B, \ldots]. \tag{12.2-21}$$

The <u>Hankel matrix of impulse responses</u>, H, is the product of the observability and reachability matrices and is a infinite-dimensional matrix with the same submatrix arranged along the counterdiagonal lines.

$$H = OC. \tag{12.2-22}$$

A Markov model is observable (A and C are an observable pair) if the rank of O is n, where n is the dimension of the state vector Z_t, while the model is reachable (A and B are a reachable pair) if the rank of C is equal to the dimension of the state vector. Aoki (1987, 61) shows that this condition will be met if $O'O > 0$ and $CC' > 0$. Define the (i,j) submatrix of H as

$$H_{|i-j|} \equiv H_k \equiv CA^{k-1}B. \tag{12.2-23}$$

H_k is a dynamic multiplier matrix of equation (12.2-2) and expresses future values of the series y_t (y_{t+1}^{+}) as a weighted average of the current and past shocks to the system u_t^{-}

$$y_{t+1}^{+} = Hu_t^{-}. \tag{12.2-24}$$

Equation (12.2-24) is the forecasting version of the VMA model given in equation (8.1-11). Another way to look at the model is to write

$$y_t = CA^{t+S}Z_{t-S} + \Sigma_{i=0}^{t+S} H_i u_{t-i}, \tag{12.2-25}$$

where $H_0 \equiv I$. Equation (12.2-25) reduces to

$$y_t = \Sigma_{i=0}^{\infty} H_i u_{t-i} \tag{12.2-26}$$

as S approaches ∞, provided A is stable such that A^i approaches the null matrix as i approaches ∞. Aoki (1987, 62) shows that

$$E(y_t u_{t-i}') = H_i \Delta, \tag{12.2-27}$$

where Δ is the covariance matrix of u_t. Define

$$\Pi = E(Z_t Z_t') \tag{12.2-28}$$

$$M = A\Pi C' + B\Delta \tag{12.2-29}$$

$\Lambda_i = E(y_{t+i}y_t') = CA^{k-1}M$ for $k \geq 1$ (12.2-30)

and

$\Lambda_0 = C\Pi C' + \Delta$,   (12.2-31)

which implies that the <u>Hankel matrix of covariance matrices</u>, H^*, can be expressed as

$H^* = O\Theta$,   (12.2-32)

where

$\Theta = (M \ AM \ A^2M \ \dots \ )$.   (12.2-33)

Θ has the same structure as the reachability matrix C. An alternative to equations (12.2-30) and (12.2-31) shows how the covariance matrix of the data is related to the Hankel matrix of the impulse responses defined in equation (12.2-22).

$\Lambda_0 = \Sigma_{k=0}^{\infty} H_k \Delta H_k'$ (12.2-34)

$\Lambda_i = \Sigma_{k=0}^{\infty} H_{k+i} \Delta H_i'$ for $i > 0$.   (12.2-35)

    Aoki (1987, 63) shows that from equations (12.2-1) and (12.2-28) we can write

$\Pi = A\Pi A' + B\Delta B'$.   (12.2-36)

Using equation (12.2-29), we substitute for $B\Delta$, and from equation (12.2-31), we factor out Δ to obtain the Riccati equation,

$\Pi = A\Pi A' + (M - A\Pi C')(\Lambda_0 - C\Pi C')^{-1}(M - A\Pi C')'$,   (12.2-37)

whose solution solves the Aoki approach to the estimation of the state space model.[7] Equation (12.2-37) links together the relationship between the covariance matrix of the data, Λ_0, which is related to the Hankel matrix (see equation [12.2-34]), the system matrices, A and C, and the covariance of the state vector Π. Since the rank of the infinite-dimensional Hankel matrix determines the dimension of the state vector Z, the KFILTER command outputs a number of measures to assist the user in determining this dimension. These include the singular values of the Hankel matrix $S(i)$, the sum of the eigenvalues of the Hankel matrix, SUMEIG, the sum of the square root of the absolute values of the eigenvalues, SUMSIN, and the incremental sums of $S(i)$ (SUMSI) and $(|S(i)|)^{.5}$ (SUMEI). From these values three measures of the "fall off" of the singular values are calculated. These include THISS = $(|S(i)|)^{.5}$ $/(|S(i-1)|)^{.5}$, REMA = (SUMSIN - SUMSI) / $(S(I-1))^{.5}$ and DROP = $(S(I))^{.5}$ / $(S(I))^{.5}$. These values are illustrated in the example section and discussed further in Aoki (1987).

The Aoki approach requires that the user experiment with various settings for the rank of the Hankel matrix (set with parameter K) and the dimension of the state vector (set with parameter NSTAR). It has been the author's experience that the results are quite sensitive to these settings. It is important to inspect the sum of squares both before and after estimation and to select models that have the greatest improvement. The autocorrelation function (ACF) of the residuals and other summary statistics are provided to test model adequacy. Some of these additional measures include optional prints of H, H'H, A, C, Π, Δ, Δ^{-1}, BΔ, B, and the <u>prediction multiplier</u>, which is defined as A-BC (Aoki 1987, 107). The prediction multiplier is useful if we use equation (12.2-2) to eliminate u_t from equation (12.2-1), giving

$$Z_{t+1|t} = AZ_{t|t-1} + By_t - BCZ_{t|t-1} = (A-BC)Z_{t|t-1} + By_t. \qquad (12.2-38)$$

Since $E(u_{t+1}) = 0$, equation (12.2-2) can be written as

$$Y_{t+1|t} = CZ_{t+1|t} = C(A-BC)Z_{t|t-1} + CBy_t \qquad (12.2-39)$$

and iterated into the form

$$Y_{t+1|t} = CBy_t + ,...,C(A-BC)^k By_{t-k} + C(A-BC)^{k+1}Z_{t-k|t-k-1} \qquad (12.2-40)$$

for k ε {1,2,...}, which converges to VAR form as k approaches ∞ since $(A-BC)^{k+1}$ approaches the null matrix. Aoki (1987, 108) shows how eigenvalue analysis of (A-BC) provides an estimate of how many lags one can use in the forecasting equation. In addition to the eigenvalues of (A-BC), diagnostic statistics include R and THETA. R_j is defined as $(\lambda^2_{jreal} + \lambda^2_{jimag})^{.5}$, while $THETA_j = \arctan(\lambda_{jreal}/\lambda_{jimag})$, where λ_j is the jth eigenvalue of (A-BC).

It should be stressed that the Aoki procedure (1987, 128) is sensitive to scaling of the data, which affects the singular values, and to alternative values for K and NSTAR. It is imperative that the user experiment with alternative models and inspect the percentage reduction in the sum of squares. Given the parameters supplied, the Aoki approach estimates an unconstrained model in that various terms in A and B are <u>not</u> constrained to zero. Its use should be an upper bound against which other forecasting approaches, such as VARMA, are tested.[8] For further detail on this approach, see Aoki (1987).

12.3 Examples

Using the Box-Jenkins (1970) gas furnace data that was used in chapter 8, the following commands were used to estimate the Geweke (1982b) measures for unconditional feedback .

```
B34SEXEC VARFREQ DATAP=4 YEARS=(1900,1)  YEARE=(1973,4)$
    VAR TIME GASIN GASOUT CONSTANT$
    VARF NLAGS=6 VAR=(GASIN,GASOUT) FEEDX=(GASIN) FEEDY=(GASOUT)
        DUMMY=CONS NREP=100
        TABLE=('GAS MODEL')
        FREQ=(1.0 .9 .85 .8 .7 .6 .5 .4 .3 .2 .1 0.0)$
    B34SEEND$

B34SEXEC VARFREQ DATAP=4 YEARS=(1900,1)  YEARE=(1973,4)$
    VAR TIME GASIN GASOUT CONSTANT$
    VARF NLAGS=6 VAR=(GASIN,GASOUT) FEEDX=(GASIN) FEEDY=(GASOUT)
        DUMMY=CONS NREP=1000
        TABLE=('GAS MODEL')
        FREQ=(1.0 .9 .85 .8 .7 .6 .5 .4 .3 .2 .1 0.0)$
    B34SEEND$
```

In the first problem NREP was set to 100. The output for running this example is shown next.[9]

```
BT CONTROL CARD READ

IOPT NSERIE IBEGIN IEND IUNIT ICON  IB34S(I),I=1...
 3    4      0     0    0    1    2   3   4

SET UP TO RUN FOR    296  OBSERVATIONS

SERIES #        B34S VARIABLE #      NAME


    1                 1             TIME
    2                 2             GASIN
    3                 3             GASOUT
    4                 4             CONSTANT


*******************    MTSM OPTION SELECTED    *******************



MTSM DATA HEADER CARD FOUND

# OF OBSERVATIONS PER YEAR =   4,  STARTING AND ENDING PERIODS =   1900    1 1973    4
FILE TO BUILD DATA ON  11  IF ZERO DEFAULTS TO 11


B34S VARIABLE X- 1  TIME      LOADED ON UNIT  11


B34S VARIABLE X- 2  GASIN     LOADED ON UNIT  11


B34S VARIABLE X- 3  GASOUT    LOADED ON UNIT  11


B34S VARIABLE X- 4  CONSTANT LOADED ON UNIT  11

NOTE: ALL DATA LOADED IN UNFORMATED FORM

   MULTIPLE TIME SERIES MANIPULATOR Edition 8302    DATE 23/ 5/90 AT TIME   8:43:47
   Copyright (c) 1983 by John Geweke.  All rights reserved.

   PROGRAM MODIFIED JUNE 1983 BY HOUSTON H. STOKES



   INPUT UNIT =  5  OUTPUT UNIT =  6  FILE INPUT UNIT = 11  STORAGE AVAILABLE =    150000
Observations per year:
    4
Maximum data range --
   First observation (GIVE YEAR AND PERIOD) :
    1900         1
   Last observation (GIVE YEAR AND PERIOD) :
    1973         4
Number of columns:
    8
 146414 REAL*8 WORDS AVAILABLE FOR WORKSPACE.
>
SCAN
   UNFORMATED/FORMATED/FREE:
UNFORMAT
   FILE UNIT #  (ENTER 11 IF UNFORMATED FROM B34S):
    11
        Series Name     Range    Obs/Yr    Mean         Minimum        Maximum
 1 TIME           1900  1 1973  4   4   1.48500E+02  1.00000E+00   2.96000E+02
 2 GASIN          1900  1 1973  4   4  -5.68345E-02 -2.71600E+00   2.83400E+00
 3 GASOUT         1900  1 1973  4   4   5.35091E+01  4.56000E+01   6.05000E+01
 4 CONSTANT       1900  1 1973  4   4   1.00000E+00  1.00000E+00   1.00000E+00
>
READ
```

```
       UNFORMATED/FORMATED/FREE:
UNFORMAT
  FILE UNIT #  (ENTER 11 IF UNFORMATTED FROM B34S):
       11
    Read from series number:
        1
    To column number:
        1
Series TIME              read from UNIT    11
    Read from series number:
        2
    To column number:
        2
Series GASIN             read from UNIT    11
    Read from series number:
        3
    To column number:
        3
Series GASOUT            read from UNIT    11
    Read from series number:
        4
    To column number:
        4
Series CONSTANT          read from UNIT    11
    Read from series number:
>
INFO
   4 observations per year
   Maximum data range 1900  1 to 1973  4 ( 296 observations)
   Current range 1900  1 to 1973  4 ( 296 observations)
   8 columns available for manipulations

        Variable            Mean        Stan. dev.      Maximum        Minimum #non-0
   1  TIME               1.48500E+02   8.55921E+01   2.96000E+02   1.00000E+00   296
   2  GASIN             -5.68345E-02   1.07277E+00   2.83400E+00  -2.71600E+00   292
   3  GASOUT             5.35091E+01   3.20212E+00   6.05000E+01   4.56000E+01   296
   4  CONSTANT           1.00000E+00   0.00000E+00   1.00000E+00   1.00000E+00   296
>
VAR
))Variables in autoregression:
      2      3
))Dummy variables --
   NONE/CONSTANT/SEASONALS/USER:
CONS
))Range of variables --
   First observation (GIVE YEAR AND PERIOD) :
      1900        1
   Last observation (GIVE YEAR AND PERIOD) :
      1973        4
))Number of lags:
       6
>>
ESTI
      Estimation time   0.29144287E-02 seconds
>>
COEF

  Equation  2  GASIN
           LAG           1             2             3             4
  2 GASIN           1.93036E+00  -1.20856E+00   1.81816E-01  -1.35104E-01
  3 GASOUT          1.33770E-03   9.31934E-03  -2.00587E-02   8.05871E-04
           LAG           5             6
  2 GASIN           3.55706E-01  -2.02320E-01
  3 GASOUT         -1.88518E-02   1.86976E-02

  Equation  3  GASOUT
           LAG           1             2             3             4
  2 GASIN           2.70203E-02  -6.77006E-03  -5.98449E-01   3.44618E-02
  3 GASOUT          1.27395E+00  -2.79406E-01  -1.86669E-01  -5.98349E-03
           LAG           5             6
  2 GASIN          -3.53191E-02   1.72608E-01
  3 GASOUT          1.00323E-01  -2.91720E-02
>>
VARM

  Equation          Innovation variance   Standard deviation
    2   GASIN           3.42197E-02          1.84986E-01
    3   GASOUT          9.52170E-02          3.08572E-01

Log[Det(Upsilon)] =   -5.74104E+00
Scaled by T/2:        -8.49673E+02
>>
FEED
  Measures of feedback
    Variables in X vector:
        2
    Variables in Y vector:
        3
  X vector
      2 GASIN
  Y vector
      3 GASOUT
      Computation time   0.11596680E-01 seconds
               F(X.Y)         F(Y to X)        F(X to Y)
        0.014 ( 1.4%)    0.005 ( 0.5%)    0.668 (48.7%)
PERIOD/FREQ:
Frequencies:
  Frequency Periodicity       f(Y to X)        f(X to Y)
     1.000pi    2.000       0.002 ( 0.2%)    0.009 ( 0.9%)
     0.900pi    2.222       0.002 ( 0.2%)    0.010 ( 1.0%)
     0.850pi    2.353       0.001 ( 0.1%)    0.012 ( 1.2%)
     0.800pi    2.500       0.001 ( 0.1%)    0.012 ( 1.2%)
     0.700pi    2.857       0.000 ( 0.0%)    0.010 ( 1.0%)
     0.600pi    3.333       0.000 ( 0.0%)    0.010 ( 1.0%)
     0.500pi    4.000       0.001 ( 0.1%)    0.027 ( 2.7%)
     0.400pi    5.000       0.003 ( 0.3%)    0.119 (11.2%)
```

```
0.300pi      6.667    0.008 ( 0.8%)    0.696 (50.1%)
0.200pi     10.000    0.015 ( 1.5%)    1.899 (85.0%)
0.100pi     20.000    0.015 ( 1.4%)    3.174 (95.8%)
0.000pi      0.000    0.013 ( 1.3%)    1.805 (83.6%)
   Number of replications:
       100
Replication   1
 One replication time     0.29922485E-01 seconds
Replication  10
Replication  20
Replication  30
Replication  40
Replication  50
Replication  60
Replication  70
Replication  80
Replication  90
Replication 100
TOTAL TIME REQ.   time     2.8371429      seconds
             Estimate     Mean    25.00%    75.00%    Adjusted    25.000%    75.000%
F(Y TO X)      0.01       0.03     0.01      0.04       0.00       0.00       0.01
F(X TO Y)      0.67       0.58     0.52      0.64       0.77       0.60       0.74
F(X.Y)         0.01       0.06     0.01      0.09       0.00       0.00       0.02


     F(Y TO X)
   PERIOD  Estimate     Mean    25.00%    75.00%    Adjusted    25.000%    75.000%
    2.000    0.002     0.033    0.003     0.043      0.000      0.000      0.000
    2.222    0.002     0.032    0.006     0.043      0.000      0.000      0.000
    2.353    0.001     0.032    0.007     0.044      0.000      0.000      0.000
    2.500    0.001     0.031    0.008     0.039      0.000      0.000      0.000
    2.857    0.000     0.029    0.005     0.035      0.000      0.000      0.000
    3.333    0.000     0.027    0.006     0.034      0.000      0.000      0.000
    4.000    0.001     0.028    0.005     0.036      0.000      0.000      0.000
    5.000    0.003     0.033    0.008     0.045      0.000      0.000      0.000
    6.667    0.008     0.043    0.010     0.059      0.001      0.000      0.002
   10.000    0.015     0.050    0.013     0.069      0.004      0.001      0.006
   20.000    0.015     0.036    0.014     0.048      0.006      0.002      0.008
    0.000    0.013     0.034    0.004     0.046      0.005      0.001      0.006


     F(X TO Y)
   PERIOD  Estimate     Mean    25.00%    75.00%    Adjusted    25.000%    75.000%
    2.000    0.009     0.010    0.001     0.011      0.009      0.001      0.010
    2.222    0.010     0.011    0.002     0.013      0.010      0.002      0.011
    2.353    0.012     0.013    0.003     0.016      0.010      0.002      0.012
    2.500    0.012     0.015    0.004     0.019      0.011      0.003      0.014
    2.857    0.010     0.013    0.004     0.019      0.008      0.002      0.011
    3.333    0.010     0.012    0.003     0.016      0.009      0.002      0.012
    4.000    0.027     0.025    0.011     0.035      0.030      0.013      0.042
    5.000    0.119     0.100    0.067     0.129      0.141      0.095      0.181
    6.667    0.696     0.530    0.420     0.630      0.913      0.724      1.085
   10.000    1.899     1.596    1.190     1.959      2.259      1.685      2.773
   20.000    3.174     2.701    2.085     3.227      3.731      2.880      4.458
    0.000    1.805     1.831    1.312     2.110      1.780      1.276      2.051
>>
TABL
  Write table on UNIT:
  Table Number (UP TO 16 CHARACTERS):

                        TABLE GAS MODEL

                Estimated Measures of Linear Feedback
                   QUARTERLY DATA   1900: 1 - 1973: 4
      6 lags   296 observations   Dummy variables: CONSTANT

     X vector: GASIN                 Y vector: GASOUT


              Estimate       Adjusted Estimate    25.0%      75.0%
F(Y TO X)    0.005 ( 0.5%)    0.001 ( 0.1%)       0.000      0.001
F(X TO Y)    0.668 (48.7%)    0.772 (53.8%)       0.695      0.850
F(X.Y        0.014 ( 1.4%)    0.003 ( 0.3%)       0.001      0.005


     F(Y TO X)
   PERIOD   ESTIMATE        ADJUSTED ESTIMATE     25.0 %     75.0 %
    2.000    0.002 ( 0.2%)    0.000 ( 0.0%)       0.000      0.000
    2.222    0.002 ( 0.2%)    0.000 ( 0.0%)       0.000      0.000
    2.353    0.001 ( 0.1%)    0.000 ( 0.0%)       0.000      0.000
    2.500    0.001 ( 0.1%)    0.000 ( 0.0%)       0.000      0.000
    2.857    0.000 ( 0.0%)    0.000 ( 0.0%)       0.000      0.000
    3.333    0.000 ( 0.0%)    0.000 ( 0.0%)       0.000      0.000
    4.000    0.001 ( 0.1%)    0.000 ( 0.0%)       0.000      0.000
    5.000    0.003 ( 0.3%)    0.000 ( 0.0%)       0.000      0.000
    6.667    0.008 ( 0.8%)    0.001 ( 0.1%)       0.000      0.002
   10.000    0.015 ( 1.5%)    0.004 ( 0.4%)       0.001      0.006
   20.000    0.015 ( 1.4%)    0.006 ( 0.6%)       0.002      0.008
 Infinite    0.013 ( 1.3%)    0.005 ( 0.5%)       0.001      0.006


     F(X TO Y)
   PERIOD   ESTIMATE        ADJUSTED ESTIMATE     25.0 %     75.0 %
    2.000    0.009 ( 0.9%)    0.009 ( 0.9%)       0.001      0.010
    2.222    0.010 ( 1.0%)    0.010 ( 0.9%)       0.002      0.011
    2.353    0.012 ( 1.2%)    0.010 ( 1.0%)       0.002      0.012
    2.500    0.012 ( 1.2%)    0.011 ( 1.1%)       0.003      0.014
    2.857    0.010 ( 1.0%)    0.008 ( 0.8%)       0.002      0.011
    3.333    0.010 ( 1.0%)    0.009 ( 0.9%)       0.002      0.012
    4.000    0.027 ( 2.7%)    0.030 ( 2.9%)       0.013      0.042
    5.000    0.119 (11.2%)    0.141 (13.1%)       0.095      0.181
    6.667    0.696 (50.1%)    0.913 (59.9%)       0.724      1.085
   10.000    1.899 (85.0%)    2.259 (89.6%)       1.685      2.773
   20.000    3.174 (95.8%)    3.731 (97.6%)       2.880      4.458
 Infinite    1.805 (83.6%)    1.780 (83.1%)       1.276      2.051

                                    100 replications
```

The preceding output shows the gas furnace data loaded into the MTSM program. A VAR model of order 6 was estimated, using the Whittle (1963) approach. The coefficients here are not in agreement with those reported in Table 8.1, which employed the joint estimation approach. The residual variance for the joint estimation for GASIN and GASOUT was .0341 and .0557, respectively. For the Whittle approach, the corresponding values were .0342197 and .095217, respectively. This is not surprising since each row of the unconstrained VAR model can be estimated with OLS, and the OLS estimators have the BLUE property or are best, linear, unbiased and efficient. As Geweke (1982a, 1982b, 1982c, 1984) notes, the Whittle approach is fast and guarantees invertibility. The order of the model was chosen to be 6 because that was what was suggested by Tiao and Box (1981). With these few lags, the minimum difference between frequencies should be .3333π since $|\lambda_0 - \lambda_1|\pi$ should be $\geq$ 2π /p. In this test problem more frequencies were estimated. The results show little contemporaneous relationship since $F_{x \cdot y}$ = 1.4%, little feedback since $F_{y \cdot x}$ = .5% and a substantial relationship from x to y since $F_{x \cdot y}$ = 48.7%. Decomposing this by frequency shows most of the relationship at low frequency. For example, at frequency .4π, 11.2%; at frequency .3π, 50.1%; at frequency .2π, 85% and at frequency .1π, 95.8%. The periods associated with these frequency measures are 5, 6.667, 10 and 20, respectively. Note that we have been reporting the results on the original data.

In order to obtain 25% and 75% confidence intervals for these measures and the adjusted results, 100 replications were calculated. These confidence bounds are the adjusted estimates of the frequency feedback effects and are reported in TABLE GAS DATA. The results are consistent with what was found with the original data; most of the effect of GASIN on GASOUT is at low frequency and there is no feedback from GASOUT to GASIN. Since there is only causality from GASIN to GASOUT, this model can be estimated with a transfer function or a VAR model. The next run estimates the same model using 1000 replications. The output for this run has been heavily edited to show just the final table. Close inspection of the table shows that while the estimated values are the same, the adjusted estimates are not the same because 900 more replications were run. The code runs quite fast. On an IBM 3090/300J, the first problem ran in 2.9 seconds, while the second ran in 28.6973 seconds. Considering that 1001 VAR models were estimated and decomposed into the frequency domain and 1000 sets of data were generated, these times are understandable. Since the times are relatively short, it suggests that the frequency decomposition of the VAR model with a substantial number of replications is practical. The output prints after every 10% of the replications are done to give the user some idea what percentage of the problem has been solved in case the problem terminates, prior to finishing, by running out of CPU time.

```
                              TABLE GAS MODEL

                      Estimated Measures of Linear Feedback
                         QUARTERLY DATA   1900: 1 - 1973: 4
           6 lags   296 observations   Dummy variables: CONSTANT

           X vector: GASIN                    Y vector: GASOUT


                    Estimate      Adjusted Estimate    25.0%    75.0%
        F(Y TO X)   0.005 ( 0.5%)    0.001 ( 0.1%)     0.000    0.001
        F(X TO Y)   0.668 (48.7%)    0.780 (54.2%)     0.707    0.857
        F(X.Y       0.014 ( 1.4%)    0.003 ( 0.3%)     0.000    0.005


          F(Y TO X)
          PERIOD      ESTIMATE      ADJUSTED ESTIMATE    25.0 %    75.0 %
          2.000     0.002 ( 0.2%)     0.000 ( 0.0%)      0.000     0.000
          2.222     0.002 ( 0.2%)     0.000 ( 0.0%)      0.000     0.000
          2.353     0.001 ( 0.1%)     0.000 ( 0.0%)      0.000     0.000
          2.500     0.001 ( 0.1%)     0.000 ( 0.0%)      0.000     0.000
          2.857     0.000 ( 0.0%)     0.000 ( 0.0%)      0.000     0.000
          3.333     0.000 ( 0.0%)     0.000 ( 0.0%)      0.000     0.000
          4.000     0.001 ( 0.1%)     0.000 ( 0.0%)      0.000     0.000
          5.000     0.003 ( 0.3%)     0.000 ( 0.0%)      0.000     0.000
          6.667     0.008 ( 0.8%)     0.001 ( 0.1%)      0.000     0.002
         10.000     0.015 ( 1.5%)     0.004 ( 0.4%)      0.001     0.005
         20.000     0.015 ( 1.4%)     0.005 ( 0.5%)      0.002     0.007
       Infinite     0.013 ( 1.3%)     0.005 ( 0.5%)      0.001     0.006


          F(X TO Y)
          PERIOD      ESTIMATE      ADJUSTED ESTIMATE    25.0 %    75.0 %
          2.000     0.009 ( 0.9%)     0.008 ( 0.7%)      0.001     0.010
          2.222     0.010 ( 1.0%)     0.008 ( 0.8%)      0.002     0.011
          2.353     0.012 ( 1.2%)     0.009 ( 0.9%)      0.002     0.013
          2.500     0.012 ( 1.2%)     0.010 ( 1.0%)      0.002     0.013
          2.857     0.010 ( 1.0%)     0.007 ( 0.7%)      0.002     0.009
          3.333     0.010 ( 1.0%)     0.008 ( 0.8%)      0.002     0.011
          4.000     0.027 ( 2.7%)     0.028 ( 2.8%)      0.012     0.038
          5.000     0.119 (11.2%)     0.144 (13.4%)      0.091     0.180
          6.667     0.696 (50.1%)     0.949 (61.3%)      0.702     1.154
         10.000     1.899 (85.0%)     2.273 (89.7%)      1.784     2.683
         20.000     3.174 (95.8%)     3.949 (98.1%)      3.041     4.581
       Infinite     1.805 (83.6%)     1.568 (79.2%)      1.045     1.871

                                                       1000 replications
  >>
  TERM
  >
  TERM


  ******************** MTSM OPTION ENDING   ********************

  B34S MTSM OPTION ENDING

  STEP ENDING. SECONDS USED   28.697372       TOTAL JOB SECONDS    49.505646
```

While the gas furnace data indicated that there was little feedback in the model, the next example, which is based on Stokes (1986b), indicates the problems of feedback. This example is based on Frankel's (1982) long-term expected price series. The Geweke (1982b) procedure is used to study the relationship between the Frankel (1982) expected price series and a representative actual price series. Building on Lovell (1986), this approach is shown to be a generalized way to test the implications of the Mills (1957) implicit expectations model and the Muth (1961) rational expectations model.

In an ingenious article, Frankel (1982, 140) proposed extracting a new measure of inflation from the interest rate term structure. During the period 1959/8 to 1979/4 he found that the market underestimated inflation in the 1970s and that his measure of expected inflation "does a slightly better job of predicting actual inflation, in terms of mean squared error, than do survey data." Stokes (1986b), from which this example was adapted, provided a further test of the dynamic implications of the proposed new inflation measure, using a test proposed by Geweke (1982b, 1984). The Geweke procedure provides additional information on the dynamics of what is being measured in the proposed inflation

measure beyond that contained in the mean squared error procedure
utilized by Frankel, which relates the new expected inflation
measure and the actual price series at only the same time period.
An underlying assumption of the proposed testing procedure is that
the appropriate way to measure the relationship between two series
in the long and short run is in the frequency domain, where short
(long) run is high (low) frequency. The usual way to relate series
is in terms of lag length with long (short) run being a long
(short) lag length. The economic reason for using the frequency
approach is that while the market place may be able to detect low-
frequency cycles, high-frequency cycles, by their very nature, are
harder to detect. The models proposed here must be related to prior
work on implicit expectations and rational expectations by Mills
(1957) and Muth (1961), which have been summarized by Lovell
(1986).

   If we assume that F_t is an expected (forecasted) inflation
measure and P_t is the actual inflation series, Lovell (1986, eq.
[4]) argues that the Mills (1975) <u>implicit expectations</u> model could
be written in terms of an OLS model of the form

$$F_t \;=\; \alpha_0 \;+\; \alpha_1 P_t \;+\; u_{1,t}, \qquad\qquad (12.3\text{-}1)$$

where it is assumed that $\alpha_0 = 0$, $\alpha_1 = 1$, $E(u_{1,t}) = 0$ and the predicted
error ($u_{1,t}$) is uncorrelated with the actual realization P_t or
$E(u_{1,t}, P_t) = 0$. The strong form of the Mills' implicit expectations
hypothesis (<u>strong implicit expectations</u>) cannot be tested in
practice since it would require that the error process of equation
(12.3-1) be uncorrelated with the entire information set available
to the researcher. A proposed weak form of the implicit
expectations model (<u>weak implicit expectations</u>), which can be
tested in practice, would require that the error process of
equation (12.3-1) be uncorrelated with past forecasts,
($E(u_{1,t}, F_{t-j}) = 0$ for $j \; \varepsilon \; \{1,..,q\}$), and past realizations,
($E(u_{1,t}, P_{t-j}) = 0$ for $j > 0$). If these added assumptions were
violated, it would imply that P_t <u>cannot</u> be used as an unbiased
proxy for F_t in empirical work, which was suggested by Mills
(1957).

   Lovell (1986) argues that the Muth (1961) <u>rational
expectations</u> model requires that the forecast error of equation
(12.3-2), $u_{2,t}$, be distributed independently of the anticipated
value, F_t. This approach reverses the orthogonality condition of
Mills (1957). According to Lovell (1986, eq. [5A]), Muth's model
in OLS terms is

$$P_t \;=\; \beta_0 \;+\; \beta_1 F_t \;+\; u_{2,t}, \qquad\qquad (12.3\text{-}2)$$

where $\beta_0 = 0$, $\beta_1 = 1$, $E(u_{2,t}) = 0$ and the error is uncorrelated with
the forecasted or anticipated value, F_t, ($E(u_{2,t}, F_t) = 0$). The strong
form of the rational expectations hypothesis (<u>strong rational
expectations</u>) is difficult to test in practice since it requires

that the errors of equation (12.3-2) ($u_{2,t}$) be "uncorrelated with the entire set of information that is available to the forecaster at the time the prediction is made" (Lovell 1986, 113). The weak form of the rational expectations hypothesis (<u>weak rational expectations</u>), which can be tested in practice, requires that the error process, $u_{2,t}$, be uncorrelated with "historical information on prior realizations of the variable being forecast" (Lovell 1986, 113), or $E(u_{2,t}, P_{t-j})=0$ for j ε {1,..,q}, and historical values of the forecasted variable, F_t, $E(u_{2,t}, F_{t-j})=0$ for j ε {1,...,q}.

Lovell (1986) makes the important point that under the Muth (1961) hypothesis concerning expectations, the variance of P_t is greater than the variance of F_t, while under the Mills (1957) hypothesis, the reverse holds. <u>Weak rational expectations</u> requires that the prediction error be uncorrelated with "historical information on prior realizations of the variable being forecast" (Lovell 1986, 113), ($E(u_{2,t}, P_{t-j})=0$ for j ε {1,..,q}) and historical values of the forecasted variable, F_t, ($E(u_{2,t}, F_{t-j})=0$ for j ε {1,...,q}). Lovell (1986) suggests using equation (12.3-3) to test the Muth (1961) model since if b_2 is significant, the weak rational expectations hypothesis will be violated.

$$P_t = b_0 + b_1 F_t + b_2 P_{t-1} \qquad\qquad (12.3-3)$$

It is important to note that equation (12.2-3) can only be used to reject the weak rational expectations hypothesis since just because b_2 is not significant does not, in and of itself, rule out that for some other lag, P_{t-k} would be significantly related to the forecast error of equation (12.2-3). To do a complete test of either of the weak implicit or the weak rational expectations hypothesis requires a general model of the form of equations (12.1-8) and (12.1-9).

Equations (12.1-8) and (12.1-9) are generalizations of equations (12.3-1) and (12.3-2), where, in this example, we substitute $x_t \equiv F_t$ and $y_t \equiv P_t$.[10] Significant terms in F_{3i} for lags 1 ... q would reject the weak implicit expectations hypothesis and call into question the suggestion of Mills (1957) that P_t can be used as a proxy for F_t in empirical work. In equation (12.1-9), a finding of significant terms in H_{3i} would reject the weak rational expectations hypothesis since it would imply that the error term of a simpler model, such as (12.3-2), is <u>not</u> orthogonal to prior information (in this case prior expectations values). These tests can be made in the frequency domain, using Geweke's approach. The objective will be to test at what frequency the data are consistent with, or reject, the weak forms of the implicit and rational expectations models. Frankel (1982) asserted he was developing a long-run measure of inflation. By decomposing into the frequency domain, we can test whether the relationship is long run (low frequency) or short run (high frequency).

Table 12.1 lists the code needed to test the Frankel data. The variable DIFFPRCE is the first difference of the Frankel (1982)

expected price change series. The series DPCZU_1, DPCZU_12 and
DPCZU_60 are first differences of the annualized percent change in
the urban CPI calculated from a monthly change, a yearly change and
a five-year change. It is not clear from theory what actual price
series to use and three models are attempted.

Table 12.1 Testing The Frankel Price Expectations Data

```
==FRANKEL
/$              RUNS CHAPTER 12 SAMPLE OUTPUT
B34SEXEC OPTIONS GETSTORAGE=300000 $ B34SEEND$
B34SEXEC DATA NOHEAD NOOB =      236
                        HEADING=('DATA FROM FRANKEL PAPER          ')$
   INPUT       DIFFPRCE DPCZU_1 DPCZU_12 DPCZU_60                  $
*   DIFFPRCE  = (1-B)F                                             $
*   DPCZU_1   = (1-B)*((PZ - LAG1(PZ))/LAG1(PZ))    * 12.          $
*   DPCZU_12  = (1-B)*((PZ - LAG12(PZ))/LAG12(PZ))                 $
*   DPCZU_60  = (1-B)*((PZ - LAG60(PZ))/LAG60(PZ))  * .2           $
*   PZ = CPI-U NSA                                                 $
COMMENT=('FILE CREATED 21/ 5/90 AT TIME 16:47:12 BY B34S          ')$
DATACARDS    CARD72   $
   0.1100000000E-02  0.5490547600E-01  0.3460242933E-02  0.1285795387E-02
  -0.1900000000E-02 -0.1409034447E-03  0.3460242933E-02  0.1292166972E-02
  -0.3000000000E-03 -0.4104944979E-01 -0.1169419566E-02 -0.2733060596E-03
   0.1000000000E-02  0.0000000000E+00  0.1169419566E-02  0.5472527160E-03
   0.8000000000E-03 -0.1363719593E-01 -0.2321563575E-02 -0.2497031108E-03
  -0.1700000000E-02  0.2728990726E-01  0.2321563575E-02  0.2497031108E-03
  -0.1000000000E-02 -0.1365271133E-01  0.0000000000E+00  0.0000000000E+00
   0.7000000000E-03  0.6818181818E-01  0.4590948895E-02  0.1248439356E-02
   0.6000000000E-03 -0.6818181818E-01 -0.1173178301E-02  0.0000000000E+00
  -0.2600000000E-02  0.2711823027E-01 -0.2375454571E-02  0.4993681224E-03
  -0.1300000000E-02 -0.2711823027E-01 -0.2322333900E-02 -0.8263587280E-03
   0.1000000000E-03  0.0000000000E+00  0.1159926995E-02  0.5502329599E-03
  -0.6000000000E-03  0.1352957479E-01 -0.2331348393E-02 -0.5758826935E-03
   0.1200000000E-02  0.4052365261E-01  0.1093499518E-02  0.9937736559E-03
   0.8000000000E-03 -0.4059949104E-01  0.1136432994E-02 -0.2681912765E-04
  -0.8000000000E-03 -0.1345373636E-01  0.0000000000E+00  0.5512478149E-03
   0.0000000000E+00  0.0000000000E+00  0.1154533298E-02  0.2766114347E-03
  -0.1300000000E-02  0.0000000000E+00 -0.1154533298E-02  0.0000000000E+00
  -0.4000000000E-03  0.0000000000E+00  0.0000000000E+00 -0.2766114347E-03
   0.8000000000E-03  0.0000000000E+00 -0.5733179446E-02 -0.2759663183E-03
  -0.9000000000E-03  0.0000000000E+00  0.0000000000E+00 -0.1096959174E-02
   0.1900000000E-02  0.1343661921E-01 -0.1147846628E-02 -0.1110381315E-02
   0.9000000000E-03  0.4025588852E-01  0.4509686235E-02 -0.6316234426E-03
   0.1100000000E-02 -0.6705635184E-01 -0.1127464565E-02  0.2323023231E-04
  -0.4000000000E-03  0.4011928960E-01  0.1113326315E-02  0.2206498768E-03
  -0.9000000000E-03 -0.2675544549E-01 -0.4539784174E-02 -0.1328898653E-02
  -0.3000000000E-03  0.0000000000E+00 -0.1128677469E-02  0.0000000000E+00
   0.1200000000E-02  0.0000000000E+00  0.0000000000E+00 -0.5270521444E-03
  -0.1000000000E-03  0.0000000000E+00  0.0000000000E+00 -0.2625912908E-03
  -0.5000000000E-03  0.2669796048E-01  0.2239778278E-02 -0.3025648634E-03
  -0.1400000000E-02 -0.6129881347E-04  0.2239607407E-02 -0.4044877109E-04
  -0.1200000000E-02 -0.5899502619E-04  0.2239607407E-02 -0.2995608467E-03
   0.5000000000E-03 -0.2657766664E-01  0.0000000000E+00 -0.5167156318E-03
   0.4000000000E-03  0.0000000000E+00 -0.1133495639E-02 -0.1281082075E-02
   0.7000000000E-03  0.2651893236E-01 -0.2282116265E-02 -0.5417124785E-03
  -0.1000000000E-03 -0.2651893236E-01  0.1126068991E-02 -0.2525715980E-03
   0.1000000000E-03  0.6615215217E-01  0.3312274210E-02  0.9259182115E-03
  -0.5000000000E-03 -0.7930884271E-01 -0.1112245289E-02 -0.2355497100E-03
  -0.4000000000E-03  0.1315669054E-01  0.0000000000E+00 -0.7556606997E-03
  -0.9000000000E-03 -0.1317314118E-01 -0.1112415020E-02 -0.2347561199E-03
  -0.5000000000E-03  0.2636075923E-01  0.1112415020E-02 -0.1012908961E-02
   0.1100000000E-02 -0.1648680201E-04 -0.1139746710E-02 -0.1472425229E-04
   0.3000000000E-03 -0.1243297268E-04 -0.1134357862E-02 -0.1244783326E-02
   0.4000000000E-03 -0.1315869827E-01 -0.2234384020E-02 -0.4881189354E-03
```

```
-0.5000000000E-03  0.0000000000E+00  0.0000000000E+00  0.0000000000E+00
 0.5000000000E-03  0.5257312812E-01  0.4419822061E-02  0.6795301296E-03
-0.2000000000E-03 -0.2273263423E-03  0.2175968326E-02  0.6779623883E-03
-0.7000000000E-03 -0.5234580178E-01  0.0000000000E+00  0.2447807936E-03
 0.8000000000E-03  0.0000000000E+00 -0.5567081344E-02  0.0000000000E+00
 0.2000000000E-03  0.1302812223E-01  0.2206020174E-02  0.2306593962E-03
-0.1000000000E-03 -0.1214303162E-04  0.1097761765E-02 -0.1461774458E-04
 0.1000000000E-03  0.1298579003E-01  0.3311212775E-02  0.7066663312E-03
 0.5000000000E-03 -0.1302800445E-01 -0.1809497415E-04 -0.1541508421E-04
 0.9800000000E-02 -0.2593351816E-01 -0.2211001605E-02  0.1541508421E-04
-0.9200000000E-02  0.2593351816E-01 -0.1561367957E-04  0.2306945952E-03
 0.3000000000E-03 -0.1598878007E-04  0.1095189938E-02 -0.1571603610E-04
-0.4000000000E-03 -0.1295777600E-01  0.0000000000E+00 -0.2457709037E-03
-0.3000000000E-03  0.2588957344E-01 -0.2247878517E-02 -0.5193818542E-03
 0.3000000000E-03 -0.5376459138E-04 -0.2228355065E-02 -0.2928879588E-04
-0.1000000000E-03 -0.3872596098E-01 -0.1085842529E-02  0.1464621979E-04
 0.0000000000E+00  0.3869620997E-01  0.2171519381E-02 -0.2719003272E-03
-0.3000000000E-03 -0.1292973508E-01 -0.1278715670E-04 -0.4972983623E-03
-0.7000000000E-03  0.1284675656E-01  0.1070397653E-02  0.4545385187E-03
-0.2000000000E-03 -0.1288807138E-01 -0.1109092054E-02  0.2272865989E-03
 0.2000000000E-03 -0.1283500794E-01 -0.1092822519E-02  0.2420253529E-03
-0.1000000000E-03  0.0000000000E+00  0.1092822519E-02 -0.2420253529E-03
 0.0000000000E+00  0.1281933823E-01 -0.1300785184E-04  0.2272519198E-03
-0.1000000000E-03  0.2560154478E-01  0.2144815829E-02 -0.5251599877E-03
 0.2000000000E-03 -0.1288935771E-01  0.2157464453E-02  0.4519705045E-03
 0.3000000000E-03  0.3816274427E-01  0.3194476583E-02  0.6474000206E-03
-0.2000000000E-03 -0.5102190125E-01 -0.1115805313E-02  0.2254929131E-03
 0.6000000000E-03 -0.3798843691E-01 -0.1055534872E-02 -0.4509514208E-03
 0.2000000000E-03  0.5068565869E-01 -0.3691867972E-04  0.2102225006E-03
 0.4000000000E-03 -0.1271252156E-01 -0.1856493373E-04 -0.7332503961E-03
 0.1100000000E-02  0.1263425536E-01 -0.3651834754E-04  0.2096653504E-03
 0.1300000000E-02  0.1256202293E-01  0.2118272816E-02  0.6718651349E-03
-0.8000000000E-03 -0.3785334684E-01  0.0000000000E+00  0.0000000000E+00
 0.2500000000E-02  0.7547247068E-01  0.6410321201E-02  0.1343798618E-02
 0.7000000000E-03 -0.3797208921E-01  0.2107239619E-02  0.6718993091E-03
-0.1600000000E-02  0.1234309315E-01  0.9751734099E-03  0.8958429626E-03
 0.4000000000E-03 -0.3743320285E-01 -0.1122456846E-02  0.2239778278E-03
 0.8000000000E-03  0.2478018802E-01 -0.2257628433E-02  0.4286674119E-03
 0.1700000000E-02 -0.1167904860E-03  0.2082776369E-02 -0.2994968927E-03
 0.2000000000E-02  0.2452797727E-01  0.7457526761E-02  0.1356677552E-02
-0.1800000000E-02 -0.3708533775E-01 -0.7343198796E-04 -0.4063987408E-04
-0.2000000000E-02  0.2441260513E-01  0.3124577173E-02  0.8898641238E-03
 0.1900000000E-02 -0.4892891396E-01 -0.2182961133E-02  0.0000000000E+00
-0.2900000000E-02  0.1218348469E-01 -0.2208666652E-02  0.2224830040E-03
-0.2500000000E-02 -0.1218348469E-01  0.0000000000E+00  0.0000000000E+00
 0.1100000000E-02  0.1216927041E-01 -0.5418138831E-02 -0.2649886853E-03
-0.2000000000E-03  0.1214646873E-01 -0.1126102558E-02 -0.4228036891E-04
 0.1900000000E-02 -0.4732020670E-04 -0.2179742271E-02 -0.4205977612E-04
 0.4000000000E-03  0.1205704316E-01  0.2040285324E-02  0.6629564485E-03
 0.2300000000E-02 -0.1077876297E-03 -0.8298562383E-04  0.6629901696E-03
-0.3000000000E-03  0.2396286900E-01  0.1971043316E-02  0.6166965522E-03
 0.1300000000E-02 -0.2425203318E-01 -0.2189690447E-02  0.6615282511E-03
-0.2000000000E-03 -0.1204827766E-01 -0.5430313802E-04 -0.7763757413E-03
 0.1800000000E-02  0.1186988386E-01 -0.1122762153E-02  0.9010089623E-03
 0.2800000000E-02 -0.1061895450E-03  0.3045716262E-02  0.6586235602E-03
-0.1400000000E-02 -0.1055605779E-03  0.1999534684E-02  0.9037501581E-03
-0.2100000000E-02  0.1170500440E-01  0.4056732979E-02  0.6330158163E-03
 0.4000000000E-03 -0.1194889409E-01  0.1991532516E-02  0.4123869353E-03
 0.1700000000E-02  0.2335654797E-01  0.2959639390E-02  0.8495554894E-03
-0.1900000000E-02 -0.2363121419E-01  0.9294004479E-03  0.6571808143E-03
 0.2000000000E-02 -0.1036775445E-03 -0.1218157757E-02  0.6571473887E-03
-.`˙˙˙˙˙˙˙900E-02  0.3471707471E-01  0.2887968931E-02  0.3206128997E-03
-0.2100000000E-02 -0.1194089992E-01 -0.2152166737E-03  0.1006218926E-03
-0.4000000000E-02 -0.2324219649E-01 -0.1281034029E-03  0.6514723819E-03
 0.2000000000E-03 -0.9861773086E-04  0.9081332359E-03  0.6514723819E-03
 0.2100000000E-02  0.3415364181E-01  0.2840389997E-02  0.1053983117E-02
 0.2000000000E-02 -0.2309255249E-01  0.8494133459E-03  0.6183316700E-03
 0.2500000000E-02 -0.1148371090E-01 -0.1400650937E-03  0.1515433589E-03
-0.5000000000E-03 -0.9393930924E-04 -0.1165570049E-02  0.3995010766E-03
```

```
  0.2000000000E-02  0.1115204024E-01  0.8424480928E-03  0.1114038831E-02
  0.1600000000E-02  0.5585267369E-01  0.3662776853E-02  0.1693742954E-02
 -0.1900000000E-02 -0.2306220783E-01  0.3732479451E-02  0.1258634268E-02
  0.2100000000E-02 -0.4465842561E-01 -0.1574362755E-03  0.6472557964E-03
  0.1800000000E-02  0.4394487113E-01  0.6489933887E-03  0.1000717661E-02
  0.2000000000E-03 -0.2236926099E-01 -0.2622376218E-03  0.5667403581E-03
 -0.4000000000E-03 -0.2481607293E-03  0.1752224703E-02  0.1329837764E-02
  0.5500000000E-02 -0.2459189882E-01  0.1742221416E-02  0.5621011407E-03
 -0.5000000000E-03 -0.1103408671E-01 -0.2221429401E-02  0.6016903718E-03
 -0.2000000000E-03  0.2134868428E-01  0.1674399542E-02  0.7716923935E-03
  0.4500000000E-02  0.1035084474E-01  0.3597387468E-02  0.1239293995E-02
  0.1600000000E-02 -0.3234950996E-01  0.7655000065E-03  0.8547203615E-03
 -0.4500000000E-02  0.2103065516E-01  0.1636216821E-02  0.1282031636E-02
 -0.6000000000E-03 -0.3331395380E-03 -0.3306760711E-02  0.1020980235E-02
  0.4300000000E-02  0.1014813411E-01 -0.3875754107E-03  0.7093567861E-03
  0.5300000000E-02 -0.2127879087E-01  0.1670252136E-02  0.5411833796E-03
 -0.5400000000E-02  0.1014720489E-01 -0.1303720733E-02 -0.2980527266E-04
  0.1100000000E-02 -0.2095859952E-01 -0.1180473482E-02  0.5847626890E-03
  0.1000000000E-02 -0.2070670065E-01 -0.2976466980E-02  0.9433312473E-03
 -0.9000000000E-03  0.4102649383E-01  0.6475045426E-03  0.7444388497E-03
 -0.1000000000E-03 -0.3145141777E-03  0.1589019155E-02  0.1003313673E-02
 -0.4000000000E-02 -0.2063431892E-01 -0.2093963066E-02  0.3177394206E-03
 -0.4300000000E-02  0.2011721158E-01 -0.1233795517E-02  0.4742228887E-03
 -0.6000000000E-03 -0.5068546796E-01 -0.2841881650E-02  0.2096244258E-03
  0.8000000000E-03  0.1005927769E-01 -0.3786109687E-02 -0.1145200503E-02
 -0.4100000000E-02  0.2006800573E-01 -0.1999738233E-02  0.5582632995E-04
  0.1000000000E-03 -0.1357616360E-03 -0.2885457332E-02 -0.2018824010E-03
  0.6000000000E-03  0.1983461167E-01  0.6767909777E-03  0.9828440829E-03
 -0.2000000000E-03  0.9635341683E-02  0.6323545298E-03  0.6706755024E-03
  0.5000000000E-03 -0.3990618789E-01 -0.1010071505E-02 -0.1547594552E-03
 -0.4000000000E-03 -0.7298086627E-04  0.7807174599E-03 -0.6644610764E-03
 -0.4600000000E-02 -0.1972984062E-01 -0.4482596362E-02 -0.3047147824E-03
 -0.2000000000E-02  0.9812525787E-02 -0.3590257087E-02 -0.6056090960E-03
 -0.7000000000E-03 -0.3059445957E-04 -0.1810509316E-02  0.4061161564E-03
  0.2100000000E-02  0.2933059779E-01 -0.1013986844E-02  0.7617147436E-03
  0.2200000000E-02 -0.3919235941E-01 -0.2817294196E-04  0.2028211735E-03
  0.2200000000E-02  0.4869487512E-01  0.3293951995E-02  0.9626510201E-03
 -0.1800000000E-02 -0.3905634405E-01 -0.1792595483E-02 -0.1028522478E-03
  0.1600000000E-02  0.9646743059E-02 -0.9485357353E-03  0.9935294938E-04
 -0.8000000000E-03  0.9583107424E-02 -0.1825151745E-02  0.4773167768E-04
 -0.9000000000E-03 -0.9746080153E-02 -0.3478132508E-02 -0.1531774160E-03
 -0.1000000000E-03  0.1913041933E-01  0.1571058130E-02 -0.2532548203E-03
  0.1100000000E-02 -0.2887678583E-01 -0.8936894637E-03 -0.3497619672E-03
  0.2200000000E-02  0.2860948388E-01  0.3249272012E-02  0.4962355052E-03
 -0.1100000000E-02 -0.9696961294E-02  0.1580601892E-02  0.4759822967E-04
 -0.2600000000E-02 -0.9600876240E-02  0.7594812157E-03 -0.1501592342E-03
  0.1000000000E-03  0.9391066146E-02 -0.9547318682E-03  0.4761997559E-04
  0.3000000000E-03 -0.1202971098E-02  0.2407398651E-02 -0.1983912556E-03
  0.1500000000E-02  0.4686845127E-01  0.2246262011E-02  0.1025253358E-02
 -0.6000000000E-03  0.2740074573E-01  0.8001981217E-02  0.1111777083E-02
 -0.1000000000E-02 -0.2877046212E-01  0.4714066148E-02  0.1011049933E-02
  0.1900000000E-02 -0.9753432185E-02  0.3042615598E-02  0.8118147089E-03
 -0.1900000000E-02  0.8677788340E-02  0.4669051267E-02  0.2633269161E-03
  0.4000000000E-03 -0.5493811042E-01 -0.1829457560E-02 -0.6440868525E-03
  0.1300000000E-02  0.1898411195E+00  0.1741080618E-01  0.3853145596E-02
 -0.2600000000E-02 -0.1815030358E+00 -0.1088722320E-02  0.2522038857E-04
 -0.5000000000E-03  0.6188882084E-01  0.5296360271E-02  0.6177274557E-03
 -0.2600000000E-02 -0.9569788027E-02  0.5329523424E-02  0.9105624535E-03
  0.1300000000E-02 -0.9359890347E-02  0.3662659651E-02  0.9604188799E-03
  0.2100000000E-02  0.2548301839E-01  0.5989124187E-02  0.1517311074E-02
  0.1600000000E-02  0.5064644730E-01  0.6340744766E-02  0.2383342014E-02
  0.5000000000E-03 -0.1892773848E-01  0.2154362612E-02  0.7609974166E-03
  0.2600000000E-02 -0.6860463618E-01 -0.1470729149E-02 -0.2346057159E-03
  0.1100000000E-02  0.6634157754E-01  0.5469255095E-02  0.2207071477E-02
  0.4000000000E-03 -0.1796309077E-01  0.3052743036E-02  0.8488501611E-03
  0.4400000000E-02 -0.2560586621E-01  0.5781068190E-02  0.7812210479E-03
 -0.1400000000E-02  0.6419601125E-01 -0.5749302252E-02  0.2219489719E-02
  0.2600000000E-02 -0.9957244961E-02  0.1000078575E-01  0.2019690625E-02
  0.1000000000E-03 -0.4126152888E-01  0.5013420579E-03  0.1351804773E-02
```

```
-0.2600000000E-02 -0.8737616651E-03  0.1307736400E-02  0.8510428095E-03
-0.2000000000E-02 -0.1641410289E-01  0.6553650733E-03  0.2432932370E-03
 0.3500000000E-02 -0.3149192197E-01 -0.4627131874E-02  0.2637667475E-03
 0.9000000000E-03  0.3050547282E-01 -0.6440442670E-02  0.4799799202E-03
 0.4100000000E-02 -0.3875847810E-01 -0.8228700868E-02 -0.3984230020E-03
 0.5700000000E-02  0.1503473927E-01 -0.5709782047E-03 -0.2859529907E-03
-0.6000000000E-03 -0.7873535725E-02 -0.7308981165E-02  0.2010172561E-04
-0.3000000000E-02  0.4496546785E-01 -0.1584573247E-02  0.8149485989E-03
 0.0000000000E+00  0.2909476349E-01  0.3360833690E-02  0.1966822324E-02
 0.3200000000E-02 -0.9005485240E-01 -0.1056420608E-01  0.3795639744E-03
 0.4000000000E-03  0.2199970679E-01 -0.7613076275E-02 -0.6058123995E-04
-0.2100000000E-02  0.1438134771E-01 -0.2627326529E-02  0.2787251598E-03
 0.4000000000E-03 -0.4456234981E-01 -0.2583055208E-02  0.7468605323E-03
-0.6000000000E-03 -0.2217959235E-01 -0.3092346337E-02 -0.2325652690E-03
-0.1300000000E-02 -0.2186135592E-01 -0.2236504134E-02  0.4368726992E-03
 0.6000000000E-03 -0.6815802083E-04 -0.4927968977E-02  0.2015334014E-03
-0.1100000000E-02 -0.7002590639E-04 -0.1506963764E-02 -0.2668079403E-03
-0.1600000000E-02  0.2142416028E-01 -0.9406206892E-03  0.2341764682E-03
 0.2900000000E-02  0.2119460472E-01  0.1617278905E-02  0.2655476547E-03
-0.1000000000E-02 -0.7513202125E-02 -0.2993679807E-02 -0.1324281547E-03
 0.2000000000E-03  0.6716296987E-02 -0.4932576385E-02  0.9523738882E-03
-0.5000000000E-03 -0.1444005337E-01  0.1676151655E-02  0.6200735645E-03
-0.1900000000E-02 -0.7240207886E-02 -0.8845257262E-03  0.9152845853E-03
-0.1800000000E-02 -0.1992481586E-03 -0.2156836339E-02  0.6822116624E-03
-0.9000000000E-03 -0.1404518318E-01 -0.3338498588E-02  0.3536912759E-03
-0.3900000000E-02 -0.9960311129E-04 -0.1411056010E-02 -0.3392511815E-03
 0.3300000000E-02  0.3432437565E-01  0.3483887672E-02  0.1393540239E-02
 0.2100000000E-02  0.5437073383E-01  0.8254682740E-02  0.1528692313E-02
 0.1000000000E-02 -0.4868400988E-01  0.4036176433E-02  0.1312723523E-02
-0.9000000000E-03  0.1974317383E-01  0.3895933464E-02  0.1558931168E-02
-0.2000000000E-03 -0.2746156991E-01 -0.4005704107E-03  0.6769082070E-03
-0.2400000000E-02  0.1291887130E-01  0.1407106525E-02  0.1224815591E-02
 0.1000000000E-03 -0.2692853272E-01 -0.1570894138E-02  0.1160207802E-03
-0.1000000000E-03 -0.6803492589E-02 -0.8944720949E-03  0.6507643162E-03
-0.1600000000E-02 -0.1756751283E-03 -0.2690523997E-03 -0.4614901333E-04
 0.1100000000E-02 -0.1321761771E-01 -0.1420835448E-02 -0.1314607051E-03
 0.8000000000E-03  0.2592749274E-01  0.2115535057E-02  0.7294057340E-03
 0.1500000000E-02 -0.1322795343E-01  0.9560558774E-03  0.1816208271E-03
 0.2100000000E-02  0.2562078011E-01  0.1842068393E-03  0.8069528052E-03
 0.9000000000E-03  0.5993867485E-02 -0.4077903735E-02 -0.1856278156E-03
 0.5000000000E-03  0.1224967800E-01  0.1289745463E-02 -0.5516110267E-03
 0.1500000000E-02  0.1830880431E-01  0.1162881863E-02  0.5875764936E-03
 0.1900000000E-02  0.5312560052E-02  0.4062816785E-02  0.9549028004E-03
 0.5000000000E-03  0.1136541094E-01  0.3936292054E-02  0.1022723871E-02
 0.1200000000E-02 -0.3813820685E-01  0.2960485545E-02  0.1443054606E-02
-0.2900000000E-02 -0.1891348566E-01  0.1887380514E-02 -0.3638054032E-02
-0.2200000000E-02  0.2389336637E-01  0.4046899944E-02  0.1349621678E-02
 0.2200000000E-02  0.5335617691E-02  0.5736665309E-02 -0.2628365436E-04
 0.1000000000E-03 -0.3063193033E-01  0.6473181407E-02 -0.5388244081E-03
 0.1100000000E-02 -0.1223971313E-01  0.7378037088E-02 -0.6082570614E-03
 0.3000000000E-03  0.5299158220E-01  0.3208929850E-02  0.6017070434E-04
 0.0000000000E+00  0.3423767075E-01  0.5774060714E-02 -0.3356950989E-03
-0.2000000000E-03 -0.2480819492E-01  0.2429031470E-02 -0.4776740350E-03
 0.8000000000E-03  0.2184674577E-01  0.2752642606E-02  0.1710964635E-02
```
B34SRETURN$
B34SEEND$

B34SEXEC VARFREQ DATAP=12 YEARS=(1959,9) YEARE=(1979,4)$
     VAR DIFFPRCE DPCZU_1$
     VARF VAR=(DIFFPRCE DPCZU_1) NLAGS=12 FEEDX=(DIFFPRCE)
          FEEDY=(DPCZU_1) DUMMY=CONS NREP=100 TABLE=('ONE')
     PERIOD=(120. 60. 40. 32. 16. 12. 10. 8. 7. 6. 5. 4. 3. 2. 0.)$
     B34SEEND$

B34SEXEC VARFREQ DATAP=12 YEARS=(1959,9) YEARE=(1979,4)$
     VAR DIFFPRCE DPCZU_12$
     VARF VAR=(DIFFPRCE DPCZU_12) NLAGS=12 FEEDX=(DIFFPRCE)
          FEEDY=(DPCZU_12) DUMMY=CONS NREP=100 TABLE=('TWO')
     PERIOD=(120. 60. 40. 32. 16. 12. 10. 8. 7. 6. 5. 4. 3. 2. 0.)$

```
        B34SEEND$

B34SEXEC VARFREQ DATAP=12 YEARS=(1959,9) YEARE=(1979,4)$
        VAR  DIFFPRCE DPCZU_60 $
        VARF VAR=(DIFFPRCE DPCZU_60) NLAGS=12 FEEDX=(DIFFPRCE)
        FEEDY=(DPCZU_60) DUMMY=CONS NREP=100 TABLE=('THREE')
        PERIOD=(120. 60. 40. 32. 16. 12. 10. 8. 7. 6. 5. 4. 3. 2. 0.)$
        B34SEEND$
==
```

Edited output from running the above problem is presented next.

```
                        TABLE ONE

              Estimated Measures of Linear Feedback
                   MONTHLY DATA   1959: 9 - 1979: 4
      12 lags  236 observations   Dummy variables: CONSTANT

      X vector: DIFFPRCE              Y vector: DPCZU_1


                  Estimate      Adjusted Estimate   25.0%    75.0%
    F(Y TO X)    0.075 ( 7.3%)     0.049 ( 4.8%)     0.036    0.062
    F(X TO Y)    0.059 ( 5.7%)     0.033 ( 3.3%)     0.026    0.039
      F(X.Y)     0.009 ( 0.9%)     0.006 ( 0.6%)     0.001    0.008


      F(Y TO X)
      PERIOD      ESTIMATE       ADJUSTED ESTIMATE   25.0 %   75.0 %
      120.000    0.018 ( 1.8%)     0.008 ( 0.8%)     0.001    0.012
       60.000    0.018 ( 1.8%)     0.009 ( 0.9%)     0.001    0.012
       40.000    0.019 ( 1.9%)     0.009 ( 0.9%)     0.001    0.012
       32.000    0.020 ( 2.0%)     0.009 ( 0.9%)     0.002    0.011
       16.000    0.026 ( 2.5%)     0.010 ( 1.0%)     0.003    0.012
       12.000    0.034 ( 3.3%)     0.013 ( 1.3%)     0.004    0.016
       10.000    0.052 ( 5.1%)     0.027 ( 2.7%)     0.009    0.038
        8.000    0.104 ( 9.9%)     0.078 ( 7.5%)     0.033    0.106
        7.000    0.151 (14.0%)     0.127 (11.9%)     0.053    0.163
        6.000    0.183 (16.7%)     0.156 (14.4%)     0.076    0.219
        5.000    0.052 ( 5.1%)     0.023 ( 2.3%)     0.006    0.034
        4.000    0.006 ( 0.6%)     0.001 ( 0.1%)     0.000    0.001
        3.000    0.393 (32.5%)     0.409 (33.5%)     0.185    0.606
        2.000    0.001 ( 0.1%)     0.000 ( 0.0%)     0.000    0.000
     Infinite    0.018 ( 1.8%)     0.008 ( 0.8%)     0.001    0.011


      F(X TO Y)
      PERIOD      ESTIMATE       ADJUSTED ESTIMATE   25.0 %   75.0 %
      120.000    0.076 ( 7.3%)     0.045 ( 4.4%)     0.008    0.067
       60.000    0.093 ( 8.8%)     0.065 ( 6.3%)     0.021    0.100
       40.000    0.112 (10.6%)     0.088 ( 8.4%)     0.043    0.124
       32.000    0.126 (11.8%)     0.104 ( 9.9%)     0.057    0.141
       16.000    0.154 (14.3%)     0.129 (12.1%)     0.075    0.171
       12.000    0.118 (11.1%)     0.085 ( 8.1%)     0.045    0.110
       10.000    0.067 ( 6.5%)     0.038 ( 3.7%)     0.015    0.048
        8.000    0.055 ( 5.4%)     0.031 ( 3.0%)     0.009    0.044
        7.000    0.087 ( 8.3%)     0.064 ( 6.2%)     0.026    0.082
        6.000    0.097 ( 9.2%)     0.072 ( 7.0%)     0.031    0.095
        5.000    0.021 ( 2.1%)     0.007 ( 0.7%)     0.002    0.010
        4.000    0.044 ( 4.3%)     0.024 ( 2.3%)     0.008    0.036
        3.000    0.013 ( 1.3%)     0.002 ( 0.2%)     0.001    0.003
        2.000    0.119 (11.2%)     0.073 ( 7.1%)     0.011    0.099
     Infinite    0.069 ( 6.7%)     0.038 ( 3.7%)     0.003    0.056

                        100 replications
```

TABLE TWO

Estimated Measures of Linear Feedback
MONTHLY DATA   1959: 9 - 1979: 4
12 lags   236 observations   Dummy variables: CONSTANT

X vector: DIFFPRCE   Y vector: DPCZU_12

	Estimate	Adjusted Estimate	25.0%	75.0%
F(Y TO X)	0.089 (8.5%)	0.062 (6.1%)	0.048	0.074
F(X TO Y)	0.074 (7.2%)	0.047 (4.6%)	0.038	0.056
F(X.Y	0.018 (1.8%)	0.015 (1.5%)	0.007	0.019

F(Y TO X)

PERIOD	ESTIMATE	ADJUSTED ESTIMATE	25.0 %	75.0 %
120.000	0.105 (10.0%)	0.087 (8.4%)	0.036	0.110
60.000	0.300 (25.9%)	0.296 (25.6%)	0.166	0.374
40.000	0.858 (57.6%)	0.942 (61.0%)	0.538	1.159
32.000	0.686 (49.7%)	0.754 (53.0%)	0.476	0.917
16.000	0.091 (8.7%)	0.084 (8.0%)	0.054	0.100
12.000	0.066 (6.4%)	0.055 (5.4%)	0.031	0.068
10.000	0.077 (7.4%)	0.058 (5.6%)	0.025	0.081
8.000	0.153 (14.2%)	0.101 (9.6%)	0.045	0.132
7.000	0.022 (2.2%)	0.007 (0.7%)	0.003	0.010
6.000	0.006 (0.6%)	0.001 (0.1%)	0.000	0.002
5.000	0.009 (0.9%)	0.000 (0.0%)	0.000	0.001
4.000	0.013 (1.3%)	0.005 (0.5%)	0.001	0.007
3.000	0.049 (4.8%)	0.031 (3.0%)	0.012	0.039
2.000	0.031 (3.0%)	0.017 (1.6%)	0.003	0.023
Infinite	0.068 (6.6%)	0.052 (5.1%)	0.011	0.069

F(X TO Y)

PERIOD	ESTIMATE	ADJUSTED ESTIMATE	25.0 %	75.0 %
120.000	0.015 (1.5%)	0.005 (0.5%)	0.001	0.006
60.000	0.037 (3.6%)	0.021 (2.1%)	0.009	0.027
40.000	0.065 (6.3%)	0.049 (4.8%)	0.023	0.063
32.000	0.087 (8.3%)	0.072 (6.9%)	0.033	0.096
16.000	0.148 (13.8%)	0.128 (12.0%)	0.056	0.174
12.000	0.099 (9.5%)	0.071 (6.8%)	0.022	0.102
10.000	0.032 (3.1%)	0.012 (1.2%)	0.003	0.015
8.000	0.063 (6.1%)	0.034 (3.4%)	0.015	0.047
7.000	0.163 (15.0%)	0.127 (11.9%)	0.076	0.178
6.000	0.262 (23.0%)	0.226 (20.2%)	0.146	0.297
5.000	0.136 (12.7%)	0.119 (11.3%)	0.047	0.175
4.000	0.008 (0.8%)	0.001 (0.1%)	0.000	0.002
3.000	0.096 (9.1%)	0.056 (5.4%)	0.020	0.080
2.000	0.064 (6.2%)	0.038 (3.7%)	0.006	0.055
Infinite	0.006 (0.6%)	0.001 (0.1%)	0.000	0.001

100 replications

TABLE THREE

Estimated Measures of Linear Feedback
MONTHLY DATA   1959: 9 - 1979: 4
12 lags   236 observations   Dummy variables: CONSTANT

X vector: DIFFPRCE   Y vector: DPCZU_60

	Estimate	Adjusted Estimate	25.0%	75.0%
F(Y TO X)	0.062 (6.0%)	0.034 (3.3%)	0.026	0.041
F(X TO Y)	0.034 (3.3%)	0.014 (1.4%)	0.010	0.018
F(X.Y	0.023 (2.3%)	0.018 (1.8%)	0.007	0.025

F(Y TO X)

PERIOD	ESTIMATE	ADJUSTED ESTIMATE	25.0 %	75.0 %
120.000	0.165 (15.2%)	0.120 (11.3%)	0.026	0.171
60.000	0.128 (12.0%)	0.090 (8.6%)	0.026	0.130
40.000	0.101 (9.6%)	0.068 (6.5%)	0.026	0.088
32.000	0.088 (8.4%)	0.058 (5.7%)	0.026	0.079
16.000	0.071 (6.8%)	0.052 (5.1%)	0.022	0.063
12.000	0.092 (8.7%)	0.070 (6.8%)	0.024	0.090
10.000	0.135 (12.7%)	0.110 (10.4%)	0.047	0.157
8.000	0.215 (19.3%)	0.173 (15.8%)	0.080	0.239
7.000	0.188 (17.1%)	0.149 (13.8%)	0.074	0.216
6.000	0.128 (12.0%)	0.093 (8.9%)	0.045	0.119
5.000	0.060 (5.8%)	0.023 (2.3%)	0.006	0.034
4.000	0.014 (1.4%)	0.004 (0.4%)	0.001	0.005
3.000	0.045 (4.4%)	0.017 (1.6%)	0.005	0.025
2.000	0.001 (0.1%)	0.000 (0.0%)	0.000	0.000
Infinite	0.187 (17.0%)	0.133 (12.5%)	0.024	0.198

F(X TO Y)

PERIOD	ESTIMATE	ADJUSTED ESTIMATE	25.0 %	75.0 %
120.000	0.006 (0.6%)	0.001 (0.1%)	0.000	0.001
60.000	0.017 (1.7%)	0.005 (0.5%)	0.002	0.007
40.000	0.035 (3.4%)	0.017 (1.7%)	0.008	0.022
32.000	0.051 (5.0%)	0.030 (3.0%)	0.014	0.040
16.000	0.125 (11.7%)	0.095 (9.0%)	0.037	0.139
12.000	0.126 (11.8%)	0.099 (9.4%)	0.043	0.131
10.000	0.099 (9.5%)	0.072 (6.9%)	0.033	0.086
8.000	0.043 (4.2%)	0.020 (2.0%)	0.006	0.025
7.000	0.013 (1.3%)	0.003 (0.3%)	0.001	0.005
6.000	0.002 (0.2%)	0.000 (0.0%)	0.000	0.000
5.000	0.006 (0.6%)	0.001 (0.1%)	0.000	0.001
4.000	0.008 (0.8%)	0.001 (0.1%)	0.000	0.001
3.000	0.025 (2.5%)	0.008 (0.8%)	0.003	0.011
2.000	0.050 (4.8%)	0.025 (2.5%)	0.003	0.035
Infinite	0.002 (0.2%)	0.000 (0.0%)	0.000	0.000

100 replications

The Frankel (1982) expected price series, F_t, runs from 1959/7 to 1979/4 and consists of 237 observations. The selection of an actual price series to relate to this series is not unique. A reasonable choice to use was the consumer price index-urban (CPI-U), which was obtained from the August 1982 version of the NBER/Citybase data tape for the period 1954/7 to 1979/4. Three transformations of this series were used in the empirical work. If we assume that ZU_t is the raw CPI-U series, then $DPCZU\_1 = (1-B) * 12 * ((ZU_t - ZU_{t-1})/ZU_{t-1})$ is a first difference of the annualized percent change in ZU_t. This transformation is comparable to a first difference of the Frankel (1982) expected long-run inflation rate, $DIFFPRCE = (1-B) * F_t$.(Both series were differenced once to achieve stationarity.) An argument can be made that since the Frankel series is an expected <u>long-run</u> inflation rate, the appropriate actual series to use would involve calculation of the percent change over a longer period. To deal with this concern, two additional transformations of ZU_t were tried. An intermediate measure, $DPCZU\_12 = (1-B)((ZU_t - ZU_{t-12})/ZU_{t-12})$ annualizes on the basis of a year, while a more-long-term measure, $DPCZU\_60 = (1-B)*(.2)*((ZU_t - ZU_{t-60})/ZU_{t-60})$, annualizes on the basis of a five-year horizon. The same data period, 1959/9 to 1979/4, was used to facilitate comparisons among alternative transformations of the price series. As was discussed earlier, the maximum order of the polynomial in Q(B) in equation (8.1-9)was selected from inspection of autocorrelations of the VAR model estimated by OLS.

The results from estimating the three models will be discussed in turn.[11] In the output labeled TABLE ONE, the results for the annualized percent change in the CPI-U (DPCZU_1) indicates strong (33.5%) high-frequency (period=3) feedback from the differenced inflation series to the differenced expected inflation series. This indicates that at this frequency the predicted error of equation (12.3-1) is not uncorrelated with the entire set of information that was available and, thus, that at this frequency the weak form of the implicit expectations hypothesis does not hold. In terms of our prior notation, we have significant terms in F_{3i} in equation (12.1-8). The only other feedback found of any note is at somewhat lower frequencies in which for periods = 8, 7, and 6, the percent explained was 7.5%, 11.9%, and 14.4%, respectively, for the estimates corrected for small-sample bias. There is less evidence of lags of the expected price series mapping to the actual price series; the only evidence of any relationship was found at lower frequencies. For example, at periods = 60, 40, 32, 16, and 12, the percentages explained are only 6.3%, 8.4%, 9.9%, 12.1%, and 8.1%, respectively. Overall, there was more of a relationship from P_t to F_t (F(Y to X) = 4.8%) than from F_t to P_t (F(X to Y) = 3.3%). We can summarize by noting that the feedback from the actual price series to the expected series was at a high frequency and much stronger than the much lower low frequency mapping from the expected price series to the actual price series. These results are more consistent with the weak form of the rational expectations model than the weak form of the implicit expectations model and are at

least consistent with Frankel's (1982) paper in which he indicated
that his expected price measure was a long-run (low frequency in
our terms) measure.

The table labeled TABLE TWO uses the yearly inflation measure
and presents a somewhat different frequency finding. The overall
measures F(Y to X) and F(X to Y) are larger than in the first case
(6.1% vs. 4.8% and 4.6% vs. 3.3%, respectively). In contrast with
the prior case, we see large low-frequency feedback, which would
indicate rejection of the weak form of the implicit expectations
hypothesis at low frequencies. For example, at periods equal to 60,
40, and 32, the percent explained is 25.6%, 61.0%, and 53.0%,
respectively. Going the other way (f(X to Y)), there is little
evidence of a relationship, except for relatively low values at
periods equal to 16, 7, and 6 in which the percentages are 12.0%,
11.9%, and 20.2%, respectively. It is worth noting that the effect
found at 16 for f(X to Y) is relatively similar across the two
tables. It is apparent that the low-frequency findings appear to
be sensitive to the construction of the actual price series. The
finding that the relationship from P_t to F_t dominates the
relationship from F_t to P_t is similar to that in the prior case. The
findings in both tables are consistent with the Muth (1961) weak
rational expectations hypothesis. Unlike the first table in which
the weak implicit expectations hypothesis was rejected at high
frequencies, here the rejection is at low frequencies.

The final table labeled TABLE THREE utilizes the longest run
measure for P_t (DPCZU_60). The findings here are more similar to
those found in the first table than in the second. The strongest
feedback was found at a very low frequency (at period = 120, the
percent is 11.3%), at several intermediate frequencies (at
periods=12, 10, 8, 7, and 6, the percentages were 6.8%, 10.4%,
15.8%, and 13.8%, respectively) and at one very high frequency (at
Inf [∞] the percentage is 12.5%). Going the other way (i. e., f(X
to Y)), there is little evidence of a relationship except for small
effects at periods 16, 12, and 10 in which the percentages are
9.0%, 9.4%, and 6.9%, respectively. The summary measures F(X to Y)
and F(Y to X) are less than in either of the prior tables but
follow the same pattern (i. e., F(X to Y) < F(Y to X)). Like the
prior two tables, the results in the final table are consistent
with the weak form of the Muth (1961) rational expectations
hypothesis and relatively less consistent with the weak form of the
Mills (1975) implicit expectations hypothesis.

It is stressed that the intention of this example is to
investigate the dynamic relationship between the proposed Frankel
(1982) expected price series and three actual price series, not to
test the Muth (1961) or Mills (1975) expectations hypothesis. To
effectively perform the latter tests requires a different
econometric setup and jointly estimating and testing the Frankel
(1982) series with appropriate cross equations restrictions. The
more modest goal was to take the published Frankel series as a

given, relate this series to three proposed price series and discuss the economic meaning of the dynamic relationships found. In contrast with the gas furnace data example, in this case there was feedback going both directions. This model would not be appropriate for a transfer function model.

The following commands were used to test the KFILTER command on the Box-Jenkins (1970) gas furnace data that were used in the prior example

```
B34SEXEC KFILTER $
        SERIESN VAR=GASIN$
        SERIESN VAR=GASOUT$
        ESTIMATE K=8 NSTAR=5 FORECAST$
    B34SEEND$

B34SEXEC KFILTER $
        SERIESN VAR=GASIN$
        SERIESN VAR=GASOUT$
        ESTIMATE K=20 NSTAR=20 FORECAST$
    B34SEEND$
```

Edited output from running this test problem is shown next.

```
KF CONTROL CARD READ

IOPT NSERIE IBEGIN IEND IUNIT ICON  IB34S(I),I=1...
   0     2      0    0     0    2      3

SET UP TO RUN FOR      296  OBSERVATIONS

SERIES #          B34S VARIABLE #      NAME

      1                    2          GASIN
      2                    3          GASOUT

THESE ROUTINES WERE OBTAINED FROM MASANAO AOKI AND WERE CONVERTED BY HOUSTON H. STOKES

FOR FURTHER DETAIL SEE 'STATE SPACE MODELING OF TIME SERIES' BY AOKI, SPRINGER(1987)


*******************    VERSION DATE 1 JANUARY 1987    *******************

*******************      AOKI1 OPTION SELECTED        *******************


STATE SPACE PROGRAM AOKI1. WRITTEN BY MASANAO AOKI.

MODIFIED FOR B34S BY HOUSTON H. STOKES JANUARY 1988.

MODEL ESTIMATED.

Y(T)    =  C * X(T)    +        E(T)
X(T+1)  =  A * X(T)    +    B * E(T)

  E(E(T)E(T)')    = DELTA
  E(X(T)X(T)')    = PI

FOR THIS PROBLEM

K (NUMBER OF LAGS ON HANKEL MATRIX) =            8
NSTAR (DIMENSION OF STATE VECTOR) =             5
MXITER (MAXIMUM NUMBER OF ITERATIONS) =       500
EPS (STEP SIZE) =                           0.50000000E-01
P (NUMBER OF SERIES) =                        2
IOLDD (= 0 IF WANT EISPACK) =                 0


DIFFERENCING OPERATOR -  NEW(T)= OLD(T) - OLD(T-DIF)

       0          0

LOG OPERATOR -  IF LOG NE 1, NEW = LOG(OLD)

       0          0
```

```
AOKI1 PROGRAM REQUIRES     40573 REAL*4 WORDS OF SPACE.    300000  WAS AVAILABLE


        SERIES #           MEAN
            1                  -0.56834459E-01
            2                  53.509122


SERIES   1 SLOPE= -0.38228485E-02 INTERCEPT=   0.51085854
SERIES   2 SLOPE=  0.15004026E-01 INTERCEPT=  51.281024

MEANS OF SERIES USED

   -0.568345E-01   0.535091E+02

SUMS OF SQUARES

    0.340450E+03   0.850540E+06

SUM (X(T) - XBAR)**2

    0.339494E+03   0.302481E+04

SERIES   1 SLOPE= -0.76147219E-03 INTERCEPT=   0.11307862
SERIES   2 SLOPE=  0.29886479E-02 INTERCEPT=  -0.44381421


VARIANCES
 1.14693790165037313       -1.65852650999815321
-1.65852650999815321       10.2189370662892367

 1 LAG
  1.0924      -1.3470
 -2.0487       9.9201

SINGULAR VALUES

   42.932      4.3061     1.5686    0.47783     0.12362    0.46122E-01  0.25228E-01  0.69604E-02  0.42498E-02  0.30743E-02
 0.23122E-02 0.18644E-02 0.15934E-02 0.94173E-03  0.37753E-03  0.10066E-03

1.0D+00/DSQRT(N)= 0.581238193719096404E-01

             100 * SUMEI / SUMEIG    100 * SUMSI / SUMSIN     THISS              REMA              DROP

      1        98.860263              86.729675         1.0000000         0.15300789        1.0000000
      2        99.854812              95.428688         0.10030031        0.52707584E-01    9.9700590
      3        99.986781              98.597480         0.36536414E-01    0.16171170E-01    2.7452149
      4        99.999027              99.562760         0.11129755E-01    0.50414142E-02    3.2827689
      5        99.999847              99.812481         0.28793032E-02    0.21621110E-02    3.8654336
      6        99.999961              99.905654         0.10742893E-02    0.10878216E-02    2.6801934
      7        99.999995              99.956618         0.58762908E-03    0.50019255E-03    1.8281760
      8        99.999998              99.970680         0.16212503E-03    0.33806752E-03    3.6245425
      9        99.999999              99.979265         0.98988110E-04    0.23907941E-03    1.6378233
     10        99.999999              99.985475         0.71607154E-04    0.16747226E-03    1.3823774
     11       100.00000               99.990146         0.53857559E-04    0.11361470E-03    1.3295655
     12       100.00000               99.993913         0.43426086E-04    0.70188611E-04    1.2402121
     13       100.00000               99.997132         0.37115144E-04    0.33073466E-04    1.1700368
     14       100.00000               99.999034         0.21935109E-04    0.11138358E-04    1.6920429
     15       100.00000               99.999797         0.87936952E-05    0.23446625E-05    2.4944131
     16       100.00000              100.00000          0.23446625E-05    0.00000000E+00    3.7505164

SUM EIGENVALUES (SUMEIG) =                    1864.4435
SUM SQRT(ABS(EIGENVAL)) (SUMSIN) =             49.501433

SUMSI(I) = SUM(S(I)), SUMEI(I) = SUM(SQRT(ABS(S(I))))

THISS(I) = SQRT(ABS(S(I)) /SQRT(ABS(S(I-1)))
REMA = (SUMSIN - SUMSI) / SQRT(S(I-1))
DROP = SQRT(S(I)) / SQRT(S(I-1))
SINGULAR VALUES OF H = SQRT(EIGENVALUES OF H'H)


EIGENVALUES OF A:
( 0.89552084  ,  0.00000000E+00)    R =  0.89552084     THETA =   0.00000000E+00
( 0.73020120  ,  0.33157203    )    R =  0.80195624     THETA =   0.42624424
( 0.73020120  , -0.33157203    )    R =  0.80195624     THETA =  -0.42624424
( 0.88546807  ,  0.40304941    )    R =  0.97288361     THETA =   0.42715518
( 0.88546807  , -0.40304941    )    R =  0.97288361     THETA =  -0.42715518

M MATRIX.
            1              2

   1  -0.116603E+01   0.302651E+01

   2   0.138955E+01   0.369718E+00

   3  -0.146956E+00  -0.505962E+00

   4  -0.318382E+00   0.234847E-01

   5  -0.119215E+00   0.420601E-01


C MATRIX.
            1              2              3              4              5

   1  -0.483775E+00   0.353517E+00   0.381781E-01  -0.177862E+00   0.987818E-01

   2   0.321275E+01   0.126089E+01   0.517491E+00  -0.588180E-01   0.256398E-01


PI  MATRIX -  DEVIATION=  0.30794017

DELTA MATRIX
```

```
           1           2
1    0.312449E-01  -0.908798E-01

2   -0.908798E-01   0.943509E+00


PI  MATRIX -  DEVIATION=  0.29506347
PI  MATRIX
           1            2             3             4             5

1    0.136975E+01  -0.100418E+01  -0.302610E-01   0.200031E+00   0.819383E-01

2   -0.100418E+01   0.291814E+01  -0.125529E+01  -0.109101E+01  -0.714530E+00

3   -0.302610E-01  -0.125529E+01   0.157200E+01   0.108565E+01   0.847441E+00

4    0.200031E+00  -0.109101E+01   0.108565E+01   0.928355E+00   0.697283E+00

5    0.819383E-01  -0.714530E+00   0.847441E+00   0.697283E+00   0.856635E+00


DELTA INVERSE
           1            2
1    0.444618E+02   0.428261E+01

2    0.428261E+01   0.147238E+01

B * DELTA MATRIX
           1            2
1   -0.627645E-01   0.237878E+00

2    0.103273E+00  -0.487073E-02

3   -0.167886E+00   0.113472E+00

4   -0.136646E+00   0.165850E+00

5   -0.147497E+00   0.148865E+00

B MATRIX
           1            2
1   -0.177188E+01   0.814506E-01

2    0.457085E+01   0.435107E+00

3   -0.697856E+01  -0.551917E+00

4   -0.536524E+01  -0.341006E+00

5   -0.592043E+01  -0.412485E+00

PREDICT. MULTIPLIER
           1            2             3             4             5

1   -0.229008E+00   0.409771E+00   0.327841E-02  -0.302584E+00   0.170687E+00

2    0.829070E+00  -0.148689E+01  -0.849630E+00   0.828095E+00  -0.477359E+00

3   -0.156183E+01   0.347228E+01   0.127325E+01  -0.106948E+01   0.626575E+00

4   -0.152149E+01   0.246815E+01   0.172808E+00  -0.864609E-01   0.722988E+00

5   -0.153426E+01   0.263242E+01   0.445790E+00  -0.161211E+01   0.154571E+01

EIGENVALUES OF PRED:
( -0.39945239    ,  0.00000000E+00)   R =   0.39945239     THETA =    3.1415927
( -0.18725967    ,  0.57444223    )   R =   0.60419372     THETA =    1.8859191
( -0.18725967    , -0.57444223    )   R =   0.60419372     THETA =   -1.8859191
(  0.89529067    ,  0.38294257    )   R =   0.97375068     THETA =    0.40418060
(  0.89529067    , -0.38294257    )   R =   0.97375068     THETA =   -0.40418060
N= 296

SUMS OF SQUARES BEFORE
339.5        3025.

SUM AFTER
16.92        303.6

PERCENTAGE REDUCTION   95.02

PERCENTAGE REDUCTION   89.96

SUM AFTER UPDATE
16.92        303.6

PERCENTAGE REDUCTION   95.02

PERCENTAGE REDUCTION   89.96
PREDICTED VALUES (OUT OF SAMPLE)
  296    -0.3710        56.18
  297    -0.5055        55.07
  298    -0.5668        54.42
  299    -0.5484        54.18
  300    -0.4642        54.26
  301    -0.3410        54.50
  302    -0.2100        54.79
  303    -0.9926E-01    55.01
  304    -0.2838E-01    55.11
  305    -0.6064E-02    55.06
  306    -0.2984E-01    54.87
  307    -0.8814E-01    54.58
  308    -0.1637        54.26
```

```
309    -0.2375      53.95
310    -0.2926      53.70
311    -0.3174      53.54
312    -0.3069      53.49
313    -0.2633      53.54
314    -0.1953      53.65
315    -0.1153      53.80
316    -0.3753E-01  53.95
317     0.2489E-01  54.06
318     0.6236E-01  54.11
```

RESIDUALS FOR SERIES   1 MEAN = -0.70324213E-04 VARIANCE =   0.57348339E-01

AUTOCORRELATIONS

```
1-12   -0.525   0.111   0.206  -0.171   0.002   0.060  -0.027   0.032  -0.063  -0.018   0.146  -0.204
13-24   0.109   0.067  -0.109   0.018   0.076  -0.059  -0.049   0.072  -0.020  -0.020   0.039  -0.008
25-36  -0.006  -0.039   0.078  -0.042  -0.021   0.028   0.014  -0.031   0.064  -0.026   0.059  -0.045
37-48   0.006   0.049  -0.091   0.032   0.023  -0.059   0.028   0.034  -0.038   0.029  -0.039   0.062
```

RESIDUALS FOR SERIES   2 MEAN =   0.59373557E-02 VARIANCE =   1.0291320

AUTOCORRELATIONS

```
1-12   -0.437  -0.045   0.286  -0.126  -0.024   0.075  -0.007   0.009  -0.091   0.036   0.154  -0.223
13-24   0.092   0.089  -0.161  -0.010   0.120  -0.073  -0.081   0.067  -0.025  -0.024   0.029  -0.002
25-36   0.003  -0.020   0.078  -0.025  -0.039   0.033  -0.004  -0.051   0.059  -0.029   0.048  -0.038
37-48   0.004   0.064  -0.070   0.046   0.021  -0.074   0.038   0.042  -0.034   0.017  -0.010   0.058
```

AUTOCOVARIANCES OF ERROR TERMS

```
          0
 0.57114E-01 -0.13944
-0.13944      1.0234
          1
-0.29952E-01  0.15901E-01
 0.21295     -0.45026
          2
 0.64185E-02  0.51681E-01
-0.12936     -0.50476E-01
          3
 0.11745E-01 -0.42681E-01
-0.15202E-01  0.29081
          4
-0.97426E-02 -0.47413E-02
 0.66436E-01 -0.13207
```

The percentage reduction in the sum of squares for GASIN and GASOUT was 95.02% and 89.96%, respectively, for the first model, which set K=8 and NSTAR=5. The second test problem, whose output is not shown, set K=20 and NSTAR=20 and was way too large. If the interested reader runs this model, it will fail. A simple model in which K=5 and NSTAR=5 results in a 95.87% and 98.77% reduction, respectively, in the sum of squares. The value 5 was chosen for the state vector because the singular values of the Hankel matrix fell off after 5. By reducing the size of the Hankel matrix from 8 to 5, the performamce of the GASOUT model improved.[12] The Hankel matrix H was not printed since the option IHANKL was not supplied.

12.4 Conclusion

This chapter has illustrated the VARFREQ and KFILTER commands, using the gas furnace data. While the VARFREQ command decomposes the VAR model into the frequency domain to study the patterns of adjustment, the KFILTER command shows how a state space model can be identified, using information in the Hankel matrix. An additional example, using price expectations data, has been presented to illustrate the problems of feedback.

NOTES

1. The author of B34S was fortunate to obtain from Geweke (1982a) the MTSM program that implements the material in Geweke (1982b, 1984). This code was converted to run under B34S. The MTSM program is unique in that it provides a way to estimate the frequency decomposition of the VAR model to measure feedback. These features have been implemented in the B34S II command language. The MTSM program also provides other useful features that are listed in Stokes (1988a), which documents the B34S native commands.

2. The author of B34S was fortunate to obtain the Aoki (1987) code and converted it to run under B34S. Aoki has recently revised his excellent book. He has been most generous in reading section 12.2 of this chapter and making a number of suggestions. He is not responsible for any remaining errors.

3. Geweke (1982b) is the major reference for the discussion of unconditional linear dependence between x_t and y_t. Geweke (1984) generalizes this to a model of conditional dependence. The discussion in this section has been adapted from these seminal articles, which should be read for additional detail.

4. The motivation for these definitions rests on the fact that the natural log of 1 is zero and the fact that, as Geweke notes, these measures can be interpreted in terms of the proportional increase in the variance of the one-step-ahead population error.

5. Harvey (1981, chap. 4) provides an introduction to the topic. While an excellent reference to state space model estimation is contained in Anderson and Moore (1979), Sargent (1987) provides economic insights into the use of the Kalman filter in economic problems.

6. This section is based on Aoki (1987) and uses his notation.

7. Aoki (1987, sec. 7.5) outlines how equation (12.2-38) is solved, using noniterative methods.

8. Aoki's code was initially REAL*4. One of the first changes was to convert all code to REAL*8. Aoki's eigenvalue routine was found to produce poor answers under some conditions. EISPACK code was substituted. Aoki accepted these changes. In order to test the effect of the change in the eigenvalue routines, the switch IOLDD is provided to allow calls to the original code. This option is <u>not</u> recommended. Occasionally the procedure will run into computational overflows if K and NSTAR are set too large. Reductions are in order. As a first approximation, it is best to set K to its default of 6 and NSTAR to 1 and gradually build up the model.

9. The MTSM program, which is called with the VARFREQ command,

actually has local-data-building capability. Since this capability is dominated by what is available in SAS or the B34S DATA procedure, these commands have not been implemented in the B34S II command language. These commands in the B34S native command form are documented in Stokes (1988a) and are accessible with use of the PGMCARDS$ sentence. The main contribution of the MTSM program is to calculate conditional and unconditional measures of feedback. These options are controlled with the VARF sentence. At first glance the command structure of the VARFREQ command seems redundant. The VAR sentence is used to load data from B34S into the MTSM program. If the VARF sentence is supplied, the local VAR parameter on the VARF sentence indicates which variables are to be used in the feedback analysis. If FEEDX and FEEDY variables are supplied, unconditional feedback analysis is performed. If, in addition, FEEDZ is supplied, conditional feedback analysis is performed.

10. In equation (12.2-8), note that if we substitute F_t for x_t, $F_t \neq F_{3i}$.

11. Because the adjusted estimates are the result of the bootstrap, if the VARFREQ command is given repeatedly, the estimates will differ since the random-number generator used to generate the artificial data does not generate the same random-number sequence.

12. These results should be compared with the sixth-order VAR model estimated in chapter 8 using the setup in Table 8.3. Here the percent reduction in the sum of squares for GASIN and GASOUT was 97.03% and 99.46%, respectively.

13. Optimal Control Analysis

13.0 Introduction

The OPTCONTROL command implements the Chow (1975, 1981) optimal control program in B34S. Because this program is well documented above, the developer of B34S decided to support both the old command syntax and the B34S II command language.[1] This chapter briefly describes what is being calculated and illustrates some of the output from running the Klein-Goldberger model.

13.1 Optimal Control Theory

Assume an economic model can be represented as

$$y_t = A_t y_{t-1} + C_t x_t + b_t + u_t, \tag{13.1-1}$$

where y_t is a vector of p endogenous variables; x_t is a vector of q control variables; A_t, C_t and b_t are matrices of known coefficients and u_t is a random vector that is serially independent and identically distributed. The problem is to specify values of the control variables such that the quadratic welfare loss function,

$$W = \Sigma_{t=1}^{T} (y_t - a_t)'K_t y_t - a_t), \tag{13.1-2}$$

is minimized where a_t is a vector of targets for y_t. The vector y_t has been augmented to include no lags > 1 on any y variable and the x_t vector as a subvector. By this device x_t does not have to be explicitly included in equation (13.1-2).

Following Chow (1981, 5-6), the first step is to calculate the expected loss in period V_T^2,

$$V_T = E_{T-1}(y_T - a_T)'K_T(y_T - a_T). \tag{13.1-3}$$

Equation (13.1-3) can be written

$$V_T = E_{T-1}(y_T'H_T Y_T - 2y_T'h_T + c_T), \tag{13.1-4}$$

where

$$K_T = H_T \tag{13.1-5}$$

$$K_T a_T = h_T \tag{13.1-6}$$

$$c_T = a_T'K_T a_T. \tag{13.1-7}$$

If V_T is minimized with respect to x_T after substitution for y_T from equation (13.1-1), the optimal policy for the control vector x_T in period T-1 is

$$\hat{x}_T = G_T y_{T-1} + g_T \qquad\qquad (13.1\text{-}8)$$

given that

$$G_T = -(C_T' H_T C_T)^{-1}(C_T' H_T A_T) \qquad\qquad (13.1\text{-}9)$$

$$g_T = -(C_T' H_T C_T)^{-1} C_T'(H_T b_T - h_T). \qquad\qquad (13.1\text{-}10)$$

An expression for V_{T-k} for $k > 1$ can be obtained by replacing T in equation (13.1-4) by T-k. This will measure the expected loss condition on information known up to period T-k. Equation (13.1-8) gives the optimal policy for the q control variables for the last period T. If this value is substituted into equation (13.1-1), we obtain

$$y_T = A_T y_{T-1} + C_T G_T y_T + C_T g_T + b_T + u_T, \qquad\qquad (13.1\text{-}11)$$

which determines the optimal vector of the p state variables for the Tth period.[3] If this value of y_T is substituted in equation (13.1-4), we obtain the minimum expected loss for the Tth period:

$$\begin{aligned}
\hat{V}_T =\ & y_{T-1}'(A_T + C_T G_T)'H_T(A_T + C_T GT)y_{T-1} - 2(b_T + C_T g_T)'h_T + \\
& 2y_{T-1}'(A_T + C_T G_T)'(H_T b_T - h_T) + c_T + E_{T-1}u_T'H_T u_T + \\
& (b_T + C_T g_T)'H_T(b_T + C_T g_T).
\end{aligned} \qquad (13.1\text{-}12)$$

The next step is to obtain x_{t-1} to minimize equation (13.1-3) for T-1. Chow (1981, 1983) shows that given equation (13.1-12),

$$H_{T-1} = K_{T-1} + (A_T + C_T G_T)'H_T(A_T + C_T G_T) \qquad (13.1\text{-}13)$$

$$h_{T-1} = K_{T-1}a_{T-1} - (A_T + C_T G_T)'(H_T b_T - h_T) \qquad (13.1\text{-}14)$$

$$\begin{aligned}
c_{T-1} =\ & a_{T-1}'K_{T-1}a_{T-1} + (b_T + C_T g_T)'H_T(b_T + C_T g_T) \\
& -2(b_T + C_T g_T)'h_T + c_T + E_{T-1}u_T'H_T u_T.
\end{aligned} \qquad (13.1\text{-}15)$$

Once the final solution has been reached, equation (13.1-8) will determine $\hat{x}_i$ and equation (13.1-12) will determine $\hat{V}_i$ for $i \ \varepsilon \ \{T,\ldots,1\}$. Chow (1975, 1981, 1983) proposes first solving equations (13.1-9) and (13.1-13) backward in time for G_i and H_{i-1}, where we initially impose the condition in equation (13.1-5). Next, we use these solutions to solve equations (13.1-10) and (13.1-14) backward for g_i and h_{i-1}. The last step is to use the four solved vectors to substitute in equation (13.1-15) backward in time to obtain the solution for the vector c_{i-1}.

The OPTCONTROL command[4] optionally outputs A_T, C_T, b_T, G_T, H_T, g_T, y_T and x_T at every time period. The covariance matrix of the optimal solution for y_t and Γ_i can be calculated at each time horizon i and can be selectively printed. Γ_i is defined as

$$\Gamma_i = V_t + (A_t + C_t \ G_t)\Gamma_{t-1}(A_t + C_t G_t)' \tag{13.1-16}$$

for $i > 1$, given that $\Gamma_1 = V_1$.

Options are available to modify the K matrix at each time period (see EXCAP command). These and other options are not discussed here in detail since they are documented in Chow (1981), who also discussed in great detail the theory behind how the system is solved. Chow (1983, chap. 12) contains additional economics examples. In the next section the OPTCONTROL program is used with the Klein-Goldberger model running a problem discussed in Chow (1981).

13.2 Examples

Table 13.1 illustrates how to code the Klein-Goldberger model in the user subroutine CH13MOD. The OPTCONTROL input commands are illustrated in Table 13.2. Inspection of this table indicates that it follows the input conventions shown in Chow (1981).[5] Table 13.3 shows the same commands, using the B34S II parser input. The advantage of the latter setup is that free-format input is allowed, extensive checking of input is performed and the syntax is machine independent.

Table 13.1 A FORTRAN Description of the Klein-Goldberger Model

```
      SUBROUTINE CH13MOD(II,NY,NX,NW,D,Y,YL,XL,X,Z,IBAD)
      IMPLICIT REAL*8(A-H,O-Z)
      DIMENSION  Y(NY),X(NX),YL(NY),XL(NX),D(NY),Z(NW)
C
C     FOR DETAIL SEE CHOW (1981 CHAPTERS 2 & 5).
C
      IBAD=0
C     IF SET NE 0  WILL MEAN NONSTANDARD RETURN
      IF(II.GT.0)GO TO 999
C
      D(22) = .0512D0*(Y(9)+X(3))
      D(21) = .248D0*(Y(14)-Y(20)-Y(3)) + .2695D0*YL(15)*(YL(14)-
     1 YL(20)-YL(3))/YL(15)
     2  + .4497D0*Y(4)-5.7416D0
      D(20) = .4497D0*Y(4)+2.7085D0
      D(19) = .1549D0*Y(6)+.131*X(1)-6.9076D0
      D(18) = .0924D0*Y(13)-1.3607D0
      D(17) = YL(17)   + Y(3)
      D(16) = YL(16)   + Y(2) - Y(5)
      D(15) = 1.062D0*Y(8)*Y(7)/(Y(6)+X(1))
      D(14) = Y(13)-Y(18)-Y(5)-Y(6)-X(1)-Y(9)-X(3)
      D(13) = Y(1) + Y(2) + X(2)
      D(12) = .26D0*Y(6)-2.55D0-.26D0*(Y(15)-YL(15))   + .61D0*YL(12)
      D(11) = .14D0*(Y(6) + X(1) - Y(19)+Y(14)-Y(21)-Y(3)+Y(9) +X(3)
     1 - Y(22))+54.083939D0
      D(10) = 1.39D0*Y(15)+32.D0
      D(9) = .054D0*(Y(6)+X(1)-Y(19)+Y(14)-Y(21)-Y(3) )
     1  + .012D0*Z(1)*Y(10)/Y(15)
      D(8) = YL(8)  +4.11D0-.74D0*(Z(3)-Y(7)-Z(4)-Z(5)) + .52D0*( YL(15)
     1 -YL(23))+ .54D0*Z(6)
      D(7) = X(4) - (Z(4)+Z(5))/1.062D0 +(26.08D0+Y(13)-X(1)-.08D0*Y(16)
     1 -.08D0*YL(16)  -2.05*Z(6) )/ 2.304537D0
      D(6) = -1.4 + .24D0*(Y(13)-X(1))+ .24D0*(YL(13)  -XL(1))
     1 + .29D0*Z(6)
      D(5) = 7.25D0+.05D0*(Y(16)+YL(16))  +.044D0*(Y(13)-X(1))
      D(4) = -7.6D0 +.68*Y(14)
      D(3) = -3.53D0+.72D0*(Y(4)-Y(20))-.028D0*YL(17)
      D(2) = -16.71D0+.78D0*(YL(14)-YL(21)+YL(9)+XL(3)-YL(22)
     1 + YL(5))    - .073D0*YL(16)  +.14D0*YL(12)
      D(1) = -22.26 + .55*(Y(6)+X(1)-Y(19)) + .41D0*(Y(14)-Y(21)-Y(3))
     1 + .34D0*(Y(9)+X(3)-Y(22)) + .26D0*YL(1)  +.072D0*YL(11)  +.26D0*
     2 Z(2)
      GO TO 99
C     THIS IS WHAT USED TO BE THE OLD MODELS PART: SEE CHOW (1981)
C
 999  CONTINUE
C
C
C     STATEMENTS FOR MODELI ARE NEXT ::::::::::::::::::::::::::
C
      D(23)=YL(15)
  99  RETURN
      END
```

Table 13.2 A Program to Simulate the Klein-Goldberger Model

```
==CH13
/$  FOR DETAIL SEE CHOW (1981, CHAPS. 2 & 5)
/$  AND "NATIVE" B34S CONTROL SYNTAX
/$
/$  ON CMS  FIRST COMPILE MODEL USING FORTVCE CH13MOD (OPT(3)
/$  NEXT GIVE  FILEDEF B34SLIB DISK CH13MOD MODULE
B34SEXEC OPTCONTROL MOD=CH13MOD $
PGMCARDS$
 &DIMENS NY=23,NX=4,NS=22,NW=6,NPD=5
 &END
 &OPT OSUP=3,DAMP=1.0,ITERL2=150
     EPS1=0.0001,EPS2=0.0001,UGZ=T
     NROUND=1,ITERL1=5,GAMMA=6
 &END
IDENTVEC I2
15
VARBLVEC 20I3
  1  2  3  4  5  6  7  8  9 10  0  0 13 14 15 16  0 18 19 20
 21 22 23  0 25  0 27  0  0 30 31  0 33 34 35 36 37 38 39  0
  0 42 43 44 45 46  0 48  0 50 51 52 53
V        9F8.4
.9718  8.6789  29.4632 .49     .4886  1.0661  1.0126  23.6293 .9120
.0003  1.6669  246.9927

KCAP    7F10.0                        Y7,Y15,Y26,Y27
  0.0       0.0       0.0       0.0       0.0       0.0       1.0
  0.0       0.0       0.0       0.0       0.0       1.0       1.0
  1.0       0.0       0.0       0.0       0.0       0.0       0.0
  0.0       0.0       0.0       0.0       1.0       0.0
Z0      8F9.0
111.4    24.3      1.9     16.51     19.35     78.65     56.0      326.2
7.3     303.0     95.2     38.10     172.0     35.17     202.4     41.5
.19     14.51     8.63     10.14     13.72      .38     197.5      15.12
0.0      .1187    9.393
ZRATE   7F10.0
1.0       1.0       1.0       1.0       1.0       1.0       1.02
1.035     1.0       1.0       1.0       1.0       1.05      1.05
1.01      1.0       1.0       1.0       1.0       1.0       1.0
1.0       1.0       1.0       1.0       1.0       1.03
Y0      7F10.0
111.4    24.3       1.9     16.51     19.35     78.65     56.0
326.2     7.3     303.0     95.2      38.1     172.0     35.17
202.4    41.5       .19     14.51      8.63     10.14     13.72
  .38    197.5     15.12      0.0      .1187    9.393
W       6F12.6
  171.859985 159.6        67.63       6.53      4.25      24.00
  171.859985 162.114990   68.629990   6.649999  4.222     25.000000
  171.859985 164.703979   69.593994   6.767999  4.203     26.000000
  171.859985 167.292984   70.557983   6.885999  4.187     27.000000
  171.859985 169.969672   71.545795   7.003061  4.173     28.000000
X       4F15.6
      15.700000    33.500000    0.117000     9.709999
      16.170996    34.504991    0.120510    10.001296
      16.656111    35.540109    0.124125    10.301326
      17.155779    36.606281    0.127849    10.610357
      17.670435    37.704432    0.131684    10.928657
Y       8F9.0/8F9.0/7F9.0
111.4    24.3       1.9     16.51     19.35     78.65     56.0      326.2
7.3     303.0     95.2      38.1     172.0     35.17     202.4     41.5
.19     14.51     8.63     10.14     13.72      .38     197.5
GAMVAR  6I5
    7   13    14    15    26    27
B34SRETURN$ B34SEEND$
==
```

Table 13.3 Revised Control Language for Klein-Goldberger Model

```
==RCH13
/$
/$  USES NEW CONTROL LANGUAGE
/$
B34SEXEC OPTCONTROL MOD=CH13MOD $
 OPTIONS NY=23,NX=4,NS=22,NW=6,NPD=5
         OSUP=3,DAMP=1.0,ITERL2=150,UGZ=T
         EPS1=0.0001,EPS2=0.0001
         NROUND=1,ITERL1=5,GAMMA=6 $
 IDENTVEC=15   COMMENT('SETS LAG OF VAR 15')$
 VARBLVEC=(1 2 3 4 5 6 7 8 9 10 0 0 13 14 15 16 0 18 19 20
           21 22 23 0 25 0 27 0 0 30 31 0 33 34 35 36 37 38 39 0
           0 42 43 44 45 46  0 48  0 50 51 52 53)
           COMMENT=('SETS PARTIALS')$
 V = (.9718  8.6789  29.4632 .49 .4886 1.0661 1.0126
      23.6293 .9120 .0003    1.6669  246.9927 0. 0. 0. 0. 0. 0. 0.
      0. 0. 0.) COMMENT('VAR-COV')$
 KCAP=(0.0 0.0 0.0 0.0 0.0 0.0 0.0 1.0 0.0 0.0 0.0 0.0 0.0 0.0 1.0 1.0
       1.0 0.0 0.0 0.0 0.0 0.0 0.0 0.0 0.0 0.0 0.0 0.0 0.0 1.0 0.0)
       COMMENT=('Y7, Y15, Y26 Y27')$
 ZO =(111.4 24.3 1.9 16.51 19.35 78.65 56.0 326.2
      7.3   303.0 95.2 38.10 172.0 35.17 202.4 41.5
      .19 14.51 8.63 10.14 13.72 .38 197.5 15.12
      0.0  .1187 9.393) COMMENT=('INITIAL TARGET VALUES')$
 ZRATE=(1.0  1.0 1.0 1.0 1.0 1.0 1.02 1.035 1.0 1.0 1.0 1.0 1.05 1.05
        1.01 1.0 1.0 1.0 1.0 1.0 1.0   1.0   1.0 1.0 1.0 1.0 1.03 )
        COMMENT=('TARGET GROWTH RATE')$
 YO =(111.4 24.3 1.9 16.51 19.35 78.65 56.0
      326.2 7.3 303.0 95.2 38.1 172.0 35.17
      202.4 41.5 .19 14.51 8.63 10.14 13.72
      .38 197.5 15.12 0.0 .1187 9.393) COMMENT=('INITIAL Y-X VECTOR')$
 W =(171.859985 159.6        67.63      6.53      4.25     24.00
     171.859985 162.114990  68.629990 6.649999 4.222  25.000000
     171.859985 164.703979  69.593994 6.767999 4.203  26.000000
     171.859985 167.292984  70.557983 6.885999 4.187  27.000000
     171.859985 169.969672  71.545795 7.003061 4.173  28.000000)
   COMMENT=('EXOGENOUS VARIABLES FOR ALL PERIODS')$
 X =(15.700000 33.500000 0.117000  9.709999
     16.170996 34.504991 0.120510 10.001296
     16.656111 35.540109 0.124125 10.301326
     17.155779 36.606281 0.127849 10.610357
     17.670435 37.704432 0.131684 10.928657) COMMENT=('POLICY GUESS')$
 Y =(111.4 24.3 1.9 16.51 19.35 78.65 56.0 326.2
     7.3 303.0 95.2 38.1 172.0 35.17 202.4 41.5
     .19 14.51 8.63 10.14 13.72 .38 197.5 15.12)
     COMMENT=('INITIAL Y')$
 GAMVAR=(7 13 14 15 26 27) COMMENT=('ROW COLS OF GAMMA TO PRINT')$
 B34SRETURN$
 B34SEEND$
==
```

The Klein-Goldberger model is given in Chow (1981, 22-24). Table 13.4 lists all input variables in the order listed in SUBROUTINE CH13MOD. With this table it is possible to reconstruct the model.[6] The user-supplied FORTRAN SUBROUTINE contains arguments:

II	- If II = 0, routine branches to NS structural equations.
	- If II $\neq$ 0, routine branches to NID identities of the lagged variables.
NY	- # of structural variables.
NX	- # of control variables.
NW	- # of uncontrolled exogenous variables.
D	- Vector of new values of endogenous variables.
Y	- Vector of endogenous variables.
YL	- Vector of lagged endogenous variables.
XL	- Vector of lagged control variables.
X	- Vector of control variables.
Z	- Vector of exogenous variables.
IBAD	- Set to 0 for normal return. Set to 1 if some endogenous variable, D(i), gets outside the acceptable range.

The control setup in Table 13.2 or 13.3 lists NS=22, NY=23. This implies that there is one identity (NID = NY-NS). The FORTRAN in Table 13.1 indicates this identity is $Y23_t = Y15_{t-1}$

Table 13.4 Variables Listed in SUBROUTINE CH13MOD

Variable	Description
Y23	Lag of one period of price index of GNP ($\equiv Y15_{t-1}$)
Y22	Taxes less transfers
Y21	Personal and corporate taxes less transfers
Y20	Corporate income tax
Y19	Personal payroll taxes less transfers
Y18	Indirect taxes less subsidies
Y17	End-of-year corporate surplus
Y16	End-of-year stock of private capital
Y15	Price index of GNP
Y14	Nonwage nonfarm income
Y13	Gross national product
Y12	End-of-year liquid assets held by businesses
Y11	End-of-year liquid assets held by persons
Y10	Index of agricultural prices
Y9	Farm income
Y8	Index of hourly wages
Y7	Number of wage and salary earners
Y6	Private employee compensation
Y5	Capital consumption charges
Y4	Corporate profits
Y3	Corporate savings
Y2	Gross private domestic capital formulation
Y1	Consumer expenditures
X4	Number of government workers
X3	Government payments to farmers
X2	Government expenditures for goods and services
X1	Government employee compensation
Z6	Time, defined as 0 for 1929 and 24 for 1953
Z5	Number of farm operators
Z4	Number of nonfarm entrepreneurs
Z3	Number of persons in the labor force
Z2	Number of persons in the United States
Z1	Index of agricultural exports

Y1-Y23 lists state variables. X1-X4 lists control variables.
Z1-Z6 lists exogenous variables

The parameter W in Table 13.3 inputs values for all six exogenous Z variables for the five periods of the simulation. For example, note that the index of agricultural exports, Z1, is held fixed at 171.859985, while the number of persons in the United States, Z2, increases from 159.6 to 169.969672 or grows at

1.586182%. The K matrix is inputed with the KCAP parameter. This
vector is all 0.0, except for Y7, Y13, Y14, Y15 and Y26, where it
is set to 1.0. The diagonal elements of the variance-covariance
matrix of the NS structural equations are inputed in V. For
example, the variance of the consumer expenditures equation, Y1, is
.9718.   The vector Z0 contains an initial guess for the targets,
while ZRATE contains the growth rates for the targets. All values
1.0 in ZRATE indicate no change in the targets. Since the seventh
element in ZRATE is 1.02, it indicates that the target for the
number of wage and salary workers, Y7, should increase from 56.0 to
57.12 (= 56 * 1.02), then to 58.2624 (= 56 * 1.02²), etc. The
graphic output of the program (displayed below) will indicate how
close the final solution is to this objective since the targets and
the fitted values are given. The situation for Y7 is shown on page
18 of the following output. Residual analysis, similar to what is
performed in the estimation phase, provides a graphic analysis of
whether there is a systematic policy error. The X vector supplies
a tentative policy for the control variables. If this initial guess
is not reasonable, the solution may have trouble converging. The
initial guesses suggest increasing X1 along the vector 15.7,
16.170996, 16.656111, 17.155779 and 17.670435. The final solution,
listed on page 17 of the program output (for row 24), suggests that
a better path would be 18.7978021, 21.5477687, 23.9961604,
26.3643654 and 28.7254491. With this solution the welfare cost from
equation (13.1-2) was found to be .473711D+03.   Edited output from
running a simulation of the Klein-Goldberger model, using this
setup, will be displayed next.

B34S OPTIMAL CONTROL OPTION CALLED. IOPT= 0

INPUT PARAMETERS SET AS:

```
                    INPUT UNIT =                    5
                    OUTPUT UNIT =                   6
                    SOLUTION UNIT =                11
                    FIRST PARTIALS UNIT            12
                    BIG AND LITTLE G UNIT          13
                    A(T), C(T)*G(T), V(T) UNIT     14
                    DDNAME FOR MODEL               B34SLIB
                    MODEL NAME                     CH13MOD
```

```
                    ---------------------------------------
                    OPTIMAL CONTROL OF NON-LINEAR SYSTEM
                    ---------------------------------------
```

PROGRAM WRITTEN BY CHOW AND BUTTERS

MODIFIED FOR B34S BY HOUSTON H. STOKES (WITH ASSISTANCE OF M. TAM) 1 JUNE 1982

FOR A FULL DESCRIPTION SEE: ANALYSIS AND CONTROL OF DYNAMIC ECONOMIC SYSTEMS - BY G. CHOW(1975)

                        ECONOMIC ANALYSIS BY CONTROL METHODS   -   BY G. CHOW(1981)

INPUT OPTIONS

OF STRUCTURAL EQ (NS) =   22
OF ENDOGENOUS VAR (NY) - NOTE: NY = NS + # OF LAGGED VAR IDENTITIES - =   23
OF CONTROL VAR (NX) =   4
OF UNCONTROLLABLE VAR (NW) =   6
OF TIME PERIODS FOR PLAN =   5

PROGRAM SWITCHES

MATRIX PRINT CONTROL (OSUP) =   3
SOLUTION PRINT CONTROL (GAUSS) = 0
COVARIANCE MATRIX SWITCH (GAMMA) =   6
SOLUTION VALUES PLOT SWITCH (PLOT) = 0
IF UGZ=T - TARGETS GROW AT CONSTANT % ... USER SUPPLIES INITIAL Z(0) AND BIG Z0 VECTOR AND RATE OF GROWTH
IF UGZ=F - USER SUPPLIES TARGETS FOR ALL PERIODS --- UGZ = T
OFDIAV=F - USER SUPPLIES ELEMENTS OF COVARIANCE MATRIX V
OFDIAV=F - USER SUPPLIES ONLY DIAGONAL ELEMENTS OF V -- OFDIAV = F
OFDIAG=F - K MATRIX IN LOSS FUNCTION HAS NONZERO OFF DIAGONAL ELEMENTS
OFDIAG=F - K MATRIX IN LOSS FUNCTION HAS ZERO OFF DIAGONAL ELEMENTS --   OFDIAG= F
DISCOUNT FACTOR FOR MODIFYING THE H MATRIX IN LOSS FUNCTION (EXKCAP) =   1.0000000
OF THE RUN TO SOLVE THE MODEL (NROUND) =   1
MAXIMUM # OF TIMES MODEL WILL BE LINEARIZED (ITERL1) =   5
MAXIMUM # OF GAUSS-SEIDEL ITERATIONS ALLOWED (ITERL2) =   150
CONVERGENCE CRITERION FOR OPTIMAL POLICY (EPS1) =   0.10000000E-03
CONVERGENCE CRITERION FOR GAUSS-SEIDEL ITERATION (EPS2) =   0.10000000E-03
STEPSIZE FOR FIRST DERIVATIVE CALCULATION (FDFRAC) =   0.10000000E-02
MINIMUM STEP (FDMIN) =   0.10000000E-02
FACTOR TO DAMPEN Y SOLUTION (DAMP) =   1.0000000   FACTOR TO DAMPEN ITERATIONS ON CONTROL VAR (DAMPX) =   1.0000000

INPUT MATRICES

IDENTVEC(NY-NS) = INDEX # OF LAGGED VAR IN IDENTITIES
VARBLVEC(NS+NY+NX+NX) LOCATION OF VARIABLES WHOSE PARTIAL DERIVATIVE IS NON ZERO
V(NS) (OR LOWER TRIANGULAR) = VARIANCE COVARIANCE MATRIX
KCAP(NY+NX) = WEIGHTING MATRIX
Z0(NY+NX)= INITIAL VALUES FOR TARGETS FOR Y
ZRATE(NY+NX) GROWTH RATE FOR TARGET
Z(NPD,(NY+NX)) = TARGETS
W(NPD,NW) = EXOGENOUS VARIABLES FOR ALL PERIODS (ONLY READ IN IF NW NE 0)
X(NPD,NX) = TENTATIVE POLICY FOR ALL PERIODS
Y(NY) = A TRIAL SOLUTION OF THE Y VECTOR
GAMVAR(N) ROW AND COL NUMBERS OF THE GAMMA N TO BE PRINTED... USED ONLY IF GAMMA=N ..

DISCUSSION OF OUTPUT

STORAGE IN VARBLVEC: Y(1,T),...,Y(NS,T),Y(1,T-1),...,Y(NY,T-1),X(1,T-1),...,X(NX,T-1),X(1,T),...,X(NX,T)

A(T), C(T), B(T), G(T), H(T), LITTLEG(T), LITTLEH(T) DEFINED IN CHOW(1975) AND CHAPTER 1 OF CHOW(1981)

BASIC MODEL: Y(T)=A(T)*Y(T-1) + C(T)*X(T) + B(T) + U(T)

OPTIMAL POLICY FOR THE LAST PERIOD: XHAT(T)=G(T)*Y(T-1) + LITTLEG(T)

GIVEN : G(T) = -((TRANS(C(T))*H(T)*C(T))**(-1))*(TRANS(C(T))*H(T)*A(T))

        LITTLEG(T)=-((TRANS(C(T))*H(T)*C(T))**(-1))*TRANS((C(T))**H(T)*B(T)-LITTLEH(T)))

&DIMENS
NY=   23,NX=   4,NW=   6,NPD=   5,NS=   22
&END
&OPT
OSUP=   3,OFDIAG=F,UGZ=T,EXKCAP= 1.0000000000000000   ,PLOT=   0,OFDIAV=F,NROUND=   1,GAUSS=   0,
GAMMA=   6,ITERL1=   5,ITERL2=   150,EPS1= 0.10000000000000001E-03,EPS2= 0.10000000000000001E-03,FDFRAC=
 0.10000000000000002E-02,FDMIN= 0.10000000000000002E-02,DAMP= 1.0000000000000000   ,DAMPX= 1.0000000000000000
&END

OPTIMAL CONTROL CALCULATIONS   PAGE   1   SEC USED =   0.00

STORAGE ALLOCATION TO THIS POINT = 2388 WORDS OUT OF 70000   (264K UNUSED)

STORAGE ALLOCATION TO THIS POINT = 2389 WORDS OUT OF 70000   (264K UNUSED)

OPTIMAL CONTROL CALCULATIONS   PAGE 15   SEC USED =   0.66

```
                                        ************
                                        ITERATION    4
                                        ************
```

STORAGE ALLOCATION TO THIS POINT = 5170 WORDS OUT OF 70000   (252K UNUSED)

STORAGE ALLOCATION TO THIS POINT = 4402 WORDS OUT OF 70000   (256K UNUSED)

C'HC

	- 1 -	- 2 -	- 3 -	- 4 -
- 1 -	7.34656383	-4.58760588	-0.31423768	-10.8790972
- 2 -	-4.58760588	5.31429387	0.24402958	7.42994091
- 3 -	-0.31423768	0.24402958	1.86973295	1.35926995
- 4 -	-10.8790972	7.42994091	1.35926995	17.3545712

C'HC

	- 1 -	- 2 -	- 3 -	- 4 -
- 1 -	7.74951715	-4.71338799	-0.33872258	-11.2928053
- 2 -	-4.71338799	5.31111773	0.24463497	7.49367077
- 3 -	-0.33872258	0.24463497	1.87011607	1.37346935
- 4 -	-11.2928053	7.49367077	1.37346935	17.6787715

C'HC

	- 1 -	- 2 -	- 3 -	- 4 -
- 1 -	8.16649985	-4.82263908	-0.35921934	-11.6907261
- 2 -	-4.82263908	5.28717645	0.24091072	7.51736169
- 3 -	-0.35921934	0.24091072	1.86965708	1.37889210
- 4 -	-11.6907261	7.51736169	1.37889210	17.9355227

C'HC

	- 1 -	- 2 -	- 3 -	- 4 -
- 1 -	8.62185460	-4.93499491	-0.38019536	-12.1145773
- 2 -	-4.93499491	5.25884377	0.23628769	7.53626497
- 3 -	-0.38019536	0.23628769	1.86901627	1.38330140
- 4 -	-12.1145773	7.53626497	1.38330140	18.1993812

C'HC

	- 1 -	- 2 -	- 3 -	- 4 -
- 1 -	9.10856136	-5.04037156	-0.40072781	-12.5494437
- 2 -	-5.04037156	5.21837413	0.22983337	7.53521216
- 3 -	-0.40072781	0.22983337	1.86809304	1.38517515
- 4 -	-12.5494437	7.53521216	1.38517515	18.4450381

OPTIMAL CONTROL CALCULATIONS   PAGE 16   SEC USED =   0.83

G(001)

	- 1 -	- 2 -	- 3 -	- 4 -
- 1 -	31.4419520	107.799588	14.1170745	46.5877755

GCAP(001)

	- 1 -	- 3 -	- 5 -	- 7 -	- 8 -	- 9 -	- 11 -	- 12 -	- 13 -	- 14 -
- 1 -	-4.4409D-16	-0.01288469	-0.03420036	0.0000D+00	0.12678420	-0.03420036	0.0000D+00	-0.00669079	-0.32666030	-0.02131567
- 2 -	-0.26000000	-0.10708050	-0.76222863	0.0000D+00	-0.00516065	-0.76222863	-0.07200000	-0.13689240	0.01056349	-0.65514813
- 3 -	4.4409D-16	-0.00198484	-0.00500387	0.0000D+00	-0.04002152	-0.00500387	4.1633D-17	-0.00084013	-0.00182659	-0.00301902
- 4 -	-6.6613D-16	-0.01074763	-0.00283066	0.0000D+00	-0.04815587	-0.00283066	-2.7756D-17	-0.00091426	-0.14661196	0.00791696

	- 15 -	- 16 -	- 17 -	- 20 -	- 21 -	- 22 -	- 23 -	- 24 -	- 25 -	- 26 -
- 1 -	0.07508160	-0.08041991	-0.00091175	-0.01287180	0.03420036	0.03420036	-0.06592778	0.32666030	0.0000D+00	-0.03420036
- 2 -	0.01070172	0.11752857	-0.00843600	-0.10697342	0.76222863	0.76222863	0.00268354	-0.01056349	0.0000D+00	-0.76222863
- 3 -	-0.02140096	-0.01279358	-0.00016783	-0.00198286	0.00500387	0.00500387	0.02081119	0.00182659	0.0000D+00	-0.00500387
- 4 -	-0.01767946	-0.00367766	-0.00077310	-0.01073688	0.00283066	0.00283066	0.02504105	0.14661196	0.0000D+00	-0.00283066

	- 27 -
- 1 -	0.0000D+00
- 2 -	0.0000D+00
- 3 -	0.0000D+00
- 4 -	0.0000D+00

STORAGE ALLOCATION TO THIS POINT = 4546 WORDS OUT OF 70000   (254K UNUSED)

OPTIMAL CONTROL CALCULATIONS   PAGE 17   SEC USED =   0.85

Y(T) FOR T = 1 TO NPD

	- 1 -	- 2 -	- 3 -	- 4 -	- 5 -
- 1 -	117.504790	120.835944	125.463204	130.562815	135.943860
- 2 -	22.9086860	24.5195696	25.6344483	27.0199442	28.4711258
- 3 -	1.38388828	1.79671545	2.22189105	2.66429616	3.12395813
- 4 -	17.3374230	18.4769645	19.6769417	20.9504407	22.2988097
- 5 -	18.7341205	19.4778710	20.3125459	21.2102510	22.1782375

```
-  6 -    82.0769771   85.1248045   88.6843869   92.5614980   96.6916413
-  7 -    56.2329801   57.0748930   57.9292772   58.8080185   59.7513996
-  8 -   345.361380   363.536550   382.270177   401.573021   421.477453
-  9 -     9.31962347    9.59117832    9.88692333   10.1950624   10.5160548
- 10 -   316.198158   319.130556   322.107641   325.133275   328.419076
- 11 -    71.1881905   71.9159822   72.7102869   73.5402907   74.4062099
- 12 -    41.4956521   44.3462764   47.0022557   49.6213754   52.2442244
- 13 -   180.738538   189.918716   199.560157   209.681609   220.290042
- 14 -    36.6726805   38.3484767   40.1131491   41.9859418   43.9688373
- 15 -   204.459107   206.568746   208.710533   210.887248   213.251134
- 16 -    45.6745616   50.7164241   56.0381765   61.8476689   68.1402398
- 17 -     1.57398008    3.37060527    5.59233174    8.25637402   11.3800612
- 18 -    15.3395382   16.1877717   17.0786500   18.0138953   18.9941216
- 19 -     8.26863892    9.10098097    9.97307901   10.8838812   11.8329501
- 20 -    10.5051893   11.0175382   11.5571250   12.1297720   12.7361200
- 21 -    14.3721927   15.5108801   16.4487224   17.4470137   18.5039291
- 22 -     0.46680903    0.47267339    0.48001950    0.48875504    0.49828459
- 23 -   202.400000   204.459107   206.568746   208.710533   210.887248
- 24 -    18.7978021   21.5477687   23.9961604   26.3643654   28.7254491
- 25 -    40.3250745   44.5630413   48.4625230   52.0989030   55.8751831
- 26 -    -0.20226710   -0.35926935   -0.51154922   -0.64905942   -0.78393650
- 27 -     9.17181458    8.51960530    7.59526813    6.48167512    5.25301898
```

TOTAL WELFARE COST =   0.4737117D+03

DETERMINISTIC COMPONENT: 0.178592D+02   STOCHASTIC COMPONENT: 0.455852D+03

OPTIMAL CONTROL CALCULATIONS   PAGE 18   SEC USED =   0.86

PLOT OF Y(7)

```
                    MEAN OF    5 RESIDUALS  =  1.49164112
                    STD. DEV. (   4 D.F.)  =  0.47463141
                    CORRECTED DURBIN-WATSON =  0.09496428
```

OBS	TARGET	FITTED	<--- TARGET(*) AND FITTED(+) VALUES --->	RESIDUAL	-3	-2	-1	0	1	2	3
1	57.1200000	56.2329801	+ *	0.88701991	.	.	.	.	.	>.	.
2	58.2624000	57.0748930	+ *	1.18750704	.	.	.	.	.	. > .	
3	59.4276480	57.9292772	+ *	1.49837081	.	.	.	.	.	.	.
4	60.6162010	58.8080185	+ *	1.80818241	.	.	.	.	.	.	.
5	61.8285250	59.7513996	+ *	2.07712542	.	.	.	.	.	.	.

OPTIMAL CONTROL CALCULATIONS   PAGE 19   SEC USED =   0.86

PLOT OF Y(13)

```
                    MEAN OF    5 RESIDUALS  = -0.45201184
                    STD. DEV. (   4 D.F.)  =  0.25111090
                    CORRECTED DURBIN-WATSON =  0.09333662
```

OBS	TARGET	FITTED	<--- TARGET(*) AND FITTED(+) VALUES --->	RESIDUAL	-3	-2	-1	0	1	2	3
1	180.600000	180.738538	+	-0.13853834	.	.	. <	.	.	.	.
2	189.630000	189.918716	+	-0.28871642	.	.	<.	.	.	.	.
3	199.111500	199.560157	*+	-0.44865652	.	.<	.	.	.	.	.
4	209.067075	209.681609	*+	-0.61453425	. <	.	.	.	.	.	.
5	219.520429	220.290042	+	-0.76961365	<	.	.	.	.	.	.

OPTIMAL CONTROL CALCULATIONS   PAGE 20   SEC USED =   0.86

PLOT OF Y(14)

```
                    MEAN OF    5 RESIDUALS  =  0.59283763
                    STD. DEV. (   4 D.F.)  =  0.26274638
                    CORRECTED DURBIN-WATSON =  0.08620211
```

OBS	TARGET	FITTED	<--- TARGET(*) AND FITTED(+) VALUES --->	RESIDUAL	-3	-2	-1	0	1	2	3
1	36.9285000	36.6726805	+*	0.25581949	.	.	.	.	>	.	.
2	38.7749250	38.3484767	+ *	0.42644826	.	.	.	.	. >	.	
3	40.7136713	40.1131491	+ *	0.60052211	.	.	.	.	.>	.	
4	42.7493548	41.9859418	+ *	0.76341303	.	.	.	.	.	>	
5	44.8868226	43.9688373	+ *	0.91798526	.	.	.	.	.	.	

OPTIMAL CONTROL CALCULATIONS   PAGE 21   SEC USED =   0.87

PLOT OF Y(15)

```
                    MEAN OF    5 RESIDUALS  = -0.22178385
                    STD. DEV. (   4 D.F.)  =  0.19151434
                    CORRECTED DURBIN-WATSON =  0.21957647
```

OBS	TARGET	FITTED	<--- TARGET(*) AND FITTED(+) VALUES --->	RESIDUAL	-3	-2	-1	0	1	2	3

```
    1    204.424000  204.459107 +                                            -0.03510660  .    .    .   <.    .    .    .
    2    206.468240  206.568746          +                                   -0.10050558  .    .   .< .    .    .    .
    3    208.532922  208.710533                       *+                     -0.17761034  .    .   <    .    .    .    .
    4    210.618252  210.887248                                 *+           -0.26899685  .    . < .    .    .    .    .
    5    212.724434  213.251134                                      *  +    -0.52669990  .<   .    .    .    .    .    .
OPTIMAL CONTROL CALCULATIONS                                                            PAGE  22           SEC USED =    0.87
PLOT OF Y( 24)
                      MEAN OF     5 RESIDUALS  = -8.76630916
                      STD. DEV. (    4 D.F.) =  3.90294058
                      CORRECTED DURBIN-WATSON =  0.08595828


   OBS    TARGET      FITTED     <--- TARGET(*) AND FITTED(+) VALUES --->   RESIDUAL   -3   -2   -1   0    1    2    3

    1    15.1200000  18.7978021 *      +                                    -3.67780209  .    .    <    .    .    .    .
    2    15.1200000  21.5477687 *             +                             -6.42776873  .    . .< .    .    .    .    .
    3    15.1200000  23.9961604 *                      +                    -8.87616045  .   .<    .    .    .    .    .
    4    15.1200000  26.3643654 *                            +              -11.2443654 .<   .    .    .    .    .    .
    5    15.1200000  28.7254491 *                                 +         -13.6054491  .    .    .    .    .    .    .
OPTIMAL CONTROL CALCULATIONS                                                            PAGE  23           SEC USED =    0.87
PLOT OF Y( 25)
                      MEAN OF     5 RESIDUALS  = -48.2649450
                      STD. DEV. (    4 D.F.) =  6.11145705
                      CORRECTED DURBIN-WATSON =  0.14298316


   OBS    TARGET      FITTED     <--- TARGET(*) AND FITTED(+) VALUES --->   RESIDUAL   -3   -2   -1   0    1    2    3

    1    0.0000D+00  40.3250745 *                             +            -40.3250745  .    .    .    .    .    .    .
    2    0.0000D+00  44.5630413 *                               +          -44.5630413  .    .    .    .    .    .    .
    3    0.0000D+00  48.4625230 *                                 +        -48.4625230  .    .    .    .    .    .    .
    4    0.0000D+00  52.0989030 *                                   +      -52.0989030  .    .    .    .    .    .    .
    5    0.0000D+00  55.8751831 *                                     +    -55.8751831  .    .    .    .    .    .    .
OPTIMAL CONTROL CALCULATIONS                                                            PAGE  24           SEC USED =    0.87
PLOT OF Y( 26)
                      MEAN OF     5 RESIDUALS  =  0.61991632
                      STD. DEV. (    4 D.F.) =  0.22989923
                      CORRECTED DURBIN-WATSON =  0.08812415


   OBS    TARGET      FITTED     <--- TARGET(*) AND FITTED(+) VALUES --->   RESIDUAL   -3   -2   -1   0    1    2    3

    1    0.11870000 -0.20226710                            +               *  0.32096710  .    .    .    .    .  .>  .   .
    2    0.11870000 -0.35926935                      +                      *  0.47796935  .    .    .    .    .   .>    .
    3    0.11870000 -0.51154922                +                            *  0.63024922  .    .    .    .    .    .  >.
    4    0.11870000 -0.64905942        +                                    *  0.76775942  .    .    .    .    .    .    .
    5    0.11870000 -0.78393650 +                                           *  0.90263650  .    .    .    .    .    .    .
OPTIMAL CONTROL CALCULATIONS                                                            PAGE  25           SEC USED =    0.87
PLOT OF Y( 27)
                      MEAN OF     5 RESIDUALS  =  2.86867838
                      STD. DEV. (    4 D.F.) =  2.05016253
                      CORRECTED DURBIN-WATSON =  0.12160049


   OBS    TARGET      FITTED     <--- TARGET(*) AND FITTED(+) VALUES --->   RESIDUAL   -3   -2   -1   0    1    2    3

    1    9.67479000  9.17181458                              +   *           0.50297542  .    .    .    .  .>  .    .    .
    2    9.96503370  8.51960530                           +        *         1.44542840  .    .    .    .    .  >.   .    .
    3    10.2639847  7.59526813                      +              *         2.66871658  .    .    .    .    .  .>   .    .
    4    10.5719043  6.48167512          +                         *         4.09022913  .    .    .    .    .    .  >  .
    5    10.8890614  5.25301898 +                                  *         5.63604240  .    .    .    .    .    .  .>.
STORAGE ALLOCATION TO THIS POINT =   3695  WORDS OUT OF  70000    (258K UNUSED)


GAMVAR  6I5

             -   1   -
   -  1  -            7
   -  2  -           13
   -  3  -           14
```

```
  -  4  -        15
  -  5  -        26
  -  6  -        27
OPTIMAL CONTROL CALCULATIONS                                      PAGE  26        SEC USED =    0.88


LIST OF GAMMA VARIABLES BEING PRINTED

                 -  1  -
  -  1  -         7
  -  2  -        13
  -  3  -        14
  -  4  -        15
  -  5  -        26
  -  6  -        27


GAMMA(001)

            -   1   -    -   2   -    -   3   -    -   4   -    -   5   -    -   6   -
  -  1  -   4.63462723   8.59572447   4.50877789  14.3812819   0.0000D+00   0.0000D+00
  -  2  -   8.59572447  20.4309578  10.7760084   24.3480583   0.0000D+00   0.0000D+00
  -  3  -   4.50877789  10.7760084   8.06542188  14.9047689    0.0000D+00   0.0000D+00
  -  4  -  14.3812819   24.3480583  14.9047689   58.4640353    0.0000D+00   0.0000D+00
  -  5  -   0.0000D+00   0.0000D+00   0.0000D+00   0.0000D+00   0.0000D+00   0.0000D+00
  -  6  -   0.0000D+00   0.0000D+00   0.0000D+00   0.0000D+00   0.0000D+00   0.0000D+00


GAMMA(002)

            -   1   -    -   2   -    -   3   -    -   4   -    -   5   -    -   6   -
  -  1  -   5.20868912   8.42155481   4.77417555  14.3605748   0.25607821   0.53270980
  -  2  -   8.42155481  20.5571154  10.7134610   24.6521625  -0.09177647  -0.19480041
  -  3  -   4.77417555  10.7134610   8.19257807  14.8999788   0.11507024   0.24240654
  -  4  -  14.3605748   24.6521625  14.8999788   57.7370935  -0.04749512  -0.10283568
  -  5  -   0.25607821  -0.09177647   0.11507024  -0.04749512   0.11693630   0.24512606
  -  6  -   0.53270980  -0.19480041   0.24240654  -0.10283568   0.24512606   0.73604116


GAMMA(003)

            -   1   -    -   2   -    -   3   -    -   4   -    -   5   -    -   6   -
  -  1  -   5.37584249   8.37755769   4.84540661  14.3790213   0.32156627   0.61064740
  -  2  -   8.37755769  20.5977542  10.7015271   24.8513332  -0.11357331  -0.22039298
  -  3  -   4.84540661  10.7015271   8.22387453  14.8949895   0.14165133   0.27253756
  -  4  -  14.3790213   24.8513332  14.8949895   56.9771264  -0.05936807  -0.11928396
  -  5  -   0.32156627  -0.11357331   0.14165133  -0.05936807   0.14299122   0.27375295
  -  6  -   0.61064740  -0.22039298   0.27253756  -0.11928396   0.27375295   0.81319835

OPTIMAL CONTROL CALCULATIONS                                      PAGE  27        SEC USED =    0.91

GAMMA(004)

            -   1   -    -   2   -    -   3   -    -   4   -    -   5   -    -   6   -
  -  1  -   5.49625024   8.34310692   4.89843840  14.3913814   0.36501079   0.65349045
  -  2  -   8.34310692  20.6383396  10.6932728   25.0308063  -0.13082514  -0.23719764
  -  3  -   4.89843840  10.6932728   8.24831817  14.8855576   0.15959164   0.28811805
  -  4  -  14.3913814   25.0308063  14.8855576   56.2708507  -0.07014937  -0.13262608
  -  5  -   0.36501079  -0.13082514   0.15959164  -0.07014937   0.15886441   0.28613189
  -  6  -   0.65349045  -0.23719764   0.28811805  -0.13262608   0.28613189   0.84418022


GAMMA(005)

            -   1   -    -   2   -    -   3   -    -   4   -    -   5   -    -   6   -
  -  1  -   5.56424561   8.32004826   4.93518530  14.3551228   0.39190433   0.66285627
  -  2  -   8.32004826  20.6771474  10.6873140   25.2032987  -0.14525485  -0.24568008
  -  3  -   4.93518530  10.6873140   8.26856703  14.8513910   0.17325081   0.29303169
  -  4  -  14.3551228   25.2032987  14.8513910   55.6345536  -0.09931796  -0.16798368
  -  5  -   0.39190433  -0.14525485   0.17325081  -0.09931796   0.17031302   0.28806279
  -  6  -   0.66285627  -0.24568008   0.29303169  -0.16798368   0.28806279   0.85007468

NORMAL ENDING OF OPTIMAL CONTROL PROGRAM
```

The next problem makes an apparently minor change in the setup to set the 26th element of KCAP to 0.0. This change removes the 26th Y variable, X3, from the objective function in equation (13.1-2). Recall that the variable X3 was set to .1187 with the Z0 sentence. In the prior problem on page 24 of the output, we see that the X3 variable, which is designated Y26, followed the path -.20336710 ,..., -.78393650, with a mean residual of .61991632. Since the 26th element of KCAP was 1.0, this "twisted" the solution. Once this constraint was removed from the objective function in equation (13.1-2), the values of Y(T) listed below exactly replicate Chow (1981, 27), which for X1, X2, Y13 and Y15 show vectors of {21.21, 26.03, 30.64, 35.38, 40.35}, {39.95, 45.40, 49.74, 53.85, 58.11}, {180.60, 189.63, 199.11, 209.07, 219.52} and {204.42, 206.47, 208.53, 210.62, 212.72}, respectively. On the output below these are shown to be rounded versions of row 24 (X1), row 25 (X2), row 13 (Y13) and row 15 (Y15).

Plots of the target variables, Y7, Y13, Y14 and Y15, now show substantially lower mean residuals than in the former problem. For these four targets the means for the first and second problems were (1.4916, .00004984), (-.45201, .00012007), (.5928, .00005721) and (-.22178, .00027585), respectively. The welfare cost of the revised program fell to .439288D+03. The above example shows how sensitive the analysis is to the specification of the problem.

Y(T) FOR T = 1 TO NPD

```
        -   1  -    -   2  -    -   3  -    -   4  -    -   5  -
-   1 -  117.737599  121.246630  126.094453  131.470757  137.191689
-   2 -   22.9086860   22.9860814   23.2779292   23.7501043   24.2143463
-   3 -    1.45291293    1.90970281    2.37839967    2.86056216    3.35614308
-   4 -   17.5114375   18.7670483   20.0848694   21.4698597   22.9228181
-   5 -   18.6270359   19.2149166   19.7921916   20.3652746   20.9393641
-   6 -   81.4636720   83.3653943   85.8354780   88.5472899   91.4046528
-   7 -   57.1200159   58.2622917   59.4276956   60.6160460   61.8284755
-   8 -  346.017799  365.053626  384.861813  405.461933  426.856546
-   9 -    9.40947692    9.72733056   10.0768404   10.4450028   10.8323876
-  10 -  316.149520  318.991050  321.859082  324.759813  327.685927
-  11 -   71.1449627   71.8497975   72.6328041   73.4595720   74.3318013
-  12 -   41.3452766   43.8141266   45.9572876   47.9635856   49.9256618
-  13 -  180.600031  189.629737  199.111621  209.066692  219.520317
-  14 -   36.9285842   38.7750707   40.7130428   42.7497932   44.8864967
-  15 -  204.424115  206.468381  208.531714  210.618570  212.723689
-  16 -   45.7816560   49.5526265   53.0385019   56.4229638   59.6979521
-  17 -    1.64278451    3.55248779    5.93082758    8.79118565   12.1470597
-  18 -   15.3267397   16.1611189   17.0371240   17.9571225   18.9229707
-  19 -    8.49024831    9.41619150   10.4024488   11.4431507   12.5373502
-  20 -   10.5833362   11.1480195   11.7406064   12.3634356   13.0168511
-  21 -   14.4783292   15.7178809   16.7480920   17.8357621   18.9828500
-  22 -    0.36041032    0.31125894    0.26063806    0.20827225    0.15425505
-  23 -  202.400000  204.424115  206.468381  208.531714  210.618570
-  24 -   21.2147388   26.0342269   30.6426403   35.3802996   40.3539907
-  25 -   39.9537382   45.3971980   49.7389226   53.8459736   58.1141764
-  26 -   -2.37019914   -3.64805832   -4.98630030   -6.37716353   -7.81956684
-  27 -   11.1714407   11.7425113   12.0278715   12.1763405   12.2286528
```

TOTAL WELFARE COST =   0.4392878D+03

DETERMINISTIC COMPONENT: 0.500894D-09   STOCHASTIC COMPONENT: 0.439288D+03

OPTIMAL CONTROL CALCULATIONS   PAGE 111   SEC USED =   1.67

PLOT OF Y(7)

```
                 MEAN OF     5 RESIDUALS  =  0.00004984
                 STD. DEV. (   4 D.F.)    =  0.00008407
                 CORRECTED DURBIN-WATSON  =  2.26344532
```

OBS	TARGET	FITTED	<--- TARGET(*) AND FITTED(+) VALUES --->	RESIDUAL	-3	-2	-1	0	1	2	3
1	57.1200000	57.1200159	+	-0.00001587	.	.	.	<.	.	.	.
2	58.2624000	58.2622917	+	0.00010829	.	.	.	.	.>	.	.
3	59.4276480	59.4276956	+	-0.00004759	.	.	.	<	.	.	.
4	60.6162010	60.6160460	+	0.00015492	.	.	.	.	.	>.	.
5	61.8285250	61.8284755	+	0.00004946	.	.	.	.	>.	.	.

OPTIMAL CONTROL CALCULATIONS   PAGE 112   SEC USED =   1.67

PLOT OF Y(13)

```
                 MEAN OF     5 RESIDUALS  =  0.00012007
                 STD. DEV. (   4 D.F.)    =  0.00020753
                 CORRECTED DURBIN-WATSON  =  2.31591298
```

OBS	TARGET	FITTED	<--- TARGET(*) AND FITTED(+) VALUES --->	RESIDUAL	-3	-2	-1	0	1	2	3
1	180.600000	180.600037	+	-0.00003711	.	.	.	<.	.	.	.
2	189.630000	189.629737	+	0.00026337	.	.	.	.	.>	.	.
3	199.111500	199.111621	+	-0.00012074	.	.	.	<	.	.	.
4	209.067075	209.066692	+	0.00038272	.	.	.	.	.	>.	.
5	219.520429	219.520317	+	0.00011210	.	.	.	.	>.	.	.

OPTIMAL CONTROL CALCULATIONS   PAGE 113   SEC USED =   1.67

PLOT OF Y(14)

```
                    MEAN OF    5 RESIDUALS  =   0.00005721
                    STD. DEV. (   4 D.F.)  =   0.00041989
                    CORRECTED DURBIN-WATSON =  3.23211874
```

OBS	TARGET	FITTED	<--- TARGET(*) AND FITTED(+) VALUES --->	RESIDUAL	-3	-2	-1	0	1	2	3
1	36.9285000	36.9285842	+	-0.00008415	.	.	.	<.	.	.	.
2	38.7749250	38.7750707	+	-0.00014565	.	.	.	< .	.	.	.
3	40.7136713	40.7130428	+	0.00062846	.	.	.	.	.>	.	.
4	42.7493548	42.7497932	+	-0.00043839	.	.	<	.	.	.	.
5	44.8868226	44.8864967	+	0.00032581	.	.	.	.	>.	.	.

OPTIMAL CONTROL CALCULATIONS   PAGE 114   SEC USED =   1.67

PLOT OF Y(15)

```
                    MEAN OF    5 RESIDUALS  =   0.00027585
                    STD. DEV. (   4 D.F.)  =   0.00066527
                    CORRECTED DURBIN-WATSON =  2.46420936
```

OBS	TARGET	FITTED	<--- TARGET(*) AND FITTED(+) VALUES --->	RESIDUAL	-3	-2	-1	0	1	2	3
1	204.424000	204.424115	+	-0.00011491	.	.	.	<.	.	.	.
2	206.468240	206.468381	+	-0.00014096	.	.	.	<.	.	.	.
3	208.532922	208.531714	+	0.00120843	.	.	.	.	>.	.	.
4	210.618252	210.618570	+	-0.00031882	.	.	.	< .	.	.	.
5	212.724434	212.723689	+	0.00074550	.	.	.	.	.>	.	.

OPTIMAL CONTROL CALCULATIONS   PAGE 115   SEC USED =   1.67

PLOT OF Y(24)

```
                    MEAN OF    5 RESIDUALS  = -15.6051793
                    STD. DEV. (   4 D.F.)  =   7.53067857
                    CORRECTED DURBIN-WATSON =  0.08916444
```

OBS	TARGET	FITTED	<--- TARGET(*) AND FITTED(+) VALUES --->	RESIDUAL	-3	-2	-1	0	1	2	3
1	15.1200000	21.2147388	* +	-6.09473882	.	.	.<	.	.	.	.
2	15.1200000	26.0342269	* +	-10.9142269	.	.	< .	.	.	.	.
3	15.1200000	30.6426403	* +	-15.5226403	.	<	.	.	.	.	.
4	15.1200000	35.3802996	* +	-20.2602996	.	<	.	.	.	.	.
5	15.1200000	40.3539907	* +	-25.2339907	.	.	.	.	.	.	.

OPTIMAL CONTROL CALCULATIONS   PAGE 116   SEC USED =   1.68

PLOT OF Y(25)

```
                    MEAN OF    5 RESIDUALS  = -49.4100018
                    STD. DEV. (   4 D.F.)  =   7.08999658
                    CORRECTED DURBIN-WATSON =  0.13538795
```

OBS	TARGET	FITTED	<--- TARGET(*) AND FITTED(+) VALUES --->	RESIDUAL	-3	-2	-1	0	1	2	3
1	0.0000D+00	39.9537382	* +	-39.9537382	.	.	.	.	.	.	.
2	0.0000D+00	45.3971980	* +	-45.3971980	.	.	.	.	.	.	.
3	0.0000D+00	49.7389226	* +	-49.7389226	.	.	.	.	.	.	.
4	0.0000D+00	53.8459736	* +	-53.8459736	.	.	.	.	.	.	.
5	0.0000D+00	58.1141764	* +	-58.1141764	.	.	.	.	.	.	.

OPTIMAL CONTROL CALCULATIONS   PAGE 117   SEC USED =   1.68

PLOT OF Y(26)

```
                    MEAN OF    5 RESIDUALS  =   5.15895762
                    STD. DEV. (   4 D.F.)  =   2.15535494
                    CORRECTED DURBIN-WATSON =  0.08989702
```

OBS	TARGET	FITTED	<--- TARGET(*) AND FITTED(+) VALUES --->	RESIDUAL	-3	-2	-1	0	1	2	3
1	0.11870000	-2.37019914	+ *	2.48889914	.	.	.	.	.>	.	.
2	0.11870000	-3.64805832	+ *	3.76675832	.	.	.	.	.	>.	.
3	0.11870000	-4.98630030	+ *	5.10500030	.	.	.	.	.	. >	.
4	0.11870000	-6.37716353	+ *	6.49586353	.	.	.	.	.	.	>
5	0.11870000	-7.81956684	+ *	7.93826684	.	.	.	.	.	.	.

PLOT OF Y(27)

```
                        MEAN OF      5 RESIDUALS  = -1.59640855
                        STD. DEV. (   4 D.F.)  =   0.18493652
                        CORRECTED DURBIN-WATSON =   0.18747593
```

```
 OBS     TARGET      FITTED     <--- TARGET(*) AND FITTED(+) VALUES --->   RESIDUAL   -3  -2  -1   0   1   2   3

  1    9.67479000  11.1714407  *                      +                   -1.49665066  .   .   .   .   .   .   .

  2    9.96503370  11.7425113  *                           +              -1.77747759  .   .   .   .   .   .   .

  3   10.2639847   12.0278715       *                           +         -1.76388679  .   .   .   .   .   .   .

  4   10.5719043   12.1763405          *                         +        -1.60443625  .   .   .   .   .   .   .

  5   10.8890614   12.2286528             *                         +     -1.33959146  .   .   .   .   .   .   .
```

STORAGE ALLOCATION TO THIS POINT =   3695 WORDS OUT OF 70000   (258K UNUSED)

GAMVAR (16I5)   ROW COLS OF GAMMA TO PRINT

```
            -  1 -
 -  1 -        7
 -  2 -       13
 -  3 -       14
 -  4 -       15
 -  5 -       26
 -  6 -       27
```

LIST OF GAMMA VARIABLES BEING PRINTED

```
            -  1 -
 -  1 -        7
 -  2 -       13
 -  3 -       14
 -  4 -       15
 -  5 -       26
 -  6 -       27
```

GAMMA(001)

```
          -  1  -     -  2  -     -  3  -      -  4  -     -  5  -     -  6  -
 -  1  -  4.63211752  8.59079487  4.50571832  14.1849719  0.0000D+00  0.0000D+00
 -  2  -  8.59079487 20.4215527  10.7701336  24.0243788  0.0000D+00  0.0000D+00
 -  3  -  4.50571832 10.7701336   8.06175740  14.6957572  0.0000D+00  0.0000D+00
 -  4  - 14.1849719  24.0243788  14.6957572  57.0478885   0.0000D+00  0.0000D+00
 -  5  -  0.0000D+00  0.0000D+00  0.0000D+00  0.0000D+00   0.0000D+00  0.0000D+00
 -  6  -  0.0000D+00  0.0000D+00  0.0000D+00  0.0000D+00   0.0000D+00  0.0000D+00
```

GAMMA(002)

```
          -  1  -     -  2  -     -  3  -      -  4  -      -  5  -      -  6  -
 -  1  -  4.64501877  8.61738985  4.51909738  14.2067211  -3.9528D-14  1.7277D-14
 -  2  -  8.61738985 20.4756613  10.7977859  24.1926932   3.9586D-15 -3.0430D-15
 -  3  -  4.51909738 10.7977859   8.07541527 14.6719438   1.2553D-14 -1.7629D-15
 -  4  - 14.2067211  24.1926932  14.6719438  55.8272213  -3.6291D-14  1.0322D-14
 -  5  - -3.9528D-14  3.9586D-15  1.2553D-14 -3.6291D-14   6.62765113 -2.95635329
 -  6  -  1.7277D-14 -3.0430D-15 -1.7629D-15  1.0322D-14  -2.95635329  1.55271435
```

GAMMA(003)

```
          -  1  -     -  2  -     -  3  -      -  4  -      -  5  -      -  6  -
 -  1  -  4.64959361  8.62734529  4.52334303  14.1915650  -2.2759D-14  2.2421D-14
 -  2  -  8.62734529 20.4972590  10.8073233  24.2795462   9.0433D-15 -5.0437D-15
 -  3  -  4.52334303 10.8073233   8.07910376 14.6115950   1.7532D-14 -9.0931D-15
 -  4  - 14.1915650  24.2795462  14.6115950  54.5882665   8.5526D-14 -5.0609D-14
 -  5  - -2.2759D-14  9.0433D-15  1.7532D-14  8.5526D-14   9.04511942 -4.89883577
 -  6  -  2.2421D-14 -5.0437D-15 -9.0931D-15 -5.0609D-14  -4.89883577  3.15056927
```

GAMMA(004)

```
          -  1  -     -  2  -     -  3  -      -  4  -      -  5  -      -  6  -
 -  1  -  4.65434085  8.63762321  4.52778437  14.1698108  -5.4673D-14  4.9016D-14
 -  2  -  8.63762321 20.5194285  10.8172082  24.3471334   1.4211D-14 -1.0443D-14
 -  3  -  4.52778437 10.8172082   8.08302933 14.5479509   2.2206D-14 -1.1657D-14
 -  4  - 14.1698108  24.3471334  14.5479509  53.4222308  -5.1879D-15  2.1435D-14
 -  5  - -5.4673D-14  1.4211D-14  2.2206D-14 -5.1879D-15  11.1677045  -6.68052338
 -  6  -  4.9016D-14 -1.0443D-14 -1.1657D-14  2.1435D-14  -6.68052338  4.66189212
```

GAMMA(005)

```
          -  1  -     -  2  -     -  3  -      -  4  -      -  5  -      -  6  -
 -  1  -  4.65930304  8.64831296  4.53246908  14.1420337   6.9509D-15  5.5325D-15
 -  2  -  8.64831296 20.5423559  10.8275405  24.3971120  -1.5601D-14  8.1974D-15
 -  3  -  4.53246908 10.8275405   8.08724314 14.4813317  -9.7033D-15  1.1635D-14
 -  4  - 14.1420337  24.3971120  14.4813317  52.3190623   2.0004D-14  8.3256D-15
 -  5  -  6.9509D-15 -1.5601D-14 -9.7033D-15  2.0004D-14  13.1526851  -8.37779556
 -  6  -  5.5325D-15  8.1974D-15  1.1635D-14  8.3256D-15  -8.37779556  6.12759541
```

NORMAL ENDING OF OPTIMAL CONTROL PROGRAM

13.3 Conclusions

This chapter has briefly surveyed the optimal control options in B34S. The earlier chapters of the book illustrated how to specify and diagnostically test a number of classes of models. A number of specification tests were discussed and illustrated with real data. This chapter has outlined how an estimated model could be used to perform policy analysis. Since the OPTCONTROL command works on linear and nonlinear models, as long as the model can be written in FORTRAN, the tools in this chapter can be used with many of the model types illustrated in the prior chapters. Econometrics has many uses. One is to characterize or summarize data. Here the specification of the model impacts the degree of fit with which a summary was achieved. Another use of econometric models is to test a hypothesis. The distribution of the coefficients is important here and must be investigated by extensive residual analysis to see if the sample residuals are distributed in a manner consistent with the assumptions of the model. Other uses of econometrics include forecasting, i. e., characterizing data in the future. A final and important use of econometrics concerns policy analysis. The OPTCONTROL command is most helpful in policy analysis since in this situation the economist is an active participant in determining the future. The brief examples in this chapter attest to the rich possibilities of control theory. It must be stressed that a structural model will do only as well as it is specified. An elegant model, whose coefficients are changing due to policy changes, will be a weak reed on which to develop economic policy. The recursive residual options in B34S were developed to investigate the stability of the estimated model over time and address this question.

Many problems remain. If, in fact, we knew in advance that the coefficients of a structural model were changing, it would be possible to put these changes in the user SUBROUTINE in the OPTCONTROL command and technically solve the system. The whole question of anticipating changes in an econometric model and correcting for these changes assumes that the changes to the coefficients are exogenous and not endogenous. If the changes are endogenous, then any attempt to "correct" for the changes will induce other changes. For the time being, the best thing is to test whether the problem really exists.

The B34S program was started many years ago and is an ongoing project. This monograph is a snapshot of the progress to date. If one knew where one was going in research, it would not be research. So it is with the B34S project. The B34S system is sufficiently flexible that other research teams can build on the foundation that the author has created, as the author, in turn, built on the excellent research of others.

NOTES

1. The author was fortunate to obtain the Chow program. This chapter draws heavily from the discussion of this program in the seminal Chow books, which document research funded by the National Science Foundation. The B34S version of the Chow optimal control program uses a dynamic link to a user subroutine in which the model is described. This change in the program facilitates multiple users all running the program simultaneously since the basic code does not have to be relinked. More discussion of the dynamic link feature in B34S is contained in chapter 11, which discusses nonlinear estimation. The B34S implementation of the Butters (1977) program discussed in Chow and Butters (1977) did not make any change in the output produced, except to echo input and document the output produced. Changes were made to increase program accuracy, to simplify input and to provide diagnostic messages to help identify errors.

2. Chow's notation has been preserved in this section since the variables in the output use these variable names.

3. Note that the notation y_t refers to the vector of p state variables in any period, while y_T refers to the vector of state variables in the last period.

4. The B34S version of the Chow program benefited from write-ups prepared by Chow and Butters (1977) and Butters (1977). Many changes were made to the code, including adding LINPACK for matrix inversion, adding BLAS and implementing the DYNCAL dynamic linking option.

5. The original input setup uses the IBM FORTRAN extension NAMELIST. While every effort will be made to keep this feature going, it will not port to B34S versions on other types of machines since the NAMELIST feature is an IBM extension to FORTRAN. For this reason, the B34S II parser commands were developed that mimic the NAMELIST input closely. The B34S parser input syntax will run on any computer system since the "native" control language could be changed to remove the NAMELIST without the user having to change the input setup. Most users feel that the B34S II input format is substantially easier to use. Extensive input checking will flag errors on input and give detailed error messages to assist the user in fixing input errors. For more detail on the B34S II input format, see the <u>B34S On-Line Help Manual</u>. For a discussion of what the variables specify see Chow (1981).

6. The Klein-Goldberger model was first published in Klein and Goldberger (1955). Further work is contained in Goldberger (1959). This model has been extensively studied. For a more modern discussion, see Theil (1971, 468-483). The variable numbers have been taken directly from Chow (1981), where the problem was initially run.

Bibliography

Abowd, J. The Bayesian Analysis Package-BRAP User's Manual. Chicago: H. G. B. Alexander Research Foundation Graduate School of Business, University of Chicago, September 1967.

Akaike, H. "Information Theory and an Extension of the Maximum Likelihood Principle." In Second International Symposium on Information Theory, edited by B. N. Petrov and F. Csaki, 267-281. Budapest, Hungary: Akademiai Kiado, 1973.

Anderson, B. D. O. and John Moore. Optimal Filtering. Englewood Cliffs, N. J.: Prentice-Hall, 1979.

Aoki, M. State Space Modeling of Time Series. New York: Springer-Verlag, 1987.

Ashley, R., Douglas Patterson, and Melvin J. Hinich. "A Diagnostic Test for Nonlinear Serial Dependence in Time Series Fitting Errors." Journal of Time Series Analysis 7, no. 3 (1986): 165-177.

Bartlett, M. S. "On the Theoretical Specification of the Sampling Properties of Autocorrelated Time Series." Journal of the Royal Statistical Society B8 (1946): 27.

Bartlett, M. S. Stochastic Processes. Cambridge, England: Cambridge University Press, 1955.

Beaton, A., Donald Rubin, and John Barone. "The Acceptability of Regression Solutions: Another Look at Computational Accuracy." Journal of the American Statistical Association 71, no. 353, (1976): 158-168.

Box, G. E. P., and G. Jenkins. Time Series Analysis, Forecasting and Control. rev. ed. San Francisco: Holden Day, 1976.

Box, G. E. P., and D. Pierce. "Distribution of Residual Autocorrelations in Autoregressive Integrated Moving Average Time Series Models." Journal of the American Statistical Association 65 (1970): 1509-1526.

Box, G. E. P., and George Tiao. "Intervention Analysis With Application to Economic and Environmental Problems." Journal of the American Statistical Association 70 (March 1975): 70-79.

Box, G. E. P., and George Tiao. "A Canonical Analysis of Multiple Time Series." Biometrika 64 (1977): 355-366.

Boyes, W., and David Kavanaugh. "Money and the Production Function: A Test for Specification Errors." Review of Economics and Statistics 61 (1979): 442-446.

Brillinger, D. R. "An Introduction to Polyspectrum." Annals of Mathematical Statistics 36 (1965): 1351-1374.

Brockett, P. L., Melvin Hinich, and Gary R. Wilson. "Nonlinear and Non-Gaussian Ocean Noise." Journal Acoustic Society of America 82, no. 4 (1987): 1386-1394.

Brockett, P., Melvin Hinich, and Douglas Patterson. "Bispectral-Based Tests for the Detection of Gaussianity and Linearity in Time Series." Journal of the American Statistical Association 83, no. 403 (September 1988): 657-664.

Brown, R., J. Durbin, and J. Evans. "Techniques for Testing the Constancy of Regression Relationships Over Time." Journal of the Royal Statistical Society B37 (1975): 149-192.

Butters, E. Nonlinear Optimal Control Program Programer's Guide. Princeton, N. J.: Princeton University, February 1977. Mimeo. Appendix: Description of Subroutines for Matrix Operations and I/O Used by the Nonlinear Optimal Control Program.

Chow, G., and Ettie H. Butters. Optimal Control of Nonlinear Systems Program User's Guide. Princeton, N. J.: Princeton University. Econometric Research Program, Research Memorandum 209, 1977. Mimeo.

Chow, G. Analysis and Control of Dynamic Economic Systems. New York: John Wiley & Sons, 1975.

Chow, G. Economic Analysis by Control Methods. New York: John Wiley & Sons, 1981.

Chow, G. Econometrics. New York: McGraw-Hill, 1983.

Christensen, L. R., and D. W. Jorgenson. "The Measurement of U. S. Real Capital Input, 1929-1967." Review of Income and Wealth. Series 15 (December 1969): 293-320.

Christensen, L. R., and D. W. Jorgenson. "U. S. Real Product and Real Factor Input, 1929-1967." Review of Income and Wealth. Series 16 (March 1970): 19-50.

Daganzo, C. Multinomial Probit: The Theory and Its Application to Demand Forecasting. New York: Academic Press, 1979.

Dongarra, J., J. Bunch, C. Moler, and G. Stewart. Linpack User's Guide. Philadelphia: Siam, 1979.

Draper, N. R., and H. Smith. Applied Regression Analysis. New York: John Wiley & Sons, 1966.

Dufour, J. M. "Methods for Specification Errors Analysis With Macroeconomic Applications." Ph.D. diss., University of Chicago, 1979.

Dufour, J. M. "Recursive Stability Analysis of Linear Regression Relationships: An Exploratory Methodology." Journal of Econometrics 19 (1982): 31-76.

Durbin, J. "Tests for Serial Correlation in Regression Analysis Based on the Periodogram of Least-Squares Residuals." Biometrika 56, no. 1 (1969): 1-15.

Epstein, R. J. A History of Econometrics. New York: North Holland, 1987.

Faddeeva, V. N. Computational Methods of Linear Algebra. New York: Dover, 1959.

Frankel, Jeffrey. "A Technique for Extracting a Measure of Expected Inflation From Interest Rate Term Structure." Review of Economics and Statistics 64, no. 1 (February 1982): 135-141.

Freiden, A. "A Program for the Estimation of Dynamic Economic Relations From a Time Series of Cross Sections." Annals of Economic and Social Measurement 2, no. 1 (January 1973): 89-91.

Freund, J. F. Modern Elementary Statistics. Englewood Cliffs, N. J.: Prentice-Hall, 1960.

Gallant, R. Nonlinear Statistical Models. New York: John Wiley & Sons, 1987.

Geweke, J. Multiple Time Series Manipulator (MTSM) Edition 8208: User's Guide. Carnegie Mellon, 1982a. Mimeo.

Geweke, J. "Measurement of Linear Dependence and Feedback Between Multiple Time Series." Journal of the American Statistical Association 77 (June 1982b): 304-313.

Geweke, J. "Feedback Between Monetary Policy, Labor Market Activity, and Wage Inflation, 1955-1978." Workers, Jobs, and Inflation. Edited by Martin Bailey. Washington D. C.: Brookings Institute, 1982c.

Geweke, J. "Measures of Conditional Linear Dependence and Feedback Between Time Series." Journal of the American Statistical Association 79 (December 1984): 907-915.

Goldberger, A. S. Impact Multipliers and Dynamic Properties of the Klein-Goldberger Model. New York: North Holland, 1959.

Goldberger, A. S. Econometric Theory. New York: John Wiley & Sons, 1964.

Granger, C. W. J. "Investigating Causal Relations by Econometric Models and Cross-Spectral Models." Econometrica 37 (1969): 424-438.

Granger, C. W. J., and Paul Newbold. Forecasting Economic Time Series. New York: Academic Press, 1977, 1986.

Greene, W. H. LIMDEP. New York: Economic Software, Inc., 1985.

Gustafson, R. L. "Partial Correlations in Regression Computations." Journal of the American Statistical Association 56 (1961): 363-367.

Harvey, A., and Patrick Collier. "Testing for Functional Misspecification in Regression Analysis." Journal of Econometrics 6 (1977): 103-119.

Harvey, A. C. Time Series Models. New York: John Wiley & Sons, 1981.

Haugh, L. D. "Checking the Independence of Two Covariance-Stationary Time Series: A Univariate Residual Cross Correlation Approach." Journal of the American Statistical Association 71 (1976): 378-385.

Haugh, L. D., and G. E. P. Box. "Identification of Dynamic Regression (Distributed Lag) Models Connecting Two Time Series." Journal of the American Statistical Association 72 (1977): 121-130.

Henry, N., John McDonald, and Houston H. Stokes. "The Estimation of Dynamic Economic Relations From a Time Series of Cross Sections: A Programming Modification." Annals of Economic and Social Measurement 5, no. 1 (January 1976): 153-155.

Hillmer, S. C., and G. C. Tiao. "Likelihood Function of Stationary Multiple Autoregressive Moving Average Models." Journal of the American Statistical Association 74 (1979): 652-660.

Hinich, M. "Testing for Gaussianity and Linearity of a Stationary Time Series." Journal of Time Series Analysis 3, no. 5 (1982): 169-176.

Hinich, M., and Douglas Patterson. "Evidence of Nonlinearity in Daily Stock Returns." Journal of Business and Economic Statistics 3, no. 1 (January 1985): 69-77.

Hinich, M., and Douglas Patterson. A Bispectrum Based Test on the Stationary Martingale Model. University of Texas, 13 August 1986. Mimeo.

Hinich, M., and M. A. Wolinsky. "A Test for Aliasing Using Bispectral Estimates." Journal of the American Statistical Association 83, no. 402 (June 1988): 499-502.3

IBM Inc. IBM System/360 and System/370 FORTRAN IV Language. 10th ed. no. GC28-6515-9. White Plains, N. Y.: IBM, 1972.

IBM Inc. VS FORTRAN Version 2, Language and Library Reference. Rel. 3. no. SC26-4221-3. White Plains, N. Y. : IBM, March 1988a.

IBM Inc. VS FORTRAN Version 2, Programing Guide. Rel. 3. no. SC26-4222-3. White Plains, N. Y. : IBM, March 1988b.

Isaacson, D., and Richard Madsen. Markov Chains Theory and Applications. New York: John Wiley & Sons, 1976.

Jenkins, G., and Donald Watts. Spectral Analysis and Its Applications. San Francisco: Holden Day, 1968.

Jennings, L. "Simultaneous Estimation - Detailed Notes Covering the Programing Package." 1973. Mimeo.

Jennings, L. "Simultaneous Equations Estimation." Journal of Econometrics 12, no. 1 (January 1980): 23-39.

Johnston, J. Econometric Methods. New York: McGraw-Hill, 1963, 1972, 1984.

Judge, G., William Griffiths, R. Carter Hill, and Tsoung-Chao Lee. The Theory and Practice of Econometrics. New York: John Wiley & Sons, 1980.

Kawasaki, S. Manual to Accompany LOGLIN 31. Northwestern University, 1978. Mimeo.

Kawasaki, S. "Applications of Log-Linear Probability Models in Economics." Ph.D. diss., Northwestern University, 1979.

Klein, L., and A. Goldberger. An Econometric Model of the United States , 1929-1952. New York: North Holland, 1955.

Klein, R., and Telma Klein. XLOGLIN, An Improved Program for Multivariate Logistic Regression. Department of Statistics University of California Riverside. Technical Report No. 169, 1988. Mimeo.

Klein, T. Manual for XLOGLIN. Department of Statistics, University of California, Riverside. 1988. Mimeo.

Kmenta, J. Elements of Econometrics. New York: Macmillan Company, 1971, 1986.

Kosobud, R., and Houston H. Stokes. "Economic Analysis of OPEC Using a Markov Chain Model." Journal of Energy and Development 3, no. 2 (Spring 1978): 378-400.

Kosobud, R., and Houston H. Stokes. "Oil Market Share Dynamics: A Markov Chain Analysis of Cunsumer and Producer Adjustments." Journal of Empirical Economics 3, no. 2 (Winter 1979): 253-275.

Kosobud, R., and Houston H. Stokes. "Simulation of World Oil Market Shocks: A Markov Analysis of OPEC and Consumer Behavior." The Energy Journal 1, no. 2 (1980): 55-84.

Leamer, E. Specification Searches: Ad Hoc Inference With Nonexperimental Data. New York: John Wiley & Sons, 1978.

Lee, T. C., G. G. Judge, and A. Zellner. Estimating the Parameters of the Markov Probability Model From Aggregate Time Series Data. New York: North Holland, 1970.

Lehrer, E., and Houston H. Stokes. "Determinants of the Female Occupational Distribution: A Log-Linear Probability Analysis," Review of Economics and Statistics 67, no. 2 (August 1985): 120-125.

Lehrer, E. "Log-Linear Probability Models: An Application to the Analysis of Timing of First Birth." Applied Economics 17, no. 3 (1984): 477-489.

Lehrer, E., and Marc Nerlove. "The Impact of Expected Child Survival on Husbands' and Wives' Desired Fertility in Malaysia: A Log-Linear Probability Model." Social Science Research 3, no. 3 (1984): 236-249.

Liu, L. M., and Dominic M. Hanssens. "Identification of Multiple-Input Transfer Function Models." Communications in Statistics-Theory and Methods 11 (1982): 297-314.

Liu, L. M., and Gregory B. Hudak, in collaboration with G. E. P. Box, Mervin Miller, and George Tiao. The SCA Statistical System. 3 vols. Lisle, Ill.: Scientific Computing Associates, 1986a.

Liu, L. M., and Gregory B. Hudak, in collaboration with G. E. P. Box, Mervin Miller, and George Tiao. Quality and Productivity Imporvement Using the SCA Statistical System. Lisle, Ill.: Scientific Computing Associates, 1986b.

Ljung, G. M., and G. E. P. Box. "On a Measure of Lack of Fit in Time Series Models." Biometrika 66 (1978): 265-270.

Longley, J. "An Appraisal of Least Squares Programs for the Electronic Computer From the Point of View of the User." Journal of the American Statistical Association 62, no. 319 (1967): 819-841.

Longley, J. Least Squares Computations Using Orthogonalization Methods. New York: Marcel Decker, 1984.

Lovell, M. "Tests of the Rational Expectations Hypothesis." American Economic Review 76, no. 1 (March 1986): 110-124.

Maddala, G. S. Econometrics. New York: McGraw-Hill, 1977.

Maddala, G. S. Limited-Dependent and Qualitative Variables in Econometrics. Cambridge, England: Cambridge University Press, 1983.

Maddala, G. S. Introductory Econometrics. New York: Macmillan, 1988.

Mandel, J. "Use of the Singular Value Decomposition in Regression Analysis." The American Statistician 36, no. 1 (1982): 15-24.

Marquardt, D. W. "An Algorithm for Least Squares Estimation of Nonlinear Parameters." Journal of the Society for Industrial and Applied Mathematics 2 (1963): 431-441.

McDonald, J., and Robert Moffitt. "The Uses of Tobit Analysis." Review of Economics and Statistics 62, no. 2 (May 1980): 318-321.

McKelvey, R., and William Zavoina. "An IBM Fortran IV Program to Perform N-Chotomous Multivariate Probit Analysis." Behavioral Science 16 (March 1971): 186-187.

McKelvey, R., and William Zavoina. "A Statistical Model for the Analysis of Ordinal Level Dependent Variables." Journal of Mathematical Sociology 4 (1975): 103-120.

McManus, W. S. "Estimates of the Deterrent Effect of Capital Punishment: The Importance of the Researcher's Prior Beliefs." Journal of Political Economy 93 (April 1985): 416-425.

Meeter, D. "Problems in the Analysis of Nonlinear Models by Least Squares." Ph.D. diss., University of Wisconsin, 1964a.

Meeter, D. Non-Linear Least Squares (GAUSHAUS). University of Wisconsin Computing Center, 1964b. Mimeo.

Miller, G. A. "Finite Markov Processes in Psychology." Psychometrika 17 (1952): 149-167.

Mills, E. "The Theory of Inventory Decisions." Econometrica 25 (April 1957): 222-238.

Muth, J. "Rational Expectations and the Theory of Price Movements." Econometrica 29 (July 1961): 315-335.

Nelson, C. Applied Time Series Analysis for Managerial Forecasting. San Francisco: Holden Day, 1973.

Nerlove, M. "Further Evidence on the Estimation of Dynamic Economic Relations From a Time Series of Cross Sections." Econometrica 39, no. 2 (March 1971a): 359-382.

Nerlove, M. "A note on Error Components Models." Econometrica. 39, no. 2 (March 1971b): 383-396.

Nerlove, M., and S. James Press. Univariate and Multivariate Log-Linear and Logistic Models. Santa Monica: RAND Corp. Report R-1306-EDA/NIA, December 1973.

Nerlove, M., and S. James Press. Multivariate Log-Linear Probability Models for the Analysis of Qualitative Data. Department of Economics Discussion paper no. 1, Northwestern University, 1976.

Neuburger, H., and Houston H. Stokes. "The Anglo-German Trade Rivalry, 1897-1913: A Counterfactual Outcome and Its Implications." Social Science History 3, no. 2 (Winter 1979a): 187-201.

Neuburger, H., and Houston H. Stokes. "The Relationship Between Interest Rates and Gold Flows Under the Gold Standard: A New Empirical Approach." Economica 46 (August 1979b): 261-279.

Pack, D. A Computer Program for the Analysis of Time Series Models Using the Box-Jenkins Philosophy. Department of Statistics, Ohio State University, 1977. Mimeo.

Phillips, G. D. A., and Andrew Harvey. "A Comparison of the Power of Some Tests for Heteroskedasticity in the General Linear Model." Journal of Econometrics 2 (1974): 307-316.

Pierce, D. "Relationships - and the Lack Thereof - Between Economic Time Series, With Special Reference to Money and Interest Rates." Journal of the American Statistical Association 72, no. 357 (March 1977): 11-21.

Pierce, D., and Larry Haugh. "Causality in Temporal Systems: Characterization and a Survey." Journal of Econometrics 5 (1977): 265-293.

Pindyck, R., and Daniel Rubinfeld. Econometric Models and Economic Forecasts. New York: McGraw-Hill, 1976, 1981, 1990.

Press, J., and Arthur Zellner. "Posterior Distribution of Population Squared Multiple Correlation Coefficient." Center for Mathematical Studies in Business and Economics, University of Chicago, 1967. Mimeo.

Priestley, M. B. Spectral Analysis and Time Series. New York: Academic Press, 1981.

Priestley, M. B. Non-Linear and Non-Stationary Time Series Analysis. New York: Academic Press, 1988.

Quenouille, M. H. The Analysis of Multiple Time Series. London, England: Griffin, 1957.

Roy, S. N. Some Aspects of Multivariate Analysis. New York: John Wiley & Sons, 1957.

Sargent, T. "Estimation of Dynamic Labor Demand Schedules Under Rational Expectations." Journal of Political Economy 86, no. 6 (1978). (Reprinted as chap. 25 in Lucas, R., and T. Sargent, eds. Rational Expectations and Econometric Practice. Minneapolis: University of Minnesota, 1981.)

Sargent, T. Macroeconomic Theory. 2nd ed. New York: Academic Press, 1987.

SAS Institute Inc. SAS/ETS User's Guide, Ver. 5. Cary NC: SAS Institute Inc., 1984.

SAS Institute Inc., SAS User's Guide: Basics, Ver. 5. Cary NC: SAS Institute Inc., 1985a.

SAS Institute Inc., SAS User's Guide: Statistics, Ver. 5. Cary NC: SAS Institute Inc., 1985b.

Schwartz, G. "Estimating the Dimension of a Model." Annals of Statistics 6 (1978): 461-464.

Sims, C. "Comment on Pierce." Journal of the American Statistical Association 72, no. 357 (1977): 23-24.

Sims, C. "Macroeconomics and Reality." Econometrics 48, no. 1 (1980): 1-48.

Sinai, A., and Houston H. Stokes. "Real Money Balances: An Omitted Variable From the Production Function." Review of Economics and Statistics 54, no. 3 (August 1972): 290-296.

Sinai, A., and Houston H. Stokes. "Real Money Balances: An Omitted Variable From the Production Function? Reply to Comments." Review of Economics and Statistics 57, no. 2 (May 1975): 247-252.

Sinai, A., and Houston H. Stokes. "Money and the Production Function - A Reply to Boyes and Kavanaugh." Review of Economics and Statistics 63, no. 2 (May 1981): 313-318.

Sinai, A., and Houston H. Stokes. "Money Balances in the Production Function: A Retrospective Look." Eastern Economic Journal 15, no. 4 (October - December 1989): 349-363.

Stokes, H. H., Donald Jones, and Hugh Neuburger. Unemployment and Adjustment in the Labor Market. Chicago: University of Chicago, 1975.

Stokes, H. H., and Hugh Neuburger. "The Effect of Monetary Changes on Interest Rates: A Box-Jenkins Approach." Review of Economics and Statistics 61, no. 4 (November 1979): 534-548.

Stokes, H. H. "Matrix Operations Using LINPACK: An Overview." In Management and Office Information Systems, edited by S. K. Chang, 415-434. New York: Plenum Publishing Corporation, 1984. (First published in 10th Annual SPEAKEASY Conference Proceedings. Chicago, SPEAKEASY Computing Corporation, 1983.)

Stokes, H. H. "Dynamic Adjustment of Disaggregate Unemployment Series." In Time Series Analysis: Theory and Practice 7, edited by O. D. Anderson, 293-311. New York: North Holland, 1985.

Stokes, H. H. "Interfacing SAS Software With the B34S System Recursive Residual Option: A Brief Look at Theory and an Example." In SUGI 12 Proceedings, 76-81. Cary NC: SAS Institute, 1986a.

Stokes, H. H. "Measuring Expected Inflation: Further tests in the Frequency Domain of a Proposed New Measure." American Statistical Association 1986 Proceedings of the Business and Economics Statistics Section (1986b): 473-477.

Stokes, H. H. The B34S Data Analysis Program: A Short Writeup. University of Illinois College of Business Administration Working Paper Series, report FY 77-1, revised repeatedly since 1977 and currently on-line as the "B34S 'Native' Command Manual," 1988a.

Stokes, H. H. B34S On-Line Help Manual. Revised repeatedly since 1987 and available on-line, 1988b.

Stokes, H. H. "Two-Level Parsing in B34S: A Large-Scale Econometric Package." In IEEE Workshop on Languages for Automation, 235-236. Los Angeles: IEEE Computer Society Press, 1987.

Stokes, H. H., and Melvin Hinich. Testing the Gas Furnace Model for Nonlinear Serial Dependence. Department of Economics, University of Illinois Chicago, 1989. Mimeo.

Stokes, H. H. "Clues in the Error Process: A Second Round Diagnostic Procedure for Transfer Function Modelling." Belgian Journal of Operations Research, Statistics and Computer Science 30, no. 1 (1990): 33-51.

Stokey, N., and Robert Lucas. Recursive Methods in Economic Dynamics. Cambridge, Mass.: Harvard University Press, 1989.

Strang, G. Linear Algebra and Its Applications. New York: Academic Press, 1976.

Theil, H. Statistical Decomposition Analysis. New York: North Holland, 1972.

Theil, H. Principles of Econometrics. New York: John Wiley & Sons, 1971.

Thornber, H. The Autoregressive Model: Bayesian vs. Sampling Theory Analysis. Technical report no. 6504, Center for Mathematical Studies in Business and Economics, University of Chicago, 1965.

Thornber, H. Manual for B34T (8 MAR 66)-A Stepwise Regression Program. University of Chicago Business School technical report 6603, 1966.

Thornber, H. BAYES Addendum to Technical Report 6603: Manual for B34T-A Stepwise Regression Program. University of Chicago Business School, 15 September 1967.

Thornber, H. BLUS Addendum to Technical Report 6603: Manual for B34T-A Stepwise Regression Program. University of Chicago Busienss School, 1 August 1968.

Tiao, G., and G. E. P. Box. "Modeling Multiple Time Series With Applications." Journal of the American Statistical Association 76 (1981): 802-816.

Tiao, G., G. Box, M. Grupe, G. Hudak, W. Bell, and I. Chang. The Wisconsin Multiple Time Series (WMTS-1) Program, A Preliminary Guide. Department of Statistics, University of Wisconsin, Madison, 1979. Mimeo.

Tobin, J. "Estimation of Relationships for Limited Dependent Variables." Econometrica 26 (1958): 24-36.

Wampler, R. "A Report on the Accuracy of Some Widely Used Least Squares Computer Programs." Journal of the American Statistical Association 65, no. 330 (June 1970): 549-565.

Whittle, P. "On the Fitting of Multivariate Autoregressions, and the Approximate Canonical Factorization of a Spectral Density Matrix." Biometrika 50 (1963): 129-134.

Wilcoxon, F., S. K. Katti, and Roberta A. Wilcox. "Critical Values and Probability Levels for the Wilcoxon Rank Sum Test and the Wilcoxon Signed-Rank Test." In <u>Selected Tables in Mathematical Statistics</u>. Vol. 1, Edited by the Institute of Mathematical Statistics, 181-259. Providence, R. I.: American Mathematical Society, 1973.

Zellner, A. <u>An Introduction to Bayesian Inference in Econometrics</u>. New York: John Wiley & Sons, 1971.

Zellner, A., and Franz Palm. "Time Series Analysis and Simultaneous Equation Econometric Models." <u>Journal of Econometrics</u> 2 (1974): 17-54.

Zellner, A., and George Tiao, "Bayesian Analysis of the Regression Model With Autocorrelated Errors." <u>Journal of the American Statistical Association</u> 59 (1964): 763-778.

Index

About the Author

HOUSTON H. STOKES is Professor of Economics at the University of Illinois at Chicago. He is author of over 60 articles and a previous book in the areas of applied econometrics, time series, monetary economics, economic history, and software design.